BEHAVIOURAL ECOLOGY
ECOLOGICAL CONSEQUENCES OF
ADAPTIVE BEHAVIOUR

BEHAVIOURAL ECOLOGY

ECOLOGICAL CONSEQUENCES OF

ADAPTIVE BEHAVIOUR

THE 25TH SYMPOSIUM OF
THE BRITISH ECOLOGICAL SOCIETY
READING 1984

EDITED BY

R. M. SIBLY AND R. H. SMITH

Department of Pure and Applied Zoology,
University of Reading

BLACKWELL SCIENTIFIC PUBLICATIONS
OXFORD LONDON EDINBURGH
BOSTON PALO ALTO MELBOURNE

First published 1985

Printed and bound in Great Britain by
The Alden Press, Osney Mead, Oxford

DISTRIBUTORS

USA and Canada
  Blackwell Scientific Publications Inc
  PO Box 50009, Palo Alto
  California 94303

Australia
  Blackwell Scientific Book Distributors
  31 Advantage Road, Highett
  Victoria 3190

British Library
Cataloguing in Publication Data

British Ecological Society: *Symposium
(25th: 1984: Reading)*
Behavioural ecology: ecological
consequences
of adaptive behaviour.
1. Population biology   2. Adaptation
(Biology)
I. Title   II. Sibly, R.M.
III. Smith, R.H.
574.5′248 QH352

ISBN 0-632-01359-1

CONTENTS

v

PREFACE

The 26th Symposium of the British Ecological Society was held at the University of Reading on 10–12 April 1984. We first suggested the symposium topic to BES Meetings Committee in May 1981 and the programme was put together during 1982 by an organizing committee made up of Tim Clutton-Brock, Tony Davy, Geoff Parker and ourselves. The meeting was attended by about 500 people, a measure of the current interest in behavioural ecology. Twenty-seven invited papers were read at the symposium, and twenty-six speakers submitted their papers for publication. Contributors to the display of about forty posters were also invited to submit short communications.

All material submitted for publication in the volume was sent to two referees, edited and revised before being accepted. The generous and rapid response of both authors and referees greatly aided and improved our editing of this volume, and we are deeply appreciative of their help. Since referees served anonymously we cannot mention them by name, but we hope they will accept our very sincere thanks. We are also very grateful to Penny Baker of Blackwell Scientific Publications for her very efficient help.

Reading,   RICHARD SIBLY
October 1984.   ROBERT SMITH

I
SELECTIVE REVIEW

.

FROM INDIVIDUAL BEHAVIOUR TO POPULATION DYNAMICS

MICHAEL P. HASSELL[1] AND ROBERT M. MAY[2]
[1]*Department of Pure and Applied Biology, Imperial College at Silwood Park, Ascot, Berks SL5 7PY, UK, and*
[2]*Department of Biology, Princeton University, Princeton, New Jersey 08544, USA*

SUMMARY

Behavioural ecologists are usually concerned with the way the behaviour of animals—as individuals or as groups—may have evolved, with little reference to the consequences such behaviour may have for the population dynamics. Population biologists, conversely, usually focus on the demographic consequences of environmental or biological changes, with little reference to behavioural mechanisms that may underlie changes in birth, death and migration rates. We survey some recent work in which the behaviour of individuals is explicitly related to the dynamics of the population: the examples are derived mainly from foraging behaviour (among parasitoids and other invertebrates, vertebrates, and disease agents), but also embrace mating, sex-ratio and territorial behaviour. Of particular interest are those situations where a phenomenological description of the way subpopulations interact in a spatially heterogeneous environment can, on the one hand, be grounded on an understanding of the behaviour of individuals and can, on the other hand, lead to insights about population dynamics and community structure.

INTRODUCTION

Students of population dynamics usually have very different objectives from those of behavioural ecology. The population ecologist deals with the fundamental demographic processes of births, deaths, immigration and emigration and the factors that affect them. The challenge is to expose the crucial factors underlying the patterns of distribution and abundance of a population over a time-scale of several generations. What is it, for example, that causes the episodic outbreaks of the larch pine moth (*Dendrolimus pini*) in forests in central Germany (Varley 1949), and what is it that drives the remarkably regular cycles of the grey larch tortrix (*Zeiraphera dineana*) in the Engadine or the 4-year small mammal cycles of boreal regions? Are they due to fluctuating physical conditions, or do they stem from interactions between

3

individuals of the same population or from different species? Behavioural ecologists, on the other hand, in focusing more on the individual or family units, are mainly concerned with the adaptive significance of behaviour patterns. The goal has been to show how they affect inclusive fitness rather than how they affect population dynamics.

The relationship between the two disciplines is thus lop-sided: the population ecologist cannot completely ignore behaviour, but the ethologist can remain unconcerned with the dynamic consequences of the behaviour studied. The level of behavioural information required by the population ecologist, however, is not great. He needs only accurate knowledge of the *end-product* of the behaviour in so far as it affects birth, deaths, and migration rates.

Part of the skill in the study of population dynamics is to collapse the essence of complex behaviour patterns into simple algebraic expressions. For example, one of the simplest insect host-parasitoid models (Nicholson 1933) merely uses the zero term of the Poisson distribution of parasitoid encounters with hosts to predict the survival f of hosts from parasitism:

$$f = \exp(-aP). \tag{1}$$

Here P is the density of searching adult parasitoids and a is a constant representing their per capita searching efficiency. This rather naive formulation, however, does translate directly into a specific foraging pattern. Parasitoid individuals roam the host habitat independently randomly, selecting hosts in an impartial way, never running short of eggs and taking a negligible amount of time to 'handle' each host parasitized.

In this paper, we illustrate the extent to which behaviour is implicit within some recent population models, chosen from a variety of contexts. First, we discuss the way foraging strategies can affect dynamics for single species, for competing species, and for predator–prey and disease–host interactions. Second, we consider some aspects of the interplay between the social structure and the overall dynamics of a population, giving attention to the way social structure is influenced by reproductive behaviour, sex ratio, territoriality, dispersal, and the like. Throughout, the argument flows from behaviour to dynamics; at the end, we show how inferences can sometimes be drawn about behaviour by considering the population dynamics (with general questions about 'prudent predation' being illustrated by observations of host–parasitoid dynamics).

FORAGING BEHAVIOUR AND POPULATION DYNAMICS

This section has two main aims: (i) to consider the extent to which the foraging behaviour of different kinds of organisms—from disease agents through leaf-feeding insects, bees and parasitoids to whales—has been captured in population models; (ii) to examine the general effects that different foraging patterns can have on the dynamics of the interactions.

Single-species system

We commence with the simple situation, based on a model by De Jong (1979), of a habitat containing n plants which serve as food for an insect species, be it caterpillar, sawfly, chrysomelid beetle, or whatever. The adult insects in generation t, N_t, are the dispersing stage and oviposit on plants such that the final egg distribution is described by a negative binomial distribution. This distribution has been widely used in insect and other studies (e.g. Bliss & Owen 1958; Harcourt 1965; Anderson 1978) and is defined by two parameters: the mean of the distribution, and a parameter k inversely defining the extent of clumping (clumping being strongest when $k \rightarrow 0$, and becoming Poisson or random as $k \rightarrow \infty$). Negative binomial distributions can arise from various biological circumstances (Boswell & Patil 1970); one that is the end result of a specific foraging strategy is discussed by May (1978) for searching parasitoids. Briefly, if the ovipositing adults distribute themselves among plants in a clumped manner (specifically, according to a Pearson Mark III or gamma distribution), but if the actual oviposition per adult on the plant is random, the resulting *overall* frequency distribution of eggs per plant exactly follows the negative binomial. Often, however, rather than invoke such a particular explanation, it is better to regard the negative binomial as a phenomenological description that broadly captures the result of complex behaviour patterns in which the patch-to-patch exploitation is not random.

We now assume that the probability of an egg surviving to give a mature adult for dispersal in the next generation, $t+1$, is density dependent. Thus, in a patch with total j eggs, the probability of any one egg surviving is:

$$\exp(-dj). \qquad (2)$$

The level of density dependence therefore depends upon d, being weak for small d and strong for large d. Equation (2) is a familiar one-parameter expression for density dependence (see, for example, May & Oster 1976). Although bettered in describing experimental and field data by some two-parameter models (Hassell 1975; Hassell, Lawton & May 1976; Bellows 1981; Stubbs 1977; Thomas, Pomerantz & Gilpin 1980), it still provides an adequate description of many different data sets, and is a convenient means of including density dependence in simple population models. The population model from generation to generation over all patches thus becomes:

$$N_{t+1} = nF\left[\sum_{i=0}^{\infty} ip(i)\exp(-dFi) \right]. \qquad (3)$$

Here the expression inside the square brackets represents the average number of surviving offspring emerging from any one of the n patches: $p(i)$ is the probability of having i adults in a patch (given by the negative binomial with mean N_t/n and clumping parameter k); F is the intrinsic fecundity per adult; and $\exp(-dFi)$ is the density-dependent probability of survival of an egg on a plant where i adults have each laid F eggs.

An attractive feature of model (3) is that it can be condensed to give a relatively simple expression for the total number of adults in generation $t+1$ as a function of the total number in generation t:

$$N_{t+1} = \lambda N_t[1 + aN_t]^{-b}. \qquad (4)$$

The heterogeneity is no longer explicit in this macroscopic population model. Here $\lambda = F\exp(-dF)$ is the usual finite net rate of increase per adult, and the population parameters a and b that determine the overall density-dependent feedback are defined in terms of the underlying microscopic parameters n, k, F and d by $a = [1 - \exp(-dF)]/nk$ and $b = k + 1$.

Conveniently, the dynamical properties of eqn (4) have already been thoroughly studied (Hassell 1975; Hassell *et al.* 1976). The stability properties are illustrated here in Fig. 1.1 and depend solely on the rate of increase of λ and the parameter b ($b = k + 1$) which characterizes the degree of density dependence; the parameter a affects the magnitude of the equilibrium population density, but not its stability properties. *Thus, any change in foraging behaviour which affects the distribution of eggs per plant—that is,*

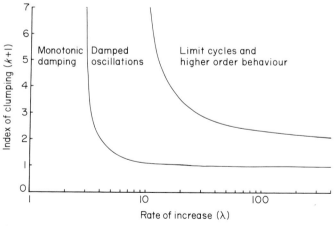

FIG. 1.1. The stability boundaries that separate the various regimes of dynamical behaviour manifested by eqn (4), as functions of the clumping parameter, $k + 1 = b$, and the population rate of increase, λ.

which affects the clumping parameter k—may be translated directly into a change in stability properties.

Equation (2) tends to represent the density-dependent survival within a patch when there is 'scramble' competition among the larvae (exploitation competition), where the adverse effects increase non-linearly with the number of competitors. Towards the opposite extreme, where the within-patch competition is a 'contest' (interference competition), the density-dependent effects tend to scale essentially linearly with the number of competitors, j, leading to a per capita survival probability of the form

$$1/(1 + dj). \tag{5}$$

An analysis similar to that of De Jong can then be carried out, to produce an equation analogous to eqn (4) relating the overall population densities in successive generations (i.e. relating N_{t+1} to N_t). This expression is given in Appendix I. In the limit when dF is small (as it usually will be in reality), the stability of this system is again found to depend only on the quantities λ and $k + 1$. As mentioned above, a variety of two-parameter expressions may be used instead of the limiting eqns (2) or (5) to describe within-patch competition: the ensuing equations that relate the total populations N_{t+1} and N_t are correspondingly more complex than eqn (4) or that given in Appendix I, but retain the essential property that the demographic parameters in these macroscopic equations are defined in terms of quantities describing microscopic, within-patch foraging and interaction.

We have, in short, clear examples of how the spatial distribution of an animal could affect population stability. For a given adult fecundity and degree of density dependence within patches, stability increases as the population becomes more clumped (i.e. as $k \to 0$ and thus as b in eqn (4) approaches unity). The underlying mechanism is the straightforward one of increased contagion leading to a greater proportion of the population confined to fewer patches in which most of the mortality occurs. The hosts in the remaining 'low density' patches suffer relatively low mortality and can thus buffer the system against large fluctuations.

In essence, this is similar to the work of Lomnicki (1978, 1980, 1982) on population regulation arising from genetic differences among individuals competing for a resource. His ranking of individuals in terms of their competitive ability is equivalent to distributing the survival probabilities by virtue of spatial location, and the mechanism of population stability is much the same. We fully concur with Lomnicki's (1980) admonishment to ecologists: 'Do not look for the average individual in a population: look for differences between the individuals and try to find out how these differences affect the individuals and try to find out how these differences affect the individual's reproduction and probability of survival. Do not look for homogeneous parts of an area: look for spatial heterogeneity and differences in reproduction and survival among . . . parts of the area.'

The above models all treat the clumping parameter k of the negative binomial distribution as a constant, independent of overall population density. In general, however, k is itself likely to be a function of N_t; Hassell (1980) has explicitly documented such effects for the winter moth (*Operopthera brumata*) in Wytham Wood. Such density-dependent clumping can obviously complicate the task of relating overall dynamics to underlying behaviour. Ultimately, the spatial distribution of individuals among patches needs to be derived directly from behavioural considerations, rather than described phenomenologically by a negative binomial or other distribution (Taylor, Woiwod & Perry 1978).

Competing species

The circumstance of a single species in a patchy environment can be readily extended to two or three different species competing for the same resource. Consider two species whose total populations, X_t and Y_t in generation t, are divided among n patches according to independently distributed negative binomials. The adults of X and Y lay F_X and F_Y eggs respectively, and in a patch with a total of x eggs of X and y eggs of Y, the density-dependent probability for an egg of species X to mature to an adult (for dispersal in generation $t+1$) is

$$\exp(-\alpha_X x - \beta_X y). \tag{6}$$

The corresponding probability for an egg of species Y to survive to maturity in the same patch is

$$\exp(-\alpha_Y y - \beta_Y x). \tag{7}$$

Here α_X and α_Y are the intraspecific competition coefficients comparable to d in eqns (2) and (5), while β_X and β_Y measure the effects of interspecific competition. As shown by DeJong (1981), the overall population dynamics of species X is now governed by an equation that is a straightforward extension of the single-species eqn (3):

$$X_{t+1} = nF_x \left[\sum_{i,j} i \exp(-\alpha_X F_X i - \beta_X F_Y j) p_X(i) p_Y(j) \right]. \tag{8}$$

There is, of course, a similar equation for Y_{t+1}. Here $p_X(i)$ and $p_Y(j)$ are the independent probabilities (both described by negative binomial distributions) that a patch contains i adults of X and j of Y. Equation (8) and the corresponding equation for Y_{t+1} can be brought to simpler form, along the lines by which eqn (3) is reduced to eqn (4) in the single-species case; these expressions relating the total populations X_{t+1} and Y_{t+1} to those in the preceding generation, X_t and Y_t, are set out in Appendix II. The conditions under which the two species may coexist overall, even when coexistence is not possible in any one patch, are also given explicitly in Appendix II.

The above model is similar to, but simpler than, that of Atkinson & Shorrocks (1981) who assume that survival within a patch follows the two-species analogue of eqn (5),

$$1/(1 + \alpha i + \beta j), \tag{9}$$

rather than the form of eqns (6) and (7). (Actually, Atkinson & Shorrocks (1981) begin formally by defining the within-patch density dependence to have the more general form $(1 + \alpha i + \beta j)^{-b}$, but all their numerical simulations—as well as subsequent analytic studies of the model by Ives & May (1984)—are restricted to $b = 1$.)

The conclusions both from the model of Atkinson & Shorrocks (1981) and from the model defined above (eqns (6)–(8) and Appendix II) are much the same. In essence, coexistence becomes more likely if the patches are more finely divided, and if the competitors exhibit an aggregated distribution among patches independently of one another. Particularly important for coexistence is the marked aggregation of the superior competitor, so providing more patches in which it is absent and in which the inferior competitor can flourish.

A rather different model has recently been proposed by Lloyd & White (1980) for competition among three species of *Cicada*. Once again much the same conclusions are reached: coexistence is markedly enhanced when each species tends to concentrate on different patches.

The validity of these models depends very much on three things. First, how well is the foraging behaviour of X and Y captured by $p_X(i)$ and $p_Y(j)$ in eqn (8) or similar equations? The use of the negative binomial has already been discussed. But there is the added behavioural problem of whether X and Y perceive the 'good' patches from the 'bad' in a similar or quite independent way. If the former, there should be a covariance in their distributions which will make coexistence harder to achieve. Second, there is the problem of how well the standard competition coefficients capture the behavioural and other inequalities between an individual of X and Y, making one the superior competitor over the other. Third, the form of the density-dependent survival within a patch can affect the outcome to some extent. As discussed earlier, the simple eqns (6) and (7)—leading to eqn (8)—may be adequate approximations if the individual competitors tend to 'scramble' for the resource, while the opposite limit, eqn (9),—leading to the results of Atkinson & Shorrocks—is likely to be a better description if the two species tend to 'contest' for the resources. More generally, one of the various two-parameter models may be required to give an adequate description of within-patch competition.

The effect of foraging behaviour on the dynamics of competing species has been well studied in bees (see Heinrich (1979) and Lawton & Hassell (1984) for reviews). Although examples of interference competition between bees have been recorded (Brian 1957; Johnson & Hubbell 1974; Morse 1977), the simple, direct exploitation of scattered nectar resources is much more likely to play an important role in structuring bee communities (Heinrich 1979). This is supported by the work of Schaffer and his colleagues on three species of bees: the domestic honey bee, *Apis mellifera*, which has small workers but very large colonies; a bumble bee, *Bombus sonorus*, with intermediate sized workers and colonies; and a larger carpenter bee, *Xylocopa arizonensis*, that provisions solitary nests (Schaffer & Schaffer 1979; Schaffer *et al.* 1983). All three species feed on the flowers of *Agave schotti*, different patches of which differ in the total amounts of nectar produced. Schaffer & Schaffer (1979) found that *Apis* predominated in the most productive patches, *Xylocopa* in the least, and *Bombus* in the patches of intermediate quality.

The explanation for this apparently rests on the fact that the individual foraging costs scale in the opposite direction to the maintenance costs of the colony. Thus, small *Apis* forage at low individual energy costs, but need to fuel very large colonies. The large *Xylocopa* expends much more energy foraging, but has no colony to maintain, and *Bombus* is intermediate in both respects. Schaffer & Schaffer (1979) developed a graphical model relating the number of consumers (X) to the available standing crop of nectar (S) where:

$$dS/dt = S[r(1 - S/K) - aX] \qquad (10)$$

$$dX/dt = aX(S - S_m) - T. \qquad (11)$$

Here r is the intrinsic rate of nectar production, K is the maximum nectar level, a is the per capita harvesting rate by bees, S_m is the minimum nectar level to make foraging energetically feasible, and T is the cost of consumer reproduction.

On this basis the model predicts the following species composition along a gradient of nectar productivity from high to low; $Apis \rightarrow Apis + Bombus \rightarrow Apis + Bombus + Xylocopa \rightarrow Bombus + Xylocopa \rightarrow Xylocopa$. Thus, in very productive patches, the large predicted number of *Apis* remove the nectar very quickly, making the average standing crop very low—too low for a *Bombus* worker to break even on an individual foraging trip, while an individual *Apis* can still make an energetic profit.

In a more recent paper, Schaffer *et al.* (1983) manipulate nectar levels by ant exclusion experiments and obtain results consistent with their theoretical model. It is a good example of how species composition is affected by the energetics of foraging, interacting with resource production and the population dynamics of the individual species.

Host–parasitoid interactions

Much has been written on how the foraging behaviour of insect parasitoids affects the dynamics of host–parasitoid interactions (e.g. Hassell & May 1973, 1974; Hassell 1978, 1979, 1980). We shall therefore be highly selective and focus primarily on foraging in the same kind of patchy environment as for the single and competing species above.

Once again, we assume a habitat divided into *n* patches (plants) upon which the host insect feeds. A population of monophagous parasitoids attacks this insect and the searching adult parasitoids allocate their available searching time amongst the *n* patches. The problem is now to define the fraction, *f*, of the total host population that survive parasitism (cf. eqn (1)). Consider, in the first place, a detailed expression that specifies both host and parasitoid distributions over the *n* patches:

$$f(P_t) = \frac{1}{\bar{N}} \sum_{j=0}^{\infty} \left[j\, p(j) \exp\left\{ -\frac{aP_t\, T(j)}{T_0 + n\bar{T}} \right\} \right]. \tag{12}$$

Here $T(j)$ is the time spent per parasitoid in a patch of *j* hosts, $p(j)$ is the probability distribution of hosts per patch, and T_0 is the total transit time between patches. $\bar{N}$ and $\bar{T}$ are, respectively, the mean number of hosts per patch and the mean time spent per parasitoid in a patch; they are related to the chosen distributions for $p(j)$ and $T(j)$ (handling time is assumed, for convenience, to be negligible). The detailed derivation and properties of model (12) are given in Hassell & May (1974).

The dynamical consequences of different foraging strategies may now be revealed by inserting eqn (12) into the familiar host–parasitoid population model:

$$N_{t+1} = \lambda N_t f(P_t), \tag{13}$$

$$P_{t+1} = cN_t[1 - f(P_t)]. \tag{14}$$

Here *c* is the average number of parasitoid progeny per host attacked and λ is the host rate of increase. Thus, if the parasitoids forage without any reference to host density per patch, parasitism overall will tend to be random and eqn (12) collapses to eqn (1). The populations then exhibit diverging oscillations.

Stability is promoted, however, by any tendency for the parasitoids to concentrate in some patches over others, so leading to a non-random distribution of parasitism. In general, stability will be enhanced by: (i) the host population becoming more clumped in its distribution; (ii) more time spent in transit between patches, T_0 (see also Murdoch & Oaten 1975; Murdoch 1977); and (iii) a large difference between the minimum and maximum time spent per patch.

For any given spatial distribution of hosts, there is an optimal allocation of parasitoid searching effort that maximizes the overall rate of encounter between parasitoids and hosts. Behaviour that leads to such searching strategies is likely to enhance fitness and hence be at a selective premium, and it is the current awareness of this that has led to the burgeoning literature on optimal foraging strategies of predators and parasitoids (e.g. Krebs, Ryan & Charnov 1974; Charnov 1976; Cook & Hubbard 1977; Krebs, Stephens & Sutherland 1983). The dynamic consequences of such optimal foraging have been explored within the framework of eqns (12)–(14) by Comins & Hassell (1979). They chose omniscient parasitoids that are able unfailingly to select the currently most profitable patches, and they showed how strongly stabilizing such behaviour can be, provided the host distribution is sufficiently uneven and the host rate of increase not too high.

Unfortunately, these host–parasitoid models become rapidly more complicated as additional details of parasitoid foraging behaviour are included. Such complications soon lead to analytically unmanageable models, particularly when dealing with more elaborate systems containing more than two interacting species. Population ecologists are continually faced with this dilemma of balancing the need to make assumptions more realistic against the need to keep the equations tractable. One solution is to seek a minimally complicated expression that may only crudely describe the outcome of the behaviour, but which can readily be used in studying the dynamics of complex systems. An example is that of May (1978) who adopted the negative binomial to describe the distribution of encounters with hosts; in this case

$$f(P_t) = (1 + aP_t/k)^{-k}. \tag{15}$$

Here a is the searching efficiency and k the clumping parameter of the distribution. Within the framework of eqns (12) and (13), the interaction is now stable for all $k < 1$.

Equation (15) makes no explicit statement about foraging behaviour. It is merely assumed that unspecified processes lead to a clumped distribution of attacks over all hosts. Non-random foraging in a patchy environment is certainly one of these as shown, for example, by Hassell (1980) for a tachinid parasitoid, *Cyzenis albicans*, of the winter moth, *Operophthera brumata*.

Figure 1.2a shows the spatial distribution of parasitism over several trees in 1965, and Fig. 1.2b the resulting negative binomial distribution of attacks amongst the total winter moth population summed over all trees. Alternatively, the process may have nothing to do with spatial patchiness, but result from variability among host individuals in their defences (Hassell & Anderson 1984). For example, Walker (1963) has found gene-dependent resistance in *Drosophila melanogaster* to its cynipid parasitoid, *Pseudeucoila bochei*, and

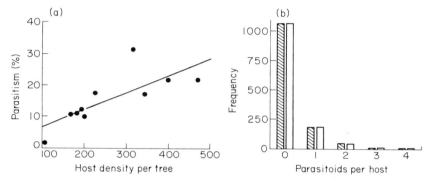

FIG. 1.2. (a) The pattern of parasitism by *C. albicans* in relation to winter moth (*O. brumata*) larval density per m² canopy area is shown for a stand of hawthorn, hazel and blackthorn in Wytham Wood in 1965. (b) The observed (□) and expected (▧) frequencies of winter moth larvae containing different numbers of *C. albicans* larvae are shown; the expected values come from a negative binomial distribution with $k = 0.547$. The data in Fig. 1.2b are from the same winter moth larvae sampled to give Fig. 1.2a, but now pooled and dissected to reveal the incidence of superparasitism. (Further details are given in Hassell 1980.)

Wellington (1960) documents variable degrees of physical defence in forest tent caterpillars, *Malacosoma disstria*, to ovipositing *Sarcophaga*.

Whatever the underlying mechanism that generates non-random parasitism, the dynamic effects are merely the consequence of some host individuals being more at risk than others. It is reminiscent of the single-species interactions discussed above where both spatial unevenness (e.g. De Jong 1979) and individual variability (Lomnicki 1980) had much the same dynamic effects.

Host–disease interactions

Another good example of how behavioural and other processes that lead to some form of heterogeneity can be followed through to the dynamics of the interacting populations comes from recent work on host–parasite systems (e.g. Anderson & May 1978, 1979, 1982; May & Anderson 1978, 1979, 1983).

Once again the notion of a habitat with n patches can be retained, but in this case each host individual is best regarded as a patch. These hosts are exposed to parasitism by the infective stages of a parasite population, whose specific distribution per host determines the extent of the spatial heterogeneity. A population model for such a system is given by Anderson & May (1978), following Crofton (1971). With a random parasite distribution per host the populations exhibit neutrally stable cycles, much as in the basic Lotka–Volterra predator–prey model. When, however, the parasite distribution is changed from random to clumped, the stability properties are altered towards damped oscillations. Specifically, if the distribution is assumed to be negative binomial (as is often observed to be the case: Anderson & May 1978), damping is most rapid for small values of k (severe clumping). In the limit $k \to \infty$, we are back to the random distribution; the damping time becomes infinite and neutral stability is recovered. The enhanced stability conferred by clumping arises because the bulk of the parasites are concentrated on or in fewer and fewer host individuals as the parasite distribution per host becomes more clumped. Since the host mortality is often a function of parasite burden, the relatively few hosts that are heavily parasitized will die, and hence a large proportion of the parasites will also fail to survive. Aggregation of the parasites thus increases the density dependence acting on the parasite population as a whole and so acts strongly as a stabilizing mechanism. Such contagion in parasite numbers per host can arise in several ways, comparable to those found in host-parasitoid systems. First, it may be due to the spatial distribution and behaviour of infective stages, as found by Keymer & Anderson (1979). Second, there may be behavioural and genetic heterogeneity among individual hosts, as discussed by Anderson (1978) for the infection of snails by miracidia, or, much more broadly, whenever resistance to infection (whether natural or by immunization) is being considered.

Prey–predator interactions

The way in which the foraging behaviour of parasitoids or the transmission behaviour of macroparasites (such as hookworms or schistosomes) translates into density-dependent reproductive success, and thence into population dynamics, is substantially simpler than is the case for most predators. Although there is a good deal of theoretical work, and an illuminating laboratory experiment (Huffaker 1958), on the way interactions between prey and predators in individual patches relate to overall population dynamics in a heterogeneous environment, there is as yet nothing like the detailed contact between individual behaviour and population dynamics that exists for host–parasitoid systems. To go from the behaviour of individual predators to the population-level functional and numerical responses to changes in prey abundance is simply more difficult for lions, or even for assassin bugs, than for parasitoids or macroparasites.

One general observation that can usefully be made, however, is that herding, shoaling or other aggregative behaviour is often found among prey populations, even in spatially uniform environments. Various mechanisms may lead to such aggregative behaviour: in some cases, per capita efficiency in foraging or in detecting predators has been demonstrated to be higher when individuals group together (see, e.g. Magurran & Pitcher 1983); in other cases, there are mechanical advantages to swimming or flying in groups (see, e.g. Lighthill 1975); and it can even be that groups are formed by 'the geometry of the selfish herd', as individuals jostle to avoid being at the exposed edge of the group (Hamilton 1971). Whatever their cause, such patterns of prey aggregation can have an important influence on the dynamics of the system.

Some practical applications of these ideas come from the harvesting of fish and whale populations. The densities of many exploited populations in the sea used to be, and some still are, estimated by assuming the density to be linearly proportional to the catch per unit (fishing) effort, CPUE. Setting aside the difficulties of estimating the relevant proportionality constant, especially when harvesting technology is changing, it is clear that any such estimate rests on the assumption that the exploited stock is distributed homogeneously and isotropically throughout the region fished, like the molecules in an ideal gas. Although this linear relation between population size and CPUE may be a workable approximation for some ground fish such as haddock, cod or whiting (where there usually do not seem to be dense concentrations, at least on any scale relating to fishing methods), it is questionable for shoaling fish like herring and for many whaling situations. Indeed, for a species that occurs in highly aggregated schools in relatively predictable locations, it can be that CPUE is almost independent of stock density; with sonar and other techniques, the effort required to catch the last 100 shoals may be not significantly greater than that required to catch the first 100. Beddington and co-workers have emphasized how prey aggregation and other behavioural factors (such as handling time, and other complications of the kind discussed in connection with eqn (12) above) can produce significant non-linearities in the relation between stock density and CPUE, and have developed more sophisticated estimation methods that take account of these behavioural complications (Beddington 1979). In particular, Beddington's work has led to revisions in the estimated magnitudes of the populations of some exploited whale species. Other broadly related studies note that the krill, *Euphausia superba*, which form the bulk of the diet of baleen whales and many other creatures in the Southern Ocean, occur in large patches rather than being distributed uniformly; this has implications for the dynamics of krill-whale interactions, for human harvesting of krill and, *a fortiori*, for any multispecies management of the Southern Ocean in which krill and whales are both harvested (May *et al.* 1979; Beddington 1984).

In summary, we have indicated some work which seeks to understand how selective forces acting on individuals produce aggregative behaviour, and other work which relates such aggregative behaviour to features of the overall population dynamics in prey–predator associations. In view of the practical importance of some of these questions, it seems likely that this area may see continuing advances toward understanding population dynamics in terms of measurable aspects of the behaviour of individuals.

SOCIAL STRUCTURE AND POPULATION DYNAMICS

Although the bulk of this article is devoted to the way foraging behaviour—broadly defined—can affect population dynamics, we now turn briefly to survey some of the ways in which mating systems, sex ratios, territoriality, and migration or dispersal patterns can affect dynamics.

Adaptive sex ratios

In this Symposium, Waage & Godfray (p. 449) have already indicated how local mate competition (LMC: Hamilton 1967) and other factors influencing sex allocation can lead to the sex ratio of progeny depending on the density of the adult population. As they mention, such density dependence in sex ratios affects the overall population dynamics. In particular, for host–parasitoid associations we note that it is female parasitoids who oviposit in hosts, so that in eqn (13) the factor $f(P_t)$ describing the probability that a host escapes parasitism depends on the density of female parasitoids, P_t. The right hand side of eqn (14), however, simply represents the total number of parasitoids produced, male and female. If the sex ratio were constant at 0·5 or some other steady value, this factor could be incorporated in the parameter c in eqn (14), whence P_{t+1} on the left hand side would represent the number of female parasitoids (only) in generation $t+1$. But if the sex ratio of offspring depends on the density of hosts and/or female parasitoids in generation t, via LMC or other mechanisms, then the factor c becomes $c(N_t, P_t)$. Hassell, Waage & May (1983) have shown explicitly how various sex ratio effects can influence both the equilibrium levels of host and parasitoid populations, and the stability of such equilibria.

More generally, it may be observed that essentially all ecology texts present the relationship between individual life histories (reflected in age-specific survival and fecundity, l_x and m_x) and population dynamics (encapsulated in a per capita population growth rate, r) as if sex ratios were age-independent constants. In particular, in human demography the fecundity schedules, m_x (which ultimately depend on male–female interactions!), are usually taken to be functions simply of female age, with no reference to the density or structure of the male and female populations (for an exception which does give a formal analysis of the way fecundity depends on male and female population structure, see Yellin & Samuelson 1977).

Models for the dynamics of baleen whale populations, for example, implicitly assume a sex ratio constant at 0·5, in which case one may equivalently compute either the number of female offspring produced per adult female, or the total number of offspring produced per adult. The resulting model for the total number of sexually mature baleen whales in generation $t+1$, N_{t+1}, thus has the basic form

$$N_{t+1} = (1-\mu)N_t + (1-\mu)^T R(N_{t-T}). \tag{16}$$

Here μ is the annual per capita mortality rate (assumed independent of age for this example, although generalization is straightforward); T is the number of years taken to attain sexual maturity; and $R(N)$ is some non-linear recruitment function, describing the total number of progeny produced by a population of size N. Although it may represent a useful first approximation thus to assume sex ratios are immutable constants in human, baleen whale, and other large mammal populations, a few studies such as that for red deer presented by Clutton-Brock and Albon (p. 557) indicate that sex ratios may depend on population density and other biological and environmental factors, and that this in turn can affect population dynamics.

Mating systems

An explicit instance where the mating system and age-dependent sex ratios have an important influence on overall dynamics arises in sperm whale populations. Sperm whales have a more elaborate social structure than do baleen whales: females attain sexual maturity at a significantly younger age than males (with the times taken being approximately $T_f = 10$ years and $T_m = 25$ years for females and males, respectively); females aggregate in 'pods', which typically contain about ten sexually mature females; sexually mature males join the pods during the breeding season but spend most of the year apart, travelling further south in the summer than do females; and, as is usual in such socially-structured systems, there is pronounced sexual dimorphism (in contrast with baleen whales). A description of the population biology of sperm whales consequently requires two equations of the form of eqn (16), one for each sex. We represent the populations of sexually mature males and females by M and N, respectively, and denote all parameters pertaining to the male and female populations by subscripts m and f, respectively, to get

$$M_{t+1} = (1-\mu_m)M_t + \frac{1}{2}(1-\mu_m)^{T_m}R(N_{t-T_m}, M_{t-T_m}),\qquad(17)$$

$$N_{t+1} = (1-\mu_f)N_t + \frac{1}{2}(1-\mu_f)^{T_f}R(N_{t-T_f}, M_{t-T_f}).\qquad(18)$$

Here $R(N,M)$ is the density-dependent recruitment function, giving the total number of progeny produced by a population of N females and M males; it is assumed that half these progeny are female (with T_f years elapsing before the survivors are recruited to the adult population), and that half are male (taking T_m years to mature). For baleen whales, the function $R(N)$ in eqn (16) is based on the assumption that the sex ratio is 50:50 at all ages, and that the pregnancy rate among females is independent of male population density. Things are more complicated for sperm whales, and we write

$$R(N,M) = N\phi(N)\pi(N,M).\qquad(19)$$

Here the 'mating probability' $\pi(N,M)$ represents the probability that a given female in oestrus will encounter (and be inseminated by) an adult male; in general, π can depend both on N and M. The quantity ϕ then represents the per capita fecundity of females, assuming $\pi = 1$ (i.e. assuming pregnancy rates are not diminished by inability to find a mate). In the computations of the International Whaling Commission, IWC, ϕ has the form

$$\phi = P + Q[1 - (N/K)^z].\qquad(20)$$

Here P is the per capita fecundity around the pristine equilibrium density of females, K, and $P+Q$ is the intrinsic per capita fecundity in the limit as population density N falls to low values. The phenomenological parameter z measures the steepness of the density-dependent response ($z = 2\cdot4$ in most IWC calculations).

Let η denote the average number of adult females in a pod. Then the 'effective sex ratio', ρ, may be defined as the number of sexually mature males per pod of sexually mature females:

$$\rho = \eta M/N.\qquad(21)$$

If we assume that one adult male will take possession of a pod of females for the entire breeding season, and that males are essentially infinitely efficient in finding 'unowned' pods, then the mating probability π takes the simple form:

$$\pi(\rho) = 1 \quad , \quad \text{if } \rho > 1,\qquad(22a)$$

$$\pi(\rho) = \rho \quad , \quad \text{if } \rho < 1.\qquad(22b)$$

For simplicity, we also assume male and female survival probabilities are equal: $\mu_m = \mu_f = \mu$. At the pristine equilibrium we have the population of adult males constant at M^*, and of females constant at $N^* = K$ (whence $\phi = P$). It follows from eqns (17) and (18) that the effective sex ratio at equilibrium is

$$\rho^* = \eta(1 - \mu)^{T_m - T_f}, \tag{23}$$

and also that the various demographic parameters are related by the so-called 'balance equation',

$$2\mu(1 - \mu)^{-T_f} = P\pi(\rho^*). \tag{24}$$

Typical IWC parameter choices are $\mu = 0.055$ year^{-1}, $P = 0.20$ year^{-1}, $Q = 0.05$ year^{-1}, $\eta = 10$, $T_f = 10$ years and $T_m = 25$ years. It follows that $\rho^* \simeq 4.3$, so that the mating probability, π, is unity in the pristine equilibrium state.

We may now study the sustainable yields that can be taken from this system. These calculations are presented in detail elsewhere (May 1980), and are summarized in Fig. 1.3 where X_f represents the female population scaled

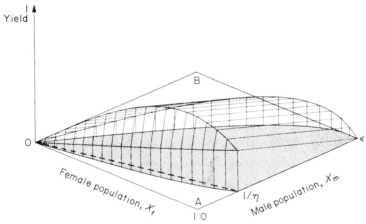

FIG. 1.3. This three-dimensional figure aims to show the sustainable yield of sperm whales as a function of the female and male population densities, X_f and X_m; the yield (vertical axis) is taken to be the unweighted sum of the yields of females and males; combinations of X_f and X_m lying in region A of the X_f–X_m plane have a male population too low to allow a sustainable harvest of females; in region B, the female population is too low to allow a sustainable harvest of males; in the pie-shaped stippled region, however, sustainable harvests of this effectively two-species system are possible. As indicated clearly in the figure, the maximum sustainable yield lies along the line $\rho = 1$ ($X_m = X_f/\eta$), corresponding to there being one adult male per pod of females. This figure is based on the equations given in the text, and the parameters are chosen to be close to those used by the IWC: $\varepsilon = 0.04$, $z = 2.4$, $Q/P = 0.5$, $\eta = 10$ (ε is the number of adult males per adult female at equilibrium, $\varepsilon = \rho^*/\varepsilon$ with ρ^* given by eqn (23)). For further discussion, see the text.

against the unharvested equilibrium density K, $X_f = N/K$ (so that without harvesting $X_f = 1$) and X_m represents the male population, also scaled against K, $X_m = M/K$ (so that without harvesting $X_m = M^*/K = \rho^*/\eta = (1 - \mu)^{T_m - T_f} \equiv \varepsilon$). For harvesting regimes that lead to combinations of X_f and X_m lying in the region A in the X_f–X_m plane, the male population is too low to allow a sustainable harvest of females. For harvesting regimes corresponding to region B, the female population is too low to allow a sustainable harvest of males. In the pie-shaped stippled region of the X_f–X_m plane, however, sustainable harvests of this effectively two-species system are possible. As indicated clearly in the figure, the maximum sustainable yield, MSY, lies along the line where the effective sex ratio is maintained at unity ($\rho = 1$, $X_m = X_f/\eta$).

Figure 1.3 is in vivid contrast with familiar single species MSY curves, in which yield is plotted as a function of stock density with no regard to sex ratio or social structure. It can be seen that in Fig. 1.3 it is possible to 'fall off a cliff' into the unsustainable harvesting regimes A or B if either male or female populations are exploited excessively heavily in relation to the other. In this way, the mating systems and social organization of animals like sperm whales can make for major complications in resource management.

Much of the above discussion, and Fig. 1.3 in particular, rests on the simple form for the mating probability given in eqn (22). This assumes males to be infinitely efficient in finding females, so that, as it were, the last male is sure to find the last pod. In practice, the IWC acknowledges the absurdity of this assumption by allowing for a 'reserve male ratio', rather arbitrarily set at 1·3; as illustrated in Fig. 1.4; this corresponds to replacing eqn (22) by

$$\pi(\rho) = 1, \qquad \text{if } \rho > 1\cdot3, \qquad (25a)$$

$$\pi(\rho) = \rho/1\cdot3, \qquad \text{if } \rho < 1\cdot3. \qquad (25b)$$

The effect is to introduce some conservatism in setting quotas, by displacing the MSY curve to higher values of X_m in Fig. 1.3. May & Beddington (1980) have provided expressions for $\pi(\rho)$ that are based on biological assumptions about the way males search for pods of females, and the way the searching efficiency may be affected by male and female population densities. This work is reviewed at length elsewhere (May 1980), but the gist of it is indicated by curves (b) and (c) in Fig. 1.4. These two curves show the mating probability, π, as a function of the number of males per pod $\rho = \eta M/N$, for two different assumptions about the searching efficiency of the males (curve a, representing eqn (22) for π, effectively corresponds to males whose searching efficiency is infinite).

All the curves in Fig. 1.4 are based on the assumption that 'harem masters' stay with their pod throughout the breeding season. This is not certain,

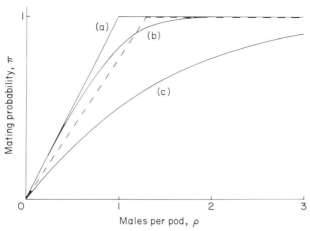

FIG. 1.4. The mating probability, π, is shown as a function of the effective sex ratio (the number of adult males per pod of females), ρ, under various assumptions. Curve (a) shows the crude model of eqn (22); the dashed curve shows the eqn (25) actually used by the IWC (with the 'safety factor' of 1·3); and curves (b) and (c) illustrate the more realistic model of May & Beddington (1980; see also May 1980), in which a parameter α measures the 'searching efficiency' of the males ($\alpha = 5$ in curve (b) and $\alpha = 1$ in curve (c)).

however, and it could be that the behavioural ecology of sperm whales is such that males stay briefly to inseminate receptive females and then move on, within the breeding season, rather than defending exclusive ownership of a single pod for the entire breeding season. Such behaviour would lead to a yet more complicated dependence of π upon M and N than is shown in Fig. 1.4 (for details, see May 1980).

We have dwelt on sperm whales because we think they typify the way social behaviour can make for a variety of complications in the overall dynamics of a species. As made plain by Fig. 1.3, many of these complications can have substantial practical implications. Sperm whales are also perhaps typical in that some of the important details—such as whether harem masters stay with their harems throughout the breeding season—are not yet described, much less understood in evolutionary terms.

Territoriality

Territorial behaviour of one kind or another can often be understood in terms of selective forces acting on the foraging or reproductive efforts of individuals, and it is in this light that territoriality is commonly studied. It is equally true, however, that territorial behaviour can be the main factor regulating population size, or otherwise influencing population dynamics (Maynard Smith 1974).

A paradigmatic recent study is that by Woolfenden & Fitzpatrick (1984) on the Florida scrub jay. These authors show, on the one hand, how helping at the nest and other aspects of the behavioural ecology of individual birds relate to the territorial social structure of the population, and, on the other hand, how this territorial social structure relates to the macroscopic dynamics of the population of jays. There is clearly room for more such studies that connect individual behaviour to population dynamics, with territoriality as the intermediate link in the chain.

Migration and dispersal

Although there is an enormous literature on migration and dispersal (e.g. Baker 1978; Swingland & Greenwood 1983), there are very few studies explicitly relating these phenomena to the magnitude and stability of the populations in question. An exception is the recent work of Taylor and collaborators (e.g. Taylor et al. 1983), which puts the general view that dispersal behaviour is the determining factor in the population dynamics of many invertebrate and other species. Another exception is the recent work on neotropical migratory birds in North-eastern America, which seeks to comprehend the population dynamics of particular species (in response to forest fragmentation in their breeding grounds) in terms of measurable parameters characterizing the migratory and reproductive behaviour of individuals (Whitcomb et al. 1981; May 1981; Wilcove 1984); these studies have obvious relevance to conservation of such neotropical migrants.

PRUDENT PREDATORS?

Up to this point, we have concentrated on situations where the dynamics of populations can be deduced, with varying degrees of explicitness, from the behaviour of individuals. Less commonly, however, it can be possible to make deductions about individual behaviour from data at the population level. An example of this inverse phenomenon follows.

Much has been written on the subject of whether natural selection is likely to cause predators to be 'prudent', with prudent usually taken to mean exploiting their prey at around MSY levels. Some conservation and wildlife management literature takes it for granted that predators are likely to have evolved to be prudent in this sense. More thoughtful authors have noted the group selectionist character of many earlier arguments, and have sought to understand how predator behaviour is in fact likely to evolve (see, for example, Slobodkin 1974; Gilpin 1975; Maiorana 1976; Mertz & Wade 1976; Schaffer & Rosenzweig 1978; Roughgarden 1979).

For many host–parasitoid associations, however, a purely empirical statement can be made about whether or not the parasitoids are exploiting their host populations at MSY. Along the general lines laid down in eqns (13) and (14), we consider a host population N whose dynamics in the absence of parasitoids obeys

$$N_{t+1} = \lambda g(N_t)N_t. \tag{26}$$

Here λ is the intrinsic finite rate of increase, as before, and $g(N)$ represents density-dependent effects that may regulate the population in the absence of parasitoids. This population will have an equilibrium density N^*, determined from the relation

$$\lambda g(N^*) = 1. \tag{27}$$

(We leave open the question of whether the population is steady at this level, or fluctuates cyclically or chaotically around it.) Suppose now that a population of parasitoids exploits this host population at MSY. Standard techniques allow us to calculate the MSY level of the exploited host population, N_{MSY}, which depends only on λ and on the functional form of $g(N)$. The calculations are outlined in Appendix III. Figure 1.5 shows the degree to which the host population is depressed below its parasitoid-free level, $q_{MSY} \equiv N_{MSY}/N^*$, as a function of λ for two opposite extreme assumptions about the functional form of $g(N)$: curve a is for $g(N)$ of the form of eqn (2), corresponding to scramble competition; curve b is for $g(N)$ of the form of eqn (5), corresponding to contest competition.

In a study altogether independent of the above considerations, Beddington, Free & Lawton (1978) have estimated the parasitoid reduction of host density below the parasitoid-free value (q-value) for ten host–parasitoid associations in the field and laboratory. These actual q-values are indicated by the horizontal lines at the left in Fig. 1.5. The six solid lines come from field studies, and the four dashed lines from laboratory studies; in all instances the λ-values are uncertain (which is why only the q-values are indicated). It will be seen that the q-values for the four laboratory situations could be consistent with the parasitoids exploiting their hosts at a MSY level, but the six field q-values are grossly inconsistent with MSY exploitation.

This population-level line of attack is quite different from studies which seek to determine whether predators are prudent on the basis of the evolution of individual behaviour. Although our answers are admittedly crude, they do appear to say that, in natural settings, at least six species of parasitoids exploit their host populations to well below MSY densities. There may well be scope for other applications of this general approach.

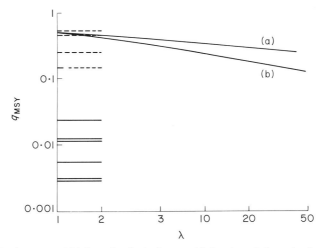

Fig. 1.5. The degree to which host density is depressed below its pristine value by a parasitoid that 'harvests' the host population for maximum sustainable yield, q_{MSY}, is shown as a function of the intrinsic growth rate of the host population, λ. Curve (a) is for the case where the parasitoid-free host population is regulated by 'scramble' competition, eqn (2), and curve (b) is for the opposite extreme case of 'contest' competition, eqn (5). The solid horizontal lines to the left show estimated q-values for six host–parasitoid associations in the field, and the broken horizontal lines are similar estimates for four laboratory populations (from Beddington *et al.* 1975). It does not appear likely that the six field populations of parasitoids exploit their host populations at MSY.

CONCLUSION

Rather than recapitulate the points we have made above, we return to focus on one aspect of the relation between foraging behaviour and population dynamics.

Much of our discussion of foraging behaviour centred around examples set within the framework either of a given number of discrete patches among which the population(s) were distributed, or of individual phenotypic or genotypic variability. In all cases the central conclusion is emphatic: the more contagious the distributions, the greater is the population stability.

In doing this, certain behavioural, and potentially important, issues have been side-stepped. For instance, there is the question of what for different animals constitutes a patch, which raises daunting problems of scale. The term 'patch' has been variously interpreted (see Wiens (1976) for a thorough review). We may in general look upon it as a spatial subunit of the habitat in which an aggregation of food items of feeding places occur, whether it be 'the prey of predators, the host of parasitoids, the leaves of caterpillars, the feeding sites for mosquitoes, the nectaries and anthers for bees, and so on' (Hassell & Southwood 1978). Such patches are most readily identified when associated with an obvious, discrete natural unit, such as a plant or a leaf harbouring insects. But as Waage (1977, 1979) has stressed, the appropriate dimensions of a patch are set not by what *we* perceive, but by the behaviour of the animals themselves. When trying to identify patch boundaries, we should thus look to specific changes in behaviour that are associated with the recognition of patch and non-patch areas. The proper recognition of patch boundaries is crucially important in studying the dynamic consequences of spatial heterogeneity, and provides a good example of how the population ecologist must lean heavily on the study of animal behaviour.

ACKNOWLEDGMENTS

This work was supported in part by the NSF under grant BSR83-03772.

REFERENCES

Abramowitz, M. & Stegun, I.A. (1964). *Handbook of Mathematical Functions*. US National Bureau of Standards, Washington D.C. [Reprinted by Dover, New York, 1965.]

Anderson, R.M. (1978). The regulation of host population growth by parasitic species. *Parasitology*, **76**, 119–158.

Anderson, R.M. & May, R.M. (1978). Regulation and stability of host–parasite population interactions. 1. Regulatory processes. *Journal of Animal Ecology*, **47**, 219–247.

Anderson, R.M. & May, R.M. (1979). Population biology of infectious diseases. Part 1. *Nature*, **280**, 361–367.

Anderson, R.M. & May, R.M. (1982). The population dynamics and control of human helminth infections. *Nature*, **297**, 557–563.

Atkinson, W.D. & Shorrocks, B. (1981). Competition on a divided and ephemeral resource: a simulation model. *Journal of Animal Ecology*, **50**, 461–471.

Baker, R.R. (1978). *The Evolutionary Ecology of Animal Migration*. Holmes and Meier, New York.

Beddington, J.R. (1979). On some problems of estimating population abundance from catch data. *Report of the International Whaling Commission*, **29**, 149–154.

Beddington, J.R. (1984). On some problems of modelling the population dynamics of krill. *Polar Biology* (in press).

Beddington, J.R., Free, C.A. & Lawton, J.H. (1975). Dynamical complexity in predator–prey models framed in difference equations. *Nature*, **255**, 58–60.

Beddington, J.R., Free, C.A. & Lawton, J.H. (1978). Characteristics of successful natural enemies in models of biological control of insect pests. *Nature*, **273**, 513–519.

Bellows, T.S. (1981). The descriptive properties of some models for density dependence. *Journal of Animal Ecology*, **50**, 139–156.

Bliss, C.I. & Owen, A.R.G. (1958). Negative binomial distribution with a common k. *Biometricia*, **45**, 37–58.

Boswell, M.T. & Patil, G.P. (1970). Chance mechanisms generating the negative binomial distribution. *Random Counts in Models and Structures* (Ed. by G.P. Patil), pp. 1–22. Pennsylvania University Press; University Park, Pa London, USA.

Brian, A.D. (1957). Differences in the flowers visited by four species of bumble-bees and their causes. *Journal of Animal Ecology*, **26**, 71–98.

Charnov, E.L. (1976). Optimal foraging: the marginal theorem. *Theoretical Population Biology*, **9**, 126–136.

Comins, H.N. & Hassell, M.P. (1979). The dynamics of optimally foraging predators and parasitoids. *Journal of Animal Ecology*, **48**, 335–351.

Cook, R.M. & Hubbard, S.F. (1977). Adaptive searching strategies in insect parasites. *Journal of Animal Ecology*, **46**, 115–125.

Crofton, H.D. (1971). A quantitative approach to parasitism. *Parasitology*, **62**, 179–194.

DeJong, G. (1979). The influence of the distribution of juveniles over patches of food on the dynamics of a population. *Netherlands Journal of Zoology*, **29**, 33–51.

DeJong, G. (1981). The influence of dispersal pattern on the evolution of fecundity. *Netherlands Journal of Zoology*, **32**, 1–30.

Gilpin, M.E. (1975). *Group Selection in Predator–Prey Communities*. Princeton University Press, Princeton, New Jersey.

Hamilton, W.D. (1967). Extraordinary sex ratios. *Science*, **156**, 477–488.

Hamilton, W.D. (1971). Geometry for the selfish herd. *Journal of Theoretical Biology*, **31**, 295–311.

Harcourt, D.G. (1965). Spatial pattern in the cabbage looper, *Trichoplusia ni*, on crucifers. *Annals of the Entomological Society of America*, **58**, 89–94.

Hassell, M.P. (1975). Density-dependence in single species populations. *Journal of Animal Ecology*, **44**, 288–295.

Hassell, M.P. (1978). *The Dynamics of Arthropod Predator–Prey Systems*. Princeton University Press, Princeton, New Jersey.

Hassell, M.P. (1979). Non-random search in predator–prey models. *Fortschritte der Zoologie*, **25**, 311–330.

Hassell, M.P. (1980). Foraging strategies, population models and biological control: a case study. *Journal of Animal Ecology*, **49**, 603–628.

Hassell, M.P. & Anderson, R.M. (1984). Host susceptibility as a component in host-parasitoid systems. *Journal of Animal Ecology*, **53**, 611–622.

Hassell, M.P., Lawton, J.H. & May, R.M. (1976). Patterns of dynamical behaviour in single species populations. *Journal of Animal Ecology*, **45**, 471–486.

Hassell, M.P. & May, R.M. (1973). Stability in insect host–parasite models. *Journal of Animal Ecology*, **42**, 693–726.

Hassell, M.P. & May, R.M. (1974). Aggregation in predators and insect parasites and its effect on stability. *Journal of Animal Ecology*, **43**, 567–594.

Hassell, M.P. & Southwood, T.R.E. (1978). Foraging strategies of insects. *Ann. Rev. Ecol. Syst.*, **9**, 75–98.

Hassell, M.P., Waage, J.K. & May, R.M. (1983). Variable parasitoid sex ratios and their effect on host–parasitoid dynamics. *Journal of Animal Ecology*, **52**, 889–904.

Heinrich, B. (1979). *Economics*. Harvard University Press, Cambridge, Mass., USA.

Huffaker, C.B. (1958). Experimental studies on predation: dispersion factors and predator–prey oscillations. *Hilgardia*, **27**, 343–383.

Ives, A.R. & May, R.M. (1984). Competition within and between species in a patchy environment: relations between microscopic and macroscopic models. *Journal of Theoretical Biology* (in press).

Johnson, L.K. & Hubbell, S.P. (1974). Aggression and competition among stingless bees: field studies. *Ecology*, **55**, 120–129.

Keymer, A.E. & Anderson, R.M. (1979). The dynamics of infection of *Tribolium confusum* by *Hymenolepis diminuta*: the influence of infective stage density and spatial distribution. *Parasitology*, **79**, 195–207.

Krebs, J.R., Ryan, J. & Charnov, E.L. (1974). Hunting by expectation or optimal foraging? A study of patch use by chickadees. *Animal Behaviour*, **22**, 953–964.

Krebs, J.R., Stephens, D.W. & Sutherland, W.J. (1983). Perspectives in optimal foraging. *Perspectives in Ornithology*, Cambridge University Press, Cambridge.

Lawton, J.H. & Hassell, M.P. (1984). Interspecific competition in insects. *Ecological Entomology* (Ed. by C.B. Huffaker & R.L. Rabb). John Wiley; New York (in press).

Lighthill, M.J. (1975). *Mathematical Biofluiddynamics.* SIAM, Philadelphia, Pa., USA.

Lloyd, M. & White, J. (1980). On recovering patchy microspatial distributions with competition models. *American Naturalist*, **115**, 29–44.

Lomnicki, A. (1978). Individual differences between animals and natural regulation of their numbers. *Journal of Animal Ecology*, **47**, 461–475.

Lomnicki, A. (1980). Regulation of population density due to individual differences and patchy environment. *Oikos*, **35**, 185–193.

Lomnicki, A. (1982). Individual heterogenity and population regulation. *Current Problems in Sociobiology* (pp. 153–167), Cambridge University Press, Cambridge.

Magurran, A.E. & Pitcher, T.J. (1983). Foraging, timidity and shoal size in minnows and goldfish. *Behavioural Ecology and Sociobiology.*, **12**, 147–152.

Maiorana, V.C. (1976). Reproductive value, prudent predators, and group selection. *American Naturalist*, **110**, 486–489.

May, R.M. (1978). Host–parasitoid systems in patchy environments: a phenomenological model. *Journal of Animal Ecology*, **47**, 833–843.

May, R.M. (1980). Mathematical models in whaling and fisheries management. *Some Mathematical Questions in Biology*, Vol. 13 (Ed. by G.F. Oster), pp. 1–64. American Mathematical Society; Providence, R.I.

May, R.M. (1981). Modelling recolonization by neotropical migrants in habitats with changing patch structure, with notes on the age structure of populations. *Forest Islands Dynamics in Man-Dominated Landscapes* (Ed. by R.L. Burgess & D.M. Sharpe), pp. 207–213. Springer Verlag, New York.

May, R.M. & Anderson, R.M. (1978). Regulation and stability of host–parasite population interactions. II. Destabilizing processes. *Journal of Animal Ecology*, **47**, 249–267.

May, R.M. & Anderson, R.M. (1979). Population biology of infectious diseases. Part II. *Nature*, **280**, 455–461.

May, R.M. & Anderson, R.M. (1983). Epidemiology and genetics in the coevolution of parasites and hosts. *Proceedings of the Royal Society*, **B219**, 281–313.

May, R.M., Beddington, J.R., Clark, C.W., Holt, S.J. & Laws, R.M. (1979). Management of multispecies fisheries. *Science*, **205**, 267–277.

May, R.M. & Beddington, J.R. (1980). The effect of adult sex ratio and density on the fecundity of sperm whales. *Report of the International Whaling Commission*, Special Issue 2, pp. 213–217.

May, R.M., Hassell, M.P., Anderson, R.M. & Tonkyn, D.W. (1981). Density dependence in host–parasitoid models. *Journal of Animal Ecology*, **50**, 855–865.

May, R.M. & Oster, G.F. (1976). Bifurcations and dynamic complexity in simple ecological models. *American Naturalist*, **110**, 573–599.

Maynard Smith, J. (1974). *Models in Ecology.* Cambridge University Press, Cambridge.

Mertz, D.B. & Wade, M.J. (1976). The prudent prey and the prudent predator. *American Naturalist*, **110**, 489–496.

Morse, D.H. (1977). Resource partitioning in bumble bees: the role of behavioural factors. *Science*, **197**, 678–680.

Murdoch, W.W. (1977). Stabilizing effects of spatial heterogeneity in predator-prey systems. *Theoretical Population Biology*, **11**, 252–273.

Murdoch, W.W. & Oaten, A. (1975). Predation and population stability. *Advances in Ecological Research*, **9**, 2–131.

Nicholson, A.J. (1933). The balance of animal populations. *Journal of Animal Ecology*, **2**, 131–178.

Roughgarden, J. (1979). *Theory of Population Genetics and Evolutionary Ecology: An Introduction.* Macmillan. New York.

Schaffer, W.M., Buchmann, S.L., Kleinhans, S., Schaffer, M.J. & Antrim, J. (1983). Competition for nectar between introduced honey bees and native North American bees and ants. *Ecology*, **64**, 564–577.

Schaffer, W.M. & Rosenzweig, M.L. (1978). Homage to the Red Queen. I. Coevolution of predators and their victims. *Theoretical Population Biology*, **14**, 135–157.

Schaffer, W.M. & Schaffer, M.V. (1979). The adaptive significance of variations in reproductive habit in Agavacease. II. Pollinator foraging behaviour and selection for increased reproductive expenditure. *Ecology*, **60**, 1051–1069.

Slobodkin, L.B. (1974). Prudent predation does not require group selection. *American Naturalist*, **108**, 665–678.

Stubbs, M. (1977). Density dependence in the life cycles of animals and its importance in *K*- and *r*-strategies. *Journal of Animal Ecology*, **46**, 677–688.

Swingland, I.R. & Greenwood, P.J. (1983). *The Ecology of Animal Movement.* Oxford University Press, Oxford.

Taylor, L.R., Taylor, R.A.J., Woiwod, I.P. & Perry, J.N. (1983). Behavioural dynamics. *Nature*, **303**, 801–804.

Taylor, L.R., Woiwod, I.P. & Perry, J.N. (1978). The density-dependence of spatial behaviour and the rarity of randomness. *Journal of Animal Ecology*, **47**, 383–406.

Thomas, W.R., Pomerantz, M.J. & Gilpin, M.E. (1980). Chaos, asymmetric growth and group selection for dynamical stability. *Ecology*, **61**, 1312–1320.

Varley, G.C. (1949). Population changes in German forest pests. *Journal of Animal Ecology*, **18**, 117–122.

Waage, J.K. (1977). *Behavioural aspects of foraging in the parasitoid,* Nemeritis canescens. Unpubl. Ph.D. thesis, University of London.

Waage, J.K. (1979). Foraging for patchily distributed hosts by the parasitoid, *Nemeritis canescens. Journal of Animal Ecology*, **48**, 353–371.

Walker, I. (1963). The relationship between *Drosophila melanogaster* and its parasite *Pseudeucoila bochei* Weld. *Proceedings of the XVI International Congress of Zoology*; *Washington*, **2**, 21.

Wellington, W.G. (1960). Qualitative changes in natural populations during changes in abundance. *Canadian Journal of Zoology*, **38**, 289–314.

Whitcomb, R.F., Robbins, C.S., Lynch, J.F., Whitcomb, B.L., Klimkiewicz, M.K. & Bystrak, D. (1981). Effects of forest fragmentation on avifauna of the Eastern deciduous forest. *Forest Island Dynamics in Man-Dominated Landscapes* (Ed. by R.L. Burgess & D.M. Sharpe), pp. 125–205. Springer Verlag, New York.

Wiens, J.A. (1976). Population responses to patchy environments. *Ann. Rev. Ecol. Syst.*, **7**, 81–120.

Wilcove, D. (1984). *A study of the causes of avian extinctions in fragmented forests in eastern North America.* Ph.D. thesis, Princeton University.

Woolfenden, G.E. & Fitzpatrick, J.M. (1984). *The Florida Scrub Jay: Demography of a Cooperative-breeding Bird.* Princeton University Press, Princeton, New Jersey.

Yellin, J. & Samuelson, P.A. (1977). Comparison of linear and non-linear models for human population dynamics. *Theoretical Population Biology*, **11**, 105–126.

APPENDIX I

This Appendix presents the equation for the overall dynamics of a patchily distributed population which obeys assumptions identical to those by De Jong

(1979), save only that the within-patch competition is governed by eqn (5) rather than De Jong's eqn (2). The equation corresponding to eqn (3) is consequently

$$N_{t+1} = nF \sum_{i=0}^{\infty} ip(i)/(1+dFi). \tag{A1.1}$$

Here the distribution $p(i)$ is negative binomial, with mean N_t/n and clumping parameter k. The series may be brought into summable form by the trick of writing

$$1/(1+dFi) = \int_{0}^{\infty} \exp[-(1+dFi)s]ds. \tag{A1.2}$$

We then have an explicit relation between N_{t+1} and N_t in terms of the parameters characterizing within-patch behaviour:

$$N_{t+1} = FN_t \int_{0}^{\infty} [1+(N_t/nk)(1-\exp(-dFs))]^{-k-1} \exp[-s(1+dF)]ds. \tag{A1.3}$$

In the limit when $dF \ll 1$, the integral in eqn (A1.3) simplifies to give

$$N_{t+1} \simeq FN_t \int_{0}^{\infty} e^{-s} [1+\psi_t s]^{-(k+1)}ds. \tag{A1.4}$$

Here ψ_t is defined as

$$\psi_t \equiv (dF/nk)N_t. \tag{A1.5}$$

The integral in eqn (A1.4) is, moreover, related to the exponential integral of order $k+1$, $E_{k+1}(z)$ (Abramowitz & Stegun 1964), whence eqn (A1.4) can be rewritten

$$\psi_{t+1} = F \exp(1/\psi_t) E_{k+1} (1/\psi_t). \tag{A1.6}$$

We therefore have an equation which relates ψ_{t+1} to ψ_t (and thus, via eqn (A1.5), N_{t+1} to N_t), and which involves only the parameters F and $k+1$. Further discussion is given in the main text.

APPENDIX II

This Appendix summarizes results for the overall dynamics of two species that compete in a patchy environment in the way discussed in the main text (see eqn

(8)). The results themselves are derived elsewhere (DeJong 1981; Ives and May 1984), and are essentially the two-species generalizations of eqn (3).

The results are

$$X_{t+1} = \lambda_X X_t [1 + (X_t/nk_X)\,(1 - \exp(-\alpha_X F_X))]^{-k_X-1}$$
$$[1 + (Y_t/nk_Y)\,(1 - \exp(-\beta_X F_Y))]^{-k_Y} \qquad (A2.1)$$

$$Y_{t+1} = \lambda_Y Y_t [1 + (X_t/nk_X)\,(1 - \exp(-\beta_Y F_X))]^{-k_X}$$
$$[1 + (Y_t/nk_Y)\,(1 - \exp(-\alpha_Y F_Y))]^{-k_Y-1}. \qquad (A2.2)$$

Here X and Y are the competing populations defined in the main text, and α_X, α_Y, β_X, β_Y are the intraspecific and interspecific competition coefficients defined in eqns (6) and (7). The populations of X and Y are distributed independently, as negative binomials with clumping parameters k_X and k_Y, respectively; likewise, F_X and F_Y are, respectively, the average number of eggs laid by individuals of each species. Finally, the intrinsic rates of increase, λ_X and λ_Y, are defined by

$$\lambda_i = F_i \exp(-\alpha_i F_i), \qquad (A2.3)$$

with $i = X, Y$.

Broadly similar, but more complicated, analytic expressions can be obtained for the circumstances explored numerically by Atkinson & Shorrocks (1981) for within-patch competition governed by the two-species analogue of eqn (5) rather than of eqn (2) (Ives & May 1984). There is a minor notational difference between the above results—in which number of adults is chosen as the population variable—and the corresponding results in Atkinson & Shorrocks (1981) and Ives & May (1984)—in which number of larvae is chosen as the population variable. The only difference is the trivial presence or absence of scaling factors F_χ and F_Y in some places in the equations. On the other hand, changing the place in the life cycle where the density-dependent effects operate can produce profound changes in the dynamical behaviour: for a full discussion, see DeJong (1981) or May et al. (1981).

Atkinson & Shorrocks (1981) study in particular the situation where intraspecific effects are the same for the two species ($\alpha_X = \alpha_Y = a$), and where X is the superior competitor (with $\beta_X = 0$ along with $\beta_Y = \beta a$ and $\beta > 1$). If $\beta_X = 0$ in eqn (A2.1), the equilibrium solution for X can be obtained; the marginal condition for species Y to be able to coexist with X then follows from eqn (A2.2) and is

$$(\lambda_Y^{1/k_X} - 1)/(\lambda_X^{1/(k_X+1)} - 1) > [1 - \exp(-\beta_Y F_X)]/[1 - \exp(-\alpha_X F_X)]. \qquad (A2.4)$$

Thus, if F_X, F_Y, α_X and α_Y (and thus λ_X and λ_Y) are specified, eqn (A2.4) enables us to find the degree of clumping in species X, k_X, necessary for the inferior competitor Y to coexist with any given value for β_Y. These results are broadly similar to those obtained by Atkinson & Shorrocks (1981) with their somewhat different model (Ives & May 1984).

APPENDIX III

This Appendix outlines the derivation of the results presented in Fig. 1.5, for parasitoids which exploit their hosts at MSY.

Suppose in generation t the parasitoids 'harvest' a fraction ϕ_t of the adult hosts. The host dynamics then obey the appropriately modified version of eqn (26):

$$N_{t+1} = \lambda g(N_t)N_t(1 - \phi_t). \qquad (A3.1)$$

We assume parasitism acts after the density-dependent factors incorporated in $g(N)$, but before reproduction: for alternative assumptions, see May *et al.* (1981). The corresponding harvest or yield, Y_t, which gives the next generation of parasitoids, can be written

$$Y_t = (\text{constant})\ \phi_t N_t g(N_t). \qquad (A3.2)$$

If a constant fraction, ϕ, is harvested in each generation, the system will settle to some new equilibrium density of hosts, N_ϕ, with ϕ and N_ϕ related by the equilibrium version of eqn (A3.1):

$$\phi = 1 - 1/[\lambda g(N_\phi)]. \qquad (A3.3)$$

The corresponding sustainable yield is

$$Y_\phi = (\text{constant})\ N_\phi[g(N_\phi) - 1/\lambda]. \qquad (A3.4)$$

The host density corresponding to MSY, N_{MSY}, is now found as the value which maximizes Y_ϕ in eqn (A3.4): N_{MSY} thus obeys

$$[g + N dg/dN]_{\text{MSY}} = 1/\lambda. \qquad (A3.5)$$

Once N_{MSY} is found from eqn (A3.5), all other quantities follow readily: q_{MSY} is of course N_{MSY}/N^* (with N^* the parasitoid-free equilibrium density, found from $\lambda g(N^*) = 1$); $\phi_{\text{MSY}} = -[N d(\ln g)/dN]_{\text{MSY}}$; and $Y_{\text{MSY}} = -(\text{constant}) [N^2 dg/dN]_{\text{MSY}}$.

To go from these general results to the curves shown in Fig. 1.5, it is necessary to make some explicit assumptions about the functional form of $g(N)$.

Example A: density dependence derived from 'scramble' competition. In this case which is discussed in the main text, $g(N)$ has the form given by eqn (2):

$$g(N) = \exp(-rN/K). \qquad (A3.6)$$

Here we have, for notational convenience, written $r = \ln\lambda$, so that $N^* = K$. There are many studies of host–parasitoid dynamics employing the density-dependent function of eqn (A3.6) (Beddington *et al.* 1975; Hassell 1978). Substituting eqn (A3.6) into eqn (A3.5), we find that q_{MSY} is given by

$$(1 - x)e^{-x} = 1/\lambda, \qquad (A3.7)$$

with x defined as $x = rq_{MSY} = (\ln\lambda)q_{MSY}$. Equation (A3.7) then gives curve (a) for q_{MSY} as a function of λ in Fig. 1.5.

Example B: density dependence derived from 'contest' competition. Here, again as discussed in the main text, $g(N)$ may be taken to have the form of eqn (5):

$$g(N) = 1/(1 + aN). \qquad (A3.8)$$

The parasitoid-free equilibrium value of N can be seen to be $N^* = (\lambda - 1)/a$. Using eqn (A3.8) in eqn (A3.5), q_{MSY} can now be seen to be related to λ by

$$q_{MSY} = 1/(1 + \lambda^{\frac{1}{2}}). \qquad (A3.9)$$

This result is displayed as curve (b) in Fig. 1.5.

2. POPULATION CONSEQUENCES OF EVOLUTIONARILY STABLE STRATEGIES

G. A. PARKER

Department of Zoology, University of Liverpool

INTRODUCTION

The evolutionarily stable strategy (ESS) concept of John Maynard Smith (1982) is one of the most important recent developments in evolutionary biology. We need ESS logic when the fitness payoffs in a biological game depend on the strategies played by other individuals, i.e. where fitnesses are frequency-dependent. Games can be between similar individuals, between and within phenotypic classes in a species, or between and within species. Several recent reviews of ESS philosophy exist (Maynard Smith 1979, 1982; Barash 1982; Riechert & Hammerstein 1983; Parker 1984; Parker & Hammerstein 1985).

A strategy is an ESS if the population adopting it is uninvadable by an initially-rare alternative strategy. For a mathematical definition, we follow Hammerstein (1985) who has suggested a general form for Maynard Smith's original conditions. Where $I, J \ldots$ etc. are the set of alternative strategies that an individual can play, strategy I will be an ESS if

$$W(I,\text{Pop}_I) \geqslant W(J,\text{Pop}_I) \quad \text{for all } J \tag{1a}$$

$$\text{and if } W(I,\text{Pop}_I) = W(J,\text{Pop}_I),$$

then for sufficiently small ε,

$$W(I,\text{Pop}_{[(1-\varepsilon)I+J\varepsilon]}) > W(J,\text{Pop}_{[(1-\varepsilon)I+J\varepsilon]}) \tag{1b}$$

To explain, in eqn (1a) $W(I,\text{Pop}_I)$ is the fitness payoff of an individual I strategist against a population of I strategists, Pop_I, eqn (1a) tells us that no rare mutant strategist J is able to spread by selection in Pop_I. However, if the payoff to the mutant J, i.e. $W(J,\text{Pop}_I)$, is equal to the payoff of I, J could proliferate by genetic drift. We therefore require the second condition of eqn (1b) to ensure that J will be eliminated by selection. This states that if the mutant J's payoff when rare is equal to that of I, then selection must act against J as it becomes commoner. Thus, in a population consisting of a small proportion (ε) of J-strategists and a large proportion ($1-\varepsilon$) of I-strategists, i.e. population $\text{Pop}_{[(1-\varepsilon)I+J]}$, the payoff to I-strategists must now exceed that of J-strategists in order for I to remain stable.

Though Maynard Smith derived the two ESS conditions independently of the work of Nash (1951), it is clear that an ESS is close to what game theorists call a Nash equilibrium, the central concept in non-cooperative game theory. This is a combination of strategies, one for each player, such that no player can profit by a unilateral deviation from the combination. As such, it is equivalent to the first ESS condition in eqn (1a). However, a Nash equilibrium is not necessarily an ESS, since it involves no restriction parallel to the second ESS condition in eqn (1b). Many of the more interesting ESSs are *mixed* strategies (e.g. I is to play pure strategy A with probability P_A, B with P_B, etc.). Here we always need to use the second ESS condition. The analogies between game theory and the logic of ESS have been considered in depth by Parker & Hammerstein (1985). The important concept in cooperative game theory is that of Pareto optimality. A Pareto optimum is a combination of strategies, again one for each player, in which no player can achieve a higher payoff by deviating without causing another player to receive a lower payoff. In general, it is difficult to envisage that Pareto optimality has relevance to biology unless kin selection or group selection are operating.

My aim in this paper is to examine some of the ways in which frequency-dependent biological games might affect the dynamics or structure of populations. The subject is not yet even in its infancy; my best hopes are that I can outline some of the ways the gametes of the two disciplines (population ecology and ESS theory) may proceed towards each other, and that the resulting zygote might be viable.

ESSs AND POPULATIONS

I see as yet no unique result of ESS theory that generates a general conclusion for all population ecology models. The immediate message of ESS theory for population ecologists is probably the same as it has been for ethologists, namely that models must not seek to maximize some species-level advantage which is in conflict with individual advantage; ecology has perhaps suffered as much as any discipline from implicit group selectionism. However, modern population ecologists are not usually concerned with evolution and adaptation so much as with population numbers and their dynamics. Accordingly, it is the implications that ESS models may have for these aspects that will be my main emphasis. It is clearly impossible to discuss the population consequences of all the many ESS models; examples chosen serve to illustrate specific points.

ESS philosophy aims to make *evolutionary* predictions under *frequency-dependent* selection, i.e. when fitnesses are related to strategy frequencies. Population ecology is sometimes concerned with *population* predictions under *density-dependent* selection, i.e. fitnesses are a function of population density. The two forms of selection should not be confused. However, the strategy that is likely to evolve may often be tuned to population density; it is under these circumstances that the links between behavioural ecology and population ecology become most interesting.

Imagine an asexually-reproducing species (males complicate the issue) of population size N. Fitness, W, (the number of surviving offspring per parent) is expected to be a function both of the population density N and the strategy S that the individuals play. The rate of change in N is

$$dN/dt = N[W(S(N), N) - 1] \qquad (2)$$

where the '-1' represents the death of the parent, and allows populations to decrease when $W < 1$. Equation (2) is a simple population dynamics equation (see e.g. MacArthur 1972). Now, if strategy S is *not* dependent on population density, then once we have established how S will affect fitness, we can concentrate largely on the effects on W of N. This is not to say that dN/dt cannot be dramatically affected by the strategy chosen (see below). However, if the strategy chosen *is* likely to be dependent on N, the population dynamics and strategies become interactive. It then becomes of particular interest to establish how the changes in S with N can affect fitness W, and what will be the characteristics of the steady-state population, if one exists.

ESSs independent of population density

There is no a priori reason why an ESS should depend on population density. The ESS sex ratio of unity (Fisher 1930; see review of Charnov 1982) is one example which, in its simplest form, is independent of population density (but not population viscosity: Hamilton 1967). When there are more males in a population than females, selection favours producing females, and vice-versa. However, it is obvious that the intrinsic rate of increase of a population is affected critically by the sex ratio. Where males contribute nothing but genes to their offspring, a population proceeds towards an equilibrium size at a rate roughly proportional to the proportion of females produced in the offspring. The final population size (assuming that males consume equivalent resources to females) is nevertheless unaffected by sex ratio. It may often be the case that adaptive behaviour affects population dynamics but not the equilibrium population size. In some instances, behaviour may not even affect the dynamics; for example the outcome of inter-male competition will usually only affect populations *via* any effect it may have on *female* reproductive success. It is hardly surprising that population ecologists have been less interested in sexual selection than behavioural ecologists.

The eventual outcome of frequency-dependent selection is unlikely to be such that mean fitness (equivalent to intrinsic rate of increase) is maximized (e.g. Dawkins 1980; O'Donald 1982). The result of conflict between individuals can often produce strategies that eventually reduce the mean number of offspring per adult, even though in reaching such an outcome each successive mutation spreads because it has a selective advantage over its alternative allele. As such, frequency-dependent competitive optimization is quite different from simple optimization (frequency-independent optimization) in which mean population fitness *is* maximized.

One might be tempted to assume that each successive form of competition and conflict added to the repertoire of a species cranks mean population fitness one notch lower, starting from the halving due to producing males, and ranging through the various forms of conflict throughout life to the eventual parent–offspring conflicts during reproduction. This 'conflict load' could be impressively high, and might add considerably to the risk of extinction. However, it is not a general rule that the outcome of conflict always acts to reduce mean population fitness. In some instances (e.g. ideal free distributions with identical phenotypes; see Sutherland & Parker, p. 255) the ESS may come close to maximizing intrinsic rate of increase. Also, it must be stressed that ESS analysis is not confined to selfish competition. It can also predict what can be stable in games of social cooperation (Axelrod & Hamilton 1981; Maynard Smith 1982), which may to some extent help to offset the 'conflict load'.

Density-dependent ESS

Most ESS models do not include the effects of population density, often because density effects will be weak or non-existent, as in the sex ratio case. The omission is sometimes pragmatic only; the models are often complicated enough without such considerations. In the classical contest models such as *hawks/doves* and *war of attrition* (see Maynard Smith 1982), N is never included. The value of winning, V, is regarded as a constant. In fact V is not the absolute value of the resource (in calories, or fertilized ova), but rather the cost of finding some alternative resource. V can therefore often be an increasing function of N. Escalation and hence contest costs are generally likely to increase as V increases; aggression should increase with N and there is evidence that it does in real populations (Moss & Watson p. 275). Contests between females (or males that show parental investment) could therefore act both to reduce the rate at which a population approaches steady-state density, and also reduce the equilibrium density.

Other ESS models do explicitly consider population density (e.g. Knowlton & Parker 1979; Parker & Knowlton 1980; Parker 1982); the example now given is a modified model from these papers. Imagine an asexual species that aggregates in resource patches; it must harvest the resource to produce babies. Each patch has a maximum carrying capacity K, defined such that if each individual were to harvest the resource in the most frugal possible way, when N (the number of competitors per patch) $= K$, fitness $= 1$ and so matches the death of the parent. But an individual can harvest the resource at a faster rate if it sacrifices some of the efficiency with which it converts resources into babies. Let strategy S be a continuous choice of efficiency E between o and 1; $E(S)$ may be 0·8, 0·5 or whatever. There may be a competitive scramble, since it can pay an individual to sacrifice efficiency in order to harvest the resource faster, and thus gain more of it. The ESS (Parker 1982) is:

$$S_* = -\frac{(N-1)}{N} \cdot \frac{E(S_*)}{E'(S_*)} \tag{3}$$

Since E is a decreasing function of S, the gradient $E'(S)$ is negative, which cancels with the negative sign of the RHS of eqn (3). How will this ESS affect the stable population size? Suppose for simplicity that $E(S)$ is linear, so that $E(S) = 1 - eS$ where e is a positive constant. Then

$$S_* = \frac{N-1}{e(2N-1)} \tag{4}$$

and it is clear that S_* is zero if $N = 1$ (be totally frugal if there are no competitors) rising to an asymptotic value of $1/2e$ when N is high. To find the steady-state population density per patch, we require from eqn (2) that fitness $W = 1$, so that dN/dt is zero. Calling

$$W(S(N),N) = \frac{K}{N}E(S),$$

we can substitute $E(S_*)$ using S_* from eqn (4) and set $W = 1$ to obtain the equilibrium density, which is independent of e:

$$N_* = (K+1)/2. \tag{5}$$

It is easy to see that the ESS population size as a proportion of K is equal to the ESS efficiency, since if $W = 1$

$$N_*/K = E(S_*) = \frac{K+1}{2K}; \tag{6}$$

population size is reduced to 50% when K is large.

This example illustrates the sort of way in which ESS technology (eqn (1)) can be merged with that of population ecology (eqn (2)) to produce conclusions both about adaptation (eqns (3), (4)), and about populations (eqns (5), (6)).

INTERACTIONS BETWEEN EVOLUTIONARY AND POPULATION DYNAMICS

Population ecologists usually disregard the effect of density-related adaptive adjustments. We have just seen how the two dimensions (adaptive change; population change) can interact and affect each other. I wish to stress this theme further by considering some games of coevolution between prey and predators.

Games that have ESSs

Imagine a predator (species 1) that specializes on a particular type of prey (species 2). We are simultaneously interested in the evolutionary dynamics of an 'arms race' game on the one hand, and on the population dynamics of the two species on the other (see Fig. 2.1). First consider the evolutionary process. When a predator sights a prey, the chances that it will be successful in catching the prey, $q(k_1, k_2)$, are a function of the expenditure k_1 on hunting specialization by the predator, and the expenditure k_2 by the prey on escape abilities. If k_1 is large relative to k_2, then the chances that the prey is captured are high, and vice versa. Let us assume that both k_1 and k_2 have some sort of cost in that they reduce the potential effort that could be expended on reproduction.

This model is essentially the 'opponent-independent costs game' (Parker 1979) to which an ESS can exist if we make q continuous with changes in k_1 and k_2 (Parker 1983). The fitnesses W_1, W_2, of the predator and prey are clearly influenced both by the *absolute* levels of armament (which affect effort remaining for reproduction) and by the *relative* levels of armament (which affect the chances of capture). However, fitnesses will also be a function of the chances or rate of encounter between the two species, which depend on the predator and prey numbers, N_1 and N_2. Call the encounter probabilities per individual $P_{12}(N_1, N_2)$ for the predator with the prey, and $P_{21}(N_1, N_2)$ for the prey with the predator; thus $P_{12} = (N_2/N_1) \cdot P_{21}$. The fitnesses W_1, W_2 interact with population numbers N_1, N_2 as explained in eqn (2) to define the rates of change in the population sizes, dN_i/dt. Prey numbers are also likely to be affected by density-dependence since the resources harvested by the prey species must be finite. The population parameters interact in a complex way with adaptation parameters, within and between the two species.

At a steady-state we must simultaneously satisfy the conditions for both

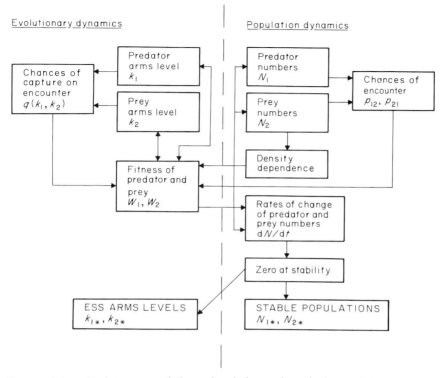

Evolutionary dynamics

Population dynamics

FIG. 2.1. Interaction between population and evolutionary dynamics in a predator–prey arms race game.

population and evolutionary stability. From eqn (2) we shall require that $W_1 = W_2 = 1$, in order that population numbers remain stationary; i.e. that $dN_1/dt = dN_2/dt = 0$. For evolutionary stability, we require the following version of the ESS condition (1a):

$$[\partial W(k_1, \text{Pop}_{[N_1k_{1*} + N_2k_{2*}]})/\partial k_1]_{k_1 = k_{1*}} = 0 \ \Big\rbrace$$
$$[\partial^2 W(k_1, \text{Pop}_{[N_1k_{1*} + N_2k_{2*}]})/\partial k_1^2]_{k_1 = k_{1*}} < 0 \ \Big\rbrace \quad (7)$$

where $W(k_1, \text{Pop}_{[N_1k_{1*} + N_2k_{2*}]})$ is the fitness payoff to a mutant predator that spends a deviant amount k_1 on armament against a 'combined' population of N_1 predators and N_2 prey that spend the ESS amounts k_{1*} and k_{2*} respectively. An exactly parallel pair of conditions must be satisfied simultaneously to ensure that k_{2*} is an ESS for the prey armament level. At first sight, the relationship of these two equations to condition (1a) may seem obscure. However, further inspection will clarify that conditions (7) mean that the payoff to all mutant strategies $k_1 \neq k_{1*}$ must always be *lower* than the payoff to an ESS-player with $k_1 = k_{1*}$, in the ESS population consisting of N_1 k_{1*}-strategists and N_2 k_{2*}-strategists. Conditions (7) are thus conditions for a Nash equilibrium under competitive optimization. Equation (3) in the model of the previous section is found by the same method (see Parker 1982).

I am fairly confident that with plausible continuous functions for P, q, and W, a steady-state ESS pair of arms levels (k_{1*} and k_{2*}) and a steady-state pair of population numbers (N_{1*} and N_{2*}) could be generated under a wide range of conditions; such an analysis will not be attempted here. The aim has been to explain the technology; I have merely amplified the approach of the last section to demonstrate how complex coevolutionary systems can be modelled to take account of the interaction between population and evolutionary dynamics. Let us hope that such 'two-dimensional' models in coevolution and population ecology may generate interesting insights for both disciplines. A second reason for elaborating this particular model in which a steady-state result is likely if $q(k_1,k_2)$ is continuous for changes in k, is to set the scene for a demonstration of what can happen when a steady state does not exist.

Games that have no ESS

Some simpler games have no ESS, and strategies show cyclical evolutionary dynamics. An example is an asymmetric game between two phenotypes (e.g. parent v. offspring; prey v. predator; host v. parasite). If we allow each phenotype, 1 and 2, just two strategies, a_1 and b_1 for 1, a_2 and b_2 for 2, such that:

$$a_1 \text{ beats } a_2 \text{ beats } b_1 \text{ beats } b_2 \text{ beats } a_1$$

there is no ESS, and the strategy dynamics can take various forms (see Maynard Smith, 1982). As suggested in the last section, an ESS could be produced by making strategy sets continuous rather than discrete and by introducing other features which allow payoffs to become continuous with continuous changes in strategy (e.g. Parker & Macnair 1979; Parker 1983), but let us continue with the 2×2 strategy case.

Imagine the predator–prey arms race game in which the predator (player 1) can play just two strategies, l_1 (low armament) and h_1 (high armament), and the prey (player 2) can play either l_2 (negligible armament) or h_2 (medium armament). The reasoning behind the choice of these four arms levels is that the predator must always play against the prey in order to survive and reproduce, whereas the prey can sometimes be lucky enough not to have to play the game at all. Armament is again assumed to have some cost, so that if the prey plays l_2 it pays the predator to play l_1, which is sufficient to win. If the predator plays l_1, it would pay a prey to have invested h_2 which would allow it to escape. An h_2 strategy can be beaten if the predator plays h_1, but now it will pay the prey to play l_2 since this is less costly. A possible payoff matrix is shown in Fig. 2.2. It is of the type for which no ESS exists.

Cyclical dynamics of strategy frequencies can bring about cyclical dynamics in populations. I have simulated a predator–prey arms race game which combines the payoff matrix in Fig. 2.2 with most of the aspects of the interaction between population and evolutionary dynamics outlined in Fig. 2.1. Details of the model are selected for heuristic purposes and qualitative correspondence with biology, not for exactness. The important feature of the model is that population cycles are driven entirely by the evolutionary cycles, not vice versa.

Call $E(l_1,l_2)$ the payoff of a predator that plays l_1 against a prey that plays l_2; $E(h_1,h_2)$ is the payoff of a predator playing h_1 against a prey playing h_2, and so on. In the simulation, payoff values were taken directly from Fig. 2.2. If r is

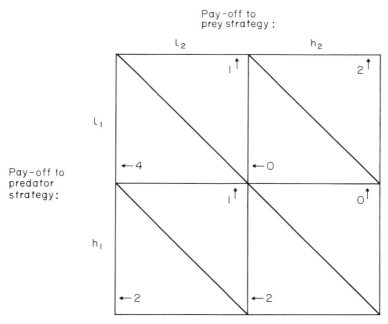

FIG. 2.2. Payoff matrix for the 2×2 strategy arms race game when a prey plays against a predator. Strategies are l_1 (low armament) and h_1 (high armament) for the predator, and correspondingly l_2 and h_2 for the prey. Payoffs to the predator are in the lower triangle of each box; payoffs to the prey are in the upper triangles.

the frequency of l_1 in the predator population, and s is the frequency of l_2 in the prey population and the alternative strategies have frequencies $(1-r)$ and $(1-s)$ respectively, the average fitnesses of each predator strategist are:

$$W(l_1) = [sE(l_1,l_2)+(1-s)E(l_1,h_2)+1]\cdot b(N_1,N_2)$$

$$W(h_1) = [sE(h_1,l_2)+(1-s)E(h_1,h_2)+\tfrac{1}{2}]\cdot b(N_1,N_2)$$

in which the constants 1 and $\tfrac{1}{2}$ give the predator some small ability to replicate independently of the strategies played by the prey (e.g. through some weak random element in prey capture). Function $b(N_1,N_2)$ scales the predator payoffs in relation to the population sizes N_1 and N_2 of the two species. I used

$$b(N_1,N_2) = a(1-\exp(-uN_2/N_1))$$

and in the simulation set $a=1$ and $u=0\cdot1$, which gives the predator a full payoff when there are vast numbers of prey and few predators, and reduces the value of the payoff with increasing severity as prey numbers decline relative to predators. The number of predators in generation $g+1$ is

$$N_1(g+1) = N_1(g)\cdot[rW(l_1)+(1-r)W(h_1)]$$

which is the product of parental numbers and mean predator fitness. It is assumed that parental mortality is already accounted for in $W(l_1)$, $W(h_1)$.

Payoffs to each individual of the prey species were calculated similarly, except that a prey plays against a predator with probability P. Thus, on $(1-P)$ occasions, it gets payoff D if it plays h_2 or alternatively $(D+1)$ if it plays the less costly l_2. So payoffs are:

$$W(l_2) = [rE(l_2,l_1)+(1-r)E(l_2,h_1)]\cdot P+(D+1)\,(1-P)$$

$$W(h_2) = [rE(h_2,l_1)+(1-r)E(h_2,h_1)]\cdot P+D(1-P)$$

and for the simulation, $D=2$. Clearly, we require P to be a function of the predator and prey numbers, and the relationship

$$P(N_1,N_2) = 1-\exp(-vN_1/N_2)$$

has the required property that P rises asymptotically to 1 when the ratio of predators to prey is high. Increasing the constant v effectively increases the probability of encounter with a predator at any given ratio N_1/N_2; v is one of the most important variables influencing the qualitative outcome of the dynamics.

The number of prey entering the next generation was subject to density-dependence, so that the prey population could not grow indefinitely. The number of prey before density-dependent selection was taken as

$$N_2'(g+1) = N_2(g) \cdot [sW(l_2) + (1-s)W(h_2)]$$

and after selection:

$$N_2(g+1) = K[1 - \exp(-N_2'(g+1)/K)] \qquad (8)$$

where $K = 1000$. Equation (8) has the property that if $N_2(g)$ is low, $N_2(g+1)$ is also low but greater than $N_2(g)$. Population size increases if $\exp(-N_2'/K) < (1 - N_2/K)$, otherwise it decreases. Thus, without any interaction with the predator, prey numbers rise to reach an asymptote where $\exp(-N_2'/K) = (1 - N_2/K)$, which represents the carrying capacity for the prey species.

In common with most ESS models, strategies were allowed to reproduce asexually. Frequencies of strategies in the next generation are proportional to payoffs in the last one.

The simulation was started with all strategies at a frequency of 0·5, which is the stationary point (non-stable equilibrium) for the payoff matrix in Fig. 2.2. However, strategies begin to cycle because frequency-independent elements have been added to the fitness payoffs. Initial population numbers were $N_1 = 3$; $N_2 = 30$. Results depend critically on the value of v selected. Increasing v means that a greater proportion of the prey population is forced into playing the game against the predator, as in Fig. 2.2. Three types of result will be summarized.

v = 1. Even at high predator/prey ratios, there is still a good chance that a prey will not play against a predator. It never pays the prey to play h_2 because of the costs; consequently, it never pays the predator to shift from l_1. Strategies l_2 and l_1 go to fixation and are stable. Population sizes stabilize at steady state with $N_{1*} = 384$; $N_{2*} = 863$. This is equivalent to the result predicted for the model in the last section.

v = 20. As v is increased towards 10 strategy frequencies begin to show marked cycling behaviour, as do population numbers. Figure 2.3a,b shows the cycles for the case where v = 20. Cycles become quite regular in amplitude and have a period of about 24 generations.

v = 100. As v increases further, cycles become more catastrophic. By v = 50, the population numbers of predators can drop to $\ln(N_2') = 0·5$, i.e. the predator would become extinct. Figure 2.4a,b shows the results of a simulation with v = 100. Cycles tend to increase in amplitude and frequency, and become irregular, suggesting that we have entered a zone of chaos (May 1975). Extinction of one or both populations is ensured (e.g. around generation 230, N_1 and N_2 crash simultaneously).

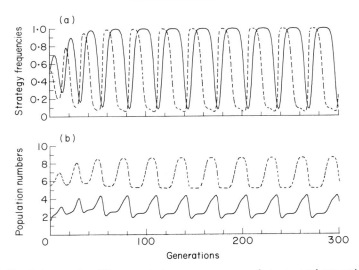

FIG. 2.3. Simulation results of the 2 × 2 strategy arms race game between predator and prey when v = 20. (a) Frequencies of the l_1 predator strategy (——) and l_2 prey strategy (– – – –). (b) Population numbers of predators, ln N_1; (——) and prey, ln $N_2 + 2$ (– – – –). Constant $a = 1$, $u = 0.1$, $D = 2$.

This heuristic model illustrates how important cyclical dynamics of strategies can be in determining what happens to populations. A rather similar sort of model in which a host can play two strategies (resistant; non-resistant) to a pathogen has been shown by May & Anderson (1983) to be capable of generating population cycles in the two species, and strategy cycles in the host. Barrett (1980; 1981) has investigated some of the ways that different genetic strategies can affect rates of population increase in host–pathogen models.

Cycles in the present model are intrinsic, because of the lack of an ESS to the game outlined in Fig. 2.2. This contrasts with the case where extrinsic population cycles can bring about evolutionary cycles in adaptive strategy. An example in nature where there may be genetic changes in behaviour due to population cycles appears to have been found by Moss & Watson (p. 275). Red grouse become more aggressive when population densities are high, and vice versa, which is concordant with current thinking on contest theory, since the value of winning a contest, V, will be an increasing function of N (see earlier). I have simulated the classical hawks/doves contest model (see Maynard Smith & Parker 1976) to include population dynamics, using a density-dependent population limitation of the same type as in eqn (8), and where V (or alternatively, $-D$, the cost of injury) increases monotonically with population size. Provided that the population can increase, it always

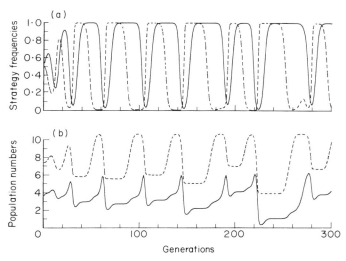

FIG. 2.4. As for Fig. 2.3, but $v = 100$. Predator numbers are $\ln N_1 + 2$, and prey numbers are $\ln N_2 + 4$.

reaches an equilibrium size N_* set by the density-dependence, and a stable frequency of hawks $= V(N_*)/D$. However, although the contest behaviour (even for the case of fighting between females) cannot generate population cycles, extrinsic population fluctuations would certainly generate adaptive changes in the frequency of hawkish behaviour, as Moss & Watson have suggested.

Cycles or stability?

It is clear that the details of how we model a particular game exert a profound influence on the sort of solution obtained; the arms race game can be modelled so as to give either an ESS or cyclical dynamics, as we have just seen. My feeling is that most games which typically give rise to evolutionary cycles can be made to give ESSs if some plausible way can be found to make *payoffs continuous for continuous changes in strategy*. Which form of model is more realistic biologically is controversial, but my instincts usually err on the side of ESSs, since (i) there are usually good reasons to imagine that strategies could be continuous, and (ii) there will usually be sufficient random elements (i.e. independent of strategy) to ensure that payoffs could be continuous functions of deviations in strategy. However, there may sometimes be reasons why (i) cannot apply, in which case neither can (ii). For instance, the allele which determines the ESS may not exist and the closest alleles prescribe strategies on either side of the ESS. Discontinuities could be brought about in other ways, e.g. there could be two quite separate biological ways in which a prey could 'arm' against a predator, and vice versa. Further, even if both (i) and (ii) do apply, an ESS might have only local stability. Big strategy deviations might thus invade, and in turn generate oscillation.

Finally, it seems important to make a distinction between games in which a density-dependent ESS can be achieved *facultatively*, by an individual shifting its strategy optimally in relation to accurate assessment of current population density, and games in which the ESS is achieved purely by selection, and without any element of assessment of current conditions. In a steady-state population, neither type of ESS would have any advantage over the other. But if population numbers are made to fluctuate by extrinsic factors, the 'facultative' ESS would always win since it is unbeatable whatever the population density. It would therefore seem rather surprising for animals to show genetic rather than facultative changes in aggressive levels with population fluctuations. Facultative responses could be produced by most behavioural games, but probably not by investment games of the arms race type, except where species can show pronounced degrees of phenotype plasticity. Since, in reality, population numbers must always fluctuate to some extent around the steady-state level, then there will be some consequent cyclical dynamics in optimum investment strategies.

Some other influences of the game structure

Other aspects of ESS models can also affect the outcome obtained, and its implications for populations. An example concerns the amount and type of information that animals have. In contests, information about asymmetries in fighting ability or resource value can dramatically reduce the extent of escalation (Maynard Smith & Parker 1976; Hammerstein 1981; Hammerstein & Parker 1982). At the ESS in the symmetric (i.e. no information about asymmetries) war of attrition game, the expected payoff is zero (Maynard Smith 1974). In an asymmetric war of attrition where opponents have near-perfect information, a maximum expected payoff of $\frac{1}{2}V_A$ can be approached in a contest in which opponents A and B differ in resource value ($V_A > V_B$) but not in fighting ability (Parker & Rubinstein 1981; Hammerstein & Parker 1982); this difference between the symmetric and asymmetric outcomes could certainly affect population dynamics.

In resource competition of the type called 'scramble' by Nicholson (1954), the ESS can be particularly influenced by information about 'self's' pheno-type; ESSs are likely to become 'phenotype-limited' (i.e. conditional strategies dependent on self's phenotype relative to the phenotype distribution of the population; see Parker 1982). Phenotype-limitation of strategies under ideal free searching (Fretwell 1972) is likely to result in the individuals with the highest competitive abilities in the best patches (Sutherland & Parker, p. 255; Parker & Sutherland, unpublished). This has important effects on the expected payoffs to each phenotype, which will not be equal as they would be under ideal free searching with identical phenotypes.

Notable changes to the predicted outcome of a given game can also be brought about if the game is played repeatedly between the same two opponents, rather than only once (see Maynard Smith 1982), or if the game is played between relatives as opposed to non-relatives (Grafen 1979; Hines & Maynard Smith 1979).

THE ROLE OF LEARNING

At least in the short term, it is adaptation by learning that will most affect populations, rather than adaptation by genetic change. Dawkins (1980) stressed that stable states in behavioural games can be arrived at by learning, and Harley (1981; see also Maynard Smith 1982) has produced a theoretical framework for such processes. The experiments of Milinski (1979) and Harper (1982) show that animals can learn ideal free distributions; the population quickly equilibrates such that the expected rates of gain are equal for all individuals wherever they search, or as close to the ideal free solution as the system can allow. Rather different outcomes can, however, be generated if individuals differ in competitive ability (Parker 1982; Sutherland & Parker, p. 255; Parker & Sutherland, unpublished).

The capacity to learn ideal free distributions has, of course, some very strong implications for the population regulation of prey species. Imagine a predator that feeds on three different prey species, A, B, and C, which each live in different parts of the habitat. If A becomes superabundant relative to B and C, then through ideal free considerations a greater number of predators will begin to exploit A, reducing the pressure on B and C. It seems possible that such a mechanism could exert a homeostatic effect on the relative abundances of the three prey species. It may not be difficult to construct a steady-state model for such processes, describing a general balance in numbers of all four species.

Such a model might still give an equilibrium if there is some overlap between A, B, and C. However if A, B, and C are randomly distributed within the habitat, the appropriate model becomes one of optimal diet rather than the ideal free distribution. Population dynamics of species under optimal foraging are discussed by Comins & Hassell (1979).

ESSs AND ANIMAL NUMBERS THROUGH TIME

Some recent work on ESS aspects of life-history strategy has implications for the seasonal distribution of animal populations, and for age structure and demography.

Seasonal incidence games

Several authors (Iwasa *et al.* 1983; Bulmer 1983; Parker & Courtney 1983) have shown independently that the variance of entry of individuals into a given life-history stage could be a mixed ESS in which a population effectively achieves an ideal free distribution in time rather than in space. The models assume that the probability distribution $i(t)$ of inputs of individuals at times t during the season is adjusted by selection so that all individuals, irrespective of their input time, achieve equal payoffs. The seasonal incidence (phenology) of a species is adaptive and stable if $i(t)$ is an ESS. Such solutions are possible where resources are seasonally distributed, and gains to each individual are a decreasing function of population density. Previous interpretations tended to be that the variation in timing of entry of individuals into seasonal populations constitutes 'maladaptive noise' around some optimal date, t_* (e.g. Fagerstrom & Wiklund 1982). So far, models have been tested exclusively on the timing of emergence of male butterflies, with the emergence distribution of the females being the seasonally-distributed resource. As yet it is not certain that the mixed ESS solution gives a better fit to the data than the optimal date model, but it is clear that an optimal date cannot be an ESS unless (i) by chance the 'noise' about t_* yields a distribution identical to $i(t)$, or (ii) it is impossible evolutionarily to achieve the distribution $i(t)$, and all that can be achieved is a pure strategy.

An illustration of the principles of the ESS model is given in Fig. 2.5, which shows the results of some simulations of parallel design to those of Parker & Courtney (1983). A resource r is unevenly distributed through time t during the season. Individuals can enter the stage of life history that exploits this particular resource at any time t, which in the simulation is divided into ten discrete intervals. Payoffs at each t to each competitor are equal to $r(t)/N(t)$, where $N(t)$ is the current population density. There is a fixed (i.e. age-independent) probability of death during each t. Thus, if survival is 100% between intervals, it must be advantageous to enter the population as early as possible. However, early entry is clearly not the best strategy when survival prospects are poorer. If survival is zero between intervals, then by ideal free theorem, $i(t)$ must match $r(t)$ exactly. Intermediate survival rates between 1 and 0 give solutions for $i(t)$ that are intermediate between the two extremes. Figure 2.5

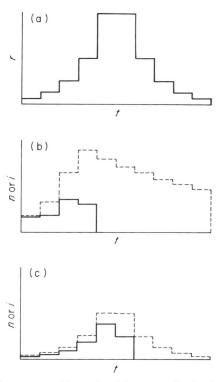

FIG. 2.5. Seasonal incidence game with a unimodal resource distribution. (a) resource distribution through time *t*. (b) inputs *i* (——) and number of competitors *N* (– – – –) with 90% survival betweeen intervals. (c) Same with 50% survival between intervals.

shows the results obtained with survival prospects of 0·9 (Fig. 2.5b) and 0·5 (Fig. 2.5c) when the resource distribution is unimodal as in Fig. 2.5a. With the higher survivorship, all input is restricted to the beginning of the season, though the relative density of competitors stays higher much longer because of the reduced mortality. Parallel results for a bimodal distribution of $r(t)$ are shown in Fig. 2.6. Bimodality has the result of restricting inputs for high survivorship even more to the start of the season; under low survivorship, the inputs become bimodal. The mean of the input distribution always precedes the mean of the resource distribution, for all survivorships greater than zero between intervals. This prediction is also true of the optimal input date model (see Fagerstrom & Wiklund 1982).

Game-like qualities of this sort are likely to be prevalent to some degree in all seasonal populations, and a more elaborate analysis of the life-history consequences is much needed. It will also be necessary to investigate

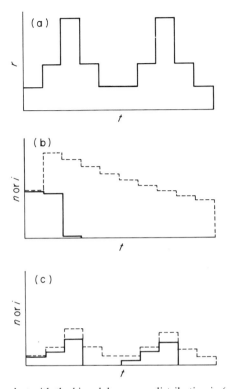

FIG. 2.6. As for Fig. 2.5, but with the bimodal resource distribution in (a).

coevolutionary models in which the resource distribution (e.g. a prey species) is not fixed, but evolves in response to the seasonal occurrence of the exploiter species (e.g. a predator). It is not yet clear whether prey–predator seasonal incidence games yield stable solutions or cyclical dynamics.

Timing of life-history switches

Population ecologists have long been interested in life-history strategy (e.g. Stearns 1976). Most models have so far not involved frequency-dependence, with the notable exception of Mirmirani & Oster (1978) in models of plant growth. Several ESS models now exist for life-history switches in animals; they indicate when an animal should change from one strategy (e.g. growth) to another (e.g. reproduction). So far there are essentially three types of model, and all relate to size and hence often also to age.

Sex switches. Ghiselin's size advantage hypothesis (1969) is that selection can favour sequential hermaphroditism when an individual's reproductive success correlates with size (or age) and where the correlation differs for the two sexes. For instance, if size is of negligible importance to female fitness, but highly important to males because of inter-male competition, selection should favour first being female then switching later to male; this switch is frequency-dependent because it affects sex ratio. Charnov (1982) has elegantly modelled such processes, and gives very convincing evidence that sex change in pandalid shrimp and labroid fish fit the predictions.

Alternative mating strategy switches. Behavioural ecologists have demonstrated the ubiquity of alternative mating strategies in which (typically) males play different strategies depending on their size or age (see Rubinstein 1980; Dunbar 1982; Davies 1982; Parker 1982; Thornhill & Alcock 1983). Large males may often act as 'guarders' in which they monopolize females aggressively against other males, and small males as 'sneaks' who can pick up matings when females escape from guarders, or other opportunist possibilities which are open to small males. There is a series of variations on this sort of theme, but most appear to involve some sort of frequency-dependence. Models for switching between the two strategies have been attempted by Gross & Charnov (1980), Rubinstein (1980) and Parker (1982).

Size games: when to become an adult. Suppose that the capacity to reproduce depends critically on self's size relative to the size of other adults in the population. An example concerns dominance; suppose that winning a female depends on some aspects of a male's size relative to that of its opponents; e.g. it wins if it is bigger. Maynard Smith (1982) has investigated an ESS model for switching to adulthood under such circumstances. Essentially the same question is analysed by Parker (1983), using a rather different approach. Size games are frequency-dependent because the success of a mutant strategy depends on the switch point of the rest of the population.

Population consequences of a simple size game

Life-history games will obviously affect the age and sex structure of a population. How will they affect population dynamics? Sex switches have an immediate effect on intrinsic rate of increase because they affect sex ratio (see Charnov 1982). The examples listed for the other two switches concerned only male strategy, and might therefore exert only weak or negligible effects. However, size games could easily be between females or hermaphrodites, in which cases the population consequences could potentially be severe. I will give an illustration, using a version of the different size games of Maynard Smith (1982) and Parker (1983), which nevertheless incorporates features from the models of both authors. It may be applicable to parasites and annual plants where resources only become limiting when competitors have grown large, as well as to more obvious cases where animals (for our present purposes females) compete over limited resources necessary for breeding. Explicit functions are chosen strictly for heuristic reasons, not for exactness.

The non-competitive case. Imagine a species in which an individual first grows, then stops growing and switches to reproduction until it dies at a fixed time T. Its reproductive rate when adult is an increasing function of its size, $s(t)$, at the time t that it stops growing to switch to reproduction. However, the time it has available for reproduction $(T-t)$ is reduced by growing for longer. Calling the reproductive rate $R(s)$, there is thus a simple trade-off in which we maximize $W(t) = R(s(t)) \cdot (T-t)$ to find the optimal switch point t_*. Setting $dW/dt = 0$,

$$t_* = T - R(s(t_*))/[R'(s(t_*)) \cdot s'(t_*)]. \tag{9}$$

For simplicity, let growth be linear as $s(t) = at$, and let reproductive rate be directly proportional to size as $R(s(t)) = b \cdot s(t)$. Then

$$t_* = T/2, \tag{10}$$

i.e. the individual should switch to reproduction half way through life. Mean fitness (equivalent to intrinsic rate of increase) is

$$W(t_*) = ab(T/2)^2. \tag{11}$$

A size game version. To convert this model into a size game with frequency-dependent payoffs, we make reproductive rate a function of both absolute *and* relative size. The idea is that abilities to convert resources into reproduction are scaled by competition between adults. The change in reproductive rate due to competition will be expressed in terms of a factor C, which is a function of the size of an adult relative to the mean size of other adults. Thus, where t_* is the ESS switch point, a mutant playing $t \neq t_*$ gets a rate of reproduction equivalent to $R(s(t)) \cdot C(\alpha)$, where $\alpha = s(t)/s(t_*)$. Mutant fitness is

$$W(t,t_*) = R(s(t)) \cdot C(\alpha) \cdot (T-t),$$

and t_* is found by setting $dW/dt = 0$ when $t = t_*$ after the principle in eqn (7). This gives

$$t_* = T - \left[\frac{R'(s(t_*)) \cdot s'(t_*)}{R(s(t_*))} + \frac{C'(\alpha) \cdot s'(t_*)}{C(1) \cdot s(t_*)} \right]^{-1}$$

c.f. eqn (9). Allowing $C(1) = 1$, and using the same linear versions of R and s as before, we obtain

$$t_* = \frac{T[1 + C'(\alpha)]}{2 + C'(\alpha)} \tag{12}$$

in which the gradient $C'(\alpha)$ tells us the relative importance of minute deviations in size about the population mean. It will always be positive if size has a competitive advantage. If minute increases in size are highly important in scaling reproductive rate, then the switch point is pushed towards T and individuals will not begin to reproduce until very late in life. In contrast, if the size effect is insignificant $C'(\alpha) \to 0$, and t_* converges towards $T/2$ as in eqn (10).

For all $C'(\alpha) > 0$, mean fitness will be reduced by the delay in the onset of reproduction. If, for example, $C(\alpha) = t/t_*$; $t_* = 2T/3$. Mean fitness is

$$W(t_*, t_*) = ab2(T/3)^2 \qquad (13)$$

and the ratio of eqns (13)/(12) is 8/9, i.e. the effect of the competition is to reduce the intrinsic rate of increase to 8/9 of its former value.

For some more detailed, and more biologically realistic models in a similar vein, the reader is referred to Mirmirani & Oster (1978).

ESSs AND ANIMAL NUMBERS IN SPACE

Some ESS models have implications for animal distributions, and their effect on populations. Three examples are given below.

Ideal free distributions

Fretwell's ideal free theory (Fretwell & Lucas, 1970; Fretwell, 1972), which states that at equilibrium, individuals are distributed such that payoffs are equal to all competitors, will be strictly true only when all individuals have equal competitive ability. For a population of phenotypes differing continuously in competitive ability, we can solve the ESS distribution using two simple rules (Parker 1984). First, at the ESS, no individual must be capable of doing better by shifting elsewhere. Second, if we arrange patch types in order of increasing tendency to amplify the competitive differences between phenotypes, for a large population of phenotypes differing continuously in competitive ability, the phenotype with the highest competitive ability in a given patch type must achieve the same payoff as the phenotype with the lowest competitive ability in the next patch type up the hierarchy. A typical result is that the most dominant phenotypes end up in the 'best' patches (highest in the hierarchy), and fitness payoffs are ranked in order of increasing competitive ability (Sutherland & Parker, p. 255; Parker & Sutherland, unpublished).

Territoriality and spite

The amount of resource guarded by each individual can affect how many individuals are excluded from resources and therefore fail to reproduce. If territoriality affects females or breeding pairs, territory size can therefore be crucial in establishing stable population sizes.

ESS models of territory size have been attempted by Maynard Smith (1982) and Knowlton & Parker (1979), Parker & Knowlton (1980). Figure 2.7 shows a version of the territory size model of Maynard Smith, altered on the assumption that displays obey the rules of the asymmetric war of attrition (Hammerstein & Parker 1982). Let V_1, V_2 be the values to opponents 1 and 2 of winning a territorial dispute at a given distance between the centres of the

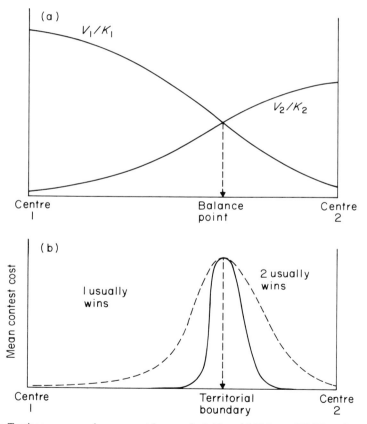

FIG. 2.7. Territory game under asymmetric war of attrition. (a) Values of V_1/K_1 and V_2/K_2 at points between the territory centres of opponents 1 and 2. (b) Mean contest costs at the start (– – –) and end (———) of territorial guarding.

two adjacent territories of 1 and 2. We expect V_1 to decline and V_2 to increase as we move towards the centre of 2, and vice versa (see Maynard Smith, 1982). Let K_1 and K_2 be the rates at which 1 and 2 accrue costs in a contest (K decreases as fighting ability increases). We plot V/K for each opponent, between the two territorial centres (Fig. 2.7a). From the asymmetric war of attrition, the contest is influenced critically by the inequality between the two values of V/K at a given point; as the magnitude of the difference increases, the risk that the opponents will make a mistake about the inequality decreases. Briefly, the prediction would be that appreciable escalation (to the level of the symmetric war of attrition) would occur at the point where $V_1/K_1 = V_2/K_2$. Outcomes of displays should here be entirely unpredictable. Disputes on either side of this balance point (territorial boundary?) will be settled with decreasing contest costs, and will usually be won by the individual with the higher V/K value (Fig. 2.7b). Initially, assessments of the inequality between the two V/K values may be relatively poor, with the result that mistakes are commoner, escalation higher, and outcomes less predictable (dotted line, Fig. 2.7) than later in the season (continuous line), when disputes may become confined almost totally to a tight zone around the balance point, which now becomes a clearly-defined territorial border. In general, bird territorial behaviour appears to fit the predictions of this model quite well. A criticism would be that an ESS analysis ought to take account of the fact that territorial disputes are typically repeated contests.

The Knowlton–Parker models use a different sort of approach, and include the effects that diminishing returns to territory size will have on population size. They also model a 'spite' component in territoriality. Verner (1977) has suggested that territory size might become larger than optimal because of a selective advantage due to excluding other individuals from breeding. In finite populations, there will always be some spiteful component to territory size, but it will be trivially small in all but the smallest populations (see also Rothstein, 1979). However, imagine some species playing a size game over resources, and so becoming larger and hence (for reasons of fixed carrying capacity) less numerous. At some point in extreme population reduction, the spiteful component could certainly come to exacerbate the decrease in population, and so increase the risk of extinction. It is possible that this effect has played a part in the extinction of large mammals and large reptiles.

Flocking and the vigilance game

Hamilton's selfish herd theory (1971; see also Williams, 1964; Vine, 1971) suggests a major advantage in social grouping which reduces individual predation risk; individual risk is diluted by being positioned close to others, which a predator might take instead. However, the chances that an individual is caught also depends on its vigilance and on the vigilance levels of the other group members. If the ESS level of vigilance per individual decreases with flock size, the potential benefits of flocking will be reduced.

Pulliam, Pyke & Caraco (1982) and Parker & Hammerstein (1985) have examined an ESS model which predicts that vigilance per individual should decline with flock size. Parker & Hammerstein also predict that in randomly-constituted groups, the *total* vigilance of the whole group should also decline with flock size (a prediction that is contradicted by field evidence), though this need not be true if groups consist of related individuals (e.g. full sibs). Paradoxically, this means that predatory attacks are more successful if prey join 'random' flocks. Does this mean that it cannot pay to join flocks, as Hamilton predicted? The answer appears to be that it nevertheless always pays to join flocks because individual fitness increases asymptotically with flock size, due both to the Hamilton effect and to the benefits of extra time spent feeding rather than being vigilant. An investigation of the predator–prey population dynamics and their effects in vigilance games would be well worthwhile.

ACKNOWLEDGMENTS

I am especially grateful to Alistair Houston for spotting an earlier error in the 'efficiency' model, and to Robert Smith for many helpful criticisms.

REFERENCES

Axelrod, R. & Hamilton, W.D. (1981). The evolution of cooperation. *Science*, **211**, 1390–1396.

Barash, J.A. (1982). *Sociobiology and Behavior*. Hodder & Stoughton, London.

Barrett, J.A. (1980). Pathogen evolution in multilines and variety monocultures. *Z. Pflkrankh. Pflschutz*, **87**, 383–396.

Barrett, J.A. (1981). The evolutionary consequences of monoculture. *Genetic Consequences of Man-Made Change* (Ed. by J.A. Bishop & L.M. Cook), pp. 209–248. Academic Press, London.

Bulmer, M.G. (1983). Models for the evolution of protandry in insects. *Theoretical Population Ecology*, **23**, 314–322.

Charnov, E.L. (1982). *The Theory of Sex Allocation*. Princeton University Press, Princeton.

Comins, H.N. & Hassell, M.P. (1979). The dynamics of optimally foraging predators and parasitoids. *Journal of Animal Ecology*, **48**, 335–351.

Davies, N.B. (1982). Behaviour and competition for scarce resources. *Current Problems in Sociobiology*. (Ed. by King's College Sociobiology Group), pp. 363–380. Cambridge University Press, Cambridge.

Dawkins, R. (1980). Good strategy or evolutionarily stable strategy? *Sociobiology: Beyond Nature/Nurture* (Ed. by G.W. Barlow & J. Silverberg), pp. 331–367. Westview Press, Boulder.

Dunbar, R.I.M. (1982). Intra-specific variations in mating strategy. *Perspective in Ethology*, Vol. 5 (Ed. by P.P.G. Bateson & P. Klopfer), pp. 385–431. Plenum Press, New York.

Fagerstrom, T. & Wiklund, C. (1982). Why do males emerge before females? Protandry as a mating strategy in male and female bufferflies. *Oecologia*, **52**, 164–166.

Fisher, R.A. (1930). *The Genetical Theory of Natural Selection*. Clarendon Press, Oxford.

Fretwell, S.D. (1972). *Populations in a Seasonal Environment*. Princeton University Press, Princeton.

Fretwell, S.D. & Lucas, H.L. (1970). On territorial behaviour and other factors influencing habitat distribution in birds. *Acta Biotheoretica*, **19**, 16–36.

Ghiselin, M.T. (1969). The evolution of hermaphroditism among animals. *Quarterly Review of Biology*, **44**, 189–208.

Grafen, A. (1979). The hawk–dove game played between relatives. *Animal Behaviour*, **27**, 905–907.

Gross, M.R. & Charnov, E.L. (1980). Alternative male life histories in bluegill sunfish. *Proceedings National Academy of Science USA*, **77**, 6937–6940.

Hamilton, W.D. (1967). Extraordinary sex ratios. *Science (Washington)*, **156**, 477–488.

Hamilton, W.D. (1971). Geometry for the selfish herd. *Journal of Theoretical Biology*, **31**, 295–311.

Hammerstein, P. (1981). The role of asymmetries in animal contests. *Animal Behaviour*, **29**, 193–205.

Hammerstein, P. (1985). *Evolutionary games with many players*. Working paper, Institute of Mathematical Economics, University of Bielefeld.

Hammerstein, P. & Parker, G.A. (1982). The asymmetric war of attrition. *Journal of Theoretical Biology*, **96**, 647–682.

Harley, C.B. (1981). Learning the evolutionarily stable strategy. *Journal of Theoretical Biology*, **89**, 611–633.

Harper, D.G.C. (1982). Competitive foraging in mallards: ideal free ducks. *Animal Behaviour*, **30**, 575–584.

Hines, W.G.S. & Maynard Smith, J. (1979). Games between relatives. *Journal of Theoretical Biology*, **79**, 19–30.

Iwasa, Y., Odendaal, F.J., Murphy, D.D., Ehrlich, P.R. & Launer, A.E. (1983). Emergence patterns of male butterflies: a hypothesis and a test. *Theoretical Population Biology*, **23**, 363–379.

Knowlton, N. & Parker, G.A. (1979). An evolutionarily stable strategy approach to indiscriminate spite. *Nature*, **279**, 419–420.

MacArthur, R.H. (1972). *Geographical Ecology*. Harper & Row, New York.

May, R.M. (1975). Biological populations obeying difference equations: stable points, stable cycles and chaos. *Journal of Theoretical Biology*, **49**, 511–524.

May, R.M. & Anderson, R.M. (1983). Epidemiology and genetics in the coevolution of parasites and hosts. *Proceedings of the Royal Society of London, B.*, **219**, 281–313.

Maynard Smith, J. (1974). The theory of games and the evolution of animal conflicts. *Journal of Theoretical Biology*, **47**, 209–221.

Maynard Smith, J. (1979). Game theory and the evolution of behaviour. *Proceedings of the Royal Society of London, B.*, **205**, 475–488.

Maynard Smith, J. (1982). *Evolution and the Theory of Games*. Cambridge University Press, Cambridge.

Maynard Smith, J. & Parker, G.A. (1976). The logic of asymmetric contests. *Animal Behaviour*, **24**, 159–175.

Milinski, M. (1979). An evolutionarily stable feeding strategy in sticklebacks. *Zeitschrift fur Tierpsychologie*, **51**, 36–40.

Mirmirani, M. & Oster, G. (1978). Competition, kin selection and evolutionarily stable strategies. *Theoretical Population Biology*, **13**, 304–339.

Nash, J.F. (1951). Non-cooperative games. *Annals of Mathematics*, **54**, 286–95.

Nicholson, A.J. (1954). An outline of the dynamics of animal populations. *Australian Journal of Zoology*, **2**, 9–65.

O'Donald, P. (1982). The concept of fitness in population genetics and sociobiology. *Current Problems in Sociobiology* (Ed. by King's College Sociobiology Group), pp. 65–89. Cambridge University Press, Cambridge.

Parker, G.A. (1979). Sexual conflict and sexual selection. *Sexual Selection and Reproductive Competition in Insects* (Ed. by M.S. & N.A. Blum), pp. 123–166. Academic Press, New York.

Parker, G.A. (1982). Phenotype-limited evolutionarily stable strategies. *Current Problems in Sociobiology* (Ed. by King's College Sociobiology Group), pp. 173–201. Cambridge University Press, Cambridge.

Parker, G.A. (1983). Arms races in evolution: an ESS to the opponent–independent costs game. *Journal of Theoretical Biology*, **101**, 619–648.

Parker, G.A. (1984). Evolutionarily stable strategies. *Behavioural Ecology: an Evolutionary Approach*, Vol. 2 (Ed. by J.R. Krebs & N.B. Davies), pp. 30–61. Blackwell Scientific Publications, Oxford.

Parker, G.A. & Courtney, S.P. (1983). Seasonal incidence: adaptive variation in the timing of life history stages. *Journal of Theoretical Biology*, **105**, 147–155.

Parker, G.A. & Hammerstein, P. (1985). Game theory and animal behaviour. *Evolution* (Ed. by P. Harvey, M. Slatkin & P. Greenwood). Cambridge University Press, Cambridge (in press).

Parker, G.A. & Knowlton, N. (1980). The evolution of territory size: some ESS models. *Journal of Theoretical Biology*, **84**, 445–476.

Parker, G.A. & Macnair, M.R. (1979). Models of parent–offspring conflict. IV. Suppression–evolutionary retaliation by the parent. *Animal Behaviour*, **27**, 1210–1235.

Parker, G.A. & Rubinstein, D.I. (1981). Role assessment, reserve strategy and the acquisition of information in asymmetric animal contests. *Animal Behaviour*, **29**, 221–240.

Pulliam, H.R., Pyke, G.H. & Caraco, T. (1982). The scanning behaviour of juncos: a game-theoretical approach. *Journal of Theoretical Biology*, **95**, 89–103.

Riechert, S.E. & Hammerstein, P. (1983). Game theory in the ecological context. *Annual Review of Ecology and Systematics*, **14**, 377–410.

Rothstein, S.I. (1979). Gene frequencies and selection for inhibitory traits, with special emphasis on the adaptiveness of territoriality. *American Naturalist*, **113**, 317–331.

Rubinstein, D.I. (1980). On the evolution of alternative mating strategies. *Limits to Action: the Allocation of Individual Behaviour* (Ed. by J.E.R. Staddon), pp. 65–100. Academic Press, New York.

Stearns, S.C. (1976). Life history tactics: a review of the ideas. *Quarterly Review of Biology*, **51**, 3–47.

Thornhill, R. & Alcock, J. (1983). *The Evolution of Insect Mating Systems*. Harvard University Press, Cambridge, Massachusetts.

Verner, J. (1977). On the adaptive significance of territoriality. *American Naturalist*, **111**, 769–775.

Vine, I. (1971). Risk of visual detection and pursuit by a predator and the selective advantage of flocking behaviour. *Journal of Theoretical Biology*, **30**, 405–422.

Williams, G.C. (1964). Measurement of consociation among fishes and comments on the evolution of schooling. *Papers of the Museum of Michigan State University, Biology Series*, **2**, 351–383.

3. INTRADEMIC GROUP SELECTION AND THE SEX RATIO

PAUL H. HARVEY*

School of Biological Sciences, University of Sussex,
Falmer, Brighton, Sussex BN1 9QG

SUMMARY

Intrademic group selection models are described. They offer a new perspective to familiar problems and processes in evolutionary biology. Whether that perspective is useful will be seen with the benefit of hindsight.

Intrademic group selection interpretations of female-biased sex ratios in a series of models are compared with individual selection interpretations of the same models. It is argued that alternative interpretations of the models are largely a matter of semantics. For example, even the definition of individual selection differs between the two perspectives.

INTRODUCTION

The renaissance of behavioural ecology has been accompanied by a shift of interest from causal to functional problems. Evolutionary questions now dominate the field. Many would argue that, compared with earlier attempts, the recent successes of this approach have resulted from an explicit recognition and avoidance of group selectionist arguments. Certainly, most current text books on the subject have been careful to emphasize the erroneous group selection interpretations found in the writings of early ethologists and ecologists. But we should not forget that it was Wynne Edwards' discussion of population regulation that led to the formulation of the particular models that most authors cite. Those models were mainly concerned with population regulation. An irony of the current situation is that behavioural ecologists tend to ignore population regulation (one of the main reasons for holding this Symposium), whereas models of that very topic form the basis for their avoidance of group selection.

What, then, is meant by group selection? It is difficult to find a definition. We generally accept that evolution by natural selection occurs if (i) there is variation, (ii) the variation is heritable, and (iii) some variants survive or reproduce better than others. It appears that selection can, therefore, be said to act at a number of levels: the gene, the individual, the group, the

* Present address: Department of Zoology, University of Oxford, South Parks Road, Oxford OX1 3PS.

population, the species, or even the ecosystem are examples. However, the source of heritable variation is the gene: if we ignore cultural transmission, the gene is *the* unit of heredity. Richard Dawkins (1976, 1982) goes beyond pointing out that the gene is the unit of heredity to arguing that the gene is also *the* unit of selection; his second book is subtitled *The Gene as the Unit of Selection*. At levels below the species (and I shall not be concerned with species selection here), genes move between groups to varying extents and it is only when that movement ceases that groups can be considered as units of heredity. Even the early group selection models acknowledged this for they actually incorporate allelic variants as their units of heredity (see below).

However, when animals with specified genotypes interact to influence each other's fitness, groups can provide a useful focus for the evolutionary biologist's attentions, as is clear from the early group selection debates. What was meant by group selection varied with context. In a most illuminating historical review, D.S. Wilson (1983a) identifies three slightly different derivations prior to 1970. They are due to Sewall Wright (1945), Wynne-Edwards (1962), and Maynard Smith (1964). As Wilson points out, they share certain features: (i) a number of groups comprise the global population; (ii) for altruistic alleles behaviour are identified which have the property of declining in frequency within groups while increasing group persistence or productivity; (iii) initially individuals are randomly distributed into groups; (iv) 'Without exception all the models identify allele frequency change within groups as individual selection and the differential contribution of the groups to the global population (whether through productivity or extinction) as group selection' (Wilson 1983a). I shall not consider these models in any detail because the issues they addressed were resolved several years ago (see Maynard Smith 1976).

In this paper I shall discuss some more recent models of structured populations that have been classified together by Wade (1978) as intrademic group selection models. These models offer a new perspective on familiar topics such as kin selection (e.g. Wade 1980), evolutionarily stable strategies (e.g. Wilson 1983a), mutualism (Wilson 1983b), the evolution of cheating (Wade & Breden 1980), and sex allocation theory (e.g. Wilson & Colwell 1981; Colwell 1981). Whether that new perspective is useful remains to be seen and the issue will, inevitably, be decided with the benefit of hindsight. Here I shall attempt to describe the approach and compare the ways that intrademic group selection and more traditional treatments interpret two cases.

INTRADEMIC GROUP SELECTION

Intrademic group selection (IGS) models were independently produced in five separate research papers (Charnov & Krebs 1975; Cohen & Eshel 1976; Matessi & Jayakar 1973; Price 1970; Wilson 1975). The five models are similar to the three produced before 1970 which are described above. Maynard Smith's (1964) 'mice in haystack' model is, in fact, a specialized IGS formulation. To qualify as an IGS model (Fig. 3.1):

   (i) a global population must be defined;
  (ii) genetic variation among individuals must be defined;
 (iii) the population (called a deme) must divide into groups (termed trait groups);
 (iv) selection must operate within trait groups so that the fitness of individuals depends in part on the genotypes of other group members;
  (v) trait groups must occasionally disperse.

If an allele is selected against within mixed groups but persists in the population as a whole, it is said to be maintained by intrademic group selection. It is important here to mention certain features of IGS models. First, trait groups can be initiated by random selection from the global population, but random selection is not necessary (Wilson 1983a). Second, trait groups can persist for a fraction of a generation or for many generations (Wilson 1983a). Third, condition (iv) above is from Wade (1978) though Wilson

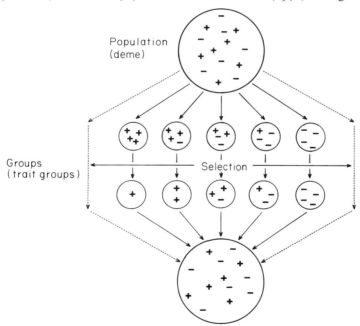

FIGURE 3.1. Intrademic group selection as defined by Wade (1978). The model works if an allele is selected against in mixed groups but increases in frequency across the population.

(1983a) preferred that groups 'must vary in their productivity in a way that correlates with allele frequencies. In other words there must be heritable variation in group fitness'. Therefore, Wilson did not *require* that individuals within groups influence each other's fitness, whereas Wade did. Wilson now prefers Wade's condition over his own (D.S. Wilson, pers. comm. 1984).

AN EXAMPLE OF INTRADEMIC GROUP SELECTION

Although IGS may seem to be firmly rooted in the classic group selection tradition, IGS does interpret familiar phenomena in new ways, as can be illustrated by adapting a well-known example of heterozygote advantage: the sickle-cell polymorphism in human populations. When genotype-dependent effects of parental care are introduced, the results can be interpreted as an example of IGS. The example is not wholly artificial (A. Fix, pers. comm. 1984), and it does focus some of the issues involved in the debate concerning the role of IGS in selecting for sex ratio bias. That will be the subject of the next section of this paper.

Human populations living in malaria-infested areas tend to be genetically polymorphic at the sickle-cell locus. The two alleles, labelled H and S, define three different genotypes: HH which is not resistant to malaria, HS which is resistant to malaria, and SS which is anaemic. HS individuals are likely to survive and reproduce since they suffer from neither malaria nor anaemia. If we assume that HH and SS individuals die before reaching reproductive age, then adults within a population are all HS. The frequency of the sickling allele S is 0·50 and this equilibrium is reached within one generation.

Now, introduce extended parental care into this system. The population is divided into family groups consisting of a father, a mother and their children. For didactic purposes, assume for the moment that every mother gives birth to four children. Each generation the families disperse and the surviving offspring from the whole population pair at random to form new family groups. We further assume that SS offspring die from anaemia but that, so long as at least one parent is resistant to malaria (the HS genotype), crops can be cultivated and HH offspring can be nourished and nursed through adulthood. There will now be two adult genotypes in the population: HS with frequency p and HH with frequency q. Three parental combinations result:

Parents	Frequency	Surviving offspring	Group productivity
$HS \times HS$	p^2	$1HH:2HS$ (:$1SS$ dies)	3
$HH \times HS$	$2pq$	$2HH:2HS$	4
$HH \times HH$	q^2	none	0

It follows that p', the frequency of HS in the next generation, is

$(2+2q)/(3+5q)$. Setting $p'=p$, the equilibrium frequency of HS is $1-\sqrt{0\cdot2}$ so that the frequency of S among adults in the population is about $0\cdot28$. It is not surprising that the equilibrium frequency of S is less when parental care is introduced. In effect, the only real difference between the two models is that with parental care some HH offspring, which would otherwise have died, survive to adulthood. If they mate with HS individuals, they produce viable offspring.

However, the parental care model is also an example of IGS. 'The model begins with a large global population . . . individuals then distribute themselves into local groups . . . selection now operates within groups . . . after selection the groups dissolve, and individuals mix throughout the global population' (Wilson 1983a). In one of the groups containing both H and S alleles, S is selected against, whereas in the other H and S are equally fit. Within-group selection therefore favours H. Since selection within groups favours H, then S is maintained in the population by intrademic group selection, i.e. the differential productivity of groups. This is evident because groups containing S have a higher productivity (3 or 4) than those without S (0).

Selection against S within groups and differential group productivity would also be apparent if groups were permanent rather than temporary associations: each generation two of the surviving offspring sib-mate to become parents of the next generation. When both parents are heterozygotes, S is selected against. But when one or both parents is a heterozygote, S can be lost through sampling between generations. The transitions that can occur are shown in Fig. 3.2. The absorbing combination is $HH \times HH$ which then goes extinct. Before extinction, however, S is lost from each group.

The conclusion that S is maintained in the population by intrademic group selection may seem contradictory because, under the individual case, the equilibrium frequency of S was higher: $0\cdot50$ compared with $0\cdot28$. But, under group selection terminology, the individual selection version was no such thing: allele frequency change within groups (rather than in the global population) would be identified with individual selection. In fact temporary groups were necessarily invoked for mating, but no selection took place within them. Following Wilson & Colwell's (1981) argument for the sex ratio, an hermaphroditic rather than asexual version might provide a plausible individual selection alternative. Here, since HS must always be the parents and their only surviving offspring would be HS, S is still maintained in the population at a frequency of $0\cdot5$. Wilson & Colwell would then argue that, in this case, the individual is also the group so we would expect S to be maintained in the global population.

Isolated groups with sib-mating

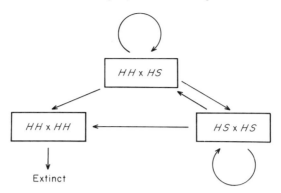

FIG. 3.2. Transitions that can occur between endogamous groups in the sickle-cell model. Note that the absorbing state is the absence of the S allele.

INTRADEMIC GROUP SELECTION
AND THE SEX RATIO

The most interesting and controversial application of IGS theory has been to the sex ratio. In the following discussion I shall assume that the sexes are equally costly to produce in terms of resource allocation so that a 50:50 sex ratio results from a 50:50 allocation of resources. In one of his seminal papers, Hamilton (1967) discussed the problem of why some sex ratios do not accord with the Fisherian expectation of 50%. For example, in several species of parasitic hymenoptera a number of females lay their eggs in a single host and their broods are often female biased. Hamilton produced a model of such systems which allowed the calculation of a female-biased equilibrium sex ratio.

Consider a large sexual population of fertilized females that divides into local groups of size n. Females within groups lay their eggs and then die. The young develop and then mate among themselves. The males die and the new generation of fertilized females disperses to re-establish the large population. Subsequently, new groups of n females are formed by random sampling from the large population. The cycle is repeated in each generation. Using a game theoretic approach, Hamilton (1967) showed that at equilibration females allocate a proportion of r_H reproductive resources to sons, where

$$r_H = (n-1)/2n \qquad (1)$$

So, when $n=2$, $r_H=0.25$ but, as n increases, r_H approaches an asymptote of 0.5. An increase in n is, of course, associated with less competition for mates among brothers. (The apparent absence of resource-allocation to males when

$n = 1$ should be interpreted to mean that a single female only allocates enough resources to sons to ensure that all her daughters are fertilized. The model assumes a very large family size, and that individual males can fertilize any number of females.)

Why should Hamilton's model lead to a female-biased equilibrium sex ratio? Following Hamilton (1967), Taylor (1981) and Grafen (1984) give particularly lucid interpretations in terms of individual advantage. They focus on the number of grandchildren produced by females who allocate different proportions of resources to the two sexes. In Hamilton's model the number of grandchildren produced per daughter remains constant, while the number of grandchildren produced per son varies with the sex ratio produced. Grafen identifies two reasons why increased resource allocation to females is selectively favoured. First, there are diminishing returns (in terms of number of grandchildren produced per son) associated with producing each additional son. To take an extreme example, if a mother produced three instead of two sons that compete for mating access to a particular female, the chances of any individual son fathering the female's offspring would be reduced from one-half to one-third. This is not the case for very large panmictic populations where the average mating success of brothers is effectively independent of their numbers. Grafen's second reason is that females can increase the number of mates for their sons by producing more daughters. One process that can cause this effect is sib-mating: if brothers mate sisters, then a mother can increase a son's mating success by producing more daughters. Of course, by producing additional daughters, the mother also increases the mating success of the sons of other females laying in the same group.

In Hamilton's model, the females disperse after they are fertilized. In some later versions (Bulmer & Taylor 1980; Wilson & Colwell 1981) groups persist for several generations before dispersing. Under such circumstances, Grafen notes a third advantage to producing a female-biased sex ratio: after the first generation, mothers who produce daughters provide additional matings for sons of relatives. This is because individuals within the groups are more related to each other than they are to individuals randomly selected from the population at large.

However, Colwell (1981) and Wilson & Colwell (1981) demonstrate that IGS also provides a ready interpretation of the female-biased sex ratio. Hamilton (1979) had previously produced a similar analysis, but did not make quite the same claims for it as do Colwell and Wilson. To fix ideas, we shall consider Hamilton's original model which is the one treated by Colwell (1981). It has all the properties of an IGS model as defined above. In mixed groups composed of 'Fisher' females who produce a 1 : 1 sex ratio and of 'Hamilton' females who produce the evolutionarily stable sex ratio, 'Hamilton' females decrease in frequency while 'Fisher' females increase in frequency. However, in the population as a whole, 'Hamilton' females increase in frequency. Clearly then, by definition, the 'Hamilton' females are increasing in frequency by IGS. A simple numerical example taken from Maynard Smith (1983) demonstrates this (Table 3.1). If we consider groups consisting of pairs of females ($n = 2$), then there are three types of groups: the pure 'Hamilton' groups produce 48 grandchildren, the mixed groups 40, and the pure 'Fisher' 32. In the mixed groups, the 'Hamilton' female produces 18·7 grandchildren compared with the 'Fisher' female's 21·3.

Maynard Smith (1983) points out that if we treat the problem as a two

TABLE 3.1. Fertilized females from a large population randomly assort into groups of two. Each has four offspring. 'Hamilton' (H) females produce three female and one male offspring, while 'Fisher' (F) females produce two of each sex. The offspring mate within the group. Each female offspring will, itself, have four children. The reproductive success of male offspring is determined by how many mates are available within the group and how many other males are competing for those mates. This numerical example is taken from Maynard Smith (1983)

Type of female:	H		H		H		F		F	F
Number of offspring	3♀	1♂	3♀	1♂	3♀	1♂	2♀	2♂	2♀ 2♂	2♀ 2♂
Grandchildren per child	4	12	4	12	4	6·7	4	6·7	4 4	4 4
Total grandchildren	12+12		12+12		12+6·7		8+13·3		8+8	8+8
	24		24		18·7		21·3		16	16

person game and draw up the payoff matrix, then pure 'Hamilton' females constitute the evolutionarily stable strategy. Despite the fact that she leaves less grandchildren than the 'Fisher' female in the same group as herself, a female playing the 'Hamilton' strategy leaves more grandchildren than she would if she played 'Fisher'. She also leaves more grandchildren if she plays 'Hamilton' rather than 'Fisher' when the other group member is a 'Hamilton' female. Although it may not pay in terms of relative fitness within mixed groups (and this is the IGS definition of individual selection), it always pays in terms of absolute fitness to play 'Hamilton' instead of 'Fisher'. The IGS interpretation points out that 'Hamilton' females lose out in terms of individual selection in mixed groups; that is only true if individual selection refers to relative rather than absolute fitness. The reason that 'Fisher' females produce more grandchildren than 'Hamilton' females in mixed groups is by way of Grafen's second effect; by producing more daughters, the 'Hamilton' females are providing their sons with extra matings. But, by so doing, they are also providing the 'Fisher' females' sons with extra mating opportunities.

Since the 'Fisher' females produce more sons than the 'Hamilton' females, the 'Fisher' females profit disproportionately.

The questions remain: does the 'Hamilton' type of female spread through (a) the diminishing returns associated with producing each additional son, (b) the production of additional daughters giving sons additional mates, or (c) both effects? In Hamilton's original formulation, both effects could be operating. We need to separate them.

Charnov (1982) shows that we still get a female-biased sex ratio when sib-mating is not allowed in Hamilton's basic model where groups dispense each generation. The evolutionarily stable sex allocation to males is

$$r_C = (n-2)/(2n-3) \qquad (2)$$

Groups must be founded by three or more fertilized females if we are to compare how a 'Charnov' female does compared with a 'Fisher' female. When $n = 3$, 'Fisher' females produce a $1:1$ sex ratio whereas 'Charnov' females produce the evolutionarily stable $1:2$ female-biased sex ratio. Table 3.2 shows how many male and female children and how many grandchildren 'Fisher' versus 'Charnov' females produce, assuming that each female produces six offspring. In agreement with the IGS interpretation, in mixed groups 'Fisher' females do better, but the productivity of pure 'Fisher' groups is lower than that of pure 'Charnov' groups.

'Charnov' females produce two sons compared with the 'Fisher' females' three sons. If diminishing returns per additional son does select for female-biased progenies, 'Charnov' females in a group with two 'Fisher' females should have more grandchildren *per son* than should 'Fisher' females that compete in a group with two other Fisher females. That is exactly what happens: the 'Charnov' female in a group with two 'Fisher' females has 7·2

TABLE 3.2. Fertilized females from a large population randomly assort into groups of three. Each female has six offspring. 'Charnov' (C) females produce four female and two male offspring, while 'Fisher' (F) females produce three of each sex. The offspring mate within the group, but not with their sibs. Each female offspring will, itself, have six children. The reproductive success of male offspring depends on how many mates are available within the group and how many other males are competing for them

Type of group	CCC	FFF	CFF	CFF	CCF	CCF
Type of female	C	F	C	F	C	F
Number of offspring	4♀ 2♂	3♀ 3♂	4♀ 2♂	3♀ 3♂	4♀ 2♂	3♀ 3♂
Grandchildren per child	6 12	6 6	6 7·2	6 7·6	6 9·3	6 9·6
Total grandchildren	24+24	18+18	24+14·4	18+22·8	24+18·6	18+28·8
	48	36	38·4	40·8	42·6	46·8

grandchildren by each son, whereas the equivalent 'Fisher' female has only 6·0 grandchildren per son. Furthermore, that same 'Charnov' female produces 38·4 grandchildren compared with the 'Fisher' female's 36 grandchildren. The results are as we would expect with diminishing returns per additional son selecting for a female-biased sex ratio.

However, by preventing sib-mating within local groups, the diminishing returns per additional son effect is increased because brothers compete more strongly among themselves for mating access to fewer females (their sisters can only be mated by non-relatives, whereas any females for which brothers compete have less potential suitors because those females' sibs are now excluded). Maynard Smith (see Appendix) has devised a suitable control where sib-mating is prevented but where competition among brothers is not increased. It is the same as Hamilton's original formulation but females lay their sons in one group and their daughters in another. (The model produces the same evolutionarily stable sex ratio for the same reasons as one produced by Werren (1983) in which females disperse before mating, while male offspring from a group remain to form a lek.) In Maynard Smith's model, groups of size n are actually contributed to by $2n$ females. I keep the notation n to describe whole clutches (containing a female and a male complement from different mothers) so that comparison can be made with formulae (1) and (2). The evolutionarily stable allocation to males is:

$$r_{MS} = (n-1)/(2n-1) \qquad (3)$$

Increased female bias in sex allocation is seen as a reduction in r_H, r_C or r_{MS}.

Grafen (1984) identified two factors selecting for female-biased sex ratios:
(i) 'diminishing returns to producing sons—each additional son creates fewer and fewer additional grandoffspring for his mother';
(ii) 'making a daughter increases the number of grandoffspring males produce for their mother, by increasing the number of mates'.

Hamilton's model has both (i) and (ii) operating, Charnov's eliminates (ii) but increases the effect of (i), and Maynard Smith's eliminates (ii) but holds the effect of (i) the same as in Hamilton's original model.

Charnov's model makes an interesting comparison with Hamilton's and Maynard Smith's (see Fig. 3.3). As with Maynard Smith's model, there is no effect due to (ii) but there is always a greater effect due to (i); as we would expect, r_C is less than r_{MS} for all n. If we compare Charnov's model with Hamilton's, there is always a greater effect due to (i) but less due to (ii) in Charnov's than Hamilton's. The two forces should select on the equilibrium

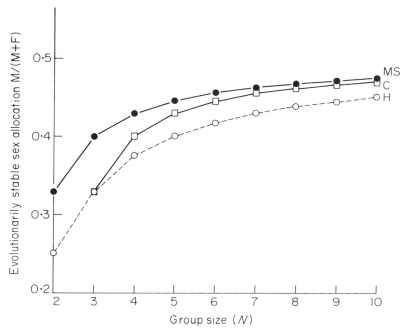

FIG. 3.3. Evolutionarily stable sex allocation (proportion of males) in three different models as a function of group size. The models are after Hamilton (H), Charnov (C) and Maynard Smith (MS); see text for details.

sex ratio in opposite directions. When n is greater than 3, r_H is always less than r_C. However, the equilibrium sex allocation is the same under both models at $n = 3$. At this group size the increased effect due to (i) in Charnov's model is exactly compensated for by the presence of (ii) in Hamilton's. At larger group sizes, $r_H < r_C$, which can be interpreted to mean that the presence of (ii) in Hamilton's model constitutes a more effective force shifting the equilibrium sex allocation towards females than does the increased effect of (i) in Charnov's model.

Nevertheless, Colwell (1981) asserts that the diminishing returns resulting from producing additional males (which can for most purposes be loosely termed local mate competition (after Hamilton 1967)) 'itself cannot select for female-biased progenies'. We can investigate this claim by adapting Maynard Smith's model. The model has no sib-mating because sons and daughters of a given female are placed in two separate patches, but there is both local mate competition among sons and a female-biased sex ratio. However, local mate competition would be eliminated and patch structure retained if each son was placed in a separate patch. Under these circumstances, the sex ratio is not biased (see Appendix). Since the essential group structure is retained but only the degree of local mate competition differs between the two versions of Maynard Smith's model, it appears that Colwell was mistaken and local mate competition itself (or Grafen's factor (i) above) *can* select for female-biased progenies.

Clearly then, the effects of both (i) diminishing returns per son associated with producing additional sons, and (ii) increased returns per son associated with producing additional daughters are apparent in these models. The IGS treatment can readily be interpreted as saying that group productivity depends on the number of females in the group at various stages. First, groups with more foundresses produce more dispersing females. Second, group productivity per female foundress depends on the number of female offspring produced by each foundress (as long as all those offspring are fertilized before dispersal). Since number of offspring per female is constant in these models, the number of female offspring per foundress depends on her resource allocation to females as opposed to males. A female-biased sex ratio results in higher group productivity (the 'group selection' component). However, within mixed groups, those foundresses that do not produce a female-biased sex ratio leave more grandchildren because their male offspring have a higher reproductive success than do the female offspring of the sex-biased foundresses (the 'individual selection' component).

There is no conflict between the IGS and more traditional ways of viewing these models (see also Grafen 1984). But there are two important caveats to such a claim. First, individual selection can mean different things to different authors. The more usual interpretation is with reference to global populations, while the group selection definition refers specifically to genetically heterogeneous local populations (trait groups). The second caveat is that when a model has been interpreted in one way, alternative interpretations are not thereby precluded. An example cited above is Colwell's (1981) claim that, because the female-biased sex ratio involves IGS, local mate competition is not relevant. It would be equally unreasonable to argue that because female-biased sex ratios involve local mate competition, IGS is not relevant.

ACKNOWLEDGMENTS

I thank Charles Godfray, John Maynard Smith, Jeff Waage and David Sloan Wilson for helpful comments on the manuscript.

REFERENCES

Bulmer, M.G. & Taylor, P.D. (1980). Sex ratio under the haystack model. *Journal of theoretical Biology*, **86**, 83–89.

Charnov, E.L. & Krebs, J.R. (1975). The evolution of alarm calls: altruism or manipulation? *American Naturalist*, **109**, 107–112.

Charnov, E.L. (1982). *The Theory of Sex Allocation*. Princeton University Press, Princeton.

Cohen, D. & Eshel, I. (1976). On the founder effect and the evolution of altruistic traits. *Theoretical Population Biology*, **10**, 276–302.

Colwell, R.K. (1981). Group selection is implicated in the evolution of female-biased sex ratios. *Nature*, **290**, 401–404.

Dawkins, R. (1976). *The Selfish Gene*. Oxford University Press, Oxford.

Dawkins, R. (1982). *The Extended Phenotype: The Gene as the Unit of Selection*. Freeman, London.

Grafen, A. (1984). Natural selection, kin selection and group selection. *Behavioural Ecology: an Evolutionary Approach* (Ed. by J.R. Krebs & N.B. Davies) (2nd edn) pp. 62–84. Blackwell Scientific Publications, Oxford.

Hamilton, W.D. (1967). Extraordinary sex ratios. *Science*, **156**, 477–488.

Hamilton, W.D. (1979). Wingless and fighting males in fig wasps and other insects. *Sexual Selection and Reproductive Competition in Insects* (Ed. by M.S. Blum & N.A. Blum.), pp. 167–220. Academic Press, New York.

Matessi, C. & Jayakar, S.D. (1973). A model for the evolution of altruistic behaviour. *Genetics*, **74**, S174.

Maynard Smith, J. (1964). Group selection and kin selection. *Nature*, **201**, 1145–1147.

Maynard Smith, J. (1976). Group selection. *Quarterly Review of Biology*, **51**, 277–283.

Maynard Smith, J. (1983). Models of evolution. *Proceedings of the Royal Society of London B*, **219**, 315–325.

Price, G.R. (1970). Selection and covariance. *Nature* **227**, 520–521.

Taylor, P.D. (1981). Intra-sex and inter-sex sibling interactions as sex determinants. *Nature*, **291**, 64–66.

Wade, M.J. (1978). A critical review of the models of group selection. *Quarterly Review of Biology*, **53**, 101–104.

Wade, M.J. (1980). Kin selection: its components. *Science*, **210**, 665–667.

Wade, M.J. & Breden, F. (1980). The evolution of cheating and selfish behaviour. *Behavioral Ecology and Sociobiology*, **7**, 167–172.

Werren, J.H. (1983). Sex ratio evolution under local mate competition in a parasitic wasp. *Evolution*, **37**, 116–124.

Wilson, D.S. (1975). A theory of group selection. *Proceedings of the National Academy of Science USA*, **72**, 143–146.

Wilson, D.S. (1983a). The group selection controversy: history and current status. *Annual Review of Ecology and Systematics*, **14**, 159–187.

Wilson, D.S. (1983b). The effect of population structure on the evolution of mutualism: a field test involving burying beetles and their phoretic mites. *American Naturalist*, **121**, 851–870.

Wilson, D.S. & Colwell, R.K. (1981). Evolution of sex ratio in structured demes. *Evolution*, **35**, 882–897.

Wright, S. (1945). Tempo and mode in evolution: a critical review. *Ecology*, **26**, 415–419.

Wynne-Edwards, V.C. (1962). *Animal Dispersion in Relation to Social Behaviour*. Oliver and Boyd, Edinburgh.

APPENDIX: BY JOHN MAYNARD SMITH

The effects of local mate competition and of sib-mating can be compared by analysing the following rather artificial model. The environment consists of patches. Each female produces all her daughters in one patch, and all her sons in another. n females contribute daughters to each patch, and a different n females contribute sons to the same patch. A female produces r offspring. Following Hamilton (1967), we seek a sex ratio S^* which is uninvadable.

Suppose that almost all females produce the sex ratio S^*. Consider a rare type of female, G, producing the ratio S. She produces $r(1 - S)$ daughters. If there are enough males to ensure that all females are mated, each daughter produces r offspring. She also produces rS sons, which breed in a patch containing $nr(1 - S^*)$ females and $(n-1)rS^* + rS$ males. Hence, each of her sons produces $nr^2(1 - S^*)/[(n-1)rS^* + rS]$ offspring.

If the population is diploid, the expected number of copies of a gene present in female G that are transmitted to her grandchildren is

$$T = \frac{r^2}{4}\left\{1 - S + \frac{nS(1 - S^*)}{(n-1)S^* + S}\right\}.$$

If the sex ratio is determined by autosomal genes acting in the mother, then S^* must be such that T is a maximum when $S = S^*$: if this were not so, then a mutant causing the sex ratio that maximizes T could invade an S^* population. That is:

$$\left.\frac{\delta T}{\delta S}\right|_{S=S^*} = 0,$$

or, after simplification,

$$S^* = \frac{n-1}{2n-1}.$$

This compares with $S^* = (n-1)/2n$, obtained by Hamilton for the case in which the sons and daughters of a female are in the same patch and can mate. For a given finite n, the stable sex ratio shows a greater female bias in Hamilton's model. This is because a female which produces an extra daughter also provides an extra mating opportunity for her sons.

The female bias in the present model is due to local mate competition only. We can see this by analysing an even more artificial model. It is identical to the one just described, except that a female contributes each of her rS^* sons to a different patch. Consider again a female G which produces rS sons and $r(1 - S)$ daughters. As before, each daughter produces r offspring. A typical patch contains $nr(1 - S^*)$ females and nrS^* males (all from different mothers). Hence, a typical male gets $(1 - S^*)/S^*$ matings. This is also the expected number of matings for a son of female G. Hence

$$T = \frac{r^2}{4}\left\{1 - S + \frac{S(1 - S^*)}{S^*}\right\},$$

and $\delta T/\delta S = 0$ when $S^* = 1/2$. That is, if there is patch structure, but no local mate competition and no inbreeding, there is no bias in the stable sex ratio.

Note. I have used a somewhat hand-waving method of finding the stationary sex ratio for these models, and have not proved stability. The same results can be obtained, with greater effort, from a sound genetic model, and stability can be proved.

4. CLASSIFICATION OF HABITATS BY SELECTION PRESSURES: A SYNTHESIS OF LIFE-CYCLE AND r/K THEORY

R. SIBLY[1] AND P. CALOW[2]

[1] *Department of Pure and Applied Zoology, University of Reading, Whiteknights, Reading RG6 2AJ, and*
[2] *Department of Zoology, University of Sheffield, Sheffield S10 2TN*

SUMMARY

High offspring survivorship selects for greater reproductive investment: towards semelparity (breed once then die) as opposed to iteroparity (repeated breeding). Better growth conditions for juveniles selects for the production of more smaller offspring, as opposed to fewer larger offspring. These predictions form the basis of a classification of habitats in terms of indices S and G related to offspring survivorship and growth conditions respectively. This classification is discussed in relation to the $r–K$ and other classifications.

INTRODUCTION

Much attention has been given to the problem of classifying habitats according to selection pressures, in the hope of being able to associate the characteristics of habitats with those of the organisms found within them. This was the basis of much of the early work on comparative ecophysiology (e.g. Chapman 1931). As evolutionary and ecological theory has matured, however, there has been a welcome shift in this programme from a posteriori description to a priori prediction (Calow & Townsend 1981) and from a concern with the particular, to the development of a general classification, the dream of an 'ecological periodic table' (Southwood 1977).

Perhaps the first rigorous attempt at such a predictive general classification was the r/K dichotomy of MacArthur (particularly well presented in MacArthur 1972). In its most basic form this is concerned with the *effects of population density* on general demographic traits (Boyce, in press), especially on fitness, F, measured by rate of increase per individual. The simplest possible relation between this measure of fitness and density is the straight line

$$\text{(rate of increase per individual)} = r - r/K \text{ (density)},$$

where r and K are parameters characterized below. Writing density $= N$ gives

$$\frac{1}{N}\frac{\mathrm{d}N}{\mathrm{d}t} = r - \frac{r}{K}N \qquad (1)$$

$$\therefore \frac{\mathrm{d}N}{\mathrm{d}t} = N\left(r - \frac{rN}{K}\right) \qquad (2)$$

which provides the starting point for contemporary population dynamics. Rate of increase per individual is a measure of fitness (F) of an organism obtained by (simplistically) ignoring all age structure. Much confusion arises because intrinsic rate of increase has been used in two different senses, both to mean $1/N\,\mathrm{d}N/\mathrm{d}t$, i.e. fitness, and to mean fitness at zero density, i.e. r_A or r_B in Fig. 4.1. The phrase 'intrinsic rate of increase' will therefore be abandoned in this paper.

Characters bringing about high F at low density might be the same as those bringing about high F at high density, in which case there is no more to say. On the other hand, if superior fitness at low density is incompatible with superior fitness at high density, then two distinct types of organisms may evolve; A being fitter than B at low density and B being fitter than A at high density. In Fig. 4.1, rate of increase per individual at zero density is labelled r, and density when rate of increase per individual is zero is labelled K (carrying capacity). A increases at a faster rate at low density ($r_A > r_B$) and is said to be r-selected. On the other hand, B increases at a faster rate at high density provided its carrying

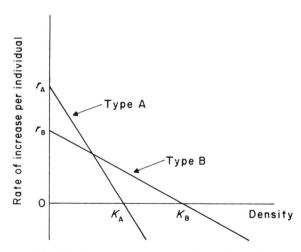

Fig. 4.1. r- and K-selection (see text for explanation). (After MacArthur, 1972.)

capacity is higher ($K_B > K_A$) (MacArthur 1972; Sibly & Calow 1983), and B is said to be *K*-selected.

However, a classification of selection pressures based only on the effects of density *N* on fitness *F* cannot be very precise because *F* is made up of a number of components (fecundity, survivorship, growth rate of offspring; see below), different values of which might maximize *F* at either low or high density. Moreover, the density effects themselves might occur in different ways (e.g. as a result of competition, predation or dispersal) and the consequences of one might not be the same as those of another (Boyce, in press). Only by the addition of a number of auxiliary hypotheses has it been possible to construct classifications rich with predictions about phenotypic traits. Thus, the 'Principle of Allocation', that organisms with finite resources have to allocate them between competing metabolic demands, ensures a trade-off between fecundity-promoting and survival-promoting traits (Cody 1966; see also Calow 1979) and the suggestion of an incompatibility between high rates and high efficiencies of production also predicts precise distinctions between traits that should evolve under conditions with and without resource limitations (Odum & Pinkerton 1955; MacArthur 1972; Smith 1976). Pianka (1970) seems to have made a number of implicit assumptions in constructing his detailed catalogue of differences between the consequences of *r* and *K* selection (e.g. his Table 1). Recognizing the limitations of a classification based on a single parameter, population density, other authors have tried to enrich the theory by incorporating other forces. Whittaker (1975), for example, pointed out that some populations occur in harsh environments and that environmental stress might have been a dominant force in shaping their evolution. Environmental stress is also incorporated into the classificatory schemes of Grime (1974, 1979), Southwood (1977) and Greenslade (1983).

The problem with such developments is not so much that they are outwith the spirit of what MacArthur intended (Boyce, in press), but that they are not defined very rigorously. However, rigorous definition is now made feasible by parallel developments in an appreciation of the way *F* is affected by age-specific schedules of survivorship, fecundity and growth rate of offspring (life-cycle or life-history theory; Charlesworth 1980; Sibly & Calow 1983). The intention here is to use life-history theory to construct an enlarged, but rigorous, classification of selection pressures, based on Pianka's classification since this has had an enormous influence on the development of research in evolutionary ecology.

We will conclude that one-dimensional classification, by population density, should be replaced by a two-dimensional scheme in which the classifying variables are those identified as being of key importance in life-cycle evolution. The two variables are: (i) an index of age-specific survivorship (S) and (ii) an index of growth rate of offspring (G). Both S and G are determined by environmental conditions (extrinsic factors) but are influenced by internal constraints and trade-offs (intrinsic factors). By definition, habitat classification is more concerned with extrinsic factors, but in practice extrinsic and intrinsic factors are often difficult to distinguish. Therefore, after defining S and G in terms of life-cycle theory we offer operational definitions as the first stage towards applying the classification in the real world. Finally, we also discuss how the classification, based on S and G, relates to the ones of Whittaker, Grime and Greenslade mentioned above.

Pianka's predictions

From the point of view of this paper, there are two main predictions about life-cycle traits in Pianka's classification (Pianka 1970).

1 At higher population densities, with more competition, the optimal strategy is to allocate less matter and energy to reproduction, and more to adult maintenance.
2 At higher population densities, with more competition, the optimal strategy is to produce fewer, larger offspring.

These will be referred to as predictions 1 and 2. They deal with the questions of how much to invest in reproduction, and how to distribute that investment between individual offspring. We shall use life-cycle theory to evaluate predictions 1 and 2, and put forward two new predictions (3 and 4) after defining fitness and hence identifying the fundamental basis of the theory.

Definition of fitness

As stated above the fitness F of phenotype p in environment E is measured as its rate of increase per individual, and is defined by the equation

$$1 = \sum_t e^{-Ft} l_t(p,E) n_t(p,E) \qquad (3)$$

where t is age in years, $l_t(p,E)$ is survivorship from birth until age t of females of phenotype p in environment E, and $n_t(p,E)$ is the number of female offspring produced per breeding female of age t with phenotype p in environment E. If the sexes have different life histories a more sophisticated approach must be used (for further discussion see Charlesworth 1980, and Bulmer 1983). If we assume that age and experience have no effect on adult rates of survival and reproduction, so that the number of female offspring produced per female is always n, then eqn (3) can be simplified. The form it takes depends on whether the costs of reproduction are incurred before the eggs are laid (here referred to as *direct costing*) or after the eggs are laid (*absorption costing*) (Sibly & Calow, in press). Costs of reproduction are in terms of increased adult mortality or increased delay before breeding again. Under direct costing eqn (3) simplifies to

$$1 = e^{-(F+\mu_1)t_1}n + e^{(F+\mu_2)t_2} \tag{4}$$

where μ_1 is juvenile mortality rate from birth to maturity (defined as the moment when costs of reproduction are first paid) at age t_1, μ_2 is adult mortality rate, and time t_2 elapses between maturity and breeding, successive breedings also being at intervals t_2 apart. It will sometimes be convenient to replace $e^{-\mu_1 t_1}$ by S_1 (juvenile survivorship) and $e^{-\mu_2 t_2}$ by S_2 (adult survivorship between breedings). Under absorption costing eqn (3) simplifies to

$$1 = e^{-(F+\mu_1)t_1}n + e^{-(F+\mu_2)t_2} \tag{5}$$

with the same notation except that first breeding occurs at maturity; successive breedings are still intervals t_2 apart.

LIFE-CYCLE THEORY AND PIANKA'S PREDICTIONS

Prediction 1

Prediction 1 was that at lower density with less competition the optimal strategy would be to put more matter and energy into reproduction each breeding season. Thus, if initial offspring size is constant, more offspring will be obtained (the trade-off between offspring number and initial offspring size will be considered in the next section). Increased investment in offspring will however be at some cost to the adult, and it will be assumed here that the cost is increased adult mortality (though it could in principle be in terms of increased time between breeding, see Sibly & Calow 1983, for a discussion). In both direct and absorption costing a trade-off is thought to exist between offspring number and adult mortality, since resources devoted to reproduction (increasing n) are denied to body maintenance (increasing μ_2), a trade-off which probably occurs generally (Williams 1966; Calow & Sibly 1983; Sibly & Calow 1983 and in press; Calow 1984; but c.f. Bell 1984a and b). The optimal strategy is characterized by

$$\frac{\partial \mu_2}{\partial n} = \frac{S_1 S_2}{t_2} e^{-Ft_1 - Ft_2} \tag{6}$$

under direct costing and

$$\frac{\partial \mu_2}{\partial n} = \frac{S_1}{t_2 S_2} e^{-Ft_1 + Ft_2} \tag{7}$$

under absorption costing (Sibly & Calow, in press). Provided that $\partial \mu_2/(\partial n)$ increases with n (i.e. μ_2 increases increasingly with n) then n_{optimal} increases with

$$\frac{S_1 S_2}{t_2} e^{Ft_1 + Ft_2} \text{ (direct costing)}$$

or

$$\frac{S_1}{t_2 S_2} e^{-Ft_1 + Ft_2} \text{ (absorption costing).}$$

In both cases the optimal strategy is to produce more offspring if juvenile survivorship is higher. The effect of the other parameters depends on whether the costs of reproduction are paid before or after the eggs are laid.

Under direct costing, higher extrinsic adult survival favours more offspring. Slightly lower values of t_2 (which might result from an improved food supply for example) favour more offspring if and only if $-F < 1/(t_2) + \mu_2$ (which is necessarily true in a stable population in which $F=0$, because $1/(t_2) + \mu_2$ is always greater than zero) (see Appendix 1). Under absorption costing, higher extrinsic adult survival favours *fewer* offspring (i.e. the reverse of the direct costing prediction). Slightly lower values of t_2 favour more offspring if and only if $F < 1/(t_2) - \mu_2$ (Appendix 1). These effects can be combined in a habitat index S; under direct costing,

$$S = \frac{S_1 S_2}{t_2} e^{Ft_1 + Ft_2} \tag{8}$$

while under absorption costing,

$$S = \frac{S_1}{t_2 S_2} e^{-Ft_1 + Ft_2} \tag{9}$$

More offspring should be produced if S is higher (we shall refer to this new result as Prediction 3). It is to be noted, though, that Prediction 3 is very sensitive to the form of the trade-off between μ_2 and n and that though the type of trade-off considered here may be plausible (Calow & Sibly 1983; Calow 1984) it has not been demonstrated beyond doubt in any organism (see also p. 77 and c.f. Bell 1984a and b). More experimental work is urgently needed here. Finally, with regard to Prediction 1 it appears that more matter and energy should be put into reproduction if and only if S is relatively high. Hence, for compatability with Pianka's scheme it is necessary that r-strategies are characterized by high S values, where S is defined by eqns (8) or (9) as appropriate.

It is our view that juvenile mortality rate is likely to be far more sensitive to environmental conditions than that of adults, and if time between breedings is fixed (as it might be in, e.g. annual breeders) then S would be proportional to S_1. S_1 might therefore turn out to be a useful operational measure of S.

Prediction 2

Initial offspring size will affect time taken to reach first breeding, since if more resources are invested in an offspring initially, fewer remain to be acquired. Thus, other things being equal, bigger offspring would breed earlier, which usually increases fitness (animals which breed once in the season after birth could provide exceptions to this rule; see Sibly & Calow 1983, for further discussion). On the other hand, if offspring are initially bigger, then fewer can be produced from a given quantity of resources. Since, other things being equal, producing fewer offspring decreases fitness, some trade-off has to be made between offspring number and initial offspring size. It turns out that the optimal strategy depends on conditions for individual offspring growth (Sibly & Calow 1982, 1983). If offspring will grow quickly then more, smaller offspring should be produced. The reason is that time to first breeding t_1 is affected both by initial offspring size (Fig. 4.2) and by individual growth rate. If growth conditions are better (as in curve (a) in Fig. 4.2) then offspring will be able to breed earlier (which is why curve (a) is below curve (b). In addition it will take less time to grow from any size X to any other size Y (dotted lines in

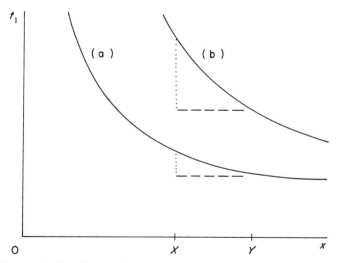

FIG. 4.2. Time to first breeding (t_1) plotted against initial offspring size ($\log_e$ scale), x. Curves (a) and (b) represent good and poor growth conditions for offspring. Dotted lines indicate times taken to grow from size X to size Y. See text for further explanation.

Fig. 4.2), so curve (a) is everywhere shallower than curve (b). (It is assumed that the time taken to grow from size X to size Y is $t_1(X) - t_1(Y)$.) Suppose that the quantity of resources available for reproduction during a particular attempt is Z and that initial offspring size is w, so that $n = Z/w$ (by the 'Principle of Allocation' discussed above). Let $x = \log_e w$. Then from eqn (5)

$$I = e^{-(F+\mu_1)t_1}\frac{Z}{w} + e^{-(F+\mu_2)t_2} \tag{10}$$

$$\therefore I = e^{-(F+\mu_1)t_1 + \log_e Z - x} + e^{-(F+\mu_2)t_2} \tag{11}$$

A necessary condition for F to be maximized is that $\partial F/(\partial w) = 0$, or equivalently $\partial F/(\partial x) = 0$. Differentiating eqn (11) with respect to x and setting $\partial F/(\partial x) = 0$ we obtain

$$-(F+\mu_1)\frac{\partial t_1}{\partial x} - I = 0$$

i.e.
$$\frac{\partial t_1}{\partial x} = -\frac{I}{F+\mu_1} \tag{12}$$

This equation can also be derived from eqn(4) (Sibly & Calow, in press). Hence, the optimal strategy is characterized by a particular slope of curve in Fig. 4.2. Other things being equal, the optimal initial size will be smaller in good growth conditions since curve (a) is shallower than curve (b). The prediction is unaffected by the actual quantity of resources allocated to reproduction, Z, since Z does not feature in eqn (12). Assuming that Z is constant, then, more smaller offspring should be produced in better growth conditions for juveniles (Prediction 4).

This prediction is somewhat sensitive to the values of F and μ_1 (eqn (12)). If F or μ_1 is higher the optimal slope of the $t_1(x)$ curve in Fig. 4.2 is shallower so the optimal strategy is to have fewer larger offspring. Thus, three independent factors favour the production of more, smaller offspring: (i) better growth conditions for the offspring, (ii) lower fitness F, (iii) lower juvenile mortality, μ_1. If these factors vary inversely with one another then the optimal compromise is determined by eqn (12) with reference to the $t_1(x)$ curve.

In assessing growth conditions for offspring in practice it will be necessary to use an index, for example

$$G = \frac{\log_e m(t_b) - \log_e m(t_a)}{t_b - t_a} \tag{13}$$

where t_a is the age at which offspring gain independence, t_b is some slightly later age, and $m(t)$ is offspring mass at age t. An index of this kind is commonly used in assessing plant growth curves (Hunt 1982).

Conclusions

As originally conceived, the theory of *r* and *K* selection was framed in terms of the effects of population density but the predictions that can be derived solely on this basis are rather limited (see Introduction). Following the lead of MacArthur, Pianka (1970) constructed a classification of life cycles, in relation to population density, in which high reproductive effort was correlated with producing small offspring. Using the techniques of life-cycle theory we have dissected this relationship into its component parts. Thus, whereas Pianka (1970) maintained that high reproductive effort is selected for by low population density (as in Prediction 1) we now conclude that high reproductive effort is selected for in environments with a high *S* index (Prediction 3), where *S* is given by eqns (8) or (9) and is likely to be dependent to a large extent on juvenile survivorship (see above). Predictions 1 and 3 are equivalent if and only if *S* reduces as population density increases. And whereas Pianka (1970) suggested that the production of fewer larger offspring is selected for by high population density (Prediction 2), we predict that the production of fewer larger offspring is selected for in environments in which juveniles can grow at a slower rate, *G* (Prediction 4). Predictions 2 and 4 are equivalent if and only if *G* reduces as population density increases. Furthermore, the correlation of high reproductive effort with the production of small offspring is only to be expected if both *S* and *G* reduce as population density increases.

CLASSIFICATION BASED ON THESE LIFE-CYCLE PARAMETERS

One-dimensional classification of selection pressures in terms of density is of limited applicability (Wilbur *et al.* 1974) since density effects are unlikely to operate unimodally on fitness and may have a variety of effects depending upon how they are applied (Boyce, in press). In this paper the focus is shifted away from population density towards two key parameters which directly affect life-cycle strategy; in particular an index *S* related to offspring survivorship, and an index *G* indicating rate at which offspring can grow in a habitat. This suggests two- rather than one-dimensional classification. If, for convenience, the two axes, *G* and *S*, are divided into high and low the matrix shown in Table 4.1 results. It is now possible to distinguish between four categories of selection: high *G*, high *S*; low *G*, low *S*; high *G*, low *S*; low *G*, high *S*. At high *S* the total investment of resources in reproduction should be high and vice versa at low *S*. Similarly, at high *G* propagule size should be small and vive versa at low *G*. Combining these two predictions, it follows that fecundity

Table 4.1. Life-cycle predictions in relation to a dichotomous classification of habitats by G, an index of growth rate of offspring, and S, an index of survivorship defined by eqns (8) or (9) as appropriate. Z = total investment in reproduction during a particular breeding attempt; w = investment per egg; n = number of eggs

	High	Z low w low n intermediate	Z high w low n very high
G			
	Low	Z low w high n low	Z high w high n intermediate
		Low	High
			S

(n) should be highest at high G, high S and lowest at low G, low S, with other habitat types favouring intermediate values. It should be noted, however, that complications may arise if resource availability for adults is higher at high G, with the probable outcome that Z (and hence n) should be increased somewhat in the top row of Table 4.1 (see p. 88). Although strictly one should discuss the two-dimensional G–S continuum it is easier to consider pairwise comparisons and to compare them with the one-dimensional r/K classification, viz:

(1) *Low* S, *low* G v. *High* S, *high* G. This dichotomy is most nearly equivalent to the r/K distinction *as perceived by Pianka* (above) and is referred to by Stearns (1977) as the 'Accepted Scheme'. According to the review by Stearns (1977) the predicted outcome (see Table 4.1) is far from universal, which Stearns took as evidence against r/K selection. However, Pianka's r/K dichotomy is only one possible consequence of density effects and hence the finding that it does not occur is not decisive in refuting their importance (Boyce, in press).

(2) *Low* S, *low* G v. *High* S, *low* G. This represents a gradient in survivorship when conditions for growth are poor. For example, British freshwater triclads all suffer resource limitations (Reynoldson 1983). Yet because of differences in the physiology of hatchlings, the juvenile survivorship of some species is better than others (Calow & Woollhead 1977;

Woollhead & Calow 1979). Absorption costing probably predominates. On this basis, triclads conform well to the predictions since species in which juveniles have good survivorship invest more in reproduction than those that have poor survivorship (Calow & Woollhead 1977; Woollhead & Calow 1979; Woollhead 1983). This kind of gradient in selection pressures is likely to be common in resource-limited top carnivores.

(3) *Low* S, *high* G *v. High* S, *high* G. This represents a gradient in survivorship when conditions for growth are good. For example gyrodactylid ectoparasites (Monogenea) of aquatic vertebrates probably experience good, reasonably stable supplies of food from their hosts, yet different species occupy different sites which differ in vulnerability. Thus, *Gyrodactylus gasterostei* from the skin of three-spined stickleback has higher adult mortality and fecundity than *Gyrodicotylus gallieni* which lives in the more protected site of the mouth of *Xenopus*. Gill parasites probably have intermediate levels of mortality and fecundity. (These data are from P. Harris, cited in Calow 1983.) High growth rates are probably typical of many parasites and so differences in S are likely to play an important part in their life-cycle evolution.

(4) *Low* S, *low* G *v. Low* S, *high* G. This represents a gradient in growth-promoting potential when conditions for survival are poor.

(5) *High* S, *low* G *v. High* S, *high* G. This represents a gradient in growth-promoting potential when conditions for survival are good. Categories (4) and (5) are conveniently treated together for, though there is a considerable amount of information on the way propagule size varies with G, the level of S is rarely specified, probably because G is more readily defined or deduced than S, and it is usually assumed (if only implicitly) that S is constant along gradients of G. G can sometimes be deduced indirectly from environmental variables. Thus, for terrestrial angiosperms seed oil content and weight increase with decreasing illumination (Levin 1974) and there is a tendency for the eggs of marine gastropods to be heavier further offshore where productivity is lower (Rex 1979). G can also be measured directly from individual growth rates. Thus, data from Grime (1979) on annual plants indicate a good negative correlation between growth rate of offspring and log seed weight (Fig. 4.3), and data from Eisenberg (1981) on mammals indicate a good negative correlation between growth rate of offspring and neonatal size (Fig. 4.4). Clearly, care has to be taken in interpreting interspecific comparisons in order not to confuse extrinsic with intrinsic effects and in all these analyses it has to be remembered that correlations do not decisively establish particular causal mechanisms (e.g. S might not be constant). Nevertheless, it is encouraging that all these examples are consistent with Prediction 4, that more smaller offspring are produced in better growth

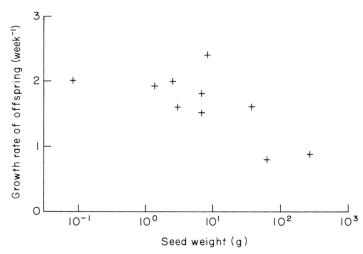

Fig. 4.3. Juvenile growth rate is negatively correlated with log seed weight in ten species of annual competitive-ruderal herbs ($r = -0.72$, $P < 0.05$). Growth rate estimated as maximum rate of dry matter production per unit weight. Data from Grime (1979, p. 59).

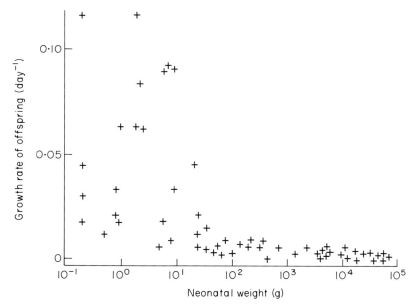

Fig. 4.4. Juvenile growth rate is negatively correlated with log neonatal size in females of fifty-eight species of mammals ($r = -0.61$, $P < 0.05$). Growth rate estimated as ($\log_e$ (adult weight) $- \log_e$ (neonatal weight))/(age at first mating). (Data from Eisenberg 1981, Appendix 4.)

conditions. Moreover, Ito (1980) has collected together a considerable amount of data on the same topic from a wide variety of sources and taxa and all are generally supportive.

(6) *High* S, *low* G *v. Low* S, *high* G. Here predictions are opposite to the 'Accepted Scheme' (comparison (1), above). It is possible that this distinction applies to endoparasites (which have good conditions for growth, but poor chances of juvenile survival) and free-living relatives (poorer conditions for growth, but better for juvenile survival (Calow 1979, 1983). It is also possibly representative of a general shift in selection pressure with trophic position from the low survival but good growth conditions for herbivores to the higher survival but poorer growth conditions for carnivores (see also Wilbur *et al.* 1974). However, caution is necessary in evaluating this comparison because differences in resource availability could mean that the absolute investment in reproduction at low S high G is equal to or greater than that at high S low G (see pp. 84 and 88).

An axis for disturbance?

In his analysis of vegetative strategies, Grime (1979) distinguishes between two major components of selection pressure—stress and disturbance—and by further distinguishing between high and low levels of each and by noting that no plant can tolerate high levels of both, develops a triangular classification system. Stress is a measure of the extent to which production is inhibited by the environment and hence is the inverse of our G. Disturbance is a measure of the extent to which organisms are killed but represents overall *not* age-specific mortality and so is equivalent to our $-S$ for direct-costing organisms (eqn (8)) but not necessarily for absorption-costing organisms (eqn (9)), for which $S = \exp((F(t_1 - t_2))S_1/(S_2 t_2)$. In the latter case S varies inversely with disturbance if and only if disturbance affects juvenile more than adult survivorship. For example, if $t_2 < t_1$ and disturbance increases both juvenile and adult mortality rates by $\Delta\mu$ then $S_1/S_2 = e^{(\mu_2 + \Delta\mu)t_2 - (\mu_1 + \Delta\mu)t_1} = e^{\mu_2 t_2 - \mu_1 t_1 - \Delta\mu(t_1 - t_2)}$ which varies inversely with disturbance (however if $t_1 > t_2$ the relationship would be reversed, i.e. S increasing as disturbance increases).

The adversity (A) selection of Greenslade (1983) occurs at low G and low *overall* survival. It is likely that mortality falls more heavily on juveniles than adults (hence low S) but this cannot be guaranteed. Hence, the theory can predict that eggs and seeds should be large, but nothing more.

Effects of other variables

Resource availability for adults is one key variable not included in the above analysis. Higher resource availability might mean that individual offspring could be obtained at lower cost to the adult, e.g. if there were less drain on adult body reserves. This would shift the trade-off curve, $\mu_2(n)$, relating offspring number to adult mortality (p. 79), and the new optimum is likely to involve the production of more offspring (unpublished analysis, see also Calow 1983). If in this case higher resource availability for adults was associated with better growth conditions for offspring, then the effect would be to increase reproductive effort, Z, and fecundity, n, on the top row of Table 4.1, though investment per egg (w) would remain unchanged. Complications for predictions about Z, due to resource availability, may therefore apply where there are gradients in G. When this happens at low S it is likely that Z will not remain constant but will be very low at low G, low S. Similarly, at high S, high G is likely to allow a very high Z and low G a lower Z. These effects accentuate the expected differences in comparison (1) above (low G, low S v. high G, high S), but blur expected differences in comparison (6) (low G high S v. high G low S). In this last instance it is difficult to know a priori whether differences in Z will occur. Comparisons along this axis must therefore be treated with caution. Another possible effect of increased resource availability for adults is a decrease in time between breeding, t_2, which also favours the production of more offspring under some conditions (Appendix 1).

It is also possible to imagine G, S and Disturbance causing evolution of traits that are not currently addressed by life-cycle theory, e.g. capacities for defence, dormancy and dispersal; these kinds of traits are incorporated into the classification tables of Pianka (1970), Southwood (1977), Grime (1979) and Greenslade (1983). Similarly, as well as evoking life-cycle responses, G and S might evoke 'direct' responses. For example, at low G there might be selection for more efficient production and at low S for better survival. In other words, under the influence of evolution, species can shift from one 'square' to another in Table 4.1. Whether and to what extent shifts occur depends on the nature of genetic variance in the population.

It has been assumed here that there are no factors preventing the predicted optima being achieved other than the trade-offs explicitly identified in the models. However, constraints associated with particular taxonomic features, especially size, may be important (Stearns 1984a, b). We would expect the predictions formulated in this paper to be most rigorously tested in comparisons between populations of the same or closely-related species. This is why we urged caution in the interpretations of Figs 4.3 and 4.4.

ACKNOWLEDGMENTS

We are very grateful to M.S. Boyce, P. Grime, T.R.E. Southwood, R.H. Smith, K. Monk and A.R. Jones for commenting on the manuscript.

REFERENCES

Bell, G. (1984a). Measuring the cost of reproduction, 1. The correlation structure of the life table of a planktonic rotifer. *Evolution*, **38**, 300–313.

Bell, G. (1984b). Measuring the cost of reproduction, 2. The correlation structure of the life tables of five freshwater invertebrates. *Evolution*, **38**, 314–326.

Boyce, M.S. (in press). Restitution of r- and K-selection as a model of density-dependent natural selection. *Annual Review of Ecology and Systematics*.

Bulmer, M.G. (1983). The significance of protandry in social hymenoptera. *American Naturalist*, **121**, 540–551.

Calow, P. (1979). The cost of reproduction—a physiological approach. *Biological Review*, **54**, 23–40.

Calow, P. (1983). Pattern and paradox in parasite reproduction. *Parasitology*, **86**, 197–207.

Calow, P. (1984). *Exploring the adaptive landscape of invertebrate life cycles. Advances in Invertebrate Reproduction*, **3**, 329–342.

Calow, P. & Sibly, R.M. (1983). Physiological trade-offs and the evolution of life cycles. *Science Progress*, **68**, 177–188.

Calow, P. & Townsend, C.R. (1981). Energetics, ecology and evolution. *Physiological Ecology: an Evolutionary Approach to Resource Use* (Ed. by C.R. Townsend & P. Calow). Blackwell Scientific Publications, Oxford.

Calow, P. & Woollhead, A.S. (1977). The relationship between ration, reproductive effort and age-specific mortality in the evolution of life history strategies—some observations in freshwater triclads. *Journal of Animal Ecology*, **46**, 765–781.

Chapman, R.N. (1931). *Animal Ecology: With Especial Reference To Insects.* McGraw-Hill, New York.

Charlesworth, B. (1980). *Evolution in Age-Structured Populations.* Cambridge University Press, Cambridge.

Cody, M.L. (1966). A general theory of clutch size. *Evolution*, **20**, 174–184.

Eisenberg, J.F. (1981). *The Mammalian Radiations.* Athlone Press, London.

Greenslade, P.J.M. (1983). Adversity selection and the habitat templet. *American Naturalist*, **122**, 352–365.

Grime, J.P. (1974). Vegetation classification by reference to strategies. *Nature*, **250**, 26–31.

Grime, J.P. (1979). *Plant Strategies and Vegetation Processes.* Wiley, Chichester.

Hunt, R. (1982). *Plant Growth Curves.* Edward Arnold, London.

Ito, Y. (1980). *Comparative Ecology* (Edited and translated by J. Kikkawa). Cambridge University Press, Cambridge.

Levin, D.A. (1974). The oil content of seeds: an ecological perspective. *American Naturalist*, **108**, 193–206.

MacArthur, R.H. (1972). *Geographical Ecology.* Harper & Row, New York.

Odum, H.T. & Pinkerton, R.C. (1955). Time's speed regulator. *American Scientist*, **43**, 331–343.

Pianka, E.R. (1970). On r- and K-selection. *American Naturalist*, **104**, 592–597.

Rex, M.A. (1979). r-selection and K-selection in a deep sea gastropod *Alvania pelagica. Sarsia*, **64**, 29–32.

Reynoldson, T.B. (1983). The population biology of Turbellaria with special reference to the freshwater triclads of the British Isles. *Advances in Ecological Research*, **13**, 235–326.

Sibly, R. & Calow, P. (1982). Asexual reproduction in Protozoa and invertebrates. *Journal of theoretical biology*, **96**, 401–424.

Sibly, R. & Calow, P. (1983). An integrated approach to life-cycle evolution using selective landscapes. *Journal of theoretical biology*, **102**, 527–547.

Sibly, R. & Calow, P. (in press). Direct and absorption costing in the evolution of life cycles. *Journal of theoretical biology*.

Smith, C.C. (1976). When and how much to reproduce: the trade-off between power and efficiency. *American Zoologist*, **16**, 763–774.

Southwood, T.R.E. (1977). Habitat, the templet for ecological strategies? *Journal of Animal Ecology*, **46**, 337–365.

Stearns, S.C. (1977). The evolution of life history traits. *Annual Review of Ecology and Systematics*, **8**, 145–172.

Stearns, S.C. (1984a). The effects of size and phylogeny on patterns of covariation in the life-history traits of lizards and snakes. *American Naturalist*, **123**, 56–72.

Stearns, S.C. (1984b). The tension between adaptation and constraint in the evolution of reproductive patterns. *Advances in Invertebrate Reproduction*, **3**, 387–398.

Whittaker, R.H. (1975). The design and stability of some plant communities. *Unifying Concepts in Ecology*. (Ed. by W.H. Van Dobben & R.H. Lowe-McConnell), pp. 169–181. Dr W. Junk, The Hague.

Wilbur, H.M., Tinkle, D.W., Collins, J.P. (1974). Environmental certainty, trophic level, and resource availability in life history evolution. *American Naturalist*, **108**, 805–817.

Williams, G.C. (1966) *Adaptation and Natural Selection*. Princeton University Press, Princeton.

Woollhead, A.S. (1983). Energy partitioning in semelparous and iteroparous triclads. *Journal of Animal Ecology*, **52**, 603–620.

Woollhead, A.S. & Calow, P. (1979). Energy-partitioning strategies during egg production in semelparous and iteroparous triclads. *Journal of Animal Ecology*, **48**, 491–499.

APPENDIX 1

Effects of a slight change in t_2 on optimal reproductive effort (Prediction 1)

The effect of a slight change in t_2 can be investigated by differentiating eqns (6) and (7) with respect to t_2. If the derivative with respect to t_2 is positive then increasing t_2 results in an increase in the optimal value of $\partial\mu_2/(\partial n)$ indicating an increase in the optimal value of n, since $\partial\mu_2/(\partial n)$ is assumed to be an increasing function of n. Writing $S_2 = e^{-\mu_2 t_2}$ and differentiating eqn (6) with respect to t_2 we get

$$\frac{\partial}{\partial t_2}\left(\frac{\partial\mu_2}{\partial n}\right) = S_1 e^{-\mu_2 t_2} e^{-Ft_1 - Ft_2}\left(\frac{-\mu_2 - F}{t_2} - \frac{1}{t_2^2}\right)$$

which is negative if and only if $-F - \mu_2 < 1/(t_2)$, i.e. $-F < 1/(t_2) + \mu_2$. Thus, slightly lower values of t_2 favour more offspring if and only if $-F < 1/(t_2) + \mu_2$ for direct-costing organisms. The same method applied to eqn (7) shows that the analogous condition for absorption-costing organisms is $F < 1/(t_2) - \mu_2$.

5. A GENERAL THEORY OF LIFE-HISTORY VARIATION

MICHAEL BEGON

*Department of Zoology, University of Liverpool, P.O. Box 147,
Liverpool L69 3BX*

SUMMARY

A simple demographic theory of life-history variation is proposed which
incorporates the cost of reproduction, reproductive value and a classification
of habitat types. It includes the r/K theory as a limited special case, and
therefore has explanatory powers which greatly exceed the r/K theory.

INTRODUCTION

Over the past 15 years there has been considerable and increasing interest in
the ecological consequences *of* reproductive behaviour ('life-history strategies'), and in the consequences that an organism's ecology has *for* its
reproductive behaviour (see, for example, Stearns 1976, 1977).

This paper describes a simple, general demographic theory of life-history
variation. It is not new in the sense of being based on new assumptions, or of
using new techniques. But it does, hopefully, provide a new synthesis and a
new degree of clarity. In particular, it includes the r/K theory (Pianka 1970;
MacArthur 1972) as a fairly limited special case. It therefore has explanatory
powers which greatly exceed the r/K theory.

THE THEORY

The cost of reproduction

It is generally accepted that observed life histories represent a compromise
allocation of limited resources (Cody 1966; Law 1979). In particular, a cost of
reproduction should be apparent in comparing individuals that reproduce
with individuals receiving the same resource-input but reproducing less or not
at all (Calow 1979; Law 1979). Individuals that restrain their reproduction to
a level less than the maximum will typically grow faster, grow larger and have
an increased quantity of resources available for maintenance and storage.
This will often express itself simply as an increase in size, but in more general

terms such individuals may be thought as having a greater 'accumulated somatic investment' or ASI. This increased ASI will often (but by no means always—see below) lead to an increased probability of future survival and an increased capacity for future reproduction (largely as a consequence of increased growth and/or development).

Reproductive value

Reproductive value is the currency in which the worth of a life-history in the hands of natural selection should be calculated (Fisher 1930; modified by Schaffer 1974; clarified by Schaffer 1981; see also Charlesworth 1980).

Reproductive value = Expected contemporary reproductive output + Residual reproductive value

Residual reproductive value (RRV) is 'the sum of all future *expected* fecundities' (Schaffer 1974) modified in a way which takes account of the *proportionate* contribution of an individual to future generations. The expected future fecundities themselves depend on expected reproductive capacity and expected future survivorship. These in their turn, as well as RRV as whole, may depend on ASI (usually size, i.e. past growth). But they will not always do so. Whether or not they do, and the extent to which they do, are of critical importance in the next section.

An increase in contemporary reproductive output is likely to lead to a decrease in ASI, and thus *perhaps* to a decrease in RRV. The compromise life-history favoured by natural selection, from amongst those available in the population, will be the one for which total reproductive value is greatest, i.e. the one for which the *sum* of contemporary reproductive output *plus* RRV is greatest (Schaffer 1974, 1981).

A classification of habitats

Habitats can be classified in terms of the effects of accumulated somatic investment (ASI) on residual reproductive value (RRV).

Type 1 habitats are defined as those in which the RRV of established individuals increases rapidly with individual size, or age, or condition, or more generally ASI.

Type 2 habitats, by contrast, are defined as those in which the RRV of established individuals is little affected by or actually decreases with ASI (Fig 5.1).

In order to define two further types of habitat, it is necessary to think of the

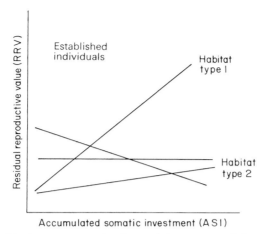

FIG. 5.1. Relationships between accumulated somatic investment and the residual reproductive value of established individuals in type 1 and type 2 habitats.

size or quality of an individual offspring as *its* ASI. In this case it is the *parent* that makes the investment.

In *type 3 habitats*, the RRV of offspring increases rapidly with ASI.

In *type 4 habitats*, the RRV of offspring is little affected by or decreases with ASI (Fig. 5.2).

Each of the four habitat types can arise for a number of different reasons.

In habitat *type 1(a)* there is *intense competition* amongst established

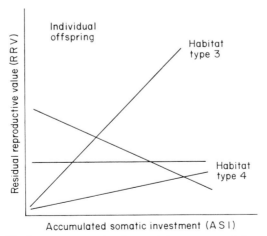

FIG. 5.2. Relationships between accumulated somatic investment and the residual reproductive value of offspring in type 3 and type 4 habitats.

individuals with only the best competitors (high ASI) surviving and reproducing.

In habitat *type 1(b)* there are, amongst established individuals, important sources of predatory or abiotically-induced mortality *against which a large ASI is the best protection.*

Habitat types 3(a) and 3(b) are analogous to 1(a) and 1(b) but 'established individuals' is replaced by 'offspring'.

In habitat *type 2(a)* mortality for established individuals is catastrophic and *unavoidable irrespective of ASI.*

In habitat *type 2(b)* mortality amongst established individuals *affects the largest disproportionately* (e.g. a predator that prefers large individuals).

In habitat *type 2(c)* conditions for established individuals are benign and competition-free and there is *plenty for all irrespective of ASI.*

Habitat types 4(a), 4(b) and 4(c) are analogous to 2(a) 2(b) and 2(c) but 'established individuals' is replaced by 'offspring'.

The expected traits in different habitats

Individuals that delay the onset of reproduction, or are iteroparous, or have a small 'reproductive allocation' (the proportion of resource-input diverted to present reproduction, sometimes called 'reproductive effort') will typically achieve a higher ASI than individuals that are precocious, semelparous, or have a large reproductive allocation. Thus, in type 1 habitats, delay, iteroparity and a small reproductive allocation will lead to large increases in RRV which are *greater* than the accompanying *de*creases in contemporary output. Delay, iteroparity and a small allocation will therefore be favoured in type 1 habitats.

In type 2 habitats, on the other hand, delay, iteroparity and a small allocation will lead to negligible increases or even decreases in RRV, which cannot outweigh the accompanying decreases in contemporary output. Precocity, semelparity and a large reproductive allocation will thus be favoured. However, semelparity in itself leads to a delay. Type 2 habitats will therefore favour *either* semelparity *or* precocious iteroparity.

The favoured alternative between 'more, smaller offspring' and 'fewer, larger offspring' depends on which group of offspring has the greater *summed* reproductive value. Thus, in type 3 habitats, fewer, larger offspring are favoured (the reproductive value of offspring rises rapidly with ASI); while in type 4 habitats more, smaller offspring are favoured (ASI has a negligible or detrimental effect on offspring reproductive value).

This association of traits with habitat types (and the different ways in which the types can arise) represents a general demographic theory of life-history variaton.

APPLICATIONS

The r/K *concept*

The celebrated and/or notorious r/K concept can now be seen as merely a special case of this more general theory. It is limited in that it proposes only two contrasting types of habitat. The first ('K-selecting') is 1(a) for established individuals and *also* 3(a) for offspring. The second ('r-selecting') alternates between 2(a) and 2(c) for established individuals and *also* between 4(a) and 4(c) for offspring. The life-history traits predicted by the r/K theory are the combined predictions from habitats 1 and 3 in the first case, and habitats 2 and 4 in the second (Pianka 1970; Stearns 1976). But the same traits could arise for quite different reasons, and the habitat types are not inextricably bound together. It is therefore not surprising that the r/K concept has been supported by a number of studies, but that a similar number of studies have failed to support the concept (Stearns 1977). Many of these will be cases in which a type 1 habitat is not associated with a type 3 habitat, or a habitat is type 1(b) rather than 1(a), and so on.

A case-study with winkles

Thus, this general theory can readily make sense of data sets which fly in the face of the r/K concept. One example is provided by the two populations of winkles (*Littorina rudis*) studied by Hart & Begon (1982). Each population combined supposedly 'r' and 'K' traits (Table 5.1). But their ecology (Hart &

TABLE 5.1. Characteristics of the 'crevice' and 'boulders' populations of *Littorina rudis* (Hart & Begon 1982) with, as appropriate, their designation as either *r* or *K* traits

Crevice	Boulders
Thinner shells	Thicker shells
Average size smaller (*r*)	Average size larger (*K*)
Maturity at smaller size (*r*)	Maturity relatively delayed to larger size (*K*)
Larger reproductive allocation (*r*)	Smaller reproductive allocation (*K*)
Fewer, larger offspring (*K*)	More, smaller offspring (*r*)

Begon 1982), couched in terms of the general theory, can fully explain the data (Fig. 5.3).

In the 'crevice' populations, there is intense competition amongst offspring for space in the limited number of crevices (habitat type 3(a)), which also applies to the smaller established individuals (type 1(a)). However, the larger, growing individuals are increasingly prone to predation and dislodgement as the number of protective crevices that are sufficiently large for them diminishes (type 2(b)). In the 'boulders' population, predation and crushing affect all offspring irrespective of size (type 4(a)). As size increases, however, large size and a thick shell become increasingly a protection against predation and crushing (type 1(b)), though as diminishing returns eventually set in, 1(b) approaches 2(a). Thus, the traits of the winkles reflect the combination of habitat types that they experience.

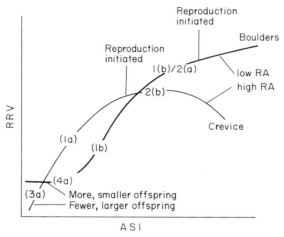

FIG. 5.3. Relationships between accumulated somatic investment and residual reproductive value for 'crevice' and 'boulders' winkles, along with the habitat types that lead to these relationships and the life-history traits that they favour.

CONCLUSION

Much of the controversy and misunderstanding surrounding the r/K concept is dissipated by the present simple analysis. The r/K concept is a useful but limited special case of a more useful, more general theory. However, the latter is only a general *demographic* theory. A list of the non-demographic factors it ignores would include: allometric and phylogenetic constraints, phenotypic responses which reflect variations in the amounts of resources obtained, responses to physiological problems, and cases where the reproductive allocation is a poor indicator of the cost of reproduction (see Begon, Harper & Townsend (1985) for a discussion of all of these).

REFERENCES

Begon, M., Harper, J.L. & Townsend C.R. (1985). *Ecology: Organisms, Populations and Communities.* Blackwell Scientific Publications, Oxford (in press).

Calow, P. (1979). The cost of reproduction—a physiological approach. *Biological Reviews,* **54,** 23–40.

Charlesworth, B. (1980). *Evolution in Age-Structured Populations.* Cambridge University Press, Cambridge.

Cody, M.L. (1966). A general theory of clutch size. *Evolution,* **20,** 174–184.

Fisher, R.A. (1930). *The Genetical Theory of Natural Selection.* The Clarendon Press, Oxford.

Hart, A. & Begon, M. (1982). The status of general reproductive-strategy theories, illustrated in winkles. *Oecologia (Berlin),* **52,** 37–42.

Law, R. (1979). Ecological determinants in the evolution of life-histories. *Population Dynamics* (Eds R.M. Anderson, B.D. Turner & L.R. Taylor), pp. 81–103. Blackwell Scientific Publications, Oxford.

MacArthur, R.H. (1972). *Geographical Ecology.* Harper & Row, New York.

Pianka, E.R. (1970). On 'r' and 'K' selection. *American Naturalist,* **104,** 592–597.

Schaffer, W.M. (1974). Selection for optimal life-histories: the effects of age structure. *Ecology,* **55,** 291–303.

Schaffer, W.M. (1981). On reproductive value and fitness. *Ecology,* **62,** 1683–1685.

Stearns, S.C. (1976). Life-history tactics: a review of the ideas. *Quarterly Review of Biology,* **51,** 3–47.

Stearns, S.C. (1977). The evolution of life-history traits: a critique of the theory and a review of the data. *Annual Review of Ecology and Systematics,* **8,** 145–171.

6. INFORMATION, NON-GENETIC CONSTRAINTS, AND THE TESTING OF THEORIES OF LIFE-HISTORY VARIATION

DAVID ATKINSON*

Department of Zoology, University of Liverpool, Liverpool L69 3BX

SUMMARY

I present a simple classification of non-genetic variation in life histories which makes explicit those non-genetic effects on the phenotype which can, and those which cannot, be interpreted by using existing life-history theory.

Theories predicting optimal life histories can be tested directly by providing organisms with misinformation about their external environment or physiological state. Adaptive phenotypic differences may also be detected when the effect of *information* on a trait runs counter to, and overrides, the effect on the trait of differences in *non-genetic constraints*.

Methods of manipulating life histories, other than by altering information only, may not allow the rigorous testing of the theories.

INTRODUCTION

Theories of life-history evolution predict what sorts of life history should evolve in specified ecological circumstances (Stearns 1976). The technique used (optimization modelling) predicts optimal *phenotypes* (Maynard Smith 1978) and therefore can be used to predict the phenotypic effects of both genetic and environmental (phenotypic plasticity) adaptive responses to environmental conditions (Caswell 1983). In this paper I consider only that component of life-history variation which is non-genetic.

Some recent studies in which the life histories of different organisms have been compared have shown how differences in the immediate environment can conceal the life-history patterns predicted by current theory (Berven 1982; Atkinson 1984). These studies highlight the importance of considering all the important influences on life-history variation and not just those explicitly

* Present address: Department of Historical and Environmental Interpretation, University of Liverpool, 1 Abercromby Square, PO Box 147, Liverpool, L69 3BX.

described by life-history theory. The problem is how to interpret life-history variation caused by non-genetic differences.

To solve at least part of the problem I produce a simple dichotomous classification which partitions non-genetic phenotypic variation to make explicit those causes which are within, and those which are outside, the explanatory scope of existing theory. I use this classification to show how differences in the effects of *constraints*, under different environmental and physiological conditions, can limit the explanatory power of existing theory, and also how optimization theories of life-history evolution can be tested directly.

CAUSES OF NON-GENETIC VARIATION (PHENOTYPIC PLASTICITY)

Non-genetic causes of phenotypic variation—whether they are measured as differences in the organism's habitat (i.e. 'external' causes) or as non-genetic differences in the organism's physiological state ('internal' causes)—may act as items of *information* which initiate or modify a phenotypic response (change in resource allocation). They may also act as *non-genetic constraints* which do not provide information but which limit the allocation of resources to some activity such as growth or reproduction. A particular environmental factor can *both* provide information and can act as a constraint, but their different effects may sometimes be difficult to separate.

That component of variation in a trait which is affected by differences in information can be described as free; it may be adaptive, neutral, or (sometimes, when selection pressures have changed in the recent past) even maladaptive.

Non-genetic constraints may arise from non-genetic differences in physiological condition (physiological constraints), stage of development (developmental constraints), and constraints on the availability of resources imposed by the external environment (external environmental constraints). Food shortage and low temperature are examples of environmental factors which can act as external environmental constraints. (Food shortage may also provide *information* about feeding conditions at some time in the future when a particular phenotypic response becomes effective (Brody & Lawlor 1984; Calow & Woollhead 1977)). In contrast to all of these, differences in phylogenetic constraints are *genetic*.

The dichotomous classification presented here, which partitions non-genetic variation in life histories can be summarized thus:

Non-genetic phenotypic variation

Free (due to differences in information)		Constrained (due to differences in the following non-genetic constraints)	
Internal	External	Internal	External
May be adaptive, neutral, or maladaptive. Only the adaptive component of the variation is predictable using existing life-history theory.		Developmental physiological	

TESTING OPTIMIZATION THEORIES OF LIFE-HISTORY VARIATION

In order to test whether a life history is optimal it should be manipulated to produce 'strategic alternatives' to that found occurring naturally. Strategic alternatives are those life histories that can be achieved by an organism with the same amount of resources and the same physiological and developmental constraints. If the naturally-occurring life history is optimal all strategic alternatives should have a lower fitness than the unmanipulated life history. The life history should be manipulated by providing the organism with misinformation about either its own physiological state or the external environment. At the same time, the overall effects (on the rate at which resources are allocated to particular activities) of differences in genotypes and non-genetic constraints should be controlled.

The most direct way of manipulating life histories by providing misinformation is by hormonal or pheromonal treatment. For example, the application of pheromones from a mature male induces young rodents to grow faster (cited in Batt 1980), and induces oestrus, blocks pregnancy, and accelerates the maturation of female rodents (Bronson 1971). Crowded female rats and humans synchronize their oestrous (menstrual) cycles; in the rats this is known to be caused by an airborne chemical (cited by Dunbar, p. 507). The application of gibberellins stimulates flowering in a number of plants (Pharis & Morf 1969; Watson, Carrier & Cook 1982). The manipulation of insect reproductive behaviour and hence of their population sizes by the use of pheromones (Tette 1974) is a well-established technique which may potentially be used to test optimization theories of life-history variation.

However, if precautions are taken to ensure that the constraints are the same, other techniques may be used, and may even be preferable because hormones can have a number of effects on a phenotype besides the one desired. By temporarily removing males, for example, egg production can be delayed or reduced in crickets (Woodring, Clifford & Beckman 1979). To use this technique, effects of male presence on the females' feeding rate and on any resources which may be acquired from the males' semen should be controlled. A female dunnock which copulates with two *different* males rather than with the same male will lay a larger clutch (Davies 1985). Because both the males which copulate with the female will help to feed the young (Davies 1985), a larger brood can be reared successfully. If this effect on clutch size is not due directly to genetic differences between the females which copulate with different numbers of males, then the enlarged clutch might result from differences only in information. Differences in non-genetic constraints due to differences in the amount of nutrients from the males' semen will be negligible (Davies 1983), although the ability of the female to attract more than one mate might also conceivably be related to her age or condition (physiological constraints and information). The breeding system in the dunnock could permit the first *rigorous* testing of the hypothesis that females producing the normal clutch sizes have a higher fitness than those producing larger-than-normal clutches: when females lay an extra egg after copulating with two different males, one of the males should then be removed so that there is only one male parent to feed the young. If the naturally-occurring clutch size is optimal, the fitness of the female which is given the misinformation (in this case, 'that there will be two males to share in the feeding of the young') will be lower than females which had not been given misinformation but which laid the number of eggs appropriate to the number of their different mates.

We need not be limited to the use of hormones or the carefully controlled use of a narrow range of environmental manipulations to show a difference in life history caused by a difference in information. The effect of the information contained in an environmental cue will be discernible if it affects a trait in the opposite way from, and overrides, the constraint contained in the environmental factor. For example, Brody & Lawlor (1984) found that the size of newborn offspring of the terrestrial isopod, *Armadillidium vulgare increased* when maternal food supply was *reduced*. Thus, the information contained in the food limitation (about conditions the offspring would face when they became independent) more than countered the direct effect of a reduction in the amount of food. For this to happen, of course, some other activity must have been reduced even more than would be expected from the direct effects of food limitation alone. Another example of the phenotypic response running counter to the direct effect of resource limitation is the *stimulatory* effect of a *decrease* of nutrients on flowering in the water hyacinth (Richards 1982).

Other forms of environmental manipulation of life histories can give ambiguous results. For example, if birds whose clutch sizes are artificially increased have a higher fitness than birds laying the normal number of eggs, the result could be interpreted as meaning that the birds normally 'hedge their bets' (Stearns 1976), i.e. lay a small clutch because feeding conditions during the period in which chicks are fed by the parents are unpredictable so that in some years, when feeding conditions during this period are good, the actual clutch size appears smaller than the optimum for that year. However, if the female had invested additional resources into producing extra eggs *as well as* into feeding additional chicks, a life history with a larger-than-normal clutch might be found to have a lower fitness in any given year than one with a clutch of normal size. The manipulated life history is not strictly a strategic alternative to the unmanipulated one because the experimental birds had been provided with extra resources in the form of additional eggs (i.e. the non-genetic constraints had been altered).

The general methodological rule is this: in order to detect those non-genetic differences in life histories which are adaptive, the effects of differences in information on the rate at which resources are allocated to different activities should be separated from the effects of differences in non-genetic constraints. These effects can be separated either when the organism is provided with misinformation about its environment or its physiological state, or when environmental or physiological information affects a trait in the opposite way from, and overrides, the effect of constraints on the trait. The traditional way of testing the adaptive significance of clutch size (by adding or removing eggs from the nest) does not produce rigorous tests because strict strategic alternatives are not produced.

ACKNOWLEDGMENTS

Mike Begon, Geoff Parker, Richard Sibly, Pérsio de Souza Santos Jr, and an anonymous referee provided helpful comments on the manuscript. This work was supported by a studentship from the Natural Environment Research Council.

REFERENCES

Atkinson, D. (1984). *A comparative study of life histories in the grasshoppers,* Chorthippus brunneus *and* Myrmeleotettix maculatus *in a sand dunes habitat.* Ph.D. thesis, University of Liverpool.

Batt, R.A.L. (1980). *Influences on Animal Growth and Development.* Edward Arnold, London.

Berven, K.A. (1982). The genetic basis of a altitudinal variation in the wood frog *Rana sylvatica*. I. An experimental analysis of life history traits. *Evolution,* **36**, 962–983.

Brody, M.S. & Lawlor, L.R. (1984). Adaptive variation in offspring size in the terrestrial isopod, *Armadillidium vulgare. Oecologia,* **61**, 55–59.

Bronson, F.H. (1971) Rodent pheromones. *Biological Reproduction,* **4**, 344–357.

Calow, P. & Woollhead, A.S. (1977). The relationship between ration, reproductive effort and age-specific mortality in the evolution of life-history strategies—some observations on freshwater triclads. *Journal of Animal Ecology,* **46**, 765–781.

Caswell, H. (1983). Phenotypic plasticity in life-history traits: demographic effects and evolutionary consequences. *American Zoologist*, **23**, 35–46.

Davies, N.B. (1983). Polyandry, cloaca-pecking and sperm competition in dunnocks. *Nature (London)*, **302**, 334–336.

Davies, N.B. (1985). Co-operation and conflict among dunnocks, *Prunella modularis*, in a variable mating system. *Animal Behaviour*, **33** (in press).

Maynard Smith, J. (1978). Optimization theory in evolution. *Annual Review of Ecology and Systematics*, **9**, 31–56.

Pharis, R.P. & Morf, W. (1969). Precocious flowering of Coastal and Giant Redwood with gibberellins A_3, $A_{4/7}$, A_{13}. *Bioscience*, **19**, 719–720.

Richards, J. (1982). Developmental potential of axillary buds of water hyacinth, *Eichhornia crassipes* Solms. (Pontederiaceae). *American Journal of Botany*, **69**, 615–622.

Stearns, S.C. (1976). Life-history tactics: a review of the ideas. *Quarterly Review of Biology*, **51**, 3–47.

Tette, J.P. (1974). Pheromones in insect population management. *Pheromones* (Ed. by M.C. Birch), pp. 399–410. North-Holland Publishing Company, Amsterdam.

Watson, M.A., Carrier, J.C. & Cook, G.S. (1982). Effect of exogenously supplied gibberellic acid (GA_3) on patterns of water hyacinth development. *Aquatic Botany*, **13**, 57–68.

Woodring, J.P., Clifford, C.W. & Beckman, B.R. (1979). Food utilization and metabolic efficiency in larval and adult house crickets. *Journal of Insect Physiology*, **25**, 903–912.

7. BEHAVIOURAL REGULATION OF BIRD POPULATIONS: A REVIEW OF HABITAT USE IN RELATION TO MIGRATION AND RESIDENCY

RAYMOND J. O'CONNOR

British Trust for Ornithology, Beech Grove, Tring, Hertfordshire

SUMMARY

Variation in breeding success is considered in relation to migratory habit and density dependence. Resident species breed earlier than migrants and produce more young under population pressure than do migrant species, probably because delayed laying results in better chick survival in better vegetated habitat or on a richer food supply. Multi-brooded species are less adversely affected by delay in laying than are single-brooded species, both amongst residents and amongst migrants. Species vary in the extent to which they successively fill a series of habitats of successively poorer quality, and the extent to which they concentrate into the best of them, and this has consequences for density-induced reduction in breeding success, but migrancy–residency habits seem to have little correlation with diversity of nesting habitat, with site fidelity or with synchrony of settlement. Nesting habitat diversity increases with delay in breeding in the most sedentary residents, is independent of delay in more migratory species and resident species, but decreases with delay in long-distance migrants, possibly because early seasonal vegetational development effectively creates additional breeding habitats of good quality. Nest habitat diversity was lower if more broods were reared in a season, so that multi-brooded species may be particularly well adapted to a narrow range of habitats, independently of their migratory status. Fledgling productivity decreases with nest habitat diversity, largely because of reduced chick survival in habitat-diverse species, and this is independent of adult survival. Despite their early start to breeding, resident species produce no more fledglings than do migrant species and may even produce fewer. Across species, more fledglings are produced where adult survival is lower, and this is independent of nesting habitat diversity but probably not of number of broods produced. Single-brooded species are therefore seen as potentially the most susceptible to competitive regulation.

INTRODUCTION

Most bird populations show far greater stability than would be expected from their maximum possible rates of increase (Lack 1954, 1966). This relative stability is, in general, brought about by density-dependent processes which intensify in their action the further the population moves either above or below the equilibrium level, thus tending to (i) check movement away from and (ii) restore the population level towards the equilibrium value. Some of these processes directly involve the behaviour of the population concerned, territorial regulation of breeding densities being a good example (Brown 1969; Davies 1978; Klomp 1970; Patterson 1980). Dominance behaviour at localized food sources during the non-breeding season, such that birds excluded are differentially likely to die (Watson & Moss 1972; Kikkawa 1980; Lomnicki & Ombach 1984), provides complementary behavioural regulation of this type. Where these types of strongly density-dependent factors regulate populations, selection favours correspondingly competitive individuals whose persistence in a given patch or habitat may be determined in large part by the degree of site dominance they can establish there (Fretwell 1981). Yet a growing body of evidence suggests that these are the characteristics only of resident species of birds and that the majority of long-distance migrants are fugitive species oriented to superabundant but sporadic or short-lived resources (Karr 1976; O'Connor 1981; Rabenold 1979). As pointed out on theoretical grounds by May (1981), the equilibrium density of migrants in a habitat patch on the breeding ground may depend on two factors that have essentially nothing to do with the patch itself, namely the year-to-year survival probability of the species and the overall rate of production of new migrant 'colonists' in the catchment area about the patch. For example, interspecific variation in the distribution of migrant species on farmland in Britain is correlated with species differences in egg production, though not with differences in survival rates (as is the case for the resident species there) (O'Connor 1981). However, May's (1981) argument is strictly valid only if the habitat patch does not impose some upper limit (=carrying capacity) to density. In the present paper, therefore, I examine the extent to which habitat dynamics and migrancy may interact in regulating population densities.

Patterson (1980), reviewing the idea of territorial behaviour as a limitation on density, considered three questions as deserving an answer: (i) can territorial behaviour limit population density; (ii) if so, does behaviour vary so as to alter density in relation to environmental resources; (iii) if so, how does behaviour determine the equilibrium density for the population in the environment concerned? In an early consideration of these questions Lack (1954) considered only cases of fixed equilibrium densities, about which the population might fluctuate. Patterson (1980), however, noted that any population limitation on potential rate of increase in density would serve to regulate population numbers. That is, if it becomes increasingly easy to recruit new individuals as population density falls, then the population densities achieved are constrained towards an equilibrium value. In principle, this equilibrium will be set by the level of environmental resources in an area and in the most simplistic models there will be a one-to-one relationship between resource level and population level. Optimal foraging theory and related ideas predict, however, that the rate of harvesting of any resource will be a balance between the benefits obtained by harvesting a particular unit of resource and the costs of harvesting that unit. This balance can vary with the ecological conditions (including local population density) prevailing, so there is unlikely to be a rigidly limited carrying capacity for a population in a given area. This source of variation was given little attention in the original consideration of population regulation in birds (Lack 1954, 1966) but has recently been reviewed by O'Connor & Fuller (in press).

If the level to which a population is regulated is determined by the outcome of some form of cost-benefit analysis, then species and groups of species with low costs are likely to achieve different equilibria (and to do so by different processes) than are species incurring high costs. Similarly, species obtaining high benefits per unit of resource harvested will attain different equilibria than will species with low benefits per unit harvested. In applying these ideas to an assessment of the impact of migration strategy upon population regulation, I note that several authors have suggested that resident species enjoy priority over migrants in access to prime breeding sites. Von Haartman (1968) suggested in particular that resident species tolerated lower survival in temperate zone winters for the sake of the higher reproductive effort they could achieve by being on station on their breeding grounds at the advent of spring. On the other hand, migrants, although enjoying a higher winter survivorship in favourable tropical climates, were seen as less successful breeders by virtue of their late return to the breeding grounds. There has been little investigation of this hypothesis; its consequences for territorial behaviour, in particular, are largely unstudied. Alerstam & Hogstedt (1981), however, have analysed nest-site utilization in relation to migrancy and foraging behaviour among Swedish birds. They found that sheltered nesting—in tree-holes, tunnels, crevices, caves, buildings and the like—is predominant among resident species, though probably at the cost of greater competitive effort in acquiring suitable sites. Amongst migrant species sheltered nesting is most common in species with exposed foraging techniques—aerial hunting, 'sit and wait' predators (flycatchers, kingfishers, etc.) and exposed gleaners (wagtails, wheatear *Oenanthe oenanthe*, etc.)—

whose feeding trips to nestlings might readily be followed by nest predators. Alerstam & Hogstedt (1981) also showed that hole-nesting migrants arrived back earlier than did species not dependent on sheltered nest sites. Garcia (1983) has also shown that between two long-distance migrants, the blackcap *Sylvia atricapilla* and garden warbler *S. borin*, the former excludes the latter from some breeding habitats by virtue of its earlier arrival.

In the present paper I examine the influence of migratory status upon population regulation. Figure 7.1 shows how the major components of behavioural regulation in the breeding season relate to migratory status, thereby illustrating the main topics to be discussed in the present paper. Factors not directly linked to the breeding season, e.g. juvenile survival and age of first breeding, are expressly omitted from consideration here. Population pressure is seen as having its primary effect upon adult survivorship, migratory status, the timing of breeding and upon habitat selection, with additional connections between these components. Habitat selection in

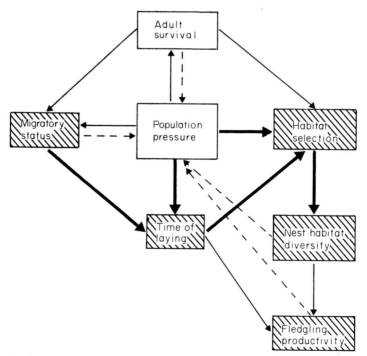

FIG. 7.1. Major components of population regulatory processes discussed in this paper. The shaded boxes and heavy arrows indicate topics to be discussed in greater detail here. Feedback paths affecting population pressure are indicated by hatched lines.

response to population pressure determines the diversity of nesting habitats used by a population and this in turn determines the overall production of fledglings by the population. This last component is additionally influenced directly, in many species, by the timing of the breeding season (Perrins 1970). Most but not all of the components shown feed back to population pressure, as indicated. In Fig 7.1 the heavy arrows and shaded boxes indicate the major discussion points for the present review. The other components and processes illustrated have been extensively reviewed by previous workers (e.g. Patterson 1970; Brown 1969; Klomp 1970). My treatment of the components reviewed here is avowedly a pilot study, and intended to bring out various implications and relationships implicit in the ideas of the major workers already cited. In particular, the restriction of my data to those obtained with a small set of species chosen to represent the migrancy–residency spectrum has meant many of the patterns discussed are supported, but not proven, by the analyses below.

MATERIALS AND METHODS

Much of my analysis is focused upon nine bird species chosen to cover the full migratory spectrum from complete residency through to long-distance seasonal migration. The species chosen are dunnock *Prunella modularis*, chaffinch *Fringilla coelebs*, bullfinch *Pyrrhula pyrrhula*, skylark *Alauda arvensis*, reed bunting *Emberiza schoeniclus*, redstart *Phoenicurus phoenicurus*, willow warbler *Phylloscopus trochilus*, spotted flycatcher *Muscicapa striata* and swallow *Hirundo rustica*. The rank ordering of these species in relation to migrancy was determined subjectively in advance of any analysis, on the basis of general understanding of the species' migratory tendencies. Empirical data in support of the rankings made may be obtained in the annual reports of the British and Irish Ringing Scheme, e.g. Mead & Hudson (1983).

Data required for the various analyses presented here were drawn from the standing enquiries of the British Trust for Ornithology (BTO). Three schemes are especially relevant here. First, for all nine species annual indices of population density are provided by the Common Birds Census scheme. The CBC is based on annual surveys of some 300–350 census plots, censused using a mapping technique (Bailey 1967). The densities estimated for each census plot are somewhat dependent upon observer census efficiency, but by pairing observer–plot combinations across years it is possible to eliminate observer variation in an index of population levels, such that year-to-year changes in species density are tracked with greater precision than the absolute densities are known (Taylor 1965; Bailey 1967; O'Connor & Marchant 1981). Separate CBC indices are available for farmland and for woodland plots for most but not all species; for some of the less numerous species, here including the redstart, all census plot data are pooled to give a scarce species index of overall population trend. Examination of the farmland census plots has shown that they broadly reflect land use practices in England and Wales but not in Scotland (R.J. Fuller *et al.* 1985).

Reproductive data for the present study were obtained from the Nest Records Scheme run by the BTO. This scheme consists of the annual collection of nest histories for nests found by participants in the scheme. Given a series of visits to the nest in the course of its cycle, it is possible to work out such parameters of reproductive effort as clutch size, hatching success, and fledging success, accompanied by information on date of egg-laying and habitat use. Not all parameters can be assessed from any given nest record but average measures for each parameter can be assessed from the large sample of cards available for each species. The present study is based on analysis of annual random samples of approximately 100 cards from those available for each species, for each of the years 1962–81 (except that 1981 data were not analysed in the case of the spotted flycatcher). For each of these cards the reproductive parameters mentioned were estimated wherever possible. In the case of dates of first egg laid for each nest, estimates were accepted if they were known to within 5 days. Frequency plots of such dates then indicate the general laying season of each species, but accuracy is greater early on because observer interest wanes seasonally, so that late nests are under-recorded. For this reason, egg-laying after day 200 (= 19 July except in leap years) was not considered (see Fig. 7.2 below).

Habitat categories were taken from the standard codes used in computerized analysis of nest record cards at the BTO. These categories are not rigorously defined because the cards are filled by volunteer participants lacking formal ecological training. Instead, each card contains a written description of the habitat in which the nest was located, together with further information on the nest site. Each nest record was subsequently assigned on the basis of these descriptions, to one of the ninety-nine possible habitat codes in use by the BTO, doing so in a consistent way for each species. The distribution of nest record cards amongst the habitat categories assigned under this treatment was subsequently used to compute a measure of nest habitat diversity given by the formula

$$D = \frac{1}{\sum_i p_i^2}$$

where p_i is the proportion of cards found in that year in habitat i. This measure is not ideal because the habitat codes are not hierarchical. Thus, where one observer may provide a description of a nest on farmland sufficiently detailed to allow recognition of the farm being under arable cultivation, a different observer may provide only a general description of the area as 'farmland', necessitating classification as 'agricultural'. Hence, the diversity index computed here should not be treated as an absolute measure of diversity.

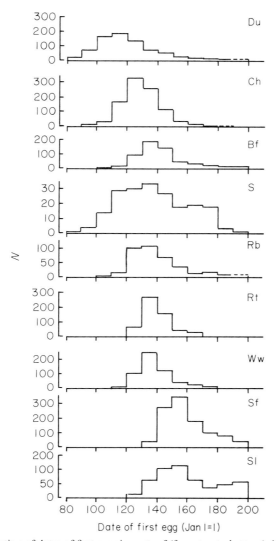

FIG. 7.2. Distribution of dates of first eggs in nests of (from top to bottom) dunnock, chaffinch, bullfinch, skylark, reed bunting, redstart, willow warbler, spotted flycatcher and swallow, a sequence corresponding to increasing migratory tendency. See Methods for details of years of observation.

Comparative use of the index is, however, more robust, in that there is no reason to expect the proportions of observers describing nest habitats at different levels of detail to vary between species.

Use of the proportion of clutches giving rise to young or of the proportion of broods giving rise to fledglings as estimators of hatching and of fledging success respectively is a biased procedure if nests are not all found during the building or egg-laying stages (because the proportion of nests that failed before they could be found by observers is then unknown). This bias was avoided here by computing all egg and chick success rates using the methods of Mayfield (1961, 1975). These methods provide unbiased estimators of the proportion of eggs or chicks surviving through each day they were known to be at risk in the nest.

More information on seasonal productivity of fledglings was obtained by using data in the appendices of Hickling (1983), who gives the normal upper and lower limits to the numbers of broods produced by each species in a given breeding season. These figures were multiplied by the known productivity of typical nests of each species in each year to obtain the upper and lower limits of seasonal productivity involved. This procedure was necessary because the information gathered by the Nest Records Scheme does not record the identity of the pairs involved with each nest, so that, on an annual basis, the incidence of repeat clutches and of second or third clutches is unknown. Where appropriate, the results using both the upper and lower estimates given by Hickling are discussed in the text below.

Estimates of annual survivorship for each of the species concerned were taken from mortality estimates provided by C. J. Mead (unpubl.). These estimates are analogous to range estimators in conventional statistics, in that they estimate average survivorship from the known minimum life-span of the oldest individual from cohorts of birds ringed. Such survival estimates are well correlated with the more complex calculations of the methods used by Lack (1943), Haldane (1955) and Seber (1972). They were used here as a standard source of survival data.

RESULTS AND DISCUSSION

Population pressure and adult survivorship

Rather little is known about how population pressure directly affects adult survival, for three reasons. First, adult survival is overwhelmingly related to body weight certainly between and probably within species, so that other factors can have, at best, only a modifying effect on survival (O'Connor 1981; Dobson 1981). Second, the large species with high survival rates are those most strongly influenced by density-dependent processes, with small species producing as many eggs as they can whilst generally unchecked by competition. Finally, rates of recruitment are inherently more sensitive to population pressure and therefore provide a more effective process through which evolutionary selection may act than do survival rates, e.g. Lack (1966). This last point is a particularly significant impediment to detecting density dependence in adult survival, for breeding activities generally expose adult birds to greater risk (particularly of predation) than do almost any other activities (Dobson 1981). Hence, skipping a breeding year in response to stress induced by high population levels can, by conserving life expectancy, yield a net increase in fitness if breeding is more successful in later years. Consequently, survival rates are likely to be well buffered against density dependence. Haukioja & Hakala (1979) have independently reached a similar conclusion. Several authors have suggested that reproductive effort is the major trade-off against survival (e.g. Cole 1954; Stearns 1976) and this appears to be true for the present species (see below).

An exception to the general pattern discussed above is the red grouse *Lagopus lagopus*. This (and related) species maintain territories throughout the winter, with the food thus safeguarded contributing to the owners' ability to survive the winter (Watson & Moss 1972). Few birds that fail to gain territories survive, so adult survival within the local population is largely set by density-dependent territoriality. Southern (1970) has described a similar situation for the tawny owl *Strix aluco*.

Newton (1980) has reviewed the evidence that food may be limiting in bird populations. Several studies, particularly of titmice (Paridae), have shown that populations may fluctuate in parallel with the availability of winter food, the factor argued by Lack (1966) as the regulating factor for tits. However, even firm evidence of limitation by food availability does not ensure that the process involved is density-dependent and capable of regulating density levels. One might infer, though, that access to a limited food supply would be controlled by dominance behaviour, such that the proportion of birds excluded was greater, on a fixed food supply, the greater the population size. Several authors have shown that supplemental feeding in winter increases over-winter survival in titmice, most so in hard winters and amongst yearlings. Species thus affected have included black-capped chicadees *Parus atricapillus* (Samson & Lewis 1979), willow tit *Parus montanus* (Ekman 1984; Jansson *et al.* 1981), great tit *Parus major* (van Balen 1975; Kallender 1981), and possibly blue tit *Parus caeruleus* (Krebs 1971). Only in Ekman's study was there direct evidence that the mortality alleviated was density-dependent.

These various studies all concern resident species over-wintering on or near their breeding grounds. They show, therefore, that resident species may pay a survivorship penalty by virtue of their residency and, by inference, that this penalty may be density-dependent in operation. Much less is known about density dependence in mortality of migrant species. Hildén (1982) provided some data to show that similar proportions of migratory and of resident goldcrests *Regulus regulus* survived from autumn to the following spring, i.e. that residents suffered no worse mortality whilst over-wintering than migrants did during two migratory journeys and their stay in the south. However, a growing body of evidence suggests that migrants may be susceptible to intraspecific competition at stop-over sites during migration (Rappole & Warner 1976; Alerstam 1978). Several species have been shown to defend territories during stop-overs (e.g. Bibby & Green 1980), thus providing a mechanism by which population regulation could be brought about. The extent to which such processes may operate on the wintering grounds is more poorly documented again.

Summarizing this section, density-dependent survival in winter may well be a feature of resident populations but the extent to which it occurs among migrants is poorly understood.

Population pressure and dispersal

Dispersal from crowded areas is one way to alleviate the effects of population pressure. What constitutes crowding depends not only on the per capita resources available in the area but on the share any individual can acquire for itself. Females and immatures are therefore often the individuals to move, reflecting their low positions in dominance rank (Greenwood 1980). Resource abundance is also critical, with rich areas supporting a greater density of birds than poor areas. Thus, Jansson *et al.* (1981) found that areas experimentally provisioned with supplemental food drew in titmice from the surrounding areas as well as increasing the survival of birds already there, but many birds departed once artificial feeding ended in early April. Direct evidence of greater dispersal in relation to population density is scarce but, where demonstrated, appears to be induced through aggressive behaviour, e.g. Kalela 1954. Density-dependent migration has been shown for several species of titmice (Greenwood, Harvey & Perrins 1979; Berndt & Henss 1967; Hildén 1977) and for the goldcrest (Hildén 1982). In this latter case, migration was the less preferred option to residency and the resident population was more stable in size than was the migratory population. Great tits similarly disperse more from their natal areas when breeding densities are high (O'Connor 1980) and willow tit autumn numbers are likewise regulated (by group territoriality among the resident birds), with forced emigration of immature birds (Ekman 1979).

On theoretical grounds density-induced dispersal is likely to play a larger part in avian population than has been demonstrated to date (Taylor & Taylor 1977). A priori, dispersal is more likely to alleviate population pressure in resident species but, in conjunction with site-imprinting, dispersal by newly-fledged young can provide an effective means of dissipating locally high densities. Thus, young pied flycatchers *Ficedula hypoleuca* disperse post-fledging and feed in habitats and areas to which they return in later years to breed (Berndt & Sternberg 1969).

Dispersal has also been linked to nesting success, which may in turn be affected by density-dependent predation. Thus, female pied flycatchers that lose nests to predators disperse farther than do successful birds (von Haartman 1949). Similarly, reed warblers *Acrocephalus scirpaceus* and great tits disperse more following predation losses (Catchpole 1972; Harvey, Greenwood & Perrins 1979).

Migratory status and population pressure

In a seasonal environment resources in winter are typically very much scarcer than in summer, with a correspondingly lower limit to the population of birds than can be supported. Consequently, the surplus must either die or move out of the area in search of resources elsewhere, as just discussed. We may therefore ask why any birds remain at all, since survival in the winter area is likely to be at the cost of increased risk to predation, to food shortage, and to inclement weather. Lack (1954) suggested that residency has evolved wherever the cost of migration, in terms of reduced survival, is higher than is the cost of residency, but von Haartman (1968) pointed out that it could also arise through differential reproduction: if the resident birds can breed more successfully by being on the breeding grounds at the start of each breeding season, the phenotype for residency will spread. Patterson (1980) and Fretwell (1981) have recently emphasized the advantages of maintaining possession of a territory at the onset of any competition, the so-called 'site dominance' advantage. In support of his hypothesis, von Haartman established that residency is commoner and breeding earlier amongst species nesting in holes, which nest sites offer high breeding success but involve increased intraspecific and interspecific competition for the limited supply available.

An alternative explanation for von Haartman's finding for hole-nesting species is that the availability of holes for winter roosting greatly increases over-winter survival, without any need for greater reproductive success. Van Balen (1980) has shown that the availability of roosting sites can be critically limiting in mid-winter for species such as the great tit. Against this explanation, von Haartman cited the general tendency amongst partially migratory species (those in which some individuals or age-classes migrate whilst others remain) for the resident individuals to resume breeding earlier than do migrant individuals and for the migrant individuals to be those with least prospect of winning superior sites even if they remained, e.g. immature males. Females can similarly afford to move where they are fewer in number than are males (see Ketterson & Nolan 1983 for a recent review). Nevertheless, direct evidence in support of von Haartman's ideas is still needed.

In a seasonal environment one would expect to find greater population pressures for dispersal with greater seasonality (Ashmole 1961, 1963; MacArthur 1959; Herrera 1978). At the time of peak resources very many birds can breed prolifically, but a large fraction of these and their offspring must subsequently migrate as resources fall to the winter low. In a less seasonal environment, proportionally fewer must leave or die at the winter low. Consequently, there is a strong correlation between the proportion of migrant individuals present in a breeding community at any site and the extent of seasonality at that site (Herrera 1978) and where densities of migrant individuals have not risen appropriately, clutch sizes of the species breeding there are correspondingly larger (Ricklefs 1980). In addition, clutch size proves to be inversely related to the extent of primary production in winter but independent of production in summer. These results are consistent with the idea that the number of breeding individuals is regulated in winter rather than by territorial behaviour during the breeding season, with population size exerting a density-dependent influence on the resources available to each individual for reproduction.

According to von Haartman's hypothesis, those species resident in an area should breed earlier than do migrants that must return from more remote wintering grounds. Figure 7.2 examines the prediction for nine common British species. The species are organized from top to bottom in order of increasing migrancy, as judged subjectively in advance of analysis (see Materials and methods). The figure shows a systematic trend for the more migratory species to breed later, as predicted by von Haartman.

Consideration of survival rate in relation to migratory tendency showed no significant correlation (Spearman rho = -0.333, ns). This is not surprising since one would expect survivorship and extent of migration to come into a balance at points at which equal fitness had been achieved (Ketterson & Nolan 1976). An earlier study of the demographic differences between migrants and residents showed that residents are no more likely to survive or to die than are migrants (O'Connor 1981). Migrant species, are, however, more likely to experience changes in territorial population level from one breeding season to the next than are residents, largely because the equilibrium population level of the matter is buffered by density-dependent processes.

Population pressure, timing of laying, and migrancy

Figure 7.3 examines how the timing of laying might affect the reproductive success of a species because of seasonal variation in resource availability. Many species utilizing seasonally increasing food supplies must wait until their resource levels have risen to a point at which the female can find not only enough energy for her own maintenance needs but enough also for the daily formation of each egg (Perrins 1970). In such species a given delay to breeding—such as might be brought about by population pressure—has a relatively large effect on the resources available to the pair for breeding, whether subsequently translated into a larger clutch size, into larger eggs, or into more effective rearing of the young. For another species breeding later in the season, nearer the time of resource peak, the same delay results in a proportionately smaller increase in resources and a correspondingly smaller increase in reproductive success (Fig. 7.3). A still later species will suffer a decrease in resource availability. This model has some implications for the interaction of migratory status with population pressure, as will now be shown.

Figure 7.4 illustrates the effect of population pressure upon date of laying in the case of the reed bunting. When populations were low, breeding was as much as 20 days earlier than it was at high populations, presumably because of the proportionately greater time spent on territorial defence under crowded conditions. Such delays then have consequences for clutch size and chick survivorship and, ultimately, the production of fledglings. The sensitivity of different species to such delays and their consequences depends upon migratory status. This is shown in Fig. 7.5, where rates of change of fledgling

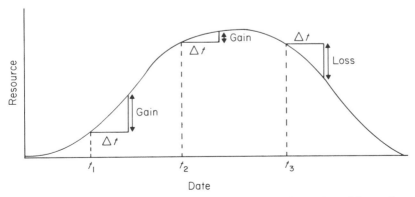

FIG. 7.3. Model showing how a given delay Δt in the start of laying leads to different changes in resource availability because of seasonal changes in resource abundance.

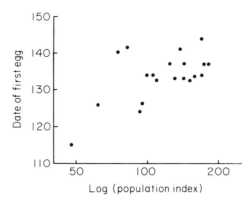

FIG. 7.4. Mean date of egg-laying in the reed bunting in relation to population density (indexed by the Common Birds Census index) $y = 24.433 \log CBC + 83.678$, $r = 0.558$, $P < 0.02$.

production in relation to population density (fledglings/CBC point) are plotted against migratory rank. The results show a clear trend from positive values amongst the resident species to negative values amongst the more migratory species. Reference to Fig. 7.3 shows that the earliest species can be expected to have the proportionately largest gains in response to delay brought about by population pressures; species breeding around the resource peak should be at most only weakly sensitive to population delay; and species

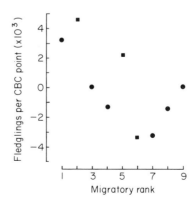

FIG. 7.5. Interspecific variation in density dependence of nest productivity in relation to rank order of migratory tendency (rank 1 = sedentary). Squares indicate species that are normally single-brooded, circles those normally multi-brooded. Spearman's rho = −0.629, $0.05 < P < 0.01$.

breeding late in the season after peak resources should decrease in productivity with further delay.

The analysis can be extended further, by examining the separate sensitivity of clutch size, egg mortality and chick mortality to delay. These different components of fledgling productivity may be expected to vary differentially (Perrins 1970). Clutch size, for example, may be held constant rather than increased in response to greater immediate availability of food if the time needed for formation of additional eggs so delays eventual hatching that chicks have to be reared on a declining food supply. In fact, in their sensitivity to delay in laying neither clutch size nor egg mortality shows any clear relationship with migratory rank. This is not the case for chick survival: Fig. 7.6 shows that the sensitivity of chick survival to laying date decreases the more migratory a species is, though the effects are modulated by differences between single-brooded and multi-brooded species. Examining multi-brooded species first, chick survival actually improves with delay in laying amongst the most resident species but the effect decreases essentially to independence in the very migratory swallow. That is, as far as chick survival is concerned, multi-brooded species lie to the left of the seasonal resource peak of Fig. 7.3 above. In contrast, the single-brooded species shown deteriorate rapidly in their sensitivity to delayed laying the more migratory they are. Chick survival in the resident chaffinch is essentially independent of egg date, but for reed bunting and redstart delay leads to sharply reducing chick survival, corresponding to positions to the right of the resource peak in Fig. 7.3. This is not altogether unexpected, in that multi-brooded species must have a very broad seasonal resource curve if they are to produce two or more

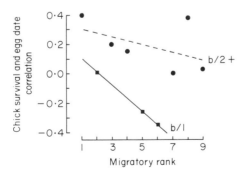

FIG. 7.6. Interspecific variation in the dependence of chick survival on date of laying, in relation to migratory tendency (rank 1 = sedentary) and to number of broods produced in a season. Spearman rho for single-brooded (b/1) species is − 1·00 and for multi-brooded species is −0·543, both non-significant.

broods in the course of a breeding season, whilst single-brood species are probably closely coupled to a sharply peaked resource curve.

Summarizing the results presented to this point, we have seen that the various species examined conform to von Haartman's expectation of earlier breeding by resident species than by migratory species, and that the resident species tend to produce more fledglings in response to nesting delay induced by population pressure; migratory species tend to produce fewer young under these conditions. This effect appears to be associated particularly with chick survival, most severely in single-brood species.

Population pressure and habitat selection

Theories of habitat selection at different population densities have been put forward by Brown (1969) and by Fretwell & Lucas (1970). Brown considered three levels of population limitation in relation to habitat suitability. As a first level he considered primary habitat in which birds prefer to settle, such that at low population densities settlement in the habitat is directly proportional to the number of potential settlers available. When the habitat eventually saturates, further settlers must move into some secondary, less preferred, habitat which they then continue to fill until it too is saturated. At a third level, further would-be settlers are unable to find suitable territories and become 'floaters' who may fill any vacancies that arise. Secondary habitat is of a poorer intrinsic quality than is the primary preferred habitat. Fretwell & Lucas (1970) extended this theory to accommodate the situation where a variety of habitats are present and where a degree of territorial compression can take place (Fig. 7.7). At low population densities (below P_1 in Fig. 7.7) all birds settle in the preferred habitat. Eventually this habitat reaches its saturation density D_1 at population size P_1. Where the Brown model would now predict the filling of habitat B (an intrinsically poorer habitat) the Fretwell and Lucas model allows some lesser or greater compression of territory size in habitat A, allowing a gradual increase in the carrying capacity of habitat A, e.g. to some new level D_2 or D_3 for a population size P_2 or P_3. Above this level further territory compression in habitat A would reduce the fitness of the territory holders in the crowded habitat A below that achievable in an uncrowded habitat B, so habitat B fills preferentially (Fig. 7.7, dotted line). The process of territorial compression can be repeated through habitats B, C, D, etc. through a hierarchy of habitats decreasing in intrinsic quality. Indeed, it is possible for still further territory compression to occur in habitat A if the alternatives are poor enough, though eventually birds may not be able to settle at all and must become floaters. The major differences between the Brown and the Fretwell–Lucas models is that the former involves exclusion of

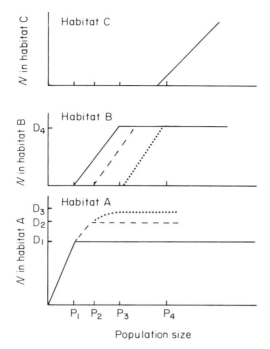

FIG. 7.7. Sequential filling of a hierarchy of preferred habitats (preference for A > preference for B > preference for C) when territory sizes within each habitat are fixed (————) or compressible to a smaller (– – – –) or larger (. . . . .) degree. Based on Brown (1969) and Fretwell & Lucas (1970).

individuals from the best habitat by despotic behaviour of the most dominant birds whilst the latter envisages that settlement can take place in all habitats at all times, within the limits of territorial compression, for equivalent fitness in the habitat chosen.

Empirical data to support these models of habitat choice are rather scarce to date but several recent studies have confirmed some of the predictions of the Fretwell–Lucas model. Thus, for the European kestrel *Falco tinnunculus* habitats colonized under population expansion were of successively poorer quality as indexed by clutch size (O'Connor 1982). A particularly detailed study of the Fretwell–Lucas effect in the yellowhammer *Emberiza citrinella* (O'Connor 1980) showed that breeding success in both preferred habitat (farmland) and less preferred habitat (woodland) is density-dependent but at different rates. The birds therefore distribute themselves between the two habitats in proportion to their relative fitness in each, as described by Fretwell and Lucas' model. For the dickcissel *Spiza americana* Zimmerman (1982) showed that males preferred the oldfield habitats where there were greater opportunities for polygynous breeding.

Figure 7.8 provides an example of habitat utilization for the redstart over the period 1961–81. The breeding population of the redstart in Britain decreased between 1965 and 1973 as a result of severe drought in the Sahelian zone of Africa. The population has subsequently recovered slowly, so that by 1981 it was about three-quarters of its 1965 level. Figure 7.8 illustrates the

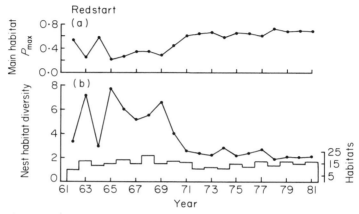

FIG. 7.8. Changes in the diversity of nesting habitat used by redstarts in Britain, 1962–81. (a) Proportion of nests found in the most frequented habitat for the year. (b) nest habitat diversity index (●————●) and total number of habitats in use (histogram) for each year. The breeding population of redstarts in Britain decreased markedly after 1968 due to drought in the African winter quarters.

corresponding changes in diversity of nesting habitat used by redstarts. Prior to 1965 habitat diversity fluctuated somewhat, in keeping with the general fluctuations of migrant species (O'Connor 1981). From 1965 until 1973 nest habitat diversity decreased sharply, thereafter levelling out to a slower rate of decrease. The upper part of the graph shows the proportion of nests found in the dominant (most frequently recorded) habitat in any one year, which measure shows a slow increase. The histogram (Fig. 7.8) shows the number of habitats in use in any given year, principally revealing a reduction in the number of habitats used between 1971 and 1975, with a slow rise thereafter. These various measures thus agree in showing that redstarts at low population densities tended to concentrate into a smaller number of habitats which were used more fully in years of low population level, as expected on these habitat models.

Rosenzweig (1981) has recently reconsidered the implications of the Fretwell–Lucas model in the light of optimal foraging theory. He points out that birds can distribute themselves in strict accordance with the Fretwell–Lucas model only if there are no costs attached to establishing their knowledge of the prevailing distribution of fitness: where there is uncertainty about the quality or degree of saturation of the available habitat, the birds incur a cost in evaluating any given vacancy. The effect is such that the higher the cost, the sooner the bird should generalize between the two habitats concerned. This idea leads to the prediction that species with high survival should be habitat generalists, broadly speaking. By virtue of their high survival, relatively few breeding vacancies are available each season, so that the cost of finding each vacancy is high. In species with poor survivorship, on the other hand, there are many vacancies each year and habitat discrimination is possible at low cost. Figure 7.9 examines this prediction for the nine species studied here and show that there is a weak but not statistically significant positive correlation between diversity and survivorship, as predicted. The test presented is not entirely satisfactory, in that the diversity measure used is the median over the 20 years of the study, during which time population densities have varied considerably. Thus, the diversity measures used in the figure are not necessarily comparable across species. Nevertheless, the analysis provides some crude evidence in support of Rosenzweig's arguments. Other supporting evidence can be adducted from the reluctance of breeding birds to move from

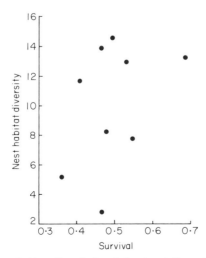

FIG. 7.9. Variation in nest habitat diversity in relation to adult survival. Spearman's rho = 0·30, not significant.

an inadequate site, as shown for Adelie penguins *Pygoscelis adeliae* by Tenaza (1971).

The validity of the Fretwell–Lucas model has been reviewed recently in the light of these studies (O'Connor & Fuller, in press). We suggested that species in fact differ in their strategies of habitat use and that the Brown and Fretwell–Lucas models reflect different strategies. For some species, hardly any density-dependent reduction of breeding success occurs and birds fill habitats in succession in line with the Brown model. For others, habitat utilization is in line with the Fretwell–Lucas model with considerable density-dependent reduction in breeding success within any single habitat. Thus, as their populations build up, species such as the chaffinch move successively into habitats of only slightly poorer breeding success whilst species such as the wren are subjected to severe reduction in clutch size. O'Connor and Fuller suggest that these models form extremes of a continuum along which the strategy used in any given species may be placed.

The influence of site fidelity

So far no consideration has been given in these models to the effects of site fidelity, yet these prove critical in understanding the origins of the continuum noted by O'Connor and Fuller (in press). For many birds there may be advantages in re-using an area frequented in previous years, even though the plot may not be held the year round. Such birds may know the best foraging places, the location of good cover against predators, and so on, and thus be able to exploit the area more effectively (Hildén 1965; Greenwood & Harvey 1976; Baker 1978). Fidelity of breeding grounds has been demonstrated for many species (e.g. Greenwood 1980; Lawn 1982) but wintering-site fidelity may also occur (e.g. Schlenker 1976; Møller 1983a, b). When Ralph & Mewaldt (1976) experimentally transported various *Zonotrichia* sparrows from their mid-winter feeding areas, the birds fairly rapidly returned over many miles. This suggests that the advantages of living in a familiar area significantly outweighed the costs of the return migration. Fretwell (1981) describes similar evidence in favour of site fidelity by birds.

How should site faithfulness affect the habitat models considered here? Consider a resident species driven by population pressure into the use of a secondary (less preferred) habitat and suppose that it survives a subsequent severe winter. Next spring it must choose between returning to its familiar territory in poor habitat or taking up residence in one of the unfamiliar territories left vacant in the good habitat by the death of the previous owners. Unless the differences in the quality of the two habitats is large enough to offset the advantages conferred by site familiarity, the bird should remain in its existing territory. Some indirect evidence in favour of this process is available in the case of the chaffinch, a species previously identified as site-tenacious (Anvén & Enemar 1975; Mikkonen 1983). Following the severe winter of 1961–62 in Britain, chaffinch densities were only about 70% of their long-term equilibrium level. During the subsequent recovery one would expect, according to the Fretwell–Lucas model, that the diversity of nesting habitats in use should increase. What actually happened, however, was that in spring of 1962 a proportion of the survivors continued to use their previous nesting habitat whilst their offspring selectively colonized the vacancies in the optimal habitat. Over the following years further mortality amongst the birds alive in 1961 further reduced the number of birds using suboptimal but familiar habitat, so that proportionately more of the population were distributed in accordance with the Fretwell–Lucas predictions. This can be examined by successively but cumulatively excluding the 1962, 1963, . . . 1971 data from calculation of diversity–density correlations over the remaining years through 1981: as the first 0–4 years data were omitted the Spearman correlation coefficients (all significant at $P < 0.05$ or better) rose from 0.469 for the full 1962–81 data through values 0.535, 0.523 and 0.521 to 0.583 for the 1966–81 data, stabilizing thereafter (e.g. 0.578 for 1968–81 data), thus showing successively closer approximation to the Fretwell–Lucas prediction as the effects of site faithfulness were removed. (With average annual mortality of about 40%, the site (= habitat) faithful birds have a mean life expectancy of only 1.2 years and only about 15% would survive to 1966).

Rather special conditions are required for philopatry to induce major deviations from the Fretwell–Lucas model's predictions. Amongst long-lived species, territorial vacancies in optimal habitat are relatively scarce since only a small proportion of the population dies in any one year. Yet because a territory holder can expect to harvest the benefits of a better territory not just in the year it changes territory but in several subsequent years, the cost of changing must be discounted over several years and a very large site dominance benefit is necessary to warrant remaining in suboptimal habitat. Møller (1982) has provided evidence to this effect for magpies *Pica pica*. He classified territories into three classes on the basis of consistency of occupation and showed that the preferred territories were composed of preferred feeding habitats (farmyards, roadside, hedgerow and pastoral areas) in which magpies could feed more efficiently. He also showed nesting was earlier and more successful in these territories and that magpies intruded more into high quality territories as birds in poor quality territories tried to move to better quality ones. Amongst short-lived birds, on the other hand, deaths are relatively numerous so survivors can expect to find vacancies in optimal habitat each spring. With a short life expectancy, however, movement will increase fitness only if the differences in intrinsic quality are large between habitats; otherwise the benefits of site dominance favour site fidelity, as with the chaffinch above. A further consideration now arises, though, in that large differences in the intrinsic quality of any two habitats will increase the likelihood that density-dependent competition for space in the better habitat will occur. If it does, the value of subsequent vacant territories will be lower for being in a crowded habitat, so movement there from the less preferred habitat will be inhibited and site faithfulness favoured. Vacancies are then likely to be filled according to the ideal free distribution of Fretwell's model. Data for the yellowhammer show that populations of this species are distributed between farmland and woodland habitat in good agreement with the relative clutch sizes anticipated in each habitat, given the prevailing densities in each (O'Connor 1980).

Throughout the above I implicitly assumed that adult mortality was similar in all habitats, with differences in intrinsic quality relating to breeding success in the various habitats. Habitats may be preferred, however, for the greater survival a bird can expect there, in which case vacancies will arise more frequently in the less preferred habitat. In such circumstances movement to the better habitat may well be favoured by the greater expectation of breeding attempts associated with high survival. It is also possible for survival to be poorer in a given habitat, yet for it to be heavily used by birds. The condition required is that reproductive success should be correspondingly greater in the riskier habitat. Batten (1977) has documented something akin to this for the blackbird *Turdus merula* nesting in rural and in suburban areas. Rural blackbirds have a high adult survival but rather poor breeding success (due to intense nest predation), to produce about 1·7 juveniles per pair annually. Suburban blackbirds do the reverse, with low adult survival due to predation yet with larger clutches producing more juveniles, averaging 2·0 annually. Thus, the two environments offer very similar overall fitness to their blackbirds. The species offers an interesting insight into Rosenzweig's (1981) hypothesis, in that one would expect the rural blackbirds to be habitat generalists to compensate for the low rate of territorial vacancies (see above). Do they then suffer the reduced nesting success described by Batten because they are not well adapted to any one habitat (cf. Fig. 7.14 below)?

Site fidelity is more likely to be of significance for resident species than for migrants, although many migrant species do return year after year to the same territory (e.g. von Haartman 1949). Järvinen (1979) in fact showed that site fidelity decreases in bird communities from south to north, i.e. as the proportion of migratory species increases. Familiarity with a breeding site should be of greatest benefit when competition is most severe and greater site fidelity in residents therefore matches my earlier conclusions, on demographic grounds, that residents are adapted to competitive situations. Competition is relatively more severe at low resource levels, so it is noteworthy that migratory chaffinches in Finland were most site faithful in years when food supplies were scarce early in spring and that they dispersed to nest more widely in years when food was superabundant (Mikkonen 1983).

Timing of territorial settlement

In considering Rosenzweig's (1981) model the assumption was made that the probability of a territory being occupied by a given bird was essentially independent of the number of potential settlers. However, Knapton & Krebs (1974) have shown experimentally for the song sparrow *Melospiza melodia* that the temporal pattern of settlement has a significant effect on the number of settlers that actually win territories. When they removed territorial owners sequentially, each vacancy was quickly taken over by one of the potential settlers, so that there was no net change in density of territorial birds. When several territory holders were removed simultaneously, however, so that a large number of adjacent territories were available together, a large number of birds settled successfully, with new territorial boundaries that differed from those defended by the previous territory owners. Spray (1978) has suggested that this effect is most important in the case of species with short-term territories. In long-term territorial systems where long-lived species are territorial throughout the year, vacancies arise only occasionally and are filled on a one-by-one basis, with maintenance of territorial boundaries. Spray showed that this was the case with the carrion crow *Corvus corone*, in which territorial boundaries are maintained even in the face of experimental supplementation of food supply. Similar behaviour has previously been recorded for the tawny owl (Southern 1970). Amongst short-term territory holders, examples of increased density due to simultaneous settlement have been given for the song sparrow by Tompa (1964) and for the great tit by Lack (1954). These two examples tend to support Spray's (1978) contention that the temporal pattern of settlement will be most significant in short-lived species and least significant in long-lived species.

Figure 7.10 presents an indirect test of the generality of temporal settlement effects. If settlement patterns are significant in determining final densities in an area, then year-to-year variation of settlement density should be greater in short-lived species in which a high proportion of the population die each year. Figure 7.10 shows how the variances of the Common Birds Census indices for a variety of species relate to adult survival. There is some suggestion that amongst species with medium to high survival population stability may increase with survival, as expected, but there are many

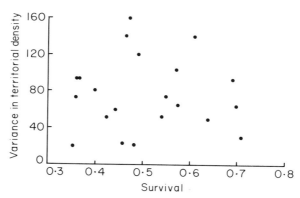

FIG. 7.10. Year-to-year variation (estimated as variance in log CBC index) in territorial densities in relation to adult survival in the species concerned. See text for details.

short-lived species with stable populations. The timing of settlement effects established by Knapton & Krebs (1974) must be over-ridden by other effects in most species and in most years.

Timing of laying and habitat selection

So far the discussion has considered nesting habitat only as a fixed variable each season (although seasonality of food was discussed earlier in relation to Fig. 7.3). In practice, vegetation and nest cover develop markedly in the course of the breeding season and may influence nesting success. This is particularly important for migrants, in that late-developing habitats unsuitable for early-nesting resident species may still be vacant on the arrival of the migrants.

Figure 7.11 shows how the diversity of nesting habitat used by two species varies in relation to the date of egg-laying in each. In the case of the resident dunnock, the diversity of nesting habitat increases with delay in egg-laying which, according to the Fretwell–Lucas theory, should result in reduced breeding success. Yet we saw earlier (Fig. 7.5) that fledgling production actually increases with population pressure in this species. In the case of the partially migratory reed bunting, nest habitat diversity shows the opposite trend, becoming more stereotyped if laying is late. If delayed egg-laying is the outcome of population pressure, as suggested earlier (Fig. 7.4), the reduced nest habitat diversity of the reed bunting in late years is consistent with the Fretwell–Lucas hypothesis if greater crowding for the best habitats is responsible for the reduced diversity. The dunnock results cannot be explained in this way. Figure 7.12 provides a broader picture of the situation: the two species of Fig. 7.11 form part of a gradient in relation to migratory

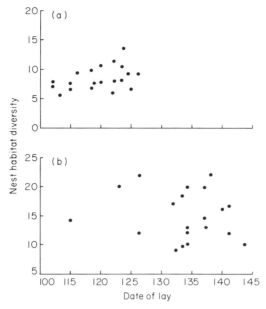

FIG. 7.11. Nest habitat diversity plotted in relation to mean date of first egg for the year: (a) dunnock and (b) reed bunting. Regression lines are (a) $y = 0.219x - 17.725$, $r = 0.478$, $P < 0.05$ and (b) $y = -0.093x + 27.755$, $r = 0.150$, ns.

status, such that the more migratory a bird is, the more likely it is to have a negative diversity–egg date relationship. Note that the pattern in Fig. 7.12 is not linear, the dunnock having a rather larger positive correlation than might be expected on the basis of the other species. These results suggest that resident species are less likely to conform to the Fretwell–Lucas model than expected, being more likely to resort to new habitats in which they achieve *greater* success (Fig. 7.5) as the season develops. One obvious explanation lies in the seasonal development of nesting habitat (Peakall 1960; Byrkjedal 1980; Bilcke 1984). Early in the season, there is little vegetation growth and only hole-nesting species and ground-nesting species utilizing the cover provided by early growth of the field layer are likely to be successful. As the season progresses, vegetational development extends to higher layers, thus increasing the availability of nest sites screened by vegetation. For the yellowhammer Peakall (1960) has shown that average nest height increases through the season, more or less in line with the development of vegetational cover. Resident species breeding earlier are more likely to be susceptible to such phenological considerations. Accepting the notion that the earliest habitat available is in some way poorer than the better vegetated sites used later (and

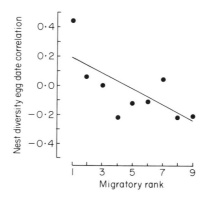

FIG. 7.12. Interspecific variation in the sensitivity of nest habitat diversity to laying date, in relation to ranked migratory tendency (rank 1 = sedentary). Spearman's rho = -0.683, $P < 0.05$.

Fig. 7.6 showed that chick survival rose the later the eggs were laid), there must be a countervailing advantage to an early start. Hence, the earliest breeders may be lengthening their breeding season to allow more broods or to have greater opportunities to relay if a given attempt fails, or they may benefit because their chicks subsequently survive better the earlier they fledge.

Correlates of habitat diversity

The pattern of habitat utilization that emerges as a result of the processes described above determines the normal spectrum of nesting habitat diversity for each species. The extent of this diversity is itself correlated systematically with the number of features to which we now turn.

Migrancy

Figure 7.13 shows the spectrum of habitat diversity for the 20 years of data for each species. The results are arranged in order of increasing migrancy and show several features of interest. First, in the case of the hole-nesting redstart habitat utilization is extremely stereotyped and diversity is low. This is almost certainly a result of the species' habit of nesting in holes, mostly in trees: Bilcke (1984) found that most of the hole-nesting species he examined had narrower habitat niches in the breeding season than at other times of year, the only exception being the coal tit *Parus ater* which can nest in ground-holes and which is therefore less constrained by the availability of tree-holes. Amongst the species considered here, the dunnock is slightly more stereotyped than are the other resident species but there is otherwise no particular pattern, except that the reed bunting is rather variable from year to year in the diversity of habitat used. There may be some suggestion of decreasing diversity with distance of migration beyond this point, through the sequence reed bunting, willow warbler, spotted flycatcher and swallow, perhaps suggesting that the

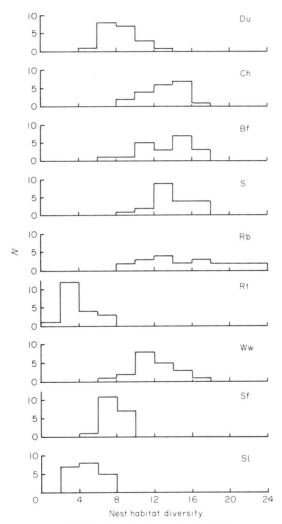

FIG. 7.13. Distribution of nest habitat diversity (annual values) for various species. Top to bottom: dunnock, chaffinch, bullfinch, skylark, reed bunting, redstart, willow warbler, spotted flycatcher and swallow.

late arrivals are more restricted in the habitats available to them. The long-distance migrants are certainly disproportionately represented in certain habitats, such as scrub and riverine habitat, compared with residents (R.J. O'Connor, unpubl.).

Number of broods

Table 7.1 summarizes the relationship between median nest habitat diversity over the years and the number of broods produced by each species. With the exception of the hole-nesting redstart, there is a clear trend towards reduced

TABLE 7.1. Nest habitat diversity in relation to numbers of broods produced per season

Broods per season	Species	Nest habitat diversity*
One, occasionally two	Reed bunting	14·5
	Chaffinch	13·0
	Redstart	2·8†
Often two	Bullfinch	13·9
	Skylark	13·2
	Willow warbler	11·8
	Spotted flycatcher	7·8
Two or more	Dunnock	8·2
	Swallow	5·1

* Median of 20 years data; see text for details.
† Hole nesting species; see text.

habitat diversity on the part of the species producing multiple broods in a single year. This cuts across the relationship with migrancy: the resident chaffinch and the partially migrant reed bunting both have high diversities but only a single brood, whilst the double-brooded resident dunnock and the double- or treble-brooded migrant swallow have fairly low diversities. Of the occasionally double-brooded species, the migrant spotted flycatcher has the lowest diversity.

Nesting success

One of the problems for birds utilizing a variety of nesting habitats is the extent to which they can specialize on any single habitat. A habitat specialist can be highly adapted to the selective pressures influencing breeding in that habitat but generalists are in general ill-adapted to any single one of the habitats in which they breed. Habitat breadths are generally smallest during the breeding season (e.g. Alatalo 1981), due to the simultaneously operating constraints of needing suitable nest-sites, song posts and feeding areas (Lack & Venables 1939; Hildén 1965). Best & Stauffer (1980) have previously presented data showing that nest-site generalists have reduced success as compared to the specialists. Examining this within the present data, there is no overall relationship between clutch size and diversity of nesting habitat used. Figure 7.14, however, shows that nesting success did decrease systematically with habitat diversity, more weakly for egg mortality (Fig. 7.14a) and more strongly for chick mortality (Fig. 7.14b). Note that in both graphs the regression slope would be steepened if the hole-nesting redstart (left-most data points) were omitted. These results thus suggest that the habitat generalists suffer more in their average rearing success than do the more specialist migrants. It is important to bear in mind, however, that for species subject to overflow into secondary and tertiary habitats in response to population pressures, average success must be expected to decrease as proportionately more of the population breed in habitats of intrinsically poor quality (see above). That is, species with high habitat diversity may be relatively more

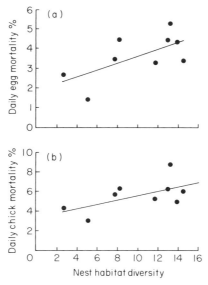

FIG. 7.14. Interspecific variation in (a) egg mortality and (b) chick mortality in relation to nest habitat diversity. Mortalities on daily basis using the method of Mayfield (1965, 1971). Regression lines are (a) $y = 0 \cdot 176x + 1 \cdot 852$, $r = 0 \cdot 612$, $P = 0 \cdot 041$ (after arc-sine transformation, one-tailed); (b) $y = 0 \cdot 220x + 3 \cdot 369$, $r = 0 \cdot 656$, $P = 0 \cdot 027$ (after arc-sine transformation, one-tailed).

saturated in population density than are species more stereotyped in habitat use. This was examined by computing an index of population saturation for each species, obtained by expressing the median CBC level over the 20 years as a fraction of the maximum CBC recorded over the same period. This assumes that all populations were equally likely to reach some degree of absolute saturation in the course of the 20 years, a view supported by subjective examination of the population trends. Hence, if a population spent much of its time near this upper equilibrium level a high index value would be obtained, whilst if the population was generally below the maximum sustainable quite a low index would prevail. The association of median habitat diversity with this index of population saturation gave a correlation coefficient of 0·529, not statistically significant. Thus, although there was some tendency for habitat diversity to be greater in the more saturated populations, the effect is probably not enough to account for the correlation with breeding success.

The final productivity of the species will be the product of its clutch size, rearing success and number of broods attempted. When seasonal productivity of fledglings was calculated in this way a negative correlation with nest habitat diversity was obtained ($r = -0·616$, $P = 0·08$). This result therefore suggests that species in the more diverse habitats tended to produce fewer fledglings over the breeding season than did birds that were more inclined towards habitat stereotypy, both because they attempt fewer broods (Table 7.1) and because the chicks survive less well (Fig. 7.14). We saw earlier (Fig. 7.6) that single-brood species were more susceptible to delay in egg-laying, though perhaps not particularly to density-induced delay (Fig. 7.5). A picture therefore emerges of single-brooded species being geared to exploit some strongly seasonal resource, so that habitat selectivity and any associated benefits for chick survival must be sacrificed to breed at the critical time. What is especially interesting is that single-broodedness is not predominantly a feature of migrants forced to arrive late and depart early. Equally, these findings suggest that the distribution of reproductive effort within a season may be as significant for birds as the better studied distribution of effort between seasons.

Productivity and migrancy

As noted earlier (Fig. 7.13) there is a somewhat complex relationship between the pattern of nesting habitat diversity and the migrancy status of species considered here. Figure 7.15 therefore plots seasonal productivity of fledglings against migratory rank. Since the exact number of broods produced in any given year was unknown in the present study two plots are presented, the first using the lower limit of the range of broods given in Hickling (1983), the second using the upper limit to brood number. The results show that if the lower limit is used to calculate numbers fledged, seasonal productivity is essentially independent of migratory rank, whilst using the upper limit gives a positive correlation. Of particular interest in this analysis is the contradiction of the negative trend expected on the basis of von Haartman's (1968) arguments, that residents should gain in productivity by virtue of being on the breeding grounds at the start of the breeding season. Figure 7.15 shows that, if anything, the reverse is true. The only way that von Haartman's hypothesis can remain true therefore is if juvenile survival is higher in compensation amongst those birds producing young early in the season. Kluyver (1966) in fact showed such an effect in the case of the great tit: when he experimentally removed the young of the first broods of the season, he found that young produced in the second broods survived exceptionally well, far better than they did in competition with the first brood young. Garnett (1981) has subsequently shown that first-brood young are dominant over second-brood young by virtue of their larger size, and for such time as the survivors of the second brood take to reach full size. Thereafter, dominance is resolved on the basis of full-grown body size. Unless some such effect operates along the

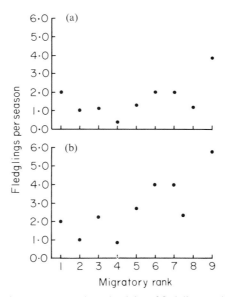

FIG. 7.15. Relationship between seasonal productivity of fledglings and ranked migratory tendency (rank 1 = sedentary), using (a) lower and (b) upper limits to broods per season. Spearman's rho = 0·329, not significant.

resident–migrant gradient considered here, von Haartman's hypothesis cannot be supported on the basis of improved breeding success.

Summarizing the analyses presented above, the more resident species are less susceptible to intraspecific competition and to delayed breeding (however caused) than are migrants. Yet the more migratory species tend to produce more fledglings than do the more sedentary species, so that any advantages to resident species must lie either in post-fledging survival or in adult survival. It is, however, possible that the trend towards greater productivity of fledglings on the part of migrant species (Fig. 7.15) is achieved at a cost in terms of adult survivorship. In an earlier paper (O'Connor 1981) I showed that migrant and resident species on British farmland are broadly similar in adult survival. Where the two groups do differ, however, is in the extent of their trade-offs between adult survivorship and reproductive efforts. Both groups conform to the theoretical expectation that species producing many eggs should have lower adult survival than species producing fewer eggs (Cole 1954; Williams 1966; Stearns 1976) but the rate of decrease of survival is much greater amongst migrants than amongst resident species. Thus, a migrant suffers heavier adult mortality in laying an extra egg each season (or otherwise producing an extra fledgling), than does a resident species with the same clutch size. Figure 7.16 examines the present species for trade-offs of this type and shows that adult survival does indeed decrease with greater breeding productivity. (Similar results to Fig. 7.16 are obtained when figures for minimum rather than for maximum broods per season are used.) The results show also a broad dichotomy between the residents and migrants, with the residents generally clustered to the upper left of the graph and the migrants clustered towards the bottom right of the graph. The partially migratory reed bunting is nicely in the middle of the graph but the skylark is well to the left. The pattern of Fig. 7.16 is potentially explicable in terms of the correlations with nest habitat diversity already described. This was examined by computing partial correlations between adult survivorship and fledgling production, with nest habitat diversity held constant: the resulting correlation ($p = 0.813$, $P < 0.02$) is very similar to that of Fig. 7.16, indicating the trade-off is maintained independently of nest habitat diversity. On the other hand, the relationship between fledgling production and nest habitat diversity is in turn largely independent of adult survival ($p = 0.585$, $P = 0.10$ against the simple correlation of -0.616). Hence, it is not possible to attribute the trade-off between survival and reproductive effort directly to nest habitat diversity.

We have therefore two questions to answer: (i) what causes this trade-off between survivorship and breeding productivity, and (ii) why do the long-distance migrants differ from the residents in their location within the trade-off plot of Fig. 7.16. One possibility is that greater reproductive effort

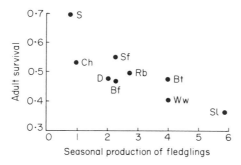

FIG. 7.16. Adult survival in relation to seasonal production of fledglings in various species. Spearman's rho $= -0.733$, $P < 0.05$. For species codes see Fig. 7.2.

leaves the migrant in poorer body condition in which to prepare for and undertake migration. Thus Bryant (1979) showed that house martins *Delichon urbica* undertaking a second brood in the season were less likely to reappear at the breeding colony the following year than were birds undertaking only a single brood. An alternative (though not mutually exclusive) explanation is that high rates of reproduction involve direct breeding risks, so that long-distance migrants are forced as a class into undertaking such risks. We return therefore to von Haartman's arguments that residents have the best choice of territories and nest sites by virtue of being on station at the start of each breeding season, and consider whether the benefits of this choice might not be taken in the form of 'safe' breeding habitats. I have previously shown that species resident on farmland can be regarded as *K*-selected, for their population levels are significantly more stable than are those of migratory species and the ubiquity of each species is strongly correlation with adult survival (O'Connor 1981). Residents may therefore be regarded as being at population levels near their carrying capacities, with reproductive effort limited by density-dependent factors and with a premium on adult survival. In contrast, migrant species show the characteristics associated with *r*-selection and it is those migrants that produce most young in a season that are the most widespread in the country, independently of adult survival. If the residents are in fact well-adapted to high densities, we have an explanation for the finding above that residents are less susceptible, i.e. are better adapted to intraspecific competition and to delay in breeding, however caused. Moreover, this explanation also accounts for the great susceptibility of single-brood species to the effects of delayed breeding: an extension of my earlier analysis (O'Connor 1981) shows that it is single-brood species that are most heavily involved in trade-offs between survival and clutch size: multi-brooded species show relatively weak trade-offs in survival for their greater productivity of young.

Implicit in the idea of r-selection is the notion that such species are fugitives breeding prolifically in habitat patches not yet colonized by the competitively superior K-strategies but being out-competed for these habitats when the K-strategies eventually arrive. Migrants on British farmland are in fact concentrated into certain habitats that are less regularly used by resident species, such as riparian vegetation and secondary growth. The reason for this need not lie with competition. For example, the later phenology of these habitats may be involved, with vegetation not providing good cover for nests until late spring, so that the migrants arriving late can use them whilst the residents starting earlier cannot. Alternatively, invertebrate populations in these habitats may peak later in the year than is the case in habitats used by residents. Resident species may therefore either have a wide spectrum of habitats available to them by virtue of their early breeding or they may be able to pre-empt a narrow spectrum of the most productive habitats, leaving the less preferred ones to the migrants. Figure 7.13 showed that the long-distance migrants tend to have narrower habitat diversities than do any of the more sedentary species except the dunnock. It is possible that this species is in turn limited by its early breeding to those habitats that provide adequate cover early in the spring. The food resource explanation finds some further evidence in the tendency for these habitats to be invaded by the new fledglings of resident species during the summer when the migrants are still breeding. Above all though, are the striking links found here between single-broodedness, use of diverse habitats and great sensitivity to delayed laying, links suggesting strong coupling to very seasonal resources. Such species may ultimately prove the most susceptible to competitive regulation.

ACKNOWLEDGMENTS

The work described here was conducted under contract HF3/03/192 from the Nature Conservancy Council to the British Trust for Ornithology, and this support is gratefully acknowledged. Nest record cards were computerized with resources provided by the Natural Environment Research Council (grant GR3/4357). Richard Sibly kindly provided a critical reading of the manuscript.

REFERENCES

Alatalo, R.V. (1981). Habitat selection of forest birds in the seasonal environment of Finland. *Annales Zoologici Fennici*, **18**, 103–114.

Alerstam, T. (1978). Reoriented bird migration in coastal areas: dispersal to suitable resting grounds? *Oikos*, **30**, 405–408.

Alerstam, T. & Högstedt, G. (1980). Spring predictability and leap-frog migration. *Ornis Scandinavia*, **11**, 196–200.

Anven, B. & Enemar, A. (1957). Om ortstrohet och medellinslandg hos bofink (*Fringilla coelebs*), några resultat av en undersökning ned hjälp av fägringmörkning. *Vår Fagelvarld*, **16**, 161–177.

Ashmole, N.P. (1961). *The biology of certain terns.* D.Phil. thesis, Oxford University.

Ashmole, N.P. (1963). The regulation of numbers of tropical oceanic birds. *Ibis*, **103**, 458–473.

Bailey, R.S. (1967). An index of bird population changes on farmland. *Bird Study*, **14**, 195–209.

Baker, R.R. (1978). *The Evolutionary Ecology of Animal Migration.* Hodder and Stoughton, London.

Balen, J.H. van. (1975). Factors affecting the size of the breeding population. *Verhandelingen-Koninklijke Nederlandse Akademie van Wetenshappen Afd Naturkunde, tweede reeks*, **66**, 80.

Balen, J.H. van. (1980). Population fluctuations of the Great Tit and feeding conditions in winter. *Ardea*, **68**, 143–164.

Batten, L.A. (1977). *Studies on the population dynamics and energetics of Blackbirds,* Turdus merula Linnaeus. Ph.D. thesis, University of London.

Berndt, R. & Henss, M. (1967). Die Kohlmeise, *Parus major*, als Invasionsvogel. *Vogelwarte*, **24**, 17–37.

Berndt, R. & Sternberg, H. (1969). Alters—und Geschlechtsunterschiede in der Dispersion des Trauerschnäppers (*Ficedula hypoleuca*). *Journal für Ornithologie*, **110**, 256–269.

Best, L.B. & Stauffer, D.F. (1980). Factors affecting nesting success in riparian bird communities. *Condor*, **82**, 149–158.

Bibby, C.J. & Green, R.E. (1980). Foraging behaviour of migrant pied flycatchers, *Ficedula hypoleuca*, on temporary territories. *Journal of Animal Ecology*, **49**, 507–521.

Bilcke, G. (1984). Seasonal changes in habitat of resident passerines. *Ardea*, **72**, 95–99.

Brown, J.L. (1969). The buffer effect and productivity in tit populations. *American Naturalist*, **103**, 347–354.

Bryant, D.M. (1979). Reproductive costs in the house martin (*Delichon urbica*). *Journal of Animal Ecology*, **48**, 655–675.

Byrkjedal, I. (1980). Nest predation in relation to snow-cover—a possible factor influencing the start of breeding in shorebirds. *Ornis Scandinavica*, **11**, 249–252.

Catchpole, C.K. (1972). A comparative study of territory in the reed warbler (*A. schoenobaenus*). *Journal of Zoology* (*London*), **166**, 213–231.

Cole, L.C. (1954). The population consequences of life history phenomena. *Quarterly Review of Biology*, **29**, 103–137.

Davies, N.B. (1978). Ecological questions about territorial behaviour. *Behavioural Ecology* (Ed. by J.R. Krebs & N.B. Davies), pp. 317–350. Blackwell Scientific Publications, Oxford.

Dobson, A.P. (1981). *Mortality rates of British birds.* D.Phil. thesis, Oxford University.

Ekman, J. (1979). Coherence, composition and territories of winter social groups of the Willow Tit *Parus montanus* and the Crested Tit *P. cristatus*. *Ornis Scandinavia*, **10**, 56–68.

Ekman, J. (1984). Density-dependent seasonal mortality and population fluctuations of the temperate-zone Willow Tit (*Parus montanus*). *Journal of Animal Ecology*, **53**, 119–134.

Fretwell, S. (1981). Evolution of migration in relation to factors regulating bird numbers. *Migrant Birds in the Neotropics.* (Ed. by A. Keast & E.S. Morton), pp. 517–527. Smithsonian Institution Press, Washington, DC.

Fretwell, S.D. & Lucas, H.L. (1970). On territorial behaviour and other factors influencing habitat distribution in birds, I. Theoretical development. *Acta Biotheoretica*, **19**, 16–36.

Fuller, R.J., Marchant, J.H. & Morgan, R.A. (1985). How representative of agricultural practice in Britain are Common Birds Census farmland plots? *Bird Study*, **32** (1).

Garcia, E.F.J. (1983). An experimental test of competition for space between blackcaps *Sylvia* *atricapilla* and garden warblers *Sylvia borin* in the breeding season. *Journal of Animal Ecology*, **52**, 795–806.

Garnett, M.C. (1981). Body size, its heritability and influence on juvenile survival among Great Tits *Parus major*. *Ibis*, **123**, 31–41.

Greenwood, P.J. (1980). Mating systems, philopatry and dispersal in birds and mammals. *Animal Behaviour*, **28**, 1140–1168.

Greenwood, P.J. & Harvey, P.H. (1976). The adaptive significance of variation in breeding area fidelity of the Blackbird (*Turdus merula* L.). *Journal of Animal Ecology*, **45**, 887–898.

Greenwood, P.J., Harvey, P.H. & Perrins, C.M. (1979). The role of dispersal in the great tit (*Parus major*): the causes, consequences and heritability of natal dispersal. *Journal of Animal Ecology*, **48**, 123–142.

Haartman, L. von. (1949). Der Trauerfliegenschnapper, I. Ortstreue und Rassenbildung. *Acta Zoologici Fennica*, **56**, 1–104.

Haartman, L. von. (1968). The evolution of resident versus migratory habit in birds. Some considerations. *Ornis Fennica*, **45**, 1–7.

Haldane, J.B.S. (1955). The calculation of mortality rates from ringing data. *Proceedings of the XI International Ornithological Congress*, 454–458.

Harvey, P.H., Greenwood, P.J. & Perrins, C.M. (1979). Breeding area fidelity of great tits (*Parus manor*). *Journal of Animal Ecology*, **48**, 305–313.

Haukioja, E. & Hakala, T. (1979). On the relationships between avian clutch size and life span. *Ornis Fennica*, **56**, 45–55.

Herrera, C.M. (1978). On the breeding distribution pattern of European migrant birds: MacArthur's theme reexamined. *Auk*, **95**, 496–509.

Hickling, R.A.O. (Ed.) (1983). *Enjoying Ornithology*. Poyser, Waterhouses.

Hilden, O. (1965). Habitat selection in birds. A review. *Annales Zoologici Fennica*, **2**, 53–75.

Hilden, O. (1977). Mass irruption of Long-tailed Tits *Aegitholos caudatus* in northern Europe in 1973. *Ornis Fennica*, **54**, 47–65.

Hilden, O. (1982). Winter ecology and partial migration of the Goldcrest *Regulus regulus* in Finland. *Ornis Fennica*, **59**, 99–122.

Jansson, C., Ekman, J. & V. Bromssen, A. (1981). Winter mortality and food supply in tits Parus spp. *Oikos*, **37**, 313–322.

Jarvinen, A. (1983). Breeding strategies of hole-nesting passerines in northern Lapland. *Annales Zoologici Fennici*, **20**, 129–149.

Jarvinen, O. (1979). Geographical gradients of stability in European land bird communities. *Oecologia (Berl.)*, **38**, 51–69.

Kalela, O. (1954). Uber den Revierbesitz bei Vogeln und Sangetieren als populations-okologischer Faktor. *Annales Zoologici Societatis Zoologicae-Botanicae Fennicae, Vanamo, Helsinki*, **16**, 1–48.

Källender, H. (1981). The effects of provision of food in winter on a population of the great tit *Parus major* and the blue tit *P. caeruleus*. *Ornis Scandinavia*, **12**, 244–248.

Karr, J.R. (1976). On the relative abundances of north temperate migrants in tropical habitats. *Wilson Bulletin*, **88**, 443–450.

Ketterson, E.D. & Nolan, V., Jr (1976). Geographic variation and its climatic correlates in the sex ratio of eastern-wintering dark-eyed Juncos (*Junco hyemalis hyemalis*). *Ecology*, **57**, 679–693.

Ketterson, E.D. & Nolan, V., Jr (1983). The evolution of differential bird migration. *Current Ornithology*, Vol. 1 (Ed. by R.F. Johnson), pp. 357–402. Plenum Press, New York.

Kikkawa, J. (1980). Winter survival in relation to dominance classes among Silvereyes (*Zosterops lateralis chlorocephala*) of Heron Island, Great Barrier Reef. *Ibis*, **122**, 437–446.

Klomp, H. (1970). The determination of clutch size in birds. A review. *Ardea*, **58**, 1–124.

Kluyver, H.N. (1966). Regulation of a bird population. *Ostrich Supplement*, **6**, 389–396.

Knapton, R.W. & Krebs, J.R. (1974). Settlement patterns, territory size, and breeding density in the song sparrow (*Melospiza melodia*). *Canadian Journal of Zoology*, 52, 1413–1420.

Krebs, J.R. (1971). Territory and breeding density in the great tit, *Parus major. Ecology*, 52, 2–22.

Lack, D. (1943). The age of the blackbird. *British Birds*, 36, 161–175.

Lack, D. (1954). *The Natural Regulation of Animal Numbers*. Oxford University Press, Oxford.

Lack, D. (1966). *Population Studies of Birds*. Oxford University Press, Oxford.

Lack, D. & Venables, L.S.V. (1939). The habitat distribution of British woodland birds. *Journal of Animal Ecology*, 8, 39–71.

Lawn, M.R. (1982). Pairing systems and site tenacity of the Willow Warbler *Phylloscopus trochilus* in southern England. *Ornis Scandinavia*, 13, 193–199.

Lomnicki, A. & Ombach, J. (1984). Resource partitioning within a single species population and population stability: a theoretical model. *Theoretical Population Biology*, 24, 21–28.

MacArthur, R.H. (1959). On the breeding distribution pattern of North American migrant birds. *Auk*, 76, 318–325.

May, R.M. (1981). Modeling recolonization by neotropical migrants in the habitats with changing patch structure, with notes on the age structure of populations. *Ecological Studies. Vol. 41. Forest Island Dynamics in Man-Dominated Landscapes* (Ed. by R.L. Burgess & D.M. Sharpe), pp. 207–213. Springer-Verlag, New York.

Mayfield, H. (1961). Nesting success calculated from exposure. *Wilson Bulletin*, 73, 255–261.

Mayfield, H. (1975). Suggestions for calculating nest success. *Wilson Bulletin*, 87, 456–466.

Mead, C.J. & Hudson, R. (1983). Report on bird-ringing for 1982. *Ringing & Migration*, 4, 281–320.

Mikkonen, A.V. (1983). Breeding site tenacity of the Chaffinch *Fringilla coelebs* and the Brambling *F. montifringilla* in northern Finland. *Ornis Scandinavia*, 14, 36–47.

Møller, A.P. (1982). Characteristics of Magpie *Pica pica* territories of varying duration. *Ornis Scandinavia*, 13, 94–100.

Møller, A.P. (1983a). Habitat selection, flocking and feeding behaviour of Hooded Crows *Corvus corone. Ornis Fennica*, 60, 105–111.

Møller, A.P. (1983b). Song activity and territory quality in the Corn Bunting *Miliaria calandra*; with comments on mate selection. *Ornis Scandinavia*, 14, 81–89.

Newton, J. (1980). The role of food in limiting bird numbers. *Ardea*, 68, 11–30.

O'Connor, R.J. (1980). Population regulation in the Yellowhammer *Emberiza citrinella. Bird Census Work and Nature Conservation* (Ed. by H. Oelke), pp. 190–200. Proceedings of the VI International Conference on Bird Census Work. Dachverbandes Deutscher Avifaunisten, Lengede.

O'Connor, R.J. (1981). Comparisons between migrant and non-migrant birds in Britain. *Animal Migration* (Ed. by D.J. Aidley), pp. 167–195. Cambridge University Press, Cambridge.

O'Connor, R.J. (1982). Habitat occupancy and regulation of clutch size in the European Kestrel *Falco tinnunculus. Bird Study*, 29, 17–26.

O'Connor, R.J. & Fuller, R.J. (in press). Bird population responses to habitat. Proceedings of the X International Conference on Bird Census Work. British Trust for Ornithology, Tring.

O'Connor, R.J. & Marchant, J.H. (1981). *A field validation of some Common Birds Census techniques*. Nature Conservancy Council Chief Scientist Team Commissioned Research Report.

Patterson, I.J. (1980). Territorial behaviour and the limitation of population density. *Ardea*, 68, 53–62.

Peakall, D.B. (1960). Nest records of the Yellowhammer. *Bird Study*, 7, 94–102.

Perrins, C.M. (1970). The timing of birds' breeding seasons. *Ibis*, 112, 242–255.

Rabenold, K.N. (1979). A reversed latitudinal diversity gradient in avian communities of Eastern deciduous forests. *American Naturalist*, 114, 275–286.

Ralph, C.J. & Mewaldt, L.R. (1976). Homing success in wintering sparrows. *Auk*, 93, 1–14.

Rappole, J.H. & Warner, D.W. (1976). Relationships between behaviour, physiology and weather in avian transients at a migration stopover site. *Oecologia (Berl.)*, **26**, 193–212.

Ricklefs, R.E. (1980). Geographical variation in clutch size among passerine birds: Ashmole's hypothesis. *Auk*, **97**, 38–49.

Rosenzweig, M.L. (1981). A theory of habitat selection. *Ecology*, **62**, 327–335.

Samson, F.B. & Lewis, S.J. (1979). Experiments on population regulation in two American parids. *Wilson Bulletin*, **91**, 222–235.

Schlenker, R. (1976). Winterplatztreue beim Bergfinken (*Fringilla montifringilla*). *Vogelwarte*, **28**, 313–314.

Seber, G.A.F. (1972). Estimating survival rates from bird-band returns. *Journal of Wildlife Management*, **36**, 405–413.

Southern, H.N. (1970). The natural control of a population of tawny owls (*Strix aluco*). *Journal of Zoology (London)*, **162**, 197–285.

Spray, C.J. (1978). *Territorial behaviour of the Carrion Crow*, Corvus corone *L., in relation to food supply. An experimental study.* Ph.D. thesis, University of Aberdeen.

Stearns, S.C. (1976). Life-history tactics: a review of the ideas. *Quarterly Review of Biology*, **51**, 3–47.

Taylor, & L.R. Taylor, R.A.J. (1977). Aggregation, migration and population mechanics. *Nature (London)*, **265**, 415–421.

Taylor, S.M. (1965). The Common Birds Census—some statistical aspects. *Bird Study*, **12**, 268–286.

Tenaza, R. (1971). Behaviour and nesting success relative to nest location in Adelie penguins (*Pygoscelis adeliae*). *Condor*, **73**, 81–92.

Tompa, F.S. (1964). Factors determining the numbers of Song Sparrows *Melospiza melodia* (Wilson), on Mandarte Island, B.C., Canada. *Acta Zoologici Fennica*, **109**, 1–68.

Watson, A. & Moss, R. (1972). *A current model of population dynamics in Red Grouse.* Proceedings of the XV International Ornithological Congress, pp. 134–149.

Williams, G.C. (1966). Natural selection, the cost of reproduction, and a refinement of Lack's principle. *American Naturalist*, **100**, 687–690.

Zimmerman, J.L. (1982). Nesting success of Dickcissels (*Spiza americana*) in preferred and less preferred habitats. *Auk*, **99**, 292–298.

II

FEEDING BEHAVIOUR AND
POPULATION DYNAMICS

8. REGULATION OF SEABIRD POPULATIONS

T. R. BIRKHEAD[1] AND R. W. FURNESS[2]

[1]*Department of Zoology, University of Sheffield, Sheffield S10 2TN and*
[2]*Department of Zoology, University of Glasgow, Glasgow G12 8QQ*

SUMMARY

The original dichotomy of views of the ways in which seabird populations may be regulated is no longer useful; other factors should be taken into consideration, e.g. colony sites may in some cases be limiting and breeding sites within colonies may regulate numbers of some species at a local level. Several lines of evidence also indicate that food availability during the breeding season may be reduced by intraspecific competition and the consequent reductions in breeding parameters may regulate populations.

Negative relationships between colony size and several breeding parameters in different seabird species support the idea of competition for food around the colony. Multiple regression analyses indicate that the influence of intraspecific competition is much stronger than interspecific competition in producing this effect.

We present population models which suggest that changes in breeding parameters could result in density-dependent regulation, but that the degree of density dependence has to be greater in fulmar-type seabirds than in shag-type seabirds for regulation to occur.

INTRODUCTION

The ways in which bird populations might be regulated have been discussed in detail by Lack (1954, 1966), who concluded that bird populations are regulated in a density-dependent manner through competition for food. An alternative and controversial view proposed by Wynne-Edwards (1962) is that social factors, such as territoriality, are of major importance in the regulation of populations. Studies have shown that territorial behaviour may limit populations, although not in the way Wynne-Edwards envisaged (see Davies 1978). The current consensus is that most bird populations are probably regulated by food, in a density-dependent way, but that territorial behaviour may sometimes also regulate populations (e.g. Newton 1980).

Seabirds share a number of demographic features which set them apart from most other birds, for example low clutch size, deferred maturity and low adult mortality rates. In addition, almost all species are colonial (Lack 1967,

1968; Ashmole 1971). Although population parameters have been estimated for several seabird species, the factors that regulate seabird populations are poorly known, because seabirds are long-lived and there have been only a few long-term population studies (e.g. fulmar *Fulmarus glacialis*, Ollason & Dunnet 1983; kittiwake *Rissa tridactyla*, Coulson & Wooller 1976; herring gull *Larus argentatus*, Coulson, Duncan & Thomas 1982). Furthermore, most seabirds come to land only to breed, and for the rest of the year are extremely difficult to study. Substantial advances in studies outside the breeding season have been made only in recent years (e.g. Brown 1980).

Ashmole (1963) suggested that tropical seabird numbers may be limited by food during the breeding season, through a density-dependent reduction in reproductive output: at high densities intraspecific competition and the depletion of food in the vicinity of the colony result in reduced rates of provisioning for chicks. Ashmole further proposed that the depletion of food around the colony would result in a reduced reproductive success long before it affected adult survival: more recent studies of life-history strategies also predict this (Goodman 1974; Stearns 1976, 1977). Lack (1966) agreed that competition for food around the colony may influence clutch size and deferred maturity, but, unlike Ashmole, considered the main factor regulating seabird numbers to be density-dependent mortality *outside* the breeding season. He argued that food is locally abundant for seabirds *throughout* the year (e.g. at upwellings) and that high numbers following breeding increased competition for food during the winter.

Both Ashmole (1963, 1971) and Lack (1966) thought that competition for breeding sites within colonies played only a minor role in the regulation of seabird numbers. However, both authors implied that suitable colony locations were often limited. Ashmole (1963) considered tropical seabirds rarely to be short of breeding sites, but suggested that species breeding at higher latitudes might be. Lack (1966) stated that even if breeding sites were limited preventing some birds from breeding, total numbers would continue to increase and ultimately be controlled by food. This view (also shared by Ashmole) is not necessarily correct since the proportion of young by pairs with sites may fail to balance the mortality of the non-breeders and breeders before numbers reach the ceiling set by food. Further, although breeding sites may not appear to be in short supply, the number of high-quality sites may be, and therefore mean nest-site quality may decline with increasing colony size such that mean breeding success falls to a level too low to support further population growth (Potts, Coulson & Deans 1980).

Lack (1954, 1966) suggested that many bird populations are regulated in part because they fluctuate only within certain limits. In fact there is little evidence of stability in seabird populations, and much evidence of large-scale changes in numbers, many of which can be attributed to climatic changes or to the activities of man. Some population declines in the past were the result of excessive exploitation, and many recent population increases may be due to subsequent protection (e.g. Ainley & Lewis 1974). Overfishing by man can result in both increases and decreases in seabird numbers, depending on the trophic relationships between the seabirds and the exploited fish (Furness 1982; Lid 1981). Even in the remote polar regions, seabird populations are influenced by man (e.g. May *et al.* 1979; Evans & Waterston 1976). Clearly, it is difficult to observe seabird populations devoid of man's influence, which in turn confounds the problem of determining how seabird numbers are regulated, if they are regulated at all.

The factors that regulate bird populations can rarely be demonstrated by experiment. However, the increased number of field studies since the accounts of Lack (1966) and Ashmole (1963, 1971) provides us with a better opportunity to examine their ideas. In the following review we consider the evidence that (i) colony sites, (ii) breeding sites within colonies, and (iii) food, either within or outside the breeding season, limit numbers. We then consider how these factors might interact.

COLONY SITES

Almost all seabirds breed colonially (Lack 1968) and colony sites must be safe from terrestrial predators, contain suitable breeding sites, and be within commuting distance of food supplies. Several authors have stated, or implied that such places are often limited (Ashmole 1963; Lack 1966, 1967; Wittenberger & Hunt, in press). However, the evidence that colony sites are limited is mainly circumstantial. Brown (1979) showed that the populations of seabirds breeding in the vicinity of the highly productive waters of Senegal are unexpectedly small and attributed this to a lack of islands or other areas where seabirds could nest safe from terrestrial predators. Some experimental evidence comes from the provision of large nesting platforms in Namibia, built for the collection of guano. The platforms were mostly constructed between 1930 and 1940 and by the 1950s were thought to hold about 500 000 pairs of Cape cormorants *Phalacrocorax capensis* (Crawford & Shelton 1978). Since breeding numbers at natural sites in Namibia are much less, it seems that the population size increased with the provision of artificial colony sites (Berry 1975). Similarly, Duffy (1983) suggested that Peruvian seabird numbers were held below the carrying capacity set by food until new breeding sites were made available by guano managers in the first half of this century.

BREEDING SITES

Most seabirds defend very small territories (Hinde's 1956, type C), which contain only the breeding site. For most seabird species the term territory and breeding site are synonymous (exceptions include some gulls and skuas). The fact that most seabirds are strongly site-tenacious and may use the same breeding site throughout their lives emphasizes the central role which this plays in reproduction. The physical characteristics of the site and its position relative to other colony members can be important in influencing the owner's fitness (Coulson 1971; Potts, Coulson & Deans 1980).

Brown (1969) presented a graphical model showing how territoriality and population density may be related in birds. If breeding sites (or territories) limit seabird population density in the manner proposed by Brown, we predict that:

    (i) breeding success is related to the quality of the breeding site;
   (ii) the mean and variance of site quality decreases with increasing population density;
  (iii) floaters (non-breeding, sexually mature birds) occur when breeding sites run out;
   (iv) competition for sites occurs.

We examine each of these in turn.

Breeding success and site quality

In a number of seabirds, reproductive success differs among individuals breeding in different types of sites (e.g. Coulson 1968, 1971; Nettleship 1972; Birkhead 1977). However, few studies have shown breeding success to be related to some independent measure of site quality because it is difficult to measure site quality other than by breeding success or to separate the effects of bird quality and site quality. A 'natural experiment' allowed Potts *et al.* (1980) to avoid these problems in a study of shags *Phalacrocorax aristotelis*. Breeding sites were ranked from poor (0) to good (4) according to various objective criteria. Breeding success at good sites was more than twice that at poor sites and breeding site quality explained over 80% of the variance in reproductive success. Following a 'red tide'—which killed a large number of shags—many good quality sites were left vacant, but these were soon occupied by birds moving from poorer quality sites, thus increasing their reproductive success.

Site quality decreases with population density

Circumstantial evidence comes from cases where birds in a depleted population or colonizing new areas take the best sites first. Nettleship (1972) showed that puffins *Fratercula arctica* breeding in sloping habitat near the cliff edge had higher breeding success than those on adjacent level ground. On Skomer Island, Wales, where puffin numbers have decreased during the present century, virtually all puffins now breed near the cliff edge on sloping ground, whereas photographs show that level ground was also utilized in the 1890s when the population was higher (Birkhead & Ashcroft 1975).

Duncan (1978) found that recruitment of herring gulls at the Isle of May was related to the density of already established conspecifics. Recruits avoided both low and high density areas, indicating that they were attracted to areas where gulls were already present but avoided crowded areas.

The clearest example, however, is that of Potts *et al.* (1980) who found that as the shag population recovered after the 'red tide' the mean quality of breeding sites decreased.

Floaters occur as breeding sites run out

The existence of floaters can be demonstrated by the removal of territory or site holders, or by the provision of extra sites. There have been very few tests for the existence of floaters in seabird populations. Floaters are distinct from immature non-breeders, but in some cases the duration of the period of immaturity may be modified by population density and site availability (Coulson *et al.* 1982). The removal of breeders has demonstrated that individuals in some populations are prevented from breeding by the territorial behaviour of established birds (Harris 1970; Krebs 1977). Among seabirds, Manuwal (1972) showed the existence of large numbers of floaters in Cassin's auklet *Ptychoramphus aleuticus* by extensive removal experiments. He also demonstrated that if large numbers of new birds were experimentally encouraged to settle into an area simultaneously, they did so at densities higher than in adjacent control areas. A similar effect has also been recorded in passerine populations (Knapton & Krebs 1974).

Evidence of competition for breeding sites

Several sources of evidence indicate that seabirds compete for breeding sites. Many seabirds are overtly aggressive, possess well developed threat and appeasement signals (Tinbergen 1959; Nelson 1970; Birkhead 1978), and frequently fight. Aggression is associated with acquisition and maintenance of two main resources: mates and breeding sites, though it is also seen within feeding associations.

There are two lines of indirect evidence of competition for breeding sites. First, several species return to breeding colonies many months before the onset of breeding, and it has been suggested that this behaviour is associated with the maintenance of the site. Some support for this comes from studies of rapidly expanding populations which tend to return earlier than stable or declining populations in which competition for sites is presumably less intense (Birkhead 1976; Coulson & Wooller 1976; Taylor & Reid 1981). Second, interspecific differences in the types of breeding site used by seabirds may reflect, in part, past competition between species for sites. Indeed, there are studies that provide evidence for interspecific competition (e.g. Belopolskii 1961; Stonehouse 1963; Williams 1974; Ashcroft 1976).

Conclusions

Some support for all four predictions is provided. Although the examples indicate that for some species in certain situations breeding sites may be limiting, or potentially so, they do not allow us to assess the relative importance of this factor in population regulation. Also, it is important to note that several authors indicate that in some areas breeding sites are clearly not in short supply. Dunnet, Ollason & Anderson (1979) noted that a total of 731 sites at Eynhallow, Orkney were used by fulmars in a period of 27 years and, on average, only 18% of these sites were occupied in any one year. Maximum occupancy was only 33%, indicating a considerable surplus of sites, at many of which successful breeding had been achieved. Croxall & Prince (1980) stated that none of the species of seabirds breeding at South Georgia could be considered to be short of potential nest sites. Limitation by nest sites appears to be an exceptional rather than a general situation.

FOOD AS A LIMITING RESOURCE

Both Ashmole (1963, 1971) and Lack (1966) regarded food to be the resource that most often limited bird populations. Newton (1980) reviewed the evidence for such an effect, and concluded that correlations between bird numbers and food supplies may provide circumstantial evidence for Lack's and Ashmole's ideas. Such correlations between food and bird numbers may be spatial or temporal, and may occur either inside or outside the breeding season. In this section we consider (a) correlations between seabird abundance and food supplies, (b) evidence for food being limited outside the breeding season, and (c) evidence for food being limited during the breeding season.

Seabird numbers and food abundance

Only in the last 10 years or so have we had good reviews of the spatial distribution of seabirds at sea. Broad correlations between densities of seabirds and some index of food availability, both during and outside the breeding season, have been recorded by several authors (e.g. Bailey 1966; Brown 1979; Bradstreet 1979, 1980). Temporal changes in seabird numbers associated with changes in the abundance of prey species are well known for those seabirds affected by El Nino (Schaefer 1970; Idyll 1973). In addition, significant correlations exist between seabird numbers and fish stocks near southern Africa over periods of 20–50 years (Crawford & Shelton 1978).

Another way of testing the idea that seabird numbers are associated with the abundance of food during the breeding season is to compare colony sizes with the size of foraging area available. One would predict that colonies located on small offshore islands would be larger than those on the mainland because the birds breeding at small islands would have twice the area of sea within their foraging range. Colonies on islands may be less susceptible to mammalian predators than those on mainland sites, so a better comparison is between mainland colonies on promontories (foraging arc of 180–360 degrees) with those on linear coastlines (foraging arc of 180 degrees). We tested this idea using data for Alaskan seabirds presented by Sowls, Hatch & Lensink (1978). In all species examined there was a significant relationship between foraging area and colony size (Fig. 8.1). Clearly this is a fairly crude analysis since it ignores several other potentially confounding variables (such as the spatial distribution of prey species), but the greater size of promontory colonies compared to those on linear coastlines argues for the importance of the size of available feeding area.

The above information suggests that seabird numbers and food abundance are positively correlated; but it says little other than, where there is more food there are more birds. The real question is whether seabirds consume enough to cause measurable food depletion and competition. Several recent studies have shown that seabird communities may annually consume as much as 20–30% of the prey production (Wiens & Scott 1975; Furness 1978; Furness & Cooper 1982; Schneider & Hunt 1982). However, information on the true availability of prey is almost non-existent, and therefore prey depletion seems plausible but cannot be demonstrated directly.

We know of no studies aimed at testing the hypothesis that competition for food increases with increasing density of conspecifics. However, we have looked at seabird colony sizes around Scotland in order to provide an indirect test. If competition for food occurs around colonies we could predict that colony size would be negatively correlated with the numbers of conspecifics breeding at other colonies within the feeding range. Few species have been censused in sufficient detail to allow such testing, but complete data exist for gannets *Sula bassana*, kittiwakes, puffins and shags. In order to minimize confounding influences of variations in food supplies between areas of

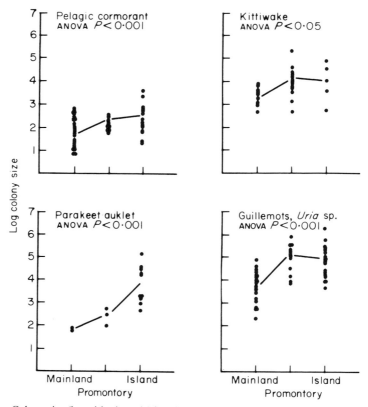

Fig. 8.1. Colony size (logarithmic scale) in relation to colony type (classified as mainland, promontory, or island) for Alaskan seabird colonies listed by Sowls *et al.* (1978); differences between types are significant (ANOVA, $P < 0.05$).

differing oceanography or productivity, we have considered populations in as limited regions as is consistent with providing adequate sample sizes. The resulting strong negative correlations (Table 8.1, Fig. 8.2.), which will be discussed in more detail elsewhere (Furness & Birkhead 1984) suggest that there is competition for food in the areas surrounding breeding colonies, and this might regulate numbers. These spatial patterns invite more direct tests of this hypothesis.

Food limitation outside the breeding season

Lack (1966) suggested that density-dependent mortality, particularly of immature birds, through competition for food outside the breeding season

TABLE 8.1. Correlations between square root of the number of breeding pairs of seabirds at colonies and square root of the number of pairs of conspecifics at other colonies within a specified distance (from Furness & Birkhead 1984)

Species	Range (km)	Correlation	Probability
Gannet	100	−0·92	<0·001
	150	−0·92	<0·001
	200	−0·47	ns
	300	−0·51	ns
Puffin	50	−0·56	<0·05
	100	−0·81	<0·001
	150	−0·88	<0·001
	200	−0·74	<0·001
	250	−0·58	<0·05
Shag	20	−0·45	<0·05
	30	−0·54	<0·01
	40	−0·48	<0·05
Kittiwake	20	−0·55	<0·01
	40	−0·67	<0·001
	60	−0·36	ns
	80	−0·32	ns
	100	−0·08	ns

regulated seabird numbers. This is a difficult idea to test since our knowledge of seabirds away from their colonies is extremely limited. Two general points emerge from the seabird literature:

(a) mortality rates of immature seabirds are greater than those of adults;

(b) in most species the main period of mortality for both adults and immatures occurs outside the breeding season.

We consider the separation of factors operating during and outside the breeding season to be artificial and misleading. Factors that operate during the breeding season may influence an individual's subsequent survival outside the breeding season as clearly illustrated by the Manx shearwater *Puffinus puffinus*, in which fledging weight is a major determinant of the probability of survival to breeding age (Perrins, Harris & Britton 1973). The chick's fledging weight is determined by factors operating during the breeding season (e.g. food availability) although the mortality actually occurs outside the breeding season. Similarly, Coulson & Wooller (1976) showed that kittiwake survival rate declined as colony size increased, although most of the mortality occurred outside the breeding season, and Parsons, Chabrzyk & Duncan (1976) showed

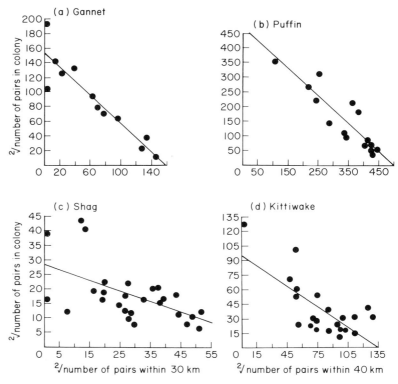

Fig. 8.2. Relationships between square root of colony size and numbers of conspecifics nesting at other colonies within a specified shortest sea distance for: (a) gannets in all colonies in Scotland Ireland and Wales formed before 1940 (range 100 km); (b) puffins (census data from Harris (1976) for colonies north of 57° 30′ N, range 150 km); (c) shags in Orkney and Shetland (data from Cramp, Bourne & Saunders (1974), range 30 km); (d) kittiwakes in Shetland (data from Richardson (1983), range 40 km) (from Furness & Birkhead 1984).

that post-fledging survival (away from the colony) in herring gulls could be related to events at the colony during the breeding season.

Evidence for food limitation during the breeding season

There is abundant evidence for food availability influencing reproduction, but in virtually every case the evidence for differences in food availability is indirect and circumstantial.

Direct evidence

Some of the most clear-cut evidence for food availability influencing reproductive performance comes from studies of alcids, particularly the puffin in the Rost archipelago, Norway, where overfishing of herring *Clupea harengus* has resulted in stocks of the fish during the 1970s being only 5–10% of those in the 1950s. The timing of the decline in herring stocks closely coincides with mass breeding failures of puffins and other seabirds. Since 1970 many or all puffin chicks from an estimated 700 000 breeding pairs have starved to death in most years and the mean body weight of breeding adult puffins has declined (Lid 1981). Anderson, Gress & Mais (1982) found that brown pelican *Pelecanus occidentalis* reproductive output is correlated with measures of local prey abundance around colonies in the Southern California Bight, both in terms of regular spatial relationships and in a temporal analysis over several years. However, they suggest that prey depletion by pelicans is unlikely since pelicans consume only a small fraction of the fish stocks (Anderson *et al.* 1980).

Puffin diet varies between colonies in different parts of Scotland and the breeding performance appears to be correlated with diet quality (Harris & Hislop 1978; Harris 1983).

Indirect evidence

Environmental factors. The short-term effects of environmental conditions on food availability have been demonstrated in several studies. For example, stormy seas break up fish shoals, thus making them more difficult for seabirds to obtain. Among common guillemots *Uria aalge* the rate at which parents provision chicks is reduced during stormy conditions (Birkhead 1976). In terns, wind-speed influences fishing success of adults and the rate at which chicks grow (Dunn 1973, 1975). Longer-term effects on food availability may be caused by the late break-up of sea ice at high latitudes. Extensive ice cover reduces the area available for foraging and may result in delayed onset of breeding, reduced egg size and several other effects (Uspenski 1956; Bianki 1967; Birkhead & Nettleship 1981).

Population change. Furness (1984) has compared the status (increasing, stable or decreasing) of seabird populations in two areas differing in the availability of food around the breeding colony. In north Britain overexploitation of gadoid and herring stocks has led to a reduction in their biomass (Hempel 1978) and a concomitant increase in the abundance of Sand-eels *Ammodytes marinus* (Sherman *et al.* 1981), the main seabird prey in this area. Seabird numbers have increased rapidly at colonies in north and north-east

Britain where these effects have been most pronounced. In contrast, stocks of mature fish have been less affected by fisheries off north-west Britain; the seabird populations at St Kilda show less sign of increasing than those in north-east Britain, and show greater evidence of food shortage and the need for longer foraging trips (Harris & Hislop 1978; Furness & Todd 1984).

Twinning experiments. Experiments in which seabirds are given additional chicks to rear have been used to provide information on food availability (Nelson 1978; Furness & Hislop 1981). In the majority of cases parents are unable to rear extra chicks, usually interpreted as evidence for limited food supplies. G.L. Hunt, Z. Eppley & D. Schneider (unpubl.) show that the ability of pairs to rear additional chicks is inversely related to colony size, and suggest that extra chicks are most easily reared in small colonies where food supply per pair is more abundant (see below). An alternative explanation for the failure to rear additional chicks may be that adults are reluctant to make the additional investment, since it might jeopardize their subsequent survival chances (see Charnov & Krebs 1974).

Experimental reduction of colony size. An experimental reduction in colony size should result in increased food availability for the individuals remaining. Removal of about 75% of the herring gull population on the Isle of May, Scotland, has given rise to several effects which strongly suggest an increased abundance of food: increased egg size, reduced age of first breeding, and an increase in both size (wing-length) and weight of adult birds (Coulson *et al.* 1982).

Colony size and breeding parameters. Perhaps some of the most interesting evidence for Ashmole's (1963) idea comes from two studies in which the relationships between colony size and various reproductive parameters have been examined. Gaston, Chapdelaine & Noble (1983) found a significant negative correlation between colony size and the mean weight at which Brunnich's guillemot *Uria lomvia* chicks leave the colony. Gaston *et al.* (1983) suggest that competition for food around large breeding colonies resulted in chicks being provisioned at lower rates, growing more slowly and fledging at lower weights.

Hunt, Eppley & Schneider (unpubl.) compared several breeding parameters of seabirds from two adjacent colonies in the Pribilofs, N. Pacific: St George Island with a population of 2·5 million birds, and St Paul with 250 000 birds. In four of the five species (black-legged kittiwake, common guillemot, Brunnich's guillemot and red-faced cormorant *Phalacrocorax urile* growth rates were significantly lower at the larger colony. The reduced growth rates resulted in significantly lower fledging weights in the two guillemot species, and protracted fledging periods for the other two species. Hunt, Eppley & Schneider (unpubl.) then went on to look at the relationship between colony size and breeding parameters in twenty-two colonies, and found consistent negative correlations. Until now we have been concerned only with intraspecific competition but we should not ignore the possibility of interspecific competition for food. We extended the approach of Gaston *et al.* (1983) and Hunt, Eppley & Schneider (unpubl.) and used multiple regression to examine the relationship between breeding parameters (dependent variables) and two independent variables: species population size (X_1) and the total number of breeding individuals of other seabird species at the same colony (X_2). This approach allows us to estimate the relative importance of intra- and interspecific competition. The results (Table 8.2) show that the addition of X_2 did not significantly improve any of the relationships between breeding parameters and X_1. In other words, the main cause of the negative relationships is likely to be intraspecific rather than interspecific competition.

Reduction in food availability in optimal foraging models. Ford *et al.* (1982) examined the influence of perturbations to food supplies around colonies in a theoretical model based on theories of central place foraging and optimal foraging, and concluded that a reduction in food supply of 10% would have little effect on guillemot fledgling production, but a 20% reduction would halve the breeding output and a 40% reduction would result in total colony

TABLE 8.2. Summary of correlation and multiple regression analyses of the relationships between population size and reproductive parameter

Species	Reproductive parameter	Correlation coefficients Species pop. (X_1)	Correlation coefficients Total pop. (X_1 & X_2 combined)	Multiple regression: does addition of X_2 improve fit?
Black-legged kittiwake	Clutch size	-0.669**	-0.590**	No
	Breeding success	-0.685**	-0.424	No
	Growth rate	-0.399	-0.186	No
Common guillemot	Fledging weight	-0.368	-0.484	No
	Breeding success	-0.429	-0.570	No
	Growth rate	-0.809	-0.838*	No
Brünnich's guillemot	Fledging weight	-0.570*	-0.561*	No
	Breeding success	-0.274	-0.567	No
	Growth rate	-0.520	-0.267	No

All relationships are between breeding parameters and log population sizes. X_1 species population size. X_2 population size (total number of individuals) of all *other* species at that colony (see text for details). Data are from Hunt *et al.* (unpubl.), Gaston *et al.* (1983), Uspenski (1956), Belopol'skii (1961), and unpubl.
* $P < 0.05$.
** $P < 0.01$.

reproductive failure. Their model is based on observed foraging rates and chick growth rates, and suggests that observed changes in fish stocks caused by environmental changes or overexploitation by man are more than sufficient to control seabird population dynamics through influences on breeding success (Furness 1982).

REGULATION OF SEABIRD NUMBERS

We have presented evidence from a number of diverse sources that intraspecific competition for food during the breeding season may influence reproductive output, as originally proposed by Ashmole (1963). Gaston *et al.* (1983) and Hunt, Eppley & Schneider (unpubl.) are the first to demonstrate the broad occurrence of density-dependent effects capable of regulating seabird numbers. In Fig. 8.3a we show the relationships between kittiwake colony size and (i) clutch size; (ii) breeding success. We have used the fitted regressions to determine if such changes in these parameters could stabilize numbers in a hypothetical kittiwake population. Data from Wooller & Coulson (1977) were used to estimate parameters for a kittiwake population increasing at 4% per annum, viz; adult annual survival 0·81, survival to breeding age 0·426, clutch size 2, breeding success 54%. For appropriate population levels we then substituted values from Fig 8.3a, and recalculated the annual rate of increase. This model (Fig. 8.3b) assumes that the changes in clutch size and breeding success observed in separate populations (Fig. 8.3a)

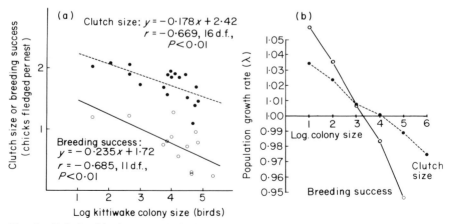

FIG. 8.3. Relationships between (a) clutch size or breeding success and log. colony size and (b) population rate of change and breeding parameters for populations of kittiwakes (see text for details and Table 8.2 for sources of data).

are the same as those which would occur within a single population over time. As Fig. 8.3b shows, with a density-dependent change in clutch size alone, numbers would stabilize at about 10 000 birds per colony, whereas with change in breeding success numbers would stabilize at about 2500 birds. The models indicate that at population levels greater than these numbers would decrease, but in this respect the models are simplistic since many natural kittiwake populations exceed these levels. Clearly, other parameters cannot remain unchanged: fecundity and survival may be inversely related, as Ricklefs (1983) suggests.

Having shown that density-dependent changes in one or more breeding parameters could regulate numbers, we next attempt to make some generalizations, by examining two extreme seabird types for which we have details of population biology. The species are the shag, an inshore feeder with a relatively high reproductive rate, and the fulmar, an off-shore feeder with a low rate of reproduction. For the shag the maximum observed rate of population increase is about 11% p.a. (Cramp, Bourne & Saunders 1974). The changes in population and breeding parameters necessary to convert this to a zero intrinsic rate of increase (i.e. where the annual loss of adult birds is exactly balanced by the production of new breeders) by altering only a single demographic parameter, are shown in Table 8.3, Model 1. Ashmole (1963) suggested that density-dependent regulation operated through breeding productivity rather than adult survival. As already mentioned, Potts *et al.* (1980) showed that among shags, breeding success was related to nest-site quality thus:

$$\text{No. chicks fledged per pair} = 0\cdot198Q + 0\cdot749$$

Where Q is an index of nest-site quality. It follows that when nest site quality is minimal ($Q = 0$) the average breeding success will be $0\cdot749$ chicks per pair. With all other parameters as in Table 8.3 we calculate that a breeding success of $0\cdot924$ chicks per pair would result in a zero rate of increase. In other words, a reduction in nest-site quality clearly would have a regulatory effect on the population.

In the fulmar the maximum observed rate of increase is 7% p.a. (Cramp *et al.* 1974). In Table 8.4 we present calculations similar to those already given for the shag, which show that the magnitude of the changes in breeding and population parameters needed to produce a stable population are much greater than for the shag. However, if we keep adult survival constant but change *all* the other parameters (Table 8.4, Model 2), the changes required are less marked and within the bounds of possibility.

Although a modest decrease in mean quality of nest sites may be sufficient to limit growth of a shag colony, as discussed above and observed by Potts *et*

Table 8.3. Population parameters* and two population models for the shag *Phalacrocorax aristotelis*

Parameter	Population increasing at maximum rate: 11% p.a.	Model 1	Model 2
Adult survival	0·82	0·722	0·82
Age at first breeding	3	or 6·5	and 3·5
1st year survival	0·58	or 0·29	and 0·48
Clutch size	3·5	or 1·75	and 3·15
Breeding success	0·525	or 0·264	and 0·425
Percentage of adults not breeding	0	or 50%	and 10%

* From Potts *et al.* 1980, Cramp *et al.* 1974.
Model 1 is the change to any one parameter to give a zero rate of increase.
Model 2 is one example of the change to all parameters except adult survival to give a zero rate of increase.

al. (1980), a much more drastic decrease in breeding success would be necessary to effect the same change to the population dynamics of a fulmar colony. Mean breeding success would have to be reduced from a presently observed 0·49 to 0·092 chicks per pair. If this were due only to nest site quality then a colony that presently contains 10 000 pairs (a fairly typical size) with breeding success of 0·49 chicks per pair would require a further 45 000 sites where breeding success was zero to be occupied before the colony ceased to grow (assuming no net emigration). Such a situation seems unrealistic and

Table 8.4. Population parameters* and two population models for the fulmar *Fulmarus glacialis*

Parameter	Population increasing at maximum rate 7% p.a.	Model 1	Model 2
Adult survival	0·97	0·902	0·97
Age at 1st breeding	8	or 60	and 11
1st year survival	0·81	or 0·152	and 0·50
Clutch size†	1	npor 1	1
Breeding success	0·49	or 0·092	and 0·20
Percentage of adults not breeding	0	or 81·3%	and 20

* From Dunnet *et al.* 1979, Cramp *et al.* 1974.
† Clutch size is fixed at 1.
Model 1 is the change to any one parameter to give a zero rate of increase.
Model 2 is one example of the change to all parameters except adult survival required to give a zero rate of increase.

suggests that seabirds with population dynamics of the fulmar-type are rather unlikely to be limited by nest-site quality in the way that some shag-type populations may be.

These simple population models show that long-lived species, with low reproductive rates and late age at first breeding, like the fulmar, require a stronger degree of density-dependent effects to stabilize numbers than species like the shag. They also show that if density dependence acted only on a single parameter it would have to have an extremely large effect. In fact, the study of Hunt, Eppley & Schneider (unpubl.) suggests that a number of breeding parameters within a single species change with increasing population size, and therefore models involving a change in several parameters (Tables 8.3 and 8.4) are probably not unrealistic.

Ashmole (1963) suggested that any density-dependent effects caused by food depletion would affect reproduction before they affected adult survival. We agree with this, and consequently excluded changes in adult survival from our models, which do suggest that regulation could occur without any change in adult survival. However, there are now good reasons for believing that adult mortality may also be affected. The costs of increased competition for food may be borne entirely by offspring, or they may be shared between offspring and their parents. Theory predicts that among long-lived species, like seabirds, offspring should bear most of the cost (Goodman 1974; Stearns 1976, 1977). Any costs that parents incur may be difficult to detect and measure. However, Gaston *et al.* (1983) found that Brunnich's guillemots breeding in large colonies had to travel further on average to obtain food for their young than those breeding in smaller colonies, and attributed this difference to competition for food. The energetic costs of travel between the colony and feeding areas may be relatively high for some species. An increased foraging range may result in an increase in mortality, either through physiological processes, or through increased risks of predation (see Ainley & DeMaster 1980), or both. Some evidence comes from Asbirk's (1979) study of Black guillemots *Cepphus grylle*, in which the average survival rate of birds that laid two eggs but did not rear the chicks was 11% higher than those rearing one or two chicks. Although the sample size was small and the difference in survival rates not significant, an 11% difference results in an increase in the further expectation of life of almost 7 years. Galbraith (1983) found that kittiwake adults at the Isle of May given artificially-manipulated larger broods left chicks unattended for longer exposing them to greater predation, and fed each chick in larger broods less, therefore growth rate was lower; they also weighed less at the end of chick-rearing than parents with smaller broods, suggesting a greater expenditure of energy and less body reserves, which might increase mortality risk. These results reinforce our view that adult survival may be affected by intra-specific competition for food during the breeding season, and that events during the breeding season may influence survival at other times.

DISCUSSION

In this review we have presented some evidence that colony sites, breeding sites within colonies and food around colonies may all potentially limit seabird populations. It is also clear that the regulation of seabird populations is complex, and most of the points we have considered clearly need to be tested in more detail. For example, the studies of Gaston *et al.* and Hunt, Eppley & Schneider (unpubl.) have produced results which, if subsequently found to be generally true, will be of great significance in understanding how seabird populations are regulated. Their ideas need to be tested with larger samples so that possible confounding variables, such as geographic area and year effects can be controlled.

Since most seabirds are colonial many workers have assumed that coloniality is adaptive (see Wittenberger & Hunt (in press) for a review), and indeed several studies have demonstrated such effects. For example, individuals breeding in small groups or at low densities suffer relatively high levels of predation (Wittenberger & Hunt, in press). However, it is clear from the present review that there may also be costs to coloniality, and individuals subject therefore to conflicting selection pressures. Decreased risks of predation may, for example, favour individuals breeding in large colonies, whereas increased risk of starvation caused by intraspecific competition for food may favour individuals breeding in smaller colonies. Wiklund (1982) recorded effects of this type in fieldfares *Turdus pilaris*, and his study emphasizes the importance of examining costs and benefits simultaneously, and should make us cautious in our interpretation of results like those of Gaston *et al.* (1983) and Hunt, Eppley & Schneider (unpubl.).

The occurrence of two or more conflicting selection pressures implies that an optimal colony size exists, at which individual fitness is maximized. Sibly (1983) showed that this would be unstable and predicts that colony size should be larger than the optimal size. This may help to explain some of the results discussed in the present paper (e.g. Table 8.2, Fig. 8.3).

The inverse relationship between colony size and various breeding parameters (Table 8.2) raises another question. If success is so much greater at a smaller colony why do individuals from larger colonies not join smaller ones as predicted by the ideal free theory (Fretwell & Lucas 1970)? There are several reasons for this. The measured reproductive parameters provide an incomplete picture of overall fitness, particularly lacking information on the effects on adult survival rates. Breeding site limitations may prevent growth of some colonies. Costs of changing colony may be high, and this may be why many seabirds are strongly philopatric and site-faithful.

It is surprising that until now no direct tests of the model proposed by Ashmole (1963) have been made. This may partly be due to a feeling that Ashmole's model may not apply to temperate and high-latitude seabird colonies where seasonal production may override influences of prey depletion around colonies. Only recently has the high impact of seabird predation on food stocks been appreciated and the idea of prey depletion needs to be examined and tested in detail.

In conclusion, we have probably raised more questions than we have answered, but we hope we have indicated the direction of promising lines of research which will help us to understand how seabird populations work.

ACKNOWLEDGMENTS

We are particularly grateful to George Hunt and Zoe Eppley for allowing us to see their unpublished results and for giving us access to their data. We would also like to thank the following for their helpful criticisms: Drs J.D. Biggins, J.C. Coulson, A.J. Gaston, A. Grafen, M.P. Harris, C.M. Perrins and C.G. Wiklund.

REFERENCES

Ainley, D.G. & DeMaster, D.P. (1980). Survival and mortality in a population of Adelie penguins. *Ecology*, **61**, 522–530.

Ainley, D.G. & Lewis, T.J. (1974). The history of Farallon Island marine bird populations. *Condor*, **76**, 432–446.

Anderson, D.W., Gress, F., Mais, K.F. & Kelly, P.R. (1980). Brown pelicans as anchovy stock indicators and their relationships to commercial fishing. *California Cooperative Oceanic Fisheries Investigations Report* **21**, 54–61.

Anderson, D.W., Gress, F. & Mais, K.F. (1982). Brown pelicans: influence of food supply on reproduction. *Oikos*, **39**, 23–31.

Asbirk, S. (1979). The adaptive significance of the reproductive pattern in the Black guillemot, *Cepphus grylle*. *Videnskabelige Meddelelser fra Dansk naturhistorisk Forening i Kjobenhavn*, **141**, 29–80.

Ashcroft, R.E. (1976). *Breeding biology and survival of puffins*. D.Phil. thesis, University of Oxford.

Ashmole, N.P. (1963). The regulation of numbers of tropical oceanic birds. *Ibis*, **103b**, 458–473.

Ashmole, N.P. (1971). Seabird ecology and the marine environment. *Avian Biology*, Vol. 1 (Ed. by D.S. Farner & J.R. King), pp. 112–286. Academic Press, London.

Bailey, R.S. (1966). The sea-birds of the southeast coast of Arabia. *Ibis*, **108**, 224–264.

Belopolskii, L.O. (1961). *Ecology of sea colony birds of the Barents Sea*. Israel Programme for Scientific Translations, Jerusalem.

Berry, H.H. (1975). History of the guano platform on Bird Rock, Walvis Bay, South West Africa. *Bokmarkierie*, **27**, 60–64.

Bianki, V.V. (1967). *Gulls, shorebirds and alcids of Kandalaksha Bay.* Israel Program for Scientific Translations, Jerusalem, 1977.

Birkhead, T.R. (1976). Effects of sea conditions on rates at which guillemots feed chicks. *British Birds*, **69**, 490–492.

Birkhead, T.R. (1977). The effect of habitat and density on breeding success in the common guillemot *Uria aalge. Journal of Animal Ecology*, **46**, 751–764.

Birkhead, T.R. (1978). Attendance patterns of Guillemots *Uria aalge* at breeding colonies on Skomer Island. *Ibis*, **120**, 219–229.

Birkhead, T.R. & Ashcroft, R.E. (1975). Auk numbers on Skomer Island. *Nature in Wales*, **14**, 222–233.

Birkhead, T.R. & Nettleship, D.N. (1981). Reproductive biology of the thick-billed murre—an inter-colony comparison. *Auk*, **98**, 258–269.

Bradstreet, M.S.W. (1979). Thick-billed murres and black guillemots in the Barrow Strait area, N.W.T., during spring: distribution and habitat use. *Canadian Journal of Zoology*, **57**, 1789–1802.

Bradstreet, M.S.W. (1980). Thick-billed murres and black guillemots in the Barrow Strait area, N.W.T., during spring: diets and food availability along ice edges. *Canadian Journal of Zoology*, **58**, 2120–2140.

Brown, J.L. (1969). The buffer effect and productivity in tit populations. *American Naturalist*, **103**, 347–354.

Brown, R.G.B. (1979). Seabirds of the Senegal upwelling and adjacent waters. *Ibis*, **121**, 283–292.

Brown, R.G.B. (1980). Seabirds as marine animals. *Behaviour of Marine Animals*, Vol. 4, *Marine Birds* (Ed. by J. Burger, B.L. Olla & H.E. Winn), pp. 1–39. Plenum, New York.

Charnov, E.L. & Krebs, J.R. (1974). On clutch size and fitness. *Ibis*, **116**, 217–219.

Coulson, J.C. (1968). Differences in the quality of birds nesting in the centre and on the edge of a colony. *Nature*, **217**, 478–479.

Coulson, J.C. (1971). Competition for breeding sites causing segregation and reduced young production in colonial animals. *Proceedings of the Advanced Institute on the Dynamics of Numbers and Populations.* Oosterbeek 1971; pp. 257–268.

Coulson, J.C. & Wooller, R.D. (1976). Differential survival rates among breeding kittiwake gulls *Rissa tridactyla* (L). *Journal of Animal Ecology*, **45**, 205–213.

Coulson, J.C., Duncan, N. & Thomas, C. (1982). Changes in the breeding biology of the herring gull (*Larus argentatus*) induced by reduction in the size and density of the colony. *Journal of Animal Ecology*, **51**, 739–756.

Cramp, S., Bourne, W.R.P. & Saunders, D. (1974). *The Sea-birds of Britain and Ireland.* Collins, London.

Crawford, R.J.M. & Shelton, P.A. (1978). Pelagic fish and seabird interrelationships off the coasts of South West and South Africa. *Biological Conservation*, **14**, 85–109.

Croxall, J.P. & Prince, P.A. (1980). Food, feeding ecology and ecological segregation of seabirds at South Georgia. *Biological Journal of the Linnean Society*, **14**, 103–131.

Davies, N.B. (1978). Ecological questions about territorial behaviour. *Behavioural Ecology* (Ed. by J.R. Krebs & N.B. Davies) Blackwell Scientific Publications, Oxford.

Duffy, D.C. (1983). Competition for nesting space among Peruvian Guano birds. *Auk*, **100**, 680–688.

Duncan, N. (1978). The effects of culling herring gulls (*Larus argentatus*) on recruitment and population dynamics. *Journal of Applied Ecology*, **15**, 697–713.

Dunn, E.K. (1973). Changes in the fishing ability of terns associated with wind speed and sea surface. *Nature*, **244**, 520–521.

Dunn, E.K. (1975). The role of environmental factors in the growth of tern chicks. *Journal of Animal Ecology*, **44**, 743–754.

Dunnet, G.M., Ollason, J.C. & Anderson, A. (1979). A 28 year study of breeding Fulmars *Fulmarus glacialis* in Orkney. *Ibis*, 121, 293–300.

Evans, P.G.H. & Waterston, G. (1976). The decline of the thick-billed murre in Greenland. *Polar Record*, 18, 283–293.

Ford, R.G., Wiens, J.A., Heinemann, D. & Hunt, G.L. (1982). Modelling the sensitivity of colonially breeding marine birds to oil spills: guillemot and kittiwake populations on the Prifilof Islands, Bering Sea. *Journal of Applied Ecology*, 19, 1–31.

Fretwell, S.D. & Lucas, H.L. (1970). On territorial behaviour and other factors influencing habitat distribution in birds. *Acta Biotheoretica*, 19, 16–36.

Furness, R.W. (1978) Energy requirements of seabird communities: a bioenergetics model. *Journal of Animal Ecology*, 47, 39–53.

Furness, R.W. (1982). Competition between fisheries and seabird communities. *Advances in Marine Biology*, 20, 225–307.

Furness, R.W. (1984). Seabird-fisheries relationships in the Northeast Atlantic and North Sea. *Marine Birds: their feeding ecology and commercial fisheries relationships* (Ed. by D.N. Nettleship, G.A. Sanger & P.F. Springer). Special Publication, Canadian Wildlife Service, Ottawa.

Furness, R.W. & Birkhead, T.R. (1984). Seabird colony distributions suggest competition for food supplies during the breeding season. *Nature* (in press).

Furness, R.W. & Cooper, J. (1982). Interactions between breeding seabird and pelagic fish populations in the southern Benguela region. *Marine Ecology Progress Series*, 8, 243–250.

Furness, R.W. & Hislop, J.R.G. (1981). Diets and feeding ecology of Great Skuas *Catharacta skua* during the breeding season in Shetland. *Journal of Zoology* (*London*), 195, 1–23.

Furness, R.W. & Todd, C.M. (1984). Diets and feeding of Fulmars during the breeding season: a comparison between St Kilda and Shetland colonies. *Ibis*, 126, 379–387.

Galbraith, H. (1983). The diet and feeding ecology of breeding Kittiwakes *Rissa tridactyla*. *Bird Study*, 30, 109–120.

Gaston, A.J., Chapdelaine, G. & Noble, D.G. (1983). The growth of thick-billed murre chicks at colonies in Hudson Strait: inter- and intra-colony variation. *Canadian Journal of Zoology*, 61, 2465–2475.

Goodman, D. (1974). Natural selection and a cost ceiling on reproductive effort. *American Naturalist*, 108, 247–268.

Harris, M.P. (1970). Territory limiting the size of the breeding population of the Oystercatcher (*Haematopus ostralegus*)—a removal experiment. *Journal of Animal Ecology*, 39, 707–713.

Harris, M.P. (1976). The present status of the Puffin in Britain and Ireland. *British Birds*, 69, 239–264.

Harris, M.P. (1983). Biology and survival of the immature Puffin *Fratercula arctica*. *Ibis*, 125, 56–73.

Harris, M.P. & Hislop, J.R.G. (1978). The food of young puffins. *Fratercula arctica*. *Journal of Zoology*, (*London*), 185, 213–236.

Hempel, G. (1978). North Sea fisheries and fish stocks: a review of recent changes. *Rapports et Proces-verbaux des Reunions. Conseil International pour l'Exploration de la Mer*, 173, 145–167.

Hinde, R.A. (1956). The biological significance of the territories of birds. *Ibis*, 98, 340–369.

Idyll, C.P. (1973). The anchovy crisis. *Scientific American*, 228, 22–29.

Knapton, R.W. & Krebs, J.R. (1974). Settlement patterns, territory size and breeding density in the song sparrow (*Melospiza melodia*). *Canadian Journal of Zoology*, 52, 1413–1420.

Krebs, J.R. (1977). Song and territory in the Great Tit. *Evolutionary Ecology* (Ed. by B. Stonehouse & C.M. Perrins), pp. 47–62. Macmillan, London.

Lack, D. (1954). *The Natural Regulation of Animal Numbers*. Oxford University Press, Oxford.

Lack, D. (1966). *Population Studies of Birds*. Oxford University Press, Oxford.

Lack, D. (1967). Interrelationships in breeding adaptations as shown by marine birds. *Proceedings of the 14th International Ornithological Congress.* **14,** 3–42.

Lack, D. (1968). *Ecological Adaptations for Breeding in Birds.* Methuen, London.

Lid, G. (1981). Reproduction of the puffin on Rost in the Lofoten Islands in 1964–1980. *Fauna Norvegica Series C, Cinclus,* **4,** 30–39.

Manuwal, D.A. (1972). *The population ecology of the Cassin's Auklet on Southeast Farallon Island, California.* Ph.D. thesis, University of California, Los Angeles.

May, R.M., Beddington, J.R., Clark, C.W., Holt, S.J. & Laws, R.M. (1979). Management of multispecies fisheries. *Science,* **205,** 267–277.

Nelson, J.B. (1970). The relationship between behaviour and ecology in the Sulidae with reference to other seabirds. *Annual Review of Oceanography and Marine Biology,* **8,** 501–574.

Nelson, J.B. (1978). *The Sulidae: Gannets and Boobies.* Oxford University Press, Oxford.

Nettleship, D.N. (1972). Breeding success of the common puffin (*Fratercula arctica* L.) on different habitats at Great Island, Newfoundland. *Ecological Monographs,* **42,** 239–268.

Newton, I. (1980). The role of food in limiting bird numbers. *Ardea,* **68,** 11–30.

Ollason, J.C. & Dunnet, G.M. (1983). Modelling annual changes in numbers of breeding Fulmars, *Fulmarus glacialis,* at a colony in Orkney. *Journal of Animal Ecology,* **52,** 185–198.

Parsons, J., Chabrzyk, G. & Duncan, N. (1976). Effects of hatching date on post-fledging survival in herring gulls. *Journal of Animal Ecology,* **45,** 667–675.

Perrins, C.M., Harris, M.P. & Britton, C.K. (1973). Survival of the Manx shearwater *Puffinus puffinus. Ibis,* **115,** 535–548.

Potts, G.R., Coulson, J.C. & Deans, I.R. (1980). Population dynamics and the breeding success of the Shag *Phalacrocorax aristotelis,* on the Farne Islands, Northumberland. *Journal of Animal Ecology,* **49,** 465–484.

Richardson, M.G. (1983). Kittiwake populations of Shetland. *Shetland Bird Report for 1982,* pp. 54–64.

Ricklefs, R.E. (1983). Comparative avian demography. *Current Ornithology* (Ed. by R.F. Johnston) Vol. 1, pp. 1–32. Plenum, New York.

Schaefer, M.B. (1970). Men, birds and anchovies in the Peru current—dynamic interactions. *Transcription of the American Fisheries Society,* **99,** 461–467.

Schneider, D. & Hunt, G.L. (1982). Carbon flux to seabirds in waters with different mixing regimes in the southeastern Bering Sea. *Marine Biology,* **67,** 337–344.

Sherman, K., Jones, C., Sullivan, L., Smith, W., Berrien, P. & Ejsymont, L. (1981). Congruent shifts in sand eel abundance in western and eastern North Atlantic ecosystems. *Nature,* **291,** 486–489.

Sibly, R.M. (1983). Optimal group size is unstable. *Animal Behaviour,* **31,** 947–948.

Sowls, A.L., Hatch, S.A. & Lensink, C.J. (1978). *Catalog of Alaskan Seabird Colonies.* United States Department of the Interior, Fisheries & Wildlife Service FWS/OBS—78/78.

Stearns, S.C. (1976). Life-history tactics: a review of the ideas. *Quarterly Review of Biology,* **51,** 3–47.

Stearns, S.C. (1977). The evolution of life-history traits. *Annual Reviews of Ecology and Systematics,* **8,** 145–171.

Stonehouse, B. (1963). The tropic birds (genus Phaethon) on Ascension Island. *Ibis,* **103b,** 124–161.

Taylor, K. & Reid, J.B. (1981). Earlier colony attendance by guillemots and razorbills. *Scottish Birds,* **11,** 173–180.

Tinbergen, N. (1959). Comparative studies of the behaviour of gulls (Laridae): a progress report. *Behaviour,* **15,** 1–70.

Uspenski, V.S. (1956). *The bird bazaars of Novaya Zemlya.* USSR Academy of Science, Moscow.

Wiens, J.A. & Scott, J.M. (1975). Model estimation of energy flow in Oregon coastal seabird populations. *Condor,* **77,** 439–452.

Wiklund, C.G. (1982). Fieldfare (*Turdus pilaris*) breeding success in relation to colony size, nest position and association with Merlins (*Falco columbaris*). *Behavioural Ecology & Sociobiology*, **11**, 165–172.

Williams, A.J. (1974). Site preferences and interspecific competition among guillemots *Uria aalge* (L.) and *Uria lomvia* (L.) on Bear Island. *Ornis Scandinavica*, **5**, 113–121.

Wittenberger, J.F. & Hunt, G.L. (in press). The adaptive significance of coloniality in birds. *Avian Biology*, Vol. VIII (Ed. by D.S. Farner and J. King). Academic Press, London.

Wooller, R.D. & Coulson, J.C. (1977). Factors affecting the age of first breeding of the kittiwake *Rissa tridactyla*. *Ibis*, **119**, 339–349.

Wynne-Edwards, V.C. (1962). *Animal Dispersion in Relation to Social Behaviour*. Oliver & Boyd, Edinburgh.

9. FORAGING BEHAVIOUR OF WADING BIRDS AND THE CARRYING CAPACITY OF ESTUARIES

J. D. GOSS-CUSTARD

Institute of Terrestrial Ecology, Furzebrook Research Station, Wareham, Dorset, BH20 5AS

SUMMARY

The foraging behaviour and dispersion of some common wading birds is discussed in relation to the numbers of birds that can use an estuary in winter. Many of the birds' activities can be understood as adaptations to increasing their immediate rate of food intake at a time of year when it is often difficult to fulfil energy requirements. Interference occurs between feeding birds in some species. The reduced rates of food intake at high bird densities may provide a feedback link from bird density to the decision of individual birds whether to remain on an estuary, or to move on. This could limit the numbers of waders using an estuary in winter, particularly in the more dispersed foragers. Depletion of the prey may be a more important feedback mechanism in those that flock as they forage.

INTRODUCTION

In late summer and autumn millions of wading birds, *Charadrii*, arrive on the estuaries of north-west Europe from their northern breeding grounds (summarized in Hale 1980). Some eventually move south to spend the winter in southern Europe and Africa, but large numbers remain until the spring. The threats to estuaries posed by various development schemes (Hale 1980; Prater 1981) have stimulated research into the ability of estuaries to support waders. Since the main activity of waders outside the breeding season is feeding, attention has focused on the birds' responses to their food supplies and to other foraging birds. This work has shown that several species of waders are particularly suitable subjects for research on foraging behaviour because their rates of food intake are relatively easy to measure in the field. Consequently, the relationships between the rate of energy intake and a variety of factors have been studied in unusual detail.

This paper reviews work done on the foraging behaviour of waders and discusses how the findings may help to predict the numbers that can use an estuary in winter. Having briefly reviewed the foraging difficulties which waders face at that time of year, I discuss the evidence that they select the food items and feeding sites on the basis of maximizing their intake rate. The extent to which their responses to conspecifics can also be understood as adaptations to increasing intake rate is then explored. Studies of colour-marked birds have shown that individuals may behave very differently. Though experience at feeding, and therefore age, accounts for some of these differences, competition between individuals plays a major role. In particular, increasing bird density may depress the intake rate of some birds and cause them to seek less contested foraging areas, perhaps on other estuaries. In effect, this could provide a feedback link from bird density to the decisions made by individuals as to whether to stay or to leave, and this clearly has consequences for the numbers of birds that use an estuary in winter, and may enable a maximum density, or 'carrying capacity' to be defined.

SEASONAL CHANGES IN FEEDING CONDITIONS

Feeding conditions deteriorate during autumn and winter for the following reasons:

1   Energy demands rise as temperature falls and wind-chill increases (reviewed by Evans 1976; Evans & Dugan 1984; Pienkowski et al. 1984).
2   At the same time foraging becomes more difficult as the density of available prey declines (a) through depletion by waders (reviewed by Goss-Custard 1980; Zwarts & Drent 1981), and other predators, (b) through a decline in the energy value of individual prey (reviewed by Goss-Custard 1981a), and (c) through a decline in the proportion of the prey that is both detectable and accessible (i.e. available) as the invertebrates (i) burrow deeper in the substrate, perhaps to reduce their own vulnerability to waders (Evans 1979), (ii) become less active and visible at low temperatures or in high winds (reviewed by Goss-Custard 1984).
3   As daylength shortens, an increasing proportion of the low water period in each 24 hours occurs in darkness when, according to most field studies (but see Dugan 1981), many waders feed at under half the daytime rate. These include several species quoted by Hale (1980) and also oystercatchers *Haematopus ostralegus* feeding on *Mytilus edulis* (Goss-Custard, unpublished; Zwarts & Drent 1981) or cockles, *Cerastoderma edule* (Sutherland 1982a); grey plover, *Pluvialis squatarola* feeding on ragworms, *Nereis diversicolor* (Evans 1976) or lugworms, *Arenicola marina* (Pienkowski 1983).

In response to these seasonal changes in the feeding conditions, waders may feed for longer at low tide (Goss-Custard et al. 1977a; Hale 1980) and at high water many may also feed on terrestrial invertebrates in fields (Goss-Custard 1969; Heppleston 1971; Townshend 1981).

The few field studies of winter mortality (Evans & Pienkowski 1984; Goss-Custard *et al.* 1977a, 1982a) and body condition (review by Davidson 1981) suggest that most birds adapt successfully and survive, except during acute periods of cold and windy weather when prey becomes less available at both low and high water (reviewed by Goss-Custard 1981a, 1983; Hale 1980) and energy demands increase (review by Evans 1976). Though birds store fat to help them survive such periods, many lose condition (Davidson 1981, 1982; Davidson & Evans 1983) and die (review by Goss-Custard 1981a; and subsequent research papers by Baillie 1980; Clarke 1982; Davidson 1982; Dugan *et al.* 1981; O'Connor & Cawthorne 1982).

DO WADERS MAXIMIZE INTAKE RATE WHILE FORAGING?

The difficult feeding conditions in winter, the need for waders to store fat rapidly in autumn and spring (reviewed by Hale 1980), along with the increasing interest in optimality models in behaviour (Krebs & Davies 1981), has led researchers to suggest that waders may usually forage so as to maximize the rate at which they collect energy. What evidence is there that they do this?

Most studies have shown that, where an obvious choice is available, waders do select the energetically more profitable kind of prey species (Hartwick 1976; Pienkowski 1981; Townshend 1981; Zwarts & Drent 1981), or size classes of one prey species (Barnard & Stephens 1981; Barnard *et al.* 1982; Goss-Custard 1977a; Hulscher 1982; Sutherland 1982a; Thompson 1983; Thompson & Barnard 1984; Wanink & Zwarts 1984; Zwarts & Drent 1981; Zwarts & Wanink 1984), or places in which to feed (Dugan 1981; Goss-Custard 1970a; Smith 1975; Sutherland 1982b; Zwarts & Drent 1981). Apparently unprofitable choices (e.g. Goss-Custard 1977d) may be explained by (i) the need for the birds to maximize the intake rate of a critical nutrient, rather than energy, or (ii) by the inability of the research worker to measure net, rather than gross, rates of energy intake: the benefit of expending less energy, for example, may explain why oystercatchers prefer feeding areas near to the high water roost (Goss-Custard *et al.* 1981; Zwarts & Drent 1981) and with a firm substrate (Goss-Custard *et al.* 1981, 1984). In a few cases, the precise predictions of early models of optimal foraging have been tested and found not to correspond exactly with the behaviour of the waders (Goss-Custard 1981b; Krebs, Stephens & Sutherland 1983; Wanink & Zwarts 1984).

Evidence that waders usually select the most profitable option does not necessarily imply that they are also foraging at the maximum possible rate. Foraging models assume certain constants which, in reality, may be variable and under the birds' control. The obvious example is walking speed: the bird may indeed make the (more-or-less) most profitable selection amongst the prey it encounters but it may be able to increase its intake rate still further by searching faster. Birds might be expected to do this, for instance, when the time available for feeding is limited or when energy demands are particularly high. However, redshank, *Tringa totanus*, did not increase their rate of foraging as the hours available declined from autumn to winter (Goss-Custard 1981b), though the mild climate may have made such a change unnecessary. In contrast, Hulscher (1982) showed that an individual oyster-catcher feeding in the same place increased its intake rate threefold during a period of 16 days as its breeding commitment increased, though possible changes in the food supply were not monitored. Goss-Custard *et al.* (1984) found that the intake rate of adult oystercatchers increased gradually during the low tide period so that the birds fed at the beginning and end of the tidal cycle in the same places but at very different rates. The clearest example is adult turnstone, *Arenaria interpres*, which increased their intake rate when fattening up for migration while the non-migratory juveniles did not (Metcalfe & Furness 1984). These studies illustrate that intake rate may not always be maximal, and that caution is required when interpreting the relationships between gross intake rates and various factors.

Submaximal rates can be reconciled with optimal foraging theory by arguing that other factors, which also affect fitness, act as constraints that change the optimal solution for foraging (Krebs *et al.* 1983). In waders, for example, large prey may be more heavily parasitized than small ones and so be rejected to reduce the risk of infection, even if intake rate is thereby reduced (Hulscher 1982). Similarly, the need to be vigilant for predators may reduce intake rate (Metcalfe & Furness 1984). If the constraints can be recognized and measured, and their effect on how to maximize intake rate worked out, the birds may still prove to be maximizing intake rate within the restrictions imposed on them by the need to do other things simultaneously. Being 'optimal' in the sense of maximizing fitness does not necessarily imply that all the individual functions, like foraging, are themselves invariably maximized.

DO THE RESPONSES OF WADERS TO CONSPECIFICS ALSO INCREASE INTAKE RATE?

Wader dispersion on the feeding grounds is very variable (Fig. 9.1). At one extreme, waders forage in compact flocks, while at the other, individuals feed solitarily in vigorously defended territories. Predation, rather than foraging, is

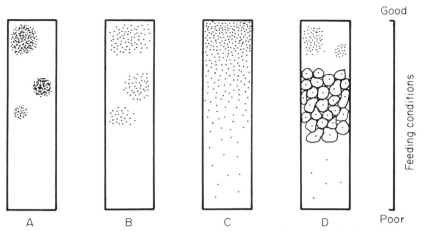

FIG. 9.1 Diagram of wader dispersion (types A–D) along a gradient in the food supply varying from good to bad. In type D, territories are occupied within the central region of the gradient, following Myers *et al.* (1979a) finding that sanderling could not defend territories in the best feeding areas and did not even attempt to in the very poor areas.

usually considered the more important selection pressure favouring flocking. There are four reasons: (i) the absence of evidence that flocking enhances foraging rates (Blick 1980)—if anything, it depresses it (see below); (ii) the mounting evidence that predators may kill many waders on the wintering grounds (Kus 1984; Page & Whittacre 1975; Townshend 1984; (iii) the increasing evidence that flocking reduces predation risk and, by reducing the need for individuals to be vigilant while remaining safe, increases the time available for feeding (reviews by Blick 1980; Myers 1984; papers by Metcalfe 1984a,b) and (iv) the observation that waders abandon feeding territories and forage in compact flocks when a predator arrives (review by Myers 1984).

But since all waders are attacked by predators, why do they not all forage in compact flocks? In developing a new, but as yet untested hypothesis, Blick (1980) argues that the feeding method of some species, particularly those that hunt for their prey visually rather than by touch and so have their heads up regularly, allows the birds to be vigilant as they forage. These birds have less need to flock to increase vigilance. In contrast, Goss-Custard (1970b) suggested that all species could benefit from flocking, but that the feeding method of some, again the visual feeders, make the birds so prone to interference in feeding that they are forced to spread out, and so forage in loose groups: in effect the birds compromise between the needs to forage and to avoid predation. What evidence is there that interference has a significant effect on the intake rates of some waders in winter?

Interference

This is defined as the immediate and reversible reduction in intake rate associated with increased bird density (Goss-Custard 1980). As predicted, visually searching redshank, oystercatchers (eating mussels) and curlew, *Numenius arquata*, showed interference, while touch-searching knot, *Calidris canutus*, and redshank did not. But contrary to expectation, oystercatchers searching visually for cockles did not show interference either (review by Goss-Custard 1980; and subsequent papers by Sutherland & Koene 1982; Zwarts & Drent 1981).

Few studies have examined the mechanism of interference. In oystercatchers eating mussels on the Exe estuary, it is probably associated with the increasing rates of food stealing that occur as bird density increases (Ens & Goss-Custard 1984a). No studies have yet demonstrated convincingly the mechanisms of interference proposed by Goss-Custard (1970b): that at high bird densities prey are less available because they retreat down their burrows or the small vulnerable fraction is depleted or individual birds are unable to pursue the optimum search path. However, the intake rate of redshank was reduced when another bird had fed recently in the same place (J. Selman & J.D. Goss-Custard, unpubl.), and the reduction lasted for several minutes, roughly the length of time for which the prey remain beneath the mud surface after a redshank walks over them (Goss-Custard 1970b). So perhaps this is a case of interference caused by reduced prey availability.

As well as encouraging flocking birds to spread out, interference may cause some waders to defend an exclusive feeding area, when the energy and time costs of defence outweigh the reduced intake rates that would otherwise result from interference (Myers *et al.* 1979a; 1980). The time spent in defence by territorial redshank was compensated by the increased intake rate that resulted from the reduced interference (J. Selman & J.D. Goss-Custard, unpubl.). Territories occupied for a short period of hours, days or weeks (review by Myers *et al.* 1979b), seem particularly likely to serve this function, especially where prey are mobile or when territories are taken up where prey are relatively scarce.

Territories taken for several months over the winter on sedentary prey may also function to conserve the food supply. Waders can have a substantial impact on the standing crop of their prey in winter (reviews by Goss-Custard 1980; Zwarts & Drent 1981, and papers by Quammen 1980; Schneider & Harrington 1981, Zwarts & Wanink 1984) and deplete their prey sufficiently to reduce their own intake rates (Goss-Custard 1980). At Teesmouth, waders take as much as 90% of the standing crop (Evans *et al.* 1979), which prompted Dugan (1982) to suggest that territories are held by some grey plovers there throughout autumn and winter to protect particularly profitable places within the territory from depletion until they are vitally needed in winter. Alternatively, holding a territory may simply reduce depletion throughout the territory. However, prey depletion over one winter was not less inside territories held by redshank from autumn to spring compared with nearby flocking areas (Goss-Custard, Nicholson & Winterbottom 1984) and Ens (1984) showed that prey depletion by curlew was too low for it to be a factor favouring territoriality. But clearly, the relative contribution played by reduction of interference and protection of food stocks in providing benefit of territorial defence throughout the winter needs further evaluation.

Variability in dispersion

Wader dispersion is strikingly characterized by flexibility and variability. Birds may change from defending territories to foraging in compact flocks during one tidal cycle according to where, and on what, the movement of the tide allows them to feed (reviewed by Myers 1984). Seasonal changes also occur. For example, dunlin on the Severn Estuary (Worrall 1984) and knot on the Wash (Goss-Custard 1977b) both foraged in compact flocks, but in winter spread out over the flats: in terms of Fig. 9.1, they changed from type A to types B or C. The very slight risk of predation is unlikely to have changed, but the food supply did. Both the ragworms eaten by dunlin (Worrall 1984), and the *Macoma balthica* eaten by the knot (Reading & McGrorty 1978) burrowed deeper in the mud in winter, substantially reducing the density of available prey. Perhaps this caused interference to become more serious, so the birds spread out to maintain their intake rate at that difficult time of year.

In conclusion, most of the variations in dispersion that are associated with meteorological, diurnal, tidal and seasonal factors seem to be responses to changes in the feeding conditions. In general, waders respond quickly to environmental changes which affect feeding profitability. With the possible exception of some long-term territory holders, the birds' responses to conspecifics, like their responses to the food supply itself, can also be understood largely as adaptations to increase immediate intake rate, within the constraints imposed by other selection pressures, notably predation.

INDIVIDUAL VARIATIONS IN RESPONSES TO FOOD SUPPLY AND OTHER BIRDS

The general tendency is for the individual bird to increase its intake rate, but individuals may vary enormously in how they respond both to the food supply and other birds. Indeed the two responses may be closely linked.

The best known example of individual variations in foraging behaviour is the oystercatcher. Individual birds tend to specialize on different prey species, e.g. mussels, or cockles, or a mixture of ragworms, the clam, *Scrobicularia plana* and earthworms. Individuals feeding on bivalve molluscs may further specialize in the technique they employ to open them (Norton-Griffiths 1968). Individual specializations are not as rigid as was once thought (Goss-Custard & Sutherland 1984; Swennen *et al.* 1983), but they are still pronounced. Little is known of the factors which cause a bird to specialize in a particular way, or to change its choice from one prey to another. Norton-Griffiths' (1968) cross-fostering experiments suggest parental training is important initially, but the possible effect of later experience when the young feed independently is unknown (Goss-Custard & Durell 1983). Nor is it known how widely individuals in other wader species specialize, though it is suspected in some cases (Prater 1981).

Individual differences in social behaviour are most obvious and most studied in the aggressive species. In species with foraging territories, only a minority of individuals hold them (review by Myers 1984). Furthermore, some defend a territory for most of the winter, while others do so for a short period in mid-winter or for only a few hours in each tidal cycle. At other times, birds forage in flocks.

Individual variations in fighting over food items and feeding sites have been studied in oystercatchers foraging in overlapping feeding ranges on a mussel bed (Ens & Goss-Custard 1984a; Goss-Custard *et al.* 1982b). Some birds, the dominants, attacked others frequently but were rather infrequently attacked themselves, stole many more mussels from other birds than they had stolen from them and boosted their intake rate considerably as a result (Goss-Custard 1983). They also spent much time in 'piping' displays, which may function to assert dominance (Ens & Goss-Custard 1984b). The subdominants were opposite in every respect. If a successful encounter is defined as one in which the victim of an attack ran away, the success of individuals varied from almost 100% down to nearly zero. As Safriel (1981) showed, such large individual differences in aggressiveness occur even in recently hatched oystercatchers.

Explanations for individual variations

There are three forms of explanation. The first is that there exist several equally effective strategies for foraging and, for reasons not yet understood, individuals specialize on one. The second is that one strategy is actually more successful than others, and birds compete for the opportunity to employ it, with the losers adopting the alternative which, though not the best possible, is the best they can employ within the constraints imposed by their poorer competitive ability. The third argues that birds differ in both competitive and foraging skills, and this determines which is the most profitable strategy for an individual, but this could change through life as a bird's skills develop.

No study has yet distinguished between these hypotheses, but the early findings of a long-term study of oystercatchers wintering on the Exe estuary may be used to illustrate some of the issues involved. Many juveniles arriving in their first autumn eat mussels, but many turn to alternative foods, particularly ragworm and clams on the estuary and earthworms in the fields: indeed many may feed on these prey from their arrival. In the following summer, when the adults have left the Exe to breed, many young birds then feed on mussels. Some continue to do so the following winter after the adults return, but many revert to the juvenile diet. Over the first few years, an increasing proportion feed more-or-less continuously on mussels, as do most of the adults (Goss-Custard & Durell 1983). But some retain the worm–clam diet, while a few others specialize on periwinkles, *Littorina* spp., or cockles.

The social environment varies with diet, and therefore with age and between individuals of the same age eating different prey. In contrast to the mussel beds, encounters are rare on the mudflats because ragworms and clams are rapidly consumed, and feeding birds are at low densities (J.S. Boates, pers. comm.). Average intake rate is also lower on the mudflats than on the mussel beds, which is presumably why the mudflat birds are several times more likely than mussel-eating birds to feed in the fields at high tide in winter (Goss-Custard & Durell 1983), and are therefore probably more at risk in freezing weather when earthworms become unavailable. In view of (i) this apparent penalty for feeding on mudflats, (ii) the differing social environment between mussel beds and mudflats, and (iii) the tendency for some young birds to switch from mussels to worms as the adults return in autumn, perhaps subdominant birds are prevented by competition from feeding on mussels, and are forced to feed on the mudflats?

Food-fighting is certainly frequent on the preferred mussel beds where most birds feed, and the least dominant birds have very low intake rates compared with the dominants (Ens & Goss-Custard 1984a; Goss-Custard *et al.* 1984). Being subdominant may itself cause low intake rates because: (i) the dominants steal many mussels from them, which reduces intake rate (Goss-Custard 1983); (ii) the rate at which they capture mussels is depressed at high bird densities, whereas it is not in the most dominant individuals (Ens & Goss-Custard 1984a); (iii) by avoiding (Vines 1980) the dominants which might attack them, they may feed more often in places where the mussels are smaller, fewer and thicker-shelled and intake rate is lower as a consequence (Goss-Custard *et al.* 1981, 1982c; Zwarts & Drent 1981). These factors might explain why the least dominant birds feed at a half or one-third of the rate achieved by the most dominant individuals.

But another possibility is that the subdominants are simply less experienced, or less skilled, at feeding as well as fighting: the correlation of intake rate with dominance may be spuriously linked *via* a third variable, bird quality or experience (Goss-Custard *et al.* 1984; Have, Nieboer & Boere 1984). This possibility is being tested, but studies on juvenile oystercatchers (unpubl.) and several other species (Burger 1980; Groves 1978; Heppleston 1971; Puttick 1979) do show that inexperienced birds feed more slowly than adults. As expected, at this age in oystercatchers inexperience at feeding and fighting go together. However, at 2 and 3 years of age birds feed much more efficiently but are still subdominant to adults. This raises the possibility that the low intake rates become increasingly associated with subdominance rather than inexperience at feeding, though more tests are required.

These results illustrate how individual differences in foraging skills and aggressiveness could influence the choice of diet. Young birds, and the less skilled adults, may find it more profitable to give up feeding on mussels and feed on the less suitable prey on mudflats which require less skill to exploit, and where the social environment is less hostile. Increasing experience at feeding and fighting may alter the balance so that the optimum strategy changes with age, but at different rates in different individuals: indeed, some may never learn the skills needed to employ the best option.

Conclusions

Laboratory workers often remark on the large individual differences in foraging and social behaviour amongst captive birds. Field studies on waders are beginning to reveal a similar diversity (see Townshend, Dugan & Pienkowski 1984, in addition to references on oystercatchers already cited). Differences in foraging and competitive abilities, both of which may change with experience and age, seem likely to be involved. Hence, the most effective strategy for increasing intake rate may differ considerably between individuals because individuals function within differing constraints. As a result, intake rates can vary considerably between individuals, and a section of the population may be doing badly even when feeding conditions are good. Whether a low intake rate necessarily implies a higher likelihood of emigrating or greater risk of dying through starvation, predation (Whitfield, in press) or disease remains to be proved, though the greater vulnerability of young oystercatchers in both mild (Goss-Custard *et al.* 1982a) and severe winters (Baillie 1980; Heppleston 1971; Swennen 1984) does suggest so.

IMPLICATIONS FOR CARRYING CAPACITY

Two questions are usually asked when the effect of the loss of a winter feeding area on wader numbers is being considered. First, will it increase mortality or emigration and so reduce the numbers of birds able to use the estuary? Second, how would an increase in winter mortality affect the total population of waders wintering on all estuaries? The two questions are concerned with very different levels of scale, with emigration likely to be most important when the number of birds on one estuary is being considered. Since recent reviews have already discussed some theoretical consequences of increased winter mortality in waders at the level of a species population (Goss-Custard 1980, 1981a), this discussion focuses on processes at the level of an individual estuary (or local group of estuaries).

One approach is to ask whether the parts of the estuary that remain can support the extra birds displaced from the areas that will be lost. If in some sense the full potential of the remaining areas is not already being used, then presumably the displaced birds would settle there. It is then necessary to ask whether all the displaced birds could fit in, or whether the number involved would exceed the maximum that the remaining area can support; in other words, the 'carrying capacity' of the remaining areas.

The term 'carrying capacity' has been criticized as inappropriate when applied to wintering wader populations (Evans 1984), mainly on the grounds that there is no reason to think that the net result of all the individuals in a population maximizing their overwinter fitness would be to produce population densities that cause the prey populations to be cropped at the maximum sustainable rate. This objection holds if carrying capacity is defined solely in terms of cropping the resources at the optimal rate. But, as the review of foraging behaviour shows, there are other feedback mechanisms operating within wintering wader populations which could set limits to density and which interact in a complex way with food abundance and other factors which affect net rates of intake. The maximum numbers of birds that can use an area may be influenced not only by the quantity of resources available in the longer term, but also by the more immediate consequences of wader density on the intake rates and behaviour of individual birds.

Carrying capacity in dispersed feeders

The first place to test the idea that increases in bird density can be restrained is amongst the dispersed foragers (types C and D in Fig. 9.1) where all of the most suitable parts of the 'food gradient' (Goss-Custard & Charman 1976) are occupied at one time. As Zwarts (1974) first showed, the density of many foraging waders does tend to reach a maximum on the most preferred feeding areas, even though the whole population continues to increase. This has been shown in oystercatchers feeding on mussels (Goss-Custard *et al.* 1981; Zwarts & Drent 1981) and cockles (Goss-Custard 1977b), redshank feeding on *Corophium* (Goss-Custard 1977c) and knot feeding on *Macoma* (Goss-Custard 1977b). Studies of oystercatchers (Goss-Custard *et al.* 1982c, 1984) and dunlin (Have *et al.* 1984) suggest that dominant birds feed disproportionately in the preferred areas, and may displace any subdominants already there. The subdominants may leave either to avoid aggression or the low intakes that result from it (Ens & Goss-Custard 1984a; Zwarts & Drent 1981). In non-aggressive species without dominance hierarchies, the depression of intake rate in all birds at high bird densities could cause some, presumably those with the poorest feeding skills or lowest tolerance, to seek new areas. Though the food supply itself may be poorer, intake rates could be higher than in the intrinsically better feeding areas with high interference. This interaction between food supply and bird density, and the attempt by individuals to secure high intake rates before the winter starts, could explain the ordered way in which bird density becomes correlated with prey abundance at several levels of scale, from along one beach to between different estuaries (Goss-Custard *et al.* 1977b; Goss-Custard 1983).

These results suggest that studying the habitat characteristics which, in conjunction with bird density, determine intake rate provides a way of measuring the maximum number of birds that can winter on an estuary. By showing that the arrival of more birds would depress the intake rates of a similar number to a level below which they could not either survive the winter or be willing to remain on the estuary, it would be possible to conclude that bird density was everywhere maximal, and the carrying capacity of the estuary reached.

This idea is expressed in two ways in Fig. 9.2. The left hand part (a) shows a hypothetical frequency distribution of the intake rates of individual birds attempting to settle on an estuary. The dashed line shows the minimum intake rate that is either acceptable to birds looking for a place to overwinter or necessary for their subsequent survival; we do not know how closely these two values are related. At low population sizes, the intake rates of most birds will exceed the minimum level, although there will be some incompetent or inexperienced birds that will not achieve this level. As the population rises, an increasing proportion will fall below the line as competition on the feeding grounds skews the distribution increasingly to the left (Begon 1984), below the threshold: it is assumed here that the top dominants can maintain their intake rates even at high densities, as do oystercatchers on the Exe. Eventually, all the

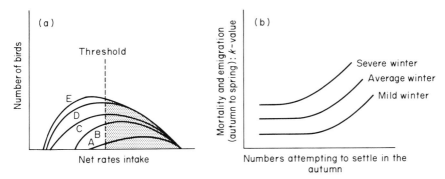

FIG. 9.2 (a) Hypothetical frequency distribution of the intake rates of individual birds in populations increasing in size from A to E. The threshold line shows the minimum intake rate required, and the shaded area the maximum numbers of birds able to achieve it and so remain and survive on the estuary. (b) Hypothetical plot of mortality and emigration in the non-breeding season as a function of bird density and annual variations in the severity of the winter.

extra increase in numbers occurs to the left of the line: the arrival of N extra birds depresses the intake rate of N birds below the threshold.

Figure 9.2b portrays the same idea but expresses the numbers of birds dying or emigrating through the non-breeding season as a k-value plotted against the logarithm of the numbers of birds attempting to settle in the autumn. At low population sizes, some birds will die, with the proportion dying or emigrating directly or indirectly as a result of food shortage varying according to the severity of the winter and food abundance. But at some point, as bird density rises (or estuary size is decreased), interference will start to further decrease the intake rates of some birds, and the proportion dying or emigrating would then be expected to increase. Bird density is maximal in all regions of the food gradient when the slope of the density-dependent part of the curve becomes one. This is another way of saying that bird numbers would be reduced by emigration or mortality to a certain number each winter, however many birds in excess of this number attempted to settle there in the autumn. If fewer than this habitually arrived, then the point at which the slope reached unity would define the carrying capacity.

The immediate disappearance of many waders from estuaries where major reclamations have occurred, well before prey depletion could have been serious (Evans 1981; Laursen, Gram & Alberto 1983), does suggest that some estuaries are near to the inflection point. Particularly in the case of the Tees, feeding time, as well as feeding area, was lost because the reclamation occurred at the top of the shore which the waders used at the start and end of the tidal cycle. In terms of Fig. 9.2a, this means the threshold was moved to the right because higher net rates of intake would have been necessary with the reduced feeding time available.

But even if the inflection point is usually reached on British estuaries, it is unlikely that the slope is one. No study has yet shown that bird density is at a maximum level in all regions of an estuary: for instance, the numbers of oystercatchers on several mussel beds of the Exe continue to increase as the numbers on the whole estuary rise, yet winter mortality is still very low. Nor is the winter mortality in waders high enough for numbers to be reduced by death to a similar level each winter. Furthermore, the increase in numbers that occurs during winter in many estuaries (Evans & Dugan 1984; Hale 1980; Prater 1981) and the small variation in the numbers of oystercatchers wintering in the Burry Inlet over many years, despite wide variations in the density of their main food (Horwood & Goss-Custard 1977), also argue that the slope would be less than one. If this is so, winter numbers can increase even if some birds already have such low intake rates that they die, and even if an increased proportion of the population is pushed off the end of the food gradient as a result. The presence of birds dying of food shortage does not necessarily imply that numbers are 'food limited' in the sense that no further increase in density is possible. Even in these circumstances, the carrying capacity cannot be said to have been reached.

Presumably, as bird numbers increase and interference becomes more severe for more birds, the slope will become one for an entire estuary, though predicting when this will happen is beyond our abilities at present. It requires information on the effect of bird density on intake rate and the effect of intake rate on a bird's decision whether to remain or emigrate that is not available at present. For the time being, studies of present densities in preferred areas may have to be used as a rough guide. This is inexact because, under increasing pressure from habitat loss, still higher bird densities may occur. For example, at very high densities, rates of aggression may decrease, as is suggested by the observations of Burger et al. (1979); Harrington & Groves (1977); Puttick (1981) and Recher & Recher (1969), or territories break down (Myers et al. 1979a), so more birds can pack into an area. While this might, in principle, be predictable from studies of the economics of foraging at high bird densities, existing knowledge does not allow it to be done.

Despite such uncertainties, foraging studies of dispersed feeders have suggested that feedback mechanisms exist which link bird density directly to the intake rates of individuals, thereby normally limiting or 'buffering' (Zwarts & Drent 1981) the density of foraging waders in the absence of serious prey depletion. Figure 9.2a illustrates this point, and also allows the many factors which affect the chances of birds achieving the required net rates of intake to be incorporated as different shaped distributions. We can only guess at these at present, but many factors apart from competition are involved. These include (i) the distribution of foraging and competitive skills through the population, both presumably depending partly on the age distribution, and (ii) the relative amounts of different quality feeding areas. In the latter case, several environmental factors other than simple food abundance may affect net rates of food intake and so how many birds feed in an area. In oystercatchers, for example, the list includes the proximity of the mussel bed to the high tide roost and the softness of the substrate and the flesh content and thickness of the shells of the mussels (Durell & Goss-Custard 1984; Goss-Custard *et al.* 1981). Several of these factors are known to affect bird density, and probably do so through their influence on intake rate. The analysis of existing population densities, and the discussion of possible maximum levels, must recognize the variety of factors other than simple food abundance which, by affecting intake rate, influence the attractiveness of a feeding area.

Carrying capacity for flock feeders

The behaviour of dispersed feeders is such that it is necessary to consider the factors in the birds' foraging and social environment which influence the intake rates of individuals and their response to them, to leave or to die. While the same considerations probably apply to individuals foraging within compact flocks, the opportunity for individuals to buffer themselves for long periods would seem to be fewer. In the presumed absence of interference, ceiling densities seem less likely to occur and flocks do not appear to defend feeding areas. In these circumstances, prey depletion over the winter may be a more important source of feedback from bird density to intake rate. However, the current impact of waders on the annual production of their prey seems so low (Hale 1980), and the reproductive rates of the prey so high, that it may normally be more appropriate to think about the effects of prey depletion during one winter as providing the main limit to density. So far, this has not been attempted in waders, and clearly represents another important gap in our knowledge.

In conclusion, the term carrying capacity has been used here in the general sense of the maximum numbers of birds the resources of an area can support, without any implication as to how it can be defined and measured in a specific case. This will depend on species adaptations and ecology. Measuring the density of birds remaining throughout the winter might be appropriate for dispersed waders, whereas measuring total bird-days, spread over a short or long time according to the numbers arriving initially, may be more appropriate for some flocking waders.

ACKNOWLEDGMENTS

I am grateful to Dr J.P. Dempster, B. Ens, Dr M.G. Morris and S.E.A. le V. dit Durell for commenting on the manuscript.

REFERENCES

Baillie, S. (1980). The effect of the hard winter of 1978/79 on the Wader populations of the Ythan estuary. *Wader Study Bulletin*, **28**, 16–17.

Barnard, C.J. & Stephens, H. (1981). Prey size selection by lapwings in lapwing/gull associations. *Behaviour*, **84**, 1–22.

Barnard, C.J., Thompson, D.B.A. & Stephens, H. (1982). Time budgets, feeding efficiency and flock dynamics in mixed species flocks of Lapwings, Golden Plovers and Gulls. *Behaviour*, **80**, 44–69.

Begon, M. (1984). Density and individual fitness: asymmetric competition. *Evolutionary Ecology* (Ed. by B. Shorrocks), pp. 175–194. Blackwell Scientific Publications, Oxford.

Blick, D.J. (1980). *Advantages of flocking in some wintering shorebirds*. Unpublished Ph.D Thesis, University of Michigan.

Burger, J. (1980). Age differences in foraging black-necked stilts in Texas. *Auk*, **97**, 633–636.

Burger, J., Caldwell Hahn D. & Chase, J. (1979). Aggressive interactions in mixed-species flocks of migrating birds. *Animal Behaviour*, **27**, 459–469.

Clarke, N.A. (1982). The effects of the severe weather in December 1981 and January 1982 on waders in Britain. *Wader Study Bulletin*, **34**, 5–7.

Davidson, N.C. (1981). Survival of shorebirds (*Charadrii*) during severe weather: the role of nutritional reserves. *Feeding and Survival Strategies of Estuarine Organisms* (Ed. by N.V. Jones & W.J. Wolff), pp. 231–249. Plenum, London.

Davidson, N.C. (1982). Changes in the body–condition of redshanks during mild winters: an inability to regulate reserves. *Ringing & Migration*, **4**, 51–62.

Davidson, N.C. & Evans, P.R. (1983). Mortality of redshanks and oystercatchers from starvation during severe weather. *Bird Study*, **29**, 183–188.

Dugan, P.J. (1981). The importance of nocturnal foraging in shorebirds: a consequence of increased invertebrate prey activity. *Feeding and Survival Strategies of Estuarine Organisms* (Ed. by N.V. Jones & W.J. Wolff), pp. 251–260. Plenum, London.

Dugan, P.J. (1982). Seasonal changes in patch use by a territorial grey plover: weather-dependent adjustments in foraging behaviour. *Journal of Animal Ecology*, **51**, 849–857.

Dugan, P.J., Evans, P.R., Goodyer, L.R. & Davidson, N.C. (1981). Winter fat reserves in shorebirds: disturbance of regulated levels by severe weather conditions. *Ibis*, **123**, 359–363.

Durell, S.E.A. le V. dit & Goss-Custard, J.D. (1984). Prey selection within a size-class of mussels, *Mytilus edulis*, by oystercatchers, *Haematopus ostralegus*. *Animal Behaviour* (in press).

Ens, B.J. (1984). Feeding territories in Curlews. *Wader Study Bulletin*, **39**, 49.

Ens, B.J. & Goss-Custard, J.D. (1984a). Interference among oystercatchers, *Haematopus ostralegus* L., feeding on mussels, *Mytilus edulis* L., on the Exe estuary. *Journal of Animal Ecology*, **53**, 217–232.

Ens, B.J. & Goss-Custard, J.D. (1984b). Piping as a display of dominance in wintering oystercatchers, *Haematopus ostralegus*. *Ibis* (in press).

Evans, P.R. (1976). Energy balance and optimal foraging strategies in shorebirds: some implications for their distributions and movements in the non-breeding season. *Ardea*, **64**, 117–139.

Evans, P.R. (1979). Adaptations shown by foraging shorebirds to cyclical variations in the activity and availability of their intertidal prey. *Cyclic Phenomena in Marine Plants and Animals* (Ed. by E. Naylor & R.G. Hartnoll), pp. 357–366. Pergamon, Oxford.

Evans, P.R. (1981). Reclamation of intertidal land: some effects on shelduck and wader populations in the Tees estuary. *Verhandling ornithologische Gesellschaft Bayern*, **23**, 147–168.

Evans, P.R. (1984). Introduction to Part 1 of: *Coastal Waders and Wildfowl in Winter* (Ed. by P.R. Evans, J.D. Goss-Custard & W.G. Hale), pp. 3–7. Cambridge University Press, Cambridge.

Evans, P.R. & Dugan, P.J. (1984). Coastal birds—numbers in relation to food resources: a review. *Coastal Waders and Wildfowl in Winter* (Ed. by P.R. Evans, J.D. Goss-Custard & W.G. Hale), pp. 8–28. Cambridge University Press, Cambridge.

Evans, P.R., Henderson, D.M., Knights, P.J. & Pienkowski, M.W. (1979). Short-term effects of reclamation of part of Seal Sands, Teesmouth, on wintering waders and shelduck. *Oecologia*, **41**, 183–206.

Evans, P.R. & Pienkowski, M.P. (1984). Population dynamics of shorebirds. *Behaviour of Marine Animals*, Vol. 5 (Ed. by J. Burger & B.L. Olla), pp. 83–123. Plenum, New York.

Goss-Custard, J.D. (1969). The winter feeding ecology of the redshank *Tringa totanus*. *Ibis*, **111**, 338–356.

Goss-Custard, J.D. (1970a). The responses of redshank (*Tringa totanus*) to spatial variations in the density of their prey. *Journal of Animal Ecology*, **39**, 91–113.

Goss-Custard, J.D. (1970b). Feeding dispersion in some overwintering wading birds. *Social behaviour in Birds and Mammals* (Ed. by J.H. Crook), pp. 3–35. Academic Press, London.

Goss-Custard, J.D. (1976). Variation in the dispersion of redshank, *Tringa totanus*, on their winter feeding grounds. *Ibis*, **118**, 257–263.

Goss-Custard, J.D. (1977a). Optimal foraging and the size selection of worms by redshank, *Tringa totanus*, in the field. *Animal Behaviour*, **25**, 10–29.

Goss-Custard, J.D. (1977b). The ecology of the Wash. III. Density-related behaviour and the possible effects of a loss of feeding grounds on wading birds (*Charadrii*). *Journal of Applied Ecology*, **14**, 721–739.

Goss-Custard, J.D. (1977c). Predator responses and prey mortality in redshank, *Tringa totanus*, and a preferred prey, *Corophium volutator*. *Journal of Animal Ecology*, **46**, 21–35.

Goss-Custard, J.D. (1977d). The energetics of prey selection by redshank, *Tringa totanus* (L.), in relation to prey density. *Journal of Animal Ecology*, **46**, 1–19.

Goss-Custard, J.D. (1980). Competition for food and interference among waders. *Ardea*, **68**, 31–52.

Goss-Custard, J.D. (1981a). Role of winter food supplies in the population ecology of common British wading birds. *Verhandlung ornithologische Gesellschaft Bayern*, **23**, 125–146.

Goss-Custard, J.D. (1981b). Feeding behaviour of redshank, *Tringa totanus*, and optimal foraging theory. *Foraging Behaviour: Ecological, Ethological and Psychological approaches* (Ed. by A.C. Kamil & T.D. Sargent), pp. 115–133. Garland, London.

Goss-Custard, J.D. (1983). Spatial and seasonal variations in the food supply of waders *Charadrii* wintering in the British Isles. *Proceedings of the Third Nordic Congress on Ornithology*, 85–96.

Goss-Custard, J.D. (1984). Intake rates and food supply in migrating and wintering shorebirds. *Behaviour of Marine Animals*, Vol. 6 (Ed. by J. Burger & B.L. Olla), pp. 233–270. Plenum, New York.

Goss-Custard, J.D. & Charman, K. (1976). Predicting how many wintering waterfowl an area can support. *Wildfowl*, **27**, 157–158.

Goss-Custard J.D. & Durell S.E.A. le V. dit (1983). Individual and age differences in the feeding ecology of oystercatchers *Haematopus ostralegus* wintering on the Exe Estuary, Devon. *Ibis*, **125**, 155–171.

Goss-Custard, J.D. & Sutherland, W.J. (1984). Feeding specialisations in oystercatchers *Haematopus ostralegus*. *Animal Behaviour*, **32**, 299–300.

Goss-Custard, J.D., Jenyon, R.A., Jones, R.E., Newberry, P.E. & Williams, R. le B. (1977a). The ecology of the Wash. II. Seasonal variation in the feeding conditions of wading birds (*Charadrii*). *Journal of Applied Ecology*, **14**, 701–719.

Goss-Custard, J.D., Kay, D.G. & Blindell, R.M. (1977b). The density of migratory and overwintering redshank, *Tringa totanus* (L.), and curlew, *Numenius arquata* (L.), in relation to the density of their prey in south-east England. *Estuary, Coastal Marine Science*, **5**, 497–510.

Goss-Custard, J.D., Durell S.E.A. le V. dit, McGrorty, S., Reading, C.J., & Clarke R.T. (1981). Factors affecting the occupation of mussel (*Mytilus edulis*) beds by oystercatchers (*Haematopus ostralegus*) on the Exe Estuary, Devon. *Feeding and Survival Strategies of Estuarine Organisms* (Ed. by N.V. Jones & W.J. Wolff), pp. 217–229. Plenum, London.

Goss-Custard, J.D., Durell S.E.A. le V. dit, Sitters, H.P. & Swinfen, R. (1982a). Age structure and survival of a wintering population of oystercatchers. *Bird Study*, **29**, 83–98.

Goss-Custard J.D., Durell, S.E.A. le V. dit & Ens, B.J. (1982b). Individual differences in aggressiveness and food stealing among wintering oystercatchers, *Haematopus ostralegus* L. *Animal Behaviour*, **30**, 917–928.

Goss-Custard J.D., Durell, S.E.A. le V. dit, McGrorty, S. & Reading, C.J. (1982c). Use of mussel *Mytilus edulis* beds by oystercatchers *Haematopus ostralegus* according to age and population size. *Journal of Animal Ecology*, **51**, 543–554.

Goss-Custard, J.D., Clarke, R.T. & Durell, S.E.A. le V. dit (1984). Rates of food intake and aggression of oystercatchers *Haematopus ostralegus* on the most and least preferred mussel *Mytilus edulis* beds of the Exe Estuary. *Journal of Animal Ecology*, **53**, 233–246.

Goss-Custard, J.D., Nicholson, A.M. & Winterbottom, S. (1984). Prey depletion inside and outside redshank, *Tringa totanus*, territories. *Animal Behaviour* (in press).

Groves, S. (1978). Age-related differences in ruddy turnstone foraging and aggressive behaviour. *Auk*, **95**, 95–103.

Hale, W.G. (1980). *Waders*. Collins, London.

Harrington, B.A. & Groves, S. (1977). Aggression in foraging migrant Semipalmated Sandpipers. *Wilson Bulletin*, **89**, 336–338.

Hartwick, E.B. (1976). Foraging strategy of the Black Oystercatcher (*Haematopus bachmani* Audubon). *Canadian Journal of Zoology*, **54**, 147–155.

Have, T.M. van der, Nieboer, E. & Boere, G.C. (1984). Age-related distribution of dunlin, *Calidris alpina*, in the Dutch Waddenzee, *Coastal Waders and Wildfowl in winter* (Eds. by P.R. Evans, J.D. Goss-Custard & W.G. Hale), pp. 160–176. Cambridge University Press.

Heppleston, P.B. (1971). The feeding ecology of Oystercatchers (*Haematopus ostralegus* L.) in winter in Northern Scotland. *Journal of Animal Ecology*, **40**, 651–672.

Horwood, J. & Goss-Custard, J.D. (1977). Predation by the Oystercatcher, *Haematopus ostralegus* (L.), in relation to the cockle, *Cerastoderma edule* (L.), fishing in the Burry Inlet, South Wales. *Journal of Applied Ecology*, **14**, 139–158.

Hulscher, J.B. (1982). The oystercatcher as a predator of *Macoma*. *Ardea*, **70**, 89–152.

Krebs, J.R. & Davies N. (1981). *An introduction to behavioural ecology*. Blackwell Scientific Publications, Oxford.

Krebs, J.R., Stephens, D.W. & Sutherland, W.J. (1983). Perspectives in optimal foraging. *Perspectives in Ornithology*, pp. 165–221. Cambridge University Press, Cambridge.

Kus, B. (1984). Age-related mortality in a wintering population of dunlin. *Auk* (in press).

Laursen, K., Gram, I. & Alberto, L.J. (1983). Short-term effect of reclamation on numbers and distribution of waterfowl at Højer, Danish Wadden Sea. *Proceedings of Third Nordic Congress on Ornithology*, 97–118.

Metcalfe, N.B. & Furness, R.W. (1984). Changing priorities: the effect of pre-migratory fattening on the trade-off between foraging and vigilance. *Behavioural Ecology and Sociobiology* (in press).

Metcalfe, N.B. (1984a). The effects of mixed species flocking on the vigilance of shorebirds: who do they trust. *Animal Behaviour* (in press).

Metcalfe, NB. (1984b). The effects of habitat on the vigilance of shorebirds: is visibility important? *Animal Behaviour* (in press).

Myers, J.P. (1984). Spacing behaviour of non-breeding shorebirds. *Behaviour of Marine Animals*, Vol. 6 (Ed. by J. Burger), pp. 271–321. Plenum, New York.

Myers, J.P., Connors, P.G. & Pitelka, F.A. (1979a). Territory size in wintering Sanderlings: the effects of prey abundance and intruder density. *Auk*, **96**, 551–561.

Myers, J.P., Connors, P.G. & Pitelka, F.A. (1979b). Territoriality in non-breeding shorebirds. *Studies in Avian Biology*, **2**, 231–246.

Myers, J.P., Connors, P.G. & Pitelka, F.A. (1980). Optimal territory size and the sanderling: compromises in a variable environment. *Mechanisms of Foraging Behaviour* (Ed. by A.C. Kamil & T.D. Sargent), pp. 135–158. Garland Press, New York.

Norton-Griffiths, M. (1968). *The feeding behaviour of the oystercatcher* Haematopus ostralegus. Unpublished Ph.D Thesis, University of Oxford.

O'Connor, R. & Cawthorne, A. (1982). How Britain's birds survived the winter. *New Scientist*, **93**, 786–788.

Page, G. & Whittacre, D.F. (1975). Raptor predation on wintering shorebirds. *Condor*, **77**, 73–83.

Pienkowski, M.P. (1981). How foraging plovers cope with environmental effects on invertebrate behaviour and availability. *Feeding and Survival Strategies of Estuarine Organisms* (Ed. by N.V. Jones & W.J. Wolff), pp. 179–192. Plenum, London.

Pienkowski, M.W. (1983). Changes in the foraging pattern of plovers in relation to environmental factors. *Animal Behaviour*, **31**, 244–264.

Pienkowski, M.W., Ferns, P.N., Davidson, N.C. & Worrall, D.H. (1984). Balancing the budget: measuring the energy intake and requirements of shorebirds in the field. *Coastal Waders and Wildfowl in Winter* (Ed. by P.R. Evans, J.D. Goss-Custard & W.G. Hale), pp. 29–56. Cambridge University Press, Cambridge.

Prater, A.J. (1981). *Estuary Birds of Britain and Ireland*. Poyser, Calton.

Puttick, G.M. (1979). Foraging behaviour and activity budgets of curlew sandpipers. *Ardea*, **67**, 111–122.

Puttick, G.M. (1981). Sex-related differences in foraging behaviour of Curlew Sandpipers. *Ornis Scandinavia*, **12**, 13–17.

Quammen, M.L. (1980). *The impact of predation by shorebirds, benthic feeding fish and a crab on the shallow living invertebrates in intertidal mudflats of two southern Californian lagoons.* Unpublished Ph.D Thesis, University of California, Irvine.

Reading, C.J. & McGrorty, S. (1978). Seasonal variation in the burying depth of *Macoma balthica* (L.) and its accessibility to wading birds. *Estuary Coastal and Marine Science*, **6**, 135–144.

Recher, H.F. & Recher, J.A. (1969). Some aspects of the ecology of migrant shorebirds. II. Aggression. *Wilson Bulletin*, **81**, 140–154.

Safriel, U.N. (1981). Social hierarchy among siblings in broods of the oystercatcher *Haematopus ostralegus*. *Behavioural Ecology & Sociobiology*, **9**, 59–63.

Schneider, D.C. & Harrington, B.A. (1981). Timing of shorebird migration in relation to prey depletion. *Auk*, **98**, 801–811.

Smith, P.C. (1975). *A study of the winter feeding ecology and behaviour of the Bar-tailed Godwit* (Limosa lapponica). Unpublished Ph.D. Thesis, University of Durham.

Sutherland, W.J. (1982a). Do oystercatchers select the most profitable cockles? *Animal Behaviour*, **30**, 857–861.

Sutherland, W.J. (1982b). Spatial variations in the predation of cockles by oystercatchers at Traeth Melynog, Anglesey. II. The pattern of predation. *Journal of Animal Ecology*, **51**, 491–500.

Sutherland, W.J. & Koene, P. (1982). Field estimates of the strength of interference between oystercatchers *Haematopus ostralegus*. *Oecologia*, **55**, 108–109.

Swennen, C. (1984). Differences in mean quality between roosting flocks of oystercatchers. *Coastal Waders and Wildfowl in Winter* (Ed. by P.R. Evans, J.D. Goss-Custard & W.G. Hale), pp. 177–189. Cambridge University Press, Cambridge.

Swennen, C., de Bruijn, L.L.M., Duiven, P., Leopold, M.F. & Marteijn, E.C.L. (1983). Differences in bill form of the oystercatcher *Haematopus ostralegus;* a dynamic adaptation to specific foraging techniques. *Netherlands Journal of Sea Research*, **17**, 57–83.

Thompson, D.B.A. (1983). Prey assessment by plovers (*Charadriidae*): net rate of energy intake and vulnerability to kleptoparasites. *Animal Behaviour*, **31**, 1226–1236.

Thompson, D.B.A. & Barnard, C.J. (1984). Prey selection by plovers: optimal foraging in mixed species groups. *Animal Behaviour*, **32**, 554–563.

Townshend, D.J. (1981). The importance of field feeding to the survival of wintering male and female curlews *Numenius arquata* on the Tees estuary. *Feeding and Survival Strategies of Estuarine Organisms* (Ed. by N.V. Jones & W.J. Wolff), pp. 261–273. Plenum, London.

Townshend, D.J. (1984). The effects of predators upon shorebird populations in the non-breeding season. *Wader Study Bulletin* (in press).

Townshend, D.J., Dugan, P.J. & Pienkowski, M.W. (1984). The unsociable plover—use of space by grey plovers, *Pluvialis squatarola*. In *Coastal Waders and Wildfowl in Winter* (Ed. by P.R. Evans, J.D. Goss-Custard & W.G. Hale), pp. 140–159. Cambridge University Press, Cambridge.

Vines, G. (1980). Spatial consequences of aggressive behaviour in flocks of oystercatchers, *Haematopus ostralegus* L. *Animal Behaviour*, **28**, 1175–1183.

Wanink, J. & Zwarts, L. (1984). The functional response of an optimally foraging oystercatcher. *Wader Study Bulletin*, **39**, 45.

Worrall, D.H. (1984). Seasonal changes in the spacing pattern of feeding dunlins. *Wader Study Bulletin*, **39**, 41.

Zwarts, L. (1974). Vogels van het brakke getijgebied. *Bondsuitgeverij*, Amsterdam.

Zwarts, L. (1978). Intra- and interspecific competition for space in estuarine bird species in a one-prey situation. *International Ornithological Congress*, **17**, 1045–1050.

Zwarts, L. & Drent, R.H. (1981). Prey depletion and the regulation of predator density: oystercatchers (*Haematopus ostralegus*) feeding on mussels (*Mytilus edulis*). *Feeding and Survival Strategies of Estuarine Organisms* (Ed. by N.V. Jones & W.J. Wolff), pp. 193–216. Plenum, London.

Zwarts, L. & Wanink, J. (1984). How oystercatchers and curlews successively deplete clams. *Coastal Waders and Wildfowl in Winter* (Ed. by P.R. Evans, J.D. Goss-Custard & W.G. Hale), pp. 69–83. Cambridge University Press, Cambridge.

10. LEARNING TO EXPLOIT PATCHILY DISTRIBUTED FOOD

A. KACELNIK and J. R. KREBS
Edward Grey Institute, Department of Zoology, University of Oxford

SUMMARY

The distribution of predators with respect to prey availability is a joint function of current prey distribution and of the history of the system. The nature of this function is likely to be related to the learning processes of individual predators. We discuss some descriptive models of learning about food availability which rely on a weighted average of past and present experience.

We argue that the widely used linear operator model of learning can give interesting insights into the exploitation of stable or gradually changing food sources. For example, in a depleting environment learning may result in a maximum spatial aggregation of predators at times when prey distribution is equal in all patches.

Three experimental examples are discussed in detail:
(a) A group of sticklebacks exploiting non-depleting patches (Milinski 1984);
(b) A group of goldfish exploiting gradually depleting patches (Lester 1984);
(c) Individual starlings exploiting patches that can deplete suddenly (Kacelnik, Krebs & Ens, in press).

Models based on simple averages of past and present experience (like the linear operator model) are insufficient to describe some important features of the way changes in food availability are detected by experimental animals. In particular these models do not show the more rapid detection of sudden depletion when the patch has a history of higher profitability. A *post hoc* descriptive model that has this property is suggested.

INTRODUCTION

The behaviour of predators, especially their level of aggregation in relation to the spatial distribution of their prey, is a crucial factor in the dynamics of predator–prey interactions (Hassell & May 1973, 1974; Murdoch & Oaten 1975).

In general, if prey are clumped and predators aggregate or otherwise intensify their rate of predation disproportionately in areas (patches) of high prey density (as indeed they are known to do, Hassell 1978), the range of values of prey rate of increase for which the interaction is stable is extended. In other words, predators' overexploitation of high prey density patches promotes stability.

This aspect of the functional response was discussed by Hassell & May (1973). Their analysis of the effect on population stability supported the idea that aggregation promotes stability: the greater the aggregation, the larger the range of prey parameters for which the system remains stable. Hassell's and May's discussion, though, was based on the very unrealistic assumption that predators would continue foraging in overexploited patches, rather than redistribute themselves tracking the changes in prey distribution. In a further development, Comins & Hassell (1979) incorporated optimality to the predators' behaviour by assuming that foraging would always be concentrated in the patch or patches of highest prey density. This pattern of predation would continuously drive the system towards spatial homogeneity, but the results for the dynamics of the system were qualitatively similar to those obtained by Hassell's and May's original model. While the inclusion of optimality at individual level increased realism, a number of serious unrealistic assumptions remained, the importance of which is hard to establish a priori. For example, predators were assumed to maximize capture rate, which is only one of a number of possible currencies (see for example Cheverton, Kacelnik & Krebs 1984; Sih 1984; Houston 1985), between-patch transit time and handling time were both assumed to be zero, and predator adjustment to changes in prey distributions was assumed to be instantaneous, i.e. predators were assumed to be omniscient. In the rest of this paper we shall restrict ourselves to this last question. The assumption of fully informed predators is a very common one, but in spite of having been acknowledged as an important source of error for some time in the optimality literature it has not yet been modified in analyses of predator–prey systems stability—nor, for that matter, in the bulk of optimal foraging models.

The problem has many facets, and can be tackled both from an optimality perspective (i.e. what rules informationally-constrained predators should use in order to maximize a given currency), and from a descriptive point of view, based on how animals are known to behave or are supposed to behave with respect to changes in food availabilities. In this paper we shall review some developments on the latter perspective, on the basis of three studies of learning in the laboratory: Milinski 1984, Lester 1984, and Kacelnik, Krebs & Ens, in press. The three studies used environments where food availability (i) did not change, (ii) changed slowly due to depletion and (iii) changed abruptly due to independent causes, respectively.

Our aim is very limited: we simply want to illustrate the difficulties that arise in modelling fairly elementary processes of learning and to point out some of the issues emerging from these attempts which may be significant at the population level.

LEARNING MODELS

Models of learning are algorithms that express behaviour as a function of previous experience. Real-life learning is a phenomenon with multiple manifestations, including acquisition of skills, improvement of sensory capabilities (as in search image formation) etc., but we will consider only one limited aspect of learning, i.e. learning about prey availability.

One obvious source of information for how models of learning can be developed is the psychological literature on operant behaviour in the laboratory. The main problem in searching the literature for suitable learning models involving situations of ecological relevance is that most models of behavioural allocation relate to equilibrium conditions, i.e. they describe how experimental animals allocate behaviour to various alternatives once this allocation becomes stable. We are mainly interested in models of *acquisition* (how predators adjust to changes in rate or reinforcement). The acquisition problem has been approached using optimality models, as in the studies of the two-armed bandit (Krebs, Kacelnik & Taylor 1978; Harley 1981; Houston, Kacelnik & McNamara 1982), and using descriptive models, aimed at representing more or less accurately how animals do behave. We are concerned here with descriptive models, but of course functional implications will be addressed.

A simple and widely used behavioural allocation model is the so-called *linear operator*, which is a linear function expressing allocation of behaviour between behavioural alternatives as a weighted average of past and present experience. The linear operator is a discrete time model first used by Bush & Mosteller (1955), and has the following general structure:

$$P_i(t+1) = aQ(t) + (1-a)P_i(t) \quad 0 < P < 1, 0 < a < 1 \tag{1}$$

where P is a variable associated with option i (P can heuristically be thought of as the predators' estimate of rate of capture in patch i); Q is a measure of present reward rate, normally the number of rewards obtained in stage t; a is the memory factor, which determines the relative weight of past and current experience.

There have been a number of versions of this model, including those considered by Bush & Mosteller themselves, and those by Pulliam & Dunford

(1980), Harley (1981), Killeen (1982, 1984), Lester (1984), Regelmann (1984), and others. In the original model, P expressed the probability of responding in alternative i on trial $t+1$ and Q was defined as either 1 or 0, depending on whether a reward was obtained or not in stage t. This was a very parsimonious, purely behaviourist attempt to describe behaviour. Most other versions have split the problem into two stages, namely:

(a) updating information about the alternatives (state updating);

(b) allocation of behaviour according to this information (decision rule).

In order to update information, models usually postulate a set of state variables, each one representing a behavioural option (e.g. feeding in a particular place). The variable corresponding to each option is updated recursively at every step according to a version of the linear operator. Behaviour is allocated using a function of these state variables, the simplest of all being to respond to the option with the highest value. Two variants of the state-updating mechanism are as follows.

1 The 'step' of the updating process can be a time interval (Killeen 1982; Lester 1984; Regelmann 1984) or one individual response (Pulliam & Dunford 1980; Houston *et al.* 1982).

2 A 'residual' value can be assigned to each option, such that the state variable associated with that option approaches this value when no rewards are obtained from a patch for a long time or the patch has never been visited by the predator (Harley 1981; Regelmann 1984).

Regarding the *decision rule* relating state variables to behaviour, the most common alternative to straightforward maximization is a form of 'matching', which postulates that the proportion of responses to each alternative equals the quotient between the state variable for that alternative and the sum of the state variables for all the available options.

Predictions from learning models can be either 'molar', when they refer to overall distribution of behaviour after a certain number of responses, or 'molecular' when the predictions are about the expected allocation of behaviour step by step. The descriptive accuracy of the sort of model described above has been tested in simple laboratory experiments, usually consisting of a choice between two feeding sites offering different schedules of reinforcement. The three cases that we discuss in this paper follow this general pattern.

EXPERIMENTAL TESTS OF THE LINEAR OPERATOR

Milinski's sticklebacks

One especially relevant learning model, which has been the focus of considerable attention in recent years, is the so-called relative pay-off sum rule, or RPS rule for short. This model was developed by Harley (1981) and discussed extensively by Maynard-Smith (1982, 1984). It was presented as a realistic approximation to an evolutionarily stable learning rule. Thus, the rule was proposed on the grounds of functional arguments, and only later was investigated as a descriptive model. There is disagreement about some aspects of the optimality arguments of Harley and Maynard-Smith (Houston *et al.* 1982; Harley 1983; Houston 1983; Krebs & Kacelnik 1984), but here we only consider the problem of how well the RPS describes the behaviour of experimental animals.

In this section we describe Regelmann's (1984) version of the RPS model and its fit to Milinski's (1984) data with sticklebacks. In Milinski's 1984 experiment, a group of six fish in a tank faced two sources of food (patches), one at each extreme of the tank. One patch was twice as good as the other in terms of food availability, and thus the prediction based on the ideal free distribution (Fretwell & Lucas 1970) is that if all fish have equal competitive abilities they ought to distribute themselves so that twice as many fish exploit the good patch as exploit the poor one. The ideal free distribution prediction had been verified for sticklebacks earlier by Milinski (1979), but in the 1984 experiment he recorded the experience of individual fish and hence the data were appropriate for testing molecular predictions of behavioural mechanisms.

The RPS rule is defined as:

$$V_i(t+1) = aV_i(t) + (1-a)R_i + Q_i(t) \qquad (2)$$

where V is the state variable for patch i at time $t+1$. V is not identical to P in eqn (1), but can be thought of as the 'subjective value' of patch i for the predator: R is the 'residual' subjective value of patch i before any reward was obtained there or a long time after the last reward in the patch; t is the unit of the updating mechanism. In Regelmann's version t is an arbitrary time interval, which was set as 2 seconds for comparisons with Milinski's data; a, Q are as in eqn (1).

The main difference between RPS and other versions of the linear operator is the presence of a 'residual' or prior estimate of reward rate. When no reward is obtained in a given patch for some time (regardless of whether the patch was visited or not), the corresponding state variable V_i drops to the value of the residual, instead of dropping to zero as in other versions. Also note that the state variable is not equivalent to a reward probability, since it can take values bigger than 1, but it still reflects the attractiveness of each patch. The range of possible values of Q, the reward during interval t, depends on how the time interval is defined. If V is updated every response, Q is either 1 or 0, but if t is an arbitrary time span, as in Regelmann's implementation, Q can take any non-negative value.

Regelmann (1984) presented Monte Carlo simulations for the conditions of Milinski's experiment, assuming that each fish behaved according to the RPS rule. Milinski used two kinds of feeding schedule, with either regular or irregular delivery of prey, and Regelmann implemented two forms of simulation, with and without the inclusion of travel times. We restrict the discussion that follows to Regelmann's simulation with travel time and Milinski's experiment with irregular supply of food, because we believe that these are the more realistic examples.

Both the RPS rule as implemented by Regelmann and the experimental fish reached equilibrium close to the predicted ideal free distribution. Furthermore, it was also true that, even though the ideal free distribution assumption of equal competitive ability between individuals was violated, both good and poor competitors ended up near the appropriate distributions, good competitors reaching equilibrium faster than poor ones (the equilibrium distribution of poor competitors is discussed further below). This delay in stabilization of the distribution of poor competitors happens because food availability for good competitors reflects food density, but food availability for poor competitors is also dependent on the distribution of dominant animals. In Regelmann's simulations, poor and good competitors were implemented by assigning a given probability of capturing a prey when several fish were present; this probability was measured directly in the experimental fish. Figure 10.1 shows the results of simulations and experiments.

A difficulty in the interpretation of these results is that predicted outcomes are very close to random expectations. Actually Regelmann's predictions for good competitors (Fig. 10.1a, top) and Milinski's results for poor competitors (Fig. 10.1b, bottom) are virtually indistinguishable from a random distribution. The near-random distribution of poor fish is not surprising: if good competitors are much better than bad ones, after good competitors have distributed themselves according to the ideal free distribution, remaining food availability in both patches ought to be equal in both patches. If this is the case, the 'ideal free' prediction for poor competitors is to exploit equally both sides. The systematic underexploitation of the better patch in the models' predictions for good competitors is more worrying, and may indicate a failure of the molar predictions of the model. Both good and bad competitors switched more often between patches in the first than in the second half of the test, in agreement with the progression from exploration to exploitation predicted on functional grounds by Krebs et al. (1978). In fact, the experimental results with good competitors show a dramatic reduction in variance as the test proceeds, and a mean which is exactly as predicted, while

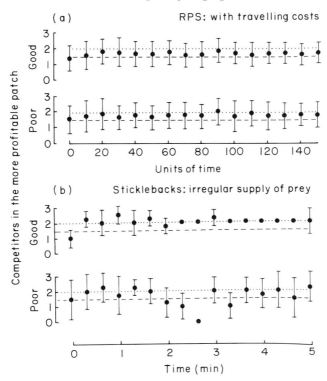

FIG. 10.1. Milinski's experiment on the distribution of six sticklebacks between two patches with a 2:1 profitability ratio, and results from Regelmann's Monte Carlo simulations for the same situation. Both model fish (a) and real subjects (b) are divided into three-fish groups of good (top) and poor (bottom) competitiveness. The dotted line shows the prediction of the ideal free distribution and the broken line is the random expectation. (From Milinski 1984; Regelmann 1984.)

the model has greater variance and a systematic bias towards under-exploitation of the better patch.

Further, even if both fish and model had reached the equilibrium distribution predicted on functional grounds, this would not be absolute evidence that both were reaching this distribution using the same rule. A number of rules would produce very similar outcomes for this problem, and thus it is necessary to compare the details of actual behaviour to test RPS as a decision mechanism. Milinski did this by calculating the probability of a switch between patches every 2 seconds according to the RPS rule and plotting this value against the observed behaviour. The linear relationship between the observed and predicted probabilities of switching is very good (see Fig. 10.2), which supports the possibility of use by the animals of a rule of this type.

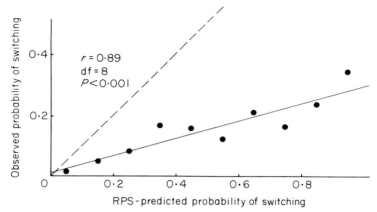

FIG. 10.2. Test of the molecular predictions of the RPS rule for Milinski's experiment. Observed probability of a switch between patches every 2 seconds (———) and expected probability of a switch from RPS rule (- - -). (From Milinski 1984.)

Nevertheless, as Fig. 10.2 shows, the absolute value of the predictions is about twice as large as the data, indicating that while the allocation rule might be related to the linear operator, it is definitely not the RPS rule. Another quite direct way of testing this point is to compare the total number of switches shown by the fish and the model. The predictions presented by Regelmann and the data from Milinski are shown in Fig. 10.3.

It can be seen that the fish switched between patches about half as many times as the model. Milinski suggested that the difference could be due to the

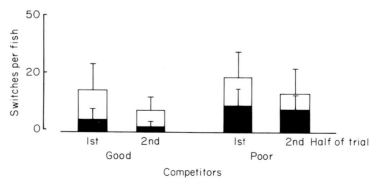

FIG. 10.3. Test of molar predictions of RPS rule for Milinski's experiment. Number of switches between patches in the first and second half of each session for the experimental fish (black bars) and the RPS rule (open bars). (From Milinski 1984 and Regelmann 1984.)

specific (arbitrary) parameters used in the simulation. But the parameters ($a = 0.97$, $R = 0.5$) were chosen because they fitted the appropriate stability criterion (Milinski 1984, p. 238), and therefore it is unlikely that a different set of parameters would behave more like the fish.

In conclusion, the RPS rule does reach a similar equilibrium distribution, but seems to use more sampling than the actual predators. Whether or not it is safe to incorporate the RPS rule into population models depends on whether we are interested in the timing of adjustment of predators to changes in prey distribution. Brian Sumida and Alasdair Houston (pers. com.) have simulated the same problem using some of the other rules discussed by Houston *et al.* (1982), and found that other rules converged to the same equilibrium distribution and in addition were closer to the actual switching behaviour than Harley's RPS rule.

Lester's goldfish

In Lester's (1984) experiments, groups of goldfish were allowed to forage for some time in a tank divided into two areas, each of them with a certain amount of food available initially. The amount of food provided at the beginning of the tests was such that the fish's feeding produced considerable depletion during the period of observation. Lester's question was 'What pattern will the movements of fish follow as depletion takes place?'. He used the classical version of the linear operator (eqn (1)), but modified so that *t* was expressed in time instead of responses, *P* was an estimate of profitability (prey/time) and *Q* was the profitability experienced in a given patch in a given interval. A peculiarity of this version is that steps of the updating mechanism are divisible in terms of behavioural allocation: instead of deciding which side to exploit, the subject is assumed to decide what fraction of the time during the next step is to be allocated to each patch. In other words, the predator can use more than one patch between two points of state updating. The decision rule used by Lester is:

$$T_i(t+1) = \frac{P_i(t)}{\Sigma_j P_j(t)} \qquad (3)$$

where *T* is the proportion of time spent in patch *i* during the time span $t+1$.

For the two-patch situation, eqn (3) becomes

$$\frac{T_1(t+1)}{T_2(t+1)} = \frac{P_1(t)}{P_2(t)} \qquad (4)$$

Lester's emphasis is on the fact that if patch choice is controlled by this kind of rule, preference cannot be predicted from knowledge of instantaneous conditions of food availability. Instead, patch preference (hence predator distribution) will depend on the history of the system. In particular, preference for a given patch (T_i) will continue to increase as long as that patch yields higher capture rate than the alternative, will remain constant (at whichever bias it has developed previously) while food availability is equal in both places, and will start to decrease as soon as the other patch becomes more profitable. This behaviour implies that when preference returns to a point of indifference, a substantial heterogeneity in food availability has been established, and the system will oscillate. Oscillations would result from a number of models involving time lags, but it is interesting that Lester's prediction was that preference should peak when food availabilities are equal. In other words, for the two-patch system with depletion, *maximum heterogeneity in predator distribution will coincide temporally with minimum heterogeneity in prey distribution*, a prediction quite opposed to expectations from considering only equilibrium conditions.

Figure 10.4 shows that the goldfish distribution did oscillate. By calculating the time that the fish took to reach these peaks in the two patches, Lester could show that the prediction of equal density at points of extreme bias was not far from the observed pattern. There are problems with Lester's study though. Perhaps the most serious is that his version of the linear operator uses an arbitrary interval during which both patches are experienced to some degree, and thus it is not really a model that can produce molecular predictions, i.e. single choices. Lester got around this problem by testing his animals in a group. In this way he could measure the number of fish-minutes in each patch for a given time interval, and implicitly assume that this global outcome describes how each fish takes decisions, perhaps not a fully watertight assumption.

Response of starlings to sudden depletion

Kacelnik *et al.* (in press) investigated whether or not the same kind of reward averaging model that was moderately successful in the previous examples might also apply to predators learning about a sudden change in the availability of resources, such as might occur for a swallow feeding on insects emerging from a pond if emergence stops, or for a touch-feeding wader if polychaetes retreat below an accessible level in the mud. In their experiment, Kacelnik *et al.* used three starlings held in individual cages and having access to two operant feeding devices ('patches'), one at each end of the cage. The birds obtained food in the patches by hopping on a perch by the feeder, as a result of which food was delivered at random on a predetermined proportion of responses. Between each response the birds had to operate a central perch

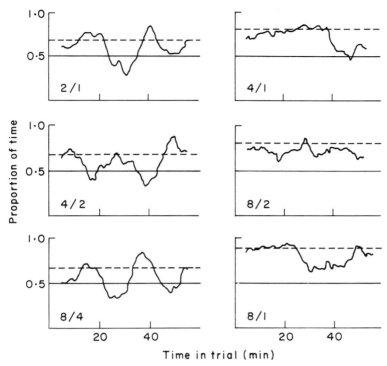

Fig. 10.4. Lester's (1984) experiment on the distribution of six goldfish between two depleting patches. The figure shows the proportion of time spent in the initially better patch. Amounts of food initially available in each patch are shown in the two numbers in each graph. The broken line represents the expected ideal free proportions at the beginning of the session.

mid-way between both patches to reload the feeders. This requirement was included to make successive choices independent: at each choice the two patches were equidistant from the bird. The birds lived continuously in the cages and during the experimental sessions they obtained all their food from the patches. The protocol for a session was as follows. At the start the two patches had reward probabilities of either 0·75 and 0·08 or (in another treatment) 0·25 and 0·08. These reward probabilities remained stable for about 1 day, until the birds had learned which of the two patches offered the higher reward probability and their choices had stabilized. At equilibrium (which was reached after more responses in the 0·25–0·08 than in the 0·75–0·08 treatment) about 98–99% of choices were made to the better patch in both treatments. After a minimum number of rewards had been obtained the reward probability in the better patch was changed to zero at an unsignalled, random moment during the second day of the session. The alternative patch remained unchanged with 0·08 probability of reward.

Figure 10.5 shows the average response of the three birds to this change. As might be expected, the birds after some time shifted their allocation of responses from the patch that was formerly the better one to the stable alternative, now the better place. In other words, the birds recognized the change in pay-off and eventually responded appropriately. The shift in preference was more rapid in the treatment with a change from 0·75 to zero than in the 0·25 to zero treatment (for statistical details see Kacelnik *et al.*, in press). This result is the opposite of the predictions from Harley's (Fig. 10.6a) and Lester's models (Fig. 10.6b).

Figure 10.6c shows the predictions of an alternative learning model which is more successful in describing the data. The model, which is described in detail elsewhere (Kacelnik *et al.* in press), has two components in determining the probability of choosing any particular patch: (a) a linear operator estimate of reward probability and (b) an estimate of 'confidence' that the value of the

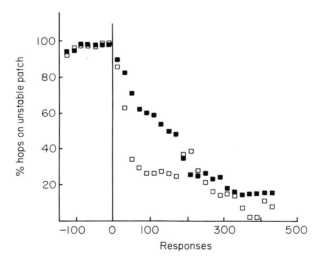

FIG. 10.5. The experiment by Kacelnik *et al.* (in press) on the changes in patch preference by starlings after the preferred of two patches suddenly ceased to deliver rewards. The points are the means of three birds with ten replicates, and represent scores for bins of ten consecutive responses. Open symbols correspond to an initial reward probability in the unstable patch of 0·75 and black symbols correspond to an initial probability of 0·25. The stable patch had a probability of reward of 0·08 in both treatments. The vertical line indicates the point when the high probability patch ceased to give rewards. The birds took longer to develop the almost exclusive preference for the unstable patch for the 0·25 than the 0·75 treatment, but this difference is not seen in this figure because all tests are synchronized at the point of the change to zero reward probability in the preferred patch.

patch has not changed to zero. The implication of the confidence component is that the birds' choices reflect the general nature of the experiment (i.e. they 'know' that a sudden drop in reward probability may occur). Each time a reward is obtained in a given patch the confidence value is set to 1 (i.e. the bird

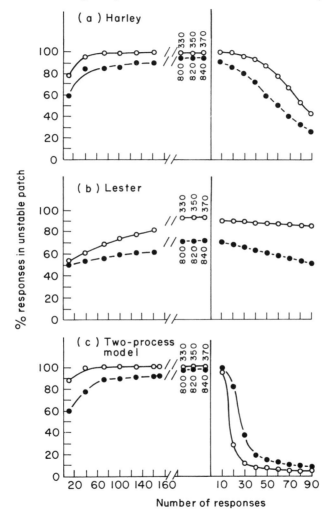

FIG. 10.6. Performance of three learning models in Monte Carlo simulations of the experiment described in Fig. 10.5. (a) Harley's RPS rule; (b) Lester's rule; (c) dual process model of Kacelnik *et al.* (in press). Each model is shown with parameters chosen to approximate the experimental results, but systematic parameter searching was not done. Amount of experience before the change was adjusted to the average experience of experimental animals.

is certain that the change to zero reward probability has not yet occurred); if no reward is obtained after a given response, the animals confidence decreases in a way that is related to the probability of failing to obtain a reward under the previous estimate of reward probability. Thus, for a patch with an estimated reward probability of 1 before the change, confidence will drop to zero after a single failure. Confidence is modelled as follows:

$$C_i(t+1) = C_i(t) \cdot (1 - P_i(t))^n \qquad (5)$$

where $C_i(t)$ is the confidence in patch i after the tth response; P_i is the estimated reward probability of that patch according to the linear operator (eqn (1)) and n is the number of successive failures during a run of bad luck: t is here measured in responses.

The 'attractiveness' A of each patch before each choice is determined by the estimated reward probability multiplied by confidence scaled with an exponent κ.

$$A_i(t) = P_i(t) \cdot C_i(t)^\kappa \qquad (6)$$

Unlike the linear operator, this model can respond rapidly to drops in reward probability: if the value of P is big, confidence diminishes rapidly as a result of a run of bad luck. In the output of the model shown in Fig. 10.6c the decision rule is to choose the patch with highest attractiveness.

DISCUSSION

What general conclusions can we draw from these three examples? We shall refer briefly to three questions: (a) what is the status of the models of learning currently being developed; (b) how successful are they in describing actual learning processes and (c) does all this matter to models of predator–prey interactions?

The first general point to be made about the models that we have presented is that they are essentially descriptive. They are neither detailed causal models of the processes that control animals' choices (c.f. Herrnstein & Vaughan 1980; Hinson & Staddon 1983; Commons, Kacelnik & Shettleworth, in press) nor functional models: they do not prescribe optimal learning strategies.

In some situations a particular learning rule obtains a nearly maximal pay-off (see Houston *et al.* 1982), but the rules are not derived a priori as rules to maximize. Harley's rule is an exception in that it has been claimed to be an evolutionarily stable learning strategy, which in the kind of problems analysed here is equivalent to a strategy maximizing pay-off (Harley 1981, 1983; Maynard-Smith 1982, 1984), but these claims have been questioned on various grounds (Houston 1983; Krebs & Kacelnik 1984). A start has been made in developing prescriptive optimal learning rules, but only for very simple learning problems (Krebs *et al.* 1978; McNamara & Houston 1980; Stephens 1982). In general, those models specify a policy for sampling alternative patches or prey in terms of the potential value of the information acquired by sampling, and not only on the basis of the immediate energetic gain. Nevertheless, from the point of view of the population biologist, descriptive models are what is required to predict the dynamics of multi-species systems (e.g. Hassell & May, p. 3).

Second, let us consider the success of the models in describing how animals adjust to exploiting patchily distributed food. Milinski's and Lester's work shows that models of the linear operator type have some success in describing the allocation of effort by individual predators when food availability is either stable or changing slowly due to depletion. Nevertheless, when the quantitative details of individual choices were analysed in the simpler of the two cases (i.e. stable environment), the particular version of the linear operator used, namely Harley's RPS rule as implemented by Regelmann (1984), performed poorly, switching between patches twice as much as the animals. In addition, neither the RPS rule nor Lester's rule predicted the more rapid rejection of a previously higher profitability patch shown by the starlings in the experiment of Kacelnik *et al*. Models that base choices on averaging past and present reward rate tend to require a longer run of failures before they abandon richer patches, the opposite of the well established psychological phenomenon known as partial reinforcement extinction effect (PREE) (see Tarpy 1982 for a review of PREE and McNamara & Houston (1980) and Houston *et al.* (1982) for a discussion of the informational problems involved). It appears from the starling experiment that starlings do more than simply average past and present reward rate with a certain relative weight: they also learn to respond to the general nature of the environmental changes that they encounter. The dual process model used by Kacelnik *et al*. is obviously not a unique way of fitting the starling data, but points to the kind of variables that successful models may need to include. To summarize, it is still uncertain how general is the descriptive power of currently available learning models, but there can be little doubt that predator distribution will somehow depend on the history of the system and not just on instantaneous prey densities. And this brings us to the final point: how relevant are these studies of learning by individual predators to the dynamics of predator–prey systems?

Current models of aggregation assume that predators distribute themselves at all times according to a given function of prey distribution, and density-dependent predation results from this distribution. It is an open question whether more realistic description of the way individual predators learn will alter qualitatively the outcome of currently available population models. A hint that the answer might be positive comes from the work by Lester (1984), analysed above. In his experiments, predators were most aggregated when the two patches were equal in food density, quite the opposite of the expected behaviour of omniscient predators.

Finally, there is one further limitation of the models discussed so far that deserves comment. Predation pressure depends not only on where predators are but also on how actively they forage, i.e. what proportion of time they allocate to foraging as opposed to other activities. Intensity of foraging does vary with local variations (spatial or temporal) in food availability, but descriptive models of the relation of rate of work to rate of reinforcement are complicated. Rate of reinforcement exerts a long-term negative feedback on rate of work (decreases hunger) but has a short-term positive effect through competition with other activities (increases the relative advantage of feeding). Learning models including positive relations between food availability and foraging rate are currently under development (Killeen 1982, 1984; B. Sumida, A. Kacelnik & A.I. Houston, unpubl.) and they too, may have something to say about predator–prey interactions.

ACKNOWLEDGMENT

We are grateful to Alasdair Houston for comments on the manuscript.

REFERENCES

Bush, R.R. & Mosteller, F. (1955). *Stochastic Models for Learning*. Wiley, New York.
Cheverton, J., Kacelnik, A. & Krebs, J.R. (1984). Optimal foraging: constraints and currencies. *Experimental Behavioral Ecology and Sociobiology*, a K. v. Frisch Memorial Symposium.
Comins, H.N. & Hassell, M.P. (1979). The dynamics of optimally foraging predators and parasitoids. *Journal of Animal Ecology*, 48, 335–351.
Commons, M.L., Kacelnik, A. & Shettleworth, S. (1985). The Harvard Symposium on quantitative analyses of behaviour (Ed. by M.L. Commons, A. Kacelnik & S. Shettleworth) Vol. 6. *Foraging*. Laurence Erlbaum Associates (in press).
Fretwell, S.D. & Lucas, H.L. (1970). On territorial behaviour and other factors influencing habitat distribution in birds. I. Theoretical development. *Acta Biotheorica*, 19, 16–36.
Harley, C.B. (1981). Learning the evolutionarily stable strategy. *Journal of Theoretical Biology*, 89, 611–633.
Harley, C.B. (1983). When do animals learn the evolutionarily stable strategy? *Journal of Theoretical Biology*, 105, 179–181.
Hassell, M.P. (1978). *Arthropod Predator–Prey Systems*. Monographs in Population Biology, Vol. 13. Princeton University Press, Princeton, New Jersey.
Hassell, M.P. & May, R.M. (1973). Stability in insect host–parasite models. *Journal of Animal Ecology*, 42, 693–726.
Hassell, M.P. & May, R.M. (1974). Aggregation of predators and insect parasites and its effect on stability. *Journal of Animal Ecology*, 43, 567–594.
Herrnstein, R.J. & Vaughan, W. Jr (1980). Melioration and behavioral allocation. *Limits to*

action: the allocation of individual behavior (Ed. by J.E.R. Staddon), pp. 143–176, Academic Press, New York.

Hinson, J.M. & Staddon, J.E.R. (**1983**). Hill-climbing by pigeons. *Journal of the Experimental Analysis of Behavior*, **39**, 25–47.

Houston, A.I. (**1983**). Comments on 'Learning The Evolutionary Stable Strategy'. *Journal of Theoretical Biology*, **105**, 175–178.

Houston, A.I. (**1985**). Maximisation of daily energy delivered to nestlings. *Biological Journal of the Linnean Society* (in press).

Houston, A.I., Kacelnik, A. & McNamara, J. (**1982**). Some learning rules for acquiring information. *Functional Ontogeny* (Ed. by D.J. McFarland), pp. 140–191. Pitman, London.

Kacelnik, A., Krebs, J.R. & Ens, B. (**1985**). Foraging in a changing environment: an experiment with Starlings (*Sturnus vulgaris*). The Harvard Symposium on quantitative analyses of behaviour (Ed. by M.L. Commons, A. Kacelnik & S. Shettleworth) Vol. 6. *Foraging*. Laurence Erlbaum Associates (in press).

Killeen, P.R. (**1982**). Incentive theory. *Nebraska Symposium on Motivation, 1981* (Ed. by D. Bernstein). Lincoln, Nebraska University Press.

Killeen, P.R. (**1984**). Incentive theory III: adaptive clocks. *Annals of New York Academy of Sciences.*

Krebs, J.R. & Kacelnik, A. (**1984**). Optimal learning rules. *The Brain and Behavioral Sciences*, **7**, 109–110.

Krebs, J.R., Kacelnik, A. & Taylor, P. (**1978**). Test of optimal sampling by foraging great tits. *Nature*, **275**, 27–31.

Lester, N. (**1984**). The feed: feed decision: how goldfish solve the patch depletion problem. *Behaviour* (in press).

McNamara, J. & Houston, A.I. (**1980**). The application of statistical decision theory to animal behaviour. *Journal of Theoretical Biology*, **85**, 673–690.

Maynard-Smith, J. (**1982**). *Evolution and the Theory of Games*. Cambridge University Press, Cambridge.

Maynard-Smith, J. (**1984**). Game theory and the evolution of behaviour. *The Brain & Behavioral Sciences*, **7**, 95–125.

Milinski, M. (**1979**). An evolutionarily stable feeding strategy in sticklebacks. *Zeitschrift für Tierpsychologie*, **51**, 36–40.

Milinski, M. (**1984**). Competitive Resource Sharing: an experimental test of a learning rule for ESSs. *Animal Behaviour*, **32**, 233–242.

Murdoch, W.W. & Oaten, A. (**1975**). Predation and population stability. *Advances in Ecological Research*, **9**, 1–131.

Pulliam, H.R. & Dunford, C. (**1980**). *Programmed to learn. An essay on the evolution of culture.* Columbia University Press, New York.

Regelmann, K. (**1984**). Competitive resource sharing: a simulation model. *Animal Behaviour*, **32**, 226–232.

Sih, A. (**1984**). Optimal behavior and density-dependent predation. *American Naturalist*, **123**, 314–326.

Stephens, D.W. (**1982**). *Stochasticity in foraging theory: risk and information.* Unpublished D.Phil. Thesis, University of Oxford.

Tarpy, R. (**1982**). *Principles of Animal Learning and Motivation.* Scott, Foresman & Co., London.

11. INTRASPECIFIC FEEDING SPECIALIZATIONS AND POPULATION DYNAMICS

LINDA PARTRIDGE and P. GREEN

Department of Zoology, University of Edinburgh, West Mains Rd, Edinburgh EH9 3JT

SUMMARY

Differences in feeding behaviour can occur between sex-classes, age-classes and individuals. Three main evolutionary causes of specializations are variable food supplies, differences in phenotype between individuals, and frequency-dependent pay-offs. These three can all occur simultaneously, and disentangling their relative effects is difficult. Feeding specializations can affect both prey and predator population dynamics.

INTRODUCTION

A casual look round a natural population of animals often reveals that the individuals are feeding differently; closer examination may show that part of the variation is attributable to sex differences (e.g. Selander 1966; Kilham 1970) and part to differences in feeding between age-classes (e.g. Clark & Gibbons 1969; Ballinger, Newlin & Newlin 1977). Individual differences can also occur (e.g. Harris 1965; Bryan 1973; Norton-Griffiths 1968), and individuals may show different specializations at different times (e.g. Heinrich 1979).

The evolutionary basis of individual feeding behaviour is in general considered in the context of optimal foraging theory. Research has been directed towards such questions as where and for how long an individual should feed, whether it should feed selectively and, if so, on which items (e.g. Krebs 1978). Optimal foraging theory has mainly been concerned with 'typical' individuals, and has not directly addressed the problem of individual differences.

A different theoretical background, that of alternative strategies, has been applied to individual differences in behaviour used to acquire scarce resources (Maynard Smith 1982). This theory explicitly recognizes the existence of individual differences and seeks to explain them in functional terms. Three main mechanisms seem to be important. First, the environment may consist of different patches where different sorts of behaviour are most appropriate. The

207

nature of the food supply may vary between areas or times, or more than one food source may be present simultaneously. Second, individuals may differ in phenotype in a way that affects the most appropriate behaviour for them to use. Third, even where individuals have otherwise identical phenotypes, the appropriate behaviour may depend on the behaviour of other individuals present, resulting in a mixture of behaviours with equal pay-offs, maintained by frequency-dependent selection.

These mechanisms are not in any sense mutually exclusive. For instance, size differences between individuals can affect their success in competition, forcing small individuals to feed on less preferred foods with whatever feeding technique is appropriate. When attempting to determine the relative importance of these effects, it is important to investigate whether different individuals experience equal pay-offs in terms of the costs and benefits associated with their feeding behaviour. These are often extremely difficult to measure.

Whatever the evolutionary explanations for particular cases where individual differences occur, these can be the product of differences in genotype, physiology and learning. It is not clear under what circumstances these pathways to individual variation evolve.

It is becoming clear that the feeding specializations of individuals can have important consequences for population dynamics, affecting all the main demographic variables. It is perhaps this aspect of feeding specializations that has received the least attention and should be the focus of future studies.

It is the aim of this paper to provide a state-of-the-art review of our understanding of the evolution and ontogeny of feeding specializations, and their effects on population dynamics. We will indicate where the major gaps occur in our understanding and knowledge, in the hope that this will stimulate future studies.

In the next section we consider the role of a patchy food supply in producing feeding specializations. Then the effects of differences in phenotype between individuals are considered. We include here those cases where phenotypic differences are the consequence of long-term selection for specialist feeding as a result of a patchy food supply and differences between individuals in their susceptibility to the effects of competition. This is followed by a brief account of feeding specializations maintained by frequency-dependent selection. Finally, we consider the consequences of feeding specializations for population dynamics. The bibliography is not intended to be exhaustive but does indicate recent work in each area.

A PATCHY FOOD SUPPLY

Sometimes variation in the food supply is such that individuals only ever encounter one type of patch. This sort of pattern can result in geographic or microgeographic differentiation in both food preferences and feeding capabilities. In other cases individuals encounter more than one food type but none the less specialize within the spectrum of food available, sometimes changing their pattern of specialization with time.

In either case, on theoretical grounds specialization of feeding capabilities and food preferences would pay if either (a) the requirements for maximum efficiency of exploitation of different foods are to some extent mutually exclusive, so that generalists are less efficient or (b) efficient generalist feeding is costly, perhaps because it requires maintenance of more sensory or digestive capabilities. We will now consider the evidence that either of these conditions holds in practice.

Does specialist feeding pay?

Evidence for benefits of feeding specialization comes from studies of digestive efficiency and the ability of animals to forage on different prey items.

Changes in the gut as a consequence of diet

There is mounting evidence that animal guts change in response to diet and that the induced changes improve digestive capability and therefore increase the nutritional value of a food that is eaten over a period of time.

Gross gut morphology can vary between areas where different diets are eaten (e.g. Myrcha 1964), and also change seasonally with diet (e.g. Al-Joborae 1980), the gut length increasing on poor quality diets in both cases. Gut length can also change in response to experimental manipulation of diet (e.g. Kenward & Sibly 1977; Miller 1975).

These changes may well lead to an improvement in the efficiency with which food is processed, although direct demonstrations of this are few. Two studies have shown that birds with long and short guts, adapted to low and high quality diets respectively, differed in digestive capability; when given the low quality diet they digested the same proportion of it but the birds with long guts processed more food per unit time (Savory & Gentle 1976; Al-Joborae 1980).

Bank voles appear to change their digestive capabilities in a slightly different way (L. Partridge & M. Lamond, unpubl.). Individuals were given various diets for periods of 3 weeks; at the beginning and end of these periods the passage rate of the food through the gut was timed by feeding the animals the experimental diet dyed with basic fuschin and recording the time of appearance of the dye in the faeces. Assimilation efficiencies were also measured, as proportion of the dry weight eaten not appearing in the dry weight of the faeces. The results are shown in Table 11.1. When eating mealworms after oats, the voles assimilated them less efficiently and had longer passage times than when they had been eating mealworms, and passage

TABLE 11.1. (a) Throughput times (min) for a pulse of food dyed with basic fuschin and fed to six bank voles kept on each diet for a period of 3 weeks. (b) Percentage dry weight of food assimilated by six bank voles kept on each diet for a period of 3 weeks (L. Partridge & M. Lamond, unpubl.)

	Experiment 1			Experiment 2	
	Oats		Mealworms	Oats	Peanuts
(a) Throughput times (min)					
Preceded by ⎧ oats	85·2	*	101·2	oats 86·8	67·2
	*		*		
⎩ mealworms	146·2	*	65·5	peanuts 73·6	57·4
(b) Percentage dry weight					
Preceded by ⎧ oats	94·5	*	85·6	oats 94·2	93·5
			*		*
⎩ meal worms	92·4		91·7	peanuts 92·1 *	96·6

* $P < 0.05$ or less.

times for oats were longer after eating mealworms than after eating oats. Peanuts were assimilated more efficiently when eaten after peanuts than after oats, while passage times were unaffected. Assimilation efficiency in this case may well have been increased by a change in enzymes or micro-organisms, as well as any changes in gut morphology. The nature of the enzymes secreted does appear to be altered in response to the nutrients in the diet (e.g. Grossman, Greengard & Ivy 1943) as well as to the toxins (e.g. Brattsten, Wilkinson & Eisner 1977; Ahmad 1983). The micro-organisms in the gut can also change in response to diet (e.g. Smith 1965; Abe & Iriki 1978).

These studies suggest that the process of digestive adaptation to one food type entails a drop in digestive efficiency on other food types, implying mutually exclusive requirements. To be sure that this, rather than the cost of maintaining several digestive capabilities, is the basis of the effect it will be necessary to compare the digestive efficiency on one diet of animals with a history of specialist and generalist feeding.

A few studies have compared specialist and generalist feeders. An interspecific comparison of larvae of *Papilio* butterflies suggested that species using several food plants digested these less efficiently than specialist species (Scriber 1979). There is some evidence that this sort of interference also goes on in bacteria (Dykhuizen & Davies 1980). If similar phenomena are general, individuals could be selected to specialize within the resource spectrum available to them, provided that a relatively steady supply of the restricted diet was available. On the other hand, if the food supply was variable, more generalist feeding might be favoured, since the gut might then be able to digest several diets reasonably efficiently. This comment applies equally to the effects of learning on foraging efficiency (see below). Either effect may account for the finding that *Peromyscus* forced to feed on a variety of foods in early life were more generalist in their feeding as adults when confronted with a choice between novel foods than were mice allowed to choose their diet in early life (Gray & Tardif 1979), suggesting that the mice had become more likely to specialize if they had experienced the opportunity for specialization.

When changes in the gut increase the nutritional value of a food over time, a corresponding change in food choice would be expected. There is evidence that a nudibranch mollusc (Hall, Todd & Gordon 1982) and several rodent species (Drickamer 1972; Partridge 1981; Partridge & Maclean 1981) show an increase in preference for a familiar food. Preference for familiarity means that common prey types will tend to suffer predation at a relatively high rate. This is a general finding, often discussed as frequency-dependent or apostatic selection (Allen 1976).

Preference for familiarity will also produce feeding specializations. The encounter rates of individuals with different food types may differ because of chance, because of the feeding specializations of other competing individuals, or because of differences in prey availability between areas. In all three cases, physiological adaptation will impose a cost to switching diet, with potential consequences for the prey populations and the residency of the predators (see p. 219).

Improvement in foraging efficiency with experience

Numerous studies have demonstrated an improvement in foraging efficiency as a result of foraging experience. For example, ability to detect prey can improve with encounter rate (Dawkins 1971a, b; Pietrewicz & Kamil 1979) as can the ability to capture and subdue it (Lawton, Beddington & Bonser 1974; Polsky 1977; Heinrich 1979; Caro 1980a, b).

There have been a few studies examining the extent to which specialized foraging pays. It has long been suspected that the different diet breadths of species represent different evolutionary compromises between the conflicting requirements of feeding efficiency and ability to deal with a variable food supply (e.g. Schoener 1971; Klopfer 1973). Work on garter snakes (Drummond 1983) has shown that, in aquatic field habitats, two specialist aquatic species foraged more efficiently than two species that fed both in water and on land. Intraspecific comparisons of a comparable kind are few. Sunfish feeding in both open water and on sediment fed less efficiently, as measured by gut contents, than did individuals specializing on one food supply or the other. It was, however, possible that the 'generalists' were at low competitive ability or were in the process of switching from one specialization to another so that their food preferences were affected (Werner, Mittelbach & Hall 1981).

We (L. Partridge & P. Green, unpubl.) have designed an experiment to test whether specialization improves the foraging efficiency of jackdaws (*Corvus monedula*). Hand-reared birds were forced to be either 'specialist' feeders on one of three artificial laboratory feeding tasks or 'generalist' feeders on all three. The 'specialist' birds were in general more efficient at extracting food from their tasks than were the generalists.

If this sort of phenomenon is general, then specialization on particular feeding skills will pay if the nature of the food supply allows it. Foraging specializations are not uncommon, the case of the oystercatcher being particularly well documented. Individual birds specialize on particular prey types and on the technique used to exploit them (Norton-Griffiths 1968; Goss-Custard & Sutherland 1984). The data in Table 11.2 indicate that turnstone *Arenaria interpres* behave rather similarly (P. Whitfield, unpubl.).

Exactly as argued for improved digestive efficiency, feeding preferences are expected to change with changes in foraging efficiency, leading to feeding specializations and switching. This has been algebraically modelled by Hughes (1979). An association between individual feeding specializations and individual foraging efficiency has been found in several studies (e.g. Heinrich 1976; Partridge 1976; Caro 1980a) and may result from an increase in preference solely as a result of encounter rate or as a result of detection of improved foraging efficiency.

Cultural inheritance

Several studies have indicated that learned feeding specializations can be transmitted to offspring through cultural inheritance from parents. For instance, when feeding on mussels, some oystercatchers stabbed through the adductor mussel while others hammered through the shell. Pairs tended to use the same technique which was transmitted to the offspring. An experiment where eggs were transferred between nests belonging to parents with different

TABLE 11.2. The feeding techniques used by individual turnstone feeding on a rocky shore in East Lothian between August 1983 and March 1984; Rout, routing seaweed; Turn, turning stones; Probe, probing for littorinids. All observations are independent. Within each sex the individual differences are significant ($P < 0.005$) on a heterogeneity χ^2 test. (P. Whitfield, unpubl.)

Sex	Feeding technique		
	Rout	Turn	Probe
m	92	0	8
m	81	0	8
m	81	2	15
f	70	0	5
f	111	0	7
m	80	0	30
f	57	12	10
f	17	4	12
m	36	21	18
f	47	77	0
f	19	48	8
m	31	0	47
m	26	0	75
m	17	1	68
m	20	1	120

techniques established that the transmission was a consequence of learning, since young adopted the feeding technique of their foster-parents (Norton-Griffiths 1968). Similar findings have been made with cats (Wyrwicka 1978). Weanling rats often prefer the same diet as that eaten by their mother during lactation, and this preference seems to be a consequence of changes in the flavour of the milk (e.g. Galef & Henderson 1972). Feeding habits can also be culturally transmitted between non-relatives (see Wilson 1975 for summary). This sort of cultural transmission can be important in rapid niche expansion (e.g. Fisher & Hinde 1949) and in long-term perpetuation of feeding specializations.

DIFFERENCES IN PHENOTYPE AND FEEDING SPECIALIZATIONS

Differences in phenotype between individuals can occur for a variety of reasons and can have a large effect on feeding. Age and sex are two major sources of phenotypic variation and both can be associated with differences in feeding (Polis 1984). Sex differences may reflect differences in parental or reproductive roles, or may have arisen partly as a consequence of natural selection in favour of individuals that overlap least in diet with members of the other sex (Selander 1966). These different selection pressures are very hard to disentangle in any one instance, but in the last case the consequent sexual dimorphism in feeding can be regarded as a long-term response to patchiness in the food supply. This is true also for trophic morphs, where individuals differ in the morphology of their feeding apparatus and show an associated difference in food preference. Cases where the differences in phenotype are related and unrelated to a history of selection for differences in feeding are considered below.

Individuals can also differ in their susceptibility to the effects of intra- and interspecific competition, and this is also considered in this section.

Age differences in phenotype

Young animals, mainly because they are growing, tend to have different nutritional requirements from adults. Young grey squirrels (Nixon 1970), black rats (Clark 1980) and several primate species (Clutton-Brock 1977) take higher protein diets than do adults. Hatchling and juvenile iguanas have higher energy and protein requirements than do adults, and select a diet higher in these constituents (Troyer 1984). Young black rats avoid plants containing secondary compounds that are consumed by adults (Clark 1980); it would be valuable to know if youngsters are in general more susceptible than adults to plant toxins.

Young animals can also differ from adults in their feeding skills. Part of this difference is attributable to lack of feeding experience (e.g. Greig, Coulson & Monaghan 1983) and part to maturation (e.g. Smith 1973; Davies & Green 1976). One obvious feature of young is that they tend to be smaller than adults, and this can affect their foraging abilities. For example, four water snake species showed an increase in the size of prey taken with age (Mushinsky, Hebrard & Vodopich 1982) and this trend may well have reflected the growth of the snakes as well as improvement in feeding skills. The change in diet appeared to be unlearned in that it occurred in the absence of experience with the prey. One corollary was that the young of the four species took more similar prey than did the adults.

Predation can also alter the picture. For example, the searching ability of sunfish increased with their size (Mittelbach 1981). Vulnerability of the fish to predation by largemouth bass also changed; sunfish over 100 mm long were almost immune and showed a seasonal habitat shift between vegetation and open water in accordance with changes in prey abundance and the predictions of optimal foraging theory. The smaller fish always stayed near vegetation, despite the often poorer feeding opportunities there, presumably because of their increased risk of predation in open water. Similar findings have been made for a lizard (Stamps 1983).

Young animals are often poor competitors, and this also can affect their feeding opportunities. For example, on the Exe estuary young oystercatchers eat mussels in the summer when the adults are absent, but most are displaced from the mussel beds when the adults return from the breedings grounds (Goss-Custard *et al.* 1982, 1984; Goss-Custard & Durrell 1983). Similarly, juvenile deer mice in high density populations are forced into low cover habitats where there are few soft-bodied arthropods of the kind that juveniles can handle; they therefore are forced to eat a diet lower in protein than are adults, despite their higher protein requirement (Van Horne 1982). In the predatory insect *Notonecta*, juveniles move around less and have depressed feeding rates in the presence of adults, this effect being particularly marked at low prey densities. *Notonecta* are cannibalistic, and juveniles may in this way be avoiding predation by adults (Murdoch & Sih 1978; Sih 1981).

Sex differences in phenotype

The nutritional requirements of the sexes are often different, especially at the time of reproduction when females tend to require a higher protein diet than do males (e.g. Jones 1976; Gautier-Hion 1980; Clark 1980). Size differences between the sexes can affect their dietary requirements: red deer hinds are smaller than stags and this seems to enable them, because of their lower absolute energy requirement, to feed on the greens where food is high in protein and low in fibre, but where intake rates are low (Clutton-Brock, Guiness & Albon 1982). Time budgets of the sexes can also be affected by overall energy requirements: male salticid spiders are smaller than females, have a lower energy need and spend less time feeding (Givens 1978).

The sexes can also differ in anatomy and behaviour in a way that affects their feeding skills (Selander 1966). Probably the most dramatic, but extinct, case was the New Zealand huia. The male had a stout, straight bill while the female had a slender, decurved one. The males hammered beetle larvae out of decaying wood while the females probed into crevices and tunnels made by the larvae. In birds of prey, females tend to be larger than males, and this often leads to a difference in foraging with females taking larger prey (Andersson & Norberg 1981). In sparrowhawks, the size dimorphism is associated with a habitat difference outside the breeding season, females foraging more in farmland and males more in forest (Marquiss & Newton 1982). The authors suggested several possible explanations for the habitat difference. Males may be more manoeuvrable than females and better able to forage in woodland, or prey size may differ between the two habitats, the thrushes, starlings and waders preferred by females being more common on farmland. Lastly, vulnerability to cannibalism could be important; ten instances of predation on male sparrowhawks by females have been witnessed, and the males may be to some extent protected in forest habitat. Predation has also been shown to affect the distribution of the sexes in a crayfish (Stem 1977).

Competition between the sexes can also be asymmetrical. For example, downy woodpecker males and females normally forage in different parts of trees. A field experiment where females were removed produced no response in the foraging of males, but if males were removed females foraged on branch sizes normally used only by males (Peters & Grubb 1983), suggesting that females restrict their foraging in the presence of males. Similar findings have been made for red deer except that here females restrict the foraging of males (Clutton-Brock *et al.* 1982).

Individual differences in phenotype

In some species there is marked variation in trophic apparatus associated with variation in feeding. Sometimes these trophic morphs are clearly genetic in origin while in other instances developmental switches may be important. These morphs may well be a long-term evolutionary response to a patchy food supply and selection for specialization as a result of increased feeding efficiency.

Genetic differentiation seems to be most likely where there is stable spatial variation in the food supply. For example, microgeographic differentiation in response to local variation in the food supply is found in a parthenogenetic moth (Mitter *et al.* 1979; Schneider 1980; Futuyma, Corti & Van Noordwijk 1984). Larvae feed on the newly-opened leaves of deciduous trees, and different tree species and individuals differ in their time of bud burst. The moths on particular tree species and even on individual trees are genetically adapted so that their emergence date is synchronized with the leaf-opening of their tree. Futuyma *et al.* (1984) have shown that feeding preferences can show microgeographic differentiation in the absence of changes in digestive capabilities, and they suggest that host specificity could arise initially as a consequence of avoidance of predation or competition, and that improved feeding efficiency would only occur secondarily. Feeding preferences may themselves indicate different sensory capabilities and hence food-finding ability. Such geographic variation in food preference also occurs in garter snakes (Arnold 1981a, b). In coastal California 90% of the diet consists of slugs, whereas inland slugs do not occur and the snakes feed mainly on frogs and fish. The food preferences are not learned; most newborn coastal snakes attack slugs on first exposure, while most newborn inland snakes refuse slugs and will starve to death if not given alternative food. It is not known if these preferences are associated with other differences in feeding efficiency.

In other instances, the ontogeny of the morphs is less certain. For instance, tropical freshwater cichlids are notorious for their endemic specializations. These have in general been assumed to be the product of multiple speciation events *in situ*. However, recent work on Mexican cichlids suggests that the apparent 'species' may in fact be morphs (Sage & Selander 1975; Kornfield *et al.* 1982). Two distinct trophic morphs exist; a 'small tooth' form has papilliform pharyngeal dentition, a narrow head, a slender pharyngeal jaw and a long intestine and feeds on plant material, while a 'large tooth' form has molariform pharyngeal teeth, a wider head, a stouter jaw and a short intestine and feeds on snails. These differences exceed those between the African lake cichlids that are assumed to be species. However, the two forms are electrophoretically similar and show parallel patterns of geographic variation and both forms occur within single broods. It is possible that these morphs result from genetic differences and from differences experienced in early life, and further work is needed to test these alternatives. Similar findings have been made in goodeid fishes (Turner & Grosse 1980; Grudzien & Turner 1984) and hook-billed kites (Smith & Temple 1982). In Darwins finches, continuous variation in bill size in several species is associated with different prey size (e.g. Grant *et al.* 1976; Boag & Grant 1981; Grant 1981). Bill size has been shown to be heritable in some species (Boag & Grant 1978; Boag 1983). However, some caution may be needed, because in red-winged blackbirds there seems to be a large and as yet unspecified environmental effect at work in determining bill size (James 1983).

Individual feeding specializations are affected by immediate competition, as well as its pattern in the evolutionary past. As has been shown for interspecific competition (Hassell 1978; Lawton & Hassell 1981), intraspecific competition is often asymmetrical in its effects, so that not all individuals are equally affected by it.

One consequence of this is that occupancy of poor feeding areas may increase at high population densities, forcing individuals of low competitive ability out of the better areas as seems to occur in oystercatchers (Ens & Goss-Custard 1984). Similar findings have been made for a coral reef fish (Coates 1980).

There is also evidence that animals alter their foraging in response to experience and anticipation of the effects of competition. For example, sticklebacks allowed to forage in pairs for *Daphnia* differed in their ability to catch them. If *Daphnia* were offered two at a time, one large and one small, then the more able foragers incorporated more of the large *Daphnia* in their diet. Subsequent tests with the competitively inferior fish revealed that their foraging preferences had become modified by their experience, so that they incorporated a higher proportion of small *Daphnia* in their diet in the absence of their foraging partner than did the superior fish (Milinzki 1982). Related findings have been made with shrews (Barnard & Brown 1981) and robins (Herrera 1978).

Several studies have shown that interspecific competition can narrow the range of feeding habits of an inferior competitor. The feeding niche in nature is often broader in the absence of the competing species (e.g. Cameron 1964; Moss 1974) and some studies have demonstrated competition directly by manipulating the presence of the competitor (e.g. Grant 1971; Werner & Hall 1979). Whether or not relaxation of interspecific competition in general leads to feeding niche expansion on islands is discussed by Williamson (1981). The effects of interspecific competition may be felt to different extents by different sections of the population (see p. 220).

Both inter- and intraspecific competition must pose some selection for flexibility in feeding, because individuals may have to respond to either by niche compression.

FEEDING SPECIALIZATIONS MAINTAINED BY FREQUENCY-DEPENDENT SELECTION

Frequency dependence may often play some role in the maintenance of feeding specializations. Where several food supplies exist in a single area, they are unlikely to be equally profitable for predators foraging alone. However, once the most profitable food starts to be exploited, its profitability will start to decline to the point where it may eventually pay new arrivals to exploit the next food down the profitability ranking. Individual specializations, rather than individuals showing a mixture of behaviours, will then be likely to occur if the conditions outlined on p. 209 apply, and could result in an ideal free distribution of specializations. Sutherland (see p. 255) has pointed out that individual susceptibility to the effects of competition can interact with frequency dependence to produce a variety of distributions of individuals and of pay-offs across resources. Detailed studies of the pay-offs experienced by different individuals are necessary to disentangle the roles of frequency dependence and competitive effects.

If an ideal free distribution is produced, the pay-offs experienced by different individuals should be the same. Demonstrating this is tricky, partly because statistically-speaking, one can only fail to reject the null hypothesis of no individual differences. In addition, where there are qualitative differences between prey items and when the costs of acquiring them include different considerations, e.g. energy, time, susceptibility to predation, etc., then comparison of pay-offs is extremely difficult.

One case where different feeding techniques may produce equal pay-offs occurs in the Harris sparrow (Rohwer & Ewald 1981). Subordinate birds differ in plumage from dominant flock members and are displaced by them from good feeding areas. No measurements of feeding rates on natural food supplies were made, but the authors suggested that equal pay-offs may have occurred, essentially because dominants protect subordinates from interferences from birds of other flocks, and lose feeding time in the process.

CONSEQUENCES OF FEEDING SPECIALIZATIONS FOR POPULATION DYNAMICS

Although the feeding specializations of individuals certainly have important consequences for population dynamics, few studies have attempted to make observations on both. The requirement for both extensive and intensive measurements is probably largely responsible for this lamentable omission. What follows is a brief account of possible points of interaction between feeding specializations and population dynamics, with an indication of those areas where empirical studies are most lacking.

Effects of specialization by predators on prey population dynamics

Theoretical work has suggested that predator switching (Murdoch, Avery & Smyth 1975; Murdoch & Oaten 1975), and type 3 functional responses (Holling 1965; Sih 1984) can regulate prey numbers, because total predation rate shows a superproportional increase with an increase in prey numbers. Individual specializations in feeding could be important in mediating these responses.

We have already seen that improvement in feeding efficiency with experience is likely to increase preference for familiar foods. McNair (1980) has considered the effects of changing preference as a result of encounter rate with prey, and concluded that type 3 functional responses and switching could be produced. The more marked the change in preference, the more pronounced was the effect. Experimental studies examining the effects of changing encounter rates on feeding efficiency and prey preference would be valuable.

The shape of the total population functional response will be affected by competitive interactions between predators. There have been very few empirical studies here. One laboratory study on *Notonecta* has shown that as prey density increases, the interference between adults and juveniles declines, and juveniles show a marked functional and developmental response to increasing prey density. More studies of this kind are needed.

We have seen that different sections of prey populations vary in their vulnerability to predation and that this can force the more susceptible to feed in suboptimal areas. A change in predator density will presumably particularly affect the feeding of those individuals. We know of no field studies examining this possibility.

Effects of feeding specializations on predator's own population dynamics

Feeding specializations can mean that the impact of changes in population numbers is felt to different extents by different sections of the predator population. Data in this area are few, but the following are the main possibilities.

The consequences of changes in prey numbers will depend upon whose food supply is affected. For example, shortage of protein-rich items could selectively affect juveniles and reproductive females. One study (Boag & Grant 1981) has shown that a shortage of small prey items brought about highly selective mortality in a finch population, large-billed birds being more likely to survive.

Changes in the numbers of competing species could also have selective consequences, those individuals whose diets overlap most with those of the competing species being likely to be worst affected. These may often be juveniles, especially in those cases where, as for example in many fish, rather similar sized eggs give rise to very different sized adults. The earlier life-history stages of different species are therefore more similar in size and hence dietary requirements than are the adults of the corresponding species. Juveniles also tend to be penalized because during growth they often have to grow through the size range of smaller competing species, and hence compete with the adults (e.g. Werner & Hall 1979; Grant & Grant 1982).

Feeding specializations can determine which individuals are most affected by a change in the level of intraspecific competition for food. Mortality patterns of the sexes may be different. For example, in red deer, hinds can crop good quality green to the point where stags, with their higher daily energy requirement, are forced to forage in poorer areas where intake rates are higher. This means that in high density populations stags will be more prone to starvation, and the best predictor of overall mortality rate will be hind density (Clutton-Brock et al. 1982).

Changes in levels of competition are also likely to have complicated effects on patterns of dispersal, residency and distribution.

Dispersal is one individual response to increasing local competition, and those individuals which most experience the adverse effects of competition are, in general, most likely to leave (Lomnicki 1978). A second consideration is that the resource value of a particular habitat may vary with length of residency in it. Individuals may acquire the appropriate feeding skills for the local conditions to the point where it no longer pays them to move, even to a habitat that would have initially been more suitable (Partridge 1978; Werner *et al.* 1981). There is abundant evidence that such shifts in habitat preference with experience do occur (Partridge 1978; Partridge & Murray, unpublished data in Table 11.3). This may mean that animals resident in an area will be more prepared to tolerate adversity or to fight to remain resident. Both factors probably mean that dispersers during times of high competition are particularly likely to be juveniles.

TABLE 11.3. Percentage of observations in which great tits were perched on oak as opposed to pine branches. The birds were hand reared and kept in aviaries with pine, oak or oak and pine branches for 5 months before testing. The tests were conducted for 2 hours and the branch on which the bird was perched was recorded in each minute. All differences significantly ($P < 0.05$ or less) different on Student–Newman–Keuls test) L. Partridge & O.O. Murray, unpubl.)

	Birds reared with	
Oak ($n = 8$)	oak + pine ($n = 5$)	pine ($n = 7$)
89	71·7	60·6

Probability of establishment in a new area, that is of successful immigration, is likely to be closely tied to feeding; individuals with the 'wrong' specialization are likely to suffer. One study has shown an association between feeding habits and dispersal. Tardif & Gray (1978) divided wild-trapped adult *Peromyscus leucopus* into three categories: residents were a random sample of mice from a large wood, contiguous immigrants were trapped from the middle of a large wood from which the inhabitants had been previously trapped and removed, and isolated immigrants were trapped in isolated woodlots (separated from adjacent habitat for *Peromyscus* by more than 100 m), from which the resident population had again been removed. The food choice of these mice was then measured in the laboratory in a four-way choice test. Both classes of immigrants were more generalist feeders than were the residents. The ontogeny of this difference was unknown, and further study of this association is required. In general, young animals are more catholic in their feeding habits than are adults, and this may make them more able to cope with the uncertainties of dispersal.

GENERAL CONCLUSIONS

Spatially and temporally variable food supplies, individual variation in phenotype and frequency-dependent pay-offs can all have an influence on the feeding behaviours shown by different individuals. Disentangling the relative contribution of these factors can be difficult, but should undoubtedly be a major focus of future research effort.

Individual feeding specializations can affect both prey and predator population dynamics. The shape of functional responses, the vulnerability both of different sections of prey populations to changes in predator numbers, and of different sections of the predator population to changes in prey numbers can all be affected. Patterns of dispersal and habitat loyalty can also be influenced. It is in this area that hard data are most lacking at present.

REFERENCES

Abe, M. & Iriki, T. (1978). Effects of diet on the protozoa populations in continuous culture of rumen contents. *British Journal of Nutrition*, **39**, 255–261.

Ahmad, S. (1983). Mixed-function oxidase activity in a generalist herbivore in relation to its biology, food plants, and feeding history. *Ecology*, **64**, 235–243.

Al-Joborae, F.F. (1980). *The influence of diet on the gut morphology of the starling* (Sturnus vulgaris L. *1758*). Unpublished D.Phil Thesis, University of Oxford.

Allen, J.A. (1976). Further evidence for apostatic selection by wild passerine birds—9:1 experiments. *Heredity*, **36**, 173–180.

Andersson, M. & Norberg, R.A. (1981). Evolution of reversed sexual size dimorphism and role partitioning among predatory birds, with a size scaling of flight performance. *Biological Journal of the Linnean Society*, **15**, 105–130.

Arnold, S.J. (1981a). Behavioral variation in natural populations, I. Phenotypic, genetic and environmental correlations between chemoreceptive responses to prey in the garter snake *Thamnophis elegans*. *Evolution*, **35**, 489–509.

Arnold, S.J. (1981b). Behavioral variation in natural populations, II. The inheritance of a feeding response in crosses between geographic races of the garter snake, *Thamnophis elegans*. *Evolution*, **35**, 510–515.

Ballinger, R.E., Newlin, M.E. & Newlin, S.J. (1977). Age-specific shift in the diet of the crevice spiny lizard, *Sceloporus poinsetti* in Southwestern New Mexico. *American Midland Naturalist*, **97**, 482–484.

Barnard, C.J. & Brown, C.A.J. (1981). Prey size and competition in the common shrew (*Sorex araneus*). *Behavioural Ecology and Sociobiology*, **8**, 239–243.

Boag, P.T. (1983). The heritability of external morphology in Darwins ground finches (*Geospiza*) on Isla Daphne Major, Galapagos. *Evolution*, **37**, 877–894.

Boag, P.T. & Grant, P.R. (1978). Heritability of external morphology in Darwins finches. *Nature*, **274**, 793–794.

Boag, P.T. & Grant, P.R. (1981). Intense natural selection in a population of Darwins finches (Geospizinae) in the Galapagos. *Science*, **214**, 82–85.

Brattsten, L.B., Wilkinson, C.F. & Eisner, T. (1977). Herbivore–plant interactions: mixed-function oxidases and secondary plant substances. *Science*, **196**, 1349–1352.

Bryan, J.J. (1973). Feeding history, parental stock, and food selection in rainbow trout. *Behaviour*, **45**, 123–153.

Cameron, A.W. (1964). Competitive exclusion between the rodent genera *Microtus* and *Clethrionomys. Evolution*, **18**, 630–634.

Caro, T.M. (1980a). The effects of experience on the predatory patterns of cats. *Behavioral and Neural Biology*, **29**, 1–28.

Caro, T.M. (1980b). Effects of the mother, object play, and adult experience on predation in cats. *Behavioral and Neural Biology*, **29**, 29–51.

Clark, D.A. (1980). Age- and sex-dependent foraging strategies of a small mammalian omnivore. *Journal of Animal Ecology*, **49**, 549–563.

Clark, D.B. & Gibbons, J.W. (1969). Dietary shift in the turtle *Pseudemys scripta* (Schoepff) from youth to maturity. *Copeia*, 1969, 704–706.

Clutton-Brock, T.H. (1977). Some aspects of intraspecific variation in feeding and ranging behaviour in primates. *Primate Ecology* (Ed. by T.H. Clutton-Brock), pp. 539–556. Academic Press, London.

Clutton-Brock, T.H., Guiness, F.E. & Albon, S.D. (1982). *Red Deer: Behaviour and Ecology of Two Sexes.* Edinburgh University Press, Edinburgh.

Coates, D. (1980). Prey-size intake in humbug damselfish, *Dascyllus aruanus* (Pisces: Pomacentridae) living within social groups. *Journal of Animal Ecology*, **49**, 335–340.

Davies, N.B. & Green, R.E. (1976). The development and ecological significance of feeding techniques in the reed warbler (*Acrocephalus scirpaceus*). *Animal Behaviour*, **24**, 213–229.

Dawkins, M. (1971a). Perceptual changes in chicks: another look at the search image concept. *Animal Behaviour*, **19**, 566–574.

Dawkins, M. (1971b). Shifts of 'attention' in chicks during feeding. *Animal Behaviour*, **19**, 575–582.

Dickinson, H. & Antonovics, J. (1973). Theoretical considerations of sympatric divergence. *American Naturalist*, **107**, 256–274.

Drickamer, L.C. (1972). Experience and selection behavior in the food habits of *Peromyscus*: use of olfaction. *Behaviour*, **41**, 269–287.

Drummond, H. (1983). Aquatic foraging in garter snakes: a comparison of specialists and generalists. *Behaviour*, **86**, 1–30.

Dykhuizen, D. & Davies, M. (1980). An experimental model: bacterial specialists and generalists competing in chemostats. *Ecology*, **61**, 1213–1227.

Ens, B.J. & Goss-Custard, J.D. (1984). Interference among oystercatchers, *Haematopus ostralegus*, feeding on mussels, *Mytilus edulis*, on the Exe estuary. *Journal of Animal Ecology*, **53**, 217–231.

Fisher, J. & Hinde, RA. (1949). The opening of milk bottles by birds. *British Birds*, **42**, 347–357.

Futuyma, D.J., Corti, R.P. & Van Noordwijk, A. (1984). Adaptation to host plants in the fall cankerworm (*Alsophila pometaria*) and its bearing on the evolution of host affiliation in phytophagous insects. *American Naturalist*, **123**, 287–296.

Galef, B.G. & Henderson, P.W. (1972). Mother's milk: a determinant of the feeding preferences of weanling rat pups. *Journal of Comparative and Physiological Psychology*, **78**, 213–219.

Gautier-Hion, A. (1980). Seasonal variation of diet related to species and sex in a community of Cercopithecus monkeys. *Journal of Animal Ecology*, **49**, 237–269.

Givens, R.P. (1978). Dimorphic feeding strategies of a salticid spider (*Phidipus audax*). *Ecology*, **59**, 309–321.

Goss-Custard, J.D., Clarke, R.T. & Durell, S.E.A. le V. dit. (1984). Rates of food intake and aggression of oystercatchers *Haematopus ostralegus* on the most and least preferred mussel *Mytilus edulis* beds of the Exe estuary. *Journal of Animal Ecology*, **53**, 233–245.

Goss-Custard, J.D. & Durell, S.E.A. le V. dit. (1983). Individual and age differences in the feeding ecology of oystercatchers *Haematopus ostralegus* wintering on the Exe estuary, Devon. *Ibis*, **125**, 155–171.

Goss-Custard, J.D., Durell, S.E.A. le V. dit., McGorty, S. & Reading, C.J. (1982). Use of mussel

Mytilus edulis beds by oystercatchers *Haematopus ostralegus* according to age and population size. *Journal of Animal Ecology*, **51**, 543–554.

Goss-Custard, J.D. & Sutherland, W.J. (1984). Feeding specialisations in oystercatchers *Haematopus ostralegus*. *Animal Behaviour*, **32**, 299–301.

Grant, B.R. & Grant, P.R. (1982). Niche shifts and competition in Darwins finches: *Geospiza conirostris* and congeners. *Evolution*, **36**, 637–657.

Grant, P.R. (1971). Experimental studies of competitive interaction in a two-species system, III. *Microtus* and *Peromyscus* species in enclosures. *Journal of Animal Ecology*, **40**, 323–350.

Grant, P.R. (1981). The feeding of Darwins finches on *Tribulus cistoides* (L.) seeds. *Animal Behaviour*, **29**, 785–793.

Grant, P.R., Grant, B.R., Smith, J.N.M., Abbott, I.J. & Abbott, L.K. (1976). Darwins finches: population variation and natural selection. *Proceedings of the National Academy of Sciences, USA.*, **73**, 257–261.

Gray, L. & Tardif, R.R. (1979). Development of feeding diversity in deer mice. *Journal of Comparative and Physiological Psychology*, **93**, 1127–1135.

Greig, S.A., Coulson, J.C. & Monaghan, P. (1983). Age-related differences in foraging success in the herring gull (*Larus argentatus*). *Animal Behaviour*, **31**, 1237–1243.

Grossman, M.I., Greengard, H. & Ivy, A.C. (1943). The effect of dietary composition on pancreatic enzymes. *American Journal of Physiology*, **138**, 676–682.

Grudzien, T.A. & Turner, B.J. (1984). Direct evidence that the *Ilyodon* morphs are single biological species. *Evolution*, **38**, 402–407.

Hall, S.J., Todd, C.D. & Gordon, A.D. (1982). The influence of ingestive conditioning on the prey species selection in *Aeolidia papillosa* (Mollusca: Nudibranchia). *Journal of Animal Ecology*, **51**, 907–921.

Harris, M.P. (1965). The food of some *Larus* gulls. *Ibis*, 107, 43–53.

Hassell, M.P. (1978). *The Dynamics of Arthropod Predator–Prey Systems.* Princeton University Press, Princeton.

Heinrich, B. (1976). The foraging specialisations of individual bumblebees. *Ecological Monographs*, **46**, 105–128.

Heinrich, B. (1979). Majoring and minoring by foraging bumblebees, *Bombus vagans*: an experimental analysis. *Ecology*, **60**, 245–255.

Herrera, C.M. (1978). Individual dietary differences associated with morphological variation in robins *Erithacus rubecula*. *Ibis*, **120**, 542–545.

Holling, C.S. (1965). The functional response of predators to prey density and its role in mimicry and population regulation. *Memoirs of the Entomological Society of Canada*, **45**, 43–60.

Hughes, R. (1979). Optimal diets under the energy maximisation premise: the effects of recognition time and learning. *American Naturalist*, **113**, 209–222.

James, F.C. (1983). Environmental component of morphological differentiation in birds. *Science*, **221**, 184–186.

Jones, P.J. (1976). The utilization of calcareous grit by laying *Quelea quelea*. *Ibis*, **118**, 575–576.

Kenward, R.E. & Sibly, R.M. (1977). A woodpigeon (*Columba palumbus*) feeding preference explained by a digestive bottleneck. *Journal of Applied Ecology*, **14**, 815–826.

Kilham, L. (1970). Feeding behaviour of downy woodpeckers, 1. Preference for paper birches and sexual differences. *Auk*, **87**, 544–556.

Klopfer, P.H. (1973). *Behavioural Aspects of Ecology.* Prentice Hall, New Jersey.

Kornfield, I., Smith, D.C., Gagnon, P.S. & Taylor, J.N. (1982). The cichlid fish of Cuatro Cienegas, Mexico: direct evidence of conspecificity among distinct trophic morphs. *Evolution*, **36**, 658–664.

Krebs, J.R. (1978). Optimal foraging: decision rules for predators. *Behavioural Ecology: an Evolutionary Approach* (1st edn) (Ed. by J.R. Krebs & N.B. Davies), pp. 23–63. Blackwell Scientific Publications, Oxford.

Lawton, J.H., Beddington, J.R. & Bonser, R. (1974). Switching in invertebrate predators. *Ecological Stability* (Ed. by M.B. Usher & M.H. Williamson). Chapman and Hall, London.

Lawton, J.H. & Hassell, M.P. (1981). Asymmetrical competition in insects. *Nature*, **289**, 793–796.

Levins, R. (1968). *Evolution in Changing Environments.* Princeton University Press, Princeton, New Jersey.

Lomnicki, A. (1978). Individual differences between animals and the natural regulation of their numbers. *Journal of Animal Ecology*, **47**, 461–475.

Marquiss, M. & Newton, I. (1982). Habitat preference in male and female sparrowhawks *Accipiter nisus. Ibis*, **124**, 324–328.

Maynard Smith, J. (1966). Sympatric speciation. *American Naturalist*, **100**, 637–650.

Maynard Smith, J. (1982). *Evolution and the Theory of Games.* Cambridge University Press, Cambridge.

McNair, J.N. (1980). A stochastic foraging model with predator training effects. 1. Functional response, switching, and run lengths. *Theoretical Population Biology*, **17**, 141–166.

Milinski, M. (1982). Optimal foraging: the influence of intraspecific competition on diet selection. *Behavioural Ecology and Sociobiology*, **11**, 109–115.

Miller, M.R. (1975). Gut morphology of mallards in relation to diet quality. *Journal of Wildlife Management*, **39**, 168–173.

Mittelbach, G.G. (1981). Foraging efficiency and body size: a study of optimal diet and habitat use by bluegills. *Ecology*, **62**, 1370–1386.

Mitter, C., Futuyma, D.J., Schneider, J.C. & Hare, J.D. (1979). Genetic variation and host plant relations in a parthenogenetic moth. *Evolution*, **33**, 777–790.

Moss, R. (1974). Winter diets, gut lengths, and interspecific competition in Alaskan ptarmigan. *Auk*, **91**, 737–746.

Murdoch, W.W., Avery, S. & Smyth, M.E.B. (1975). Switching in predatory fish. *Ecology*, **56**, 1094–1105.

Murdoch, W.W. & Oaten, A. (1975). Predation and population stability. *Advances in Ecological Research*, **9**, 1–131.

Murdoch, W.W. & Sih, A. (1978). Age-dependent interference in a predatory insect. *Journal of Animal Ecology*, **47**, 581–592.

Mushinsky, H.R., Hebrard, J.J. & Vodopich, D.S. (1982). Ontogeny of water snake foraging ecology. *Ecology*, **63**, 1624–1629.

Myrcha, A. (1964). Variations in the length and weight of the alimentary tract of *Clethrionomys glareolus* (Schreber 1780). *Acta Theralogica*, **9**, 10, 139–148.

Nixon, C.M. (1970). Insects as food for juvenile grey squirrels. *American Midland Naturalist*, **84**, 283.

Norton-Griffiths, M. (1968). *The feeding behaviour of the oystercatcher* Haematopus ostralegus. Unpublished D. Phil. Thesis, University of Oxford.

Partridge, L. (1976). Individual differences in feeding efficiencies and feeding preferences in captive great tits. *Animal Behaviour*, **24**, 230–240.

Partridge, L. (1978). Habitat selection. *Behavioural Ecology: an Evolutionary Approach* (1st edn). (Ed. by J.R. Krebs & N.B. Davies), pp. 351–376. Blackwell Scientific Publications, Oxford.

Partridge, L. (1981). Increased preferences for familiar foods in small mammals. *Animal Behaviour*, **29**, 211–216.

Partridge, L. & Maclean, R. (1981). Effect of nutrition and peripheral stimuli on preferences for familiar foods in the bank vole. *Animal Behaviour*, **29**, 217–220.

Peters, W.D. & Grubb, T.C. (1983). An experimental analysis of sex-specific foraging in the Downy Woodpecker, *Picoides pubescens. Ecology*, **64**, 1437–1443.

Pietrewicz, A.T. & Kamil, A.C. (1979). Search image formation in the blue jay (*Cyanocitta cristata*). *Science*, **204**, 1332–1333.

Polis, G.A. (1984). Age structure components of niche width and intraspecific resource partitioning: can age groups function as ecological species? *American Naturalist*, **123**, 541–564.

Polsky, R.H. (1977). The ontogeny of predatory behaviour in the golden hamster (*Mesocricetus a. auratus*). 1. The influence of age and experience. *Behaviour*, **61**, 26–57.

Pond, C.M. (1977). The significance of lactation in the evolution of the mammals. *Evolution*, **31**, 177–199.

Rohwer, S. & Ewald, P.W. (1981). The cost of dominance and advantage of subordination in a badge signalling system. *Evolution*, **35**, 411–454.

Sage, R.D. & Selander, R.K. (1975). Trophic radiation through polymorphism in cichlid fishes. *Proceedings of the National Academy of Sciences, USA*, **72**, 4669–4673.

Savory, C.J. & Gentle, M.J. (1976). Changes in food intake and gut size in Japanese quail in response to manipulation of dietary fibre content. *British Poultry Science*, **17**, 571–580.

Schneider, J.C. (1980). The role of parthenogenesis and female aptery in microgeographic, ecological adaptation in the fall cankerworm, *Alsophila pometaria* Harris (Lepidoptera: Geometridae). *Ecology*, **61**, 1082–1090.

Schoener, T.W. (1971). Theory of feeding strategies. *Annual Review of Ecology and Systematics*, **2**, 369–404.

Scriber, J.M. (1979). The effects of sequentially switching food plants upon biomass and nitrogen utilization by phytophagous and stenophagous *Papilio* larvae. *Entomologia Experimentalis et Applicata*, **25**, 203–215.

Selander, R.K. (1966). Sexual dimorphism and differential niche utilization in birds. *Condor*, **68**, 113–151.

Sih, A. (1981). Stability, prey density and age-dependent interference in an aquatic insect predator *Notonecta hoffmanni*. *Journal of Animal Ecology*, **50**, 625–636.

Sih, A. (1984). Optimal behavior and density-dependent predation. *American Naturalist*, **123**, 314–326.

Smith, S.M. (1973). A study of prey attack behaviour in young loggerhead shrikes *Lanius ludovicianus*. *Behaviour*, **44**, 113–141.

Smith, T.B. & Temple, S.A. (1982). Feeding habits and bill polymorphism in hook-billed kites. *Auk*, **99**, 197–207.

Smith, W.H. (1965). Observations on the flora of the alimentary tract of animals and factors affecting its composition. *Journal of Pathology and Bacteriology*, **89**, 95–122.

Stamps, J.A. (1983). The relationship between ontogenetic habitat shifts, competition and predator avoidance in a juvenile lizard. *Behavioural Ecology and Sociobiology* **12**, 19–33.

Stem, R.A. (1977). Selective predation, optimal foraging, and the predator–prey interaction between fish and crayfish. *Ecology*, **58**, 1237–1253.

Tardif, R.R. & Gray, L. (1978). Feeding diversity of resident and immigrant *Peromyscus leucopus*. *Journal of Mammalogy*, **59**, 559–562.

Troyer, K. (1984). Diet selection and digestion in *Iguana iguana*: the importance of age and nutrient requirements. *Oecologia (Berlin)*, **61**, 201–207.

Turner, B.J. & Grosse, D.J. (1980). Trophic differentiation in *Ilyodon*, a genus of stream-dwelling goodeid fishes: speciation versus ecological polymorphism. *Evolution*, **343**, 259–270.

Van Horne, B. (1982). Niches of adult and juvenile deermice (*Peromyscus maniculatus*) in seral stages of coniferous forest. *Ecology*, **63**, 992–1003.

Werner, E.E. & Hall, D.J. (1979). Foraging efficiency and habitat switching in competing sunfishes. *Ecology*, **60**, 256–264.

Werner, E.E., Mittelbach, G.G. & Hall, D.J. (1981). The role of foraging profitability and experience in habitat use by the bluegill sunfish. *Ecology*, **62**, 116–125.

Williamson, M. (1981). *Island Populations*. Oxford University Press, Oxford.

Wilson, E.O. (1975). *Sociobiology*. The Belknap Press of Harvard University Press. Cambridge, Massachusetts.

Wyrwicka, W. (1978). Imitation of mother's inappropriate food preference in weanling kittens. *Pavlovian Journal of Biological Science*, **13**, 55–72.

12. INVERTEBRATE BEHAVIOUR AND THE STRUCTURE OF MARINE BENTHIC COMMUNITIES

K. H. MANN

Marine Ecology Laboratory, Department of Fisheries and Oceans,
Bedford Institute of Oceanography, Box 1006, Dartmouth, Nova Scotia,
Canada B2Y 4A2

SUMMARY

Sea urchins of the genus *Strongylocentrotus* provide spectacular examples of the way in which the adaptive behaviour of individual animals can profoundly affect the structure of whole communities. They have three modes of feeding: passive detritivore, aggressive herbivore and a browsing mode. Change from one to the other is seen as a response to changing population density and the need to protect themselves against predators. A case history of progression through the three modes of feeding is given from the Atlantic coast of Nova Scotia. It is associated with a change from highly productive kelp beds (*Laminaria* spp.) to relatively unproductive coralline communities. The whole phenomenon is considered in the context of other work on the mechanisms structuring marine benthic communities.

Particular attention is given to the paradigm which states that in every benthic community there is a hierarchy of competitive dominance, so that if conditions remain constant a small number of species use more and more of the resources. Factors which oppose this tendency, reducing the numbers of the competitive dominants and freeing resources for other species, are referred to as disturbance factors. In the North Pacific it is clear that sea urchins are competitive dominants and that sea otter predation is the main factor preventing their complete domination. The situation in Nova Scotia does not fit this paradigm and several factors, including urchin disease and interannual variations in temperature appear to play a part.

INTRODUCTION

During the last two decades, the study of marine benthic communities has shifted its emphasis from pattern recognition to experimental investigation of community dynamics. The great pioneers like Thorson (1957) and Stephenson & Stephenson (1972) took vast amounts of descriptive material from disparate areas and showed that for a given set of environmental conditions the same functional groups of invertebrates tend to occur, no matter where in the world you may look. Like many good ideas in science, it was pushed beyond the limits of the evidence, and a reaction set in, so that Mills (1975) was moved to refer to benthic ecology as 'a rather shabby and intellectually suspect branch of biological oceanography'.

Fortunately, by the time he wrote this, an alternative and much more dynamic approach to the understanding of marine benthic communities was already well under way, and it involved consideration of many aspects of animal behaviour. It was becoming apparent to careful observers that marine benthic communities, far from being static assemblages amenable to very detailed classification, are in a constant state of flux. New propagules, such as settling planktonic larvae, compete with established organisms for limiting resources, such as space and food. Those that succeed in establishing themselves intensify the competition as they grow, and may succeed in replacing their neighbours by crushing them, overgrowing them or intercepting their food. While these competitive interactions are in process, the community is disturbed from time to time by physical events or by the actions of predators, and uninhabited spaces are formed, in which the competitive processes begin anew. Some of this activity has a seasonal rhythm and some of it is random in its occurrence. If the sequence of events is studied in very fine detail, an impression is created of infinite complexity and great variability. But if controlled manipulations are performed and the results observed on an appropriate scale of time and space, clear patterns are seen.

Stated in its simplest form, without the qualifications that will be introduced later, the current paradigm of marine benthic community ecology may be stated as follows. In any community, there is a hierarchy of competitive dominance so that, if competition continues for an extended period, the top species use more and more of the resources, and species diversity is reduced. The factors which oppose this tendency all come under the general heading of 'disturbance'. Disturbance factors reduce the number of the competitive dominants, freeing resources for species lower in the hierarchy. Sometimes the disturbance factors are purely physical, like wave action or desiccation, but of particular interest in the present context are the behavioural disturbance factors, especially predation.

Early work in this field (Connell 1961; Paine 1966; Dayton 1971) was carried out on the intertidal communities of rocky shores. Subsequently, manipulations were carried out on the permanently submerged 'fouling' communities characteristic of the undersides of floating structures, dock piles, etc. (Sutherland 1974). Observations made by diving indicated that the grazing sea urchins on seaweed beds in the subtidal nearshore zone was producing phenomena analogous to those seen in the intertidal, and attempts were made to make the observations fit the paradigm (Mann 1972; Estes & Palmisano 1974). On the Pacific rim there seems to be little doubt that sea urchins are a competitive dominant in the rocky nearshore subtidal environment, and that predation is the disturbance factor which tends to prevent them from monopolizing the resources. In Eastern Canada the ecological interactions of the sea urchin *Strongylocentrotus droebachiensis* have been studied intensively for more than 15 years, and we are still not sure that the facts fit the paradigm. From the point of view of this symposium, however, it is very clear that the behaviour of *S. droebachiensis* has profound and far-reaching effects on the structure of the nearshore benthic community.

This paper is concerned with the development of current ideas on the structure and function of marine benthic communities, and with attempts to find a coherent explanation for the 'sea urchin phenomenon.'

EFFECT OF GRAZERS ON MARINE PLANT COMMUNITIES

There is no doubt that grazers dramatically affect marine plant communities. Paine (1977) reviewed the evidence showing that manipulation of populations of limpets, littorines, chitons, sea urchins or fish produce major changes in the resident flora. In what follows we consider some more recent developments.

Effect of Littorina *grazing*

Lubchenco (1978) found that in rock pools near high tide level on the New England coast, the green alga *Enteromorpha intestinalis* was the competitive dominant, and in the absence of grazers she found only three species in the community (Fig. 12.1a). However, by manipulating densities of the snail *Littorina littorea* she was able to show that the biomass of *Enteromorpha* could be reduced and communities of eight to twelve species could develop. Maximum species diversity was obtained at densities of 100–200 snails m^{-2}. Above this density, the whole community was impoverished by overgrazing, so that there was a humped curve relating herbivore density to algal species diversity (Fig. 12.1a).

This relationship does not hold if the competitive dominant is selectively avoided by the grazer. On the exposed rock surface between tide pools in the lower intertidal level, Lubchenco (1978) found that desiccation favoured the perennial brown algae *Fucus* and *Ascophyllum* rather than *Enteromorpha*. *Littorina* lived in this situation, but it foraged in the understorey between the *Fucus* and *Ascophyllum*. At low population densities of the snails up to twelve

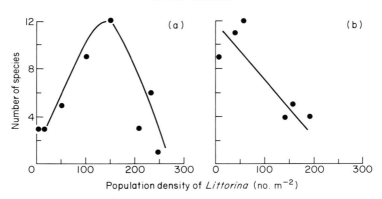

FIG. 12.1. (a) Effect of *Littorina* density on number of algal species presents in pools near tide level. (From Lubchenko 1978.) (b) Effect of *Littorina* density on number of algal species on rocky surfaces between pools in low intertidal zone. (From Lubchenco 1978.)

species of algae co-existed with the dominants, but as *Littorina* numbers increased, more and more species were eliminated. Hence, the effect of *Littorina* on the community was quite different when the competitive dominant was selectively avoided (Fig. 12.1b).

On the other hand, predation can increase species diversity even when the predator shows no particular preference for the competitive dominant. In work that will be discussed later (p. 234) Menge (1976, 1978) found that the gastropod *Thais* controlled the abundance of the competitively dominant mussels (*Mytilus*) even though it showed no preference between mussels and barnacles as food. Caswell (1978) and Hanski (1981) put forward theoretical models in which predators increased species diversity in a community without showing a strong preference for the competitive dominant.

Calcareous deposits as a defence against herbivores

Recent work (e.g. Steneck 1982, 1983) has shown very clearly that, in communities with heavy grazing, red algae have adopted two protective strategies: (i) a low encrusting form and (ii) thick calcareous tissue over growth zones and reproductive organs. For example, the limpet *Acmaea testudinalis* on the coast of Maine, USA, is found most abundantly attached to the coralline alga *Clathromorphum circumscriptum* and its radula is clearly adapted to browsing on the calcareous tissue. The alga appears to need browsers for its survival, for in their absence it quickly becomes colonized by epiphytic algae which cut off the light and kill it. This seems to be a clear case of coevolution, an example of the herbivore evolving an adaptation to more efficient browsing and the food organism evolving its defences, and so on—the 'evolutionary arms race'. An interesting perspective on the coevolution of corallines and their grazers is given by Steneck (1983). He shows that in molluscs, echinoderms and fish there has been since the mid-Mesozoic era a spectacular increase in the number of groups and species capable of excavating calcareous substrata, and a parallel adaptive radiation of corallines.

When sea urchins overgraze seaweed beds, denuding the rocks of fleshy algae, the algal assemblage that remains is dominated by encrusting corallines which are resistant to the grazing of the urchins. Many of these ward off epiphytes by sloughing surface cells or by emitting chemical defence substances. The situation in which the coralline has no defence against epiphytes except an obligatory association with a herbivore appears to be the exception rather than the rule (Littler, Taylor & Littler 1983).

Sea urchins: their three patterns of feeding behaviour

The ability of sea urchins to control algal populations was first documented in an experimental way by Kitching & Ebling (1961) in Lough Ine. There have been many subsequent examples, but in Nova Scotia in the last decade we have witnessed destruction of algal beds by the sea urchin *Strongylocentrotus droebachiensis* over an extremely large area (Wharton & Mann 1981).

The sea urchin *Strongylocentrotus droebachiensis* is approximately spherical in shape, has well developed jaws and is capable of devouring large seaweeds at a great rate. Nevertheless, it has been observed many times to live in equilibrium with dense kelp beds which persist for long periods. Under these circumstances its population density is low ($\sim 0\cdot1$ m^{-2}) and the urchins live in crevices from which they seem never to emerge (Bernstein, Williams & Mann 1981; Hagen 1983). The source of food is probably pieces of algae which break off and drift into the crevices. This may be called the passive detritivore mode.

Sometimes there develops a temporary phase in which the urchins are much more abundant (30–100 m^{-2}), and aggregate in the open. The aggregations form around the bases of kelp plants (*Laminaria*) on which they feed voraciously. These aggregations have been seen on the North American coast (Breen & Mann 1976; Garnick 1978) and on the Norwegian coast (Hagen 1983), and similar aggregations have been noted for other species in many parts of the world. The aggregations may be isolated clumps of urchins, associated with one or two kelp plants, or they may form lines, or 'fronts', extending for tens of metres along the edges of dense kelp beds, into which they may advance steadily at a rate of 1–2 m per month, eating everything in their path. We may call this the 'aggressive herbivore mode'. Garnick (1978) documented a situation in New England in which there were feeding aggregations in exposed places and non-feeding aggregations in more sheltered places. Although the aggregations persisted in the same places for many days, their composition changed on a daily basis, with the urchins shuttling between the feeding and non-feeding aggregations. The average duration of stay was 1 day in a feeding aggregation and 6 days in a non-feeding aggregation.

The third mode develops slowly after a kelp bed has been completely destroyed by urchin grazing. When we first observed kelp bed destruction we assumed that there would be a mass mortality of the urchins as a result of starvation. This was not the case. In the places where dense kelp beds had stood there were large areas of rocky substrate to which were attached crustose coralline algae. The urchins distributed themselves over these areas and maintained high population densities ($30-100$ m^{-2}) for a decade. The almost complete destruction of kelp in St. Margarets bay (140 km^2) was observed in the early 1970s (Breen & Mann 1976), but the urchin populations persisted until the early 1980s. Meanwhile, a survey in 1978–1979 showed that similar kelp bed destruction had occurred along 500 km of the Nova Scotia coast (Wharton & Mann, 1981).

Lang & Mann (1976) showed that after kelp bed destruction the urchins had greatly reduced growth rates and gonad production. The urchins fed on drift algae from the intertidal and sublittoral fringe (where wave action protected the algae from the urchins), on diatom films which coated the rocks, on seasonal growths of ephemeral algae, and on corallines, but the total plant productivity was two orders of magnitude lower than in the original kelp beds (Chapman 1981). What was particularly interesting was the way in which the urchins alternated between coming out on top of the rocks to feed and going down under the rocks to hide from potential predators. Bernstein, Williams & Mann (1981) observed that in summer, the majority were living cryptically by day and foraged only at night, whereas in winter the majority were out in the open both by day and by night. This correlated with the tendency of predatory fish to move into shallow water in summer, but to move offshore in winter.

The underwater community that replaces kelp beds after destruction by sea urchins is known from many parts of the world. The Japanese call it 'Isoyake' and have studied it since the turn of the century (Hagen 1983); coralline specialists call it 'coralline flats' (Ayling 1981) and echinoderm specialists call it 'urchin-dominated barren grounds' (Lawrence 1975). The feeding behaviour of the urchins in these situations may be called the browsing mode.

It is interesting to note that *Strongylocentrotus droebachiensis* has flexibility to live for long periods in two quite different modes, and in a third mode during a transitional period. In the passive detritivore mode they live a solitary, cryptic existence. In the aggressive herbivore mode they live in aggregations. (There are two variants, one of which has them shuttling between discrete feeding aggregations and non-feeding aggregations, while in the other they form extended 'fronts' from which they have not been observed to depart (Garnick 1978; Bernstein, Williams & Mann 1981). Finally, when the kelp has been overgrazed, they live in a disaggregated manner, moving between the tops of rocks where they browse, and the crevices where they hide. The question of what controls these behaviour patterns will be discussed after we have reviewed relevant work from other habitats.

Lawrence (1975) reviewed what is known about the feeding habits of sea urchins on a world-wide basis. He found almost forty published descriptions of 'urchin-dominated' barren grounds, so the browsing mode of life is clearly widespread. The aggressive herbivore mode has been reported many times, often in association with the transition from dense kelp to barren grounds, but in South Africa (Fricke 1979) and in Chile (Castilla & Moreno 1982) the sea urchins are apparently incapable of destroying the kelp plants among which they live. Under these circumstances, passive detritivory is an important feeding mode. Lawrence (1975) also records many times that animal remains have been found in urchin guts, emphasizing that they are not exclusively herbivorous.

PREDATOR–HERBIVORE INTERACTIONS

Mussel communities

We saw in the introduction that work in the intertidal zone suggested that predators may have a strong influence on community structure. Paine (1966) observed that in some parts of the coast of the State of Washington, *Mytilus californianus* forms intertidal mussel beds that are almost continuous over large areas. In other places the same intertidal zone had a more diverse community including starfish, snails, chitons, limpets, nudibranchs, mussels, barnacles, anemones, sponges and four species of benthic algae. When Paine removed all the starfish *Pisaster ochreus* from an experimental area, and maintained that condition for 3 years, the mussels came to dominate the community, forcing out the benthic algae, the barnacles, the nudibranchs and the sponges. He proposed that the starfish, by preying on the mussels, were preventing them from reaching complete dominance, thus permitting coexistence of a number of other species. In its general form, this has become known as the keystone predator hypothesis.

On the Atlantic coast of the USA, Menge (1976) obtained analogous results. He found that the gastropod *Thais* reduced the abundance of *Mytilus* and permitted algae, limpets and three species of *Littorina* to enter the community. A complicating factor was the effect of wave action on the abundance of *Thais*. In sites less exposed to wave action *Thais* was more abundant and more effective in reducing the competitive dominance of mussels (Menge & Sutherland 1976).

Intertidal communities in Australia

Underwood, Denley & Moran (1983) reported on their experimental manipulations of mid-shore intertidal communities in New South Wales. They concluded that there was no clear competitive dominant, and that the competitive success of various species was dependent on chance events such as the settlement of planktonic larvae of a species which happened to come along soon after a space had been opened in a community. They observed the following competitive interactions. Recruitment of limpets (*Cellana*) was negatively associated with increasing density of adult limpets, and with increasing density of barnacles (*Tesseropera*). Growth and survival of juvenile limpets was decreased by increasing density of barnacles. Adult limpets migrated away from dense populations of barnacles and if confined to such areas starved and lost weight. Conversely, the settlement and survival of barnacles was affected sometimes positively, sometimes negatively by the activities of limpets, depending on the relative density of barnacles and limpets, the height on the shore and the weather. Predatory whelks, *Morula*, had no effect on the recruitment or survival of the limpets (*Cellana*), but for a smaller limpet, *Patelloida*, survival was poor in areas where whelks were active.

While it seems reasonable to expect that in any given community, under a particular set of environmental conditions, there will always be a competitive dominant, it is conceivable that in some situations the environmental conditions are so variable that the potential competitive dominant is constantly changing. It is also conceivable that the random nature of recruitment processes makes it necessary to observe a situation over a long period before a clear competitive dominant emerges as a statistical trend. We shall return to this point in the next section.

'Fouling' communities on submerged surfaces

Permanently submerged hard surfaces within the euphotic zone are often colonized by characteristic assemblages of sessile organisms. If they are isolated from the predatory or grazing activities of bottom-living inverte-brates, as is often the case on the undersides of ships or other man-made structures, they may develop a particularly large biomass and have a nuisance value. Hence, they have come to be known as 'fouling communities'. Sutherland (1974) developed an experimental method for non-destructive sampling of such communities. He suspended ceramic tiles at a depth of 0·3 m below low tide level, and retrieved them for observation at regular intervals.

From the first 4 years of observation it was clear that larval recruitment was very variable and unpredictable (Sutherland & Karlson 1977). It was also seen that each resident adult tended to inhibit the recruitment and development of other species though with varying degrees of success. Finally, Sutherland & Karlson (1977) found that larvae differed in their ability to colonize occupied substrate. The tunicates *Styela* and *Botryllus* and the sponges *Haliclona* and *Halichondria* were common invaders of fully occupied space, whereas the larvae of many other species failed to do so. After 4 years of study the authors concluded that there was no evidence of competitive dominance.

However, the conclusions changed significantly when Sutherland (1981) was able to review 7–8 years' data. *Styela*, which we have seen could colonize mature communities, was able to then resist further colonization by other species. It commonly invaded a community in the spring, grew to a large size in the summer, then sloughed off in the autumn, taking much of the adjacent community with it. Next spring, it was almost always the successful colonist of the space it had created, displacing anything that had arrived during the intervening period. Statistically, over the whole period, it was the most dominating species. On a sufficiently long time scale, it appeared to be the competitive dominant after all.

It is now possible to argue that in the fouling communities and perhaps also in the Australian intertidal communities the paradigm is not violated. There really is some competitor which is best adapted to the average environmental conditions, so that in some sense it is the competitive dominant. If this signal is obscured by the noise of environmental variability, by random events such as the arrival of planktonic larvae just at the time when space is made available, or even by very intense predation then it is necessary to continue the observations over a longer period in order to find out which species, in a statistical sense, is the competitive dominant. On the other hand, chance events and/or disturbance may be so intense that a competitive dominant, even if it exists, never emerges.

Communities living in sediment

The fact that sediment-dwelling animals inhabit a three-dimensional world while hard-bottom communities compete for space on a two-dimensional surface may mean that the rules for competitive displacement are quite different in the two environments. Woodin (1978) showed that on an intertidal sand flat in Virginia there were two predators which preyed extensively on the infauna and also caused important physical disturbance of the community. The blue crab *Callinectes* and the horseshoe crab *Limulus* dug pits in the sediment at high tide, as they searched for food organisms. If stranded by the falling tide they buried themselves completely. Their activities are modified by a polychaete worm *Diopatra*, which forms a tube about 1 m long projecting about 5 cm above the sediment surface. A cluster of these tubes is a barrier to the activities of the crabs, so that within the cluster the population density of prey organisms is higher. This is indirect evidence that predation is a significant factor in structuring a sediment community.

OTHER FORMS OF DISTURBANCE IN COMMUNITIES

In all of the situations in which a competitive dominant is identified, and can be observed to be expanding its share of the resources, circumstances arise which cause a reversal of this trend. We have discussed the role of predation in this context, but there are many cases documented where physical forces play an analogous role. Dayton (1971) showed that the impact of wave-driven floating logs could restrict the competitive dominance of barnacles, and Connell (1978) suggested that storms and other forms of disturbance are essential to maintaining the species diversity of coral reefs. Sousa (1979) showed that overturning intertidal boulders by wave action led to increased species diversity among the organisms colonizing the boulders. Paine & Levin (1981) documented and modelled the formation of gaps in mussel beds on the Washington coast, these gaps being formed mainly by severe wave action. In some situations, however, there is a two-step interaction, in which wave action is strong enough to remove the predators but not strong enough to damage the competitive dominant, so that physical disturbance actually favours the dominant (Menge & Sutherland 1976).

SEA URCHINS AS COMPETITIVE DOMINANTS

The evidence already presented makes it clear that under some circumstances urchins are the dominant invertebrates on rocky bottoms in the nearshore subtidal zone. The occurrence of 'urchin-dominated barren grounds' has been noted from both eastern and western shores of the North Atlantic, and both sides of the North Pacific (Himmelman 1969; Paine & Vadas 1969; Leighton 1971; Mann 1972; Estes & Palmisano 1974; Breen & Mann 1976; Duggins 1980; Hagen 1983). An indication of the relative biomasses of urchins and other invertebrates can be obtained from the energy flow model for St Margaret's Bay, Nova Scotia, constructed by Miller, Mann & Scarratt (1971) at a time when the kelp beds were still more or less intact but the sea urchins had clearly begun their population explosion. The urchin biomass was twice that of all other invertebrates combined. The question to be examined next is: Are sea urchin populations controlled by keystone predators?

Sea otters as controlling predators

The sea otter, *Enhydra lutris* was once abundant around the North Pacific rim from northern Japan to California, (Fig. 12.2) but is now reduced to isolated populations on the Kuril, Commander and Aleutian Islands, parts of south eastern Alaska, and to some places in British Columbia, Washington, Oregon and California where populations have been reintroduced. It is known to feed

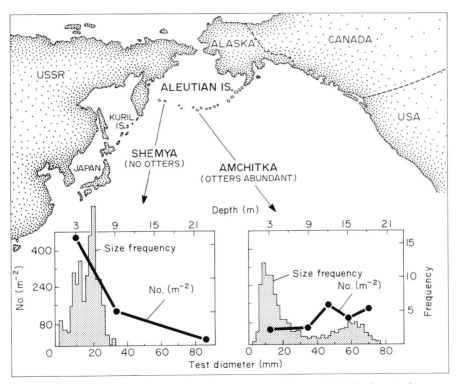

FIG. 12.2. Map to show Aleutian Islands and to show sea urchin population density at various depths and sizes frequency of sea urchins (all depths combined) on islands with and without otters. (After Estes & Palmisano 1974.)

voraciously on sea urchins. An investigation of two Aleutian islands, one with otters and one without, showed that at the island with otters there were far fewer sea urchins (*Strongylocentrotus* spp.) and those that were present grew to larger size (Estes & Palmisano 1974). The island with otters and fewer urchins had an extremely dense, almost complete cover of kelps, while the other one had very little macrovegetation subtidally. Dayton (1975) investigated competitive interactions between the three kelps *Alaria, Laminaria* and *Agarum* on the island of Amchitka and confirmed that sea otters, by their predation on urchins, had a powerful influence on the structure of nearshore kelp communities. These results have been amply confirmed by subsequent work in the Aleutians (Estes, Smith & Palmisano 1978; Simenstad, Estes & Kenyon 1978; Estes, Jameson & Rhode 1982) and by studies of situations where the otters have been reintroduced, e.g. south east Alaska (Duggins 1980), southern British Columbia (Breen *et al.* 1982).

This example clearly fits the paradigm discussed in the introduction. Sea urchins are capable of becoming the dominant invertebrates, and in doing so they radically change the whole nearshore community from one dominated by highly productive fleshy algae to one dominated by the urchins themselves. The factor which in some areas prevents the urchins from 'taking over' is the predatory action of sea otters. The relationship is analogous to that between the mussels and their predators in the intertidal zone, except that when mussels are controlled by their predators there is a less spectacular growth of primary producers, and much of the space is occupied by sub-dominant invertebrates like barnacles, limpets, etc.

Other controls on sea urchin numbers in the Pacific

Dayton & Tenger (1984) pointed out that sea otters have been functionally absent from southern California for 150 years, but luxuriant kelp forests have persisted. They showed that the two important sea urchins, *Strongylocentrotus franciscanus* and *S. purpuratus* are largely controlled by predation from spiny lobster *Panulirus interruptus* and a fish known as sheepshead *Semicossyphus pulcher* (Tegner & Dayton, 1981). It seems that in Alaska the sea urchins have no other important predators except sea otters, and the role of otters as 'keystone predators' in the system is clear cut. But as one moves south along the Pacific coast the situation becomes more complex, with other predators playing a part, and other environmental changes having an effect.

For example, the Peruvian upwelling failure ('El Nino') of 1957–1959 resulted in abnormally high water temperatures in the Californian Current, an increase in salinity and decreased southward flow. In other words, large amounts of tropical water intruded into the California system. No detailed studies of kelp and urchins were in progress, but it is known that sea urchin densities vastly increased and most of the kelp forests virtually disappeared (Dayton & Tegner, 1984).

What controls Strongylocentrotus *in the North Atlantic?*

In 1972, with Paine's keystone predator hypothesis in mind, Mann & Breen (1972) proposed that the great increase in sea urchin numbers observed in St Margarets Bay was the result of release from predation. It was known that urchins were preyed upon by a variety of fish as well as by crabs and lobsters, but of these, only the lobsters were known to be subject to heavy fishing mortality. It therefore seemed possible that lobsters were keystone predators analogous to sea otters. Breen & Mann (1976) published evidence showing a decrease of 50% in the catch of lobsters in St Margaret's Bay at the time of kelp bed destruction, and Wharton & Mann (1981) documented a clear correlation between declining lobster stocks and destruction of kelp beds by sea urchins along 500 km of Nova Scotia coastline (Fig. 12.3). In a review of the situation, Mann (1977) stated: 'There are two hypotheses which are not fully substantiated, although both seem likely to be true. These are: (1) that the basic cause of kelp bed destruction is removal of lobsters from the system, and (2) that urchin-dominated barren grounds represent a stable system rather than a short interlude between two peaks of kelp biomass'.

A totally unexpected turn of events caused us to rethink both of these hypotheses. Beginning in 1980, there were widespread mass mortalities of the urchins, clearly caused by an outbreak of a communicable disease (Miller & Colodey 1983; Moore & Miller 1983; Scheibling & Stephenson 1984). The causative agent is only communicated effectively when the water temperature is above 12°C. The summers of 1980, 1981 and 1982 were associated with above average water temperature, and resulted in virtual elimination of sea urchin populations to a depth of about 25 m along some hundreds of km of the Nova Scotia coast (Fig. 12.3). Populations of algae quickly regenerated so that now we are approaching the completion of an outbreak cycle begun 15–20 years ago when the urchins first began to overgraze the kelp. If sea temperature can have such a drastic effect on the whole inshore community, precipitating an abrupt switch from barren grounds to kelp beds, what other effects may it have?

Foreman (1977) reported on an outbreak of *Strongylocentrotus droeba-chiensis* in the Straits of Georgia, British Columbia. In a survey of 200 km of coastline, twenty-one sites were located where *S. droebachiensis* was very abundant (average 322 m⁻²) and eight of those sites had urchin populations extending for more than 2 ha. It appears that most of the urchins had recruited

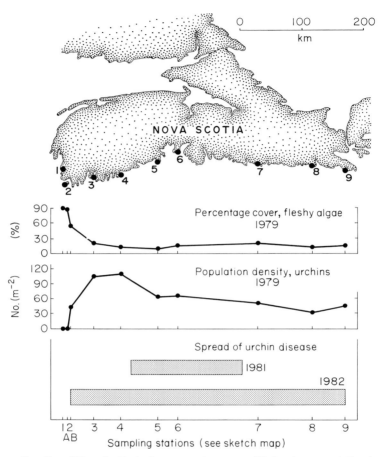

FIG. 12.3. Coastline of Nova Scotia, to show percentage cover of fleshy algae, population density (no. m^{-2}) of urchins in 1979 and geographical extent of urchin mortality in subsequent years. (From Wharton & Mann 1981; Scheibling & Stephenson 1984.)

in one year, 1969, in which there was a favourable spring plankton bloom, the spring water temperatures constituted a 20-year record low, and the duration of cool water temperature was unusually extended. He concluded that since *S. droebachiensis* is a cold water species and the Straits of Georgia are near the southern end of its range, unusually cold conditions may well favour outbreaks of the species.

Coming back to the Nova Scotia coast, we may note that low temperatures are unfavourable for the development of lobsters (Harding, Drinkwater & Vass 1983) and may be expected to reduce the predatory activities of the fish, many of which enter the nearshore zone only during the summer period. Hence, we plan in Nova Scotia to investigate further the possibility that the build up of *S. droebachiensis* populations occurs in cooler than average years, while population collapse occurs in warmer than average years.

To summarize to this point, it now seems likely that the control of sea urchin populations in Nova Scotia is not analogous to the control of sea urchins by sea otters in Alaska, i.e. attributable to the activities of a single keystone predator. Instead, the situation seems to be closer to that found in southern California, where the occurrence of a suite of predators and long-term fluctuations in oceanographic conditions cause the situation to be much less simple and clear cut than in Alaska.

Sea urchin behaviour determines community structure

Since a simple keystone predator hypothesis was not adequate to explain the changes observed in the kelp–urchin system of Nova Scotia, we tried to give an explanation in terms of the three types of feeding behaviour of *Strongylocentrotus*. Our working scenario was: Destruction of kelp beds is the result of a switch from the passive detritivore mode of feeding to the aggressive herbivore mode. The passive detritivore mode, in which the urchins live in crevices, is adopted by them as a defence against predators. When urchins become very abundant they are unable to find enough crevices and enough detrital food, so they adopt an alternative predator defence mechanism, which is to form fully exposed aggregations. Kelp plants which are 1–2 m long and kept in constant motion by wave action are relatively immune to the attacks of single urchins, but an aggregation can cut through the stipe, hold down the plant, and completely devour it before passing to the next. In time, whole kelp communities are destroyed by this feeding process.

To investigate this scenario, we tested the following hypotheses (Mann *et al.* 1984; Bernstein, Schroeter & Mann 1983).

(a) Sea urchins are capable of detecting the presence of predators and of kelp and of reacting appropriately to each.

(b) Increasing the population density increases the tendency to aggregate.

(c) The presence of predators increases the tendency to aggregate.

(d) The responses of urchins on barren grounds are different from the responses of urchins in kelp beds.

To demonstrate reaction to water-borne stimuli from predators we set up a chamber with two converging currents of water and found that at temperatures of 10–12°C, 80% of the urchins responded within 5 min by moving away from the stream of water that had passed over one lobster or two crabs. When the temperature was lowered, a much higher proportion of the urchins remained inactive but of those that responded within 5 min, the same proportion, about 80%, moved away from the scent of a predator.

Keeping the temperature in the 10–12°C range, we tested other organisms. There was no significant response to starfish, or to other urchins, but when an urchin was crushed, the test animals moved away. When urchins were allowed to eat kelp in the stimulus chamber, the experimental animals moved towards that side but since they had not moved towards intact urchins we inferred that the attractant emanated from the kelp. When urchins were placed in one stimulus tank, and kelp in the other, the urchins moved towards the kelp.

The response of the urchins to various extracts of kelp was also investigated. The attractant substance was very powerful, for when 75 g of *Laminaria* was left in 500 ml of distilled water for 10 min, an optimum response was obtained from the urchins when that solution was effectively diluted 7500 ×, and significant responses were obtained at twice that dilution.

To experiment with the factors influencing aggregation, an underwater multi-factorial experiment was designed (Bernstein *et al.* 1983). Flexible netting cages were designed that would withstand the strong wave surge characteristic of the kelp bed habitat. Each had a floor area of 1 m² and thirty-six of these were deployed by anchoring them to large boulders. In the factorial experiment the following variables were controlled: (i) source of urchins (kelp bed or barrens), (ii) population density of urchins (high, 20 per cage, or low, 4 per cage), (iii) location of experiment (kelp bed or barrens), (iv) presence or absence of invertebrate predators (crabs or lobsters), and (v) season (winter or summer). One may ask why the design was so complex. Why not elegantly simple experiments, holding all conditions constant except one? The answer is found in Underwood (1981); in nature many factors change simultaneously, and it is important to investigate first, second and even third order interactions in order to understand what is going on in natural populations. For details, the interested reader should consult the original publication, but the result of analysis of variance was to show that urchins aggregate more at high density than at low density, and that the tendency to aggregate was enhanced by the presence of lobsters when the experiments were conducted in kelp beds, and by the presence of crabs in experiments on the barrens. For urchins that did not aggregate, the presence of lobsters increased the tendency to hide in crevices under rocks, or to move away from the predator to the periphery of the cage.

From these experiments, we are able to see how the behaviour of the sea urchins leads to major changes in community structure along hundreds of km of the Nova Scotia shoreline. At low population density, in the presence of predators, the sea urchins live cryptically. When population density increases the sea urchins aggregate in relatively exposed situations and this may happen either if there are more urchins than crevices or if the supply of detrital food to the crevices is limiting. With their demonstrated awareness both of the presence of predators and of the presence of *Laminaria* the urchins form aggregations large enough to attack and destroy whole kelp plants.

After all the fleshy algae in an area have been destroyed, the plant community remaining is dominated by encrusting coralline algae that are resistant to urchin grazing. Under these conditions the urchins maintain a relatively high population density for a decade or more, browsing on the tops of the rocks for part of the time, especially at night, and hiding from predators during the day, particularly in summer.

Predators such as lobsters thus perform two opposite roles. At low urchin population densities they keep the urchins in hiding and thereby contribute to kelp bed persistence. At higher urchin densities, predators trigger the formation of large, exposed urchin aggregations that graze destructively on kelp. The large-scale change in community structure, from kelp bed to barrens, can thus be understood in terms of the adaptive behavioural response of individual organisms.

The missing piece of the puzzle is the answer to the question, 'What causes urchin numbers to increase dramatically?' Is it simply release from predator pressure, or is it some factor or combination of factors that leads to one or more highly successful year-classes? Since the scale of the phenomenon was about 500 km, and 20 years, it will be necessary to look at oceanographic phenomena on comparable scales.

ACKNOWLEDGMENTS

The work on the kelp–urchin system of Nova Scotia was made possible by grants from the Natural Science and Engineering Research Council of Canada, and by funds from the Department of Fisheries and Oceans and the Department of Supply and Services. Of the colleagues whose publications are mentioned, the author owes a particular debt to Paul Breen, Brock Bernstein, Robert Miller, Richard and Barbara Welsford and Gary Wharton. Robert Paine, Craig Johnson, Nils Hagen, Paul Johns, Robert Stephenson and Robert Miller provided valuable criticism.

REFERENCES

Ayling, A.M. (1981). The role of biological disturbance in temperate subtidal encrusting communities. *Ecology*, **62**, 830–847.

Bernstein, B.B., Schroeter, S.C. & Mann, K.H. (1983). Sea urchin (*Strongylocentrotus droebachiensis*) aggregating behaviour investigated by a subtidal multifactorial experiment. *Canadian Journal of Fisheries and Aquatic Sciences*, **40**, 1975–1980.

Bernstein, B.B., Williams, B.E. & Mann, K.H. (1981). The role of behavioural responses to predators in modifying urchins' (*Strongylocentrotus droebachiensis*) destructive grazing and seasonal foraging patterns. *Marine Biology*, **63**, 9–49.

Breen, P.A., Carson, T.A., Foster, J.B. & Stewart, E.A. (1982). Changes in subtidal community structure associated with British Columbia sea otter transplants. *Marine Ecology Progress Series*, **7**, 13–20.

Breen, P.A. & Mann, K,H. (1976). Destructive grazing by sea urchins in Eastern Canada. *Journal of the Fisheries Research Board of Canada*, **33**, 1278–1283.

Castilla, J.C. & Moreno, C.A. (1982). Sea urchins and *Macrocystis pyrifera*: experimental test of their ecological relations in Southern Chile. *Echinoderms* (Ed. by J.M. Lawrence), pp. 257–263. Proceedings of the International Conference, Tampa Bay, A.A. Balkema, Rotterdam.

Caswell, H. (1978). Predator-mediated coexistence: a non-equilibrium model. *American Naturalist*, **112**, 127–154.

Chapman, A.R.O. (1981). Stability of sea-urchin dominated barren grounds following destructive grazing of kelp in St. Margarets Bay, eastern Canada. *Marine Biology*, **62**, 307–311.

Connell, J.H. (1961). Effects of competition, predation by *Thais lapillus*, and other factors on natural populations of the barnacle *Balanus balanoides*. *Ecological Monographs*, **31**, 61–104.

Connell, J.H. (1978). Diversity in tropical rain forests and coral reefs. *Science*, **199**, 1302–1310.

Dayton, P.K. (1971). Competition, disturbance and community organizations: the provision and subsequent utilization of space in a rocky intertidal community. *Ecological Monographs*, **41**, 351–389.

Dayton, P.K. (1975). Experimental studies of algal canopy interactions in a sea-otter dominated kelp community at Amchitka Island, Alaska. *Fishery Bulletin of the U.S. Fish and Wildlife Service*, **73**, 230–237.

Dayton, P.K. & Tenger, M.J. (1984). The importance of scale in community ecology: a kelp forest example with terrestial analogs. *A New Ecology: Novel Approaches to Interactive Systems* (Ed. by P.W. Price, C.N. Slobodchikoff & W.S. Gaud). pp. 457–481. John Wiley & Sons, New York.

Duggins, D.O. (1980). Kelp beds and sea otters: an experimental approach. *Ecology*, **61**, 447–453.

Estes, J.A. & Palmisano, J.F. (1974). Sea otters: their role in structuring nearshore communities. *Science*, **285**, 1058–1060.

Estes, J.A., Smith, N.S., & Palmisano, J.F. (1978). Sea otter predation and community organization in western Aleutian Islands, Alaska. *Ecology*, **59**, 822–833.

Estes, J.A., Jameson, R.J. & Rhode, E.B. (1982). Activity and prey selection in the sea otter: Influence of population status on community structure. *American Naturalist*, **120**, 242–258.

Foreman, R.E. (1977). Benthic community modification and recovery following intensive grazing by *Strongylocentrotus droebachiensis*. *Helgoländer wissenschaftliche Meeresuntersuchungen*, **30**, 468–484.

Fricke, A.H. (1979). Kelp grazing by the common sea urchin *Parechinus angulosus* Leske in False Bay, Cape. *South African Journal of Zoology*, **14**, 143–148.

Garnick, E. (1978). Behavioural ecology of *Strongylocentrotus droebachiensis* (Muller) (Echinodermata: Echinoidea): aggregating behaviour and chemotaxis. *Oecologia (Berlin)*, **37**, 77–84.

Hagen, N.T. (1983). Destructive grazing of kelp beds by sea urchins in Vestfjorden, northern Norway. *Sarsia*, **68**, 177–190.

Hanski, I. (1981). Coexistence of competitors in a patchy environment with and without predation. *Oikos*, **37**, 306–312.

Harding, G.C., Drinkwater, K.F. & Vass, W.P. (1983). Factors influencing the size of the American Lobster (*Homarus americanus*) stocks along the Atlanitic coast of Nova Scotia, Gulf of St. Lwrence and Gulf of Maine: A new synthesis. *Canadian Journal of Fisheries and Aquatic Sciences*, **40**, 168–184.

Himmelman, J.H. (1969). *Some aspects of the ecology of* Strongylocentrotus droebachiensis *in eastern Newfoundland.* M.Sc. Thesis, Memorial University, St John's, Newfoundland.

Kitching, J.A. & Ebling, F.J. (1961). The ecology of Lough Ine, XI. The control of algae by *Paracentrotus lividus* (Echinoidea). *Journal of Animal Ecology*, **30**, 373–383.

Lang, C. & Mann, K.H. (1976). Changes in sea urchin populations after destruction of kelp beds. *Marine Biology*, **36**, 321–326.

Lawrence, J.M. (1975). On the relationship between marine plants and sea-urchins. *Oceanography and Marine Biology, Annual Review*, **13**, 213–286.

Leighton, D.L. (1971). Grazing activities of benthic invertebrates in Southern California kelp beds. *The Biology of Giant Kelp Beds* (*Macrocystis*) *in California* (Ed. by W.J. North), pp. 421–453. Nova Hedwigia Supplement, 32.

Littler, M.M., Taylor, P.R. & Littler, B.S. (1983). Algal resistence to herbivory on a Caribbean barrier reef. *Coral Reefs*, **2**, 111–118.

Lubchenco, J. (1978). Plant species diversity in a marine intertidal community: importance of herbivore food preference and algal competitive abilities. *American Naturalist*, **112**, 23–39.

Mann, K.H. (1972). Ecological energetics of the seaweed zone in a marine bay on the Atlantic coast of Canada. I. Zonation and biomass of seaweeds. *Marine Biology*, **12**, 1–10.

Mann, K.H. (1977). Destruction of kelp beds by sea urchins: cyclic phenomenon or irreversible degradation? *Helgoländer wissenschaftliche Merresuntersuchungen*, **20**, 455–467.

Mann, K.H., & Breen, P.A. (1972). The relation between lobster abundance, sea urchins & kelp beds. *Journal of the Fisheries Research Board of Canada*, **29**, 603–609.

Mann, K.H., Wright, J.L.C., Welsford, B.E. & Hatfield, E. (1984). Responses of the sea urchin *Strongylocentrotus droebachiensis* to water-borne stimuli from potential predators and potential food algae. *Journal of Experimental Marine Biology and Ecology*, **79**, 233–234.

Menge, B.A. (1976). Organization of the New England rocky intertidal community: Role of predators, competition and environmental heterogeneity. *Ecological Monographs*, **46**, 355–393.

Menge, B.A. (1978). Predation intensity in a rocky intertidal community: Relation between predator foraging activity and environmental harshness. *Oecologia*, **34**, 1–16.

Menge, B.A. & Sutherland, J.B. (1976). Species diversity gradients: Synthesis of the roles of predation, competition and temporal heterogeneity. *American Naturalist*, **110**, 351–369.

Miller, R.J. & Colodey A.G. (1983). Widespread mass mortalities of the green sea urchin in Nova Scotia, Canada. *Marine Biology*, **73**, 263–267.

Miller, R.J., Mann, K.H. & Scarratt, D.J. (1971). Production potential of a seaweed-lobster community in Eastern Canada. *Journal of the Fisheries Research Board of Canada*, **28**, 1733–1738.

Mills, E.L. (1975). Benthic organisms and the structure of marine ecosystems. *Journal of the Fisheries Research Board of Canada*, **32**, 1657–1663.

Moore, D.S. & Miller, R.J. (1983). Recovery of macroalgae following widespread sea urchin mortality with description of the nearshore hard-bottom habitat on the Atlantic Coast of Nova Scotia. *Canadian Technical Report of Fisheries and Aquatic Sciences*, 1230. 94p.

Paine, R.T. (1966). Food web complexity and species diversity. *American Naturalist*, **100**, 65–75.

Paine, R.T. (1977). Controlled manipulations in the marine intertidal zone and their contributions to ecological theory. *Changing Scenes in the Natural Sciences 1776–1976* (Ed. by C.E. Goulden). Special Publication 12, Academy of Natural Sciences, Philadelphia.

Paine, R.T. & Levin, S.A. (1981). Intertidal landscapes: Disturbance and the dynamics of pattern. *Ecological Monographs*, **51**, 145–178.

Paine, R.T. & Vadas, R.L. (1969). The effect of grazing by sea urchins *Strongylocentrotus* spp. on benthic algal populations. *Limnology and Oceanography*, **14**, 710–719.

Peterson, C.H. (1979). Predation, competitive exclusion, and diversity in the soft-sediment benthic communities of estuaries and lagoons. *Ecological Processes in Coastal and Marine Systems* (Ed. by R.J. Livingstone), pp. 233–264. Plenum Press, New York.

Scheibling. R.E. & Stephenson, R.L. (1984). Disease-related mortality of *Strongylocentrotus droebachiensis* (Echinodermata: Echinoidea) off Nova Scotia, Canada. *Marine Biology*, **78**, 153–164.

Simenstad, C.A., Estes, J.A. & Kenyon, K.W. (1978). Aleuts, sea otters, and stable-state communities. *Science*, **200**, 403–411.

Sousa, W.P. (1979). Disturbance in marine intertidal boulder fields: The nonequilibrium maintenance of species diversity. *Ecology*, **60**, 1225–1239.

Steneck, R.S. (1982). A limpet-coralline alga association: adaptations and defences between a selective herbivore and its prey. *Ecology*, **63**, 507–522.

Steneck, R.S. (1983). Escalating herbivory and resulting adaptive trends in calcareous algal crusts. *Palaeobiology*, **9**, 44–61.

Stephenson, T.A. & Stephenson, A. (1972). *Life Between Tidemarks on Rocky Shores*. W.H. Freeman & Co., San Francisco.

Sutherland, J.P. (1974). Multiple stable points in natural communities. *American Naturalist*, **108**, 859–873.

Sutherland, J.P. (1981). The fouling community at Beaufort, North Carolina: A study in stability. *American Naturalist*, **118**, 499–519.

Sutherland, J.P. & Karlson, R.H. (1977). Development and stability of the fouling community at North Carolina. *Ecological Monographs*, **47**, 425–446.

Tenger, M.J. & Dayton, P.K. (1981). Population structure, recruitment and mortality of two sea urchins (*Strongylocentrotus franciscanus* and *S. purpuratus*) in a kelp forest near San Diego, California. *Marine Ecology Progress Series*, **5**, 255–268.

Thorson, G. (1957). Bottom communities. *Geological Society of America, Memoir*, **67**, 461–534.

Underwood, A.J. (1981). Techniques of analysis of variance in experimental marine biology and ecology. *Oceanography and Marine Biology, Annual Review*, **19**, 513–605.

Underwood, A.J., Denley, E.J. & Moran, M.J. (1983). Experimental analyses of the structure and dynamics of mid-shore rocky intertidal communities in New South Wales. *Oecologia (Berlin)*, **56**, 202–219.

Wharton, W.G. & Mann, K.H. (1981). Relationship between destructive grazing by the sea urchin *Strongylocentrotus droebachiensis* and the abundance of American lobster *Homarus americanus* on the Atlantic coast of Nova Scotia. *Canadian Journal of Fisheries and Aquatic Sciences*, **38**, 1339–1349.

Woodin, A.S. (1978). Refuges, disturbance and community structure: a marine soft-bottom example. *Ecology*, **59**, 274–284.

13. WHAT DOES A SHREW DO IN AN ENERGY CRISIS?

ILKKA HANSKI

Department of Zoology, University of Helsinki, P. Rautatiekatu 13, SF-00100 Helsinki 10, Finland

SUMMARY

Shrews (Soricinae) ranging from 2 to 15 g have approximate starving times of 4–12 hours. A simple stochastic model suggests that this difference in starvation times is enough to cause different responses to an energy crisis in small and large species, with the small but not the large shrews increasing their foraging activity in randomly occurring, short-term food shortages. In an experiment imposing 5% loss in body weight but rewarding both increased and decreased activity, small shrews (*Sorex minutus* 3 g and *S. caecutiens* 5 g) increased, but large species (*S. araneus* 9 g and *S. isodon* 12 g) decreased their activity within 24 hours.

INTRODUCTION

An energy crisis arises from low food availability. I have limited this paper to a consideration of short-term fluctuations in food availability, and to energy crises caused by them. Behavioural and physiological adaptations to long-lasting (e.g. seasonal) food scarcity require a different approach (e.g. Hyvärinen 1984).

Northern shrews Soricinae have exceptionally high metabolic rates (Vogel 1980) and therefore cannot survive many hours without food. Perhaps their only option is to increase foraging activity in an energy crisis to secure what little food is available?

Crocidurinae, the tropical–southern temperate subfamily of Soricidae, have somewhat lower metabolic rates than Soricinae, and unlike them can enter torpor in times of food scarcity (Vogel 1980). In certain situations it is advantageous to enter torpor as an effective method for saving energy; why should it otherwise have evolved. However, the difference between normo-thermic rest and torpor is quantitative, not qualitative, and one cannot conclude from this comparison that Soricinae should always become more active in food shortages.

A shrew in an energy crisis may be expected to do whatever is most likely to keep it alive. What matters is the kind of food shortages shrews meet and have met in their natural environment. An extreme example is hummingbirds, which have exceptionally high metabolic rate like Soricinae but do enter torpor; their torpor, of course, occurs nightly when foraging is presumably impossible. Soricinae do not have such a constraint, and the availability of their food (small arthropods in forest litter) is likely to vary less predictably than nectar production in hummingbirds' flowers.

The size of a shrew's energy reserves is another crucial ingredient; torpor is a means of making the reserves last longer. Assuming that the size of the reserves increases with body size faster than metabolic rate, larger animals take longer to starve than smaller animals. Here I report theoretical and experimental results confirming that the shorter the period the animal can survive without food the more likely it is to increase its activity in an energy crisis.

MODEL

Let us assume an environment which is always in one of two states, good (G) or bad (B), the latter corresponding to an energy crisis for the shrew. Time is discrete and measured in hours. Let a transition from G to B occur at time $t = 0$. The shrew's task is to stay alive until the next transition from B to G. Let p denote the probability that, given B at time t, the transition from B to G occurs before $t + 1$.

Our model shrew has two options, to rest or to be active. If it chooses to rest, it survives the energy crisis if the transition from B to G occurs before $t = T$, where T is the number of hours the shrew's energy reserves will last. If the shrew chooses to be active, q is the probability of death in each hour until the transition from B to G takes place. Probability q includes increased risk of predation, starving, etc. Constant q is not an unreasonable assumption because I do not assume food availability to be nil in B. Should the shrew rest or be active in B?

Option rest. The probability that the transition from B to G does not occur in T hours is $(1-p)^T$, which is the probability of a resting shrew starving. The probability of a resting shrew surviving an energy crisis is thus $1 - (1-p)^T$.

Option active. Consider the following three-state Markov model with two absorbing states, alive in G and dead:

			Transition probabilities		
	States				
States					
Environment	Shrew		1	2	3
1	G	alive	1	0	0
2	B	alive	p	$(1-p)(1-q)$	$(1-p)q$
3	B	dead	0	0	1

The probability of absorption in state (G, alive) is $p/(p+(1-p)q)$ (Cox & Miller 1965).

In conclusion, the shrew should rest if

$$1-(1-p)^T > \frac{p}{p+(1-p)q}. \qquad (1)$$

If R is the size of the shrew's energy reserves (Joules), and M is its resting metabolic rate (in Jh^{-1}), then $T = R/M$. In Soricinae, $M = 2 \cdot 47 W^{0 \cdot 52}$, in which W is the body fresh weight (g) (Hanski 1984). R is not known, but a reasonable guess is $R = aW$, where a is a constant. T is thus roughly equal to a constant times the square root of the body fresh weight, $T = cW^{0 \cdot 5}$. c is roughly 3 (I. Hanski, unpubl.).

Expression (1) was evaluated for three values of T: 4, 10 and 20 hours, which are realistic starving times for a small soricin (e.g. *Sorex minutus*), a large soricin (e.g. *Sorex isodon*), and a crocidurin entering food shortage-induced torpor (e.g. *Crocidura russula*), respectively.

For small values of q, and where p is less than $0 \cdot 5$ (reasonable parameter ranges in nature), the shrew's response to an energy crisis should be sensitive to changes in T in the range of 4–20 hours (Fig. 13.1). Small species with small

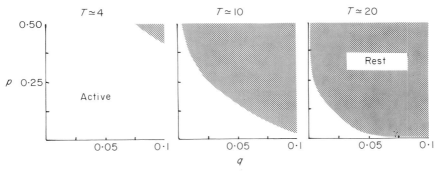

FIG. 13.1. Expression (1) was evaluated for three values of T: 4, 10 and 20 h. The model shrew's predicted response to an energy crisis is to rest in the shaded part of the parameter space. q = probability of not surviving from t to $t+1$ if active, p = transition probability from bad to good environment, and T = starvation time.

energy reserves should be active in the kinds of energy crises modelled; larger species with larger energy reserves should do better by resting until food availability improves. To test this prediction an experiment was conducted.

EXPERIMENT

Experiments were conducted using the following apparatus: a metabolic chamber; an automatic feeder attached to the lid of the chamber; an infra-red gas analyser used to measure the carbon dioxide production by a shrew in the chamber; and a microcomputer used to record the CO_2 output and to control the feeder (for details see Hanski 1984). With this arrangement, and knowing the shrew's food utilization efficiency (Hanski 1984), one can accurately calculate its energy budget throughout the experiment, and adjust the feeding schedule to control the shrew's energy budget.

An activity index—a measure of the shrew's time budget—was calculated by first averaging the instantaneous metabolic rate for periods of c. 75 s, then determining the proportion of these values higher than a predetermined value Q during the past 200 time units, or c. 4 h (200 × 75 s). Resting metabolic rate is about half of the active rate (Hanski 1984). Ideally, the Q value distinguishes between periods of rest and activity, and the activity index gives the proportion of time rested during the past 4 h.

The experiments consisted of two parts, each lasting c. 24 h. In the first part food was supplied to match expenditure regardless of activity, so that body weight was held constant. Feeding rate was controlled by the microcomputer, which recorded the shrew's instantaneous energy budget (calculated from the known food availability, estimated food utilization efficiency, and measured CO_2 production). In the second part, starting immediately after the shrew had been weighed and the chamber cleaned, the Q value was selected as the median of all values in the first part of the experiment. This scaling eliminates the effects of individual differences in activity. Thus, if the shrew behaved in the second part as it had behaved in the first part, its activity would hover around 0·5. In the second part, however, food was supplied by the microcomputer in such a way as to make an activity index of 0·5 the worst possible, resulting in 5% loss in body weight, while becoming either more or less active would restore a positive energy budget (see left-hand part of Fig. 13.3). The experiment thus poses the question: Does the shrew change its activity in an energy crisis causing 5% loss of body weight?

Figure 13.2 is a summary of the results of fifteen experiments with eight individuals of four species. There is little difference between the animals during the first 5 h but thereafter a difference begins to emerge between large (*Sorex araneus* and *S. isodon*) and small (*S. minutus* and *S. caecutiens*) species. At 15–20 h these two groups of shrews show little or no overlap: large species are less active and small species more active than they were in the first part of the experiment (the previous 24 h). There is, in fact, a significant negative correlation between body weight and the activity index calculated for 15–20 h from the beginning of the second part of the experiment (Fig. 13.3). No correlation was found in control experiments, consisting of two 'first parts' of the experiment (no imposed energy crisis; $b = -0.0080$, $t = -0.86$, NS, $n = 10$).

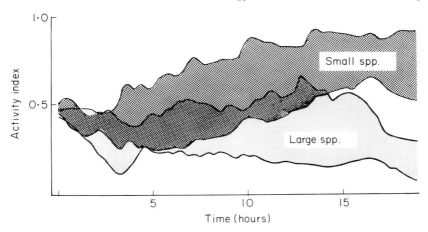

FIG. 13.2. The course of shrews' activity in the second part of the experiment. The lightly shaded region (plus the overlap region) delimits the observations for large species, excluding the largest and smallest value for each hour, and the strongly shaded region (plus the overlap region) delimits the observations for small species, again excluding the largest and smallest values. The large species are *Sorex isodon* (1 individual, 2 experiments) and *S. araneus* (4 individuals, 6 experiments), the small species are *S. minutus* (1 individual, 2 experiments) and *S. caecutiens* (2 individuals, 5 experiments). The activity index gives the proportion of the past 4 h that the shrew has been active.

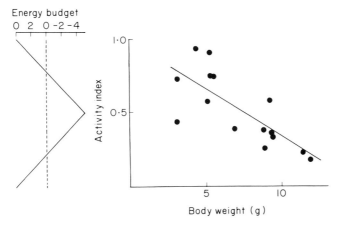

FIG. 13.3. A plot of the activity index calculated as the average of values at 15, 16, . . . , 20 h against body fresh weight (15 experiments). The regression is significant ($y = 0.978 - 0.0642x$, $t = -4.08$, $P < 0.01$) and accounts for 56% of the variance in y. On the left is shown the function that determined the shrew's energy budget as a function of its activity index in the second part of the experiment (in the first part this function was simply 'energy budget' = 0). The unit is gain/loss of body weight as a percentage of the initial weight. Feeding was controlled by a microcomputer.

Percentage change in average metabolic rate was also negatively related to body weight, but in this case the correlation was non-significant ($r = -0.323$), perhaps because the metabolic rate was calculated for the whole second part of the experiment. What shrews do after the 24 h (Fig. 13.2) has not yet been studied.

DISCUSSION

Do food shortages select for larger shrews? Very severe shortages, in which increased activity would be of no help, would undoubtedly favour larger individuals (and species) with larger energy reserves. In the real world, however, food availability does not vary from nought to plenty; the changes are more subtle. Boyce's (1979) explanation of Bergmann's Rule—that acute food shortages in northern latitudes select for larger individuals—is problematic because low average food availability selects for smaller individuals with smaller energy demands; we do not yet know which is more important, a decrease in the mean or an increase in the variance of food availability with increasing latitude. Both presumably occur for most animals. In shrews, Soricinae, the very northern species tend to be small (I. Hanski, unpubl.), which disagrees with Bergmann's rule.

In this paper it is suggested that short-term energy crises exist in which it pays some shrews to rest, others to be active, depending on how long their energy reserves will last. This is not to say that very hungry shrews, regardless of their size, would not start, ultimately, to search for food.

ACKNOWLEDGMENTS

I thank C. Barnard, J. Gibbs, P. Harvey, O. Järvinen and R. Sibly for their advice and comments on the manuscript. The study was funded by the Academy of Finland.

REFERENCES

Boyce, M.S. (1979). Seasonality and patterns of natural selection for life histories. *American Naturalist*, 114, 569–583.
Cox, D.R. & Miller, H.D. (1965). *The Theory of Stochastic Processes*. Chapman & Hall, London.
Hanski, I. (1984). Food consumption, utilization and metabolic rate in six species of shrews (*Sorex* and *Neomys*). *Annales Zoologici Fennici*, 21, 157–165.
Hyvärinen, H. (1984). Wintering strategy of voles and shrews in Finland. *Bulletin of the Carnegie Museum of Natural History* (in press).
Vogel, P. (1980). Metabolic levels and biological strategies in shrews. *Comparative Physiology: Primitive Mammals* (Ed. by K. Schmidt-Nielsen, L. Bolis & C.R. Taylor), pp. 170–180. Cambridge University Press, Cambridge.

III

SPACING BEHAVIOUR AND POPULATION DYNAMICS

14. DISTRIBUTION OF UNEQUAL COMPETITORS

WILLIAM J. SUTHERLAND[1] AND G. A. PARKER[2]
[1]*School of Environmental Sciences, University of East Anglia,*
Norwich NR4 7TJ, and
[2]*Department of Zoology, University of Liverpool,*
Liverpool L69 3BX

INTRODUCTION

Understanding the distribution of animals is interesting for both applied and academic reasons. Attempts to conserve animals (such as birds on estuaries or the predators of pests) or destroy animals (such as pests) require an understanding of the factors determining their distribution. This subject provides a good opportunity to develop and test simple game theory models.

In many species there are considerable individual differences in competitive ability and the major aim of this review is to consider the implications of these differences. We shall review the literature on how individuals differ in competitive ability, produce models incorporating such differences into previous game theory, and assess the role of these differences in determining dispersion, dispersal and carrying capacity.

INDIVIDUAL DIFFERENCES IN COMPETITIVE ABILITY

Evidence for individual differences

Individuals may differ in the amount of food they acquire whilst competing. Rubinstein (1981) showed that everglades pygmy sunfish *Elassoma evergladei* showed considerably greater individual differences in growth rate whilst under competition. Some fish were little affected yet others suffered considerably. Comparable results have been obtained for tadpoles (Wilbur & Collins 1973) and plants (e.g. Obeid, Machin & Harper 1967).

Milinski (1982) showed that captive sticklebacks *Gasterosteus aculeatus* of equal sizes showed considerable differences in their abilities to compete for water fleas *Daphnia magna* which were added to the tank at regular intervals. There was no aggression observed but the most successful fish caught three times as many *Daphnia* as the least successful ones. The least successful thus suffered considerably in the presence of others, while the more successful were shown to be little hindered by competition. Milinski also showed that the good

255

competitors not only took a disproportionate share of the numbers of *Daphnia* but also usually took the larger ones.

Further experiments by Milinski (1984) showed that those sticklebacks which were infected with parasites were the poorer competitors: when competing for prey of two different sizes, the unparasitized sticklebacks went for the larger ones; fish parasitized only by the cestode *Schistocephalus solidus* or only by the sporozoan *Glugea anomala* attacked both prey size-classes equally often, while sticklebacks infested by both species of parasite preferred to attack the less profitable prey. Milinski argues that parasitized individuals are poor competitors and gain a higher intake by going for the small prey than they would by attempting to compete for larger prey. The role of parasites in determining the competitive abilities of different species is well known; for example, the classic experiments on flour beetles by Park (1948) or those on competing grasses by Burdon & Chilvers (1977). It may be that parasites also play a considerable role in creating individual differences in competitive ability within a species. Jenkins, Watson & Miller (1963) showed that the level of infection of a red grouse *Lagopus lagopus* with the nematode *Trichostrongylus tenuis* was correlated with the animal's ability to gain a territory. This correlation does not demonstrate a causal relationship but changing the parasite load of male mice does change their dominance (Freeland 1981; Rau 1983).

The best field evidence for individual differences in competitive ability comes from the work of Goss-Custard and his co-workers who studied oystercatchers *Haematopus ostralegus* on the Exe Estuary. Ten birds studied in detail by Ens & Goss-Custard (1984) showed a stable linear dominance hierarchy. Of the eight for which adequate data were obtained, six showed a reduced food intake at high oystercatcher densities due to the direct and indirect effects of mussels being stolen from them. By contrast, the two top dominant birds did not eat less in the presence of others and may even have increased their intake from the food they stole. All of the individuals in this study were adults or near adults. Other work (Goss-Custard, Durell & Ens 1982) has shown an age difference in competitive ability.

Why do these differences persist?

Parker (1982) has reviewed the similar explanations for the maintenance of variability in mate-finding strategies. Variation in strategy can come about in two quite separate ways.

1 Different strategies are equally good in the long term: 'a mixed evolutionarily stable strategy'. For differences in competitive ability to coexist as a mixed evolutionarily stable strategy (i) all individuals must have the same

long-term fitness, and (ii) pay-offs must be frequency-dependent so that if the evolutionarily stable distribution of competitive abilities is disrupted, selection can restore it. Condition (i) is perhaps supported by the limited evidence available from studies of flocking birds (see Maynard Smith 1982) but not by most studies of mammals (Dewsbury 1982). Various workers have shown that birds become more dominant after testosterone implant (Arnold 1975; Rowher & Rowher 1978). If dominance hierarchies are mixed evolutionarily stable strategies, the increased dominance should yield no long-term advantage. Silverin (1980) has shown that there may be costs associated with high levels of testosterone, which could balance any advantage of dominance. No studies are yet adequate to test whether condition (ii) operates.

2 There can be considerable individual variation in competitive ability caused by chance differences in phenotype. An individual's strategy then depends upon the behaviour of others of both similar and different phenotypes. It is then necessary to work out the stable conditions for a 'phenotype-limited evolutionarily stable strategy' (Parker 1982). We suspect this is the more important cause of differences in competitive ability. In contrast with (1), the long-term fitness of individuals with different competitive abilities need not now be equal.

So it seems that there may often be considerable differences in competitive ability which may be caused by differences in age, sex, size, parasite burden, parents' ability or alternative strategies. Models of dispersion must take into account these differences.

INTERFERENCE

Interference is the more or less immediate, and reversible, reduction in feeding rate when the density of competitors increases (Goss-Custard 1980).

The amount of interference (m) is the extent to which an increase in the number of competitors (N) results in a reduction in the rate of food intake (I). As in Fig. 14.1, it is conventional to express both axes on log scales (Hassell & Varley 1969). The equation for any of the relationships shown in Fig. 14.1 is

$$\log I = \log a - \log N\, m$$

removing logarithms gives

$$I = a\, N^{-m} \tag{1}$$

$\log a$ is the intercept and m is the interference constant of Hassell & Varley (1969). In the field, interference can be determined if the intake can be measured in an area in the presence of varying numbers of competitors. Intake must be expressed as the number of prey items found divided by the time spent searching (i.e. handling time is excluded). The slope of log intake against log

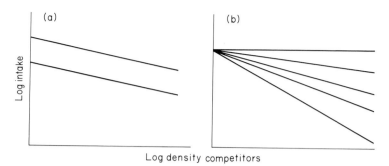

Fig 14.1. Suggested ways in which individuals may differ in the interference they experience: (a) different individuals with different searching efficiencies; (b) different individuals experiencing different interference.

competitor density is the interference constant m. The antilogarithm of the intercept divided by prey density is the 'Quest constant'. An alternative method is to include handling time in the measure of intake—the slope is then an overestimate of the value of m, although the discrepancy is usually likely to be small. We shall use the second method for models II and IV because of its greater simplicity and shall then refer to the intercept as the 'foraging efficiency' and the slope as the 'interference experienced'.

The approach of Hassell and Varley leads to a useful general way of expressing differences in competitive ability. Rather than assuming that all animals are equal and thus all find the same amount of food when in the same area, it is possible to assess the interference sustained by different individuals (Fig. 14.1). Individual's differences in competitive ability will be expressed as differences in either their 'foraging efficiency' (see Fig. 14.1a) or in their 'interference experienced' (see Fig. 14.1b) or both.

MODELS OF DISPERSION

In this section we consider models which describe the dispersion of the population using the assumption that each individual behaves so as to maximize its rate of food intake. The distribution of competitors will then be the sum of all the individual decisions. These models are summarized in Table 14.1. For some species, such as parasitoids, interference is probably unimportant in determining dispersion and the models developed by Comins & Hassell (1979) and Hassell (1980) are more appropriate.

The ideal free distribution assumes that all animals have equal capabilities and requirements and in the resulting models (I and IV) all individuals receive the same gains. In three other models (II, III and IV) individuals differ in capabilities or requirements and it is then necessary to work out where each

TABLE 14.1. Summary of models relating to dispersion. All models assume each individual goes where it can get the highest reward

A DISPERSION WITH INTERFERENCE

I. Ideal free distribution
Assumption: all animal are equal.
Expectations: reward the same in all sites and for all individuals.
Proportion of competitors in site = constant × proportion prey$^{1/m}$ where m expresses the strength of interference.
Examples: none known

II. Individuals differ in interference experienced
Assumption: individuals differ in the value of m they would experience within a site.
Expectations: strongest competitors in best sites; mean reward highest in best sites.
Examples: herring gulls (Monaghan 1980) and oystercatchers (Ens & Goss-Custard 1984).

III. Individuals differ in foraging efficiency
Assumption: Individuals differ in intercepts (see Fig. 15.1a)
Expectations: any distribution which conforms to eqn (1). Within this limitation, individuals can go anywhere so the highest mean intake can be anywhere.
Examples: could contribute to the site differences in intake shown in studies of herring gull and oystercatcher (see above).

DISPERSION WITH RENEWAL

IV. Ideal free distribution
Assumptions: continuous replenishment of food; all individuals equal.
Expectations: density of competitors proportional to input rates; mean rewards the same in all sites.
Examples: none known

V. Individuals differ in competitive ability
Assumptions: continuous replenishment of food; Individuals differ in competitive ability; ratio of competitive abilities constant in all sites.
Expectations: any distribution as long as the sums of competitive abilities are proportional to the input rates; density may be highest anywhere; intake may be highest anywhere.
One possible solution mimics the ideal free case (IV) with equal mean rewards in each site and the density of competitors proportional to the input rate. This solution may be favoured by chance or as a consequence of the different sampling speeds of good and poor competitors.
Examples: dungflies (Parker 1978) mallard (Harper 1982), sticklebacks (Milinski 1984), cichlids (Godin & Keenleyside 1984)

DISPERSION WITH SPACE COMPETITION

VI. Territorial defence
Assumption: residents defend territories and exclude newcomers ('ideal despotic').
Expectations: reward highest in best sites; density highest in best sites.
Example: territorial cichlids (Patterson, p. 393).

individual should go so as to maximize its rate of food intake. Although better competitors will gain more than poor competitors, all individuals of a given competitive ability should have the same intake, otherwise they would move. The resulting solution is known as a phenotype-limited evolutionarily stable strategy (Parker 1982).

We have classified the models into three categories. The first category assumes the prey are not continually replenished but that interference is important (e.g. oystercatchers searching for mussels). The second assumes that there is a continuous renewal of resources (e.g male dungflies scrambling for arriving females). The third assumes that some individuals can defend territories and exclude others.

MODELS OF DISPERSION WITH INTERFERENCE

All the models in this category assume that the number of prey present is approximately constant but that the presence of competitors reduces the ease with which prey can be found.

I. The ideal free distribution

This theoretical approach suggested by Fretwell & Lucas (1970) assumes that all individuals are equally good competitors and each behaves in such a way as to maximize the rate at which it feeds. The theory aquires its name from the authors' assumptions that individuals are free to move wherever they want, and that each individual is ideal in having perfect knowledge of the relative profitability of each site. The profitability of a site depends upon just two factors: the food intake possible in the absence of competitors and the extent to which intake is affected by the presence of competitors. For predators searching for prey, it is possible to achieve an ideal free distribution of predators amongst the different prey intake rate by interference. The basic idea behind the interference model of ideal free distribution is that, as a consequence of all individuals acting to maximize their feeding rate, the feeding rate will be the same in all sites—any discrepancies in food density will be equalized by interference. Thus, if the feeding rate proves better in one site then further individuals are expected to move there to exploit it and the resulting increase in interference will remove the discrepancy.

It is easy to produce a simple model describing the predator distribution expected if individuals follow the ideal free distribution. Two factors are assumed to influence feeding rate. These are the density of food and the interference caused by competitors. The effect of food density can be described by the disc equation (Holling 1959), while the effect of competitors is described by Hassell & Varley's (1969) interference equation. Combining these equations and simplifying by using the assumption that feeding rate is the same in all sites and is thus a constant gives the following relationship between the proportion of predators (b_i) in the ith site and the proportion of prey (α_i) for a given strength of interference m.

$$b_i = c\,\alpha_i{}^{1/m} \qquad (2)$$

where c is a normalizing constant (Sutherland 1983).

Hassell & May (1973) proposed an aggregative constant μ which describes the aggregation shown in field and laboratory studies. They suggested that

$$b_i = c\,\alpha_i{}^{\mu}$$

which has the same form as eqn (2) making it clear that $\mu = 1/m$. In other words, aggregation in Hassell & May's model is equivalent to the reciprocal of interference in the ideal free model; which makes biological sense since it suggests that species which aggregate are those with little interference.

II. Individuals differ in interference experienced

Ens & Goss-Custard (1984) showed that individual oystercatchers differ in the interference which they experience, and Fig. 14.1b illustrates what the individual interference relationships may look like. The dominant birds have shallower slopes than do the subdominants.

It is not easy to incorporate individual differences, because the interference experienced by one individual is likely to depend upon the phenotypes of the others present nearby. In the absence of more detailed information we shall use the following modification of eqn (1) to describe the intake I of an individual in the presence of N competitors

$$I = aN^{-mR} \qquad (3)$$

where R is the relative competitive ability, i.e. the average competitive ability of all individuals in that site divided by the competitive ability of the individual under study. Thus, a weakling will suffer particularly severe interference when surrounded by strong competitors yet experience average interference for the population when surrounded by equals.

This model was explored by simulation of three habitats containing equal numbers of ten phenotypes with competitive abilities ranging from 1 to 10. The phenotypes were assumed to feed where their intake would be highest. The standard solution to such game theory problems is to assume relative reproductive rate is proportional to intake. The simulation continues until the population remains static. This technique ensures that the intake for a given phenotype is the same in all the sites it inhabits.

Figure 14.2 shows the result of this simulation. As would be expected, the intake is highest for the strong competitors which feed at the sites with the most food. If a strong competitor moved it would do badly because there is less food in the poor sites. If a weak competitor moved to a good site it would do worse because it would suffer from extreme interference. There is a strict truncation of the phenotype distribution between the different habitats.

Figure 14.2 also shows how intake is greatest in the best sites. This runs contrary to the expectation of the ideal free distribution that intake is equal in all sites. It is also a possible explanation of the widespread observation that intake is highest in the best sites. Sibly & McCleery (1983) conclude their paper by saying 'thus the ideal free distribution predicts some features of the distribution of gulls but leaves as a paradox the low energy returns obtained by herring gulls feeding at other sites when the tip was open'. The model presented here is compatible with their suggestion that this paradox may be caused by individual differences in competitive ability. It may well be that subdominant individuals obtain even less food if they move to the tip.

Monaghan's (1980) observations of herring gulls *Larus argentatus* at a refuse tip conform to our model. She distinguished two feeding areas: a main area in which most of the rubbish was directly dumped and a secondary area surrounding this. In the main tip the density of gulls and their average intake

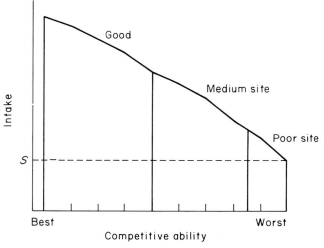

FIG. 14.2. Dispersion expected for individuals experiencing different interference. Intake is determined by eqn (3) and each individual goes where its intake is highest. This simulation assumes three different habitats (good, medium and poor) in which the foraging efficiencies are 6, 4 and 2 respectively. Competitive ability runs from 1 to 10 with equal numbers of each. The average interference m is 0·1. As described on p. 268 S is the amount of food necessary for survival.

was about five times better but there were also three times as many aggressive encounters. More immatures fed in the secondary area and, as the total number of gulls increased, a higher proportion of the immatures used the secondary area, which she interpreted as immatures being forced out of better areas by dominant adults.

Figure 14.2 suggests that the better the site, the higher the density of competitors. However, this conclusion appears to be dependent upon the mean level of interference. With a mean level of 0·2 there were more individuals in the poor site than in the good one and with exceedingly high levels of interference such as 1·0 the poorest site held about 80% of the population. We certainly accept that these values are wildly speculative. The expected result will depend critically upon the range of phenotypes present and the exact way in which relative competitive ability affects interference. But this result warns us that it does not always follow that the density of competitors is highest in the best site or, as Fretwell & Lucas (1970) and Ens & Goss-Custard (1984) proposed, that the site with the most competitors will also be the site with the highest mean intake.

The average reduction in feeding rate due to interference amongst wading birds appears small (Goss-Custard 1980) and the same is true for parasitoids (Free, Beddington & Lawton 1977; Hassell 1978). In the absence of strong interference we would expect from the ideal free distribution and eqn (2) that practically all individuals collect in the best sites, yet this is not what happens for many individuals ignore the good sites. With the model developed here the average level of interference may be low yet certain individuals would do very poorly in the best sites and so move elsewhere.

This model has assumed that all individuals have the same intercept or 'foraging efficiency' as shown in Fig. 14.1b. It may be that some individuals (e.g. adults) are likely to be efficient feeders yet also suffer little interference whilst others (e.g. juveniles) have both a low foraging efficiency and high interference. This will further increase the differences in intake recorded in Fig. 14.2.

III. Individuals differ in foraging efficiency

As illustrated in Fig. 14.1a, individuals may differ in their intercepts or foraging efficiencies but suffer equally from interference. For example, adults may be better at finding food than juveniles. As the plot is log–log, it can be seen that interference reduces intake by the same proportion. As they respond exactly in unison they will respond to the density of competitors and prey availability in the same way. The best decision for one individual is the same as the best decision for another. So the different types can be combined and fitted into eqn (2).

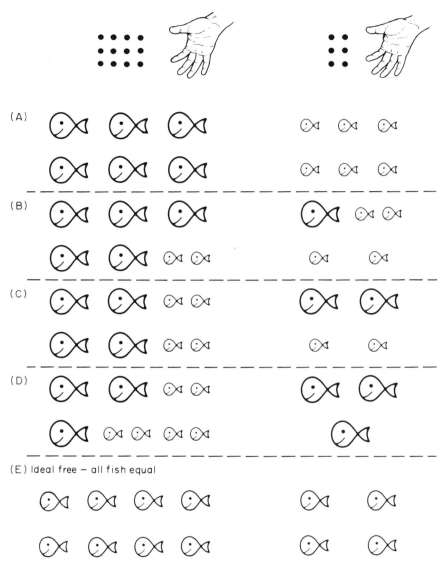

FIG. 14.3. The range of possible solutions for individuals differing in competitive ability. For this example food is added at rates of 6 and 12 items per unit time in the two sites. In A, B, C and D the twelve fish differ in their competitive abilities such that each of the six big fish always capture twice as much as each of the six small fish. Note that (i) in none of the cases could any individual gain by moving, (ii) the sums of competitive abilities always equals 12:6, (iii) the number of individuals and the mean intake in each site differs considerably between the different solutions.

Just as in the fish example illustrated in Fig. 14.3, there are a range of possible solutions to eqn (2). If the efficient feeders go into the best site then intake will be highest there: if they go into the worst site then the mean intake will be highest in the worst site.

The above argument applies only when the ratios of competitive abilities are constant everywhere. If the ratios of competitive ability vary between sites then the best competitors go into the sites where competitive ratios are greatest, which will usually be the best sites (G.A. Parker & W.J. Sutherland, unpubl.).

MODELS OF DISPERSION WITH RENEWAL

In this section we assume that prey arrive continually from outside and each individual competes for its share. Many of the tests of the ideal free distribution have involved experimentally manipulating the renewal rates (=prey arrival rates) and there are some field situations which involve renewal, such as fish competing for food drifting downstream or waders competing for worms rising to the surface of the mud. It is probably most useful as a description of mate competition where the arrival of the other sex can be considered as a renewing supply (e.g. Parker 1970, 1974).

IV. The ideal free distribution

As described earlier (I) the ideal free distribution assumes all individuals are equally good competitors and so everyone obtains the same intake. In the case of renewing resources, an individual's share is the total divided amongst n competitors so that intake is proportional to $1/n$. The resultant slope of log intake against log competitor density is minus one. The prediction from eqn (2) for $m = 1$ is that the density of competitors should be proportional to the input rates: Parker (1978) has suggested the term 'input matching'. In the four available studies the density of competitors was proportional to the input rate (Parker 1978; Milinski 1979; Harper 1982; Godin & Keenleyside 1984) but this result is also compatible with model V.

V. Individuals differ in competitive ability

What if some individuals are better competitors than others? Suppose that individuals have constant competitive abilities, e.g. big fish do twice as well as small ones in all patches. There seem to be a whole range of suitable distributions. *Any solution seems acceptable as long as the sums of the competitive abilities are held in fixed proportion to the input rates.* This rule has been proved more formally by G. A. Parker & W.J. Sutherland (unpubl.) and is similar to Harper's (1982) idea of 'bird units'.

Figure 14.3 illustrates the above rule. The large fish are assumed to be twice as good at competing for food. In each case the sums of competitive abilities are equal in the two sites. In the examples illustrated no individual could do better by moving. Note how the distribution and mean intake vary between these solutions. In solution A there are equal numbers in each site whilst in solution D there are three times as many in the good site as in the poor. When a mix of individuals occurs in a site, the big fish always do twice as well as the small ones, but the *mean* intake varies from being highest in the bad site (solution D) to being twice as good in the best (solution A). With such diversity of possible outcomes it will be difficult in field studies to tell if animals are actually conforming to this rule.

Solution C is curious for it mimics the ideal free distribution. If all animals were equal (as in E) then the only stable solution would be eight fish in the good site and four in the bad—the same as solution C. The average intake rates for solution C are also just the same as expected from the ideal free distribution (E). With equal competitors the average intake in each site would be 1·5 prey per minute (i.e. 12/8 and 6/4). With solution C the average intake is also 1·5 (i.e. half the fish get 2 and the rest 1). Without marked individuals it would be very difficult to separate a solution like C (with the same ratio of good to poor competitors within each patch) from the ideal free distribution E.

When food is supplied at different rates as in Fig. 14.3 the animals do seem to opt for solution C: the mimic of the ideal free distribution. Both Milinski's (1984) study of sticklebacks and Harper's (1982) study of mallards *Anas platyrhyncos* showed considerable differences between individuals yet they conformed to solution C. If Milinski and Harper had not been able to recognize individuals they could have wrongly concluded that this was an ideal free distribution. Harper showed that other solutions were possible, for in some experimental trials the best competitors went into the good site whilst the majority of the population went into the poor site (as in solution A).

Why should animals often opt for solution C (the mimic of the ideal free distribution)? Regelman (1984) provides a possible explanation. He argues that good competitors can sample more quickly as a consequence of their faster food intake and thus are the first to decide where to settle. They then conform to their own ideal free distribution (which in our example would be four in the best patch and two in the worst). When the poor competitors subsequently decide where to feed they are only left with conforming as in solution C. Regelman used Harley's (1981) learning rule to show how this comes about. For transitory patches Regelman's explanation is possible, but for long-lived patches the speed of sampling will be irrelevant and any of the possible outcomes seems equally good. Another problem with Regelman's explanation is that animals achieve their solution very quickly (Harper 1982; Godin & Keenleyside 1984; Milinski 1984); in fact faster than seems possible by sampling.

Although Regelman's model may provide a partial explanation for the occurrence of solutions similar to C (Milinski 1984) it is probably not the complete explanation. We suggest chance may also play a role. If individuals behave randomly within the constraint of our rule then on average we should expect solution C. It is very unlikely that one site would be occupied by either all the best or all the worst individuals. Although Harper (1982) describes cases in which the four best competitors went into the poor site, this was during a period when these four acted as a cohesive subflock. Having all four best competitors in the poor site would be statistically unlikely if each individual behaved independently. It also seems likely that an individual's competitive ability is not constant but depends upon which other individuals are present.

SPACE COMPETITION AND DISPERSION

VI. Territorial defence

In many species, individuals defend areas and exclude others. Fretwell & Lucas (1970) referred to this as 'despotic behaviour' and called the resulting dispersion the 'ideal despotic distribution'. Their argument is that the first individuals to settle go into the best habitat and defend territories, so that residents will be at an advantage over otherwise identical newcomers. Newcomers then have the choice between squeezing into any remaining room in the best site or having a free choice in a poorer site. A result of territorial behaviour is that the average rewards may be considerably higher in the best sites which contrasts with the ideal free distribution in which the rewards are the same everywhere. Patterson's (p. 393) study of cichlids is an example of how territoriality influences dispersion.

DISCUSSION

Dispersal

Dispersal is a crucial and often neglected component of population dynamics (Taylor & Taylor 1979; Łomnicki 1982; Pienkowski & Evans, p. 331). One function of dispersal is for individuals to find their best possible feeding conditions under the prevailing circumstances. We shall consider how this is affected by differences in competitive ability. There are of course other good reasons for dispersing, such as avoiding inbreeding (Greenwood, Harvey & Perrins 1979).

Subdominants in dense areas may suffer considerably from the presence of competitors. In a stable environment it would make sense for weak competitors to disperse from good, dense areas to poor uncrowded areas (see Fig. 14.2). In a fluctuating environment, the numbers of competitors may not always accord with the food density. The poor competitors would gain most by seeking areas with proportionately few competitors. Dispersal is usually of juveniles (Baker 1978) and there is limited evidence that even among this class it is the subdominants which are involved, e.g. dispersing house sparrows *Passer domesticus* are smaller than the ones which stay (Cink 1977). Studies of the great tit *Parus major* in England and Belgium have provided evidence that dispersal is related to competitive ability and the number of competitors. Birds leaving the nest later in the season tend to be smaller and lose a disproportionate number of disputes (Garnett 1981). These young birds disperse further than the earliest fledglings who will be larger and dominant (Dhont & Huble 1968). Kluijver (1971) showed that these later broods of great tits did not move as far if he removed 90% of the first brood. Young birds at Wytham Wood, England, disperse over a greater number of territories in years of high population density (Greenwood *et al.* 1979).

Implications for carrying capacities

It is interesting to know, for both economic and conservation reasons, how many animals a certain area can sustain. This term has been called the carrying capacity but, apart from its use in the logistic equation, this concept is rather nebulous. The approach we have described leads to a way of looking at carrying capacities. Goss-Custard (p. 169) reviews the ideas and literature concerning the carrying capacity of wading birds on estuaries.

We assume that a certain daily intake (S in Fig 14.2) is necessary for survival, and if an individual's intake falls below this level then it either emigrates or starves. The population remaining can be considered as the carrying capacity (strictly this is just an approximation for the population may be capable of sustaining further good competitors). This shows that the average individual can be doing very well despite the population being at the carrying capacity. It is probably, therefore, insufficient to use the proportion of the day spent feeding as a measure of whether a population is limited by food supply. To understand the carrying capacity and population dynamics of many vertebrates it is probably necessary to concentrate on the facts affecting the intake of the poorest feeders.

What effect does the range of values of interference have on the carrying capacity? If interference is low then the species is likely to aggregate and deplete the food supply in the best site and then disperse *en masse* (Goss-Custard & Charman 1976). Brent geese *Branta bernicla* appear to do this as they feed extensively upon *Zostera* and having depleted this shift to *Enteromorpha* (Charman 1979). In species in which different individuals experience very different amounts of interference the subdominant individuals are expected to disappear one by one due to death or emigration. Goss-Custard *et al.* (1984) document the gradual disappearance of subdominant oystercatchers from a mussel bed in the manner expected by such a model.

Winter distribution

With the model illustrated by Fig. 14.2, it may pay subdominant individuals to leave the best areas. The examples we have considered are all small-scale, such as an oystercatcher leaving one mussel bed for another or gulls moving between piles of rubbish. It is possible that the same argument may apply on a much larger scale and explain the distribution of birds within continents. Pienkowsi & Evans (p. 331) discuss this subject further.

Various authors, especially Gauthreaux (1978, 1982), have argued that the distribution patterns of birds in winter can be explained by dominance. In general, males tend to be dominant over females, and adults of both sexes tend to dominate young. This correlates with observations that, in the northern hemisphere, adult males tend to winter further north than adult females, and that juveniles winter further south than both. Gauthreaux's argument is thus that, in the absence of competition, the best wintering grounds are in the north and these are exploited by the males. The females and juveniles avoid competition by wintering in the poorer areas further south.

Another model of differential dispersal due to Fretwell (1980) also assumes that behavioural dominance results in considerable differences in food intake. Both Fretwell and Gauthreaux suggest that experience in a habitat contributes to dominance status there and that this is a cause of site fidelity. Fretwell differs from Gauthreaux in his suggestion that residents stay in order to push up their position in the dominance hierarchy on the breeding grounds. These residents could achieve a higher intake elsewhere but sacrifice this short-term advantage for the long-term gain in obtaining access to the best breeding sites.

There are yet other explanations for these observations (Ketterson & Nolan 1983). It could be that males are usually the larger sex and thus can winter in more rigorous climates. Another possible interpretation is that males need to be first to return to the breeding grounds in order to obtain a territory and thus do not fly as far south.

A useful test to distinguish these hypotheses is to consider those species in which the females are dominant over the males. Myers (1981) reviews the literature on wading birds and gives four such species. In three of these (least sandpiper *Calidris minutilla*, western sandpiper *C. mauri* and sanderling *C. Alba*) the males still winter further north than the females. For the fourth species (grey phalarope *Phalaropus fulicarius*) males and females winter at the same latitude. Myers concludes that winter distribution is best explained by the need of males to be close to the breeding area.

Gauthreaux (1982) reviews the literature on birds of prey which are another group known for their reversed size dimorphism and comes to exactly the opposite conclusion. He found sufficient detail on three species: sparrowhawk *Accipiter nisus* (Belopol'skij 1972), goshawk *Accipiter gentilis* (Sulkova 1964) and rough-legged buzzard *Buteo lagopus* (Russell 1981). In each case the evidence suggests that males winter further south than females. This seems to support the suggestion that dominance is important (although it is known that males and females have different diets and thus may be expected in different areas). As Ketterson & Nolan (1983) suggest, it seems likely that there is no single explanation for differential winter distributions although from what we know about small-scale distributions (e.g. Monaghan 1980; Goss-Custard *et al.* 1984) it would be surprising if dominance had no role to play.

ACKNOWLEDGMENTS

This paper owes much to numerous discussions with John Goss-Custard and Bruno Ens in the cafe at Dawlish Warren. We thank Duncan Brooks and two referees for very detailed comments.

REFERENCES

Arnold, A.P. (1975). The effects of castration and androgen replacement on song, courtship and aggression in Zebra Finches (*Poephila guttata*). *Journal of Experimental Zoology*, **191**, 309–325.

Baker, R.R. (1978). *The Evolutionary Ecology of Animal Migration.* Hodder & Stoughton. London.

Belopol'skij, K. (1972). Ecological pecularities in *Accipiter nisus* migrations. *Ekologiya*, **3**, 58–63.

Burdon, J.J. & Chilvers, G.A. (1977). The effect of barley mildew on barley and wheat competition in mixtures. *Australian Journal of Botany*, **25**, 59–65.

Cink, C. (1977). *Winter behaviour of the house sparrow.* Unpublished Ph.D. thesis, University of Kansas.

Charman, K. (1979). Feeding ecology and energetics of the dark-bellied brent goose (*Branta bernicla bernicla*) in Essex and Kent. *Ecological Processes in Coastal Environments*. (Ed. by R.L. Jefferies & A.J. Davy), pp. 451–465. Blackwell Scientific Publications, Oxford.

Comins, H.N. & Hassell, M.P. (1979). The dynamics of optimally foraging predators and parasitoids. *Journal of Animal Ecology*, 48, 335–351.

Dewsbury, D.A. (1982). Dominance rank, copulatory behaviour and differential reproduction. *Quarterly Review of Biology*, 57, 135–159.

Dhondt, A. & Huble, J. (1968). Fledging date and sex in relation to dispersal in young tits. *Bird Study*, 15, 127–134.

Ens, B. & Goss-Custard, J.D. (1984). Interference among oystercatchers *Haematopus ostralegus*, feeding on mussels *Mytilus edulis* on the Exe Estuary. *Journal of Animal Ecology*, 53, 217–231.

Free, C.A., Beddington, J.R. & Lawton, J.H. (1977). On the inadequacy of simple models of mutual interference for parasitism and predation. *Journal of Animal Ecology*, 46, 543–554.

Freeland, W.J. (1981). Parasitism and behavioral dominance amongst male mice. *Science*, 213, 461–462.

Fretwell, S.D. (1980). Evolution of migration in relations to factors regulating bird numbers. *Migrant Birds in the Neotropics* (Ed. by C.A. Keast & E. Morton), pp. 517–527. Smithsonian Institution Press, Washington.

Fretwell, S.D. & Lucas, H.L. (1970). On territorial behaviour and other factors influencing habitat distribution in birds. *Acta Biotheoretica*, 19, 16–36.

Garnett, M.C. (1981). Body size, its heritability and influence on juvenile survival amongst great tits *Parus major*. *Ibis*, 123, 31–41.

Gauthreaux, S.A. (1978). The ecological significance of behavioural dominance. *Perspectives in Ethology*. (Ed. by P.P.G. Bateson & P.H. Klopper), pp. 17–54. Plenum, New York.

Gauthreaux, S.A. (1982). The ecology and evolution of avian migration systems. *Avian Biology*, Vol IV (Ed. by D.S. Farner, J.R. King & K.C. Parkers), pp. 93–168. Academic Press, New York.

Godin, J.-G.,J. & Keenleyside, M.H.A. (1984). Foraging on patchily distributed prey by a cichlid fish (Teleostei: Cichlidae): a test of ideal free distribution theory. *Animal Behaviour*, 32, 120–131.

Goss-Custard, J.D. (1980). Competition for food and interference amongst waders. *Ardea*, 68, 31–52.

Goss-Custard, J.D. & Charman, K. (1976). Predicting how many wintering waterfowl an area can support. *Wildfowl*, 27, 157–158.

Goss-Custard, J.D., Durell, S.E.A. Le V. dit & Ens, B. (1982). Individual differences in aggressiveness and food stealing among wintering oystercatchers *Haematopus ostralegus* L. *Animal Behaviour*, 30, 917–928.

Goss-Custard, J.D., Clarke, R.T., & Durell, S.E.A. Le V. dit (1984) Rates of food intake and aggression of oystercatchers *Haematopus ostralegus* on the most and least preferred mussel *Mytilus edulis* beds of the Exe Estuary. *Journal of Animal Ecology*, 53, 233–245.

Greenwood, P.J., Harvey, P.H. & Perrins, C.M. (1979). The role of dispersal in the great tit (*Parus major*): the causes, consequences and heritability of natal dispersal. *Journal of Animal Ecology*, 48, 123–142.

Harley, C.B. (1981). Learning the evolutionarily stable strategy. *Journal of Theoretical Biology*, 89, 611–633.

Harper, D.G.C. (1982). Competitive foraging in mallards: ideal free ducks. *Animal Behaviour*, 30, 575–584.

Hassell, M.P. (1978). *The Dynamics of Arthropod Predator–Prey Systems*. Princeton University Press, Princeton.

Hassell, M.P. (1980). Foraging strategies, population models and biological control: a case study. *Journal of Animal Ecology*, 49, 603–628.

Hassell, M.P. & May, R.M. (1973). Stability in insect host–parasite models. *Journal of Animal Ecology*, **42**, 693–726.

Hassell, M.P. & Varley, G.C. (1969). New inductive population model for insect parasites and its bearing on biological control. *Nature*, **223**, 1133–1136.

Holling, C.S. (1959). Some characteristics of simple types of predation and parasitism. *Canadian Entomologist*, **91**, 385–398.

Jenkins, D., Watson, A. & Miller, G.R. (1963). Population studies on red grouse. *Lagopus lagopus scoticus* (lath.) in north-west Scotland. *Journal of Animal Ecology*, **32**, 317–376.

Ketterson, E.D. & Nolan, V. Jr (1983). The evolution of differential bird migration. *Current Ornithology* Vol. 1 (Ed. by R.F. Johnston), pp. 357–402.

Kluijver, H.N. (1971). Regulation of numbers in a population of great tits (*Parus m. major*). *Dynamics of Numbers in Populations* (Ed. by P.J. den Boer & G. R. Gradwell), pp. 507–523. Centre for Agricultural Publishing and Documentation, Wageningen.

Łomnicki, A. (1982). Individual heterogeneity and population regulation. *Current Problems in Sociobiology* (Ed. by King's College Sociobiology Group), pp. 153–167. Cambridge University Press, Cambridge.

Maynard Smith, J. (1982). *Evolution and the Theory of Games*. Cambridge University Press, Cambridge.

Milinski, M. (1979). An evolutionarily stable feeding strategy in sticklebacks. *Zeitschrift für Tierpsychologie*, **51**, 36–40.

Milinski, M. (1982). Optimal foraging: the influence of intraspecific competition on diet selection. *Behavioural Ecology and Sociobiology*, **11**, 109–115.

Milinski, M. (1984). Competitive resource sharing: an experimental test of a learning rule for ESSs. *Animal Behaviour*, **32**, 233–242.

Milinski, M. (in press). Parasites determine a predator's optimal feeding strategy. *Behavioural Ecology and Sociobiology*.

Monaghan, P. (1980). Dominance and dispersal between feeding sites in the herring gull (*Larus argentatus*). *Animal Behaviour*, **28**, 521–527.

Myers, J.P. (1981). A test of three hypothesis for latitudinal segregation of the sexes in wintering birds. *Canadian Journal of Zoology*, **59**, 1527–1534.

Obeid, M., Machin, D. & Harper, J.L. (1967). Influence of density on plant to plant variation in Fiber Flax *Linum usistatissimum*. *Crop Science*, **7**, 471–473.

Park, T. (1948). Experimental studies of interspecies competition, 1. Competition between populations of the flour beetle *Tribolim confusum*, Duval and *Tribolium castaneum* Herbst. *Ecological Monographs*, **18**, 265–308.

Parker, G.A. (1970). The reproductive behaviour and the nature of sexual selection in *Scatophaga stercoraria* L., II. Spatial distribution of fertilisation rates and evolution of male search strategy within the reproductive area. *Evolution*, **28**, 93–108.

Parker, G.A. (1974). The reproductive behaviour and the nature of sexual selection in *Scatophaga stercoraria* L., IX. The fertilisation rate and the spatial and temporal relationships of each sex around the site of mating and oviposition. *Journal of Animal Ecology*, **39**, 205–228.

Parker, G.A. (1978). Searching for mates. *Behavioural Ecology: an Evolutionary Approach* (1st edn) (Ed. by J.R. Krebs & N.B. Davies), pp. 214–244. Blackwell Scientific Publications, Oxford.

Parker, G.A. (1982). Phenotype-limited evolutionarily stable strategies. *Current Problems in Sociobiology* (Ed. by Kings College Sociobiology Group), pp. 173–201. Cambridge University Press, Cambridge.

Rau, M.E. (1983). Establishment and maintenance of behavioural dominance in male mice infected with *Trichinella spiralis*. *Parasitology*, **86**, 319–322.

Regelmann, K. (1984). Competitive resource sharing: a simulation model. *Animal Behaviour*, **32**, 226–232.

Rowher, S. & Rowher, F.C. (1978). Status signalling in Harris sparrows: experimental deceptions achieved. *Animal Behaviour*, **26**, 1012–1022.

Rubinstein, D.I. (1981). Individual variation and competition in the everglades pygmy sunfish. *Journal of Animal Ecology*, **50**, 337–350.

Russell, K. (1981) *Differential winter distribution by sex in birds*. Unpublished MS thesis. Clemson University, South Carolina.

Sibly, R.M. & McCleery, R.M. (1983). The distribution between feeding sites of herring gulls breeding at Walney Island, UK. *Journal of Animal Ecology*, **52**, 51–68.

Silverin, B. (1980). Effects of long-acting testosterone treatment on free-living pied flycatchers *Fideaula hypoleuca*. *Animal Behaviour*, **28**, 906–912.

Sulkova, S. (1964). Zur nahrungsbiologie des habichts. *Accipiter gentilis* (L.) Aquilo. *Ser. Zool*, **3**, 1–103.

Sutherland, W.J. (1983). Aggregation and the 'ideal free' distribution. *Journal of Animal Ecology*, **52**, 821–828.

Taylor, R.A.J. & Taylor, L.R. (1979). A behavioural model for the evolution of spatial dynamics. *Population Dynamics* (Ed. by R.M. Anderson, B.D. Turner & L.R. Taylor), pp. 1–27. Blackwells Scientific Publications, Oxford.

Wilbur, H.M. & Collins, J.P. (1973). Ecological aspects of amphibian metamorphosis. *Science*, **182**, 1305–1314.

15. ADAPTIVE VALUE OF SPACING BEHAVIOUR IN POPULATION CYCLES OF RED GROUSE AND OTHER ANIMALS

R. MOSS AND A. WATSON

Institute of Terrestrial Ecology, Banchory, Scotland

SUMMARY

Red grouse numbers are affected by the amount and quality of their food, cover, weather, predation, parasites and disease. Increases from low densities occur when such extrinsic constraints are weak enough to allow them. Declines from high densities are sometimes associated with an increase in the severity of one or more extrinsic constraints. However, the main demographic cause of some intensively studied declines has been a change in patterns of movement associated with a change in spacing behaviour.

In north-east Scotland, where we study red grouse, populations show cycles with a period of about 6 years. Superimposed on this cyclic pattern are non-cyclic variations in numbers which we attribute to extrinsic factors. The cyclic component can be explained as a result of fairly regular changes in the birds' spacing behaviour and rate of dispersal, associated with changes in density. We have tested the idea that these regular changes in behaviour are genetically determined. The results confirm that genetic changes in aggression take place during a population fluctuation; but they are not consistent with such changes being the cause of the fluctuation. Rather, they seem to be the result of the fluctuation and suggest that selection against aggressive types occurs during the increase and for them during the decline phase of a fluctuation.

In this paper we suggest that these regular changes in behaviour can be considered adaptive. During the increase phase, tolerance of close neighbours, and a consequent increase in density, can be explained in terms of increased fitness for the individual and its kin. At peak densities and after they have been reached, intolerance is seen to become more advantageous; as a result, levels of aggression and rates of dispersal increase and density declines. We develop the idea that cycles in animal populations are a special case of adaptive irruptions. Whilst this offers a satisfying evolutionary framework for understanding population cycles, the idea remains to be tested.

INTRODUCTION

The main aim of our work on red grouse (*Lagopus lagopus scoticus* Lath.) has been to understand the behavioural and other mechanisms which limit populations and cause changes in numbers. We have intentionally restricted ourselves to looking at behaviour as a mechanism of population limitation and avoided any work based on the assumption that the patterns of behaviour seen by us have adaptive value.

The assumption that a trait is adaptive is often made in behavioural ecology. It has the drawback that it is not usually testable by experiment, and can lead to teleological rationalizations. The value of the approach is that it can provide a useful theoretical framework for organizing past observations and predicting future ones. We now apply it to red grouse, speculating about evolution with the aims of rationalizing past observations and defining questions for new research.

Analyses of shooting bags show that red grouse numbers exhibit cycles, i.e. a tendency for fluctuations to recur more regularly than expected by chance (Watson & Moss 1979; Rothery, Moss & Watson 1984). (We avoid the use of terms such as phase remembering and phase forgetting quasi-cycles (Nisbet & Gurney 1982), regarding these as classifications of mathematical models rather than of types of biological population fluctuations.) Williams (1974) re-analysed fourteen series of bag data from Middleton (1934) and MacKenzie (1952), finding strong evidence of 6-year cycles in six of them, including north-east Scotland where we work. Serial correlations showed damped oscillations, with statistically significant values at lags of 3 and 6 years. In series from other areas, there were suggestions of cycles from 4 to 10 years in length.

We are interested in the role of spacing behaviour in randomly fluctuating and fairly stable populations, as well as in cyclic ones. Our main work at the moment involves an experimental test of the hypothesis that cyclic populations are limited by regular, intrinsic variations in the animals' spacing behaviour, consequent rate of emigration and hence density. Even so, all cyclic populations must also be affected by extrinsic constraints such as weather, food, disease and predation. We therefore start by reviewing evidence on extrinsic processes that cause changes in numbers; we then discuss our current thinking which involves an integration of the effects of extrinsic and intrinsic processes on demography, and summarize a predictive mathematical model based on this integration. After summarizing evidence on the role of spacing behaviour in cyclic population fluctuations, we end with an openly speculative account of the adaptive value of population cycles in red grouse, with extrapolations to other animals. This account is based on the well established idea that spatial and temporal variations in density result in a lower incidence of starvation, disease, parasitism and predation. We make the inference that this lower incidence is an ultimate cause as well as an immediate consequence of population fluctuations (Taylor & Taylor 1978) or, in short, that cycles are adaptive.

BACKGROUND TO STUDY

Red grouse are territorial, monogamous gallinaceous birds. In autumn, old and young cocks compete for territories; old cocks which lose their territories and young cocks which fail to become territorial have usually died or emigrated by the spring. Hens which fail to pair with a cock also die or leave the study area. Not all cocks get hens, and in some springs over half the cocks may remain unmated despite the presence of many unattached hens in winter.

In years of high breeding density some territorial pairs may emigrate in spring, shortly before egg-laying. The remaining hens hatch about seven eggs each. In some years, much chick mortality occurs in the first week or two after hatching. After 2 weeks of age, chick mortality is generally low. After the hatching, territorial boundaries are defended no longer but broods are usually reared fairly near to where they were hatched. In some years, however, entire families may leave the study area in summer, the parents returning by autumn without their young.

The demographic parameters measured in intensive studies include: the spring density of each sex before breeding, spring emigration of adults, clutch size, hatchability of eggs, some measure of breeding success such as the number of chicks per hen, proportion of families which emigrate in summer, density of young and old birds in autumn, and overwinter loss between autumn and spring. In some studies it has proved possible to distinguish between losses of fully-grown birds due to mortality on the study area and losses due to birds leaving the area. In less intensive studies, it has been common to measure spring density and breeding success only.

EXTRINSIC FACTORS AFFECTING GROUSE POPULATIONS

To rule out extrinsic constraints as the sole proximate causes of population fluctuations, we must understand how and when these constraints operate. Variations in food, cover, weather, predation, parasitism and disease have all been shown to affect grouse demography. One may be the main factor limiting a population or several may act together. Their relative importance probably differs over the birds' range; most of our work has been done in north-east Scotland.

Food

Grouse numbers vary, within and amongst areas, in parallel with food supplies. The main food is heather (*Calluna vulgaris* L.), an evergreen dwarf shrub which dominates the moors of north-east Scotland, forming extensive swards managed by rotational burning. When we consider differences amongst areas, grouse are on average more abundant where the cover of heather is greater (Miller, Jenkins & Watson 1966), where it is more nutritious (Moss 1969) and where the sward is a fine-grained patchwork of young and old heather due to burning many small fires (Picozzi 1968).

These simple associations are not simple to explain, because the birds eat only a minute fraction of the green heather available to them: commonly 2–3% and rarely 10% (Miller & Watson 1978; Savory 1978). However, they are selective feeders, choosing to graze upon the heather patches richest in nitrogen (Lance 1983) and, within a patch, choosing the richest shoots (Moss 1972; Savory 1983). Furthermore, they prefer to graze heather which is easy of access and at a height (20–30 cm) convenient for feeding (Moss, Miller & Allen 1972). It has therefore been argued that they are limited by the amount of good quality food readily available to them (Moss 1969).

Grouse are unlikely to run short of food, however, because they can lengthen their guts in response to poorer food (Moss 1983) and mean gut length differs between populations (Moss 1967). Birds with short guts could therefore increase the amount of food that can effectively be used by the population, by lengthening their guts.

Although long guts enable a bird to digest poorer food they make it heavier and presumably less able to fly and fight. So birds with short guts may be fitter than birds with long guts, as long as enough food is available for them to select a rich diet (Moss 1983). Taking a large territory could ensure a rich food supply, increasing the quality of the bird's diet and so its competitive ability. Optimum territory size would then be the result of a balance between the advantages of better food and the penalties of defending a bigger area. Variations in food may cause alterations in the optimum territory size, and so the mean population density, even when very little of the food available is actually eaten. If so, the population is limited (in the sense of Watson & Moss 1970) by both food and territorial behaviour at the same time.

Can variations in food supply within areas explain year-to-year fluctuations in numbers? Experiments involving burning (Miller, Watson & Jenkins 1970) and fertilizing (Watson *et al.* 1977) showed that grouse numbers increase following improvement of their heather food. Hence, numbers might vary in parallel with the small fraction of the food supply rich enough to meet their needs. This simple idea, however, could not explain a recent major population decline at Kerloch in 1973–77 when neither the amount nor quality (N and phosphorus content) of food available decreased; also, the application of fertilizer failed to halt the decline, which continued to extinction on the experimental area (Watson, Moss & Parr 1984).

A more subtle idea is that an increase in population density may reduce the quality of the birds' diet because the area available to each bird for selection of food decreases. If such a reduction in food quality were followed by an increase in the population's level of aggression and increase in mean territory size, then population density might decline again. If a time-lag of a year or two occurred in this response, this could form the basis of a population cycle. One such hypothesis—the 'maternal nutrition' hypothesis (Watson & Moss 1972)—has been refuted as an explanation for the recent decline at Kerloch. This hypothesis predicted that, in years of population decline, brood sizes should be smaller and chicks inherently less viable but more aggressive than in years of population increase. Smaller brood sizes did occur in the decline phase of the fluctuation but these were not due to poorer chick viability. Also, inherent variations in our main measure of aggression were not related inversely to brood size (Moss, Watson & Rothery 1984). This refutation, however, did not exclude more general hypotheses about food, such as a reduction in food quality triggering population declines without involving maternal nutrition.

Cover

Tall old heather provides cover for nesting and hiding from predators. If fires are too big, there may be plenty of nutritious, accessible heather but very few grouse, as in western Scotland (Watson & Miller 1976). When feeding on young heather, which is both short and nutritious, grouse prefer to keep near the edge of the short patch, close to taller heather, and rarely use the middle (Savory 1974).

Uneven ground also provides cover. Within an area, territory size is inversely related to the cover from vegetation and uneven ground (Watson 1964). Thus, the association between high average grouse densities and a fine-grained patchwork of burned areas, both amongst (Picozzi 1968) and within (Miller, Watson & Jenkins 1970) areas, may depend on the provision of well-distributed cover as well as making good quality food accessible.

Changes in burning can affect grouse numbers but are not frequent enough to explain big annual fluctuations in density. Also, fluctuations occur on moors with unaltered management.

Predation

Almost all birds which fail to get territories in autumn have died by spring (Watson 1967). The proximate cause of death is often predation but most non-territorial birds would die anyway, either from leaving their moorland habitat after being chased by territory owners, from the stress of chases, or from stress-associated disease. Hence, winter predation may have little effect on populations in north-east Scotland (Jenkins, Watson & Miller 1964).

Egg-robbing by crows and foxes may affect numbers. Many grouse re-lay if their first clutch is lost, thus compensating for some robbing (Moss *et al.* 1984). Nonetheless, heavy robbing can reduce chick numbers and in our demographic model (below) this reduces subsequent breeding density.

On western Irish moors which are overgrazed by sheep and cattle, carrion from numerous dead sheep supports many crows and foxes (Watson & O'Hare 1980) which outnumber the scarce grouse. Their predation on red grouse can be heavy and may well be a major factor limiting grouse numbers.

Disease and parasites

Louping ill, a virus disease of sheep, is transmitted to grouse by sheep ticks *Idoxes ricinus* L. It is usually fatal to grouse and can depress populations to very low levels (Duncan *et al.* 1978). It probably expanded onto Scottish moors along with the expansion of hill sheep in the 1700s and 1800s (Reid *et al.* 1978) and red grouse have not yet developed much resistance. Its incidence is patchy and confined to a minor part of the moors in north-east Scotland.

The classic 'grouse disease', trichostrongylosis, is caused by the nematode *Trichostrongylus tenuis* which lives in the birds' caeca. Most grouse have some worms and are usually little affected by them. There are, however, outbreaks of disease when many birds are found dead and dying, usually in spring and early summer, in poor condition and containing thousands of worms. The best documented examples, at Glen Esk in 1958 and 1959 (Jenkins, Watson & Miller 1963), were associated with winter browning of the birds' heather food; possibly the parasites multiplied as a result of the birds' low resistance to larval infection following the poor diet. After both outbreaks, grouse breeding densities declined. Nonetheless, the number dying due to poor food and disease was insufficient to account for these declines. The entire moor was occupied by territory owners each autumn and there were many non-territorial birds. Hence, breeding densities could have been higher had territories been smaller.

The 'maternal nutrition' hypothesis (Watson & Moss 1972) suggested that birds become more aggressive and take bigger territories following a period of poor food. It might be argued that worms have a similar effect, by competing with the birds for scarce nutrients and, by damaging gut walls, impairing their digestive abilities. In theory at least, a big build-up of worms alone could reduce grouse numbers when food is good. Furthermore, worm burdens show a delayed density-dependent relationship with grouse densities with a lag of 1–2 years (Jenkins *et al.* 1963; A. Watson *et al.*, unpubl.) and so one might speculate that parasite burdens cause grouse cycles. To model this one simply needs to multiply delayed density-dependent worm burdens by some mortality factor (cf. Anderson & May 1978). The biological mechanism causing this mortality could include, for example, an effect of worms on levels of aggression causing increased territory size, and so leading to more non-territorial birds and reduced population density.

However, although they show delayed density dependence within one fluctuation, mean worm burdens vary considerably from one fluctuation to another (Watson *et al.*, unpubl.). Hence, worm burdens alone cannot explain all fluctuations. Most grouse declines in Scotland are not associated with outbreaks of trichostrongylosis. Also, Wilson (1979) detected no lasting effect of worm burdens on the dominance and aggressiveness of captive birds.

In northern England, Potts, Tapper & Hudson (1984) have placed more emphasis on worms as a cause of regularity in fluctuations of grouse numbers than have we in north-east Scotland. This may reflect real differences because grouse densities are higher there and the milder English climate allows worm larvae a longer active season. Other differences are that shooting pressures are probably greater in northern England, and that grouse bags there do not show as clear a cyclic pattern as in north-east Scotland.

The model of Potts *et al.* (1984) for fluctuating grouse populations rests upon largely random variations in density, with a slight degree of regularity imposed by delayed density-dependent worm burdens. Our population model (Watson *et al.* 1984) is outlined later in this paper; unlike that of Potts *et al.* it is based empirically on detailed demographic data from a long-term population study. It shows oscillations whose period is largely unaffected by random variations in breeding success and it does not invoke parasite burdens as the main cause of regularity. We agree with Potts *et al.* that *T. tenuis* is not the sole or major cause of population fluctuations in red grouse but reject their conclusion that cyclic or 'quasi-cyclic' fluctuations could not occur without the parasite.

Shooting

Grouse bags indicate past population trends. The 6-year periodicity of bags from 1850 onwards (Middleton 1934; MacKenzie 1952; Williams 1974) in north-east Scotland, shows that the three fluctuations studied intensively by us (6, 6 and 8 years in length) were a continuation of past patterns. Bags from MacKenzie's 'England West' region from 1900 onwards differed, with a less well marked period of about 4 years, as confirmed by more bag data analysed by Potts *et al.* (1984).

Bag data should nonetheless be interpreted with care because shooting itself can be a major cause of mortality: the number shot on an area sometimes exceeds the number counted there before the shooting. Jenkins *et al.* (1963) argued that the shooting which they observed each autumn was unlikely to have reduced breeding stocks in spring because a further natural decline in numbers usually followed the shooting season, due to birds without territories dying over winter. However, very heavy shooting is likely to kill so many territory owners that the pattern of territories would be broken up, and thus the one-for-one replacement of shot territory owners by previously non-territorial birds would become less likely. Two further points also suggest that shooting may affect numbers. First, demographic modelling (below) implies that the number of birds in autumn is a determinant of breeding density the next spring and hence of its inverse—territory size. Shooting reduces the number in autumn, and models fitted the number observed in the next spring better when shot birds were subtracted from the number reared on the study area. Second, fluctuations which depend on changes in spacing behaviour (below) are also likely to depend on the nature of individuals, not just on their numbers. Shooting is likely to kill a different set of birds than would have died from natural causes in the absence of shooting. For example, some dominant birds may be shot, so allowing some subordinates, which would otherwise have died or emigrated, to remain in the population.

We have avoided these problems by doing our main work since 1964 on unshot areas, so our conclusions may have to be modified before being applied to shot populations. There is some evidence that the amplitude of fluctuations on lightly shot or unshot moors may exceed that on heavily shot areas (Watson & Miller 1976).

MAIN DEMOGRAPHIC PROCESSES IN RECENT STUDIES

So far we have summarized ways in which extrinsic constraints to population growth may act separately. We now show how extrinsic and intrinsic processes can be integrated to explain population fluctuations. At Kerloch moor, breeding densities fluctuated about twofold in 1963–69, and fivefold in 1969–77. Losses of eggs and chicks occurred in spring and summer, and losses of fully-grown birds throughout the year. Of these losses, winter loss was the one best correlated with changes in spring numbers, and the largest single loss. It was only partly due to deaths on the area and in most years involved much emigration. In the second, bigger fluctuation, many birds emigrated in summer during decline years, and summer and winter losses were correlated: the main cause of the decline was an increased rate of emigration (Watson *et al.* 1984).

During the first, smaller fluctuation, winter losses tended to compensate for poor breeding, so that spring numbers increased from 1965 to the peak in 1966 despite poor breeding. We concluded that the first fluctuation resulted from an intrinsic cyclic process modified by extrinsic factors including considerable egg-robbing by crows. The second fluctuation, when egg-robbing was light, was thought to reflect largely the intrinsic cyclic process. Intrinsic processes within the population caused losses more by emigration, and extrinsic processes imposed on the population more by death.

DEMOGRAPHIC MODEL

We constructed a predictive mathematical model based on the demographic processes observed at Kerloch (Watson *et al.* 1984 and Fig. 15.1). Winter loss could not be used to predict spring numbers because we could calculate it only after the spring counts. However, three other major causes of loss—the failure of cocks to pair with a hen, the extent of summer emigration, and egg and chick losses—were all correlated with each other and with winter loss. We combined all three in a single measure, the chick production ratio, which was the ratio of the number of young birds present in August to the number of adults in spring. Changes in spring numbers from one spring to the next could be predicted from the observed chick production ratio each year. Such predictions have been reasonably good at Rickarton, our new study area.

The two sexes were modelled separately. The incorporation of data on the cocks' spring density improved the fit of the hen model to the observed data, suggesting that the hens' density depended on the cocks. Predictions of the cocks' density, however, were not improved by data on the hens. This indicated that cocks played a leading role in determining densities, as was to be expected because cocks often maintain territories without a mate, as hens never do; and because the experimental removal of cocks results in the disappearance of the hens that were paired with them (Watson & Jenkins 1968).

The chick production ratio showed delayed density dependence because it was related to spring numbers 2 years previously. We could therefore predict it 2 years ahead. We could then put the predicted ratio into the model and predict grouse numbers next spring, and so on indefinitely, assuming an

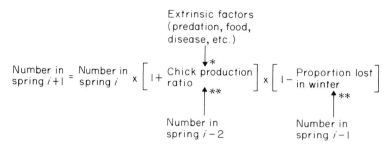

*Mortality
**Relationship due largely to emigration

FIG. 15.1. Scheme of processes in demographic models. The simplest model for cocks was

$$Y_{i+1} = \alpha + Y_i + b_i + e_i$$

where Y was the natural logarithm of breeding density, subscripts indicated the year, b was $\log_e (1 + \text{chick production ratio})$, α mean winter survival and e varied randomly with zero mean. However, winter survival was correlated with Y_{i-1} and b with Y_{i-2} giving

$$Y_{i+1} = 3 \cdot 1 + Y_i - 0 \cdot 18 Y_{i-1} - 0 \cdot 50 Y_{i-2}$$

In addition, extrinsic factors modified b. All this is illustrated in linear form in the figure, where arrows indicate correlations which affect the target parameter. Correlations occur both with extrinsic factors and with past spring densities; we attribute the latter to intrinsic factors.

absence of extrinsic effects on the population. The model was entirely empirical and incorporated no prior assumptions causing it to cycle. Nonetheless, when it was allowed to run freely into the future, it showed clear oscillations. The oscillatory pattern was unaffected by the random imposition of poor breeding, and so was consistent with our idea of an intrinsic cyclic process in grouse fluctuations which remains operative and detectable despite extrinsic factors.

SPACING BEHAVIOUR IN GROUSE CYCLES

This section begins by summarizing evidence for changes in spacing behaviour during population fluctuations of red grouse and goes on to speculate why such changes should occur.

Population limitation by territorial behaviour in red grouse

There is good evidence from studies of red grouse populations at Glen Esk and Kerloch that density is limited by territorial behaviour. Each year, cocks take up territories in autumn and usually hold them until spring. Young and old compete on roughly equal terms and about half get territories in autumn; most of the remaining non-territorial birds emigrate or die over winter but some take over territories whose owners have died.

Each increase in breeding numbers on the intensive study area at Kerloch between the trough in 1969 and the peak in 1973 followed a decrease in mean territory size. To find whether this was accompanied by inherent changes in behaviour, we studied the behaviour of captive birds hatched from eggs laid by wild hens near the intensive study area. Our main measure was a dominance ranking (Moss *et al.* 1979) similar to a pecking order in poultry. Each autumn we had a cohort of fully-grown cocks which had hatched from eggs taken from the hill that year. A linear dominance ranking was determined for each cohort. Most cocks still survived from the previous year's cohort and so we could compare the dominance of the two cohorts by testing one against the other. An index of change was calculated for each pair of years and these changes were added together to indicate changes in relative dominance throughout the study.

Differences in dominance were inherent, and probably genetically inherited. Relative dominance declined as densities increased, and continued to decline for 1 year after the peak (Fig. 15.2). During the rest of the population decline, it increased until the next trough. This and other evidence (Moss *et al.* 1984) was consistent with genetic selection against the traits underlying dominance during years of population increase and peak, and for them during decline years.

Chitty (1967) suggested that natural selection for and against aggressive and presumably dominant genotypes should occur during population cycles. Our data were consistent with this for the 1969–77 fluctuation. However, they refuted the idea that such selection is the main cause of grouse declines, as the birds' level of dominance increased only after the decline in numbers was under way. Indeed, the pattern observed by us (Fig. 15.2) is more or less the inverse of that postulated by Krebs (his Fig. 16.1, p. 297) on the basis of Chitty's hypothesis. Instead, we concluded that selection for dominance occurred as a consequence of the demographic processes which caused the population to fluctuate. The main cause of the 1969–77 fluctuation was a low rate of emigration during the increase and a high rate during the decline (Watson *et al.* 1984). We suggested that subordinate birds dispersed more readily than dominant ones—more subordinates tending to remain in the increasing population and more tending to leave the declining one. Unable to explain the decline as a consequence of poor food (Watson *et al.* 1984), predation (Watson & Moss 1980) or parasitism (Watson *et al.*, unpubl.), we attributed it largely to a change in spacing behaviour at high densities. The population

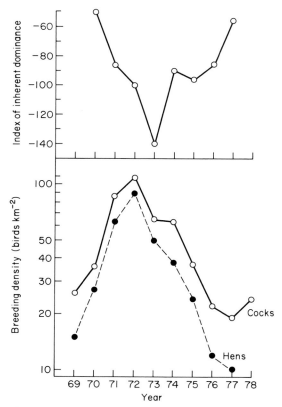

FIG. 15.2. Index of inherent dominance (ability to dominate others) and population density on parts of Kerloch adjacent to intensive study area. Note that numbers here reached a peak in 1972, a year earlier than on the intensive area (Fig. 15.3); this does not affect our interpretation.

increase had occurred, we thought, because birds were relatively tolerant and the decline because they became and remained intolerant (Moss *et al.* 1984).

Adaptive significance of tolerance and intolerance

We have not yet published any functional explanation of these suggested changes in tolerance. They can be explained in terms of kin selection. The essential feature of kin selection for a gene is that animals in the set embodying that gene co-operate to increase their representation in the population. A possibility (which we are now analysing) is that changes in tolerance occur as a consequence of neighbours tending to be closely related during the increase phase: a group of neighbouring cocks might comprise father, sons and brothers (Lance 1978). During declines this pattern might be disrupted due to more emigration.

It seems reasonable that kindred neighbours should tolerate each other. At relatively low densities, a father could increase his genotype's fitness by allowing his sons to take parts of his old, large territory. If birds were more tolerant this would allow recruitment of less dominant individuals. It would be consistent with the observed reduction in inherent dominance during the population increase (Fig. 15.2) and with the parallel observation that successive cohorts of young cocks took smaller territories than old cocks in the same year (Watson & Moss 1980).

Following peak densities in 1973, so many hens emigrated over winter in 1973–74 and subsequently that roughly half the cocks had territories but no hens in 1974–76, as opposed to a quarter in 1970–73 (Fig. 15.3). In 1973 and 1974 young cocks were less successful than old ones in getting hens, although equally or more successful earlier and later. Furthermore, they were less successful in recruiting from 1974 onwards, forming about 50% of the breeding population in years of increase; but only 20–35% in the main decline years. Also, inherent dominance increased again during the decline (Fig. 15.2).

At peak densities many territories, particularly those of young cocks, were

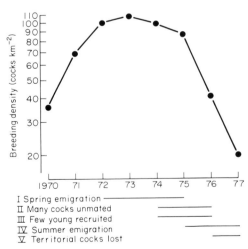

FIG. 15.3. Diagram of the timing of different aspects of spacing behaviour during the recent population fluctuation of red grouse on the intensive study area at Kerloch. The solid line connecting the years 1970–77 shows the density of cocks (number per km²) in spring. I. Pre-laying emigration of adults > 20% 1972–75. II. Proportion of unmated cocks in the territorial male spring population > 50% 1974–76. III. Proportion of young in the territorial male spring population < 35% 1974–76. IV. Summer emigration of adults > 30% 1975–77. V. Late-winter loss of territorial cocks > 30% 1976–77.

small and had no hen. This may have meant that the fitness of a family's genotype could no longer be increased by successive generations taking yet smaller territories. There seem to have been three options. First, emigrate and attempt to breed elsewhere; emigration did increase at the peak and during the decline, and spring and summer emigration, which previously had been unusual, became frequent. Second, increase one's fitness by excluding competitors; this could result from the observed increases in territory size during the decline, when the most dominant birds would presumably be the best competitors and selection for dominant types would ensue (Fig. 15.2). Third, some representatives of a genotype could emigrate and some stay. The observed summer emigration of entire families could achieve this. In autumn the parents returned without their young, presumably having reared them elsewhere. Another way might be for the least dominant birds of a given genotype to emigrate readily, thus leaving the most dominant in possession of a large area without their chances of survival being reduced by excessive competition.

Why did the sex ratio favour cocks during the decline? Even at low densities, many cocks had no hens even though their territories were large by the standards of previous years. Breeding may reduce a cock's chances of survival and the chances of offspring being recruited were small during the decline. Thus, the extra cost of breeding added to that of defending a territory against intolerant birds during the decline may have outweighed the benefits of attempting to rear young. Such a cock might thereby increase his chances of breeding in a later year, when his offspring had a better chance of recruitment. Unlike unmated cocks, unmated hens did not defend territories. A hen had no option of remaining and not breeding. She had to pair with a cock to ensure her survival, but the chances of this or of rearing young may have been better elsewhere. Hence, hens may have more reason to emigrate during declines than during increases.

At the end of the decline, the few remaining cocks had very large territories. In late winter 1975–76 and 1976–77 over a third of the territorial cocks lost their territories and later died or emigrated (Fig. 15.3). At high densities, neighbours usually expand their territories to take in deserted ground but in 1977 and 1978 a small fraction of the study area remained unoccupied in spring. This observation is paralleled in cyclic troughs of populations of ruffed grouse (*Bonasa umbellus* L.) (Gullion 1981) and willow grouse (*Lagopus lagopus* L.) (Myrberget 1983); similarly voles and lemmings desert a large proportion of their habitat during cyclic low densities (Clough 1968). In spring 1978 the sex ratio of red grouse at Kerloch returned to what it had been during the previous increase phase, and the next population increase then began. Presumably, tolerance had again become adaptive.

Adaptive value of synchronous dispersal and decline

To judge from shooting bags on other moors, declines as at Kerloch in the mid 1970s also occurred over hundreds of square miles of moorland, although numbers on adjacent areas were not always exactly in phase. Such approximate synchrony in many local populations could result from widespread extrinsic effects, such as catastrophic damage to food by weather. Another mechanism might be the triggering of social intolerance, and consequent decline, by immigrants from neighbouring populations which have reached a peak or are already in decline (Abramsky & Tracy 1979; Charnov & Finerty 1980).

Whatever the proximate mechanism, synchronous dispersal from a large area in a short period may swamp predators and improve the dispersing individual's chances of survival. Synchronous declines to low densities, even the desertion of parts of the range, may prevent increases of predators and diseases such as trichostrongylosis.

Individuals dispersing at a different time from most may have a poorer chance of survival, so synchrony might be maintained by selection (Lloyd & Dybas 1966). Maintenance of low densities over large areas for long enough for disease organisms and predators to die or disperse is also likely to increase an individual bird's chances of leaving descendants there during the subsequent increase.

EXTRINSIC AND INTRINSIC CYCLES

A predator/prey cycle is conceptually similar to a disease/host cycle. People who tender these hypotheses as explanations for cycles do not usually support the hypothesis that changes in spacing behaviour cause cycles. However, a behavioural cycle may result from a predator/prey cycle. We turn for evidence of this to work on birds other than red grouse.

One hypothesis explains the 3–4 year cycle in autumn densities of several grouse species in Scandinavia as a consequence of predators switching from small rodents to grouse in years when rodents crash in density. Small rodents show a 3–4 year cycle, and so do the grouse, which breed poorly in the year following each rodent peak. Evidence for this timing and the switch in diet is mounting (Myrberget 1974; Angelstam 1983).

During decline years, when grouse breed poorly, predators may rob many nests. Myrberget, Olsvik & Sæther (1981), however, made an observation on a cyclic, migratory island population of willow grouse which cast doubt on the necessity of the predator-switch hypothesis. Rodents reached a peak on the nearby mainland in 1978 but not on the island. On the island many nests were lost in 1979, apparently to crows, but predator numbers showed no change. This appears to show that neither an increased number of predators nor a rodent peak and decline on the breeding grounds is necessary for the cyclic grouse decline.

We can speculate that predation has been involved in the evolution of an intrinsic 3–4 year cycle in willow grouse performance. When the chances of hen, eggs and chicks being eaten are high, hens may put less effort into protecting their nest and be readier to desert. This may improve their chances of survival in such years.

What cue might the willow grouse use to determine breeding effort? Do they estimate rodent abundance, or some sign of it, before the breeding season; or else have a completely intrinsic 3–4 year cycle which is kept in phase with the rodent cycle by predation? In principle, these possibilities could be distinguished by experiment. For example, one might increase rodent numbers earlier than usual by releasing individuals, or reduce rodent numbers by removals.

Thus, adaptations of prey to predator, or host to disease, may involve the evolution of such an intrinsic cycle from an extrinsic one. This may be more general. In red grouse in north-east Scotland, for example, densities usually decline before trichostrongyle worm burdens build up to a point where fresh outbreaks of grouse disease occur. The avoidance of disease may be one cause of the bird's intrinsic cyclic decline to low densities.

CYCLES AS IRRUPTIONS

Many species show irruptions, short periods of great abundance followed by longer periods of relative scarcity, and break out of their usual limits of abundance when food is plentiful. White (1976) suggests that most animals are limited by nitrogenous food for their young and that plants stressed by unusually high or low rainfall contain more nitrogen than usual.

Such weather is likely over wide areas, so ensuring many dispersing animals which will swamp predators and have a good chance of founding new populations. An effective predator-swamping mechanism might involve maintaining very low densities or irrupting, and avoiding intermediate densities which would support many enemies. If this mechanism is optimum and has evolved, then we might expect from it a threshold of food quality below which an animal breeds at a slower rate than the food would allow (this prediction is not, of course, exclusive to this hypothesis). The occurrence of good food, probably over a large area, should provide both raw material and trigger for an irruption.

In some biotopes, such an extrinsic trigger may not be dependable, food quality may not vary much, and yet the irruptive stratagem may be adaptive, allowing animals to avoid predators or parasites. To co-ordinate large-scale irruptions from adjacent local populations we might have to substitute an intrinsic trigger for an extrinsic one. One possibility is a biological clock which triggers irruptions at regular intervals and hence produces cycles. This clock could be internal or work through a delayed density-dependent mechanism. In this light, cycles might be regarded as irruptions triggered by temporal rather than nutritional cues.

CURRENT TEST OF MECHANISMS INVOLVED IN POPULATION CYCLES

Our numerical model of grouse populations (Fig. 15.1) provides reasonable predictions of grouse density but tells little about the biological mechanisms involved. The linear delayed density-dependent relationships in the model may reflect parallel biological processes. Or, grouse numbers may rise and fall every 6 years or so irrespective of density, as a result of an internal biological clock or an undiscovered extrinsic cyclic process. A third, our favoured, hypothesis implies a stepwise delayed density-dependent relationship. Tolerance is thought to change to intolerance above a certain threshold of density, when the strategy of taking smaller territories becomes maladaptive; the rate of emigration then increases and numbers decline.

An experiment that we are doing at present is designed to distinguish predictions from these three possibilities (Fig. 15.4). The control population

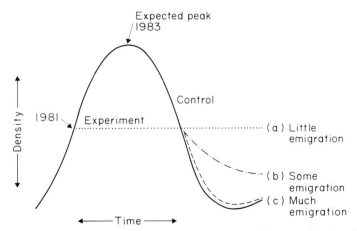

FIG. 15.4. Scheme of possible results of current experiment at Rickarton, where breeding densities on the experimental area are not being allowed to exceed the 1981 level: (a) expected from stepwise delayed density dependence (threshold > 1981 density); (b) expected from linear delayed density dependence; (c) expected from cyclic process independent of density.

should have reached its peak in 1983; on an experimental area we are holding breeding densities down to 1981 levels. We expect the control population to decline, with much emigration, whilst the experimental population remains constant.

CONCLUSION

We do not pretend to have uncovered the evolutionary pressures which have shaped population cycles. Rather, our speculations about evolution contribute to a rationale which helps to organize and predict observations on cyclic populations. They also add interest and motivation to the testable question of whether the mechanisms underlying grouse cycles show linear or stepwise delayed density dependence, or operate independently of density.

REFERENCES

Abramsky, Z. & Tracy, C.R. (1979). Population biology of a 'noncycling' population of prairie voles and a hypothesis on the role of migration in regulating microtine cycles. *Ecology*, **60**, 349–361.

Anderson, R.M. & May, R.M. (1978). Regulation and stability of host–parasite population interactions. I. Regulatory processes. *Journal of Animal Ecology*, **47**, 219–247.

Angelstam, P. (1983). *Population dynamics of tetraonids, especially the black grouse* Tetrao tetrix L., *in boreal forests*. Ph.D. thesis, University of Uppsala.

Charnov, E.L. & Finerty, J.P. (1980). Vole population cycles: a case for kin-selection? *Oecologia*, **45**, 1–2.

Chitty, D. (1967). The natural selection of self-regulatory behaviour in animal populations. *Proceedings of the Ecological Society of Australia*, **2**, 51–78.

Clough, G.C. (1968). Social behaviour and ecology of Norwegian lemmings during a population peak and crash. *Papers of the Norwegian State Game Research Institute*, 2nd series, No. 28, pp. 1–50.

Duncan, J.S., Reid, H.W., Moss, R., Phillips, J.D.P. & Watson, A. (1978). Ticks, louping ill and red grouse on moors in Speyside, Scotland. *Journal of Wildlife Management*, **42**, 500–505.

Gullion, G.W. (1981). Non-drumming males in a ruffed grouse population. *Wilson Bulletin*, **93**, 372–382.

Jenkins, D., Watson, A. & Miller, G.R. (1963). Population studies on red grouse, *Lagopus lagopus scoticus* (Lath.) in north-east Scotland. *Journal of Animal Ecology*, **32**, 317–376.

Jenkins, D., Watson, A. & Miller, G.R. (1964). Predation and red grouse populations. *Journal of Applied Ecology*, **1**, 183–195.

Lance, A.N. (1978). Survival and recruitment success of individual young cock red grouse *Lagopus l. scoticus* tracked by radio-telemetry. *Ibis* **120**, 369–378.

Lance, A.N. (1983). Selection of feeding sites by hen red grouse *Lagopus lagopus scoticus* during breeding. *Ornis Scandinavica*, **14**, 78–80.

Lloyd, M. & Dybas, H.S. (1966). The periodical cicada problem. II. Evolution. *Evolution*, **20**, 466–505.

MacKenzie, J.M.D. (1952). Fluctuations in the numbers of British tetraonids. *Journal of Animal Ecology*, **21**, 128–153.

Middleton, A.D. (1934). Periodic fluctuations in British game populations. *Journal of Animal Ecology*, **3**, 231–249.

Miller, G.R., Jenkins, D. & Watson, A. (1966). Heather performance and red grouse populations. I. Visual estimates of heather performance. *Journal of Applied Ecology*, 3, 313–326.

Miller, G.R. & Watson, A. (1978). Heather productivity and its relevance to the regulation of grouse populations. *Ecological Studies*, 27 (Ed. by O.W. Heal & D.F. Perkins), pp. 277–285. Springer-Verlag, Berlin.

Miller, G.R., Watson, A. & Jenkins, D. (1970). Responses of red grouse populations to experimental improvement of their food. *Animal Populations in Relation to their Food Resources* (Ed. by A. Watson), pp. 323–334. Symposia of the British Ecological Society, 10. Blackwell Scientific Publications, Oxford.

Moss, R. (1967). *Aspects of grouse nutrition*. Unpublished Ph.D. thesis, University of Aberdeen.

Moss, R. (1969). A comparison of red grouse (*Lagopus l. scoticus*) stocks with the production and nutritive value of heather (*Calluna vulgaris*). *Journal of Animal Ecology*, 38, 103–112.

Moss, R. (1972). Food selection by red grouse (*Lagopus lagopus scoticus* (Lath.)) in relation to chemical composition. *Journal of Animal Ecology*, 41, 411–418.

Moss, R. (1983). Gut size, body weight, and digestion of winter foods by grouse and ptarmigan. *Condor*, 85, 185–193.

Moss, R., Kolb, H.H., Marquiss, M., Watson, A., Treca, B., Watt, D. & Glennie, W. (1979). Aggressiveness and dominance in captive cock red grouse. *Aggressive Behavior*, 5, 59–84.

Moss, R., Miller, G.R. & Allen, S.E. (1972). Selection of heather by captive red grouse in relation to the age of the plant. *Journal of Applied Ecology*, 9, 771–781.

Moss, R., Watson, A. & Rothery, P. (1984). Inherent changes in the body size, viability and behaviour of a fluctuating red grouse (*Lagopus lagopus scoticus*) population. *Journal of Animal Ecology*, 53, 171–189.

Myrberget, S. (1974). Variations in the production of the Willow Grouse *Lagopus lagopus* L. in Norway, 1963–72. *Ornis Scandinavica*, 5, 163–172.

Myrberget, S. (1983). Vacant habitats during a decline in a breeding population of Willow Grouse *Lagopus lagopus*. *Fauna Norvegica*, Series C, Cinclus 6, 1–7.

Myrberget, S., Olsvik, O. & Sæther, T. (1981). On a 'crash' in a population of Willow Grouse *Lagopus lagopus*. *Fauna Norvegica*, Series C, Cinclus 4, 64–68.

Nisbet, R.M. & Gurney, W.S.C. (1982). *Modelling Fluctuating Populations*. John Wiley & Sons, Chichester.

Picozzi, N. (1968). Grouse bags in relation to the management and geology of heather moors. *Journal of Applied Ecology*, 5, 483–488.

Potts, G.R., Tapper, S.C. & Hudson, P.J. (1984). Population fluctuations in red grouse: analysis of bag records and a simulation model. *Journal of Animal Ecology*, 53, 21–36.

Reid, H.W., Duncan, J.S., Phillips, J.D.P., Moss, R. & Watson, A. (1978). Studies on louping-ill virus (Flavivirus group) in wild red grouse (*Lagopus lagopus scoticus*). *Journal of Hygiene*, 81, 321–330.

Rothery, P., Moss, R. & Watson, A. (1984). General properties of predictive population models in red grouse (*Lagopus lagopus scoticus*). *Oecologia*, 62, 382–386.

Savory, C.J. (1974). *The feeding ecology of red grouse in N.E. Scotland*. Unpublished Ph.D. thesis, University of Aberdeen.

Savory, C.J. (1978). Food consumption of red grouse in relation to the age and productivity of heather. *Journal of Animal Ecology*, 47, 269–282.

Savory, C.J. (1983). Selection of heather age and chemical composition by Red Grouse in relation to physiological state, season and time of day. *Ornis Scandinavica*, 14, 135–143.

Taylor, L.R. & Taylor, R.A.J. (1978). The dynamics of spatial behaviour. *Population Control by Social Behaviour* (Ed. by F.J. Ebling & D.M. Stoddart), pp. 181–212. Institute of Biology, London.

Watson, A. (1964). Aggression and population regulation in red grouse. *Nature* (London), 202, 506–507.

Watson, A. (1967). Social status and population regulation in the red grouse (*Lagopus lagopus scoticus*). *Abstracts of the Proceedings of the Royal Society Population Study Group*, No. 2, 22–30.

Watson, A. & Jenkins, D. (1968). Experiments on population control by territorial behaviour in red grouse. *Journal of Animal Ecology*, **37**, 595–614.

Watson, A. & Miller, G.R. (1976). *Grouse Management*. The Game Conservancy, Fordingbridge.

Watson, A. & Moss, R. (1970). Dominance, spacing behaviour and aggression in relation to population limitation in vertebrates. *Animal Populations in Relation to their Food Resources* (Ed. by A. Watson), pp. 167–218. Symposia of the British Ecological Society, 10. Blackwell Scientific Publications, Oxford.

Watson, A. & Moss, R. (1972). A current model of population dynamics in red grouse. *Proceedings of the International Ornithological Congress*, 15, 134–149.

Watson, A. & Moss, R. (1979). Population cycles in the Tetraonidae. *Ornis Fennica*, **56**, 87–109.

Watson, A. & Moss, R. (1980). Advances in our understanding of the population dynamics of red grouse from a recent fluctuation in numbers. *Ardea*, **68**, 103–111.

Watson, A., Moss, R. & Parr, R. (1984). Effects of food enrichment on numbers and spacing behaviour of red grouse. *Journal of Animal Ecology*, **53**, 663–678.

Watson, A., Moss, R., Phillips, J. & Parr, R. (1977). The effect of fertilizers on red grouse stocks on Scottish moors grazed by sheep, cattle and deer. *Ecologie du Petit Gibier et Aménagement des Chasses* (Ed. by P. Pesson & M.G. Birkan), pp. 193–212. Gauthier-Villars, Paris.

Watson, A., Moss, R., Rothery, P. & Parr, R. (1984). Demographic causes and predictive models of population fluctuations in red grouse. *Journal of Animal Ecology*, **53**, 639–662.

Watson, A. & O'Hare, P.J. (1980). Dead sheep and scavenging birds and mammals on Mayo bog. *Irish Birds*, **1**, 487–491.

White, T.C.R. (1976). Weather, food and plagues of locusts. *Oecologia*, **22**, 119–134.

Williams, J.C. (1974). *Mathematical analysis of red grouse populations*. Unpublished B.Sc. thesis, University of York.

Wilson, G.R. (1979). *Effects of the caecal threadworm* Trichostrongylus tenuis *in red grouse*. Unpublished Ph.D. thesis, University of Aberdeen.

16. DO CHANGES IN SPACING BEHAVIOUR DRIVE POPULATION CYCLES IN SMALL MAMMALS?

CHARLES J. KREBS

Department of Zoology, University of British Columbia, Vancouver, BC, Canada

SUMMARY

The general hypothesis that *changes in the spacing behaviour of individuals are necessary to cause cyclic fluctuations in population density* is consistent with observations and experiments on small rodent populations. Spacing behaviour causes dispersal, reproductive inhibition, and mortality, the three demographic processes that generate cyclic population fluctuations. Both laboratory and field approaches have been used to study the role of spacing behaviour in rodent population dynamics. One promising approach is through standarized laboratory tests of agonistic and exploratory behaviour. Agonistic scores obtained from such tests for male and female *Microtus townsendii* correlate with demographic changes in field populations.

The mechanics of how spacing might drive cyclic density shifts are less clear and we lack a general model. Spacing behaviour leads to dispersal, which is maximal in increasing populations and absent in declines. Thus, dispersal losses cannot be the delayed density-dependent factor that generates cycles. I postulate that in vole populations spacing behaviour produces an unstable equilibrium at high density which is caused by reproductive inhibition and mortality due to aggressive encounters. Spacing behaviour in voles and lemmings may thus depend on the frequency of aggressive individuals, and we must find out what genotypic and other conditions determine an individual's spacing behaviour. The genetic structure of field populations is likely to affect the expression of spacing behaviour and we need to know how relatives are distributed in natural populations.

Spacing behaviour is sex-specific in voles and the limiting resource for males is thought to be *breeding females* and for females *space* free from intruders. Spacing behaviour can link intrinsic hypotheses of regulation with extrinsic hypotheses.

INTRODUCTION

Small mammal populations show a bewildering variety of changes in density over time, and great faith is required to hope that a unified theory will arise to explain these changes. Some small mammal populations show cycles more or less regularly, and others fluctuate only annually or irregularly (Elton 1942; Chitty 1952; Hansson & Henttonen 1984; Taitt & Krebs 1984). During the past 10 years most authors have agreed that spacing behaviour is at least one component of the mechanism driving population cycles in small mammals (Finerty 1980) but its exact role is far from clear.

In this paper I will summarize the evidence that spacing behaviour drives population cycles, present some new data on agonistic behaviour of *Microtus townsendii* in relation to demography, and speculate on the adaptive value of spacing behaviour for small mammals. *Microtus townsendii* populations fluctuate irregularly and not cyclically (Krebs 1979), but spacing behaviour may limit population density in stable, cyclic, and irregularly-fluctuating populations. Consequently the same general predictions can be made for the relationship between spacing behaviour and demographic variables for all types of cyclic and non-cyclic populations.

We begin with the following hypothesis: *Changes in the spacing behaviour of individuals are necessary to cause cyclic fluctuations in population density* (Chitty 1967). Spacing and territorial behaviour can be regarded as forms of dominance and have recently been reviewed by Kaufmann (1983). We assume here that spacing behaviour occurs in small mammals because it allows priority of access to resources, and this raises the problem of what resources are limiting (which I discuss later, p. 310). Note that our starting hypothesis is quantitatively vague and Fig. 16.1 shows one attempt to make the hypothesis more specific. We need to address two difficult questions:

(i) How can we measure *spacing behaviour*?

(ii) How does spacing behaviour affect density changes?

AN OVERVIEW OF METHODS

Spacing behaviour is a form of social behaviour, and we have suspected since the pioneering works of Calhoun (1949) and Clarke (1955) that spacing behaviour could be a potent force in population regulation. Table 16.1 lists the six general approaches that have been used to study the role of spacing behaviour in small mammal populations, and the general conclusions that have followed from these approaches.

It is relatively easy to quantify the aggressive, submissive, and avoidance components of spacing behaviour in dyadic encounters under controlled conditions (Eisenberg 1966; Healey 1967, and many others). But as we move into the field we are less able to measure such behaviour directly and must rely on indirect variables (such as wounding) to see the effects of spacing behaviour on populations. To students of small mammals it seems curiously perverse

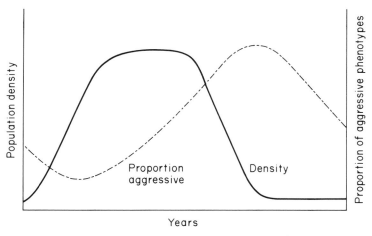

FIG. 16.1. A simplified diagram of the hypothesis that spacing behaviour changes with population density in cyclic populations. This is Krebs' version of one model of the Chitty hypothesis if aggressiveness is genetically determined. Not all spacing behaviour is aggressive, and any relevant form of spacing behaviour for the species in question is implied.

that in herbivorous large mammals, whose behaviour can be seen readily in the field, spacing behaviour is not deemed important in population regulation (Caughley & Krebs 1983). In small mammals we cannot observe spacing behaviour easily in the field, yet we think that it limits breeding density (Tamarin 1983).

If spacing behaviour is to cause density changes, it must affect the animals' rates of reproduction, mortality, emigration or immigration. Spacing behaviour can produce dispersal (Lidicker 1975) and can also block reproduction and increase mortality (Watson & Moss 1970).

The most empirical model that is useful for demonstrating that spacing behaviour limits population density is that of Watson & Moss (1970). There has been no explicit challenge to the Watson & Moss model (Tamarin 1983) although their criteria are difficult to demonstrate conclusively in field populations. I will assume that the Watson & Moss criteria provide the operational definition of population limitation through spacing behaviour.

SPACING BEHAVIOUR IN *MICROTUS TOWNSENDII*

In this section I present some results from an attempt to relate social behaviour measured in standardized laboratory tests to population changes in

TABLE 16.1. Methods used to study the role of spacing behaviour in population dynamics of small mammals, and some general conclusions

Approach	Type of data obtained	General conclusions for voles and lemmings	References
Laboratory colonies	Observations on individuals in confinement, demography	(a) Adult voles can be highly aggressive, particularly to strangers. (b) Adult voles of both sexes may kill juveniles, nestlings and other adults. (c) Subordinate individuals are restricted in spatial movements and do not breed.	Chitty (unpubl.) Clarke (1955) Lidicker (1980) Getz & Carter (1980) Gipps & Jewell (1979)
Standard laboratory tests	Open field activity, maze exploration, dyadic bouts	(a) Some populations show cyclic changes in activity measures and in agonistic behaviour. (b) Cyclic and non-cyclic populations of the same species vary in activity and exploration measures. (c) Agonistic behaviour measures correlate with demographic changes in field populations.	Krebs (1970) Rasmuson et al. (1977) Hofmann et al. (1982) This study Reich et al. (1982)
Indirect field observations	Home ranges, wounding	(a) Home ranges of breeding females do not overlap. Male home ranges may or may not overlap. (b) Some species are monogamous at least at low densities, and the social system may be density dependent.	Madison (1980) Jannett (1980) Getz & Carter (1980) Lidicker (1980) Gaines & Johnson (1982)

Field experiments manipulating density	Density, survival, growth, reproduction	(c) Wounding is more severe in breeding males than in breeding females.	Taitt & Krebs (1981) Viitala (1977)
		(a) If breeding residents are removed, large numbers of new individuals colonize the empty area and breed.	Krebs (1966) Myers & Krebs (1971) Gaines *et al.* (1979) Boonstra (1977) Baird & Birney (1982) Redfield *et al.* (1978)
		(b) If only breeding males are removed, females are unaffected. If females are removed, males may or may not be affected.	
		(c) The fence-effect suggests that spacing behaviour is the immediate control of local population density.	
Field observations on spacing behaviour	Dominance and territorial behaviour	(a) At low densities adult females may abandon the young at weaning. At high densities extended maternal families may be formed.	Jannett (1980) Crawford (1971) Colvin (1973)
		(b) Severe fighting may be observed in natural populations.	
Field manipulations of spacing behaviour	Chemical implants of individuals, demographic parameters	(a) Passive, drugged males survive better than control males in the spring breeding period.	Gipps *et al.* (1981) Taitt & Krebs (1982)
		(b) Testosterone-implanted females survive worse than control females during the spring breeding period.	
		(c) No one has been able to stop a population decline by chemical manipulation of spacing behaviours.	

Microtus townsendii. The basic approach was to remove individuals for 2 days from a field population, test them in the laboratory for open field activity, maze exploration, and aggressive behaviour, and then return them to their home range (Krebs 1970; Krebs, Halpin & Smith 1977; Myers & Krebs 1971). In addition, open field tests were conducted as described in Myers & Krebs (1971), and linear maze exploration was measured as described in Fairbairn (1978). I did agonistic bouts on 2714 voles and activity tests on 1270 of them.

Since both sexes were tested, as well as both breeding and non-breeding individuals, the first question I asked was whether the behaviour of these groups differed. I tested this hypothesis with stepwise discriminant analysis and found highly significant differences between groups (Table 16.2). Therefore, sexes and breeding groups are segregated in the analysis that follows. I used factor analysis to reduce the number of variables. Four factors were extracted to describe agonistic behaviour and three to describe activity and exploratory behaviour. A factor stability check was run on randomized subsets of the data, and the same factors were always extracted in the same order.

Table 16.3 gives the matrix of factor loadings which summarize the twelve agonistic variables. Factor 1 is a defensive factor with heavy loadings on pounces and vocalizations. Factor 2 weights approaches and general activity, and Factor 3 is almost entirely an avoidance score. Factor 4 is an aggressiveness measure which weights boxing and wrestling heavily.

Table 16.4 gives the matrix of factor loadings which summarize the eight activity and exploration variables. Factor 1 contains most of the detailed variables from the linear maze exploration. Factor 2 measures activity within the maze, and Factor 3 measures open field activity.

We can now ask the critical question: *Can we correlate standardized behaviour tests with the demographic performance of field populations?* Voles were tested from seventeen trapping grids scattered in three geographical areas just south of Vancouver, B.C. during 1974–76. Four trapping areas were sampled more intensively than the others. Demographic data and behavioural data were averaged for summer and winter periods of each year for each area, corresponding in general to the breeding and non-breeding seasons. Because more breeding voles were tested than non-breeding voles, I used only data from dyadic encounters between breeding animals.

Table 16.5 presents the results of stepwise multiple regression analysis to predict fourteen demographic variables by the use of sixteen agonistic behaviour factor scores. The results are highly encouraging: we can predict thirteen of the fourteen demographic variables of field populations from data obtained from standard laboratory bouts. The four agonistic factors do not

TABLE 16.2. Mean scores for six behaviour variables recorded during 10-min dyadic encounters in *Microtus townsendii*. All variables were transformed by log (x + 1) before analysis. All trapping areas and years combined. Stepwise discriminant analysis (program BMD 07M) was used to test for differences between groups. Almost every group could be statistically distinguished from every other group at $P < 0.01$

Variable	♂ Breeding v.				♂ Non-breeding v.				♀ Breeding v.				♀ Non-breeding v.				Weighted Standard Deviation
	♂ breeding	♂ non-br.	♀ breeding	♀ non-br.	♂ breeding	♂ non-br.	♀ breeding	♀ non-br.	♂ breeding	♂ non-br.	♀ breeding	♀ non-br.	♂ breeding	♂ non-br.	♀ breeding	♀ non-br.	
Time to first contact	1·41	1·38	1·25	1·51	1·34	1·39	1·52	1·29	1·26	1·52	1·52	1·54	1·48	1·30	1·54	1·46	0·66
Wrestling, chasing	0·09	0·08	0·09	0·04	0·09	0·08	0·05	0·07	0·05	0·03	0·04	0·04	0·03	0·06	0·02	0·02	0·18
Vocalizations	0·63	0·55	0·42	0·38	0·68	0·63	0·46	0·54	0·90	0·68	0·62	0·57	0·84	0·73	0·53	0·60	0·52
Upright	0·39	0·41	0·34	0·48	0·43	0·35	0·31	0·34	0·42	0·34	0·37	0·34	0·58	0·39	0·37	0·36	0·38
Activity	1·59	1·59	1·84	1·79	1·58	1·55	1·77	1·82	1·72	1·74	1·82	1·74	1·67	1·78	1·65	1·87	0·52
No. of bouts	495	174	236	94	209	329	79	113	229	82	209	74	103	108	78	102	2714

TABLE 16.3. Rotated factor loadings matrix for the factor analysis of twelve agonistic behaviour variables in *Microtus townsendii*. The loadings for the most important variables are in bold face for each factor. Factors were extracted using orthogonal rotation with program BMD X72

Variable	Factor			
	1	2	3	4
Time to first contact	−0·226	−0·212	0·040	−0·060
No. approaches	0·100	**0·964**	−0·077	0·073
No. boxing	0·483	0·164	−0·017	**0·405**
No. wrestling	0·088	0·148	−0·037	**0·556**
No. pounces	**0·764**	−0·012	0·016	0·234
Vocalizations	**0·734**	−0·120	0·045	0·271
No. uprights	**0·676**	0·015	0·059	−0·009
No. avoidances	0·042	−0·043	**0·996**	0·065
No. submissions	0·085	−0·131	0·084	0·122
No. groom other	−0·143	0·214	−0·032	−0·057
No. groom self	−0·105	0·123	−0·111	−0·281
Activity score	0·140	**0·877**	0·054	0·067

TABLE 16.4. Rotated factor loadings matrix for factor analysis of eight activity and maze exploration variables in *Microtus townsendii*. The most important variables for each factor are in bold face. Factors were extracted using orthogonal rotation with program BMD X72

Variable	Factor		
	1	2	3
Open field activity	0·062	0·002	**−0·894**
Latency to leave home cage	**−0·846**	−0·192	−0·182
Latency to enter strange cage	**−0·846**	−0·279	−0·052
Time in home cage	−0·191	**−0·940**	−0·025
Time in strange cage	0·614	0·492	−0·320
No. maze section entered	**0·811**	0·068	−0·182
No. of exits from home cage	**0·813**	0·138	−0·320
No. of entrances into strange cage	0·723	0·391	−0·396

all share equally in the prediction equations. A simple tally of the number of times that each appears in Table 16.5 gives:

Factor 1 ('defensive')	9 times
Factor 2 ('activity')	3 times
Factor 3 ('avoidance')	10 times
Factor 4 ('aggressiveness')	11 times

Clearly Factor 2 is of little use statistically.

TABLE 16.5. Results of stepwise multiple regression analyses to correlate fourteen demographic variables with agonistic behaviour factor scores broken down by sex. Variables listed in order of importance to the predictive regression. All variables could be predicted significantly ($P < 0.05$) except for weight at maturity of males

Variable	Percentage of variance explained (R^2)	Variables used in multiple regression and partial correlations
Average density of males	26	Factor 3 male v. female (−0.51)
Average density of females	46	Factor 3 male v. female (−0.51), Factor 2 female v. female (+0.51)
Rate of population change: males	60	Factor 3 male v. male (−0.46), Factor 4 female v. female (+0.40), Factor 1 male v. female (−0.03)
Rate of population change: females	77	Factor 3 male v. male (−0.52), Factor 2 female v. female (+0.41), Factor 4 female v. female (+0.33), Factor 1 male v. female (−0.06)
Index of juvenile survival	92	Factor 4 male v. female (+0.60), Factor 4 male v. male (−0.14), Factor 3 male v. female (+0.42), Factor 4 female v. female (+0.54)
Male survival rate	21	Factor 4 female v. male (+0.46)
Female survival rate	58	Factor 3 male v. male (−0.49), Factor 4 male v. male (+0.19), Factor 3 female v. male (+0.23)
Dilution rate	23	Factor 1 male v. male (−0.48)
Weight at sexual maturity: males	0	—
Weight at sexual maturity: females	53	Factor 1 male v. male (+0.63), Factor 4 male v. female (+0.29)
Percentage adults lactating	43	Factor 3 male v. female (−0.51), Factor 4 male v. male (−0.50)
Percentage adult males scrotal	56	Factor 1 male v. male (−0.53), Factor 3 male v. female (−0.50)
Average no. of wounds in males	78	Factor 4 male v. female (−0.54), Factor 1 male v. male (−0.45), Factor 3 male v. female (−0.47), Factor 1 male v. female (+0.16)
Intensity of spring decline*	93	Factor 1 male v. female (−0.76), Factor 4 female v. female (−0.36), Factor 1 male v. male (−0.39), Factor 2 male v. female (−0.03)

* Measured by the rate of population change per week.

Some of the relationships given in Table 16.5 agree with our ecological prejudices, which is also encouraging. For example, the intensity of the spring decline in density was more severe when male defensive scores are high and female aggressiveness scores are high. To check further on the validity of these correlations, I did a more restricted analysis on only the summer data ($n = 13$) and the Factor 4 ('aggressiveness') scores. Eleven of the fourteen demographic variables could be predicted successfully from Factor 4 scores alone. Hence, I am encouraged to believe that this is not simply the usual multivariate statistical obfuscation syndrome.

Table 16.6 presents the results of stepwise multiple regression analysis to predict demographic variables from six activity factor scores. The results are less significant than those in Table 16.5. Only five of fourteen demographic variables were correlated with the activity data, almost all from the Factor 1 scores for breeding males. Adding the exploratory and activity factor scores to the multiple regressions in Table 16.5 produced no increase in the variation accounted for in the demographic parameters. I conclude that measuring exploratory activity is less useful than measuring agonistic behaviour if one is interested in predicting demographic trends in field populations.

Individuals in peak populations of cyclic voles and lemmings are 10–30% larger than individuals in other phases of the cycle—the *Chitty effect* (Boonstra & Krebs 1979). Two alternative explanations have been put forward for these large individuals: they are *r*-selected, docile, individuals or they are α-selected, aggressive, individuals (Stenseth 1978). I have analysed the agonistic behavioural data to test whether body size is a determinant of aggressiveness in *Microtus townsendii*. Only breeding individuals were used for this analysis. There were no significant correlations between any of the

TABLE 16.6. Results of stepwise multiple regression to predict fourteen demographic variables from exploratory activity factor scores broken down by sex. Demographic variables are the same as those in Table 16.5, but are omitted if not statistically significant

Dependent variable	Percentage of variance explained (R^2)	Independent variables used in multiple regression (correlation)
Rate of population change: males	43	Factor 1, males (0·65)
Rate of population change: females	38	Factor 1, males (0·61)
Male survival rate	37	Factor 1, males (0·61)
Female survival rate	27	Factor 1, males (0·52)
Intensity of spring decline*	34	Factor 1, females (0·58)

* Measured by the average rate of population decline per week for adults during the first 6–12 weeks of the spring breeding period.

four agonistic factors and body weight for any of the sex combinations on any of the areas. Within the range of weights studied (52–56 g mean, SD 8·0) there was no obvious relationship of size to agonistic behaviour for either males or females.

OTHER ATTEMPTS TO TEST THE MODEL

There have been three other attempts to test the specific model of Fig. 16.1 with standardized laboratory tests on field animals. Figure 16.1 implies a linear relationship between the population growth rate and the percentage of aggressive phenotypes. Krebs (1970) found that male agonistic behaviour changed significantly over the population cycle in *Microtus ochrogaster* and *M. pennsylvanicus* but maximum aggression occurred in the peak phase not in the decline phase. Hofmann, Getz & Klatt (1982) reported no systematic change in levels of male aggressiveness over the cycle in these same two species, but their conclusions are confounded by a poor classification of 'cyclic phase', which includes a mix of seasonal and cyclic changes in density. For example, they classified 1973, a year in the decline and low phase of the 1971–74 cycle, as an increase and peak year. Mihok (1981) found a significant drop in attack behaviour in female *Clethrionomys gapperi* between peak and decline years but no change in adult male aggressiveness. He noted that this pattern, similar to the one described by Krebs (1970) for *Microtus ochrogaster* and *M. pennsylvanicus*, was at variance with Krebs' interpretation of Chitty's original predictions (Fig. 16.1) that individuals should be most aggressive in the decline phase. Table 16.5 shows that in *M. townsendii* aggressiveness is positively related to population growth rate, the opposite to that predicted in Fig. 16.1. Insofar as one can extrapolate laboratory behaviour to field behaviour, voles in decline phase seem to be 'docile' or 'solitary' rather than aggressive. These results support Stenseth's (1978) interpretation of large-size voles in peak populations as α-selected types, and reject the original simple model shown in Fig. 16.1.

A CONCEPTUAL MODEL

How can spacing behaviour drive a population cycle? There are two quite different conceptual models that are commonly used. The *moving equilibrium* model is the classical time-lag model for generating cyclic population traces (May 1981). If spacing behaviour sets carrying capacity and adjusts only with a time lag of one generation or more, cycles may be the result. The second model is the *multiple equilibrium* model in which (in the simplest case) the system has two equilibrium points and moves between them (Clark & Holling 1979).

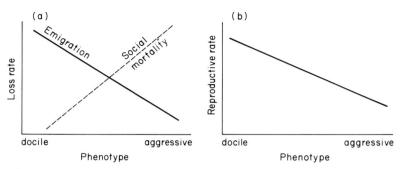

FIG. 16.2. Hypothesized relationship between spacing behaviour phenotypes and (a) losses, (b) reproduction. There is reasonable correlation-type evidence for the emigration and the reproductive curves, but no direct evidence regarding socially-induced mortality.

By combining the two models, we can construct a conceptual model for the vole cycle that is based on spacing behaviour. First, I assume that the range of phenotypes that exists in these populations can be defined by two extremes, *docile* and *aggressive*, which differ in their per capita rates of emigration, social mortality, and reproductive inhibition (Fig. 16.2). Second, I assume that there is some conversion mechanism by which docile phenotypes can produce aggressive phenotypes and vice versa; the mechanism of conversion could be genotypic or phenotypic. Third, I assume that aggressive voles tend to win against docile voles in competition for breeding space. Finally, I assume that there is a time lag in the response of these losses to population density (Fig. 16.3): a time lag produced both by seasonality and by the conversion mechanism of dociles to aggressives and vice versa.

These assumptions produce the schematic model in Fig. 16.4. The low or

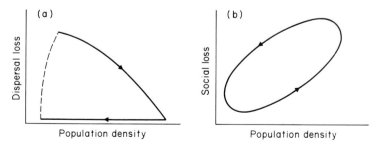

FIG. 16.3. Assumed time-lag relationships between population density and (a) dispersal loss, and (b) social mortality. There is good evidence for the dispersal curve (Stenseth 1983) but no data on the social mortality curve.

trough phase might be a lower equilibrium point determined by emigration of docile phenotypes (Fig. 16.4a). As density grows in the increase phase, the amount of emigration falls because docile animals are being replaced by aggressive individuals. In the peak phase a single equilibrium exists, dominated by a declining reproductive rate and rising socially-induced

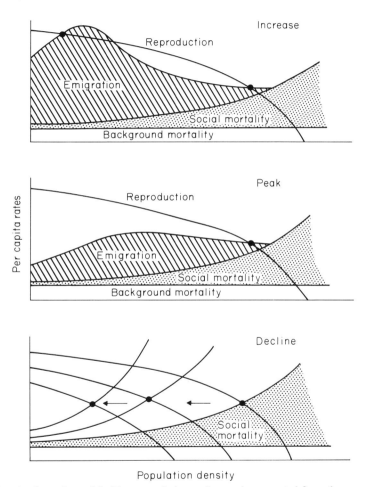

FIG. 16.4. A schematic model of how population cycles can be generated from the relationships shown in Figs 16.2 and 16.3. This diagram shows how a sample of voles from the three phases of a population cycle would respond to living at a range of population densities. (a) In the low phase and increase phase docile voles predominate, and dispersal losses are most significant. (b) In the peak phase aggressive voles are replacing the dociles and socially-induced mortality is critical. (c) In the decline the equilibrial density collapses because aggressive voles depress reproduction and increase mortality.

mortality (Fig. 16.4b). But this upper equilibrium is not stable because of continuous replacement of docile voles with aggressive ones, and the population declines from rising socially-induced mortality coupled with reduced reproduction (Fig. 16.4c).

The decline phase in this schematic model is similar to that shown in Fig. 16.1 and is at variance with the observation that declining voles are docile in laboratory tests. If aggressive phenotypes predominate in declining populations, their spacing behaviour must be achieved by some other method than direct aggression. The conceptual model in Fig. 16.4 is consistent with the observed events in the increase and peak phases, but is weak in providing an explanation for the decline without *ad hoc* assumptions.

Other factors such as food and cover could be added to this simple model of Fig. 16.4. There is no shortage of models for cycles (Stenseth 1984) but most of them have unrealistic assumptions (Hestbeck 1982). Unfortunately, there has been little feedback between models and field research. We clearly need to answer some simple questions.

What determines spacing behaviour?

This question is central to all modelling efforts, and is the key unknown. A quantitative genetics model seems to be an approximate first model to study this question for voles and lemmings. Krebs (1979) suggested a direct correlation between the amplitude of population changes and the heritability of spacing behaviour. Cyclic populations would thus be predicted to have a high heritability of aggressive behaviour. It is a mistake to assume that higher heritabilities of aggressive behaviour cannot occur in field populations. Singleton & Hay (1982) estimated the narrow heritability of aggressiveness to be 0·56–0·75 for wild house mice. I do not know why heritability of aggressiveness should be high in some populations and low in others.

Inheritance is one way of adding a time lag to the system, and inherited spacing behaviour may be sufficient to drive a population cycle (Anderson 1975). Additional time lags are produced by seasonality and the inherent time lags built into a mammalian life cycle, and Stenseth (1981) has shown how to incorporate these fluctuations into a model of the Chitty hypothesis.

If spacing behaviour has low or zero heritability in cyclic populations, we must determine the environmental conditions that produce aggressive and docile individuals. It is possible that early experience or other events could also introduce a time lag in the response of spacing behaviour to population density. If no time lags occur, population size will be stable.

What is the genetic structure of vole and lemming populations?

Spacing behaviour has rather different effects if one is surrounded by relatives than if one is surrounded by genetic strangers. Charnov & Finerty (1980) suggested that kin selection could contribute to cycles if aggression is minimal between relatives and maximal between strangers, and if the relatedness of individuals in the same neighbourhood is inversely correlated with population density. This model is very similar to the model of Smith, Garten & Ramsey (1975), who invoked heterozygosity of individuals in place of relatedness. There are at present no published data on the genetic architecture of vole or lemming populations. The Charnov–Finerty model is consistent with the fence effect observed by Krebs, Keller & Tamarin (1969), who showed that voles enclosed in a mouse-proof fence increased to a high density and were unable to regulate their numbers below the limit set by starvation.

What role does dispersal play in generating cycles?

Spacing behaviour may lead to reproductive inhibition (Getz & Carter 1980), mortality, or dispersal. I have in the past emphasized the role of dispersal in cycles (Krebs 1979). But dispersal is predominant in the increase phase of the cycle (Gaines & McClenaghan 1980) and we are left trying to explain the obviously increased mortality that occurs in the peak and decline phases. Dispersal losses do not seem to be the delayed density-dependent factor that generates cycles. I have been reluctant to invoke spacing behaviour as a direct cause of death by fighting because of the belief that an individual would more likely flee and thus disperse than stay and be killed; this assumption needs to be reconsidered. If spacing behaviour does not lead to direct mortality in peak and declining populations, we must invoke some variant of the Errington model (predators feeding on a doomed surplus) of compensatory mortality. It is clear from enclosure studies that *in situ* mortality is the cause of cyclic declines in voles (Getz *et al.* 1979; Beacham 1980). One possibility is that general viability is impaired during the decline phase. Chitty (1967) abandoned the idea that the viability of individuals in peak and declining populations was adversely affected. What happens to individuals which disappear from natural declining populations remains a central mystery in need of study.

EVOLUTIONARY STRATEGIES OF SPACING

Why should small mammals space themselves out? An emerging belief is that spacing behaviour is sex-specific and the limiting resources differ for the two sexes (Boonstra 1977, 1978; Redfield, Taitt & Krebs 1978; Boonstra & Rodd 1983; Hannon 1983). The limiting resource for males may be *breeding females*, so male spacing behaviour is oriented toward maximizing fitness by obtaining priority of access to breeding females. The limiting resource for females may be *space*, space free from intruding adults who will kill nestlings and juveniles. Space is clearly a complex variable, because it must include an adequate food supply and cover to escape from predators and to rear young. Females will thus be expected to adjust their spacing behaviour to manipulations of food and cover (Taitt & Krebs 1983) and males will be less concerned with these habitat variables. In this way, spacing behaviour can be considered the mechanism through which intrinsic hypotheses of population regulation are linked to extrinsic hypotheses in a multifactor model of population regulation (Taitt & Krebs 1984).

REFERENCES

Anderson, J.L. (1975). *Phenotypic correlates among relatives, and variability in reproductive performance in populations of the vole,* Microtus townsendii. Ph.D. thesis, Univ. British Columbia, Vancouver, 207 pp.

Baird, D.D. & Birney, E.C. (1982). Pattern of colonization in *Microtus pennsylvanicus. Journal of Mammalogy,* **63,** 290–293.

Beacham, T.D. (1980). Dispersal during population fluctuations of the vole, *Microtus townsendii. Journal of Animal Ecology,* 49, 867–877.

Birney, E.C., W.E. Grant & Baird, D.D. (1976). Importance of vegetative cover to cycles of *Microtus* populations. *Ecology,* **57,** 1043–51.

Boonstra, R. (1977). Effect of conspecifics on survival during population declines in *Microtus townsendii. Journal of Animal Ecology,* **46,** 835–851.

Boonstra, R. (1978). Effect of adult Townsend voles (*Microtus townsendii*) on survival of young. *Ecology,* **59,** 242–248.

Boonstra, R. & Krebs, C.J. (1979). Viability of large- and small-sized adults in fluctuating vole populations. *Ecology,* **60,** 567–573.

Boonstra, R. & Rodd, F.H. (1983). Regulation of breeding density in *Microtus pennsylvanicus. Journal of Animal Ecology,* **52,** 757–780.

Calhoun, J.B. (1949). A method for self-control of population growth among mammals living in the wild. *Science,* **109,** 333–335.

Caughley, G. & Krebs, C.J. (1983). Are big mammals simply little mammals writ large? *Oecologia,* **59,** 7–17.

Charnov, E.L. & Finerty, J. (1980). Vole population cycles: a case for kin-selection. *Oecologia,* **45,** 1–2.

Chitty, D. (1952). Mortality among voles (*Microtus agrestis*) at Lake Vyrnwy, Montgomeryshire in 1936–39. *Philosophical Transactions of the Royal Society of London, Series B,* **236,** 505–552.

Chitty, D. (1967). The natural selection of self-regulatory behaviour in animal populations. *Proceedings of the Ecological Society of Australia,* **2,** 51–78.

Clark, W.D. & Holling, C.S. (1979). Process models, equilibrium structures, and population dynamics: on the formulation and testing of realistic theory in ecology. *Fortschritte der Zoologie,* **25,** 29–52.

Clarke, J.R. (1955). Influence of numbers on reproduction and survival in two experimental vole populations. *Proceedings of the Royal Society of London, Series B* 144, 68–85.

Colvin, D.V. (1973). Agonistic behavior in males of five species of voles *Microtus*. *Animal Behaviour*, 21, 471–480.

Crawford, R.D. (1971). High population density of *Microtus ochrogaster*. *Journal of Mammalogy*, 52, 478.

Eisenberg, J.F. (1966). The social organization of mammals. *Handbuch der Zoologie*, 10, 1–92.

Elton, C. (1942). *Voles, Mice and Lemmings*. Clarendon Press, Oxford.

Fairbairn, D.J. (1978). Dispersal of deer mice, *Peromyscus maniculatus*: proximal causes and effects on fitness. *Oecologia*, 32, 171–193.

Finerty, J.P. (1980). *The Population Ecology of Cycles in Small Mammals*. Yale University Press, New Haven.

Gaines, M.S. & Johnson, M.L. (1982). Home range size and population dynamics in the prairie vole, *Microtus ochrogaster*. *Oikos*, 39, 63–70.

Gaines, M.S. & McClenaghan, L.R. Jr (1980). Dispersal in small mammals. *Annual Review of Ecology and Systematics*, 11, 163–196.

Gaines, M.S., Vivas, A.M. & Baker, C.L. (1979). An experimental analysis of dispersal in fluctuating vole populations: demographic parameters. *Ecology*, 60, 814–828.

Getz, L.L. & Carter, C.S. (1980). Social organization in *Microtus ochrogaster* populations. *The Biologist*, 62, 56–69.

Getz, L.L., Cole, F.R., Verner, L., Hofmann, J.E. & Avalos, D. (1979). Comparisons of population demography of *Microtus ochrogaster* and *M. pennsylvanicus*. *Acta Theriologica*, 24, 319–349.

Gipps, J.H.W. & Jewell, P.A. (1979). Maintaining populations of bank voles, *Clethrionomys glareolus*, in large outdoor enclosures, and measuring the response of population variables to the castration of males. *Journal of Animal Ecology*, 48, 535–555.

Gipps, J.H.W., Taitt, M.J., Krebs, C.J. & Dundjerski, Z. (1981). Male aggression and the population dynamics of the vole, *Microtus townsendii*. *Canadian Journal of Zoology*, 59, 147–158.

Hannon, S.J. (1983). Spacing and breeding density of willow ptarmigan in response to an experimental alteration of sex ratio. *Journal of Animal Ecology*, 52, 807–820.

Hansson, L. & Henttonen, H. (1984). Geographic differences in cyclicity and reproduction in *Clethrionomys* species: are they related? *Annales Zoologici Fennici* (in press).

Healey, M.C. (1967). Aggression and self-regulation of population size in deermice. *Ecology*, 48, 377–392.

Hestbeck, J.B. (1982). Population regulation of cyclic mammals: the social fence hypothesis. *Oikos*, 39, 157–163.

Hofmann, J.E., Getz, L.L. & Klatt, B.J. (1982). Levels of male aggressiveness in fluctuating populations of *Microtus ochrogaster* and *M. pennsylvanicus*. *Canadian Journal of Zoology*, 60, 898–912.

Kaufmann, J.H. (1983). On the definitions and functions of dominance and territoriality. *Biological Reviews*, 58, 1–20.

Jannett, F.J. Jr (1980). Social dynamics of the montane vole, *Microtus montanus*, as a paradigm. *The Biologist*, 62, 3–19.

Krebs, C.J. (1966). Demographic changes in fluctuating populations of *Microtus californicus*. *Ecological Monographs*, 36, 239–273.

Krebs, C.J. (1970). *Microtus* population biology: behavioural changes associated with the population cycle in *Microtus ochrogaster* and *M. pennsylvanicus*. *Ecology*, 51, 34–52.

Krebs, C.J. (1979). Dispersal, spacing behaviour, and genetics in relation to population fluctuations in the vole *Microtus townsendii*. *Fortschritte der Zoologie*, 25, 61–77.

Krebs, C.J., Keller, B.L. & Tamarin, R.H. (1969). *Microtus* population biology: demographic changes in fluctuating populations of *M. ochrogaster* and *M. pennsylvanicus* in southern Indiana. *Ecology*, **50**, 587–607.

Krebs, C.J., Halpin, Z.T. & Smith, J.N.M. (1977). Aggression, testosterone, and the spring decline in populations of the vole, *Microtus townsendii*. *Canadian Journal of Zoology*, **55**, 430–437.

Lidicker, W.Z. (1975). The role of dispersal in the demography of small mammals. *Small Mammals: Their Productivity and Population Dynamics* (Ed. by F.B. Golley, K. Petrusewicz & L. Ryszkowski), pp. 103–128. Cambridge University Press, London.

Lidicker, W.Z. Jr (1980). The social biology of the California vole. *The Biologist*, **62**, 46–55.

Madison, D.M. (1980). An integrated view of the social biology of *Microtus pennsylvanicus*. *The Biologist*, **62**, 20–33.

May, R.M. (1981). Models for single populations. *Theoretical Ecology: Principles and Applications* (Ed. by R.M. May), pp. 5–29. Blackwell Scientific Publications, London.

Mihok, S. (1981). Chitty's hypothesis and behaviour in subarctic red-backed vole *Clethrionomys gapperi*. *Oikos*, **36**, 281–295.

Myers, J. & Krebs, C. (1971). Genetic, behavioural, and reproductive attributes of dispersing field voles *Microtus pennsylvanicus* and *Microtus ochrogaster*. *Ecological Monographs*, **41**, 53–78.

Rasmuson, B., Rasmuson, M. & Nigren, J. (1977). Genetically controlled differences in behaviour between cycling and noncycling populations of field vole (*Microtus agrestis*). *Hereditas*, **87**, 33–42.

Redfield, J.A., Taitt, M.J. & Krebs, C.J. (1978). Experimental alteration of sex ratios in populations of *Microtus townsendii*, a field vole. *Canadian Journal of Zoology*, **56**, 17–27.

Reich, L.M., Wood, K.M., Rothstein, B.E. & Tamarin, R.H. (1982). Aggressive behaviour of male *Microtus breweri* and its demographic implications. *Animal Behaviour*, **30**, 117–122.

Singleton, G.R. & Hay, D.A. (1982). A genetic study of male social aggression in wild and laboratory mice. *Behavior Genetics*, **12**, 435–448.

Smith, M.H., Garten, C.T. & Ramsey, P.R. (1975). Genic heterozygosity and population dynamics in small mammals. *Isozymes, IV. Genetics and Evolution* (Ed. by C.L. Markert), pp. 85–102. Academic Press, New York.

Stenseth, N.C. (1978). Demographic strategies in fluctuating populations of small rodents. *Oecologia*, **33**, 149–172.

Stenseth, N.C. (1981). On Chitty's theory for fluctuating populations: The importance of genetic polymorphism in the generation of regular density cycles. *Journal of Theoretical Biology*, **90**, 9–36.

Stenseth, N.C. (1984). Mathematical models of microtine cycles. *Annales Zoologici Fennici* (in press).

Taitt, M.J. & Krebs, C.J. (1981). The effect of extra food on small rodent populations. II. Voles (*Microtus townsendii*). *Journal of Animal Ecology*, **50**, 125–137.

Taitt, M.J. & Krebs, C.J. (1982). Manipulation of female behaviour in field populations of *Microtus townsendii*. *Journal of Animal Ecology*, **51**, 681–690.

Taitt, M.J. & Krebs, C.J. (1983). Predation cover, and food manipulations during a spring decline of *Microtus townsendii*. *Journal of Animal Ecology*, **52**, 837–848.

Taitt, M.J. & Krebs, C.J. (1984). Population dynamics and cycles. *Biology of New World Microtus* (Ed. by R.H. Tamarin). Special Publication, American Society of Mammalogists (in press).

Tamarin, R.H. (1983). Animal population regulation through behavioral interactions. *Advances in the Study of Mammalian Behavior* (Ed. by J.F. Eisenberg & D.G. Kleiman), pp. 698–720. American Society of Mammalogists Special Publication No. 7.

Viitala, J. (1977). Social organization in cyclic subarctic populations of the voles *Clethrionomys rufocanus* (Sund.) and *Microtus agrestis* (L.). *Annales Zoologici Fennici*, **14**, 53–93.

Watson, A. & Moss, R. (1970). Dominance, spacing behaviour and aggression in relation to population limitation in vertebrates. *Animal Populations in Relation to their Food Resources* (Ed. by A. Watson), pp. 167–218. Blackwell Scientific Publications, Oxford.

17. EXPERIMENTAL ANALYSIS OF SPACING BEHAVIOUR IN THE VOLE, *MICROTUS TOWNSENDII*

MARY J. TAITT

Department of Zoology, University of British Columbia,
Vancouver BC, Canada V6T 1W5

SUMMARY

Populations of *Microtus townsendii* show tendencies towards both cyclic and non-cyclic changes in numbers. Spring breeding densities may be portents of the form of population dynamics. Experimental studies indicate that breeding density in *M. townsendii* populations may be limited by both spacing behaviour and food. However, chemical manipulation of male and female behaviour in spring did not result in substantial changes in breeding density. The prevention of predation in early spring, and experimental increases in cover and food resulted in a high breeding density, particularly of female voles. It is suggested that spacing behaviour may determine which voles are surplus, but the state of extrinsic factors may control the 'fate' of the surplus and whether the population is cyclic or not.

INTRODUCTION

Field data collected on *Microtus* species in North America indicate that populations may be non-cyclic more often than cyclic (Taitt & Krebs 1985). Long-term population data for *Microtus townsendii* (Bachman) show both patterns in sequence (Fig. 17.1). Further, field data indicate that a substantial spring decline in density is associated with years of annual fluctuations in numbers, while little or no spring decline occurs in years of multi-annual cycles (e.g. Fig. 17.1). The spring decline coincides with the onset of breeding and establishment of the breeding population. What is the role of spacing behaviour and extrinsic factors at this time and how do they interact to produce the two types of spring decline?

METHODS

Populations of *M. townsendii* were studied in grasslands on Westham Island in the Fraser River Delta, BC, Canada. The voles were live-trapped every 2 weeks on grids with trapping stations placed 7·6 m apart.

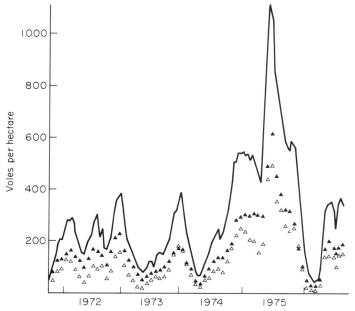

FIG. 17.1. *Microtus townsendii* population data for Westham Island, British Columbia.
——Total, △ males, ▲ females. (After Krebs 1979.)

Male and female behaviours were manipulated by subcutaneous implants
(Gipps *et al.* 1981; Taitt & Krebs 1982). Both sexes were made aggressive by
implants of testosterone. Males were made passive by implants of scopolamine HBr, and females by oral administration of a chemosterilant, mestranol.

Predation, cover and food were manipulated separately and in combination (Taitt & Krebs 1983). Predation was reduced by hanging netting over
populations. Cover was increased by spreading straw and decreased by
mowing. Food was added by placing containers of whole oats at each trapping
station.

RESULTS AND DISCUSSION

Watson & Moss (1970) suggested four conditions for determining whether
breeding density is limited by spacing behaviour. Previous research indicates
that populations of *M. townsendii* may fulfil conditions A–D (Table 17.1) and
that populations with extra food increase in density (Taitt & Krebs 1981,
1983). The effect of extra food on density appears to be mediated by a change
in spacing behaviour; home ranges are reduced in proportion to the amount of
extra food available. Thus, populations of *M. townsendii*, by the criteria in
Table 17.1, appear to be limited by spacing behaviour and food.

TABLE 17.1. Summary of research on *Microtus townsendii* that has attempted to test the criteria of Watson & Moss (1970)

Condition	Criteria and suggested result	Reference
A	If residents are removed, new voles colonize: there are surplus voles.	Krebs *et al.* 1976 Krebs, Redfield & Taitt 1978
B	New colonizers can establish breeding populations: the presumed surplus voles can breed.	
C	A fenced population supported a higher density than a control: resources do not directly limit open vole populations.	Boonstra & Krebs 1977
D	Voles disappeared from populations in spring in proportion to population density: vole spacing behaviour may have compensatory demographic effects.	Taitt & Krebs 1983
E	Conditions A–D appear to be fulfilled *and* numbers change when food is added: both spacing behaviour and food limit the number of breeding voles.	Taitt & Krebs 1981, 1983

Behaviour experiments

Manipulation of behaviour during the spring decline did not result in large changes in density. When large males were made 'passive' by scopolamine implants, male density declined more slowly than in a control population (Gipps *et al.* 1981). 'Aggressive' females (testosterone implants) had larger home ranges, high wounding and lower survival than control females (Taitt & Krebs 1982). However, high immigration made up for the reduced survival, and therefore, the 'aggressive' female population had a similar density to the control. Both males and females survived better in a population of 'passive' females compared with a control population.

Madison (1980), using radiotelemetry, found that reproductively active females *M. pennsylvanicus* (Ord) had small, exclusive territories. He suggested that such females may force males to forage in the interstices of these territories. Perhaps female voles may be considered equivalent to male territorial birds: they secure an area free of intruders to raise their young (Frank 1957), the area contains food for their lactation, and pheromones act as the advertising currency equivalent to bird song. This could explain why voles survived well in populations of 'passive' (anoestrus) females. It would also explain why juvenile survival and female recruitment are strongly influenced by female density (Boonstra 1978; Redfield, Taitt & Krebs 1978), and why female numbers increase immediately when food is provided (Taitt & Krebs 1981, 1983). The high level of blood steroids observed in reproductively active females in spring may enable them to dominate both males and immature females (McDonald & Taitt 1982).

Extrinsic experiments

It has been suggested that winter flooding imposes temporal and spatial restrictions on space and food for *M. townsendii* populations (Taitt & Krebs 1981). Voles are forced into unflooded patches, they lose weight, stop breeding and reach peak densities in early winter. Population numbers then decline gradually until spring. Experiments have shown that if cover is poor, predation can be substantial in winter. However, when predation is prevented, winter densities remain high (Taitt & Krebs 1983).

In spring, flooded areas dry out and grass begins to grow. Voles now gain weight and start breeding. If food is experimentally improved early in spring, breeding can be earlier. As voles are not aggressive until they become reproductive (Turner & Iverson 1973), I suggest that spacing behaviour at the onset of breeding, initially between males and then between mature females and all voles, may determine which voles are potential residents and which are surplus. However, visibility to predators, availability of food and the extent of temporary suitable habitat may control the fate of the surplus (as prey, subordinates or dispersers). The state of extrinsic factors may then drive the population towards either a cyclic tendancy (little or no spring decline especially in females, see Fig. 17.1) or else an annual fluctuation (large male and female decline) in numbers. Simultaneous settlement (Van den Assem 1967) of many 'territorial' females in response to very good extrinsic conditions may also contribute to the high female density observed in the spring of a cyclic year.

ACKNOWLEDGMENTS

I thank the National Science and Engineering Research Council of Canada for financial support.

REFERENCES

Boonstra, R. (1978). Effect of adult Townsend voles (*Microtus townsendii*) on survival of young. *Ecology*, **59**, 242–248.

Boonstra, R. & Krebs, C.J. (1977). A fencing experiment on a high density population of *Microtus townsendii*. *Canadian Journal of Zoology*, **55**, 1166–1175.

Frank, F. (1957). The causality of microtine cycles in Germany. *Journal of Wildlife Management*, **21**, 113–121.

Gipps, J.H.W., Taitt, M.J., Krebs, C.J. & Dundjerski, Z. (1981). Male aggression and the population dynamics of the vole, *Microtus townsendii. Canadian Journal of Zoology*, **59**, 147–158.

Krebs, C.J. (1979). Dispersal, spacing behaviour, and genetics in relation to population fluctuation in the vole *Microtus townsendii. Fortschritte der Zoologie*, **25**, 61–77.

Krebs, C.J., Redfield, J.A. & Taitt, M.J. (1978). A pulsed-removal experiment on the vole, *Microtus townsendii. Canadian Journal of Zoology*, **56**, 2253–2262.

Krebs, C.J., Wingate, I., Redfield, J.A., Taitt, M. & Hilborn, R. (1976). *Microtus* population biology: dispersal in fluctuating populations of *Microtus townsendii. Canadian Journal of Zoology*, **54**, 79–95.

Madison, D.M. (1980). Space use and social structure in meadow voles, *Microtus pennsylvanicus. Behavioural Ecology and Sociobiology*, **7**, 65–71.

McDonald, I.R. & Taitt, M.J. (1982). Steroid hormones in the blood plasma of Townsend's vole (*Microtus townsendii*). *Canadian Journal of Zoology*, **60**, 2264–2269.

Redfield, J.A., Taitt, M.J. & Krebs, C.J. (1978). Experimental alteration of sex ratios in populations of *Microtus townsendii*, a field vole. *Canadian Journal of Zoology*, **56**, 17–27.

Taitt, M.J. & Krebs, C.J. (1981). The effect of extra food on small rodent populations. II. Voles (*Microtus townsendii*). *Journal of Animal Ecology*, **50**, 125–137.

Taitt, M.J. & Krebs, C.J. (1982). Manipulation of female behaviour in field populations of *Microtus townsendii. Journal of Animal Ecology*, **51**, 681–690.

Taitt, M.J. & Krebs, C.J. (1983). Predation, cover, and food manipulations during a spring decline of *Microtus townsendii. Journal of Animal Ecology*, **52**, 837–848.

Taitt, M.J. & Krebs, C.J. (1985). Population dynamics and cycles. *The Biology of New World Microtus* (Ed. by R.H. Tamarin), in press. American Mammal Society.

Turner, B.N. & Iversen, S.L. (1973). The annual cycle of aggression in male *Microtus pennsylvanicus* and its relation to population parameters. *Ecology*, **54**, 967–981.

Van den Assem, J. (1967). Territory in the three-spined stickleback *Gasterosteus aculeatus. Behaviour*, Suppl. 16, 1–164.

Watson, A. & Moss, R. (1970). Dominance, spacing behaviour, and aggression in relation to population limitation in vertebrates. *Animal Populations in Relation to their Food Resources* (Ed. by A. Watson), pp. 167–218. Blackwell Scientific Publications, Oxford.

18. RANGING BEHAVIOUR AND POPULATION DYNAMICS IN GREY SQUIRRELS

R. E. KENWARD

Institute of Terrestrial Ecology, Monk's Wood Experimental Station,
Abbots Ripton, Huntingdon, Cambs. PE17 2LS

SUMMARY

Seasonal and annual variation in grey squirrel range sizes, recorded by radio tracking, was more closely linked to sexual activity than to food supply. Male ranges increased greatly at the start of the mating period for summer litters, in May, and remained larger than female ranges until August. Female range size varied little throughout the year, although ranges of both sexes were smallest in March. In late winter and spring, large individual range size was associated with loss of yearlings from the population and with poor breeding in females. It is suggested that density was the main factor determining the average size of squirrel ranges, despite their considerable overlap, through the use of exclusive core ranges in autumn, when most emigration was recorded.

The male range increase associated with sexual activity in summer was not found when mating for spring litters is thought to occur in winter, even when the males were fed artificially, which suggests that their mating strategy may differ between seasons. In fact, the males with the largest testes showed most range decrease when fed, possibly because sexually dominant males were displacing subordinates.

INTRODUCTION

Social behaviour determines whether individuals compete for resources in a 'contest, or a 'scramble', in the sense of Nicholson (1954). An exclusive territorial system may be seen as a contest for sites, after which a site holder's intrinsic foraging ability (its individual genetic or learned competence in finding and handling food) will determine its survival and productivity. In a system of overlapping ranges, an individual's intrinsic foraging ability may be the sole determinant of its survival in a scramble for food, although interference from conspecifics may become important if they meet frequently. Since the extent of contest or scramble in a species' feeding competition can influence its population dynamics (Hassell 1975), a species' social behaviour has consequences for its population dynamics.

The grey squirrel (*Sciurus carolinensis* Gmelin) is generally considered to

319

lack territoriality, since the ranges of marked individuals overlap extensively (e.g. Thompson 1978). Moreover, Don (1983) showed that ranges based on live-trapping are about ten times as large as would permit exclusive territories, across a wide range of densities recorded in six North American and three British projects. Although comparing these areas gave an inverse relationship between range size and density, which is also characteristic of territorial species, Don pointed out that inter-area differences in food supply could produce this result for the squirrels. Grey squirrel breeding, first year survival and overall density have all been related to annual variations in tree seed crops, which are the squirrels' main winter food (Gurnell 1983).

Range size could be linked to squirrel density and food in three ways. The first is that good feeding conditions could result in small squirrel ranges, which reduce social pressures, energy expenditure or predation risks and thus allow a high squirrel density (Fig. 18.1a). In this case, ranging behaviour would provide the mechanism relating squirrel numbers to their food supply. Secondly, small range size could result from increased social pressures (Fig. 18.1b) when abundant food leads to high squirrel density. Although grey squirrels do not defend exclusive territories, they might nevertheless be avoiding each other in more subtle ways. In this case range size would be causally related to population density. A third possibility is that good feeding results in both small range size and high population density (Fig. 18.1c), such that range size and density are correlated but not causally related.

This paper describes how a radio-tagging study of seasonal, individual and annual variation in ranging behaviour, complemented by feeding experiments, is starting to reveal the mechanisms which determine range size in grey squirrels. It concludes by discussing the possible consequences of these mechanisms for squirrel population dynamics.

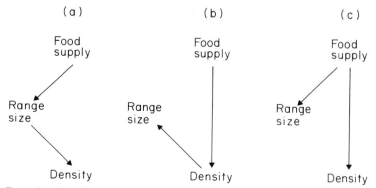

FIG. 18.1. Possible relationships between food resources, range size and density.

SEASONAL, INDIVIDUAL AND ANNUAL
VARIATION IN RANGING BEHAVIOUR

Methods

Up to twenty-two squirrels at a time were radio-tracked in mature oak–ash woodland at Monk's Wood, and in similar woodland at Elton Estate. All tracking was on foot with a three-element Yagi receiving antenna, and positions were recorded as sightings or by triangulation, normally from within 100 m. Each squirrel was checked in turn three times a day during 10-day periods, to give comparable thirty-position ranges for different times of year in both these Cambridgeshire woods. There was little increase in measured range size if more than thirty positions were taken (Kenward 1982a).

Since squirrel range positions tend not to fit circular or bivariate normal distributions, thus violating the assumptions of circular and ellipsoid range models (Don 1983), convex polygons were used to estimate range areas and to investigate spatial relationships between ranges. The ranges included one to six dreys, but were based mainly on locations where squirrels were active: squirrels were tracked at times of day when they were likely to be foraging, and each drey's position was used once only in the analysis. Only 14% of 234 Monks' Wood ranges were obviously multinuclear. The strong impression of multinuclearity in data used for the model of Don & Rennolls (1983) depends mainly on multiple use of the same drey positions.

Taking the logarithm of the convex polygon areas effectively normalized range-size distributions, and also minimized the distorting effect of any extreme peripheral positions. A BBC BASIC program (available from the author on request) was written to produce probabilistic polygons by focusing on a decreasing percentage of the densest positions. Exclusion of peripheral points often produced discontinuous changes in the slope of a range's utilization distribution (Ford & Krumme 1979). However, the slope of the distribution was always regular for the densest 60% of the positions, which were therefore used as a core range. Non-parametric, two-tailed tests were used to compare range sizes.

The squirrel density at Elton was based on the number trapped in 6-day sessions four times a year (Kenward 1982a) throughout the 36-ha wood. In the 157 ha of Monk's Wood, the trap grid covered 15 ha. To estimate female squirrel density there, the grid was assumed to trap an area larger at the sides by half one female trap range. Since some males had radio ranges which were larger than the trap grid, the total squirrel density on the trap grid was estimated as twice the female density.

The acorn crop at Monk's Wood was estimated by throwing a 0·25 m quadrat under the canopy of a random fifty oaks in February or March, and counting the number of fallen acorn cups. At Elton, squirrels also had access to pheasant feed sites from July to February.

Results

There was considerable variation in range size between individual squirrels (Fig. 18.2). In both sexes the range size tended to decrease to a minimum from September to March, although the trend was significant, for females in 1983–84 ($P = 0.021$), only if sign test probabilities for September–November, November–December and December–March were combined. Otherwise, female range size showed no significant variation through the year at Monk's Wood, and the same was true at Elton (Kenward 1982b).

This contrasts with the considerable seasonal changes in foraging (Fig. 18.3). The squirrels in both woods fed extensively on flowers and ripening samaras of deciduous trees between April and July, but spent most of the autumn and winter on the ground, caching and later recovering the acorns and smaller hazel crops (see Kenward 1982b for Elton). In late winter, food must have been less abundant than in the autumn, and one might therefore have expected a range increase. In fact, average ranges sizes were at a minimum. This was associated with a marked decline in the duration of daily activity (see

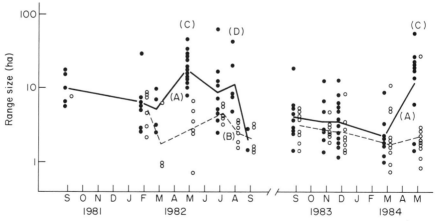

FIG. 18.2. The range of squirrels at Monk's Wood in different months of 1981–84. Solid lines join means for males (●), dashed lines for females (O). The significance of changes is: (A) the male range increase from March to May, $P < 0.01$ both years; (B) the female decrease July–September 1982, $P = 0.062$; (C) the difference in male and female May ranges, $P < 0.01$ in 1982, $P < 0.02$ in 1984; (D) the difference between male and female ranges in August 1982, $P < 0.01$.

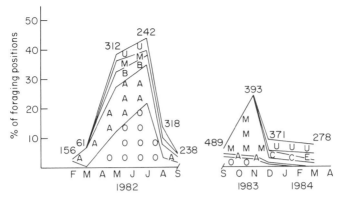

FIG. 18.3. The percentage of records which were in various tree species at Monk's Wood, during February–September 1982 and September 1983 to March 1984. The numbers of foraging observations are shown, for 6–19 squirrels in the first period and 14–22 in the second. Tree species were: (O), Oak (*Quercus robus*); (A), ash (*Fraxinus excelsior*); (B), birch (*Betula pendula*); (M), field-maple (*Acer campestre*); (C), hawthorn (*Crataegus monogyna*); (E), elm (*Ulmus procera*) and unknown (U). Squirrels not foraging in trees were on the ground.

also Tonkin 1983), from an autumnal 10–12 hours each day to only 3–4 hours a day between January and March, suggesting that the squirrels adopted an energy conservation strategy at a time of poor weather and reduced food abundance.

The most dramatic seasonal range change was an average threefold increase in male range area between March and May ($P < 0.01$ each year, Wilcoxon test). Males tended to have larger ranges than females throughout the summer, the differences being significant both years in May ($P < 0.02$, U-test) and in August 1982 ($P < 0.01$). Since there were no sex differences in the feeding observations, the male range expansion apparently reflected sexual activity, coinciding with a peak in testis development (Webley & Johnson 1983; R.E. Kenward & T. Parish, unpubl.) during the mating period for summer litters. On seven occasions males outside their normal ranges were found gathered in one place, apparently engaged in mating chases. The sexes did not differ significantly in range size between September and March, and despite recording ranges between December and late February in 4 years for a total of twenty adult male squirrels, at least six of which had enlarged testes, no dramatic range increases were recorded during the mating period for spring litters.

Some large ranges were recorded for males (and females) in late winter, but these individuals were not sexually active. A range increase at that time, which was contrary to the general trend, appeared to reflect feeding requirements:

TABLE 18.1. December–June range sizes and fate of squirrels in Monk's Wood

	Remained in population		Left population within 3 months
Adult			
n	13		5
Geometric mean	4·47 ha	ns	3·76 ha
95% CL	2·07–9·62 ha		1·68–8·40 ha
1st year			
n	7		7
Geometric mean	4·40 ha	$P = 0·019$	12·78 ha
95% CL	3·07–6·32 ha		5·25–31·13 ha

Probabilities were estimated with the Mann–Whitney U-test.

several Monk's Wood squirrels travelled each day to a conifer plantation well outside their autumn range, and one adult female commuted daily to a pheasant feed site 1·2 km from her drey. Moreover, there was evidence that range sizes sometimes reflected intrinsic foraging ability, or range quality, or both factors. First-year squirrels which remained in the Monk's Wood population for less than 3 months in late winter and spring had significantly larger ranges than other yearlings (Table 18.1). Moreover, the ranges of lactating females which failed to rear a spring litter were larger than those which eventually reared their young (Table 18.2).

As well as seasonal and individual variation in range size, there were inter-year differences in average range size at Monk's Wood. Combining data from both sexes, average range sizes differed between 1981, 1982 and 1983 in September ($P < 0·05$, U-tests), between the 1980–81 and 1983–84 winters in December–January ($P < 0·02$), and between 1982 and 1984 in February–March ($P < 0·02$). Population mean range sizes recorded between December

TABLE 18.2. April–May range sizes of lactating females which weaned litters or failed, and of non-breeding females

	Successful		Failed		Non-breeding
n	6		5		6
Geometric mean	1·61 ha	$P = 0·041$	3·47 ha	ns	4·72 ha
95% CL	0·72–3·59 ha		2·24–5·37 ha		1·83–12·14 ha

Probabilities were estimated with the Mann–Whitney U-test.

and March in different years were more closely related to squirrel density than to their food supply (Table 18.3). At Monk's Wood range size decreased with increasing squirrel density, and neither varied systematically with winter food.

In conclusion, the evidence is that seasonal and annual variation in the average range sizes of these squirrels could be linked to sexual activity but not to food supply, whereas variation of individual ranges within a season sometimes reflected differences in individual foraging ability or range quality. Variation in the size of 60% core ranges, which correlated strongly with total range sizes ($r = 0.853$, $N = 186$, $P < 0.001$), followed the same pattern. To see

TABLE 18.3. Squirrel density, range size and winter food during December–March at two sites over 4 years

Site & year	Winter food (acorn index)	Squirrel density	Range size (N)
Monk's Wood			
1980–81	Fair (6·4)	0·67 ha^{-1}	5·66 ha (10)
1981–82	Good (10·4)	0·73 ha^{-1}	5·63 ha (14)
1983–84	Poor (3·3)	1·53 ha^{-1}	3·09 ha (20)
Elton			
1979–80	Good*	2·33 ha^{-1}	1·79 ha (16)

* All radio-tagged squirrels used pheasant feed sites during winter at Elton.

whether an artificial abundance of food might enable squirrel ranges to contract or, on the other hand, allow sexually active males to expand their ranges during the mating period for spring litters, feeding experiments were conducted in Monk's Wood in 1982 and 1984.

FEEDING EXPERIMENTS

Methods

The ranges of fourteen radio-tagged squirrels were recorded in February 1982, after which seven squirrels were given *ad lib.* maize at sites within 50 m of their dreys. Maize was heaped inside multiple-capture traps with their doors kept open, which made it inaccessible to pigeons and pheasants; the maize was replenished on alternate days so that it did not run out before the traps were set to catch the squirrels at the end of the experiment. Seven squirrels remained unfed, with ranges well away from the feeding sites. All ranges were recorded again in the second and third weeks of feeding.

The experiment was repeated in 1984, in case the artificial feeding in 1982 had been inadequate for a major effect on ranging behaviour. The squirrels were given more nutritious food for longer than in 1982, by providing *ad lib.* wheat from late December to early March, in a winter with a relatively poor acorn and hazel crop (Table 18.3). Feeding sites were up to 100 m from dreys, and were replenished two to three times a week so that they did not run out until the end of the experiment. Traps were set to catch the squirrels after feeding for 1 month, and after recording March ranges, so that the sexual status of males could be determined by examining the scrotum. Testis size was scored on a 0–10 scale, which correlated strongly with testis weights in dead squirrels from other woods ($r = 0.945$, $N = 44$, $P < 0.001$, Kenward & Parish, unpubl.).

Results

The decreases in total range sizes in females were not significantly different from those of controls in either experiment (Table 18.4), but the core range decrease was significant ($P = 0.008$) if probabilities from both experiments were combined. The total range sizes of the fed squirrels were almost all considerably larger than expected if squirrels simply went from drey to feeding

TABLE 18.4. Changes in late winter range sizes of squirrels which were given supplementary food, and of unfed controls

Year, sex & treatment		N	Total range area (ha)			60% core range area (ha)		
			First range	Second range	P, for difference in change	First range	Second range	P, for difference in change
1982, short-term feeding								
Females:	fed	6	3·7	1·6	0·440	0·9	0·2	0·057
	unfed	4	4·8	2·3		1·5	0·6	
Males:	fed	5	9·2	10·1	0·657	2·3	1·0	0·155
	unfed	5	4·0	4·8		0·6	1·1	
1984, long-term feeding								
Females:	fed	3	3·3	1·1	0·313	1·0	0·1	0·071
	unfed	5	2·1	1·0		0·4	0·4	
Males:	fed	5	4·3	1·0	0·008	0·7	0·1	0·008
	unfed	5	2·3	4·8		1·1	1·1	

Probabilities were estimated with the Mann–Whitney 'U'-test

site and back. This, and the lack of any absolute difference in total range size between fed and unfed squirrels, indicated that total range size was not solely related to food, even when this remained very abundant for more than 2 months. However, the change in their core range sizes showed that the squirrels were modifying their intensive foraging according to food abundance.

In 1982, two of four fed males quite markedly increased their range sizes, one of them changing his overnight drey to a position 400 m from the feeding site. In 1984 the ranges of fed males showed a very significant decrease, compared with those of unfed controls.

Male range size changes in 1984 were related not only to feeding but also to their testis score in March ($r = -0.804$, $P < 0.01$): the males with the largest testes had the greatest reduction in range size. Feeding and testis size together explained 89% of the variation in male range size changes, significantly more than testis size alone ($F_{1/7} = 15.46$, $P < 0.01$): feeding had the greatest range-reducing effect on the males with the largest testes. There were no testis scores for the 1982 experiment.

The feeding experiments showed that the size of total winter ranges was markedly affected by artificial food abundance only in males, where the effect was modified by sexual status. The tendency for males with large testes to respond most to feeding may well have been effected through social interactions, with sexually active males displacing the others away from their normal foraging areas for some of the time (though they still used the feeding sites).

DISCUSSION

Since average ranges were not linked to food supply seasonally, and since winter range size was more closely related to squirrel density than to autumn seed crop abundance (Table 18.3), it seems that squirrels were adjusting their range size less to their food supply than to their population density. This counts against a direct causal relationship between resources and range size (Fig. 18.1a,c). The failure of supplementary feeding to reduce female total ranges supports this view (Table 18.4); the reduction in their core ranges is probably an artefact of using a point food source. However, the effect of artificial feeding on male range size is contradictory evidence, unless the range reductions are a product of social factors and not a direct response to food abundance. Some squirrels were drawn to feeding sites outside their normal ranges, which would increase local density at feed sites, and perhaps thereby increase social pressures to which males were more responsive than females.

If the pathways in Fig. 18.1a,c are excluded, squirrel density is limited directly by food supply (Fig. 18.1b), but not necessarily each winter. Unless the nut and mast crop is very poor in relation to squirrel density, the population size may be less closely linked to immediate winter food than to food during the preceding spring and summer (through mortality of spring young), to food during the preceding winter (through direct mortality or failure of spring breeding), or even to a limiting seed crop more than a year ago. When seed crops fail while squirrel density is high in extensive woodland, there may even be the irruptive mass emigrations which have occasionally been recorded in North America (Christian 1969). Such intermittent population limitation may be seen as an ecological consequence of feeding on tree seeds (Newton 1972), and means that food supply levels must be taken into account when seeking density-dependent relationships.

If squirrel density is limited directly by food supply, there remains the problem of explaining how density determines range size (Fig. 18.1b). Since squirrel ranges overlap so extensively and since squirrels are active more or less from dawn to dusk through the autumn, there is little opportunity for the temporal separation found in chipmunks (*Tamias striatus*) by Getty (1981). However, 60% core ranges were very much smaller than the total ranges (Table 18.4), and a preliminary analysis for the 1983–84 autumn and winter showed that they were generally exclusive (Kenward & Parish, unpubl.). With ranges recorded by radio-tracking twenty-seven of the thirty-nine squirrels resident on the Monk's Wood trap grid that winter, core ranges within each sex fell into two categories. For most squirrels they were exclusive, but for four same-sex pairs and one trio there were extensive overlaps; these squirrels also tended to share dreys. One same-sex pair was of mother and daughter, while one other pair may have come from the same autumn litter, because they were close in size and weight when first caught, in the same trap in mid-winter. The relationship between squirrels in the other three groups was unknown.

There are at least two ways in which core ranges could become exclusive. The squirrels might defend their main foraging areas, or they might simply avoid foraging where resource depletion or scent cues (Taylor 1977) indicate that another squirrel is concentrating its activity. In contrast to the spring, when many squirrels congregate in one or two flowering trees for a few days at a time, the autumn is a period of widespread food availability. Thus, defence of a small area containing food for several months is more practical in autumn than in spring, and the continuous squirrel activity throughout autumn days might be the result of a need to deter conspecifics. Moreover, the ten radio-tagged juvenile and yearling squirrels which emigrated from the dense Elton population all left between 25 August and 10 October. This autumn emigration could result from some young squirrels failing to secure exclusive areas when density is high; alternatively, squirrels might be especially sensitive to food shortage in autumn, and therefore disperse if constrained to exclusive ranges in which the food supply would later become inadequate for survival. In either case the autumn dispersal would be a consequence of social behaviour, and the reduced survival or breeding success of squirrels with large late winter ranges (Tables 18.1 and 18.2) a consequence of poor foraging in the ranges to which they had been constrained.

Increased sensitivity to food shortage could provide a mechanism for ensuring dispersal while food is still relatively abundant, for instance as fuel for long distance travel. A response to food shortage, rather than social behaviour, is the most probable trigger for autumn dispersal in goshawks (*Accipiter gentilis* L.), because their overlapping autumn–winter ranges differ from those of grey squirels in (i) lacking exclusive high-use areas and (ii) being related in size to food and habitat content (Kenward 1982c).

A few squirrels moved well outside their autumn ranges in late winter, to feeding sites and to the conifer plantation adjacent to Monk's Wood. Perhaps defensive or avoidance behaviour relaxes as winter progresses and the squirrels reduce their period of activity each day. Defence of an area would be more advantageous in autumn, while tree seed crops are available to be cached, than after the nuts and acorns have been scatterhoarded in sites familiar only to the squirrel which buried them.

The failure of sexually active males to expand their ranges when fed, contrasting with the substantial range expansion when males were sexually active in summer, suggests an evolved difference in mating strategy between the two seasons. There are several pressures which might select against wide-ranging in winter, including unfamiliarity with food caches outside a squirrel's autumn range, high energy loss outside dreys in cold weather, and perhaps an increased vulnerability to predation when deciduous leaves and ground cover are gone. Intense competition for the few local females could result in displacement of subordinate males from the main foraging areas of sexually dominant ones, thus explaining the reduced effect of feeding on the ranges of males with small testes. In this light, the summer range expansion of males may be a consequence of competition for mates at a time when squirrels are less constrained to one area, rather than an outbreeding adaptation (Thompson 1978).

There is still much to do before the mechanisms linking squirrel food, ranging behaviour and density can be determined unambiguously. To investigate social effects, the ranges of almost all the squirrels in an area need to be determined. This requires radio-tracking rather than trapping, which cannot measure ranges in sufficient detail or at all times of year. Ideally, experiments should be done in several small woods with similar winter food supplies, to avoid local movement and immigration effects when squirrels are removed to reduce density, fed throughout a wood, or left as controls.

ACKNOWLEDGMENTS

I am very grateful to J.L. Holm and T. Parish for considerable help with trapping and radio-tracking. Sir Peter Proby and the Nature Conservancy Council kindly gave permission for their words to be used in the study. I thank J.P. Dempster, B.A.C. Don, and I. Newton for discussion and comments at all stages of the work. R.M. Sibly and the anonymous referees helped greatly in revising the original manuscript.

REFERENCES

Christian, J.J. (1969). Gray squirrels. *Bioscience*, **19**, 106.
Don, B.A.C. (1983). Home range characteristics and correlates in tree squirrels. *Mammal Review*, **13**, 123–132.
Don B.A.C. & Rennolls, K. (1983). A home range model incorporating biological attraction points. *Journal of Animal Ecology*, **52**, 69–81.
Ford, G. & Krumme, D.W. (1979). The analysis of space use patterns. *Journal of Theoretical Biology*, **76**, 125–155.
Getty, T. (1981). Territorial behaviour of eastern chipmunks (*Tamias striatus*): encounter avoidance and spatial time-sharing. *Ecology*, **62**, 915–921.
Gurnell, J. (1983). Squirrel numbers and the abundance of tree seeds. *Mammal Review*, **13**, 133–148.
Hassell, M.P. (1975). Density dependence in single-species populations. *Journal of Animal Ecology*, **44**, 283–295.
Kenward, R.E. (1982a). Techniques for monitoring the behaviour of grey squirrels by radio. *Symposia of the Zoological Society, London*, **49**, 175–196.
Kenward, R.E. (1982b). Bark stripping by grey squirrels—some recent research. *Quarterly Journal of Forestry*, **76**, 108–121.
Kenward, R.E. (1982c). Goshawk hunting behaviour, and range size as a function of food and habitat availability. *Journal of Animal Ecology*, **51**, 69–80.
Newton, I. (1972). *Finches*. Collins, London.
Nicholson, A.J. (1954). An outline of the dynamics of animal populations. *Australian Journal of Zoology*, **2**, 9–65.
Taylor, J.C. (1977). The frequency of Grey squirrel (*Sciurus carolinensis*) communication by use of scent marking points. *Journal of Zoology (London)*, **183**, 543–545.
Thompson, D.C. (1978). The social system of the grey squirrel. *Behaviour*, **64**, 305–328.
Tonkin, J.M. (1983). Activity patterns of the Red squirrel (*Sciurus vulgaris*). *Mammal Review*, **13**, 99–111.
Webley, G.E. & Johnson, E. (1983). Reproductive physiology of the Grey squirrel (*Sciurus carolinensis*). *Mammal Review*, **13**, 149–154.

19. THE ROLE OF MIGRATION IN THE POPULATION DYNAMICS OF BIRDS

M. W. PIENKOWSKI* AND P. R. EVANS

Department of Zoology, University of Durham,
South Road, Durham DH1 3LE

SUMMARY

Some implications of migration for population dynamics are explored, drawing examples particularly from coastal birds. In a single non-breeding area (e.g. migration, moulting or wintering site), individuals of a species may be present from a variety of breeding areas. There is evidence for competition amongst juveniles, and between juveniles and adults, for winter sites which minimize the distance juveniles have to migrate from their birth-places. Some juveniles are displaced from near areas, implying lower survival. Most of the difference in survival rates between juveniles and adults appears to arise during the period before juvenile shorebirds established themselves on a wintering area. Subsequent survival of young and adults is high.

For many shorebird species, individuals return in later years to sites where they wintered as young. Thus, distributions observed in any one year may be the result of conditions experienced and behaviour patterns established in previous years. A few shorebird species which are less site-faithful generally feed on young age-classes of prey animals which vary irregularly in their distribution and abundance.

INTRODUCTION

Migration, a term restricted in this paper to the regular seasonal movements of birds between breeding and non-breeding ('wintering') ranges more than a few hundred kilometres apart, is a behaviour which considerably complicates the study of a species' population dynamics. For only a few migrants, such as the barnacle goose *Branta leucopsis*, is it possible to study an isolated breeding population which is also confined to an isolated and restricted winter range. For most, even those few individuals present within a workable study area in the breeding range are likely to migrate to a variety of different wintering sites; and, conversely, individuals which might be studied in a typical site within the wintering range almost certainly originate from a variety of breeding areas.

Although density-dependent processes, e.g. of the type discussed by

---

* Present address: Chief Scientists Team, Nature Conservancy Council, Northminster House, Peterborough PE1 1UA.

Goss-Custard in this volume (p. 169), may be shown to operate at a site in one part of the non-breeding range, it is not obvious that they will operate equally in all parts of that range. Nor have the costs associated with migration over different distances been quantified. To model the dynamics of such a population, one requires measurement of survival rates of birds wintering in each site, and how these depend quantitatively upon (i) numbers of conspecifics; (ii) possible interspecific competitors; (iii) predators; (iv) weather conditions. At the moment, such data are scarce for migrant species, but indications of the *relative* rates of survival in different parts of the non-breeding range are obtainable by examining the various hypotheses that have been advanced to account for variation amongst individuals in the distance travelled between breeding and non-breeding sites. In this paper, we review these hypotheses with particular reference to shorebirds breeding in arctic and northern temperate areas. Arctic-breeding shorebirds are obligate migrants. Some individuals travel as far as southern Australia, whilst others of the same species remain within the mid-latitudes of the northern hemisphere in winter. This extreme variability in migratory performance assists tests of the validity of the hypotheses proposed to account for it. We aim to show that the limited data available are consistent with the proposal that shorebirds in the eastern Atlantic settle in autumn as near to the breeding grounds as possible, but that some are prevented from doing so by competition.

WHY DO SOME BIRDS MIGRATE FURTHER FROM THEIR BREEDING AREAS THAN OTHERS?

Hypotheses on this question can be divided according to whether or not they invoke competition on wintering grounds nearest the breeding grounds. These categories resemble (but do not correspond exactly to) the 'ideal-despotic' and 'ideal-free' models invoked with respect to local distributions (e.g. Sutherland & Parker, p. 255). First we shall discuss those which do not invoke competition at wintering sites.

Group A: 'non-competition' models

(i) A long-standing 'non-competition' model suggests that large birds should be able to winter further north, because large bodies are energetically more efficient than small ones in keeping warm in cold surroundings ('Bergman's Rule', e.g. Salomonsen 1955). Various workers differed as to which of the two factors, size and wintering location, was cause and which effect. The model has found little support in recent years, largely because so many exceptions to its predictions have been reported (e.g. Hale 1980;

Myers 1981a; Ketterson & Nolan 1983). Consequently, we shall not discuss it further.

(ii) More recently, Greenberg (1980) proposed a 'trade-off' between time spent on the breeding grounds, devoted to reproduction, and time spent on the non-breeding site, devoted to maximizing survival. Greenberg suggested that the length of the profitable breeding season (during which reproductive output exceeds mortality) determines the length of the wintering season. He supposed that non-breeding sites progressively further away from (and usually to the south of) the breeding area are progressively more 'benign', so that survival is higher, but that there is an increasing cost of migration to and from more distant sites. The longer the period of the year that birds spend away from the breeding area, the greater the accumulated improvement in their chances of survival in a distant wintering site, by comparison with a site closer to the breeding area. Greenberg supposed that natural selection would lead to choice of a non-breeding area in which the benefits of improved survival maximally exceed the costs of migration to and from it.

Group B: 'competition' models

The other group of hypotheses supposes that birds try to winter as near to the breeding grounds as is habitable but that some are displaced by competition (see Cox 1968; Gauthreaux 1978, 1982). The advantage to individuals of wintering as close as possible to the breeding grounds have been variously suggested as:

(i) they should be in a better position than are longer-distance migrants to obtain limited resources on the breeding grounds, such as holes for protected nest-sites (von Haartman 1968) or territories (Myers 1981a).

(ii) by remaining in the same climatic region as their breeding grounds, they should be able to respond to variations in weather in different years so as to return and commence breeding as soon as this is possible (Alerstam & Högstedt 1980).

(iii) migration itself is so costly that birds should minimize the distance moved. This might relate mainly to the first migration of inexperienced birds (see Greenberg 1980; Gauthreaux 1982; Pienkowski & Evans 1984).

Some selection pressures concerning migration could act together; this makes investigation more difficult. Baker's (1978) model allows for a multiplicity of factors but, as noted by Ketterson & Nolan (1983), it does not generate testable predictions.

Until recently the question concerning differing migration distances was directed towards the comparison of migrant with non-migrant species, or migrant with resident individuals within a species, rather than towards differences in distance travelled by individuals of a migrant species from a certain breeding area. Even in the last few years, hypotheses concerning the ultimate factors responsible for differential migration patterns have had to be tested by comparisons between the non-breeding ranges of different age and sex categories, different geographical populations or even different species (e.g. Greenberg 1980; Myers 1981a,b; O'Connor 1981; Ketterson & Nolan 1983). This approach has proved valuable and is used here also, but it has limitations. The fact remains that a change of species, sex or age-class is not a behaviour open to an individual bird.

There is a further practical difficulty. To test their ideas, theoreticians have frequently calculated survival rates from bird-ringing recoveries. However, the assumptions of the underlying mathematics may not be met (e.g. Lakhani & Newton 1983); and there are doubts as to the representativeness of the samples of birds ringed (Swennen 1984; Evans & Pienkowski 1984). Measures of survival based on returns or recaptures of individually marked birds from intensively studied populations are much more reliable. Shorebirds provide a group of species in which individuals tend to be sufficiently site-faithful to make such studies feasible (Evans 1981), and are large enough and occupy sufficiently open habitats for unique marking with colour-rings to be visible.

The behaviour of birds as they arrive on potential wintering areas in autumn, and identification of the proximate factors that determine whether an individual settles or migrates further, could also be used to test the various hypotheses. Displacement by competition would provide clear evidence against hypotheses of group A. Observations, within the possible winter range, that first arrivals move on before the arrival of conspecifics, presumably as part of a time-programmed migration (see review by Berthold 1984), would seem to go against those of group B. However, in this case, differences in behaviour between different populations may not be a good guide to the reasons for individual differences in behaviour. If, within a single species, birds of one breeding population tend to be outcompeted in a particular area by birds of another breeding population, perhaps because of consistent size differences, the migration patterns may have evolved so that one population now avoids direct competition with the other by consistently migrating further and perhaps at different times in all years.

Evaluation of the hypotheses as they apply to shorebird migration

Greenberg's time allocation model

Several assumptions underlie Greenberg's model. One is that the chances of survival of a migrant on a wintering area progressively improve with distance from the breeding site. Another is that the costs of migration are affected only by the distance travelled and not by the time of year at which the flights are made. If we accept the model and its assumptions, it follows that more pronounced seasonality in the breeding area (i.e. a short duration of favourable conditions for reproduction and consequent longer non-breeding seasons) should lead to longer migrations, to more distant non-breeding sites. This would provide an explanation for the phenomenon of leap-frog migration, whereby northern breeding populations of a species migrate further and winter in more southerly areas than southern breeding populations of the same species (see Salomonsen 1955). Whilst the model was apparently designed to provide predictions on the interpopulation or interspecific level, it is difficult to see how such a model could account for individual variation in distance travelled from a single breeding area, particularly variation on the scale seen in many shorebird species.

What of the assumptions which underline the model? Greenberg does not specify the factors leading to increased survival at more distant wintering areas. For arctic-breeding shorebirds, the assumption that tropical wintering areas are more benign than temperate ones is in doubt. On the principal West African non-breeding area, the Banc d'Arguin, Mauritania (latitude 20°N), prey densities are surprisingly low, and shorebirds forage for a large proportion of the period of tidal exposure but achieve a low food intake, compared with that in Europe (Altenburg *et al.* 1982). Dugan (1981) argued that it is because of these unfavourable foraging conditions that some adult grey plovers *Pluvialis squatarola* and bar-tailed godwits *Limosa lapponica* return northwards to western Europe as early as January and February, before departing to the arctic in May.

For at least some groups of birds, the risk of mortality associated with a given migration varies with the time of year. Hirundines on migration through Europe and north Africa are likely to suffer mass mortality more often late in the autumn (e.g. in October) than earlier, because of the increased risk of cold spells and resulting scarcity of flying insects (Elkins 1983). Certain weather systems change track with season, on average in a predictable way, and if they are associated with particularly strong winds, they could be important (and seasonally varying) sources of mortality for migrants. Thus some species, particularly the weaker fliers, may have been selected to curtail their stays on what might otherwise have been still-profitable breeding areas.

What evidence is available for or against the time-allocation hypothesis? Greenberg (1980) claimed that migrant passerines breeding in N. America generally had higher survival rates than residents (although he recognized that his methods of estimation had various faults), whilst residents tended to have higher productivity, probably because they had more clutches per season.

However, O'Connor (1981) was unable to find significant differences in survival rates or productivity between migrant and non-migrant species in a British sample, again mainly of passerines. Generally, breeding productivity of shorebirds (as for many migrants that attempt to produce only one brood of young per year) increases towards the arctic, probably due to lower rates of predation on eggs and young (Larson 1960; Boyd 1962; Goss-Custard 1981; Pienkowski 1984). Consequently, increased length of migration tends to be associated with increased hatching and fledging success. However, there is little evidence as to how, within one breeding area, resident species (or individuals) compare with migrant species (or individuals) in terms of total annual production. Productivity to the fledging stage has been studied directly in few shorebird species (Pienkowski 1984). Most workers have used indirect methods to estimate this, usually assuming constant population size.

Greenberg suggested a test between his hypothesis and those based on competition. If more distant wintering populations comprised birds displaced from preferred sites closer to the breeding areas by competition, the annual survival rates of the displaced birds should not exceed those of the birds remaining. In the time-allocation model, the more southern or more distant winterers should have a higher survival.

No data are yet available for intraspecific comparisons of survival in relation to migration distance for individual shorebirds from the same breeding area. However, information is available (from temperate breeding and non-breeding areas) on survival rates of a range of populations and species which move to very different extents to winter quarters. These data from individually colour-marked birds indicate (Fig. 19.1) that those wintering further south survive less well (which agrees with data from Mauritania reviewed above). It is, therefore, difficult to reconcile Greenberg's predictions with shorebird migrations in the Palaearctic. The same is true if we assume that the survival rates calculated from ringing recoveries by Boyd (1962) are mutually comparable (even though underestimates of the true values, for the reasons discussed by Evans & Pienkowski 1984). The mean annual survival rate of seven resident or partial migrants was 63%, of eight longer-distance migrants 59%, and of thirteen long-distance migrants 62%.

Hypotheses involving competition for non-breeding sites close to the breeding areas

If competition does take place for wintering areas close to the breeding areas, one would expect sequential filling of decreasingly profitable feeding sites within each wintering area, as numbers arriving there increase in autumn. This has been found by, e.g. Zwarts (1974) Goss-Custard (1977), and Meire &

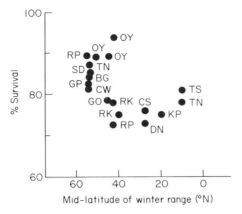

FIG. 19.1. Average minimum annual survival rates of adult shorebirds (estimated by return of individually marked birds) in relation to mid-latitude of winter quarters. OY, oystercatcher *Haematopus ostralegus*; RP, ringed plover *Charadrius hiaticula*; KP, Kentish plover *C. alexandrinus*; GP, grey plover *Pluvialis squatarola*; GO, golden plover *P. apricaria*; SD, sanderling *Calidris alba*; TS, Temminck's stint *C. temminckii*; DN, dunlin *C. alpina*; BG, bar-tailed godwit *Limosa lapponica*; CW, curlew *Numenius arquata*; RK, redshank *Tringa totanus*; CS, common sandpiper *Actitis hypoleucos*; TN, turnstone *Arenaria interpres*. Several values are shown for some species in which winter ranges are known to differ between local populations whose survival rates have been measured (sources listed in Goss-Custard 1981; Evans & Pienkowski 1984). The two parameters are significantly correlated (using the arcsine transformation to normalize the survival percentages, $r = 0.49$, $P < 0.05$).

Kuyken (1984), and there is increasing evidence that some birds are excluded from the best feeding sites (see Goss-Custard, p. 169).

Direct evidence of competition has been gathered also by Townshend (1985). In an important study, he found that juvenile grey plovers (from Siberian breeding grounds) compete in autumn for winter feeding territories on intertidal mudflats at Teesmouth, and that some unsuccessful birds leave the estuary, some continuing migration at least as far as France. Townshend found that juveniles obtaining winter territories in competition with other juveniles were, on average, larger. However, juveniles could be displaced from territories they had acquired in early autumn by adults when these arrived in late autumn, provided that the adults had held territories in those places in previous years.

At present, Townshend's is the only evidence relating extended migration to competition at a site closer to the breeding area. However, there is evidence that sites at the furthest extremes of migration routes tend to be used extensively only when populations are high after a series of successful breeding seasons. For example, numbers of shorebirds reaching Tasmania, the southern extreme of the non-breeding range of birds breeding in eastern Siberia, vary greatly between years (Thomas 1970). Similarly in South Africa, the numbers of young shorebirds of species breeding in the Siberian high Arctic varied greatly between years, apparently in parallel with weather conditions on the breeding grounds (Robertson 1981). Within the NW European region, several wader species from arctic breeding grounds migrate first to moulting centres around the North Sea, and then they move on in directions between NW and S to wintering sites (Pienkowski & Pienkowski 1983). The furthest sites, for example in Scotland and France, were used less in winters when populations were low (Symonds, Langslow & Pienkowski 1984; R. Mahéo in Evans & Pienkowski 1984). Populations of both knot *Calidris canutus* and dunlin *C. alpina* wintering in western Europe declined during the late 1970s (Fig. 19.2), probably as a result of several years of poor breeding success in the Arctic (see Green, Greenwood & Lloyd 1977; Evans & Pienkowski 1984; Mason 1984). For both species, the numbers wintering in the less distant part of the non-breeding area, mainly around the North and Irish Seas, were less variable than those in western Europe as a whole, while those in a southern part, France, were most variable (Fig. 19.2). Indeed, the numbers of several shorebird species in Britain and Ireland were less variable than those in France (Table 19.1).

We suggest that these changes in distribution in dunlins result from changes in the settlement pattern of young birds, rather than changes in

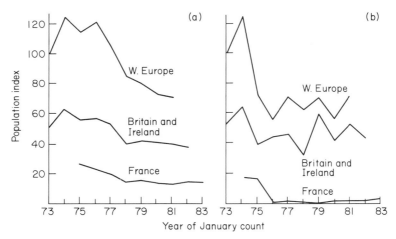

FIG. 19.2. The numbers of (a) dunlin *Calidris alpina* and (b) knot *C. canutus* in Britain & Ireland, France and the whole of western Europe in January in different years. The numbers of each species are scaled so that the total number in western Europe in 1973 equals index 100. Index 100 corresponds for dunlin to about 1·5 million birds, and for knot to about 0·6 million birds. (Sources: Mahéo 1978–83; Marchant 1982; Prater 1974–82).

TABLE 19.1. Coefficients of mid-winter variation of numbers of common shorebird species in Britain & Ireland and France (sources as for Fig. 19.1)

Species	Coefficient of variation in:	
	Britain & Ireland	France
Oystercatcher *Haematopus ostralegus*	0·18	0·28
Grey plover *Pluvialis squatarola*	0·21	0·24
Knot *Calidris canutus*	0·21	1·35
Dunlin *Calidris alpina*	0·19	0·29
Curlew *Numenius arquata*	0·19	0·29
Bar-tailed godwit *Limosa lapponica*	0·34	0·58
Redshank *Tringa totanus*	0·15	0·42

wintering areas of those adults that had already used France in previous years. The gradual decline in numbers wintering in France (Fig. 19.2) would be compatible with this, on the assumption that it reflected chiefly the mortality of adults, with little compensation from arrivals of those juveniles that could not be accommodated in wintering areas nearer the breeding grounds. (Adult dunlins are known to return to the same site in successive winters in several areas (e.g. Minton 1975; Symonds *et al.* 1984), including France (pers. obs.).)

Individual knots are markedly more mobile, both within and between winters, than other waders so far investigated (Dick *et al.* 1976; Dugan 1981; Symonds *et al.* 1984). The more rapid redistribution in France of knots than of dunlins, between 1975 and 1976 (Fig. 19.2), is compatible with this, and could not be explained otherwise except if catastrophic mortality of adults had occurred.

Thus the data, while far from conclusive, seem more compatible with the competition hypotheses than the time-allocation hypothesis. However, whether competition occurs within the whole population of the species, or only amongst juveniles and between juveniles and adults, probably varies from species to species.

Townshend (1985) has shown that the locations of the winter quarters of individual grey plovers are determined, in most cases, by the site in which each finally settles in its first winter of life. Faithfulness to a wintering site in successive years has been shown by adult shorebirds of several species, but the method of selection of the site has been established only for grey plover. Sutherland (1982) gave evidence that chiefly young oystercatchers *Haematopus ostralegus* took advantage of an increase in cockles *Cardium edule* on one estuary in one year, and speculated that these are the mobile, dispersing age-groups (although his procedures to sample age-ratios may have involved biases; see Pienkowski & Dick 1976).

Itinerancy

If there is competition for wintering sites nearest to the breeding areas, why do individuals of some species move about during a winter, as remarked above for the knot? Changes of wintering site occur in individuals of some other species, both from year to year and within a single winter (see, e.g. Evans 1981 (in Britain) and Myers 1980 (in California) for sanderling).

Movements within a single year occur throughout the winter. They are most conspicuous in those shorebird species that depend for food on small intertidal invertebrates that occur (i) in the upper layers of sediments liable to be washed away, and (ii) attached to rocks from which they may be dislodged, in both cases by severe wave action at unpredictable dates during the winter. In Europe, the invertebrates concerned include in particular the recently settled spat of bivalves such as *Macoma balthica* in the upper layers of estuarine muds and *Mytilus edulis* on rocky shores. When these animals grow older and larger, they bury deeper in soft sediments or attach more firmly to hard substrates, respectively. Thus, individuals of larger shorebird species (such as curlew *Numenius arquata*) which feed only on the larger invertebrates, whose abundance is not likely to decline at unpredictable times, do not move about within a winter (although they may switch foods if some types become less accessible or detectable in cold weather). Little is known of the differences between individuals that stay the whole winter in a particular site, risking the unpredictable loss of their food resources, and those that move about or patrol different lengths of coastline. Preliminary analysis of sanderling behaviour at Teesmouth indicates that those that move are no different in age composition from those that stay, but that (for a given body-size) they tend to be heavier in mid-winter. This may reflect greater fat reserves. Sedentary sanderlings do not appear to show greater flexibility in diet than mobile birds, which move between areas with similar ranges of prey species to those in areas used by sedentary birds.

The reasons for change of wintering location between years are probably to be found in the irregularity of successful spat settlement by bivalves in a particular site. *Mya arenaria* or *Cardium edule* may recruit successfully only at intervals of 5 or more years (see e.g. Zwarts & Wanink 1984). This is probably not too serious for the larger shorebird species that feed upon them, since the long-billed birds may be able to exploit the bivalves profitably for several seasons before they bury too deep or become too large. However, for knot, which can take only small prey (chiefly 1- or 2-year-old bivalves—and then only if they are at high densities), irregular spat settlement could pose problems if birds relied on a return to the same wintering site in successive years. After adult knots have moulted in a few large estuaries in western Europe in early autumn, the degrees of mobility shown in the subsequent winter may depend on the extent of spat settlement of estuarine bivalves at these sites in the previous summer(s) though this has not been proven.

Thus, individuals of itinerant species may not move further from their breeding areas than necessary to maximize their chances of survival.

WHY COMPETE FOR WINTERING GROUNDS NEAR TO THE BREEDING GROUNDS?

We now consider the fine details of the competition hypotheses.

Resource competition on the breeding grounds

The resource competition model (van Haartman 1968) proposes that residents gain an advantage over migrants in competition for limiting nesting resources, particularly nest cavities (but presumably also territories, if such are held). Strictly, this model of resource competition on the breeding grounds does not need to invoke competition in the wintering area. Rather than competition, increased environmental risks from wintering in northern areas could provide the counter pressure, by lowering survival of birds wintering there. The evidence runs counter to this in comparisons between species and populations (e.g. for shorebirds see Fig 19.1), and in intersexual comparisons: in many species males winter further north but there is still a surplus of males in the breeding season (see below). Furthermore, the evidence reviewed in the previous section points towards competition in the winter quarters. Therefore, we treat this hypothesis here as one of the competition group.

Aspects of this model relating specifically to hole-nesting (for discussion see references cited by Alerstam & Högstedt 1983) are clearly inapplicable to open-nesting species such as most shorebirds. For these, an abundant summer food supply (e.g. Holmes 1970) and reduced risk of nest-predation (e.g. Larson 1960; Pienkowski 1984) favour arctic breeding in many populations. Competition for space either for feeding purposes (e.g. Holmes 1970) or in which to hide a nest (e.g. Pienkowski 1983b, 1984) possibly prevents some males from obtaining a mate. However, territory holders from previous seasons can generally regain their territories from newcomers however late they return from migration. In coastal birds, this applies both to breeding season territories (e.g. shelducks *Tadorna tadorna*; Pienkowski & Evans 1982) and winter feeding territories (e.g. grey plovers; Townshend 1985). It also holds for several passerines, e.g. song sparrow *Melospiza melodia* (Nice 1943), prairie warbler *Dendroica discolor* (Nolan 1978). Possibly, early arrival (which might be favoured by a shorter migration) could be advantageous to first-time breeders trying to obtain a territory in competition with other first-time breeders. Yet there would be little advantage in arriving before adults which could then readily displace newcomers from territories the adults had held previously, rather than waiting to find gaps left by non-returning older birds. However, when the possible breeding season is short, it is important to reach the breeding area at the right time; too early imperils survival, too late does not allow time for successful breeding and, especially for recruits, to obtain territories where there are gaps (see Pienkowski & Evans 1984).

Testing this idea is difficult, because its predictions would depend on a complex quantitative analysis of the interactions between seasonal factors in numerous different areas. Generally, however, the earlier that a bird needs to reach the breeding area, the nearer it should over-winter, because feeding conditions (and hence the ease of storing fat for migration) will be more difficult at sites along migration routes early in the spring (see below). In species in which males migrate north before females (and subsequently compete for territories on the breeding grounds), males winter further north than females (Myers 1981a). This finding, and other material reviewed by O'Connor (p. 105), support the hypothesis (Group B (i)) that competition for near wintering grounds results from competition for resources on the breeding grounds, provided that they are considered in combination with the evidence, reviewed earlier, for the existence of competition on the winter grounds. However, two problems arise.

(a) In Myers' (1981a) comparison, for two species in which the females are larger than the males and which show sequential polyandry, the females do not precede the males on migration nor (possibly with an exception in one species) do they winter closer. However, whilst in many species males may require a territory in order to have a chance of breeding, this does not appear to apply to females, even in species showing reversal of sexual roles (Evans & Pienkowski 1984). Even in species showing sequential polyandry, 'excess' males failed to secure mates (Hildén & Vuolanto 1972; Hildén 1979).

(b) Myers (1981a) asked why individuals did not winter further away and depart earlier. It is clear, however, that spring migration is difficult because of (i) the need to arrive at the breeding grounds at the right time (see above); (ii) the predominant headwinds in spring for migrants from southern areas (Moreau 1972); and (iii) the difficulty in time-tabling a migration schedule to cope with both these complications and with the need for time to feed and deposit fat (e.g. Dick 1979; Davidson 1984). The main period of productivity of prey animals, for shorebirds at least, occurs later in the summer, and by April and May food stocks are low after over-winter depletion (e.g. Evans *et al.* 1979; Dugan 1981). At this time of year, many shorebirds which have wintered in northwest Europe move (before their main long-distance migration) to sites further east where winter depletion of prey has been less, and where spring availability of prey is probably higher than in their winter quarters, due to a more rapid rise in temperature and consequent increased prey activity (Dugan 1981; Pienkowski & Prokosch 1982; Pienkowski 1983a; Pienkowski & Evans 1984).

Because high-arctic breeding species generally have later breeding seasons than those breeding in temperate areas, and since conditions in the temperate staging areas should improve rapidly in spring, one would expect less strong selection for high-arctic breeding species to stay close to the breeding areas in winter. Accordingly, one would expect leap-frog migration to be fairly common and, within a species, an inverse interpopulation correlation between breeding latitude and wintering latitude. Myers (1981b) did indeed find a Spearman coefficient of -0.37 ($P < 0.04$) in such an interspecific comparison.

Prediction, from the winter quarters, of the onset of suitable conditions on the breeding grounds

Alerstam & Högstedt (1980) proposed an alternative model to account for leap-frog migration. They postulated that there was competition for northern wintering grounds but that the benefits to temperate breeding shorebirds of remaining at northern sites was greater than to arctic breeding birds, so that they would be prepared to invest more to stay there. These benefits were thought to result because birds wintering in the same climatic zone as their breeding areas could monitor weather conditions indicative of those at the breeding grounds, enabling them to return as soon as possible to the breeding grounds and benefit from an early start to nesting. Slagsvold (1982) and Pienkowski, Evans & Townshend (1984) cast doubt on the validity of this model partly because of its assumptions (including that the timing of arctic seasons is less variable than temperate ones), and partly because evidence runs counter to the prediction that individual shorebirds vary the timing of their migrations from year to year. Pienkowski, Evans & Townshend (1984) agreed that there were advantages in shorebirds generally wintering as near to their breeding grounds as possible but suggested that differences in competitive ability, rather than differences in potential benefits, determined which birds stayed and which migrated further. As mentioned earlier, in grey plovers competitive ability amongst juveniles is related to size (Townshend 1985; see also Gauthreaux 1978, 1982 for general discussion). Within populations, size could of course be influenced by both genetic and environmental factors. The latter may be particularly important in view of the variability and shortness of the arctic growing season. In a comparison between populations of the same species in the east Atlantic region, Pienkowski *et al.* (1984) found that those with individuals of larger size generally wintered further north, so that leap-frog migration resulted simply when birds in a southern-breeding population were generally larger than those in a northern one.

The costs of migration select for short migration distances

The remarkable lengths of regular migratory journeys made by many birds are now so well established that some biologists seem to discount their costs. For example, apart from a single passing comment, Fretwell (1980) did not consider the risks of migration in his discussion of why birds migrate. However, reports of mass deaths of migrants, or of birds arriving in very weak and vulnerable condition, are fairly frequent, despite the obvious difficulty in making such observations (Dick & Pienkowski 1979; Greenberg 1980; Morse 1980; Evans & Pienkowski 1984).

If migration costs are important in minimizing migration distance, survival rates would be expected to decrease with increasing migration distance. Figure 19.1 lends some support to this expectation: because most of the estimates there (except some of those between 50° and 60°N) were based on work in temperate breeding areas, the scale of latitude of wintering areas approximates to one of migration distance.

It is possible that the costs of migration are experienced mainly in the first migration of young birds. Certainly they are low in adults, even of the smaller species (see Fig. 19.1 for annual survival rates; mortality over the period of spring and autumn migrations and the breeding season averaged 7% and 9% in turnstone *Arenaria interpres* and sanderling, respectively; Evans & Pienkowski 1984). Most of the anecdotal reports of high casualties during migration relate to young birds, and young individuals are more frequently found in a wider spread of areas and habitats than are adults (e.g. Gromadzka 1983; Pienkowski & Evans 1984), but some would argue that this behaviour is adaptive (Baker 1978). Unfortunately, very few direct measures of first-year survival are available, especially for migratory populations of shorebirds. The situation is even worse for most other migratory bird species, possibly with the exception of geese—whose restricted winter ranges make a comparative approach impracticable.

Some evidence that the higher annual mortality of young birds than adults occurs primarily during their first migration comes from studies of sanderlings that settled for the winter at Teesmouth. Having arrived after long migration, overwintering adults and juveniles had similar rates of survival (Table 19.2). In contrast, juvenile dunlins ringed during migration through Poland

TABLE 19.2. Overwinter mortality of juvenile sanderlings *Calidris alba* marked at Teesmouth in autumn, compared with those of adults in the same year (for methods of estimation see Evans & Pienkowski 1984)

Year	Season of marking	Juveniles		Adults	
		No. marked	% mortality	No. with marks	% mortality
1979–80	early Oct	10	0	48	8
1980–81	early Nov	12	0	106	11
1981–82	Oct/Nov	9	11	132	15
	late Dec/Jan	21	14		

produced four times more recoveries in September per bird ringed than did adults (Gromadzka 1983). The chance of recoveries of juveniles decreased in later months, approximating to the rate for adults by December. This marked difference in the ringing recovery rate during the migration period occurred despite the fact that most juvenile dunlins ringed in Poland had already migrated from breeding grounds in northern USSR.

The fact that, at least for some species, adults appear not to attempt to compete for winter quarters, but simply return to those used in their first year, lends support to the view that it is conditions and decisions taken in the first year of life which are critical. This is especially so, if one follows Myers (1984) in arguing that, rather than optimizing their behaviour, birds exhibit 'behavioural inertia: do something as long as it works' and 'drift through routines that meet each requirement but optimize none.'

Why should there be such a high premium for young birds to settle as far north as possible? Since most shorebirds delay breeding until their second or third year of life, and many spend their first summer(s) south of the breeding range, the answer cannot be to gain access to breeding resources. However, the risks of migration reviewed above apply particularly to young birds. Those in the arctic have to deposit fat reserves almost simultaneously with (or even before) completing growth. They generally migrate later and have less suitable weather for migration than adults; and probably inherit only a direction of travel so that they do not know exactly where their target lies. Indeed, at each stage of their journey (once they have reached the nearest environmentally acceptable wintering area, a minimal distance which is presumably achieved by genetically controlled, time-programmed migrations; see Berthold 1984), they are unlikely to know the distance to the next suitable piece of habitat. Consequently, they may always deposit relatively large fat reserves as an insurance against the possibility of long flights to the next possible wintering site. For example, a bird leaving an estuary on the shores of the North Sea may have only a few kilometres to travel before the next suitable site; leaving a site in Morocco, it may have several thousand. This situation will have changed rapidly in geological time. At its worst, during glacial maxima and shortly afterwards, estuaries would have been very restricted sites along the edge of the continental shelf. Thus, once within the general wintering area of its population, the major factor influencing a young shorebird to try to stay at the first sites reached may be that, from its viewpoint, there might not be any other sites or, if there are, these could be very distant.

There is no doubt that shorebirds are adapted to extend their winter range as far northwards as possible, by carrying fat reserves as an 'insurance' against periods of several days when weather is too severe to allow them to meet their energy requirements. The size of these reserves is greater in places where the risk of prolonged severe weather is higher (Pienkowski, Lloyd & Minton 1979; Davidson 1982; Dugan et al. 1981; Pienkowski et al. 1984). Survival rates of a variety of species of shorebirds at Teesmouth (54°N), north-east England, close to the northern limit of the non-breeding range, are high (Fig. 19.1) in spite of the cold winter climate. The annual cycles of shorebirds also show adaptations according to their main wintering areas. Those populations wintering in the north temperate zone finish their moult early and rapidly in autumn. Those 'wintering' in the tropics or southern hemisphere spread moult into the 'winter' or even throughout the non-breeding season (Pienkowski et al. 1976).

IMPLICATIONS OF MIGRATION FOR POPULATION DYNAMICS IN SHOREBIRDS

In this paper, we have tried to account for the presence in a single non-breeding area of individuals of any one shorebird species from a variety of breeding areas and of different ages and sexes. The limited data are most consistent with the view that there is competition for winter quarters as near to the breeding grounds as is habitable, probably because young birds gain a strong advantage by settling in the first suitable site they reach within their (presumably inherited) winter range. For most species, in subsequent years, an individual gains other advantages by returning to a site with which it has become familiar, and at which it was able to overwinter safely as an inexperienced bird, even if this site was not as near to the breeding grounds as possible. Even though the conditions to which an individual must respond at a particular site vary greatly in different years, not least because of variations in numbers of conspecifics, the patterns of distribution observed at any one time may be the consequence of behaviours of individuals established in response to a variety of conditions over the past several years. A further reason for wintering close to the breeding grounds may be that this also reduces the difficulties of return migration at a time of year when the nesting areas become habitable, and so increases the chance of breeding successfully. Our conclusions concerning selective factors acting on migrant shorebirds show some parallels with those of Ketterson & Nolan (1983), who studied a passerine species, the dark-eyed junco *Junco hyemalis*, in the USA, even though their study species apparently showed a shift of winter quarters between its first and later years of life.

Competition implies that there are density-dependent processes restricting juvenile settlement in a given area, and thereby affecting the chances of survival of those that have to travel further. We suspect that major losses of young occur during their first migratory flights and in securing a suitable wintering site; certainly survival of both adults and juveniles after settlement in winter quarters appears to be very high.

There is abundant evidence that intra-specific interactions, between individuals from different breeding sites, could occur at many different places along the first migration route of juveniles, and not only on potential wintering grounds. Before migration, small parties of birds gather on good feeding areas to lay down fat reserves for the long migratory flights. In Greenland, these parties include birds from valleys where reproduction may have been early and good, and from adjacent valleys where, because of the vagaries of precipitation the previous winter, breeding was later and less successful (Green *et al.* 1977). Birds from many breeding areas may assemble on a common moulting site, e.g. redshanks *Tringa totanus* from Iceland and continental Europe on the Waddensea (Boere 1976). This also happens at important refuelling sites on autumn migration, e.g. dunlins from Iceland at The Wash, alongside moulting dunlins that had bred in northern Russia. Juveniles late to arrive at refuelling sites may be faced with considerable reductions in prey density, possibly to levels at which intraspecific interactions during foraging could reduce chances of survival (Schneider & Harrington 1981).

Thus, it is not only at potential wintering sites that the chances of survival of juveniles from one breeding area might be affected by the presence of birds from other breeding areas. If we are to look for population regulation in shorebirds, then studies in a single breeding area or wintering site are unlikely to be sufficient. Attention should rather be focused on the migratory losses of juveniles and the causes of these. Amongst these should be included interspecific as well as intraspecific interactions, for it is clear that, under adverse foraging conditions, large species sometimes oust smaller species from feeding sites (see e.g. Smith 1975).

Even for shorebirds, for which there are better data on survival rates than for most seasonally migratory animals, the data with which to test ideas of the adaptive advantages of different patterns of migration are sadly few. More studies are needed of the survival values of different migratory strategies by birds using a single breeding area, of productivities in arctic areas, and of survival rates measured at arctic and low-latitude sites, to compare with those available from the temperate zone. Valid estimates of survival rates need studies in at least 2 years, and if any investigations are to be made of annual fluctuations, which may be crucial to the strategies adopted by long-lived animals, extended periods of study are essential.

ACKNOWLEDGMENTS

Our debt to Dr David Townshend, both for allowing us to make extensive use of the results of his studies before publication and for constructive criticism of our ideas, will be apparent. We are also most grateful to present and past colleagues, particularly Dr Nicholas Davidson, Dr Patrick Dugan and Mrs Ann Pienkowski, for their contributions which have allowed us to begin to test some of the ideas discussed in this paper. Work at Teesmouth was made possible by permission for access to important intertidal sites by the Tees and Hartlepool Port Authority and the British Steel Corporation. Many persons from the Zoology Department at Durham University and the Teesmouth Bird Club assisted in the programme of catching and marking shorebirds, and in the subsequent observations of colour-marked individuals. Observations from elsewhere in Europe have been co-ordinated through the Wader Study Group. We gratefully acknowledge the financial support for various aspects of our studies on shorebirds from Nature Conservancy Council, Natural Environment Research Council, Science and Engineering Research Council, Nuffield Foundation, and the Commission of the European Communities.

REFERENCES

Alerstam, T. & Högstedt, G. (1980). Spring predictability and leap-frog migration. *Ornis Scandinavica*, **11**, 196–200.
Alerstam, T. & Högstedt, G. (1983). Reply to Wesolowski. *Ornis Scandinavica*, **14**, 246–247.
Altenburg, W., Engelmoer, M., Mes, R. & Piersma, T. (1982). *Wintering waders on the Banc d'Arguin*. Comm. No. 6 of the Wadden Sea Working Group, Leiden.
Baker, R.R. (1978). *The Evolutionary Ecology of Animal Migration*. Hodder & Stoughton, London.
Berthold, P. (1984). The endogenous control of bird migration: a survey of experimental evidence. *Bird Study*, **31**, 19–27.
Boere, G.C. (1976). The significance of the Dutch Waddenzee in the annual life cycle of arctic, subarctic and boreal waders. Part 1. The function as a moulting area. *Ardea*, **64**, 210–291.
Boyd, H. (1962). Mortality and fertility of the European Charadrii. *Ibis*, **104**, 68–87.

Cox, G.W. (1968). The role of competition in the evolution of migration. *Evolution*, **22**, 180–192.

Davidson, N.C. (1982). Changes in the body-condition of redshanks during mild winters: an inability to regulate reserves? *Ringing & Migration*, **4**, 51–62.

Davidson, N.C. (1984). How valid are flight range estimates for waders? *Ringing & Migration*, **5**, 49–64.

Dick, W.J.A. (1979). Results of the WSG project on the spring migration of Siberian knot *Calidris canutus* in 1979. *Wader Study Group Bulletin*, **27**, 8–13.

Dick, W.J.A. & Pienkowski, M.W. (1979). Autumn and early winter weights of waders in north-west Africa. *Ornis Scandinavica*, **10**, 117–123.

Dick, W.J.A., Pienkowski, M.W., Waltner, M.A. & Minton, C.D.T. (1976). Distribution and geographical origins of knots *Calidris canutus* wintering in Europe and Africa. *Ardea*, **64**, 22–47.

Dugan, P.J. (1981). *Seasonal movements of shorebirds in relation to spacing behaviour and prey availability*. Ph.D. thesis, University of Durham.

Dugan, P.J., Evans, P.R., Goodyer, L.R. & Davidson, N.C. (1981). Winter fat reserves in shorebirds: disturbance of regulated levels by severe weather conditions. *Ibis*, **123**, 359–363.

Elkins, N. (1983). *Weather and Bird Behaviour*. T. & A.D. Poyser, Calton.

Evans, P.R. (1981). Migration and dispersal of shorebirds as a survival strategy. *Feeding and Survival Strategies of Estuarine Organisms* (Ed. by N.V. Jones & W.J. Wolff), pp. 275–290. Plenum Press, New York.

Evans, P.R. & Pienkowski, M.W. (1984). Population dynamics of shorebirds. *Behavior of Marine Animals. Vol. 5. Shorebirds. Breeding Biology and Populations* (Ed. by J. Burger & B. Olla), pp. 83–123. Plenum Press, New York.

Evans. P.R., Henderson, D.M., Knights, P.J. & Pienkowski, M.W. (1979). Short-term effects of reclamation of part of Seal Sands, Teesmouth, on wintering waders and Shelduck. *Oecologia (Berlin)*, **41**, 183–206.

Fretwell, S.D. (1980). Evolution of migration in relation to factors regulating bird numbers. *Migrant Birds in the Neotropics* (Ed. by A. Keast & E. Morton), pp. 517–527. Smithsonian Institution Press, Washington, D.C.

Gauthreaux, S.A., Jr. (1978). The ecological significance of behavioral dominance. *Perspectives in Ethology* (Ed. by P.P.G. Bateson & P.H. Klopfer), pp. 17–54. Plenum, New York.

Gauthreaux, S.A., Jr. (1982). The ecology and evolution of avian migration systems. *Avian Biology. Vol. 6*. (Ed. by D.S. Farner, J.R. King & K.C. Parkes), pp. 93–168. Academic Press, New York.

Goss-Custard, J.D. (1977). The ecology of the Wash. III. Density-related behaviour and the possible effects of a loss of feeding grounds on wading birds (Charadrii). *Journal of Applied Ecology*, **14**, 721–739.

Goss-Custard, J.D. (1981). Role of winter food supplies in the population ecology of common British wading birds. *Verhandlungen der Ornithologischen Gesellschaft in Bayern*, **23**, 125–146.

Green, G.H., Greenwood, J.J.D. & Lloyd, C.S. (1977). The influence of snow conditions on the date of breeding of wading birds in north-east Greenland. *Journal of Zoology*, **183**, 311–328.

Greenberg, R.S. (1980). Demographic aspects of long-distance migration. *Migrant Birds in the Neotropics*. (Ed. by A. Keast & E. Morton), pp. 493–504. Smithsonian Institute Press, Washington, D.C.

Gromadzka, J. (1983). Results of bird ringing in Poland: migrations of Dunlin *Calidris alpina*. *Acta Ornithologica (Warszawa)*, **19**, 113–136.

Hale, W.G. (1980). *Waders*. Collins, London.

Hildén, O. (1979). Territoriality and site tenacity of Temminck's Stint *Calidris temminckii*. *Ornis Fennica*, **56**, 56–74.

Hildén, O. & Vuolanto, S. (1972). Breeding biology of the Red-necked Phalarope *Phalaropus lobatus* in Finland. *Ornis Fennica*, 49, 57–85.

Holmes, R.T. (1970). Differences in population density, territoriality, and food supply of Dunlin on arctic and sub-arctic tundra. *Animal Populations in Relation to their Food Resources* (Ed. by A. Watson), pp. 303–317. Blackwell Scientific Publications, Oxford.

Ketterson. E.D. & Nolan, V., Jr. (1983). The evolution of differential bird migration. *Current Ornithology. Vol. 1.* (Ed. by R.F. Johnston), pp. 357–402. Plenum Press, New York & London.

Lakhani, K.M. & Newton, I. (1983). Estimating age-specific bird survival rates from ring recoveries—can it be done? *Journal of Animal Ecology*, 52, 83–92.

Larson, S. (1960). On the influence of the arctic fox, *Alopex lagopus*, on the distribution of arctic birds. *Oikos*, 11, 276–305.

Mahéo, R. (1978–83). *Limicoles séjournant en France.* Reports by BIROE France and Office National de la Chasse.

Marchant, J.H. (1982). Waders. *Wildfowl and Wader Counts 1981–82* (Ed. by D.G. Salmon), pp. 31–50. The Wildfowl Trust, Slimbridge, Glos.

Mason, C.F. (1984). The passage of waders at an inland reservoir in Leicestershire. *Ringing & Migration*, 5, 133–140.

Meire, P. & Kuyken, E. (1984). Relations between the distribution of waders and the intertidal benthic fauna of the Oosterschelde, Netherlands. *Coastal Waders and Wildfowl in Winter* (Ed. by P.R. Evans, J.D. Goss-Custard & W.G. Hale), pp. 57–68. University Press, Cambridge.

Minton, C.D.T. (1975). *The Waders of The Wash—Ringing and Biometric studies.* Report of Scientific Study G of The Wash Storage Scheme Feasibility Study, to the Natural Environment Research Council.

Moreau, R.E. (1972). *The Palaearctic–African Bird Migration Systems.* Academic Press, London.

Morse, D.H. (1980). Population limitation: breeding or wintering grounds? *Migrant Birds in the Neotropics.* (Ed. by A. Keast & E. Morton), pp. 505–516. Smithsonian Institution Press, Washington, D.C.

Myers, J.P. (1980). Sanderlings *Calidris alba* at Bodega Bay: facts, inferences and shameless speculations. *Wader Study Group Bulletin*, 30, 26–32.

Myers, J.P. (1981a). A test of three hypotheses for latitudinal segregation of the sexes in wintering birds. *Canadian Journal of Zoology*, 59, 1527–1534.

Myers, J.P. (1981b). Cross-seasonal interactions in the evolution of sandpiper social systems. *Behavioural Ecology and Sociobiology*, 8, 195–202.

Myers, J.P. (1984). Spacing behavior of nonbreeding shorebirds. *Behavior of Marine Animals. Vol. 6. Shorebirds. Migration and Foraging Behavior* (Ed. by J. Burger & B. Olla), pp. 271–321. Plenum Press, New York.

Nice, M.M. (1943). Studies in the life history of the song sparrow. Vol. 2. *Transactions of the Linnean Society of New York*, 6, 1–328.

Nolan, V., Jr. (1978). The ecology and behavior of the prairie warbler *Dendroica discolor*. *Ornithological Monographs*, 26, 1–595.

O'Connor, R.J. (1981). Comparisons between migrant and non-migrant birds in Britain. *Animal Migration* (Ed. by D.J. Aidley), pp. 167–195. University Press, Cambridge.

Pienkowski, M.W. (1983a). Surface activity of some intertidal invertebrates in relation to temperature and the foraging behaviour of their shorebird predators. *Marine Ecology Progress Series*, 11, 141–150.

Pienkowski, M.W. (1983b). Habitat specialization in breeding shorebirds: a defence against egg-predation? *Wader Study Group Bulletin*, 39, 50.

Pienkowski, M.W. (1984). Breeding biology and population dynamics of Ringed plovers *Charadrius hiaticula* in Britain and Greenland: nest-predation as a possible factor limiting distribution and timing of breeding. *Journal of Zoology*, 202, 83–114.

Pienkowski, M.W. & Dick, W.J.A. (1976). Some biases in cannon- and mist-netted samples of wader populations. *Ringing & Migration,* **1,** 105–107.

Pienkowski, M.W. & Evans, P.R. (1982). Breeding behaviour, productivity and survival of colonial and non-colonial Shelducks *Tadorna tadorna. Ornis Scandinavica,* **13,** 101–116.

Pienkowski, M.W. & Evans, P.R. (1984). Migratory behavior in the western Palearctic. *Behavior of Marine Animals. Vol. 6. Shorebirds. Migration and Foraging Behavior* (Ed. by J. Burger & B. Olla), pp. 73–123. Plenum Press, New York.

Pienkowski, M.W. & Pienkowski, A.E. (1983). WSG project on the movements of wader populations in western Europe: eighth progress report. *Wader Study Group Bulletin,* **38,** 13–22.

Pienkowski, M.W. & Prokosch, P. (1982). Wanderungsmuster von Watvögeln zwischen de Küsten-Ländern West-Europas—Bericht über ein laufendes Projekt. *Seevögel,* **3,** 123–128.

Pienkowski, M.W., Evans, P.R. & Townshend, D.J. (1984). Leap-frog and other migration patterns of waders: a critique of the Alerstam and Hogstedt hypothesis, and some alternatives. *Ornis Scandinavica,* **15** (in press).

Pienkowski, M.W., Lloyd, C.S. & Minton, C.D.T. (1979). Seasonal and migrational weight changes in Dunlins. *Bird Study,* **26,** 134–148.

Pienkowski, M.W., Knight, P.J., Stanyard, D.J. & Argyle F.B. (1976). The primary moult of waders on the Atlantic coast of Morocco. *Ibis,* **118,** 347–365.

Pienkowski, M.W., Ferns, P.N., Davidson, N.C. & Worrall, D.H. (1984). Balancing the budget: problems in measuring the energy intake and requirements of shorebirds in the field. *Coastal Waders and Wildfowl in Winter* (Ed. by P.R. Evans, J.D. Goss-Custard & W.G. Hale), pp. 29–56. University Press, Cambridge.

Prater, A.J. (1974). The population and migration of Knot in Europe. *Proceedings of the International Waterfowl Research Bureau Wader Symposium, Warsaw 1973,* pp. 93–113. IWRB, Warszawa.

Prater, A.J. (1974, 1976, 1977, 1982). Wader Research Group report. *International Waterfowl Research Bureau Bulletin,* **37,** 102–104; **41/42,** 60–65; **43/44,** 47–50; **47,** 74–78.

Robertson, H.G. (1981). Annual summer and winter fluctuations of Palaearctic and resident waders (Charadrii) at Langebaan Lagoon, South Africa, 1975–1979. *Proceedings of the Symposium on Birds of the Sea and Shore* (Ed. by J. Cooper), pp. 335–345. African Seabird Group, Cape Town.

Salomonsen, F. (1955). The evolutionary significance of bird migration. *Det Kongelige Danske Videnskabernes Selskab, Biolgiske Meddelelser,* **22,** 1–62.

Schneider, D.C. & Harrington, B.A. (1981). Timing of shorebird migration in relation to prey depletion. *Auk,* **98,** 801–811.

Slagsvold, T. (1982). Spring predictability and bird migration and breeding times: a comment on the phenomenon of leap-frog migration. *Ornis Scandinavica,* **13,** 145–148.

Smith, P.C. (1975). *A study of winter feeding ecology and behaviour of the Bar-tailed Godwit* Limosa lapponica. Ph.D. thesis, University of Durham.

Sutherland, W.J. (1982). Food supply and dispersal in the determination of wintering population levels of oystercatchers, *Haematopus ostralegus. Estuarine, Coastal and Shelf Science,* **14,** 223–229.

Swennen, C. (1984). Differences in quality of roosting flocks of Oystercatchers. *Coastal Waders and Wildfowl in Winter* (Ed. by P.R. Evans, J.D. Goss-Custard & W.G. Hale), pp. 177–189. University Press, Cambridge.

Symonds, F.L., Langslow, D.R. & Pienkowski, M.W. (1984). Movements of wintering shorebirds within the Firth of Forth: species differences in usage of an intertidal complex. *Biological Conservation,* **28,** 187–215.

Thomas, D.G. (1970). Fluctuations of numbers of waders in south-eastern Tasmania. *Emu,* **70,** 79–85.

Townshend, D.J. (1985). Decisions for a lifetime: establishment of spatial defence and movement patterns by juvenile grey plovers (*Pluvialis squatarola*). *Journal of Animal Ecology*, **54** (in press).

von Haartman, L. (1968). The evolution of resident versus migratory habit in birds, Some considerations. *Ornis Fennica*, **45**, 1–7.

Zwarts, L. (1974). *Vogels van het brakke getijgebied.* Amsterdam.

Zwarts, L. & Wanink, J. (1984). How Oystercatchers and Curlews successively deplete clams. *Coastal Waders and Wildfowel in Winter* (Ed. by P.R. Evans, J.D. Goss-Custard & W.G. Hale), pp. 69–83. University Press, Cambridge.

20. TERRITORY SIZE, REPRODUCTIVE SUCCESS AND POPULATION DYNAMICS IN THE GREAT TIT, *PARUS MAJOR*

R. H. McCLEERY AND C. M. PERRINS

Edward Grey Institute, University of Oxford, Oxford

SUMMARY

Great tits defend territories. The size of the territory, estimated from the Dirichlet tesselation on the occupied nest boxes, affects the nesting success. Small territories have smaller clutches and lower hatching and fledging success than large territories; the reduced hatching and fledging success may be the result of higher predation. Territory size is necessarily inversely correlated with nesting density; predation tends to be more severe in years of high nest density, but there is also evidence that smaller territories suffer more losses than larger territories within the same year.

The key factor determining fluctuations in the population is mortality during the late summer and autumn. While nesting losses do not appear to have important consequences for population size they may be important for individuals, who would be more successful if they were able to maintain large territories. Recruitment into the breeding population is density-dependent, but there is no evidence that settlement is ever prevented completely because there is no more space available.

INTRODUCTION

There has been much discussion of the factors affecting animal numbers. Many factors have been related to density, showing greater effects at high than at low densities. The extent to which such factors may regulate numbers at the levels observed in nature has also been of considerable interest (Lack 1966).

Particularly amongst higher animals, intraspecific spacing is potentially capable of setting a limit to the numbers which can live in any given area; many birds and mammals show strong territorial behaviour either all the year round or during the period prior to and during breeding. The possible functions of territory have been much discussed (see, for example, Davies & Houston 1984) and one or more of the following are commonly thought to be important:

(i) a secure place in which pair formation can occur and where the pair are able to get on with breeding with the minimum of disturbance from other conspecifics;

(ii) a place in which the pair are relatively free from intraspecific competition and can expect to be able to obtain the necessary food for their growing family;

(iii) increasing the spacing between pairs may reduce the risk of disease or predation (Krebs 1971; Dunn 1977).

It is not our aim here to discuss the relative merits of the evidence relating to the general advantages of territorial behaviour; we are concerned only with the effects of territorial spacing on the breeding biology and breeding success of the great tit, *Parus major*.

A number of aspects of great tit breeding biology have been shown to vary in relation to breeding density.

(i) Clutch size decreases with increasing density (e.g. Lack 1966; Perrins 1965; Dhondt 1977).

(ii) The proportion of the population which has second broods decreases with increasing density (Kluijver 1951; Dhondt 1977). This feature is very important on the European mainland where second broods are common, but is not very important in Britain where, for some reason, second broods are not common in most habitats.

(iii) Hatching success is density-dependent (Krebs 1970), largely because predators (mainly weasels, *Mustela nivalis*), take more nests when the tits are nesting at high density than at low (Krebs 1971; Dunn 1977).

(iv) Nestling mortality is density-dependent, probably because of competition for food between the adults feeding their young (Dhondt 1977).

The observations that, other things being equal, birds breeding at low densities have more young per nesting attempt, have more nesting attempts per year and are more likely to raise their young than birds nesting at high densities are mostly based on comparisons of nesting success between years when the breeding densities are different. However, it could be advantageous for a pair of birds to have a large territory at any time. In this paper we try to see whether any of the observed density effects occur within, as well as between, years. In addition, we briefly consider the evidence as to whether the proportion of birds able to settle in the wood depends on the number of birds present in mid-winter, which is an indication of the number seeking to establish territories and breed.

METHODS

Great tit population data

The data on which this paper are based come from a study of great tits carried out on the Wytham Estate near Oxford. The study was started in 1947 by Drs

D. Lack and J.A. Gibb, in a 26 ha section of the estate, known as Marley Wood, which was reasonably separate from most of the other wooded areas. Between 1958 and 1963 the study was gradually expanded to cover all the woodland areas of the estate, with some 950 nest boxes throughout the woodland. The nest boxes are not moved unless minor shifts of position are necessitated by, for example, tree fall. Nest box positions are all mapped against a system of grid poles erected at 100 m intervals throughout the wood.

Most of the analyses presented here are based on the data for Marley wood which has longer runs of data than any other area. The density of nesting boxes over many of the other areas of the wood is lower than in Marley and, perhaps because the pairs are spaced further apart as a result, there seem to be fewer signs of effects of density. We are currently carrying out an analysis of the population data for the whole wood since 1960 which will be published separately.

The data are derived from regular visits to the nesting boxes throughout the breeding season. Weekly visits were sufficient to provide the information on: (i) date of laying, (ii) clutch-size, (iii) number of young hatched and (iv) number of young fledged; eggs or young taken by predators could normally easily be recognized. Most of the parent birds were trapped while they were feeding young, making it possible to establish the number of young birds from any cohort which survived to reach breeding age. By trapping in the winter (and using those birds caught breeding for a mark–release–recapture estimate) it was possible to estimate the number of young which survived from fledging to mid-winter. All the data are stored in the Oxford University computer as a network database using the ICL/Cullinane Integrated Database Management System (IDMS). For further details of methods used see Perrins (1965, 1979).

Measuring the breeding density at a nest site

The most commonly used method for measuring local density for an array of points such as occupied nest sites is to use the distance to the nearest occupied point (nest box). However, we feel that there are disadvantages to this approach; for example, two points close together but at some distance from others may have the same nearest neighbour distance (to each other) as points that lie at the centre of a dense cluster. Partly to circumvent this problem, and partly because it seems a more realistic measure of the area around each box, we decided to use a measure based on the Dirichlet tesselation (Mead 1971) formed from the positions of occupied boxes in each year. We used all occupied nest sites including probable re-lays of failed nests (judged by date) for the tesselation, though the re-lays were not used in the subsequent analyses. In Wytham, great tits occupying nest boxes are in one to one correspondence with the territories detected by playback; there is no evidence that pairs occupy boxes but do not hold territories, though this has been seen elsewhere (Eyckerman 1974).

The area of the Theissen polygon (Rhynsburger 1973) containing each nest box was used as the measure of breeding density for that box in that year. The Theissen polygon is the area containing all points that are closer to the generating point than to any other. The tesselation corresponds to a very simple model of territory in which once birds have selected a nest site the strength of their defensive behaviour is proportional to the distance from the nest, all birds being assumed to have the same fighting ability. A minor complication is that the tesselation procedure we used requires that the area to be tesselated should be convex, which is not true of the boundary of Marley Wood. Hence, it was necessary to form the tesselation in a rectangle enclosing the wood and then find the area of intersection between any polygon which cut the wood boundary and the polygon defining the wood edge. The manipulations were carried out on the Oxford University computer using a library of routines originating from the Geographical Algorithm Group (GAG), University of East Anglia.

We checked the relationship between the Theissen polygons and the actual territory boundaries for 1983, using a map kindly provided by Dr P.K. McGregor for the locations of territories at the end of May based on song playback results. Not surprisingly, the fit between the actual boundaries and the polygon edges was not strikingly good; two reasons for the poor fit are that some areas within the wood boundary are not suitable habitat and are not occupied by great tits and that great tits are not idealized equally competitive animals living in a uniform space. There are also uncertainties about the precise positions of some territory boundaries near the edge of the wood. We found that the correlation coefficient for polygon areas with real territory areas was between 0·4 and 0·5, depending on how much special pleading was allowed for uncertainties in the real territory boundaries and the existence of no-man's land; for comparison, the correlation between actual territory area and nearest neighbour distance was between 0·2 and 0·3. Polygons which cut the wood boundary tend to be larger than those which do not ($F_{1,973}$) = 33·8; $P < 0·001$); Krebs (1971) found that real territories on the edge of the Marley wood tended to be larger than those nearer the centre.

RESULTS

Temporal changes in the density dependence of clutch size

As a preliminary to the main analysis we decided to check the relationship between clutch size and population density previously reported for Wytham

TABLE 20.1. Regression analysis of mean clutch size on (a) population size (b) median laydate and population size: Marley 1947–83; df for *t*-tests are 35 in (a) and 34 in (b)

	Const	Population size	*t*	Median laydate	*t*	$\bar{R}^2$
(a)	10·04	−0·03	3·05	—	—	0·19
(b)	12·82	−0·04	4·30	−0·09	4·24	0·48

great tits by Lack (1966) and Perrins (1965). Clutch size is particularly interesting since it represents in some sense a 'decision' by the birds as to how many young they should try to raise in a particular season, unlike brood size or fledging success which are affected to a large extent by factors outside the control of the adults.

A regression analysis using the now much longer run of data from Marley Wood (37 years) appears to confirm that the clutch size of the great tit varies in relation to density. As noted by Perrins (1965) the relationship is complicated by the fact that the clutch size is also markedly affected by the data of laying; the earlier the lying starts in any year, the larger the average clutch tends to be. A regression of clutch size on both laying date and density of breeding pairs shows that both factors are significant and together explain about 50% of the variation in clutch size between 1947 and 1983 (Table 20.1).

However, as can be seen by looking at Fig. 20.1, there seems to be a difference between the years 1947–61 and 1962–83. Table 20.2 shows the effect of fitting the two-parameter regression model separately to the two sets of data. In the early period, which roughly corresponds to the data used by Lack (1966) and Perrins (1965), the density-dependent effect is strong and the model accounts for a high proportion of the total variance ($\bar{R}^2 = 0.78$); this result is

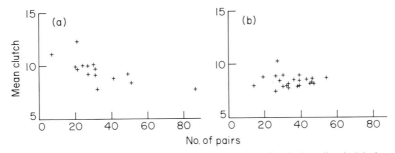

FIG. 20.1. Scatter plot of mean clutch size against a number of pairs breeding in Marley wood: (a) 1947–61; (b) 1962–83.

TABLE 20.2. Regression analysis of mean clutch size on population and median laydate: Marley (a) 1947–61, (b) 1962–83; d.f. for *t*-tests are 12 in (a), 19 in (b)

	Const	Population size	t	Median laydate	t	$\bar{R}^2$
(a)	13·82	−0·06	6·63	−0·09	4·52	0·78
(b)	9·56	0·00	0·01	−0·04	1·15	0·00

robust, even when outlying points such as 1961, which had an exceptionally high population (86 pairs), are eliminated. In the later period there is no sign of a relationship; again this result is robust against outlier effects. The mean clutch sizes for the earlier period have a higher standard error than the later ones, and the mean of the yearly means for the earlier period is significantly higher than for the later years (mean clutch size 9·5 against 8·4, two-sample *t*-test: $t = 3·43$, d.f. $= 18·8$, $P < 0·01$). There seems little doubt that some unidentified change has occurred since the early years of the study.

Prior to 1958 the only part of Wytham wood containing boxes was Marley, but during the years 1958–63 boxes were introduced to the surrounding woodland, thus providing increased nesting opportunities. No obvious effect can be seen in the population of Marley itself (Fig. 20.2); for

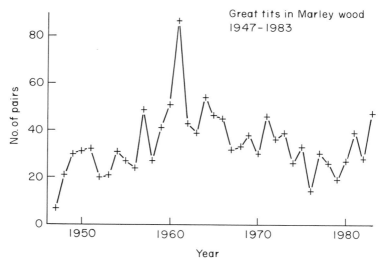

FIG. 20.2. Breeding population of Marley wood (no. of pairs) for the years 1947–83.

example, there is no sudden drop in numbers such as might have occurred if it had previously been overcrowded and part of the population had moved out to nest in the newly created nest sites elsewhere. However, it is possible that the existence of a much larger area in which potential recruits to the population could settle has altered the balance of factors which previously resulted in the relationship between clutch size and population size. The problem remains under investigation.

Nest site density and reproductive output

Although the negative density dependence between clutch size and population size may have disappeared since the early 1960s we will present some evidence that reproductive output may be related to nest site dispersion. The most likely mechanism for such an effect is predation, which seems to affect nests which are close together more frequently than those which are widely spaced (Krebs 1971; Dunn 1977). That such effects may be important to great tits is suggested by the observation that nest sites are overdispersed (Krebs 1970, 1971). In this part of our paper we look again at the effects of nest site dispersal on reproductive success.

Clutch size, brood size and number fledged

Figure 20.3 shows the mean clutch sizes for five levels of polygon size in increments of 3500 m^2. The means differ significantly between the area classes ($F_{(5,1153)} = 5.85$; $P < 0.001$). The effect is not very marked, and seems to be mainly that polygons of 3500 m^2 or less tend to be associated with smaller than average clutches. However, Fig. 20.3 was obtained by pooling all the data for all years. Since mean polygon area in any year is bound to be correlated with population size the relationship between mean clutch size and polygon area probably reflects the between-years density effect which was significant overall (Table 20.1) even though it petered out half way through the study.

In order to separate the two effects we carried out a two-way analysis of variance with repeated measures (as implemented in BMDP2V; Dixon 1981) using year and polygon size class as grouping variables. We split polygon areas into those above and below 7000 m^2 on the basis of Fig. 20.3. Analysis of variance (Table 20.3) shows that the between-years effect was indeed causing the apparent relationship between clutch size and polygon area, there being no significant effect due to polygon size alone. We repeated the analysis using only data for 1947–61, thinking that a within-years effect might have existed during the time that the between-years density effect on clutch size was

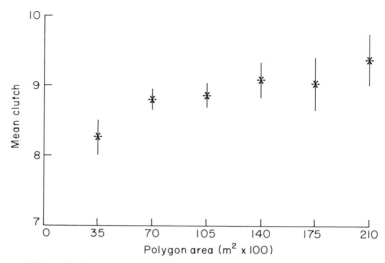

Fig. 20.3. Mean clutch size plotted against the area of the Theissen polygon containing the nest box (expressed in increments of 3500 m²). All data for 1947–83; the vertical lines are 95% confidence intervals.

present, but the results were essentially identical; there was no effect of polygon area alone.

Figure 20.4 and Table 20.4 show an identical analysis for brood size (i.e. number of hatched eggs). Again small polygon areas are associated with small broods, but the difference between the smallest polygons and the rest is even more marked ($F_{(5,989)} = 4.95$; $P < 0.01$). The two-way ANOVA shows that in this case there is a just significant effect of polygon area within years ($P = 0.02$), and there is no interaction between year and polygon area; therefore the effects of polygon area and year on brood size are independent.

TABLE 20.3. Two-way analysis of variance showing the effect of calendar year (YEAR) and polygon area (AREA) on clutch size

Source of variance	Sum of squares	d.f.	Mean square	F	P
YEAR	318·81	32	9·96	4·66	0·00
AREA	0·19	1	0·19	0·09	0·77
Y × A	47·46	32	1·48	0·69	0·90
MEAN	31908·49	1			
ERROR	1758·88	822			

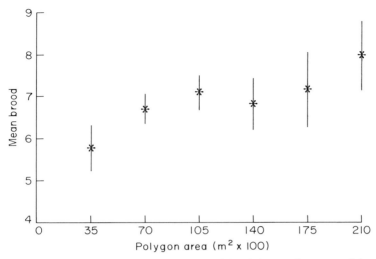

FIG. 20.4. Mean brood size plotted against the area of the Theissen polygon containing the nest box (expressed in increments of 3500 m²). All data for 1947–83; the vertical lines are 95% confidence intervals.

Figure 20.5 shows a similar analysis for number fledged. Again, small territories did worse than the rest ($F_{(5,988)} = 18\cdot13$; $P < 0\cdot01$) and the independent effect of polygon area in the two-way ANOVA is just significant ($F_{(1,869)} = 4\cdot69$; $P = 0\cdot03$), with no interaction between polygon area and year ($P = 0\cdot53$). As before, we can conclude that there is a consistent independent effect of polygon area on number fledged within years.

Hatching success and fledging success

So far we have shown that two measures of reproductive output, brood size and number fledged, are inversely related to the absolute size of the area

TABLE 20.4. Two-way analysis of variance showing the effect of calendar year (YEAR) and polygon area AREA on brood size

Source of variance	Sum of squares	d.f.	Mean square	F	P
YEAR	849·24	32	26·54	2·61	< 0·001
AREA	53·35	1	53·35	5·25	0·02
Y × A	398·99	32	12·47	1·23	0·18
MEAN	20580·98	1			
ERROR	88837·03	869			

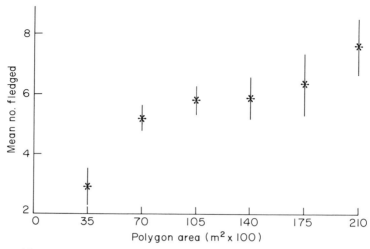

FIG. 20.5. Mean number fledged plotted against the area of the Theissen polygon containing the nest box (expressed in increments of 3500 m²). All data for 1947–83; the vertical lines are 95% confidence intervals.

surrounding the nest box within years. To gain an understanding of the processes which might be involved we need to look at the hatching success (i.e. chicks produced per egg) and fledging success (young fledged per chick) for nests on polygons of different sizes. Figure 20.6 shows the relationship between polygon area and (a) hatching success and (b) fledging success. There is a significant effect of polygon area on both hatching success ($F_{(5,922)} = 2.63$; $P < 0.05$) and fledging success ($F_{(5,847)} = 14.78$; $P < 0.01$).

However, the distributions of hatching success and fledging success (Fig. 20.7) reveal that the majority of nests either succeed or fail, and that the all-or-nothing effect is more marked in fledging success than hatching success. Thus, variations in hatching and fledging success are probably mainly due to predation rather than starvation, because in a bird of this type one would expect deaths in the nest to be in proportion to food supply rather than all or nothing (O'Connor 1978). We therefore split the data into two groups and, classifying nests as successful if they hatched more than half their eggs or fledged more than half their chicks, we asked whether successful nests differed from unsuccessful ones in respect of their polygon area. The answer, for all years together, is shown in Fig. 20.8. Nests which are unsuccessful at hatching tend to have smaller mean polygon areas than those which are successful ($F_{(1,921)} = 9.35$; $P < 0.01$), as do nests which are unsuccessful at fledging compared with successful nests ($F_{(1,847)} = 27.71$; $P < 0.01$). We again used a two-way ANOVA to look at within-year effects, but this time with polygon area

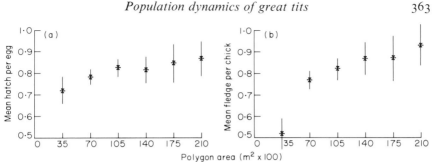

FIG. 20.6. (a) Mean hatching success (chicks/egg) and (b) mean fledging success (fledgings/chick) plotted against Theissen polygon areas (3500 m² increments); bars are 95% confidence interval.

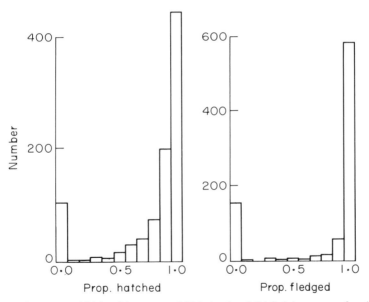

FIG. 20.7. Histograms of (a) hatching success (chicks/egg) and (b) fledging success for all pairs 1947–83.

as the dependent variable, and year and hatching or fledging success as grouping variables. For hatching success we found a weak within-year effect ($F_{(1,784)} = 4\cdot73$; $P < 0\cdot05$); for fledging success the effect was more significant ($F_{(1,676)} = 7\cdot66$; $P < 0\cdot01$).

An obvious interpretation of both results would be that they are due to a predator which uses high density areas more intensively than low density

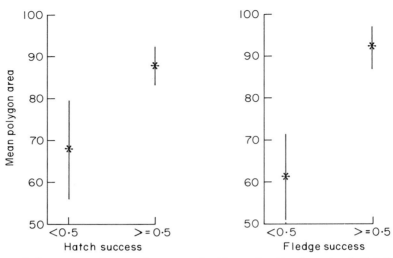

FIG. 20.8. Comparison of mean polygon areas for (a) nests hatching fewer than half their eggs ('failed') and those hatching more than half ('succeeded'), and (b) those fledging fewer than half their chicks and those fledging more than half; the bars are 95% confidence intervals.

areas, and predates whole broods. To look at this we divided the data into years of high weasel predation (1956–75) and those where weasel predation was low (1950–55, 1976–83) based on Dunn 1977. The data for 1947–49 could not be used for this analysis. We carried out a two-way ANOVA on each set of data for hatching success and year, and for fledging success and year. The results are summarized in Table 20.5. There is evidence of a relationship between polygon area and hatching success only in years of high predation, as would be expected on the basis of previous work. However, for fledging success the effect is most marked in years of low predation. We do not suggest that fledging success was higher in high predation years, indeed the reverse is clearly the case (Table 20.6), but it does mean that the within-year effect of density is only seen when losses are lower, possibly because the effect of polygon area is swamped in years of heavy predation. Thus, the process mediating the effect of density on hatching success seems to be different from that involved in the density effect on fledging success.

INFLUENCE OF DENSITY-MEDIATED EFFECTS ON POPULATION DYNAMICS

The dynamics of the Wytham great tit population have been studied previously by Krebs (1970) who used the method devised by Varley &

TABLE 20.5. Two-way analyses of variance showing the effect of calendar year (YEAR) hatching success (H/EGG) or fledging success (F/CHICK) on polygon area in high predation years (1956–75) and low predation years (1950–55, 1976–83)

Source of variance	Sum of squares	d.f.	Mean square	F	P
Hatching success in high predation years					
YEAR	99543·20	19	5439·12	4·70	0·00
H/EGG	6176·68	1	6176·68	5·54	0·02
Y × H	37371·82	19	1966·94	1·76	0·02
MEAN	1077413·56	1			
ERROR	579709·40	520			
Fledging success in high predation years					
YEAR	148985·68	19	7841·35	6·92	0·00
F/CHICK	2363·22	1	2363·22	2·08	0·15
Y × F	23544·01	19	1239·16	1·09	0·35
MEAN	1224113·24	1			
ERROR	528261·88	466			
Hatching success in low predation years					
YEAR	173617·52	11	115783·41	6·47	0·00
H/EGG	1802·13	1	1802·13	0·74	0·39
Y × H	19656·37	11	1786·94	0·73	0·71
MEAN	1132552·21	1			
ERROR	643898·91	264			
Fledging success in low predation years					
YEAR	41265·45	9	4585·05	1·67	0·10
F/CHICK	12238·89	1	12238·89	4·46	0·04
Y × F	15439·34	9	1715·48	0·63	0·78
MEAN	603248·75	1			
ERROR	576330·71	210			

Gradwell (1960) to analyse mortality acting at different stages in the yearly cycle. The losses in numbers during any phase in the life cycle can be expressed as the ratio of numbers entering the phase to those left at the end of it; the logarithm of this quantity is called a *k*-value and these have the useful property that the *k*-value for a sequence of phases in the life cycle is the sum of the *k*-values for each phase. The yearly fluctuations in population are expressed as

$$K = \log_{10} (\text{population in year } x - 1/\text{population in year } x) \quad (1)$$

which is equal to the sum of the component *k*-values (see Table 20.7 for definitions). The *k*-value which is most highly correlated with *K* is said to be the key factor, i.e. the mortality factor most closely related to annual changes

Table 20.6. Numbers of nests fledging fewer than half their nestlings ('failed') or more than half ('succeeded') in years of high and low predation

	Low predation	High predation
Failed	24	148
Succeeded	206	358

in population size (Morris 1959). By correlating the k-values with density (i.e. number present at the beginning of the phase), density-dependent mortality can be located.

The results presented in this section are a preview of an analysis for the whole of Wytham for the years 1964–83 (C.M. Perrins & R.H. McCleery, unpubl.). Some of the inferences are tentative in that they depend on how we deal with some problems in the data—such as missing values for clutch sizes and manipulated broods and whether or not immigrant birds are included in a cohort—and cannot be regarded as definitive. We use the same methods and data as Krebs (1970), and we have retained his terminology, but we differ from him slightly in using the actual numbers of eggs, young hatched and young fledged for each year rather than using the mean for each value multiplied by the breeding population. In an ideal world this would make no difference, but in practise the numbers differ slightly due to missing data.

Table 20.7. Definitions of k-values. This terminology is that used by Krebs (1970)

Numbers	k-value	Interpretation
Maximum clutch size + adults	$k1$	Reduction in clutch size
Actual clutch size + adults	$k2$	Hatching mortality
Eggs hatched + adults	$k3$	Fledgling mortality
Young fledged + adults	$k4$	Overwinter mortality
Birds breeding in next season		

We found that $k4$ was highly correlated with K ($r = 0.84$); $k1$ was also significantly correlated with K ($r = 0.44$), but $k1$ and $k4$ were not correlated with one another. Neither $k2$ nor $k3$ were significantly correlated with K. $k4$ is significantly correlated with the logarithm of total number fledged plus the adults ($r = 0.61$) and thus shows signs of density dependence. The regression of $k4$ on the logarithm of summer population is

$$k4 = -1.51 + 0.66 \log_{10} (\text{no. fledged} + \text{adults}) \qquad (2)$$

the slope differing significantly from 0 ($t = 3.57$, 21 d.f., $P < 0.01$). Our results differ from those of Krebs (1971) in that neither k_1 nor k_2 are correlated with density. Krebs (1971) was doubtful whether k_4 showed density dependence, but in our results it does.

By using data from captures during the winter we were able to arrive at an estimate of the mid-winter population of Wytham born juveniles, which we define as:

$$\text{Winter estimate} = \frac{\begin{array}{cc}\text{No. caught} & \text{No. caught}\\ \text{Dec--Mar} \times \text{breeding}\end{array}}{\text{No. caught both periods}} \qquad (3)$$

Because of the way in which the data have been collected, this estimate can only be made reliably for birds hatched in Wytham, but the breeding population contains a high proportion of birds originating from outside the wood. There is no evidence that the population is buffered by immigration (Webber 1975); the numbers of Wytham-born first years and immigrant first years are highly correlated ($r = 0.73$). It is thus possible to split k_4 (mortality outside the breeding season) into two components: $k_4.1$ mortality from the end of the breeding season to mid-winter (late summer/autumn mortality), and $k_4.2$, mortality from mid-winter to the beginning of the breeding season (winter mortality), but there are several ways in which $k_4.2$ might be calculated.

$k_4.1$ is significantly correlated with $K(r = 0.61)$ but not with log density (i.e. no. fledged + adults). Thus, late summer/autumn mortality does not show density dependence but does have an important influence on fluctuations in the population.

We used two different methods of calculating $k_4.2$

(a) $k_4.2$ is defined as

$$k_4.2(a) = \log_{10} \frac{\text{Wytham pulli in midwinter}}{\text{Wytham pulli breeding}} \qquad (4)$$

effectively ignoring immigration. The correlation of $k_4.2(a)$ with K verges on significance ($r = 0.42$, $n = 23$), but it is not correlated with mid-winter estimated population, so it can not be said to show density dependence.

(b) $k_4.2$ is defined as

$$k_4.2(b) = \log_{10} \frac{\text{Wytham pulli in midwinter}}{\text{All first years breeding}} \qquad (5)$$

This version of $k_4.2$ can take negative values, if the total number of first years breeding happens to be greater than the number of Wytham juveniles alive the previous midwinter. $k_4.2(b)$ is not correlated with K but is correlated with the log of the mid-winter estimate ($r = 0.61$) and can thus be said to show density dependence. Neither of these estimates of $k4.1$ and $k4.2$ include the adults so they do not necessarily add up to $k4$ as we have defined it above.

Although there are some problems of interpretation, we conclude that mortality in late summer/autumn is a key factor *sensu* Morris (1959) in determining population size. There is some evidence that density-dependent 'mortality' (more accurately, failure of recruitment into the breeding population) occurs during the latter part of the winter.

It is interesting that $k2$ (hatching failure) and $k3$ (fledging failure) are not significantly correlated with K or with density, and hence can be said to have little effect on changes in the population. Thus, although we seem to have some evidence for within-year effects of nest site density (territory size) on reproductive success, largely mediated by predation, the effects on population change are minimal compared with other effects. Of course, such effects are far from unimportant for individual birds in that they govern who contributes descendants to the breeding population. Further, we should emphasize that since, in other studies, clutch size has been related to breeding density and to be capable of having an influence on population regulation, the apparent lack of importance in this situation should not be taken as general.

RECRUITMENT PRESSURE AND POPULATION

The observation that when a breeding pair are removed from the wood their territory is rapidly taken over by a new pair (Krebs 1971, 1977) strongly suggests that space is a limiting factor, as does the finding by O'Connor (1980) that an increase in woodland densities was accompanied by a disproportionate increase in farmland densities. The observation that less favoured habitat acts as a kind of buffer zone (Kluijver & Tinbergen 1953; Krebs 1971; Dhondt 1971) suggests that there is no fixed limit to numbers but rather that, as density increases it becomes increasingly difficult for new pairs to establish a territory. Detailed observations of territory formation tend to support this view (Drent 1983; Eyckerman 1974).

Klomp (1980) suggested that the effect of territory on settlement of new pairs in great tits might be a non-linear process. At low densities there may be no dependence of recruitment on population density. Above some threshold density settlement may become increasingly difficult, perhaps as a linear function of density until an upper threshold is reached above which no further settlement is possible. Klomp shows that the slope of the relationship between $\log_{10}$ (candidates for settlement/number breeding), which is equivalent to our $k4.2$, and $\log_{10}$ (candidates for settlement) indicates which phase the population is in. If the slope is 0 then there is no density-related effect on settlement; if the slope is 1 the upper limit on settlement has been reached and if the slope is between 0 and 1 territoriality may be producing a density-dependent effect on recruitment. In Fig. 20.9 we plot $k4.2(b)$ against the logarithm of the winter population estimate. The regression is

$$k4.2(b) = -1 \cdot 05 + 0 \cdot 48 \log \text{ (Wytham juveniles in mid-winter)} \quad (6)$$

As before, note that $k4.2(b)$ can take negative values, but the effect of having a figure for total winter population would probably be to move the whole figure up without changing the slope. The slope differs from 0 ($t = 3 \cdot 87$, 18 d.f., $P < 0 \cdot 01$) and from 1 ($t = 4 \cdot 23$, 18 d.f., $P < 0 \cdot 01$).

Some caution is required in interpreting this result, since it does not take account of the adult population, nor is immigration represented correctly. Its validity depends on the accuracy of the mid-winter population estimate as an indicator of the actual number of birds trying to set up territories. We have given above our reasons for thinking that it is accurate, but further work is needed to check this assumption.

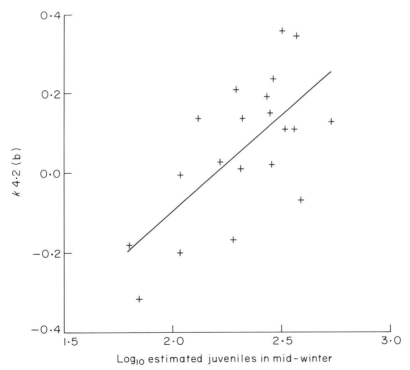

FIG. 20.9. Recruitment of juvenile great tits measured by $k4.2(b)$ plotted against $\log_{10}$ (estimated winter juveniles) (see text for definitions).

We conclude, somewhat tentatively, that territoriality has a restraining effect on settlement of great tits in Wytham, but that the population does not normally reach a size where further settlement is completely prevented.

DISCUSSION

Our analysis of factors determining the population size in Wytham great tits differs in two important respects from the earlier analysis of the same population carried out by Krebs (1970). He found that both k_1 (clutch size reduction) and k_2 (hatching failure) were density-dependent. He also found that k_4 plotted against log summer population had a steep slope, though because of the high variance there was some doubt as to whether this really represented density dependence. From a simulation study he concluded that it was not necessary to invoke density dependence in k_4 to account for the observed fluctuations in population size, bearing in mind that if k_4 *was* density-dependent then the regression slope showed it to be strongly so. While we reiterate the provisional nature of our analysis, for reasons outlined above, some comparisons are in order. In our results neither k_1 nor k_2 show density dependence, but we have rather stronger grounds for thinking that k_4 is density-dependent, and that this density dependence operates in the late winter/early spring. Late summer/autumn mortality ($k_{4.1}$) in contrast appears to be the key factor determining the fluctuations in population; this explains the fact that k_4 is both density-dependent and a key factor. The density dependence of $k_{4.2}$ is consistent with the view that territorial behaviour is acting as a regulator of the population, as might be expected on the basis of detailed studies of the process of setting up territories.

The improvement in the regression relationship between k_4 and density in our results compared with those of Krebs (1970) may simply be due to the fact that we have nearly twice as much data as he had. The different result concerning k_1 is another way of expressing the disappearance of the density dependence of clutch size which seems to have occurred since 1961; the significance of the lack of density dependence of k_2 is less clear and remains under investigation, but it could be that the dynamics of the population have undergone a change such that regulation which formerly acted *via* clutch size and hatching success has disappeared and been replaced by regulation acting *via* territorial behaviour. Klomp's (1980) model does suggest that a population might, by growing slightly, move from a phase where territory had no regulatory effect into a phase where it did; in most of the years 1947–61 (not counting the exceptional 1961 itself) the population of Marley wood is slightly lower than most of the years 1962–83. A further k-value analysis using only the data 1962–83 would probably clarify matters.

The conclusion that over-winter mortality is the key factor in controlling numbers is consistent with other observations. In an analysis of the factors accounting for variance in the life-time reproductive success of individual great tits we find that most of the variance between individuals was accounted for by the recruitment rate of fledged individuals into the breeding population. (R.H. McCleery and C.M. Perrins, unpubl.). A.J. van Nordwijk (pers. comm.) found an exactly similar result for the Netherlands population of great tits, and a result similar to our key factor analysis is reported by Ekman (1984) for willow tits in southern Scandinavia. A corollary of our results is that, although predation acts in a density-dependent way, insofar as it is related to the spacing out of nests, it does not have a regulating effect on the population as a whole since k_2 and k_3 do not show density dependence.

While the results presented here suggest that variations in clutch size, hatching success and fledging success may not be important in population dynamics, they do show that territory size may have important consequences for individual birds since it has an effect on individual reproductive success. It should be noted that the reasons for the differences in breeding success of individuals in relation to territory size shown in this paper result from different underlying causes. The reduced hatching and fledging success found in small territories comes about mainly from losses due to predation. These are largely outside the control of the tits, but nevertheless contribute strongly to the reduction in reproductive output. The other factor which lowers reproductive output is the reduction in clutch size (together with, on the Continent, a reduction in the tendency to have second broods). Clutch size and tendency to have a second brood, in contrast with losses due to predators, are potentially within the control of the birds. It is unlikely that clutch size was related to the amount of food which the birds could find when forming eggs and therefore outside the birds' control since a bird, if it loses a partly-laid clutch to a predator, may almost immediately lay another clutch in an adjacent nest box; the combined total of eggs in the two nests is often markedly in excess of the normal clutch (Perrins 1970, 1979). In addition, feeding experiments in which parts of a population of passerine birds (including tits) have given extra food at the time of laying have, with one exception, had the effect of bringing forward the time of laying, but not of increasing the size of the clutch (see review by Davies & Lundberg 1985). In view of these facts, it is probably not surprising that territory area, as estimated by the polygon method, has little effect on clutch size within a year.

If the birds are not laying a clutch which matches the availability of food to them at the time of laying, then it seems likely that the variations in clutch size are related to the numbers of young which the birds are likely to be able to rear. Reduction of clutch size in years of high density or in territories which are small or of poor quality would have two advantages. First, there would be fewer mouths to feed and therefore a greater chance that the parents could raise young which would fledge at a reasonable weight with a reasonable chance of survival (Perrins 1965). Second, by reducing their clutch size, the parents would reduce the time spent laying the clutch and hence the time which the nest was at risk to predators; it should be noted that the advantages of the latter 'strategy' are not as great in a nidicolous bird with a large clutch as in other birds (Perrins 1977).

It appears that the effects of nest site density within years are due mainly to predation rather than competition for food, but there is a complication in interpreting the benefit of spacing out as reducing the likelihood of predation. Blue tits, *Parus caeruleus* also nest in the nest boxes in some numbers and do so within great tit territories. Reproductive success of great tits is negatively density-dependent on the density of blue tits as well as that of other great tits (Dhondt 1977; Minot 1978), and in any case it seems unlikely that predators differentiate between the two species, so why do great tits not try to defend their territories against blue tits? While this question remains unresolved at present, it may be that we are looking at an unnatural situation since we are talking of nests of both species in the same type of nest site (nest boxes). Under natural conditions the two species have different nest site preferences so it may be that predators do search for them separately.

In our results the pattern of hatching and fledging and its relation to territory is probably due mainly to predation, rather than some policy of brood reduction related to the food supply. If there are any such effects then they are masked by predation in our analysis, partly because we are effectively treating the wood as being of uniform quality. A more sophisticated analysis taking nest site quality (e.g. by using the mean reproductive output of each box over a number of years) might show up some different effects, as might use of fledgling weights, which are correlated with the survival of young (Perrins 1965). These analyses remain to be done.

REFERENCES

Davies, N.B. & Houston, A.I. (1984). Territory economics. *Behavioural Ecology* (2nd edn) (Ed. by J.R. Krebs & N.B. Davies), pp. 148–169. Blackwells Scientific Publications, Oxford.

Davies, N.B. & Lundberg, A. (1985). The influence of food on time budgets and timing of breeding. *Ibis*, **127** (in press).

Dhondt, A.A. (1971). The regulation of numbers in Belgian populations of great tits. *Proceedings of the Advanced Study Institute on 'Dynamics of Numbers in Populations'*, pp. 522–547. Oosterbeek 1970.

Dhondt, A.A. (1977). Interspecific competition between Great and Blue tits. *Nature*, **268**, 521–523.

Dixon, W.J. (Ed.) (1981). *BMDP statistical software*. University of California Press, Los Angeles.

Drent, P.J. (1983). *Functional ethology of territoriality in the great tit, Parus major L.* Ph.D. thesis. University of Groningen.

Dunn, E.. (1977). Predation by weasels (*Mustela nivalis*) on breeding tits (*Parus* spp.) in relation to the density of tits and rodents. *Journal of Animal Ecology*, 46, 633–652.

Ekman, J. (1984). Density dependent seasonal mortality and population fluctuations of the temperate zone willow tit (*Parus montanus*). *Journal of Animal Ecology*, 53, 119–134.

Eyckerman, R. (1974). Some observations on the behaviour of intruding great tits, *Parus major*, and on the success of their breeding attempts in a high density breeding season. *Die Giervalk*, 64, 29–40.

Kluijver, H.N. (1951). The population ecology of the great tit *Parus m. major* L.. *Ardea*, 39, 1–135.

Kluijver, H.N. & Tinbergen, L. (1953). Territory and the regulation of density in titmice. *Netherlands Journal of Zoology*, 10, 265–289.

Klomp, H. (1980). Fluctuations and stability in great tit populations. *Ardea*, 68, 205–224.

Krebs, J.R. (1970). Regulation of numbers in the great tit (Aves: Passeriformes). *Journal of Zoology (London)*, 162, 317–333.

Krebs, J.R. (1971). Territory and breeding density in the great tit, *Parus major*. *Ecology*, 52, 2–22.

Lack, D. (1966). *Population Studies of Birds*. Clarendon Press, Oxford.

Mead, R. (1971). Models for interplant competition in irregularly spaced populations. *Statistical Ecology*, Vol. 2, (Ed. by G.P. Patil), pp. 13–30. Penn State University Press,

Minot, E. (1978). Interspecific competition in tits. *Nature (London)*, 275, 463.

Morris, R.F. (1959). Single factor analysis in population dynamics. *Ecology*, 40, 580–588.

O'Connor, R.J. (1978). Brood reduction in birds: selection for fratricide, infanticide and suicide. *Animal Behaviour*, 26, 79–96.

O'Connor, R.J. (1980). Pattern and process in great tit populations in Britain. *Ardea*, 68, 165–183.

Perrins, C.M. (1965). Population fluctuations and clutch-size in the great tit, *Parus major* L. *Journal of Animal Ecology*, 34, 601–647.

Perrins, C.M. (1970). The timing of bird's breeding seasons. *Ibis*, 112, 242–255.

Perrins, C.M. (1977). The role of predaton in the evolution of clutch-size. *Evolutionary Ecology* (Ed. by B. Stonehouse & C.M. Perrins). Macmillan, London.

Perrins, C.M. (1979). *British Tits*. Collins, London.

Rhynsburger, D. (1973). Analytic delineation of Theissen polygons. *Geographical Analysis*, 5, 133–144.

Varley, G.C. & Gradwell, G.R. (1960). Key factors in population studies. *Journal of Animal Ecology*, 29, 399–401.

Webber, M.I. (1975). *Some aspects of the nonbreeding population dynamics of the great tit* (Parus major). D.Phil thesis, University of Oxford.

21. DOMINANCE AND AGGRESSION IN JUVENILE GREAT TITS, *PARUS MAJOR MAJOR* L. IN RELATION TO DISPERSAL

JENNY V. De LAET

Laboratorium voor Oecologie der Dieren, Zoögeografie en Natuurbehoud, Ledeganckstraat 35, 9000 Ghent, Belgium

SUMMARY

Great tits were ranked by dominance scores based on interactions at an artificial feeder from the end of June until the end of August. Juvenile males were dominant over juvenile females, and resident juveniles that disappeared during the dispersion period were dominated by non-dispersers of the same sex. More females than males dispersed.

Aggression in the population increased from about 50% in June to about 90% in November. Post-fledging dispersal did not start before August with an explosive dispersal at the end of October. These results suggest that during the summer of 1983 intraspecific competition over food was important and responsible for a high juvenile mortality in the first month after fledging. Although aggression was more intense in September than in the summer, due to an increasing territorial behaviour of mainly resident adult males, most dispersing resident juveniles did not leave their birthplace before mid-October when aggression increased to a maximum and territorial behaviour had ceased.

This demonstrates an important role of agonistic behaviour in relation to dispersal in juvenile great tits.

INTRODUCTION

In studies of the dispersal of young great tits (*Parus major major* L.) away from their birthplaces (Krätzig 1939; Plattner & Sutter 1946–1947; Koskimies 1948; Kluyver 1951, 1970; Goodbody 1952; Hinde 1952; Perrins 1963, 1965; Dhondt 1979; Dhondt & Hublé 1968; Greenwood, Harvey & Perrins 1978, 1979) two hypotheses have been proposed to explain the high rate of disappearance of juvenile birds in late summer, i.e. elimination by (i) food shortage or (ii) territorial behaviour. For practical reasons it is difficult to assess how much of the summer losses are due to mortality and how much can be accounted for by dispersal.

According to Goodbody (1952) an explosive dispersal of juvenile birds seems to occur about 1 month after fledging. This was also found by Dhondt (1979) in Sweden where a second dispersal phase was found at the beginning of September. The ultimate factors causing dispersal may be related to a reduction of inbreeding (Kluyver 1951; Dhondt 1979), since inbreeding in great tits reduces breeding success (Greenwood *et al.* 1978; van Noordwijk *et al.* 1981). Although inbreeding depression was detected by both Kluyver (1951) and Dhondt (1979), neither author found any evidence of behavioural avoidance of inbreeding. According to Moore & Ali (1984) invoking inbreeding avoidance is 'inadequate and unnecessary' and the major cause of natal dispersal is competition.

Holleback (1974) found an increased intolerance particularly of adult males towards juveniles in the black-capped chickadee (*Parus atricapillus*), and of the young among each other once they start to feed independently. Dhondt (1979) suggested that dominance relationships in the summer flocks can be responsible for the dispersal of subordinate individuals before winter.

During the summer of 1983 a great tit population in Belgium was studied in their birthplace. In this paper I present data in support of Holleback's results and the suggestion of Dhondt. The dominance scores of great tits that dispersed and those that did not are compared, while the timing of dispersal is related to changes in aggression.

MATERIAL AND METHODS

Field work was conducted between June and November 1983 at Zwijnaarde near Ghent (Belgium), in a 27 ha mature beech wood (*Fagus sylvatica*) with an understorey of *Rhododendron praecox* in which a surplus of great tits nest boxes has been available since 1964.

During the breeding season nestlings were banded with a metal ring of the Belgian Ringing Scheme and colour rings, the same colour being used for each sex in a family. From 20 June onwards the birds were baited with sunflower seeds at a feeder that followed the design of Blurton-Jones (1968). Aggressive and neutral behavioural interactions between great tits, observed from a hide located approximately 8 m from the feeder, produced data for ranking the birds in several ways. The proportions of wins in its total interactions revealed the *dominance relationship* of each bird. Birds were also ranked by *the proportion of encounters which were aggressive*. The *dominance score* of each bird was determined as the number of individuals dominating it subtracted from the number of individuals it dominated. The dominance relationship was correlated with the second and the third measure ($r_s = 0.793$ and 0.878

TABLE 21.1. Dominance of juvenile males over juvenile females and of adult males over adult females (Mann–Whitney U-Test)

Dominance relationship	$\bar{X}$	se	n		$\bar{x}$	se	n	U
Juvenile males	48·56	7·42	19	Adult males	59·25	6·37	19	151	ns
Juvenile females	19·49	3·46	29	Adult females	17·01	4·16	16	180	ns
$Z = -2·75$	$P < 0·0003$				$U = 29·5$	$P < 0·002$		

respectively) which were also correlated with each other ($r_s = 0·683$; all $P < 0·01$ and $N = 37$).

Great tits were mist-netted regularly to change the colourband combination of males and females of the same nest, while immigrants were newly colourbanded so that each bird had a unique colour combination.

RESULTS

Until the end of August resident juvenile males dominated juvenile females, although they lacked the black breast of adult males. Juveniles were not dominated by adults of the same size (Table 21.1). Juveniles that disappeared during the dispersion period had previously been dominated by juveniles of the same sex which then stayed in their birthplace until the end of February (Table 21.2). Of all females (29) 58·62% disappeared during the dispersal period while only 30% of all males (20) disappeared. Analysed over several years, significantly more females disappeared during this period ($U = 8, n = 7$, $P < 0·05$).

In Figs 21.1 and 21.2, the proportion of encounters which were aggressive

TABLE 21.2. Juvenile males (females) that disappeared were dominated by juvenile males (females) that spent the winter in their birth place (Mann–Whitney U-test)

Dominance relationship	$\bar{x}$	se	n
Juv. males disappeared	22·59	12·83	6
stayed	57·77	7·19	14
$U = 15$			$P < 0·05$
Juv. females disappeared	13·75	3·09	17
stayed	31·22	4·60	12
$U = 41$			$P < 0·05$

378   J. V. De Laet

and the cumulative number of individuals trapped, were plotted in relation to date. This shows that the proportion of encounters which were aggressive increased gradually from the end of June to the end of November (Fig. 21.1). Until November encounters between juvenile birds were more aggressive than those between adults and juveniles ($z = -2.25$, $P = 0.012$, $n = 30$, $\bar{x}_{j-j} = 60.54$, $\bar{x}_{A-J} = 52.06$). The number of immigrant juveniles (Fig. 21.2) increased

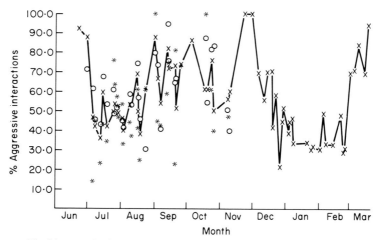

FIG. 21.1. The % aggressive interactions in each observation period of 3 hours: aggression between juveniles (O); aggression from adults to juveniles (∗); total aggression (×).

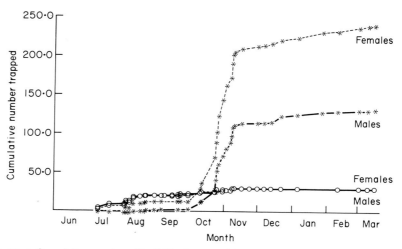

FIG. 21.2. Cumulative number of individuals trapped during the study period: resident juveniles (O); immigrants into the study area (∗).

rapidly between the end of September and the beginning of November, while more females than males were trapped. During this period levels of aggression were at their highest, though they decreased in December when immigration had ceased. Throughout the winter period 44% of the encounters between great tits were aggressive on average, but the proportion rose rapidly at the end of February.

DISCUSSION

Aggression in this great tit population reached high levels (53%) a few weeks after fledging (Fig. 21.1) about 2 months before the explosive immigration of juveniles from outside the study area (Fig. 21.2). Simultaneously, great tits were easily attracted by sunflower seeds while rather few juvenile residents—20% (315)—were observed both on the feeder and in the study area. Both results suggest a high mortality shortly after fledging caused by intraspecific competition for food that could be in short supply during this particular summer. During the summer of the previous year (1982) great tits were not attracted by sunflower seeds and the aggression in the population (field observations) did not increase until the end of August (J.V. De Laet, unpubl.). In both years the number of immigrants was negligible between July and September but increased rapidly in October.

This means that most dispersal occurred after autumn territorial behaviour, which shows a second peak in September (Hinde, 1952; Eyckerman, 1979). Levels of aggression increased slowly from the end of June to a maximum at the beginning of November. I suggest there was intense intraspecific competition for food in June and July of 1983, responsible for a high mortality among subdominant and weak resident juveniles. Dominant resident juveniles still present at the end of August tended to stay for the winter in their birthplace while subdominant birds tended to disappear during the period when dispersal was most intense.

Since juvenile males are dominant over juvenile females, and since juvenile males that remain close to their birthplace will obtain better quality territories and survive better after their first breeding season (Dhondt 1971b), females should disperse more than males, as supported by my data. On the other hand, in periods of intense intraspecific competition (for food and/or space) it might be to the advantage of subdominant juvenile birds to leave their birthplace and find areas in which food is available but competition less intense. In the future this might be investigated by obtaining data on subdominant dispersed birds.

ACKNOWLEDGMENTS

I am very grateful to Dr Jan Hublé as promotor of my study. To Sir X. de

Ghellinck for permission to work in his forest. I am grateful for comments
made by an anonymous referee and by Dr Richard Sibly.

REFERENCES

Blurton-Jones, N.G. (1968). Observations and experiments on causation of threat displays of the
Great Tit *Parus major. Animal Behaviour Monograph* 1, part 2.

Dhondt, A.A. (1971b). Some factors influencing territory in the Great Tit, *Parus major* L. *Giervalk*,
61, 125–135.

Dhondt, A.A. (1979). Summer dispersal and survival of juvenile Great Tits in Southern Sweden.
Oecologia, **42,** 139–157.

Dhondt, A.A. & Hublé, J. (1968). Fledging-date and sex in relation to dispersal in young Great
Tits. *Bird Study*, **15,** 127–134.

Eyckerman, R. (1979). Oecologische functies van het koolmeesvocabularium (*Parus m. major* L.).
Verhandeling tot het behalen van de graad van doctor in de Wetenschappen, Rijksuniversi-
teit Gent.

Goodbody, I.N. (1952). The post-fledging dispersal of juvenile Titmice. *British Birds*, **45,** 279–285.

Greenwood, P.J., Harvey, P.H., Perrins, C.M. (1978). Inbreeding and dispersal in the Great Tit.
Nature, **271,** 53–54.

Greenwood, P.J., Harvey, P.H. & Perrins, C.M. (1979). The role of dispersal in the Great Tit
(*Parus major major*) the causes, consequences and heritability of natal dispersal. *Journal of
Animal Ecology*, **49,** 123–142.

Hinde, R.A. (1952). The behaviour of the Great Tit (*Parus major*) and some other related species.
Behaviour, Suppl. 2, 1–201.

Holleback, M. (1974). Behavioral interactions and the dispersal of the family in Black-capped
Chickadees. *Wilson Bulletin*, **86,** 466–468.

Kluyver, H.N. (1951). The population ecology of the Great Tit, *Parus major major* L. *Ardea*, **39,**
1–135.

Kluyver, H.N. (1970). Regulation of numbers in populations of Great Tits (*Parus m. major*). *Proc.
Adv. Study Inst. Dynamics Numbers Popul.* (Oosterbeek 1970), pp. 507–523.

Koskimies, J. (1948). Talitiaisen, *Parus major* L. vaellusgista Suomessa. *Ornis Fennica*, **25,** 28–35.

Krätzig, H. (1939). Untersuchungen zur Siedlungsbiologie waldewohnender Hohlenbruter.
Ornithologische Abhandlungen. Beihefte der Zeitschrift Deutsche Vogelwelt.

Moore, J. & Ali, R. (1984). Are dispersal and inbreeding avoidance related? *Animal Behaviour*, **32,**
94–112.

Noordwijk, A.J. van & Scharloo, W. (1980). *Inbreeding in an island population of the Great Tit.*
PhD thesis, University of Utrecht, The Netherlands.

Perrins, C.M. (1963). Survival of the Great Tit (*Parus major*). *Proceedings of the 13th International
Ornithological Congress*, 717–728.

Perrins, C.M. (1965). Population fluctuations and clutch size in the Great Tit (*Parus major* L.).
Journal of Animal Ecology, **34,** 601–647.

Plattner, J. & Sutter, E. (1946–1947). Ergebnisse der Meisen und Kleiberberingung in der Schweiz
(1929–1941). *Ornithologische Beobachtungen*, **43,** 136–188.

22. EVIDENCE FOR RANDOM MATING IN THE GREAT TIT, *PARUS MAJOR* (L.)

A. J. VAN NOORDWIJK[1], P. H. VAN TIENDEREN[2],
G. DE JONG[2] AND J. H. VAN BALEN[3]

[1]*Zoologisches Institut der Universität Basel, Rheinsprung 9,
CH-4051 Basel, Switzerland,*
[2]*Department of Population and Evolutionary Biology, University of Utrecht,
P.O. Box 80.055, 3508 TB Utrecht, The Netherlands, and*
[3]*Institute for Ecological Research, P.O. Box 40, 6666 GA Heteren,
The Netherlands*

SUMMARY

The mating pattern in the great tit population on the island of Vlieland is not different from random. The average degree of relatedness of mates is very similar to the relatedness of neighbours and to the relatedness of randomly chosen contemporaneous birds. Males are more closely related to other males in the population ($F = 0.0143$) than to females in the population ($F = 0.0114$), while the average degree of relatedness between females is again lower ($F = 0.0088$). It is possible that this is a consequence of differences in dispersal (measured as immigration into the population) between sexes.

INTRODUCTION

In a previous study, van Noordwijk & Scharloo (1981) observed that the occurrence of inbreeding in the great tit population on the island of Vlieland was at least three times as high as expected in a random mating population of the same size. They attributed this high rate of inbreeding mainly to the variance in the number of offspring, since this variance is higher than in an ideal population. These findings were surprising in the light of a widely held belief that inbreeding-avoidance mechanisms must have evolved to counteract the deleterious effects of close inbreeding (see May 1979). It is thus important to study the occurrence of inbreeding in more detail. Independent of this, the average degree of relatedness can also be seen as a convenient summary of the population structure and of the net effects of dispersal within the study area (*cf.* van Noordwijk 1984).

The data from the great tit population on the island of Vlieland are unique in the extent to which the family trees of the birds are known. Since 1955 all nestlings have been ringed and both parents have been identified in virtually all nests that produced fledglings (see Kluyver 1971). Some 80–90% of all breeding birds are autochthonous (i.e. born on the island), so that for about one-third of the breeding pairs all eight grandparents are known. Here we report the results of a further analysis in which we test more directly whether or not inbreeding occurs as frequently as expected in a random mating population. We have expressed all degrees of relatedness as Wright's coefficient of inbreeding F (see e.g. Falconer 1981), to aid comparisons with previous studies on inbreeding (e.g. Bulmer 1973; Greenwood, Harvey & Perrins 1978; Ralls, Brugger & Ballou 1979). Our average F is equal to the parameter α that has been used in many studies on inbreeding in humans (see Cavalli-Sforza & Bodmer 1971).

The main problem in testing the randomness of the matings that take place is to decide from what group of potential partners every individual bird could have chosen a partner. This set is constrained by the effects of dispersal and also by which birds were available at the right time. We think that the degree of relatedness of the breeding birds to their neighbours is a good reference for judging the amount of inbreeding that occurs. The constraints on the set of potential mates work very similarly on the set of potential neighbours. A second reference is the relatedness with a randomly chosen bird. If we compare the degree of relatedness between partners with that to a randomly chosen bird instead of with that to the neighbour, we should be able to detect whether the dispersal pattern *within* the study area limits the group of potential partners from which a bird can choose.

Even if we limit the comparison to the nearest neighbour pair and one randomly chosen pair, there are, next to the relationship within the pair, eight different relationships to evaluate for every pair, namely the degrees of relatedness of the focal female with the female nearest neighbour and with the male nearest neighbour, and of the focal male with the female nearest neighbour and with the male nearest neighbour, and similarly the degrees of relationship of the focal female and the focal male with the randomly chosen pair instead of the neighbour pair. Of these relationships, the female–male and the male–female relationships will be largely, but not entirely, overlapping. This is because, in several cases, nestbox A is the nearest to B, while a different nestbox C is the nearest to A. In the comparisons with a randomly chosen pair the male–female and the female–male comparisons are two independent estimates of the same parameter.

RESULTS AND DISCUSSION

In this report we will limit ourselves to the subpopulation in the wood near the village Oost-Vlieland (area 2·4 km²), which occupies a continuous wooded area to the west, north and east of the village and also includes the village itself. The subpopulation contains about 70% of the breeding pairs on the island. Exchange of birds with the four smaller wooded areas to the west is much less than expected, probably because of the width of the gap between the most easterly of the small woods and the main wood (van Noordwijk & Scharloo 1981).

In the period 1964–82 both female and male parents were identified in 834 true first broods. Assuming that all inbreeding that occurred has been detected, the average degree of relatedness within pairs was $F = 0.0120$ which is very close to the two estimates (starting from the females or from the males) of the degree of relatedness between neighbours ($F = 0.0122$ and $F = 0.0119$) and the two estimates of the average degree of relatedness with a randomly chosen bird ($F = 0.0120$ and $F = 0.0114$). In all cases the degree of relatedness is measured between birds of opposite sex. In contrast, much lower values are found for the relatedness of female neighbours (see Table 22.1), and also with randomly chosen females, while the degree of relatedness between two neighbouring (or randomly chosen) males is higher. In general the degrees of relatedness are highest between two males and lowest between two females.

TABLE 22.1. The degree of relatedness, expressed as Wright's F, within pairs, with nearest neighbours and with a randomly chosen pair. Data from true first clutches in the wood near the village on Vlieland 1964–82 (see text)

	Overall value	Mean of annual values	s.d. of annual values
Pairs	0.0120	0.0120	0.0043
Neighbours (F–M)	0.0122	0.0130	0.0082
Neighbours (M–F)	0.0119	0.0124	0.0078
Neighbours (F–F)	0.0064	0.0064	0.0041
Neighbours (M–M)	0.0160	0.0172	0.0091
Random (F–M)	0.0120	0.0129	0.0075
Random (M–F)	0.0114	0.0132	0.0082
Random (F–F)	0.0088	0.0090	0.0056
Random (M–M)	0.0143	0.0162	0.0085
Number of observations	834	44	18
Total number of pairs*		54	22

F, female; M, male.
* Also includes pairs that were not identified, e.g. due to early nest failure.

In order to assess the significance of the above differences, we calculated all parameters separately for each year (the means and standard deviations of the annual estimates are given in Table 22.1). The estimates for subsequent years are not entirely independent, since about a quarter of the pairs are identical, and will thus be included twice. Furthermore, sampling errors are not likely to be randomly distributed, so that some caution is necessary in interpreting the results of statistical analyses. Using paired comparison tests, only the degrees of relatedness between two females are clearly significantly different from the comparisons between two males or between two birds of opposite sex. The P-values found in comparing the relatedness between two males and the relatedness between opposite sexes are all less than 0.2, while the P-values for comparisons within all degrees of relatedness involving the same sexes are always greater than 0.5 and mostly greater than 0.8. Paired comparisons were used because many of the annual estimates were positively correlated, although the correlations are not very high. Nevertheless, the means of the annual estimates (column 2) are very close to the overall mean values (column 1). In several cases the mean of the annual estimates is slightly higher than the overall value, because of the effect of population size. Observations from years with a low population density are weighted more heavily in the mean of the annual estimates. It is expected that relatively more relationships are observed at low density.

Further research is in progress. We hope to explain the differences in relatedness between sexes in terms of their different dispersal behaviour and to make a more detailed analysis of the frequencies of different degrees of relatedness. Initial results (to be published elsewhere) indicate that the population structure can not be distinguished from a random mating population.

ACKNOWLEDGMENTS

We thank Dr M.G. Bulmer for pointing out a serious error in a previous version.

REFERENCES

Bulmer, M.G. (1973). Inbreeding in the Great Tit. *Heredity*, **30**, 313–325.
Cavalli-Sforza, L.L. & Bodmer, W.F. (1971). *The Genetics of Human Populations*. Freeman, San Francisco.
Falconer, D.S. (1981). *Introduction to Quantitative Genetics* (2nd edn). Longman, London.
Greenwood, P.J., Harvey, P.H. & Perrins, C.M. (1978). Inbreeding and dispersal in the Great Tit. *Nature*, **278**, 52–54.

Kluyver, H.N. (1971). Regulation of numbers in populations of Great Tits (*Parus m. major*). *Dynamics of Populations* (Ed. by P.J. den Boer & G.R. Gradwell), pp. 507–523. Pudoc, Wageningen.

May, R.M. (1979). When to be incestuous. *Nature*, **279**, 192–194.

Noordwijk, A.J. van (1984). Problems in the analysis of dispersal and a critique on its heritability in the great tit. *Journal of Animal Ecology*, **53**, 533–544.

Noordwijk, A.J. van & W. Scharloo (1981). Inbreeding in an island population of the Great Tit. *Evolution*, **35**, 674–688.

Ralls, K., Brugger, K. & Ballou, J. (1979). Inbreeding and juvenile mortality in small populations of ungulates. *Science*, **206**, 1101–1103.

23. WINTER SURVIVAL, HOME RANGES AND FEEDING OF FIRST-YEAR AND ADULT BULLFINCHES

P. W. GREIG-SMITH

*Ministry of Agriculture, Fisheries and Food, Agricultural Science Service,
Worplesdon Laboratory, Tangley Place, Worplesdon, Surrey*

SUMMARY

Higher winter mortality of juvenile than adult birds is often attributed to
poorer competitive ability. A population of bullfinches was studied to
determine whether first-year birds suffered restricted access to fruiting ash
trees, one of their most important winter foods. Field and laboratory
observations of foraging behaviour, gut content analysis, and radio-tracking
to plot home ranges together suggested that juveniles were not excluded from
trees, but may have been less efficient foragers.

INTRODUCTION

In many bird populations, juveniles suffer disproportionately high mortality
in their first few months of life (e.g. Krebs & Perrins 1978; Ekman 1984). This
is often accounted for as a consequence of young birds' inferiority in some
form of competition, restricting their access to critical resources. For example,
winter territoriality may exclude juvenile pied wagtails *Motacilla alba* from
high quality areas (Davies & Houston 1981), while dominance hierarchies
among silvereyes *Zosterops lateralis* and some tits *Parus* spp. determine their
order of precedence at feeding sites (Kikkawa 1980; Ekman, Cederholm &
Askenmo 1981). In addition, inexperienced juveniles may be less efficient than
adults in foraging (e.g. Quinney & Smith 1980).

This paper examines the winter ranging behaviour of bullfinches *Pyrrhula
pyrrhula* (L), to determine whether first-year birds suffer restriction of access
to ash trees *Fraxinus excelsior* (L) bearing seeds. Ash seed is particularly rich
in fat and protein (Greig-Smith & Wilson 1985) and forms a major part of
bullfinches' winter diet (Newton 1964; Summers 1981; P.W. Greig-Smith,
unpubl.), probably because it enables birds to form the large stores of fat
needed for overnight survival in winter (Newton 1969). This work forms part
of a broader study of the feeding behaviour of bullfinches in relation to
damage caused by bud-feeding in orchards (Greig-Smith & Wilson 1984).

METHODS

Bullfinches were caught in mist-nets in an area of orchards, woods and fields in Kent, between September 1980 and March 1984 (see Greig-Smith & Wilson 1984). First-year birds were recognized by the presence of unmoulted, brown-tipped wing covert feathers (Newton 1966). Home ranges were plotted by locating signals from birds carrying miniature radio-transmitters (weight 2·0–2·5 g, with a range up to 0·75 km, and battery life 3–6 weeks). Feeding in ash trees was studied directly by continuous observation of focal birds in foraging bouts that averaged 4·5 min (Greig-Smith & Wilson 1985), and indirectly by examining the gut contents of bullfinches shot in and around the study area.

Observations on captive first-year bullfinches were made to assess their skill in extracting ash seeds from fruits. The behaviour of four 'experienced' birds, which had regularly eaten ash seed for 5 months, was compared with that of four 'inexperienced' birds, which had not.

RESULTS AND DISCUSSION

Figure 23.1 shows that the proportion of first-year birds among bullfinches caught in mist-nets declined steadily from three-quarters in September to one-half in the following summer. While this pattern may reflect a combination of juveniles' higher mortality, greater net dispersal, and increasing ability to avoid nets, data on the recapture of marked individuals at several sites

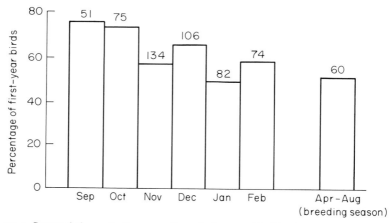

FIG. 23.1. Seasonal change in the proportion of mist-netted bullfinches that were first-year birds. Data from 4 years are combined; sample sizes are above the columns. Test for a linear trend in winter: $\chi_1^2 = 7·8$, $P < 0·01$.

suggested that the latter two causes are relatively unimportant (unpublished data). Consequently, Fig. 23.1 implies greater mortality of first-years throughout the winter.

The use of radio-tracking to determine winter home ranges revealed that most birds remained largely within small areas (1–2 ha) for periods of a few weeks, making only occasional brief excursions to distances of a few hundred metres (e.g. Fig. 23.2a). Over longer periods, there were occasional shifts of range, sometimes more than 1 km, before settling again in a small area. Some changes could be related to human disturbance, or the appearance of new food resources (e.g. ripening catkins of aspen *Populus tremula* (L)), but no obvious reason could be adduced in many cases. Among twelve first-year birds and fifteen older birds for which ranges were plotted, there were no significant differences between the patterns of the two age-classes.

There was extensive overlap of ranges. Figure 23.2b shows that at one site in January 1983, all four radio-tracked birds shared an area containing a large number of ash trees, at which up to ten birds often fed together, though they travelled between trees independently. At another site, a single ash tree was visited by at least twelve marked birds (five first-year and seven adult) over 3 weeks in February. These results suggest that first-year bullfinches were not excluded from feeding in ash trees used by older birds, and they appeared to have the flexibility to change their ranges to exploit trees over a wide area. In addition, aggression between feeding bullfinches was very infrequent, averaging 1·6 incidents per bird per hour (see also Wilkinson 1982), and caused only momentary interruptions of foraging.

Despite apparently equal opportunities to eat ash seed, first-year bullfinches did so less than adults. The stomach and oesophagus contents of all seventeen adults killed in periods of high ash seed availability (November–December 1981 and November 1982–February 1983) contained fragments of seeds, whereas only sixty-one of eighty first-year birds did (Fisher exact test, $P = 0·017$).

Bullfinches obtain ash seed by plucking fruits in the tree canopy, and manipulating them in the beak to remove the fruit coat, before eating the seed within. Many fruits are rejected or dropped accidentally during handling (over 50% in November, when ash seed is first included in the diet; see Greig-Smith & Wilson 1985), so that the skills of foraging include not only the speed with which seeds are husked and eaten (conventional 'handling time'), but also the ability to avoid dropping fruits (Greig-Smith 1984). Observations on captive birds showed that the 'inexperienced' first-year bullfinches, which had not eaten ash seed before, attacked as many fruits as 'experienced' first-years (224 *v.* 221), but they dropped a higher proportion (95·8% *v.* 87·6%; $\chi_1^2 = 6·6$, $P < 0·02$) and ate seeds from a smaller proportion

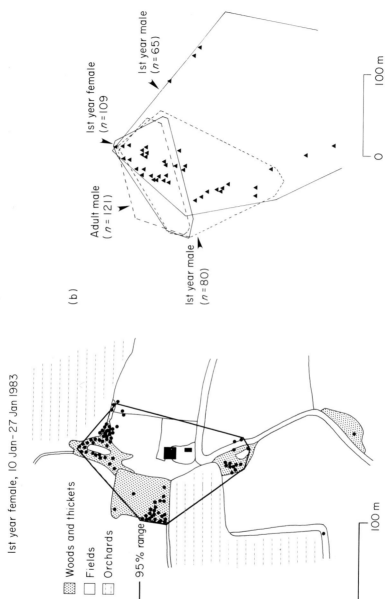

Fig. 23.2. (a) Example of the ranging behaviour of a bullfinch during 18 days in January, shown by radio-tracking. Points indicate positions determined at intervals of at least 30 min, on 11 observation days. The bold line encloses the 95% range. (b) Overlap of bullfinches' 95% ranges in January 1983, determined by radio-tracking. The triangles mark positions of ash trees bearing fruit crops, in which the birds frequently foraged. Sample sizes are numbers of fixes of position, at intervals of at least 30 min.

($10 \cdot 7\% \, v. \, 27 \cdot 6\%$; $\chi_1^2 = 22 \cdot 7$, $P < 0 \cdot 001$). There were no significant differences in the average times (s) spent handling fruits before dropping them ($5 \cdot 3 \pm 0 \cdot 4 \, v.$ $7 \cdot 2 \pm 1 \cdot 2$), removing the husks ($26 \cdot 1 \pm 4 \cdot 2 \, v. \, 21 \cdot 7 \pm 2 \cdot 2$), or ingesting the seeds ($87 \cdot 9 \pm 18 \cdot 3 \, v. \, 84 \cdot 7 \pm 8 \cdot 4$) (all $P > 0 \cdot 20$, Kolmogorov–Smirnov tests). These results suggest that previous experience allows bullfinches to exploit ash seed more efficiently, so that first-years might be less adept than older birds, at least at the start of the winter. This interpretation is supported by the fact that first-years formed smaller energy reserves (chiefly fat, but also muscle protein; see Newton 1969) than adults when ash-feeding began in autumn (average body weights in November were $23 \cdot 2 \pm 0 \cdot 2$ g ($N = 71$) and $24 \cdot 0 \pm 0 \cdot 2$ g ($N = 57$) respectively; t-test, $P < 0 \cdot 02$), but did not differ in previous or later months. However, other factors, such as an aversive reaction by naive birds to the taste of phenolic constituents in ash seed (Greig-Smith & Wilson 1985) might also contribute to young birds' lower consumption.

CONCLUSION

This study suggests that first-year bullfinches were not seriously restricted in their access to ash trees, and suffered no direct interference while feeding. Consequently, their poor winter survival is not obviously attributable to competition with adults, but is more likely to involve relative incompetence in foraging, avoiding predators, or other activities. While inefficient handling of ash fruits owing to lack of experience seems a plausible mechanism underlying first-year birds' lower weights in November, it is unlikely to persist longer than a few weeks after the start of ash feeding. Whatever mechanism is involved, differential survival of first-year and adult birds continued throughout the winter, implying that learning of survival skills continues well beyond the first few weeks after fledging (cf. Smith 1983).

The results are also relevant to damage caused by bullfinches in orchards. First, since bud-feeding usually ensues when ash and other seeds are no longer available (Newton 1964; Summers 1981; P.W. Greig-Smith, unpubl.), the lower ash seed consumption by first-year birds suggests that they may be responsible for a disproportionate amount of early damage. Second, the flexible overlapping ranges mean that orchards may not suffer immediate damage when local seeds are depleted, but when damage does ensue, it may involve large numbers of bullfinches.

ACKNOWLEDGMENTS

I am very grateful to Colin Mackenzie for help with radio-tracking and observations of foraging bullfinches, and to Kate Hill for examining the gut contents of numerous carcasses.

REFERENCES

Davies, N.B. & Houston, A.I. (1981). Owners and satellites: the economics of territory defence in the pied wagtail, *Motacilla alba. Journal of Animal Ecology*, **50**, 157–180.

Ekman, J. (1984). Density-dependent seasonal mortality and population fluctuations of the temperate-zone willow tit, *Parus montanus. Journal of Animal Ecology*, **53**, 119–134.

Ekman, J., Cederholm, G. & Askenmo, C. (1981). Spacing and survival in winter groups of willow tit *Parus montanus* and crested tit *P. cristatus*—a removal study. *Journal of Animal Ecology*, **50**, 1–9.

Greig-Smith, P.W. (1984). Food-handling by bullfinches in relation to the risks associated with dropping seeds. *Animal Behaviour*, **32**, 929–931.

Greig-Smith, P.W. & Wilson, G.M. (1984). Patterns of activity and habitat use by a population of bullfinches, *Pyrrhula pyrrhula*, in relation to bud-feeding in orchards. *Journal of Applied Ecology*, **21**, 401–422.

Greig-Smith, P.W. & Wilson, M.F. (1985). Influences of seed size, nutrient composition and phenolic content on the preferences of bullfinches feeding in ash trees. *Oikos* (in press).

Kikkawa, J. (1980). Winter survival in relation to dominance classes among silvereyes, *Zosterops lateralis chlorocephala*, of Heron Island, Great Barrier Reef, *Ibis*, **122**, 437–446.

Krebs, J.R. & Perrins, C.M. (1978). Behaviour and population regulation in the great tit, *Parus major. Population Control by Social Behaviour* (Ed. by F.J. Ebling & D.M. Stoddard), pp. 23–47. Institute of Biology, London.

Newton, I. (1964). Bud-eating by bullfinches in relation to the natural food-supply. *Journal of Applied Ecology*, **1**, 265–279.

Newton, I. (1966). The moult of the bullfinch, *Pyrrhula pyrrhula. Ibis*, **108**, 41–67.

Newton, I. (1969). Winter fattening in the bullfinch. *Physiological Zoology*, **42**, 96–107.

Quinney, T.E. & Smith, P.C. (1980). Comparative foraging behaviour and efficiency of adult and juvenile Great Blue Herons. *Canadian Journal of Zoology*, **58**, 1168–1173.

Smith, S.M. (1983). The ontogeny of avian behaviour. *Avian Biology*, Vol. VII (Ed. by D.S. Farner, J.R. King & K.C. Parkes), pp. 85–160. Academic Press, New York.

Summers, D.D.B. (1981). Bullfinch, *Pyrrhula pyrrhula*, damage in orchards in relation to woodland bud and seed feeding. *Pests, Pathogens and Vegetation* (Ed. by J.M. Thresh), pp. 385–391. Pitman, London.

Wilkinson, R. (1982). Group size and composition and the frequency of social interactions in bullfinches, *Pyrrhula pyrrhula. Ornis Scandinavica*, **13**, 117–122.

24. LIMITATION OF BREEDING DENSITY THROUGH TERRITORIAL BEHAVIOUR: EXPERIMENTS WITH CONVICT CICHLIDS, *CICHLASOMA NIGROFASCIATUM*

I. J. PATTERSON

Department of Zoology, University of Aberdeen, Culterty Field Station, Newburgh, Aberdeenshire

SUMMARY

The limitation of breeding density through territorial behaviour in relation to habitat preference was investigated in experiments with captive populations of convict cichlids *Cichlasoma nigrofasciatum*, given a simultaneous choice of two breeding habitats (caves versus stones). The habitat expected to be preferred (cave) was settled at the faster rate and eventually supported higher densities. There was no difference between habitats in the territorial aggression of the initial settlers but intrusion frequency was highest in the preferred habitat, suggesting that this was the major factor affecting final density. Fish holding preferred sites increased their territorial aggressiveness after a few days' residence, possibly in relation to the higher value of a cavity nest.

INTRODUCTION

If individual animals vary their territorial behaviour in response to variations in a resource such as their food supply (Davies 1978), population density will be adjusted to resource level as a direct consequence. Two main behavioural variables are likely to be important in such adjustment (Patterson 1980): (a) the territorial aggression of the initial settlers in an area (which could for example vary between year classes or with habitat quality) and (b) the number and behaviour of subsequent potential settlers (which could also vary with habitat quality). The density established in any particular patch of habitat will be a compromise between these two variables. One of them may, however, be more important than the other in a given situation; density might be determined principally by variations in the territorial aggressiveness of the initial settlers, as has been suggested for red grouse *Lagopus lagopus* (Moss & Watson 1980; Watson & Moss 1980) or might be affected more by the number and behaviour of subsequent arrivals (Patterson 1980).

This paper is concerned with the latter possibility, which emphasizes the role of habitat preferences and 'immigration pressure' in density limitation. Habitats should vary in the degree to which they are preferred by settlers (in relation to habitat 'suitability' (Fretwell 1972), reflecting the fitness which can be achieved in each in terms of reproductive success and survival). The initial settlers in each habitat need not differ in their territorial aggressiveness but the preferred habitat should attract most of the subsequent potential settlers, leading to squeezing of the initial territories and consequently to a higher density than in less preferred habitats. The frequency of interaction between territorial residents and non-territorial animals should be highest in the preferred area, since most intruders should be attracted there. A number of studies (e.g. Glas 1960; Kluyver & Tinbergen 1953; Pitelka 1973) have shown that densities were higher and less variable in apparently preferred habitats and Vines (1979) found that intrusions were most frequent in higher density populations of oystercatchers *Haematopus ostralegus*.

The aim of the present work was to study the effects of habitat preference on density, territorial aggression and number of intrusions, during the establishment of territorial systems in different habitats. Since this is difficult to achieve with wild populations the initial experiments were carried out on small territorial fish in captivity.

MATERIALS AND METHODS

The study animal

The convict or zebra cichlid *Cichlasoma nigrofasciatum* forms monogamous pairs which defend small territories, both sexes showing complex parental care from egg-laying until the young are 6–8 weeks old. Both sexes also show vigorous territorial defence, mainly by rapid attack rushes with raised opercula. When kept at 25°C, convict cichlids are continuously territorial.

An adult male, obtained from a local dealer, was paired with three successive females to produce stocks of young, which were reared in 2×1 m fibreglass tanks and fed on standard 'Tetramin' tropical fish food. At maturity (5–8 months), when the sexes could be distinguished by gold scales on the females' sides and blue irridescence in their fins, the fish were used in trials.

The fish were anaesthetized with Benzocaine (Laird & Oswald 1975), measured to 1 mm and marked for individual recognition by injecting Alcian Blue dye under the scales, using a modified (low power) 'Panjet' needle-less injector (Wright Dental Co., Kingsway West, Dundee). Spots of dye on one or more of the eight pale stripes on the fishes' sides (Fig. 24.1) gave a large number of combinations. The spots gradually faded but were clearly visible for 8–12 weeks.

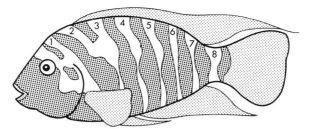

FIG. 24.1. Male convict cichlid, showing dye mark positions.

Apparatus

The test arena (Fig. 24.2) was a large tank 2·5 m square filled to 25 cm with water at 25°C. The floor was covered with 2–3 cm of washed sand and two blocks of nest sites were laid out on a grid system (Fig. 24.2), with an area of bare sand at one side of the tank. An automatic feeder delivered food once each day into the sand-floored area, where most fish congregated to feed before returning to their territories. The food quickly drifted round the whole arena. Between the five replicate trials the tank was cleaned, the water

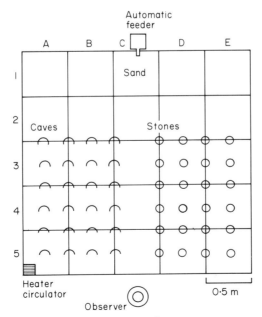

FIG. 24.2. Layout of test arena.

replaced and the positions of the two habitat blocks were interchanged. Four sets of naive fish were used; fish from sets I and II were re-used as set III after 3 months 'rest period' in a large stock tank.

Nesting habitats

Since wild convict cichlids nest in cavities, usually in rocky substrates (Meral 1973), two types of stone nest site were used: (a) cave, formed from a flat stone (c. 15×10 cm) placed on top of two cuboid stones (c. 8 cm side) set 5 cm apart; (b) stone, a flat rounded stone (c. 10×15 cm). The sites were spaced at $12 \cdot 5$ cm centres in two blocks of 24 (Fig. 24.2), with a 50-cm channel left clear between the blocks. This number and density of sites, in relation to the number of fish used, ensured that there was a clear surplus of sites in most territories while a substantial proportion of the fish remained non-territorial.

RESULTS

Habitat preferences

The experimental fish preferred the cave sites; two pairs given a choice of stone versus bare sand laid their eggs on the stone and four pairs each given a stone and a cave all laid in the cave. This preference was also tested by order and speed of settlement in the main trials.

Settlement

When new stocks of fish were put in the test arena they swam rapidly around it in a tight shoal for the first hour or so before beginning to spread out. Within about 2 hours some males began to show territorial behaviour by restricting themselves to small parts of the nesting habitat and by making attack rushes at passing fish. They dug pits in the sand and neighbouring males displayed frontally at each other with raised opercula, making it easy to determine when and where individual males had become territorial. Most were joined quickly by females, which immediately became territorial also.

The territorial males and pairs were counted and their positions plotted at 2-hour intervals on the first day, twice on the second day and once per day on most days thereafter. In all five trials the caves were occupied at a faster rate than the stones (e.g. trial III, Fig. 24.3, first 9 days). However, fish usually began settling on the stones well before the number in the caves reached its maximum (c.f. Fretwell 1972); the only exception to this was trial I, when the fish took 3 weeks to reach maximum density in the cave area and settlement on stones was very slow until then.

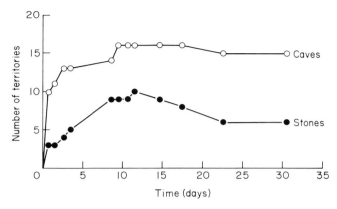

FIG. 24.3. Number of territories in the two habitats in trial III. Where more than one count was made in one day (days 1–3), the maximum is plotted.

Density in the two habitats

In each trial the number of territorial pairs reached an asymptote (e.g. trial III, Fig. 24.3, after 9 days), which was maintained until the end of the test (usually after 30 days). The final densities were dynamic equilibria, with fish occasionally giving up or being displaced from territories and others taking their places. In all but one of the trials the density in the cave habitat was almost twice that in the stones (Table 24.1). Trial IV was an exception, with the stone density reaching 73% of that in the caves; however, after these fish were netted for re-marking, the densities changed to become similar to those in

TABLE 24.1. Final number of territories in the two habitat blocks

Trial	Number introduced males	females	Territories* caves	stones	Stones as % of caves
I	43	29	13·1	7·6	57·5
II	32	32	14·5	8·3	56·9
III	40	40	16·0	8·0	50·0
IV	40	40	14·1	10·3	73·2
V	20	20	7·9	4·7	59·2
IV (re-run)	40	40	13·9	7·4	53·2

* Mean number over 8–10 counts, after the totals had levelled off. Five results all in same direction, $P < 0.05$, one-tailed Sign Test.
Author's note: a further trial with twenty pairs gave mean values of 8·7 territories in caves and 5·0 on stones (57·4% of cave density).

the other trials. Trial III, with thirty-two pairs, had territorial densities within the range of those with forty pairs, but trial V, with only twenty pairs, had considerably lower final densities. Here, however, the ratio between the two habitats remained the same as in the other trials.

In three of the trials, the males which had territories when numbers reached their maxima were significantly larger than the non-territorial males, but there was no significant or consistent difference between males with caves and those with stones (Table 24.2).

TABLE 24.2. Male lengths

| | Mean length of males (mm) | | | | | | | | |
| | Cave | | | Stone | | | Non-territorial | | |
Trial	Mean	SE	N	Mean	SE	N	Mean	SE	N
I	89·3	1·1	7	91·9°	0·9	10	89·3°	0·9	11
II	86·9	0·8	13	87·4	1·1	9	87·0	1·1	9
III	93·4°	1·6	18	97·0*	1·2	11	88·4*°	1·9	11
IV	81·2†	1·3	16	78·4	1·0	13	75·6†	1·3	11
V	78·4	1·5	10	75·3	1·5	8	73·5	6·5	2

t-tests; ° $P<0.05$; † $P<0.01$; * $P<0.001$.

Removal experiments

In two of the trials (I and IV), when densities had been stable for at least 15 days, all the fish in the cave habitat were removed, after dropping a barrier net around the whole block of cave sites. In both cases the caves were quickly recolonized and the density again became higher than in the stone habitat, although lower than it had been in the caves prior to the experiment (e.g. trial IV, Fig. 24.4). The total number of pairs in the arena had, of course, been reduced from forty to twenty-six, so this result is consistent with that of trial V.

Surprisingly, of the eleven pairs which recolonized the cave area in trial IV, only one moved from the stones (out of seven pairs previously there). The remaining ten colonists were non-territorial or were defending small parts of the open sand area at the time of the removal. Nine of them, however, had been territorial in the 7 weeks prior to the experiment but had left or been displaced from their territories.

The failure of fish to move from the stone habitat, and the consequent maintenance of the same density there, resulted in a higher relative density in the stones after the removal than before (61·4% of cave density compared to 53·2%, Fig. 24.4).

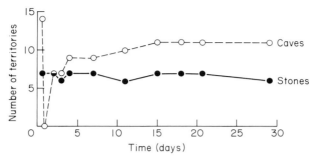

FIG. 24.4. Removal experiment after trial IV; number of territories in the two habitats before and after removal of all the fish in the cave area.

Territorial aggression

The aggressiveness of territorial males (their tendency to attack conspecifics) was tested using two measures: (a) the distance at which approaching non-territorial fish were attacked and (b) the frequency of attack on a decoy fish near the nest site. Both were measured soon after each male became territorial (usually within 2–6 hours and always within 24 hours), before aggressiveness was likely to have been modified by interactions with neighbours or by experience specific to each habitat.

Attack distance

The position of each intruding fish, at the instant when a territorial male charged at it, was plotted on a map of the arena and its distance from the nest site measured later. There were small variations in mean attack distance between trials but no difference between males in the two habitats (Table 24.3). The attack distances of males in trial V, where the final densities were

TABLE 24.3. Attack distances immediately after settlement

| | Attack distance (cm) | | | | | |
| | Cave | | | Stone | | |
Trial	Mean	SE	N	Mean	SE	N
III	24·8	1·0	86	24·4*	1·1	68
IV	27·6	0·9	76	27·4	1·0	62
V	28·7	1·8	36	29·8*	2·1	24
Combined (III–V)	26·6	0·7	198	26·4	0·7	154

* $d = 2·26$, $P < 0·05$. No other significant differences.

lower than in the other tests, were slightly longer than those in the other two trials (Table 24.3), although significantly so only between stone males in trial V and those in trial III.

Attack frequency

A decoy male, taken from a separate stock of fish, was placed in a small transparent polythene bag weighed down by a Petri dish and positioned 5 cm from each occupied nest site in turn. After allowing 1 minute for the residents to settle down, the attack rushes made by the male towards the decoy were counted each minute for five consecutive minutes.

Again there was no difference between habitats, with mean attack frequencies of about eight or nine attacks per minute in both (Fig. 24.5a). However, when the same males were tested again 3 days after settlement, the males with caves had increased their attack frequencies significantly and attacked the decoy about three times more frequently than did the males with stones (Fig. 24.5b). A similar difference was found in another set of fish, tested 3 weeks after settlement.

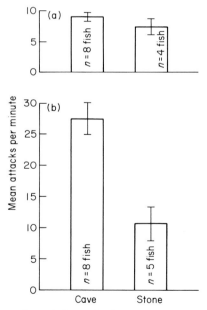

FIG. 24.5. Frequency of attacks made by territorial males on a decoy male placed 5 cm from the nest (a) when newly settled, (b) 3 days after settlement. Bars are standard errors. (Cave fish, newly settled v. later, Mann–Whitney $U=0$, $P<0.001$; cave v. stone fish after 3 days, $U=1$, $P=0.002$; no other significant differences.)

Five individual males which moved from one type of site to the other changed their frequency of attack correspondingly, with a mean of $25.8 \pm$ (SE) 4.7 attacks per min. at cave sites and 8.7 ± 1.8 on stones. Another five males which remained at stone sites and were re-tested with decoys after the same interval showed no change in attack frequency (first test mean, 9.9 ± 4.0 attacks per min; second test, 9.5 ± 2.1).

In contrast to the response to the decoys, there was no significant difference between habitats in the frequency of attack rushes towards territorial neighbours (caves, 5.04 ± 0.64 attacks per min; stones, 4.44 ± 0.63; Mann–Whitney $U = 66$, $N = 16$, 10).

Interaction between territorial and non-territorial fish

Once the densities in the two habitats had reached their maxima, interactions between the territorial fish and the remaining non-territorial ones became infrequent, as the latter avoided the nesting habitat and stayed mainly in the open sand area. However, in three periods just after densities levelled off the number of intruders entering the two blocks of habitat were compared; the duration of each intrusion and the number of attacks on the intruder before it

TABLE 24.4. Intrusion frequency and duration, and attacks per intruder, in the two habitats

	Cave			Stone		
	Mean	SE	(n)	Mean	SE	(n)
Intrusions per 10 min	30.7	7.2	(3)*	3.0	1.0	(3)
Duration of intrusion (sec)	11.6	2.9	(26)	6.2	1.1	(7)
Attacks per intruder	1.4	0.2	(26)	1.4	0.5	(7)

* Mann–Whitney $U = 0$, $P = 0.05$. No other significant differences.

fled back to the non-territorial area were measured using a stopwatch and counter.

Intrusions into the cave habitat were considerably and significantly more frequent than those into the stone habitat (Table 24.4). The intrusions into the cave area lasted about twice as long as those into the stone area but there was no difference between habitats in the number of attacks suffered by each intruder (Table 24.4). Most intrusions ended immediately the intruder was attacked, although some fish received further attacks while escaping to the sand area through other territories.

DISCUSSION

Habitat preference and settlement

The rate of settlement confirmed the prediction from field observations and preliminary tests; the cave habitat, which was expected to be preferred, was indeed settled fastest (Fig. 24.3). Settlement in the stones, however, occurred earlier than expected from Fretwell's (1972) model, which would predict that the less preferred habitat should only begin to be settled when density in the preferred one has risen enough to decrease its suitability for subsequent settlers. This result may be an artefact of the experimental design, in which a large number of fully mature (and probably already paired) fish were released simultaneously into breeding habitat, leading very rapid and highly competitive settlement. In these circumstances, some fish may not have been very selective in their initial choice and may have settled at a stone without having surveyed the whole area.

The preference for cave sites may confer benefits to the survival of eggs and young fry, since most fish laid their eggs inside the cavity and kept the fry there, where they were much less exposed than at open stone sites. The survival of the brood was not, however, tested directly in this study, in the absence of inter-specific predators.

Final densities

The results confirmed the hypothesis that density should be higher in the preferred habitat, with a consistent ratio between the densities in the two areas over the five trials (Table 24.1), and rapid re-establishment of the difference after removal of all the fish from the caves (Fig. 24.4). The reality of this difference was emphasized by the maintenance of fairly constant densities over long periods, even though individual fish left their territories and were replaced by others.

The lower numbers of territories in the cave area after the removal experiments, and in both habitats in trial V (with fewer fish in the arena), suggest that density was affected by the number of potential settlers available in the area. The maintenance of the same ratio between the densities in the two habitats in trial V is, however, difficult to explain, but little can be concluded from this single result.

The higher proportion of fish than expected remaining in the stone habitat after the removal experiments, when pairs might have been expected to move to caves, can perhaps be explained by their continuing with current breeding attempts. It may well be advantageous to stay to rear a part-grown brood than to change to a new site, even if it might be better in the long term. However, this cannot explain why the higher relative density in the stone habitat was maintained for several weeks, even after many of the original fish there had lost their broods. Partridge (1978) suggested that experience of successful breeding in a particular habitat may increase an individual's preference for it, e.g. in hedgerow-nesting great tits *Parus major* (Krebs 1971). Possibly higher fitness can be achieved by staying in a habitat where breeding has been shown to be possible, than by incurring the risks and costs of moving and establishing a territory in a new, unknown habitat.

Territorial aggression

The difference in density between habitats was not due to variation in the initial levels of aggression of the settling males, which attacked at the same distance (Table 24.3), and with the same frequency (Fig. 24.5a) in both areas. This is in contrast to red grouse (Moss & Watson 1980; Watson & Moss 1980) where differences in density were related to the aggression of different stocks.

The increase in aggressiveness of cave males towards decoys after 3 days emphasized the lack of correlation between aggression and territory size; the smaller territories of males in the higher density cave habitat were not associated with lower levels of aggression, as might have been expected. Individual males which changed from one habitat to the other also changed their behaviour appropriately, suggesting that the difference was a response to the environment and not a characteristic of the fish settling in each area.

There was no difference between habitats in the frequency of interactions between neighbours (which might condition the fish to respond differently to non-territorial intruders). Males in the cave area would, however, have been exposed to more frequent intrusion by non-territorial fish than would males with stones, particularly just after first settlement (see next section, below).

It is possible that a cavity site allows more successful reproduction than a stone site. If so, this would justify the expenditure of more time and energy, and the taking of greater risks in aggression, in the defence of a more valuable site. It was not possible to test this without information on breeding success in different types of site in the wild. However, Riechert (1979) has shown that the energetic cost of territorial encounters in a sheet-web spider *Agelenopsis aperta* increased sharply with the value of the site in terms of its potential for food capture and reproductive success. Assessment of site quality seemed to occur only after a period of residence, since new arrivals did not vary their behaviour significantly with site value.

Interaction between territorial and non-territorial fish

There was evidence of greater intruder 'pressure' (frequency of intrusions) in the preferred habitat, as predicted (Table 24.4). This is likely to have been the major factor causing the observed difference in final density between the habitats, since there was no difference in initial territorial aggression (Fig. 24.5a).

The longer duration of intrusions in the cave area may also reflect greater interest by the non-territorial fish in this habitat compared to the stones. However, the caves provided more cover than the stones and cave pairs also spent some of their time inside the cavity, so that intruders may well have remained undetected for longer.

Limitation of breeding density

The results in general support the specific hypothesis of the limitation of breeding density in relation to habitat preference. The higher density and smaller territories found in the preferred habitat were apparently not due to the initial residents being less aggressive but were associated with higher immigrant pressure there, suggesting that more fish were trying to settle in the preferred habitat. There is also support for the more general hypothesis that breeding density is adjusted by an interaction between the territorial aggression of the initial settlers in an area and the number and persistence of later potential settlers. The trial using fewer fish (trial V) and the removal experiments give some support for such an interaction, since final densities were lower when there were fewer potential settlers in the whole arena.

Although this study is a valid experimental test of the original hypothesis, it might be argued that the results are not relevant to wild populations in natural habitats. The densities established in the present experiments were higher (up to 8 pairs per m²) than those measured in the field by Meral (1973), who found pairs 'evenly distributed (0·5–1 m apart) . . .' (i.e. 1–4 per m²). However, he also noted that 'most pairs kept conspecifics more than 0·2 m from the nest, usually attacking at 0·4 m', distances fairly similar to those found in the present study (0·2–0·3 m, Table 24.3). The density differences between field and laboratory situation may thus be due to differences in the distribution of suitable nest sites or in the number of potential settlers, neither of which was measured in the field study. The enclosure used in the present study was large relative to the size of the fish and their territories, and the nesting habitats approximated to those apparently used in the wild. It thus seems likely that the animals' territorial behaviour and the relationship between habitat preference and density might be similar to that found in nature.

The experimental design used in this study could also be used to test whether variations in the territorial aggressiveness of different stocks could lead to differences in density. Territory systems could be set up with fish of different aggressiveness, to test whether final densities differed in the predicted direction, with the more aggressive stock having larger territories and consequently a lower density.

REFERENCES

Davies, N.B. (1978). Ecological questions about territorial behaviour. In *Behavioural Ecology: An Evolutionary Approach* (Eds J.R. Krebs & N.B. Davies), pp. 317–350. Blackwell Scientific Publications, Oxford.

Fretwell, S.D. (1972). *Populations in a Seasonal Environment.* Princeton University Press, Princeton.

Glas, P. (1960). Factors governing density in the chaffinch (*Fringilla coelebs*) in different types of wood. *Archives Néerlandaises de Zoologie*, **13**, 466–472.

Kluyver, H.N. & Tinbergen, L. (1953). Territory and regulation of density in titmice. *Archives Néerlandaises de Zoologie*, **10**, 265–286.

Krebs, J.R. (1971). Territory and breeding density in the great tit *Parus major* L. *Ecology*, **52**, 2–22.

Laird, L.M. & Oswald, R.L. (1975). A note on the use of benzocaine (ethyl P-aminobenzoate) as a fish anaesthetic. *Journal of the Institute of Fish Management*, **6**, 92–94.

Meral, G.H. (1973). *The adaptive significance of territoriality in New World Cichlidae.* Unpublished Ph.D. thesis, Berkeley, California.

Moss, R. & Watson, A. (1980). Inherent changes in the aggressive behaviour of a fluctuating red grouse *Lagopus lagopus scoticus* population. *Ardea*, **68**, 113–119.

Partridge, L. (1978). Habitat selection. In Krebs, J.R. & Davies, N.B. (eds) *Behavioural Ecology. An Evolutionary Approach* (Eds J.R. Krebs & N.B. Davies), pp. 351–376. Blackwell Scientific Publications, Oxford.

Patterson, I.J. (1980). Territorial behaviour and the limitation of population density. *Ardea*, **68**, 53–62.

Pitelka, F.A. (1973). Cyclic pattern in lemming populations near Barrow, Alaska. In *Alaskan Arctic Tundra* (Ed. M.E. Britton), pp. 199–215. Arctic Institute of North America technical paper no. 25.

Riechert, S.E. (1979). Games spiders play. II. Resource assessment strategies. *Behavioural Ecology and Sociobiology*, **6**, 121–128.

Vines, G. (1979). Spatial distributions of territorial aggressiveness in Oystercatchers, *Haematopus ostralegus* L. *Animal Behaviour*, **27**, 300–308.

Watson, A. & Moss, R. (1980). Advances in our understanding of the population dynamics of red grouse from a recent fluctuation in numbers. *Ardea*, **68**, 103–111.

IV

BREEDING BEHAVIOUR AND POPULATION DYNAMICS

25. SEXUAL SELECTION OF POPULATION DYNAMICS IN AQUATIC CRUSTACEA

MARK RIDLEY AND DAVID J. THOMPSON

Departments of Zoology, Universities of Oxford and Liverpool

SUMMARY

A characteristic of the population dynamics of aquatic Crustacea is a seasonal cycle of the frequency distribution of individual sizes. Average size typically peaks early in the breeding season and then declines. Size in these species is influenced by sexual selection. Because of their female reproductive cycle, selection favours male choice. Males prefer larger mates because of their high fecundity. Samples recurrently demonstrate homogamy (i.e. assortative mating) for size; but the explanation of homogamy is controversial: it may be due to sexual selection, geography, or mechanics. Size, at least in *Asellus*, is heritable. The combination of heritability and sexual selection may drive the seasonal cycle of population dynamics.

Our aim in this review is to discuss how our growing knowledge of sexual selection in aquatic Crustacea might provide some understanding of their population dynamics. This understanding may come in any of three main forms. One is that sexual selection, over evolutionary time, may have influenced the value of parameters that control population dynamics—a relatively modest kind of illumination. Second, sexual selection would be of more direct importance if sexual selection itself drove the dynamical changes we observe in ecological times. A third interest is that an understanding of how sexual selection operates on a population might enable predictions to be made about how the population would respond to a change; furthermore, different hypotheses on the action of sexual selection might lead to different predictions. As we consider the subject, we shall see which of these three kinds of understanding can be gained.

POPULATION DYNAMICS OF AQUATIC CRUSTACEA

What do we know about the population dynamics of aquatic Crustacea in nature? When the pond net emerges from the water, the first thing the population ecologist sees is that the individuals of a population vary continuously in size. It is possible to count individuals over a certain time and plot their changes in abundance, but it is not very informative compared with a plot of the size–frequency distribution. Figure 25.1 shows a typical plot for the amphipod *Gammarus pulex* (Hynes 1955). This seasonal cycle of the size–frequency distribution, which is nearly always found, is at least as important for predicting population dynamics as the population abundance because (as we shall see) almost all reproductive parameters are affected by size.

If we want to understand the population dynamics of the seasonal size cycle and predict its future course, we must decide which parameters to measure. We should start with the relation of reproductive rate and size. We

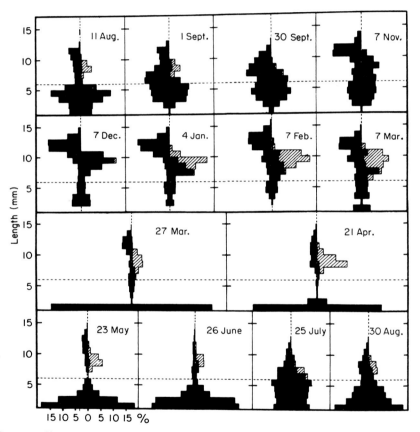

FIG. 25.1. Size and sex distribution in samples of *Gammarus pulex* from Shotwick, 1949–50. The length of the shrimps is given by the vertical scale, and the length of each horizontal size-group block represents the percentage of the total in that size-group. The horizontal dotted line (at 6 mm length) shows the lower limit of sex distinction: below this line the blocks are centred; above it males are shown on the left and females on the right. Females shown by the cross-hatched areas had fully bristled oostegites (from Hynes 1955).

should also want to know the relation of size with the time to maturity, the adult life span, how many times a female breeds, mate choice, and the mating rate. We should also need to know the heritability of size. If we knew all those factors for a population, we could predict its future size–frequency distribution. In the following section, we shall examine what we do know about them.

SEXUAL SELECTION IN CRUSTACEA

It has been well proved that within a species of aquatic Crustacea, larger females lay more eggs than smaller ones; this is known for many species (see Ridley & Thompson, 1979 for *Asellus* and Birkhead & Clarkson, 1980 for *Gammarus*). Although unsurprising, it is important. As we move on to the other factors, we shall concentrate on the two species that have been studied most. They are the isopod *Asellus aquaticus* and the amphipod *Gammarus pulex*. Both are widespread in freshwater in the UK and elsewhere. In *Asellus*, larger females (which lay more eggs than smaller females) reach maturity earlier in the season (Fig. 25.2). Larger males also mature earlier (Fig. 25.3). The seasonal cycle is at least partially caused by the higher death rate of larger males earlier in the season (which manifests itself in a female-biased sex ratio).

Let us turn now to mate choice. In a (so to speak) 'normal' animal, in which the male does little more than simply fertilize the female's eggs, mate choice can be practically ignored in population dynamics. The males will be selected to search for and mate with females as rapidly as possible, and it is

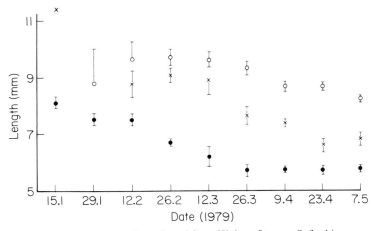

FIG. 25.2. The sizes of female *Asellus* collected from Hinksey Stream, Oxford in 1979 against the date of collection. Standard errors ($\pm$ 1 SE) are attached. ●, all females; X guarded females; o, brooding females. (From Ridley & Thompson 1979.)

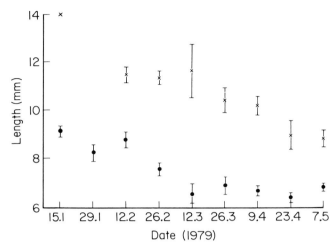

FIG. 25.3. The sizes of male *Asellus* collected from Hinksey Stream, Oxford in 1979 against the date of collection. Standard errors ($\pm$ 1 SE) are attached. ●, all males; X, guarding males. (From Ridley & Thompson 1979.)

reasonable to assume that all the females are mated as rapidly as they become ready to reproduce. In such a species the only possible effect of sexual selection on population dynamics would be through 'eugenics', i.e., female choice (or male competition) favouring males with better than average genes. Eugenic female choice can only operate if fitness is heritable. It is, of course, controversial whether fitness is at all heritable in natural populations. We shall return to that.

Aquatic Crustacea do not have that 'normal' mating system. The male does more than just inseminate the female. Typically, the male also 'guards' (Parker 1974) the female for a period of several days beforehand (see Ridley, 1983). This behaviour will change the kind of sexual selection. The male now invests a substantial amount of time in each mating. In a species in which the male invests no more than his sperm, males are selected to mate indiscriminately with all females; there is no advantage to being choosy. But in these crustaceans, males may be selected to discriminate, if mating with some kinds of females gives a higher rate of reproduction. Females vary in two relevant ways. Larger females lay more eggs; other things being equal, therefore, males are selected to mate with larger females. Secondly, because the moult cycles of the females are not synchronized, at any one time some females will be nearer to their next moult than others; males are selected to enter precopula with females that are nearer to their moult. Both predictions have been tested in *Asellus*.

Manning (1975) first demonstrated that, when given the choice, males entered precopula preferentially with larger females (Fig. 25.4). Subsequently, Thompson & Manning (1981) showed that males enter precopula preferentially with females that are closer to their moult. They also suggested that males were able to trade off the virtues of small versus large size, with time from the moult.

Other factors, we can predict, should affect the male's decision of whether to enter precopula with a particular female. One is the sex ratio. If it is more female-biased, a male should be choosier than if it is more male-biased. Manning (1980) has tested this prediction too, also in *Asellus*. He varied the sex ratio experimentally in laboratory populations of *Asellus*, and discovered that, as the sex ratio was made more female-biased, the mean duration of precopula decreased (Table 25.1). Ward (1983a) has shown that the absolute number of mates and competitors also influences the male's guarding

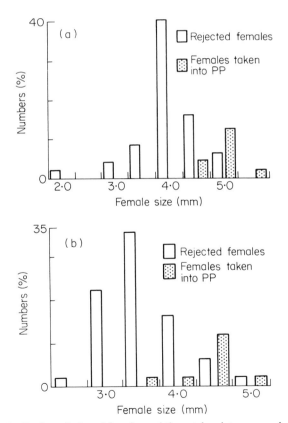

FIG. 25.4. Size distribution of rejected females and those taken into precopula by (a) *Asellus aquaticus*, (b) *A. meridianus*. (From Manning 1975.)

Table 25.1. Precopula durations at three different sex ratios in *Asellus*. Experiments by Manning (1980)

Sex ratio	*A. aquaticus*		*A. meridianus*	
♂:♀	Precopula duration (days)	Sample size	Precopula duration	Sample size
35:70 (0·5:1)	5·1	30	5·1	17
70:70 (1:1)	6·1	21	7·7	21
105:70 (1·5:1)	7·7	19	9·4	18

decision. When there are more competitors, males guard for longer both because they are more likely to lose a female per unit time and a female becoming available is more likely to be taken into precopula by another male. When there are more females in the population, a male will be more likely to find one within any given fraction of the moult cycle if the females remain unpaired, as the females do not appear to be synchronized in their breeding, and so the mean guarding time decreases.

Another factor is size. A male's size matters because, in *Asellus*, larger males can take over females from precopula with smaller males (Ridley & Thompson 1979). That makes the sex ratio effectively female-biased for large males, because the smaller males effectively do not exist; a female paired to a smaller male is like an unpaired female if it is costless to take over. Accordingly, the prediction is that larger males should have shorter precopulas than smaller males (Grafen & Ridley 1983). Disconcertingly they do not (Fig. 25.5, Table 25.2). The result is quite clear, and highly significant. The same results has been obtained by Ward (1983a) for *Gammarus* and again goes against theory. We do not fully understand this result.

There is a general point here. Size controls fecundity in females. It is also sexually selected in males. Any selection on males results in a correlated response in females. Therefore, sexual selection in males will result (evolutionarily speaking) in higher fecundity. Similarly there can be conflict between sexual and natural selection which may reduce fecundity. For example, natural selection works against large size, both through selective predation on larger sized individuals (Berglund, 1968), and the effects of current speed; larger *Gammarus* males suffer higher mortality than smaller ones at high current speeds (Ward 1983a). Sexual selection, at least, must have influenced the evolution of some of the parameters (such as female fecundity and survivorship) governing population dynamics.

Predation is one more factor (and the last for now). If the rate of predation is different on precopulatory pairs to that on individuals, then duration of precopula should vary with predation rate. This has been tested by Strong

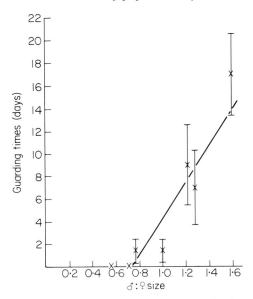

FIG. 25.5. The relation between guarding time (days) and ratio of male to female size for *Asellus aquaticus* (see also Table 25.2). (From Ridley & Thompson 1979.)

(1973) for the amphipod *Hyalella azteca*, which is similar to *Gammarus*. Precopulatory pairs of *Hyalella* are taken more by predators, and Strong found that where predation was higher, precopula was shorter.

Let us now turn to population-level consequences of these sexually selected factors. One consequence is obvious. Because larger females lay more eggs, the peak time of reproduction corresponds to the time when the average sizes of the female population is largest. The disproportionate reproduction of larger males has a more subtle effect, for it reduces the 'effective population number', that crucial variable of population genetics (see Partridge 1983).

But the scheme of sexual selection that we have outlined leads to a less obvious prediction. Males (as we have seen) prefer larger females, nearer their time of moult, and larger males can take females over from the smaller males. Put these two factors together, and the prediction of homogamy (or assortative mating) for size comes out. All the males would prefer to mate with larger females, but only the larger males can capitalize on their preference because smaller males will generally be dispossessed (Fig. 25.6). They are left with the smaller females. We have tested this prediction in *Asellus*, and it has been confirmed.

We have been tempted to generalize the prediction. If the factors we have

TABLE 25.2 (a) Mean guarding times (days) for *Asellus* pairs of various male and female sizes and (b) an analysis of variance of the guarding times. (From Ridley & Thompson 1979.)

(a)

		Female size (mm)	
		7	9
	5	0	0
Male size (mm)	7	0·33	1·33
	9	7	2·33
	11	17	9

(b) Analysis of variance

Source of variation	Degrees of freedom	Sum of squares	Mean square	F	P
Subgroups	7	902·54	128·93		
Female size	1	42·67	42·67	1·79	NS
Male size	3	796·83	265·61	11·18	<0·001
F × M interaction	3	63·04	21·01	0·89	NS
Within groups	16	379·96	23·75		

been discussing were the whole story (and they probably are not) then, in any species in which there is a precopula (or some other sizable male investment in mating), and larger females lay more eggs, and larger males can take over females from smaller males, mating should also be homogamous for size. The predicted comparative trend exists and is statistically significant (see Ridley 1983) for details).

Before we can take the story to the next stage we must meet some criticism. The interpretation of sexual selection in aquatic Crustacea that we have just been through is controversial. The main evidence has come from the isopod *Asellus*; it has been challenged mainly with evidence from the amphipod *Gammarus*. *Gammarus* has a similar reproductive cycle to *Asellus* and, like *Asellus*, it is homogamous for size.

We should explain its homogamy by sexual selection: because larger females are more fecund and it has a precopula, males will be selected to choose larger females. The third variable in the theory is the competitive superiority of larger males. All studies agree that, in samples, larger males are disproportionately represented in precopulatory pairs, which suggests that larger males enjoy a competitive advantage; but the direct evidence is more conflicting. Ward (1983a,b) reported two experiments in which paired *Gammarus* were placed in containers with at least one other male. In the first experiment, when only one other male was present 9% of paired males lost

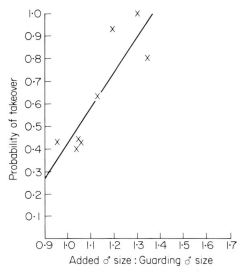

FIG. 25.6. The probability of takeover for various ratios of added male/original male size when single males are added to pairs already in precopula. (From Ridley & Thompson 1979.)

their female to the second male. In the other experiment with more single males present, 22% of males lost their female before her moult. Though Ward has not seen a takeover, he (pers. comm.) and one of us (DJT) has witnessed single males attacking precopula pairs.

Birkhead & Clarkson (1980) proposed that homogamy is caused by random mating with microgeographic variation for size. Larger individuals, they suggest, inhabit microhabitats that differ in substrate particle size from the microhabitats of smaller individuals. Larger individuals occur in one place, smaller individuals in another. The individuals pair up locally at random and homogamy only appears when the samples from more than one locality are mixed. We disagree with them for reasons that one of us has discussed at length elsewhere (Ridley 1983) and from evidence provided by Thompson & Moule (1983). Thompson & Moule (1983) confirmed that large *Gammarus* prefer substrates with larger particle size than small *Gammarus*; however, in choice experiments in artificial streams in the laboratory, *Gammarus* males and females showed homogamy within each of three substrates differing in mean particle size (Table 25.3). But Birkhead and Clarkson's study does strongly suggest a geographical contribution to homogamy in *Gammarus*.

Mechanical constraint is another kind of explanation of homogamy. Homogamy for size was first demonstrated in *Gammarus* by Crozier & Snyder (1923, cf. Ridley 1983). They supposed that small males were physically

TABLE 25.3. The correlation coefficient of length between male and female *Gammarus pulex* in precopula on three different substrate types (from Thompson & Moule 1983)

Substrate type (determined by sieving)	Correlation coefficient	Sample size	Probability
Fine gravel	0·49	58	<0·001
Medium	0·53	46	<0·001
Coarse	0·38	115	<0·001

incapable of holding on to large females and large males to small females. They provided no evidence, and Birkhead & Clarkson (1980) refuted them by a simple experiment. More recently Adams & Greenwood (1983) have provided evidence of another kind of mechanical constraint in *Gammarus*. 'Where the male in a pair is relatively larger than the female the swimming performance is superior to those pairs in which the males and female are of similar sizes'. They tested *Gammarus* pairs in artificial streams and demonstrated that pairs in which the male was relatively large swam more powerfully (Fig. 25.7).

They actually only used their result to explain why the male *Gammarus* has evolved to be larger than the females, but also suggested, as an 'implication', that the 'pattern of [homogamy] found in *G. pulex* may be a compromise for

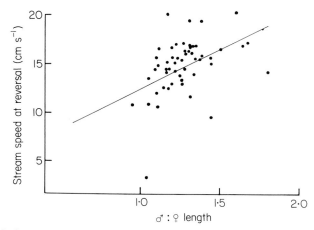

FIG. 25.7. Maximum stream speeds at which precopula pairs of *Gammarus pulex* were able to make forward progress; $r = 0.43$; $P < 0.002$. (From Adams & Greenwood 1983.)

the male between minimizing the risk of swimming impairment and maximizing the number of eggs he fertilizes'. This is another possible explanation of homogamy for size. Adams and Greenwood would predict a larger size ratio of male to female in fast moving streams than in still water, and have subsequently confirmed their prediction (Greenwood & Adams 1984). Ward, however, has obtained the opposite result (see Table 25.4). According to your prior bias, you may conclude that sexual selection is here under assault, or yet to be confirmed.

In any event, the swimming performance of pairs will affect the population dynamics of the species. Downstream drift is a most important phenomenon in the ecology of most stream-dwelling invertebrates, and gammarids have figured prominently in studies on drift (Elliott 1965; Marchant 1981; Müller 1963, 1966). All studies have shown that the amount of drift increases at night, particularly in the period soon after sunset. Müller's (1966) study of a small spring-stream in Germany is of particular interest for he showed that the maximum drift of *Gammarus* occurred in summer, which is the time of maximum breeding. In artificial streams in the laboratory, Ward (1983a) has shown that female survivorship is unaffected by current speed but increasing current decreased male survivorship and increased precopula duration. Here is another relation of population dynamics and sexual selection through the common factor of stream drift.

The sexual selection upon males to choose larger females may well reduce population growth rate because individuals are swept away downstream. But whether or not there is such male choice, the evolution of the precopula habit alone will have reduced population growth, because pairs swim more than single *Gammarus* (Adams & Greenwood 1983) and swimming more, they are more liable to be lost downstream. The increase in mortality will, in turn, have selected against the evolution of precopula. Sexual selection is here again setting the variables that govern population dynamics.

In the evolution of those variables, it will have mattered whether homogamy was caused by sexual selection, microgeographic differentiation,

TABLE 25.4. Size ratios of pairs of *Gammarus pulex* in still and running water

Size measured by	Average size ratio ♂/♀			Location	Authority
	Still water		Running water		
Length	1·4	NS	1·3	Liverpool	Ward (pers. comm.)
Weight	2·12		2·78	Newcastle	Greenwood &
		$P < 0.005$			Adams (1984)

or mechanical constraint. But, for the stronger question of whether the homogamic habit influences population dynamics in ecological time it does not matter which process is responsible for homogamy. If homogamy did turn out to be important, the question of its cause might become important again, for different causes would predict different responses to changes in the population. If, for example, homogamy were caused purely by sexual selection, and microgeographic differentiation and downstream drift had no effect, then changing the stream current or bottom particles should not alter the population dynamics; conversely, if they did matter such changes should affect the population dynamics.

   If homogamy for size is to have much effect on population dynamics, size must be heritable. Then the larger parents will produce proportionally larger offspring, which will have higher fecundities, and increase population growth. *Asellus* (as we have seen) is homogamous for size, and one of us (DJT) has measured the heritability of size in this species. For males $h^2 = 0.40$ (± 0.18, $P < 0.05$) and for females, $h^2 = 0.49$ (± 0.19, $P < 0.01$). At first sight this is a rather surprising result for a character that closely determines fitness (Falconer 1981). By contrast, other authors have found very low or zero heritabilities of size in species in which size is closely related to fitness (e.g. Sigurjonsdottir (1980) for *Scatophaga stercoraria* and Solbrig & Solbrig (1984) for two species of plants). It is, at present, a question of theoretical and empirical controversy whether fitness in natural populations is strongly heritable (Eshel & Hamilton 1984; Hamilton 1980, 1982; Lande 1976; Maynard Smith 1982; and several papers in Bateson 1983). We cannot therefore say whether the conflicting results for *Asellus* and other species are paradoxical.

SEXUAL SELECTION OF POPULATION DYNAMICS IN AQUATIC CRUSTACEA

Let us now return to the original problem, the seasonal cycle of the size–frequency distribution. We cannot explain this pattern, but we can summarize some of the ways in which sexual selection is influencing it. In *Asellus*, at least, the larger pairs breed first. At any one time, in addition, mating is homogamous for size. The larger males pair with the larger females; because larger females are more fecund, they will leave more offspring than average; because size is heritable, they will leave larger offspring than average. Their offspring probably grow to reproduce early in the next season. The larger individuals suffer a higher mortality rate, and the average size decreases. Now it is the turn of the smaller individuals to breed, although there is still homogamy superimposed on the seasonal change.

The factors that we have been discussing cannot alone control the population dynamics of aquatic Crustacea. There must be other factors, external environmental ones, that set the breeding season in the late winter (see Andersson 1969; Økland 1978). But however that may be, for any detailed understanding of the population dynamics, individual variation cannot be ignored (see also Begon 1984). One must know what traits control differences in fitness, and what those differences are. In aquatic Crustacea, the main such trait that has been identified is size. Within the context of the crustacean mating system, size controls fecundity, mating rate, time of maturation, and mortality rate. The sexual selection of size may well be the factor controlling population dynamics. At all events, it cannot be ignored. Whatever the ecological fruits of such research, it has taught us a lot about the natural selection of reproductive behaviour.

ACKNOWLEDGMENT

We are grateful to Paul Ward for permitting us to use his unpublished data in Table 25.4, and to him and Tim Birkhead for their critical and constructive comments on an earlier version of the manuscript.

REFERENCES

Adams, J. & Greenwood, P.J. (1983). Why are males bigger than females in precopula pairs of *Gammarus pulex*? *Behavioural Ecology and Sociobiology*, **13**, 239–241.

Andersson, E. (1969). Life cycle and growth of *Asellus aquaticus* (L.) with special reference to the effects of temperature. *Institute of Freshwater Research Drottingholm Reports*, **49**, 5–26.

Bateson, P. (Ed.) (1983). *Mate Choice*. Cambridge University Press, Cambridge.

Begon, M. (1984). Density and individual fitness; asymmetric competition. *Evolutionary Ecology* (Ed. by B. Shorrocks). Blackwell Scientific Publications, Oxford.

Berglund, T. (1968). The influence of predation by brown trout on *Asellus* in a pond. *Institute of Freshwater Research Drottingholm Report*, **48**, 77–101.

Birkhead, T. & Clarkson, K. (1980). Mate selection and precopulatory guarding in *Gammarus pulex*. *Zeitschrift für Tierpsychologie*, **52**, 365–380.

Crozier, W.J. & Snyder, L.H. (1923). Selective coupling in gammarids. *Biological Bulletin*, **45**, 97–104.

Elliott, J.M. (1965). Daily fluctuations of drift invertebrates in a Dartmoor stream. *Nature*, **205**, 1127–1129.

Eshel, I. & Hamilton, W.D. (1984). Parent–offspring correlation in fitness under fluctuating selection. *Proceedings of the Royal Society of London B*, 222, 1–4.

Falconer, D.S. (1981). *Introduction to Quantitative Genetics* (2nd edn). Oliver & Boyd, Edinburgh.

Grafen, A. & Ridley, M. (1983). A model of mate guarding. *Journal of Theoretical Biology*, **102**, 549–567.

Greenwood, P.J. & Adams, J. (1984). Sexual dimorphism in *Gammarus pulex*: the effect of current flow on precopula pair formation. *Freshwater Biology*, **14**, 203–209.

Hamilton, W.D. (1980). Sex versus non-sex versus parasite. *Oikos*, **35**, 282–290.

Hamilton, W.D. (1982). Pathogens as causes of genetic diversity in their host populations.

Population Biology of Infectious Diseases (Ed. by R.M. Anderson & R.M. May), pp. 269–296. Springer-Verlag, Berlin.

Hynes, H.N. (1955). The reproductive cycle of some British freshwater Gammaridae. *Journal of Animal Ecology*, **24**, 352–387.

Lande, R. (1976). The maintenance of genetic variability by mutation in a polygenic character with linked loci. *Genetical Research*, **26**, 221–235.

Manning, J.T. (1975). Male discrimination in *Asellus aquaticus* (L.) and *A. meridianus* Racovitza (Crustacea: Isopoda). *Behaviour*, **55**, 1–14.

Manning, J.T. (1980). Sex ratio and optimal male time investment strategies in *Asellus aquaticus* (L.) and *A. meridianus* Racovitza. *Behaviour*, **74**, 264–273.

Marchant, R. (1981). The ecology of *Gammarus* in running water. *Perspectives in Running Water Ecology*. (Ed. by M.A. Lock & D.D. Williams), pp. 225–249. Plenum Press, New York.

Maynard Smith, J. (1982). *Evolution and the Theory of Games*, Cambridge University Press, Cambridge.

Müller, K. (1963). Diurnal rhythm in 'organic drift' of *Gammarus pulex*. *Nature*, **198**, 806–807.

Müller, K. (1966). Die Tagesperiodik von Fliesswasserorganismen. *Zeitschrift für Morphologie der Tiere*, **56**, 93–142.

Økland, K.A. (1978). Life history and growth of *Asellus aquaticus* (L.) in relation to environment in eutrophic lakes in Norway. *Hydrobiologia*, **59**, 243–259.

Parker, G.A. (1974). Courtship persistence and female-guarding as male time investment strategies. *Behaviour*, **48**, 157–184.

Partridge, L. (1983). Non-random mating and offspring fitness. *Mate Choice* (Ed. by P. Bateson), pp. 227–256. Cambridge University Press, Cambridge.

Ridley, M. (1983). *The Explanation of Organic Diversity*. Clarendon Press, Oxford.

Ridley, M. & Thompson, D.J. (1979). Size and mating in *Asellus aquaticus* (Crustacea: Isopoda). *Zeitschrift für Tierpsychologie*, **51**, 380–397.

Sigurjonsdottir, H. (1980). *Evolutionary aspects of sexual dimorphism in size: studies on dungflies and three groups of birds*. Unpublished Ph.D. thesis, University of Liverpool.

Solbrig, O.T. & Solbrig, D.J. (1984). Size inequalities and fitness in plant populations. *Oxford Surveys in Evolutionary Biology*, **1**, 139–157.

Strong, D.L. (1973). Amphipod amplexus, the significance of ecotypic variation. *Ecology*, **54**, 1383–1388.

Thompson, D.J. & Manning, J.T. (1981). Mate selection by *Asellus* (Crustacea: Isopoda). *Behaviour*, **78**, 178–187.

Thompson, D.J. & Moule, S.J. (1983). Substrate selection and assortative mating in *Gammarus pulex* L. *Hydrobiologia*, **99**, 3–6.

Ward, P.I. (1983a). Advantages and a disadvantage of large size for male *Gammarus pulex* (Crustacea: Amphipoda). *Behavioural Ecology and Sociobiology*, **14**, 69–76.

Ward, P.I. (1983b). *Sexual selection in* Gammarus *and* Sepsis. Unpublished Ph.D. thesis, University of Liverpool.

26. OVIPOSITION, OVICIDE AND LARVAL COMPETITION IN GRANIVOROUS INSECTS

R. H. SMITH[1] AND C. M. LESSELLS[2]

[1]*Department of Pure and Applied Zoology, University of Reading, Reading RG6 2AJ, and*

[2]*Department of Pure & Applied Biology, Imperial College at Silwood Park, Ascot SL5 7PY*

SUMMARY

The larvae of internally feeding granivores are generally unable to migrate between seeds. Competition between larvae reduces both survival and the expected fecundity of the larvae. In this paper, we discuss three problems that arise because larvae are confined within seeds selected for them by their mother. The first two concern the behaviour of the mother. (i) How should the mother distribute eggs between seeds? (ii) Should she attempt to reduce the competition faced by her offspring by some form of ovicide? The third problem concerns the behaviour of larvae within a seed. (iii) Should a larva coexist peacefully or attempt to find and kill competitors within the seed? The last problem relates to the traditional ecological dichotomy between 'scramble' and 'contest' competition, and we discuss different meanings of the terms.

INTRODUCTION

Competition between animals for limited resources is a major functional determinant of life-history strategies and behaviour. Competition is particularly a problem for those granivorous insects (mainly beetles and moths) whose immature stages spend their lives within a single seed. In this paper we develop models to predict the optimal behaviour in relation to ecological features of the different granivore species and the species of seed that they infest. The ecology of the granivore species, in terms of both population structuring and the effects of larval competition, has important effects on the evolution of behaviour, while the behaviour has consequences for the rate of population growth and stability. Thus, ecology and behaviour are intimately linked.

The adults of internally feeding granivores lay eggs on or inside a seed, the larvae and pupae feed and grow within that seed, and adults emerge to mate

[2] *Present address: Department of Zoology, University of Sheffield, Sheffield S10 2TN.*

and lay their eggs. We will consider three problems that arise because a larva is confined within a seed chosen by its mother.

    (i) *Oviposition*: how should a female distribute eggs between seeds to maximize her fitness?

    (ii) *Ovicide*: should a female attempt to reduce the competition faced by her offspring by killing eggs already present?

    (iii) *Larval competition*: should a larva coexist with other larvae in a seed, or alternatively attempt to seek out and attack them?

The data presented in support of our models are from studies of stored product pests which are more tractable experimentally than most animals. Specifically we will refer to bean weevils of the family Bruchidae and true weevils of the family Curculionidae (the two families contain about 50 000 known species), but some of our models have a wider application to other animals whose young compete within discrete patches of a resource.

Problems (i) and (ii) concern the behaviour of the adult female and (iii) that of the larva, but the optimal solutions all depend critically on the effects of larval competition on survival and fecundity. Our approach is based on four main concepts, defined as follows.

Larval fitness (s): the probability of a larva emerging successfully multiplied by its potential fecundity.

Female fitness (F): the number of female offspring surviving to emerge multiplied by their potential fecundity (see next section).

Most productive clutch size (N^*): the number of eggs per seed which maximizes the number of adults emerging from a seed (called the 'Lack solution' by some authors, e.g. Charnov & Skinner 1984; Waage & Godfray, p. 450).

Optimal clutch size ($\hat{N}$): the number of eggs that an individual female should leave on a seed to maximize the incremental addition to her fitness F.

Because the female's fitness is the product of the larval fitness and the number of larvae, maximization of the female's fitness does not necessarily imply maximization of the fitness of individual larvae. In the next section, we justify our definitions of fitness by considering observed relationships between larval density, survival and fecundity.

THE LARVAL COMPETITION CURVE

Generally, weevil larvae are not able to migrate between seeds. Hence there is competition between larvae within a seed and survival decreases with increasing density (Fig. 26.1). Not only larval survival but also the weight of adults at emergence will be affected by competition (Fig. 26.2b). Both fecundity (Fig. 26.2a) and longevity (Fig. 26.4) are related to weight, and these

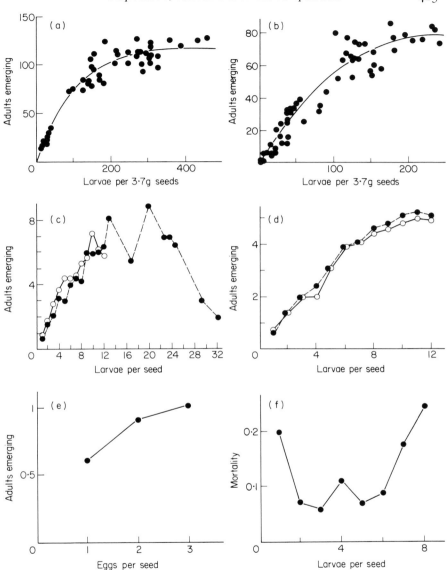

FIG. 26.1. Effects of larval competition on numbers surviving to emergence in some granivorous insects: (a) *Callosobruchus chinensis* and (b) *C. maculatus* on cowpeas (after Bellows 1982a); (c) *C. maculatus* (O) and *C. rhodesianus* (●) on cowpeas (after Giga 1982); (d) *C. chinensis* (●) and *C. maculatus* (O) on azuki beans (after Umeya, Kato & Kocha 1975); (e) *C. maculatus* on mung beans (after Mitchell 1975); (f) *Zabrotes subfasciatus* on azuki beans (after Utida 1967; a plot of mortality rather than survival). Other relationships are described by Booker 1967; Crombie 1944; Giga 1978; Fujii 1968; Howard 1983; Nakamura 1967; Nwanze & Horber 1975; Utida 1942, 1972.

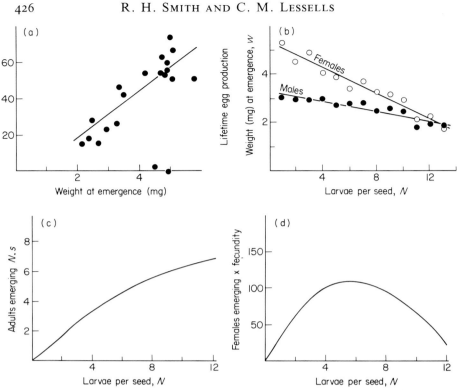

FIG. 26.2. Effects of larval competition on emergence weight and fecundity of adult bean weevils on cowpeas: (a) *C. chinensis* (C.M. Lessells, unpubl.); (b)–(d) *C. maculatus* (after Giga 1982). Giga's fitted curves related: (b) emergence weight w to initial larval density N ($w = 5\cdot50 - 0\cdot28N$ for females); (c) survival s to initial larval density N (when $N = 1$, $s = 0\cdot79$, when $N = 2$, $s = 0\cdot85$, when $N > 2$, $s = 0\cdot96 - 0\cdot031N$); (d) female fecundity f to weight w ($f = 24w - 44\cdot8$), giving the larval competition curve shown.

effects should be included in any measure of fitness (Andersson 1978). Figure 26.2c,d, show the effect of including fecundity as well as larval survival when measuring larval fitness in relation to larval density. A plot of total larval fitness ($N.s$) as a function of larval density (N) will be referred to as a *larval competition curve* (e.g. Fig. 26.2d).

Unfortunately, including the potential fecundity of female larvae in our definition does not give a complete measure of fitness because we do not know how reproductive success varies with weight in males. Weight at emergence must be particularly important in those granivorous moths and beetles (e.g. *Callosobruchus* species) whose adults cannot feed on seed and rely for survival and reproduction on energy reserves accumulated during the larval stage.

We shall assume that the larval competition curve is generally of the form derived for *Callosobruchus maculatus* in Fig. 26.2d. However, although survival usually decreases monotonically with density, a few species show an Allée effect where survival initially increases with increasing density (e.g. Fig. 26.1f; also Giga & Smith 1981).

FEMALE OVIPOSITION BEHAVIOUR: OPTIMAL CLUTCH SIZE

At the simplest level, we expect females to choose to oviposit on the seeds which offer their larvae the best prospects in terms of survival and fecundity. Other things being equal (including seed quality), females should choose to oviposit on those seeds which currently have fewest eggs, which will result in a distribution of eggs over seeds that is more uniform than random. Uniform distributions are found in the genus *Callosobruchus* (Utida 1943; Yoshida 1961; Nakamura 1967; Umeya *et al.* 1975; Mitchell 1975), but the egg distributions of some other species, notably weevils of the genus *Sitophilus*, tend to be clumped (Richards 1947; Segrove 1951; Umeya 1966; Utida 1967; Umeya & Kato 1970; Dobie 1974; Arbogast & Miller 1978; Shazali 1982; Holloway 1984).

Previous models

Mitchell (1975) investigated the effect of seed quality on larval survival, and showed that single larvae survived better in larger seeds, although survival was independent of seed weight for higher larval densities. Mitchell proposed that the optimal oviposition strategy for a single female would be to produce a uniform distribution in which the first egg per bean is added to the largest seeds first, and the second to the smallest seeds first; in fact, the beans with most eggs were always the heaviest in distributions with up to three eggs per bean (Mitchell 1975). Mitchell's model constrains both the total number of seeds and eggs; he did not consider whether females would have achieved greater lifetime fitness by laying more (or fewer) eggs on more (or fewer) seeds.

A number of general models (e.g. Charnov & Skinner 1984; Iwasa, Suzuki & Matsuda 1984; Parker & Courtney 1984) consider the optimal oviposition strategies of insects. The constraints they consider are the amount of resource (oviposition sites), the total time available, or the number of eggs that the female can lay. The constraints can act alone or in combination and may or may not be independent. For instance, both time and egg load may be limiting but independent of each other. On the other hand, an increase in the number of eggs laid may decrease life expectancy so that time for oviposition and number of eggs are interdependent (e.g. Fig. 26.4).

All such models include some kind of resource (nest, host or seed) into which eggs are laid, and offspring survival and fecundity are a function of the number of eggs per resource unit. In common with the above models, we seek the clutch size which will maximize the female's lifetime reproductive success. We do not consider the advantages of early reproduction (Cole 1954), the effects of variation in reproductive success (Gillespie 1977), the effects of variation in resource quality (cf. Högstedt 1980; Mitchell 1975; Iwasa *et al.* 1984), or problems of sex allocation (cf. Charnov 1982; Waage & Godfray, p. 449).

Single oviposition

We consider first the case in which a single female is ovipositing and does not revisit beans.

When the amount of resource (seed) is the sole constraint, females should maximize their reproductive success per resource unit (Lack 1947; Charnov & Skinner 1984; Parker & Courtney 1984). If there is a trade-off between the number of offspring and their expected survival, then there will be a most productive clutch size (*sensu* Charnov & Krebs 1974) N^* which maximizes the product of clutch size and offspring survival (Fig. 26.3a) (Lack 1947). Clearly it never pays a single female to lay more than the most productive clutch size on a single seed, since her fitness decreases when N exceeds N^*; hence the optimal clutch size must lie between 0 and N^*.

However, females may be constrained by time rather than resource availability, and by laying smaller clutches females can increase the time available to visit other resource units. The trade-off between number of resources visited and the time spent at each can be examined by considering time as the constraint instead of amount of resource. Charnov & Skinner (1984) use the graphical version of the marginal value theorem (Charnov 1976) to show that when time is a constraint, females should lay less than the most productive clutch size and that clutch size should increase with time spent searching for resource units (Fig. 26.3b).

The above model assumes that the total time available for foraging is independent of the number of eggs laid. However, an increase in reproductive effort is likely to reduce a female's life expectancy (Williams 1966; Charnov & Krebs 1974); this cost of reproduction is particulary important in those moths and weevils whose reserves are not renewable. Reserves are used either for egg production or for maintenance (Fig. 26.4), and a conversion rate can be specified between eggs laid and life-span. The trade-off can be modelled using the marginal value theorem with 'egg equivalents' replacing time as the constraint. Search time is expressed as the number of eggs T (energy content

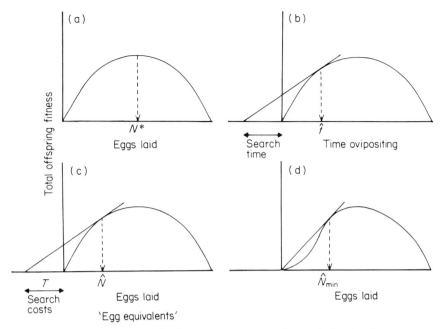

FIG. 26.3. Prediction of optimal clutch size from curves relating total offspring fitness to oviposition effort. (a) *Resource units limiting*: offspring fitness as a function of eggs laid. The optimal clutch size $\hat{N}$ is the most productive clutch size N^* (*sensu* Charnov & Krebs 1974); (b) *Time limiting*: offspring fitness as a function of time spent ovipositing. Clutch size is assumed to be proportional to time t spent ovipositing. The optimal time $\hat{t}$ (and hence $\hat{N}$) is found by constructing the tangent to the curve from the point representing the time taken to search for and find new resource units; (c) *Energetic reserves limiting*: as (b) except that offspring fitness is shown as a function of clutch size, and search costs (T) are expressed in egg equivalents; (d) *An Allée effect* implies a lower limit to optimal clutch size, N_{min}.

divided by conversion efficiency plus maintenance energy during oviposition) that must be metabolically sacrificed to provide the energy (including maintenance) to search for a new resource unit (Fig. 26.3c).

The qualitative predictions are the same as those when time is the constraint: *as search costs* (T) *increase, so does the optimal clutch size.* Since T (expressed as egg equivalents) will be small for most granivores infesting seed stores or crop monocultures, females should lay few eggs per seed (perhaps only one). (Note that an Allée effect will set a lower limit $\hat{N}_{min}$ to the optimal clutch size, even when travel costs are zero (Fig. 26.3d; Parker & Courtney 1984).)

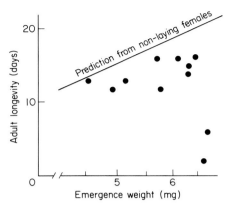

FIG. 26.4. Cost of reproduction in *Callosobruchus analis*: females who lay eggs live less long than non-laying females. Females were weighed at emergence, kept with males for 24 hours to allow mating, and then placed singly on azuki beans. The solid line (————) is a least squares regression fit for those females which failed to lay eggs plus a control group of unmated females; data points (●) are for females which laid eggs, and all points fall below the line (R.H. Smith & P. King, unpubl.).

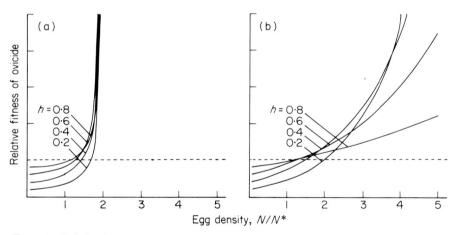

FIG. 26.5. Relative fitness of non-selective ovicidal behaviour plotted against egg density for: (a) linear larval survival function; (b) exponential larval survival function. A female lays an egg and applies an ovicide which kills with probability $(1-h)$ each of the N eggs and larvae in the seed; N includes her own egg. The relative fitness plotted is the ratio of the expected fitnesses of ovicidal and non-ovicidal behaviour and can only exceed 1 when N exceeds the most productive clutch size N^*. If some eggs were invulnerable to ovicide, the curves would be of similar shape but the relative fitness of ovicide would be lower. Relative fitness is given by: (a) $h \cdot (1 - h \cdot N/2N^*)$ for the linear survival function; (b) $h.\exp (N \cdot (1-h)/N^*)$ for the exponential survival function.

Multiple oviposition

So far we have only discussed the problem of oviposition tactics when one female is exploiting a resource. The optimal oviposition behaviour may change when other females are ovipositing on the same seeds (Andersson & Eriksson 1982; Parker & Courtney 1984). Empirical data show that females are able to respond to eggs already laid on a seed; oviposition markers (oviposition deterring pheromones) are produced by bean weevils including *Callosobruchus chinensis*, *C. maculatus* (Yoshida 1961), *C. rhodesianus* (Giga 1982), *Zabrotes subfasciatus* and *Acanthoscelides obtectus* (Szentesi 1981). Surprisingly, there is no evidence that females of *Sitophilus* species respond to the protein plugs with which they seal their eggs into oviposition holes.

As Parker & Courtney have shown, the female's optimal behaviour depends on whether early ovipositing females know at the time they oviposit how many other females have oviposited or will oviposit on the same seed. In order to examine the effect of multiple ovipositions we will discuss two extreme alternatives. In the first, a female assesses how many eggs the seed bears already and assumes that she is the last female to lay there. In the second, we assume that a group of females lay on the seed, and that each knows, at the time of oviposition, how many other females will lay there. We use the two models to examine how the clutch size laid by an individual female, and the total number of eggs laid on a seed, should vary with the number of females. Is there, for instance, an upper limit to the total number of eggs that females should oviposit on seeds?

Model 1a. We model the effects of multiple oviposition under an 'egg equivalents' constraint using the marginal value theorem, and ask first how many eggs, N, a female should add to a seed that already contains x eggs if she will be the last female to oviposit. The fitness (including fecundity effects) of each of the $(N+x)$ eggs is given by a function $s(N, x)$. Hence, the total fitness of surviving offspring is

$$F(N, x) = N \cdot s(N, x)$$

Differentiating with respect to N:

$$\frac{dF}{dN} = s(N, x) + N \cdot s'(N, x) \tag{1}$$

where primes denote derivatives with respect to N. Using the marginal value theorem (Charnov 1976), the female's optimal clutch size, $\hat{N}$, is found at the point where the tangent from $(-T, 0)$ meets the curve $F(N, x)$ (Fig. 26.3c), i.e. when

$$\frac{\hat{N} \cdot s(\hat{N}, x)}{T + \hat{N}} = s(\hat{N}, x) + \hat{N} \cdot s'(\hat{N}, x)$$

or by rearrangement,

$$-\frac{s(\hat{N}, x)}{s'(\hat{N}, x)} = \frac{\hat{N} \cdot (\hat{N} + T)}{T} \tag{2}$$

For analytical convenience we consider a linear fitness function (Perrins & Moss 1975):

$$s(N, x) = a - b \cdot (N + x) \tag{3}$$

and an exponential fitness function (Bellows 1981; Waage & Godfray, p. 455):

$$s(N, x) = \exp[-c \cdot (N + x)] \tag{4}$$

Both of these functions decrease monotonically with increasing N. The essential difference between the functions is that fitness is always greater than zero for the exponential function, but is equal to zero for the linear function when $N = a/b$.

Substituting for the linear function into eqn (2) and ignoring the negative root gives the solution for $\hat{N}$:

$$\hat{N} = -T + \sqrt{T^2 + T \cdot (2N^* - x)} \tag{5}$$

$\hat{N}$ decreases monotonically with increasing x and is equal to zero when $x = 2N^*$ (because larval fitness becomes zero). Thus, $2N^*$ is the maximum number of eggs expected on a seed.

Similarly for the exponential function, the positive root is:

$$\hat{N} = \frac{-T + \sqrt{T^2 + 4N^* \cdot T}}{2} \tag{6}$$

That is, $\hat{N}$ is independent of x, the number of eggs already on the seed, and there is no upper limit to the total number of eggs expected on a seed (because larval fitness never drops to zero). The contrast between the predictions of the linear and exponential fitness functions emphasizes the caution that should be exercised in choosing functions a priori and in drawing general conclusions from a specific model.

Model 1b. The above analysis solves for the optimal clutch size when all the seeds carry the same number (x) of eggs, and asks how optimal clutch size varies *between environments* with different x. Alternatively, we can consider how clutch size should vary with x *within an environment*. It follows from the marginal value theorem that the optimal clutch size for a seed already bearing x eggs occurs when

$$\frac{dF(N, x)}{dN} = k \tag{7}$$

$$= F'(N, x)$$

where k is some constant for all x. Since both $dF'(N, x)/dx$ and $F''(N, x)$ are negative for all values of N of the linear fitness function and for $N < N^*$ for the exponential function ($\hat{N}$ cannot exceed N^*), optimal clutch size decreases with increasing x. Thus, given an environment in which seeds vary in the number of eggs they already bear, optimal clutch size will always be smaller for those seeds which already have most eggs.

Model 2. Finally, we consider how many eggs a female should lay given that she is one of i females each of whom acts as though $(i-1)$ other females will lay on that seed. Given that the evolutionarily stable (*sensu* Maynard Smith 1982) clutch size will be the same for all females (Parker & Courtney 1984), the optimal clutch size $\hat{N}$ may be found by substituting $(i-1)\cdot\hat{N}$ for x in eqns (1)–(4).

For the linear function:

$$\hat{N} = -T + \sqrt{T^2 + 2N^* \cdot T/i} \qquad (8a)$$

Thus, $\hat{N}$ decreases monotonically with i. The total number of eggs per seed,

$$i\cdot\hat{N} = -i\cdot T + \sqrt{i^2 T^2 + 2N^* \cdot i \cdot T} \qquad (8b)$$

increases monotonically with i (and also with T). In the limit when either i or T approach infinity, $[(i\cdot T)^2 + 2N^* \cdot i \cdot t]$ approaches $[(i\cdot T)^2 + 2N^* \cdot i \cdot T + (N^*)^2]$, and $i\cdot\hat{N}$ approaches N^*. Thus, as the number of females increases, the optimal clutch size per female decreases, and the total number of eggs laid should increase to a maximum of N^*.

Similarly for the exponential function:

$$\hat{N} = [-T + \sqrt{T^2 + 4T\cdot N^*/i}]/2 \qquad (9a)$$

$$\hat{N} = [-T + \sqrt{i^2 T^2 + 4i\cdot T\cdot N^*}]/2 \qquad (9b)$$

and in the limit when either i or T approaches infinity, $i\cdot\hat{N}$ approaches N^*.

Summary

Clearly neither of the extremes represented by Model 1 and Model 2 is realistic. In most cases a female cannot assume that she is the last female to lay on a seed, but neither can a coalition of i females behave as though they are the only females ovipositing on a seed; another female who arrives at the seed after the coalition has completed laying should behave as predicted by Model 1. We therefore do not expect to find the upper limit (N^*) to the number of eggs on a seed predicted by Model 2, but if the fitness function is linear we do expect to find the upper limit ($2N^*$) predicted by Model 1, since the female's fitness will not be increased by adding eggs above that limit. In practice, larval fitness functions tend not to intersect the abscissa over the observed range of larval densities (see Larval Competition Curve, p. 424), and we therefore do not expect an upper limit to the number of eggs on a seed. Combining the predictions of Model 1 and Model 2, we expect clutch size to decrease with both adult density and with egg density.

As yet, there are no data available for testing our models quantitatively. Qualitatively, the decrease in realized fecundity with increasing adult density found in many species (Crombie 1942, 1943; Ullyett & van der Merwe 1947; Umeya & Kato 1970; Bellows 1982b) is consistent with our predictions, but also with simple energetic models (Wightman 1978). In addition, female *C. chinensis* and *C. maculatus* will lay up to 100 eggs on a single seed (pers. obs.) without reaching any apparent upper limit.

FEMALE OVIPOSITION BEHAVIOUR: OVICIDE

In the previous section we considered how females could increase their fitness *F* by choosing seeds in which there were fewest competitors for their offspring. We now consider whether it is possible for females to increase their fitness by destroying any eggs or larvae that are already present. For instance, the eggs of *Callosobruchus* species are in a vulnerable position on the outside of the seed during the several days that they take to hatch. Another example of an opportunity for ovicide is provided by *Sitophilus* species; females bore a hole into a seed, lay the egg inside and seal the hole with a gelatinous plug. In theory, a later female could both reduce larval competition and the energy expended in boring a hole in the seed by removing the plug from a previous hole and replacing the egg inside with her own.

In *Callosobruchus* species there is some evidence for ovicide; the oviposition marker of *C. chinensis* is ovicidal at high concentrations (Oshima, Honda & Yamamoto 1973; Honda, Oshima & Yamamoto 1976) and the hatching success of eggs of both *C. chinensis* and *C. maculatus* decreases with increasing adult and egg density (Utida 1941a,b; Bellows 1982a,b; J. Addison, pers. comm.), although whether the increased mortality is caused by an oviposition marker or some other factor such as increased trampling (Utida 1941c) is unknown.

In modelling the effects of ovicide by females it is important to distinguish situations in which the female's own egg is affected (*non-selective ovicide*) from those in which it is not (*selective ovicide*). Chemical ovicide applied after laying an egg may be as likely to damage the female's own egg as other eggs. On the other hand a female might chew, or otherwise mechanically damage, all the unhatched eggs on the seed before laying her own egg. We do not wish to imply that chemical ovicides will always be non-selective; the important distinction is whether the female's own egg is at risk from her ovicidal behaviour.

A game theory model (Maynard Smith 1982) of ovicidal behaviour needs to consider how the relative pay-offs of *ovicidal* and *non-ovicidal* strategies vary with the frequency of each strategy. The pay-off is simply the expected fitness of an egg (defined as for larvae in the Introduction), and may be altered by the presence of ovicidal strategists in the population in one of three ways.

(a) Eggs may be killed by ovicidal activity other than that of their mother at the time they were laid. Provided that ovicidal females lay their eggs randomly among the available seeds, the eggs of ovicidal and non-ovicidal females are equally likely to be destroyed.

(b) Larvae may benefit from reduced competition as a result of ovicidal activity other than that of their mother at the time they were laid. Larval survival is increased because of a reduced larval density.

(c) Eggs may be killed or larvae benefit from reduced competition as a result of the ovicidal activity of their mother at the time they were laid.

We will assume that eggs are laid singly and consider the fate of a focal egg. (a) and (b) have equal effects on the fitness pay-offs to ovicidal and non-ovicidal females at any frequency of the ovicidal strategy, provided that ovicidal and non-ovicidal females lay their eggs independently of the maternal phenotype of eggs already present. Thus, the strategy with the higher pay-off can be found by considering whether the net effect of (c) is an increase or decrease in the fitness of the egg.

Non-selective ovicides

When the female finds the seed, it contains N_{vul} eggs and larvae vulnerable to ovicide, and N_{inv} invulnerable to ovicide. By applying an ovicide at the time of laying the focal egg, the female kills with probability $(1 - h)$ the focal egg and each of the N_{vul} vulnerable eggs and larvae. If she doesn't apply the ovicide, her offspring from the focal egg will be a fraction

$$\frac{1}{1 + N_{vul} + N_{inv}}$$

of those hatching from the seed. If she does apply the ovicide, the focal egg will contribute a fraction

$$\frac{h}{h \cdot (1 + N_{vul}) + N_{inv}} = \frac{1}{1 + N_{vul} + (N_{inv}/h)}$$

of those hatching. Since $0 \leqslant h \leqslant 1$, a non-specific ovicide will always reduce the *proportional* contribution of the focal egg to the insects that emerge from that seed, provided $N_{inv} > 0$.

If the larval competition curve increases monotonically, the overall fitness of survivors will be reduced by ovicide or remain the same. The focal egg will give rise to a smaller proportion of a smaller total fitness, and ovicidal behaviour will lower the pay-off of ovicidal strategists. Non-ovicidal behaviour is therefore evolutionarily stable.

On the other hand, if the larval competition curve is domed (e.g. Fig. 26.2d), there may be some initial number N of eggs and larvae such that killing some of the competitors will produce a sufficient increase in the total fitness of survivors to offset the ovicidal effect on the focal egg itself. Figure 26.5 shows the pay-off of an ovicidal strategy relative to that of a non-ovicidal female. In both cases, the relative pay-off increases with the initial egg density, but only exceeds one (and is therefore selected for) at some density above the most productive clutch size N^*. The proportion of eggs killed by the ovicide, $(1 - h)$, that yields the largest increase in fitness increases with increasing egg density (see Fig. 26.5).

Selective ovicides

When ovicidal activity does not affect the focal egg laid by the female, the fitness of the focal egg will always be increased (unless there is an Allée effect). Hence, the pay-off to ovicidal females will always be greater than that of non-ovicidal females for *all* frequencies of ovicidal strategists. Our conclusion is that *selective ovicidal behaviour should be an evolutionarily stable strategy (ESS)*, yet we know of no documented examples of selective ovicide in weevils. We can think of two possible explanations.

(i) We have not included any costs of ovicidal behaviour, other than the risk of killing one's own eggs ((a) above). Other costs of ovicide might include the need for specialized morphological structures, or the time and energy spent on the behaviour. We have no way of quantifying these.

(ii) We have assumed that ovicidal and non-ovicidal females' eggs are independently distributed among the seeds (see also Maynard Smith 1982). Random mixing of eggs may be the case in small patches of seeds, but it is unlikely to be true when all seeds being laid on by the whole of the population are considered. Thus, the effects of (a) and (b) on the pay-offs to ovicidal and non-ovicidal females will no longer be equal. Non-independent distribution of eggs may be particularly true of stored product insects in which the population is divided among seed stores. Parker (p. 33) has emphasized that an ESS may have a lower fitness than alternative strategies, which is likely to apply to ovicidal behaviour since ovicide will increase generation time and hence decrease the rate of increase.

When an ESS does have lower fitness and a population is also subdivided, the fitness of individuals in one subpopulation relative to that of individuals in other subpopulations with different proportions of ovicidal females must be taken into account (Wilson 1983). However, without knowledge of the structure of the population, we have no way of assessing whether population subdivision could have been sufficient to prevent selective ovicide from evolving.

LARVAL COMPETITION STRATEGIES

We now consider how a larva within a seed should react to the presence of other larvae if it is to maximize its expected fitness. We will again use a game theory approach, and first we define the alternative larval strategies.

In some species, for example *Bruchus pisorum* (Baranyovits 1948), only one larva will normally emerge from a seed no matter how many entered; larvae seem to treat each encounter as a fight to the death, and we call such behaviour the *Attack* strategy. In contrast, larvae of most granivorous insects seem to coexist and suffer the costs of crowding within a seed (Figs 26.1 and 26.2); direct contact with other larvae seems to be avoided, and we call such behaviour the *Avoid* strategy. Sometimes both types of response are found in closely related species, as in bean weevils of the genus *Callosobruchus* (Umeya, Kato & Kocha 1975); in most of the species, including *C. chinensis* and *C. maculatus*, the larvae make separate cells just under the surface of the seed, and at high density the cells may be separated by only paper-thin walls. In contrast, *C. analis* larvae burrow to the centre of the seed and meet any other larvae present. In azuki beans, usually only one adult emerges and dead larvae, bearing the mandible marks of the victor, may be found in the central cell (Umeya *et al.* 1975).

The evolution of larval competition strategies can only be explained by considering larval fitness in relation to alternative strategies, and we will use a simple game theory model (Maynard Smith 1982) to focus attention on some of the important variables. The game we develop is for non-relatives since the number of eggs contributed by individual females to any seed is likely to be small (see above).

The game with two larvae

For simplicity, fitness is defined relative to the expected fitness of an *Avoid* larva on its own in a seed, and the expected fitnesses of different sorts of larvae playing different sorts of opponent in a seed are summarized in the pay-off matrix (Table 26.1). The main assumptions implicit in Table 26.1 are that there is only one survivor if a seed contains one or more *Attack*, and that the survivor of a contest suffers no cost of having fought that contest. We also assume that, if *Attack* meets *Avoid*, *Attack* will be at least as likely to survive as *Avoid* ($1/2 \leqslant W \leqslant 1$). When there are two *Avoid* larvae in a seed, there is no

TABLE 26.1. Pay-off matrix in the two-larvae game. The matrix shows the expected pay-off to an individual playing a particular strategy against different sorts of opponent

Player	Opponent	
	Avoid	*Attack*
Avoid	$(1-E)$	$(1-W)$
Attack	W	$1/2$

direct conflict but each suffers a cost E of exploiting the same resource. The game is analysed by calculating the average fitnesses of *Avoid* (s_{avoid}) and *Attack* (s_{attack}) in a population containing a proportion p of *Avoid* and $(1-p)$ of *Attack*. The average fitnesses are as follows:

$$s_{avoid} = p \cdot (1-E) + (1-p)(1-W) \qquad (10)$$

$$s_{attack} = p \cdot W + (1-p)/2 \qquad (11)$$

The average fitnesses therefore depend on the phenotypic composition of the population as shown in Fig. 26.6. In the game defined in Table 26.1 and Fig. 26.6, *Attack* is an evolutionarily stable strategy (ESS) provided that $W > 1/2$, and *Avoid* is an ESS if $(1-E) \geqslant W$.

Table 26.2 assumes that there is only one survivor when *Attack* meets *Avoid*. If the pay-offs are modified to allow for a specified probability (q) of *Avoid* being successful in avoiding contact with *Attack*, the game may have a different outcome. As q increases, *Attack* may no longer be an ESS; eventually a mixed strategy may be the only ESS (C.M. Lessells & R.H. Smith, unpubl.). The qualitative effect of increasing q is to make *Attack* less likely as an ESS.

N *larvae in a seed*

As the number of larvae in a seed increases, the pay-offs will change according to the types of larvae present in a seed. Here we demonstrate that the outcome

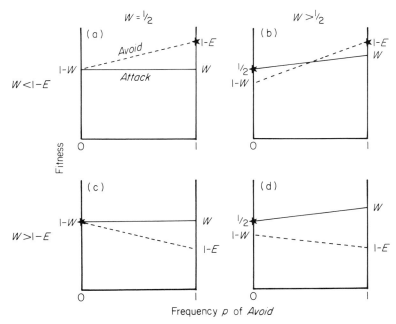

FIG. 26.6. The fitness versus frequency curves for the two larvae game. Fitnesses of *Avoid* (– – –) and *Attack* (———) are plotted against frequency of *Avoid*. If both strategies are present, the strategy with the higher average fitness will increase in the population. Evolutionarily stable strategies (ESSs) are indicated by stars. *Attack* is an ESS if $W > 0.5$ ((b) and (d)). *Avoid* is also an ESS if $W < (1 - E)$ ((a) and (b)). Both pure strategies may be ESSs if $(1 - E) > W > 0.5$ as in (b). No mixed strategy is stable; the intersection of the fitness curves in (b) is unstable because an initial frequency p to the left of the intersection will move to $p = 0$, while one to the right will move to $p = 1$.

TABLE 26.2. Pay-off matrix for the three-larvae game. The two opponents that a player meets are either both *Avoid*, both *Attack* or one of each, with frequencies as shown in the bottom line of the table

Player	Opponents		
	2 *Avoid*	1 *Avoid* + 1 *Attack*	2 *Attack*
Avoid	$s(3)$	$(1 - W) \cdot (s(2) + W/2)$	$(1 - W) \cdot (1 - 2W/3)$
Attack	W^2	$W/2 + W \cdot (1 - W)/3$	$1/3$
Frequency	p^2	$2p \cdot (1 - p)$	$(1 - p)^2$

for three or more larvae is not qualitatively different from the two larvae game, and then we show how the predictions can be generalized for different larval competition curves. We assume a fitness per individual larva of $s(N)$ for N *Avoid* in a seed, and consider only the case where $q = 0$ (only one survivor when there is one or more *Attack* larva present). The pay-offs for three larvae in a seed are shown in Table 26.2. The pay-offs are derived by considering encounters as a sequence of events whose order is random, using path analysis to evaluate the probabilities of different sequences (Wilson 1975) and hence to give the expected pay-offs to *Avoid* and *Attack* in the three different categories of seed. We also assume that the costs to *Avoid* occur only after any encounters with *Attack* larvae. The frequencies of the different categories of encounter in the bottom row of Table 26.2 give the average pay-offs to *Avoid* and *Attack* as quadratic functions of p. Considering $p = 0$ and $p = 1$, *Attack* is again an ESS if $W > 1/2$ and *Avoid* is an ESS if $s(3) \geqslant W^2$.

A similar treatment for $N = 4, 5 \ldots$ larvae per seed shows that *Attack* is an ESS if $W > 1/2$, and that *Avoid* is an ESS if $s(N) \geqslant W^{N-1}$. In practice, seeds will contain different numbers of larvae. Therefore, both the larval fitness function for *Avoid* ($s(N)$) and the frequency distribution of larvae per seed are needed to give the average fitnesses of *Atack* and *Avoid*. However, we will now show that the larval competition curve can be used to make broad predictions about evolutionary stability.

For N larvae hatching in a seed, *Avoid* is stable to invasion by *Attack* provided $s(N) \geqslant W^{N-1}$, or (multiplying through by N) $N \cdot s(N) \geqslant N \cdot W^{N-1}$. Thus, a plot of $N \cdot W^{N-1}$ against larval density N can be divided into regions where (depending on the value of W) *Avoid* is or is not stable according to where the $N \cdot s(N)$ curve lies (Fig. 26.7a). But the *larval competition curve* is a plot of $N \cdot s(N)$ against N (Fig. 26.2d). In Fig. 26.7b we have superimposed on Fig. 26.7a Giga's (1982) empirical larval competition curve for *C. maculatus* (from Fig. 26.2d; the only species for which we can take fecundity effects into account). The curve lies in the region where we would expect *Avoid* to be an ESS provided $W \geqslant 0.7$. The method used in Fig. 26.7b requires the larval competition curve, which can be observed for species using an *Avoid* strategy but cannot be obtained directly for species with the *Attack* strategy.

Population structure and evolution

Unless $W = 1/2$, *Attack* is always an alternative to *Avoid* as an ESS, yet *Avoid* is the more common larval strategy found in internal seed feeders. Two factors may affect which of the two alternative ESSs is found; both depend on a population structure with temporary patches of seed resource colonized by a small number of individuals. First, founder effects may make it relatively easy

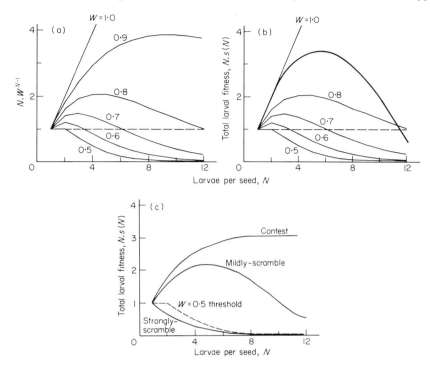

FIG. 26.7. Threshold curves for the N larvae game. (a) *Avoid* is an ESS if the total larval fitness $N \cdot s(N)$ is above the $N \cdot W^{N-1}$ curve (shown for different values of W), and evolutionarily unstable if total larval fitness is below the curve. *Attack* is always an ESS if $W > 0.5$. The dashed line shows the total larval fitness (1, by definition) for *Attack*. (b) The thick line is the larval competition curve for *C. maculatus* scaled to fitness = 1 for 1 larva in a seed (see Fig. 26.2(d); after Giga 1982) and superimposed on the threshold curves in (a). (c) The curves show different outcomes of a scramble (e.g. *Avoid*) process.

for the population to switch between alternative strategies (cf. Riechert & Hammerstein 1983). When both strategies are stable, a local population will move to fixation of *Attack* or *Avoid* depending on whether the initial frequency of *Avoid* lies to the left or right of the intersection of the fitness curves (see Fig. 26.6b). Second, the ESS with the higher fitness will give rise to proportionately more potential colonizers during the migration/colonization phase. Thus, the frequency of the ESS with the higher fitness will increase in the global population (cf. Wilson 1983; Harvey, p. 59). In the two-larvae game, *Avoid* always has greater fitness than *Attack* when the two strategies are alternative ESSs. When there are three or more larvae, *Avoid* will have the higher fitness if $s(N) > 1/N$, i.e. if $N \cdot s(n) > 1$; this threshold is shown as the dashed line in Fig. 26.7.

Figure 26.7 also allows us to make general predictions about the effects of seed size on the evolution of larval competition strategies. As seed size decreases, the peak in the larval competition curve (Fig. 26.2d) is likely to be lower and displaced to the left. Such a pattern is found in *C. maculatus* where the total mass of adults emerging (a crude measure of fitness) from seeds with two larvae relative to seeds with one larva decreases with decreasing seed size (cowpeas, 1·79; azuki beans, 1·54; mung beans, 1·41; C.M. Lessells, pers. obs.). As a result, *Attack* is more likely to be found in species developing in smaller seeds. Unfortunately, the original host species is not known for many stored product pests, but if our prediction is true, selective breeding by man for larger seed size may have favoured *Avoid*.

DISCUSSION

Table 26.3 summarizes the aspects of population dynamics that determine and are determined by the behaviours we have examined in this paper. Although each of these behaviours has been analysed separately, the optimal strategy for one behaviour must depend to some extent on that for the other behaviours. For instance, oviposition and ovicidal behaviour affect the mean and variance of the number of larvae per bean, which has some effect on what form (*Attack* or *Avoid*) of larval competition is stable. Conversely, the form of larval competition will determine the shape of the larval competition curve which is a critical determinant of the oviposition and ovicidal strategies.

Clearly the strategies adopted by individuals will have consequences for

TABLE 26.3. Interdependence of behaviour and population dynamics in weevils

Behavioural strategy	Aspect of dynamics which determines optimal strategy	Aspect of behaviour which determines population dynamics
Clutch size	Larval competition curve	Mean and variance of number of eggs laid in relation to adult numbers
Ovicide	Larval competition curve	Eggs hatching in relation to eggs laid per seed
Larval competition	Larval competition curve under *Avoid* strategy	Adults emerging in relation to eggs hatching per seed

the dynamics of populations, affecting both the rate of population increase and population stability (Parker, p. 33) has emphasized that a strategy that is evolutionarily stable may have a lower fitness than an alternative strategy. All of the three behaviours that we have considered may have ESSs for which this is true: for oviposition behaviour, Model 2 suggests that a group of i females will lay, in combination, a monotonically increasing number of eggs, but never exceed the most productive clutch size. However, sequential oviposition (Model 1) can lead to the most productive clutch size being exceeded, and hence the total productivity decreasing with group size. Similarly, selective ovicide can lead to a reduction in the rate of increase of a population; in contrast, non-selective ovicides will only be favoured by natural selection when they increase productivity per seed (although they may increase generation time). Finally, the *Attack* larval competition strategy always leads to one adult emerging per seed (by definition) whereas Fig. 26.7 shows that *Avoid* may be stable even when a smaller mean number of adults hatches per seed. However we have argued that, when the population is subdivided, strategies that lead to a reduction in fitness are less likely to be found than in an undivided population.

The second component of the dynamics that will be affected is stability. The implication of Model 1b for multiple oviposition is that, after a period of oviposition, all seeds should offer equal pay-offs to ovipositing females. The result is similar to models of parasitoid foraging (Cook & Hubbard 1977; Hubbard & Cook 1978) based on the premise that optimally foraging parasitoids will reduce all patches of hosts to equal oviposition rates. In parasitoids, such behaviour confers stability on the parasitoid–host interaction through the aggregation of parasitoids in high density patches (Comins & Hassell 1979), in contrast with granivores. In the parasitoid model, the pay-off to females decreases with the exploitation of a patch (of hosts) because the search time for successive healthy hosts increases, while the survival prospects of each egg laid in a healthy host remain constant. The optimal behaviour always results in spatially density-dependent parasitism (Lessells 1984). However, in granivores the pay-off to females decreases with the exploitation of a patch (a seed) because larval survival is density-dependent. Females can, potentially, oviposit at a constant rate within a patch (Charnov & Skinner 1984). The optimal behaviour results in eggs being distributed homogeneously with respect to the resource, and hence the stability that can be conferred by heterogeneity (de Jong 1979) is not introduced.

Our model of larval competition relates to the traditional dichotomy between *scramble* and *contest* competition (Nicholson 1954). We have avoided using the terms scramble and contest to describe the alternative larval strategies because of confusion in the literature over their definition.

Nicholson (1954) originally defined scramble and contest in terms of *resource use*: in scramble competition 'success is commonly incomplete, so that some, and at times all, of the requisite secured by the competing animals takes no part in sustaining the population, being dissipated by individuals which obtain insufficient for survival'. In contest competition 'the individuals are either fully successful, or unsuccessful; and the whole amount of the requisite obtained collectively by the animals is used effectively and without wastage in maintaining the population' (Nicholson 1954, p. 20). At the same time, Nicholson also mentions the *process* by which competition takes place: 'Scramble is the kind of competition exhibited by a crowd of boys striving to secure broadcast sweets' (Nicholson 1954, p. 19) and 'With contest on the other hand, the individuals may be said to compete for prizes . . .' (Nicholson 1954, p. 20). Our definitions of *Avoid* and *Attack* correspond to a *scramble process* and a *contest process*. However, scramble and contest are now frequently defined by their *outcome* in terms of the relationship between the numbers (or fitness) of survivors versus the initial numbers (Varley, Gradwell & Hassell 1973, Fig. 2.11; Bellows 1982b, p. 273); a contest outcome gives stable population dynamics, and a scramble outcome less stable dynamics (Varley *et al.* 1973). The three methods of defining scramble and contest unfortunately do not coincide, particularly when fecundity effects (Varley *et al.* 1973) are included. As an example, a scramble process might result in a reduction in fecundity but no mortality. Hence, it would be classified as contest in terms of resource use. Whether there was a scramble or contest outcome would be dictated by the magnitude of the reduction in fecundity.

In our model of larval competition, we ask what process of competition we expect to be evolutionarily stable. The model makes predictions from the larval competition curve, i.e from the outcome of a scramble process. If the larval competition curve represents a contest outcome (e.g. Fig. 26.1a) or a mildly-scramble outcome (e.g. Fig. 26.1c), then our model predicts that the scramble process (*Avoid* strategy) should be evolutionarily stable. However, the observed outcome of the scramble process may appear as either a contest or a mildly-scramble outcome (see Fig. 26.7c). In contrast, if the scramble process leads to a strongly-scramble outcome, then the contest process (*Attack*) may be the only stable strategy (see Fig. 26.7c); we therefore expect to observe both a contest process and a contest outcome (Table 26.4) as is apparently the case in *C. analis* (Umeya *et al.* 1975).

Our distinction between behavioural process and ecological outcome allows us to draw two general conclusions. First, observed contest outcomes may be the result of a scramble process (e.g. *C. chinensis*; Fig. 26.1a) or of a contest process (e.g. *C. analis*) which can both arise from opposite ends of the ecological continuum governing the evolution of scramble or contest

TABLE 26.4. The effect of the outcome of a scramble process (see Fig. 26.7c) on which process (scramble or contest) is evolutionarily stable, and the observed outcome of the stable process

Outcome of scramble process:	contest	mildly-scramble	strongly-scramble
Evolutionarily stable process:	scramble	scramble	contest
Observed outcome of stable process:	contest	mildly-scramble	contest

processes (the continuum being the outcome of a scramble process; see Fig. 26.7c); an observed scramble outcome is intermediate (see Table 26.4). Thus, contest and scramble outcomes should only be regarded as opposites insofar as they tend to be associated with stable and unstable population dynamics respectively (Varley *et al.* 1973). Second, we rarely expect to observe strongly-scramble outcomes in nature because the causal process will often be evolutionarily unstable, particularly when resources are finely subdivided as in our examples.

Our second conclusion may have some relevance to the interpretation of patterns of single-species population dynamics. Hassell, Lawton & May (1976) and Bellows (1981) have noted that density dependence in insect populations usually acts in an undercompensatory manner associated with stable population dynamics; undercompensatory density dependence means a contest outcome or a mildly-scramble outcome (Fig. 26.7c) leading to monotonic damping or damped oscillations around an equilibrium (see Fig. 9 of Bellows 1981). Their observation is ecologically important, but we do not believe that natural selection has acted directly on stability which is clearly a property of a population, not of an individual. Rather, we suggest that the ecological stability may be a consequence of the evolutionary instability of behaviour processes which give rise to strongly-scramble outcomes.

ACKNOWLEDGMENTS

We are grateful to the following for their comments on an earlier version of the manuscript: Charles Godfray, Alan Grafen, Mike Hassell, Geoff Parker and Richard Sibly. The work was in part supported (C.M.L.) by a NERC grant to Professor M.P. Hassell.

REFERENCES

Andersson, M. (1978). Natural selection of offspring numbers: some possible intergeneration effects. *American Naturalist*, **112**, 762–766.

Andersson, M. & Eriksson, M.O.G. (1982). Nest parasitism in Goldeneyes *Bucephala clangula*: some evolutionary aspects. *American Naturalist*, **120**, 1–16.

Arbogast, R.T. & Miller, M.A. (1978). Spatial distribution of eggs of ovipositing Indian meal moths, *Plodia interpunctella* (Hübner). *Research on Population Ecology*, **19**, 148–154.

Baranyovits, F. (1948). Der Erbsenkafer (*Bruchus pisorum* L.) *Reviews of Applied Entomology Series A*, **36**, 61–62.

Bellows, T.S.Jr. (1981). The descriptive properties of some models for density dependence. *Journal of Animal Ecology*, **50**, 139–156.

Bellows, T.S.Jr. (1982a). Analytical models for laboratory populations of *Callosobruchus chinensis* and *C. maculatus* (Coleoptera. Bruchidae). *Journal of Animal Ecology*, **51**, 263–287.

Bellows, T.S.Jr. (1982b). Simulation models for laboratory populations of *Callosobruchus chinensis* and *C. maculatus*. *Journal of Animal Ecology*, **51**, 597–623.

Booker, R.H. (1967). Observations on three bruchids associated with cowpea in northern Nigeria. *Journal of Stored Products Research*, **3**, 1–15.

Charnov, E.L. (1976). Optimal foraging: the marginal value theorem. *Theoretical Population Biology*, **9**, 129–136.

Charnov, E.L. (1982). *The Theory of Sex Allocation*. Princeton University Press, Princeton, N.J.

Charnov, E.L. & Krebs, J.R. (1974). On clutch size and fitness. *Ibis*, **116**, 217–219.

Charnov, E.L. & Skinner, S.W. (1984). Evolution of host selection and clutch-size in parasitoid wasps. *Florida Entomologist*, **67**, 5–21.

Cole, L.C. (1954). The population consequences of life-history phenomena. *Quarterly Review of Biology*, **29**, 103–137.

Comins, H.N. & Hassell, M.P. (1979). The dynamics of optimally foraging predators and parasitoids. *Journal of Animal Ecology*, 335–351.

Cook, R.M. & Hubbard, S.F. (1977). Optimal foraging by parasitoid wasps. *Journal of Animal Ecology*, **46**, 115–125.

Crombie, A.C. (1942). The effect of crowding upon the oviposition of grain infesting insects. *Journal of Experimental Biology*, **19**, 311–340.

Crombie, A.C. (1943). The effects of crowding on the mortality of grain infesting insects. *Proceedings of the Zoological Society of London, Series A*, **113**, 77–98.

Crombie, A.C. (1944). On intraspecific and interspecific competition in larvae of granivorous insects. *Journal of Experimental Biology*, **20**, 135–111.

de Jong, G. (1979). The influence of the distribution of juveniles over patches of food on the dynamics of a population. *Netherlands Journal of Zoology*, **29**, 33–51.

Dobie, P. (1974). The laboratory assessment of the inherent susceptibility of maize varieties to post-harvest infestation by *Sitophilus zeamais*. *Journal of Stored Products Research*, **10**, 183–187.

Fujii, K. (1968). Studies on interspecific competition between the azuki bean weevil and the southern cowpea weevil. III. Some characteristics of strains of two species. *Research on Population Ecology*, **10**, 87–98.

Giga, D.P. (1978). *Studies on interspecific competition and varietal resistance in relation to survival of weevils* Callosobruchus maculatus *and* C. chinensis *on cowpeas*. M.Sc. thesis, University of Reading.

Giga, D.P. (1982). *The comparative biology of four Callosobruchus species with particular reference to competition in* C. rhodesianus *and* C. maculatus. Ph.D. thesis, University of Reading.

Giga, D.P. & Smith, R.H. (1981). Varietal resistance and intraspecific competition in the cowpea weevils *Callosobruchus maculatus* and *C. chinensis* (Coleoptera: Bruchidae). *Journal of Applied Ecology*, **18**, 755–761.

Gillespie, J.H. (1977). Natural selection for variance in offspring numbers: a new evolutionary principle. *American Naturalist*, **111**, 1010–1014.

Hassell, M.P., Lawton, J.H. & May, R.M. (1976). Patterns of dynamical behaviour in single-species populations. *Journal of Animal Ecology*, **45**, 471–486.

Högstedt, G. (1980). Evolution of clutch size in birds: adaptive variation in relation to territory quality. *Science*, **210**, 1148–1150.

Holloway, G.J. (1984). *Genetic differentiation and life history variation in the rice weevil,* Sitophilus oryzae. Ph.D. thesis, University of Reading.

Honda, H., Oshima, K. & Yamamoto, I. (1976). Oviposition marker of azuki bean weevil, *Callosobruchus chinensis* (L.). *Proc. of the Joint United States–Japan seminar on stored product insects*, Kansas State University, Manhattan, Kansas (December 1976).

Howard, D.C. (1983). *The population biology of the greater grain borer* Prostephanus truncatus (Horn). Ph.D. thesis, University of Reading.

Hubbard, S.F. & Cook, R.M. (1978). Optimal foraging by parasitoid wasps. *Journal of Animal Ecology*, **47**, 593–604.

Iwasa, Y., Suzuki, Y. & Matsuda, H. (1984). Theory of oviposition strategies of parasitoids. 1. Effect of mortality and limited egg number. *Theoretical Population Biology* (in press).

Lack, D. (1947). The significance of clutch size. *Ibis*, **89**, 309–352, and **90**, 25–45.

Lessells, C.M. (1985). Parasitoid foraging: should parasitism be density dependent? *Journal of Animal Ecology*, **54**, 27–42.

Maynard Smith, J. (1982). *Evolution and the Theory of Games*. Cambridge University Press, Cambridge.

Mitchell, R. (1975). The evolution of oviposition tactics in the bean weevil, *Callosobruchus maculatus* (F.). *Ecology*, **56**, 696–702.

Nakamura, H. (1967). Comparative study of adaptability to the density in two species of *Callosobruchus*. *Japanese Journal of Ecology*, **17**, 57–63.

Nicholson, A.J. (1954). An outline of the dynamics of animal populations. *Australian Journal of Zoology*, **2**, 9–65.

Nwanze, K. & Horber, E. (1975). How seed size affects the occurrence of 'active' and 'miniature' forms of *Callosobruchus maculatus* (F.) in laboratory populations. *Environmental Entomology*, **4**, 729–732.

Oshima, K., Honda, H. & Yamamoto, I. (1973). Isolation of an oviposition marker from azuki bean weevil. *Agricultural and Biological Chemistry*, **37**, 2679–2680.

Parker, G.A. & Courtney, S.P. (1984). Models of clutch size in insect oviposition. *Theoretical Population Biology*, **26**, 27–48.

Perrins, C.M. & Moss, D. (1975). Reproductive rates in the Great Tit. *Journal of Animal Ecology*, **44**, 695–706.

Riechert, S.E. & Hammerstein, P. (1983). Game theory in the ecological context. *Annual Reviews of Ecological Systematics*, **14**, 377–409.

Richards, O.W. (1947). Observations on grain weevils, *Calandra* (Col. Curculionidae). I. General biology and oviposition. *Proceedings of the Zoological Society of London*, **117**, 1–43.

Segrove, F. (1951). Oviposition behaviour in the two strains of the rice weevil, *Calandra oryzae* (L.). *Journal of Experimental Biology*, **28**, 281–297.

Shazali, M.E.H. (1982). *The biology and population ecology of four insect pests of stored sorghum with particular reference to competition and succession*. Ph.D. thesis, University of Reading.

Szentesi, A. (1981). Pheromone-like substances affecting host-related behaviour of larvae and adults in the dry bean weevil *Acanthoscelides obtectus*. *Entomol. Exp. Appl.*, **30**, 219–226.

Ullyett, G.C. & van der Merwe, J.S. (1947). Some factors influencing population growth of *Ephestia kuhniella* Zell. (Lep., Phycitid.). *Journal of the Entomological Society of South Africa*, **10**, 46–63.

Umeya, K. (1966). Studies on the comparative ecology of bean weevils. I. On the egg distribution and the oviposition behaviours of three species of bean weevils infesting azuki beans. *Research Bulletins of Plant Protection, Japan*, **3**, 1–11.

Umeya, K. & Kato, T. (1970). Studies on the comparative ecology of bean weevils. V. Distribution of eggs and larvae of *Acanthoscelides obtectus* in relation to its oviposition and boring behaviour. *Research on Population Ecology*, **12**, 35–50.

Umeya, K., Kato, T. & Kocha, T. (1975). Studies on the comparative ecology of bean weevils. VI. Intraspecific larval competition in *Callosobruchus analis* (F.). *Japanese Journal of Applied Entomology and Zoology*, **19**, 47–53.

Utida, S. (1941a). Studies on experimental population of the azuki bean weevil, *Callosobruchus chinensis* (L.). III. The effect of population density upon the mortalities of different stages of life cycle. *Memoirs of the College of Agriculture, Kyoto University*, **49**, 21–42.

Utida, S. (1941b). Studies on experimental population of the azuki bean weevil, *Callosobruchus chinensis* (L.). IV. Analysis of density effect with respect to fecundity and fertility of eggs. *Memoirs of the College of Agriculture, Kyoto University*, **51**, 1–26.

Utida, S. (1941c). Studies on experimental population of the azuki bean weevil, *Callosobruchus chinensis* (L.). I. The effect of population density on the progeny populations. *Memoirs of the College of Agriculture, Kyoto University*, **48**, 1–31.

Utida, S. (1942). Studies on experimental population of azuki bean weevil, *Callosobruchus chinensis* (L.). VII. Analysis of the density effect in the preimaginal stage. *Mem. Coll. Agric., Kyoto Univ.*, **53**, 19–31.

Utida, S. (1943). Studies on experimental population of azuki bean weevil, *Callosobruchus chinensis* (L.). VIII. Statistical analysis of frequency distribution of the emerging weevils on beans. *Mem. Coll. Agric., Kyoto Univ.*, **54**, 1–22.

Utida, S. (1967). Collective oviposition and larval aggregation in *Zabrotes subfasciatus* (Boh.) (Coleoptera: Bruchidae). *Journal of Stored Products Research*, **2**, 315–322.

Utida, S. (1972). Density-dependent polymorphism in the adult of *C. maculatus* (F.). *J. Stored Prod. Res.*, **8**, 111–126.

Varley, G.C., Gradwell, G.R. & Hassell, M.P. (1973). *Insect Population Ecology*. Blackwell Scientific Publications, Oxford.

Wightman, J.A. (1978). The ecology of *Callosobruchus analis* (Coleoptera: Bruchidae): energetics and energy reserves of adults. *Journal of Animal Ecology*, **47**, 131–142.

Williams, G.C. (1966). Natural selection, the costs of reproduction, and a refinement of Lack's principle. *American Naturalist*, **100**, 687–690.

Wilson, D.S. (1983). The group selection controversy. History and current status. *Annual Reviews of Ecological Systematics*, **14**, 159–187.

Wilson, E.O. (1975). *Sociobiology: the Modern Synthesis*. Harvard University Press, Cambridge, Mass.

Yoshida, T. (1961). Oviposition behaviour of two species of bean weevil and interspecific competition between them. *Memoirs of the Faculty Lib. Arts Education, Miyazaki University.*, **2**, 41–65.

27. REPRODUCTIVE STRATEGIES AND POPULATION ECOLOGY OF INSECT PARASITOIDS

J. K. WAAGE AND H. C. J. GODFRAY
Imperial College at Silwood Park, Ascot,
Berkshire, SL5 7PY

SUMMARY

When a foraging parasitoid finds a host or patch of hosts, it must decide (i) how many eggs to lay and (ii) what sex ratio to produce. We examine models for optimal progeny allocation in parasitoids and compare their predictions with data from different parasitoid species. We do the same for optimal sex allocation, and develop some models for optimization of both sex and progeny allocation where sexual asymmetries apply. Some population dynamic consequences of variation in progeny and sex allocation are considered, and we discuss their importance to the efficiency of parasitoids as biological control agents.

INTRODUCTION

There are over 200 000 species of flies and wasps that develop as parasitoids of other insects. Some develop as larvae within their hosts (endoparasitoids) while others consume their prey from the outside (ectoparasitoids). In solitary species, only one adult emerges from a single host, while in some gregarious species, up to several thousand individuals can develop on the same host (Askew 1971). A typical adult female parasitoid forages actively for hosts distributed patchily in the environment. When she finds a host, she must make two decisions: how many eggs to lay and what sex ratio to produce. The last question arises because most parasitoids belong to the Hymenoptera and are arrhenotokous haplodiploids which exhibit maternal control of the sex ratio.

These two decisions we shall call a parasitoid's reproductive strategy (Waage & Ng 1984). To understand how natural selection will act on it, we must delve into a number of topics in behavioural ecology: sex ratio theory, optimal foraging theory, clutch size theory and the theory of life-history strategies. In this paper, we examine the different adaptive responses parasitoids make in progeny and sex allocation under changing ecological conditions and their consequences for the distribution and dynamics of

449

parasitoid populations. The majority of models to date have considered either progeny or sex allocation. We will attempt, in a stepwise manner, to consider both decisions in order to gain a realistic understanding of parasitoid reproductive ecology.

OPTIMIZING BROOD SIZE

To begin, we will consider the first decision of the reproductive strategy: how many eggs to lay per host. Let us initially assume that natural selection acts on parasitoids to maximize brood productivity, measured in some appropriate function of fitness; brood productivity is analogous to the maximum clutch productivity in ornithology (Lack 1947) and we will refer to it as the Lack solution. If the fitness of an individual larvae in a brood is some function $f(c)$ of brood size c, the fitness gain to a female per brood will be $cf(c)$ and the Lack solution will be $c_L = -f(c)/f'(c)$, where f' is the first derivative of f (assuming no mathematical impropriety in the function f). This model provides a simple yardstick for investigating brood size and brood mortality in parasitoids.

Progeny allocation in parasitoids shows considerable variability. For solitary species, supernumerary larvae in a host are eliminated by competition, and often by combat (Salt 1961) such that only one larva survives. There are possible advantages of larger clutches, in particular the tendency of mortality due to host immune responses to decrease when several larvae are present (Askew 1968; Puttler 1974), but the majority of solitary parasitoids studied have been found to lay one egg per oviposition.

The case of gregarious parasitoids is more complex. From a very large literature on variation in brood size, we have selected those exceedingly few studies which actually measured both eggs going in and parasitoids coming out. Figure 27,1a,b is for two endoparasitoids of insect eggs, while Fig. 27.1c–e is for two larval and one pupal ectoparasitoid, respectively. In all experiments, large clutches were obtained by creating conditions for superparasitism (see below). For each species, survivorship decreases with increasing progeny allocation, as expected.

In gregarious parasitoids, differences in the intensity of within-brood mortality will be related to the size of the particular host and the food requirements of a single parasitoid. There may be an Allee effect, with a minimum brood size below which no larvae survive (Taylor 1937; DeLoach & Rabb 1972), and a maximum brood size, above which the host and all its inhabitants die (Johannson 1951; Walker 1967; Fig. 27.1a). Overall, however, it is clear from Fig. 27.1f, that typical brood sizes are larger for species with lower levels of density-dependent, within-brood mortality; a pattern which is in accord with the Lack solution.

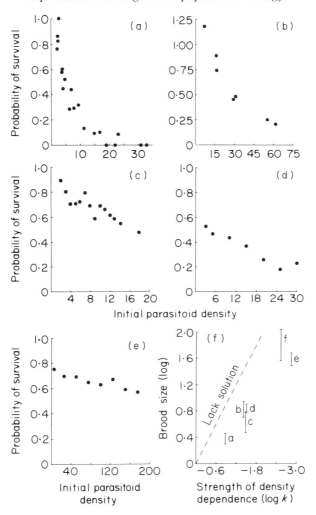

FIG. 27.1. Within-brood density-dependent mortality in (a) *Trichogramma evanescens* (N. Pallewatta, unpubl.), (b) *Telenomus fariai* (Escalante & Rabinovich 1979), (c) *Bracon hebetor* (Benson 1973), (d) *Bracon gelechiae* (Narayanan & Subba Rao 1955), (e) *Dahlbominus fuliginosus* (Wilkes 1963). Data for (b) were obtained by sequentially sacrificed replicates, hence it is possible for the estimate of the probability of surviving to be above 1. For (f), the function $f(c) = \exp(-kc)$ (see text) was fitted to the data set for each species by the method of non-linear least squares estimation, and a value for k was obtained. On the abcissa, $\log k$ is plotted as a measure of the strength of within-brood density dependence (decreasing from left to right). On the ordinate is plotted the typical range of brood sizes produced by each species, obtained from the literature. A sixth data set is included (marked *f*); *Apanteles congregatus* (Beckage & Riddiford 1978). The Lack solution ($1/k$) is plotted as a dashed line.

Offspring mortality is only one of several factors affecting parasitoid fitness. Over a range of brood sizes where all offspring survive, those wasps from larger broods are usually smaller and display reduced fecundity, longevity and searching ability (Klomp & Teerink 1967; Waage & Ng 1984), all important components of fitness. Consider, for instance, the trichogrammatid egg parasitoid, *Trichogramma evanesens*. If we take offspring fecundity as a measure of fitness, we can describe fitness per host as the total egg load of all daughters produced, and represent it in terms of brood size, as in Fig. 27.2a (these data are for all-female broods, to avoid the complications of sex ratio, to be considered later). In this species, an intermediate brood size is fittest, and indeed, the mean size of all-female broods in *T. evanescens* is two, as predicted (J.K. Waage, unpubl.).

Figure 27.1f shows that the brood size commonly observed in nature is below the Lack solution, something also noted for parasitoids by Charnov & Skinner (1984) and Waage & Ng (1984) in considering wider fitness criteria than just mortality. Charnov & Skinner (1984) suggest the most likely reason for this is that maximization of fitness per host may not maximize lifetime fitness.

In order to explore this possibility, we consider a model for optimal clutch size with respect to lifetime fitness. Assume that a parasitoid ecloses with a fixed total of M eggs (e.g. a pro-ovigenic parasitoid; Flanders 1950), and lays c eggs in each host encountered. Thus, the maximum number of hosts which it can attack is M/c. Suppose that the probability that she survives between one host and the next is a constant p and that fitness of the parasitoid's progeny is a function $f(c)$ of the number of siblings developing in the same host. We can then write an expression for her lifetime fitness.

$$W = cf(c) + pcf(c) + p^2cf(c) + \ldots + p^{\frac{M}{c}-1}cf(c) \qquad (1)$$

Which is a geometric series and sums to

$$W = cf(c)\left(\frac{p^{\frac{M}{c}}-1}{p-1}\right) \qquad (2)$$

Selection will act on the brood size to maximize W. The optimal brood size ($\hat{c}$) is thus found by solving for c when the derivative of W with respect to c is zero. As an example, let $f(c) = \exp(-kc)$; fitness declines monotonically with brood size at a rate set by the constant k. The relationship between $\hat{c}$ and k for different values of p is shown in Fig. 27.2b for $M = 60$, and the Lack solution is $1/k$. In general, the optimal brood size is not very sensitive to changes in M (cf. Parker & Courtney 1984).

When the probability of surviving to find another host is small ($p \to 0$), the model reduces to the Lack solution, where fitness is maximized per host. At

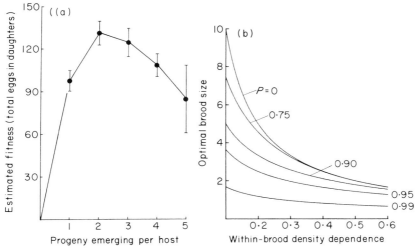

FIG. 27.2. (a) Estimated fitness to a female *Trichogramma evanescens* of different sized
all-female broods. Large broods were obtained by encouraging superparasitism on the host
Mamestra brassicae (see Waage & Ng Sook Ming (1984) for details). (b) The relationship
between optimal brood size and within-brood density dependence (k), for different values of
p, the probability of survival between hosts. Optimal brood size is determined from eqn (2),
where $f(c) = \exp(-kc)$ and $M = 60$ (see text for further explanation).

the other extreme ($p \to 1$), the parasitoid should lay a single egg in each host it
encounters. Note that optimal brood size does not decrease substantially until
p is relatively large.

This type of model has been used by Weiss, Price & Lynch (1983) to
understand the oviposition behaviour of gregarious gall midges and by
Godfray (1985) for a gregarious leaf-miner. Though herbivores, these species
make a decision on progeny allocation analogous to that of parasitoids. One
simplifying assumption of these models is that brood size does not vary over
the insect's life time. If the assumption is relaxed—for example, by replacing
M by $M - \Sigma c_j$ where the summation is the total eggs laid in previous hosts—it
is found that the optimal clutch size drops as the egg limit is approached. The
same conclusion has been reached by Parker & Courtney (1984) and Iwasa,
Suzuki & Matsuda (1984), in their more sophisticated and general models for
clutch size optimization.

What ecological factors will influence p? In the simplest case, p might be
expressed as the product of an instantaneous mortality rate and the time taken
to find another host, which will be a function of host density, the rate of search
of the parasitoid, and the handling time for each host (Hassell & May 1974).
Thus, differences between species in searching rate or handling time should

lead to different optimal brood sizes. The fact that, compared with solitary species, many gregarious species are small, and that small parasitoids have relatively lower searching efficiency and longer handling time, is in accord with this hypothesis. However, the relatively smaller size of gregarious species may also reflect the constraint that large, gregarious parasitoids are unlikely to evolve on insect hosts, which are generally small.

Within species, an increase in the rate of host finding (e.g. with host density) should lead to smaller broods, as has been found in some parasitoids (Jackson 1966; Ikawa & Suzuki 1982; Glas *et al.* 1981; Waage & Ng 1984), although patterns of sex allocation can complicate the interpretation of the data. A more striking line of support is to be found in the tendency of some wasps to attack a host, resume search and then, if no other hosts are found, return to lay more eggs in the host before leaving the patch. This behaviour suggests that a wasp may adjust her brood size following assessment of host finding rate, and has been observed in *Trichogramma evanescens* foraging on leaves (J.K. Waage, unpubl.) and in the bethylid, *Cephalonomia gallicola* (Kearns 1934).

When time associated with egg laying (e.g. handling time, time for egg maturation) becomes a significant fraction of searching time, the expenditure in time of laying a large brood must be discounted against any benefits (Charnov & Skinner 1984; Iwasa *et al.* 1984). Parker & Courtney (1984) and Skinner (1985) have explored in more detail the theoretical relationship between brood size and foraging using gain-rate maximization techniques.

SEXUAL ASYMMETRIES

So far, we have ignored the sex ratio of the progeny allocated per host. This has not mattered as none of the models developed so far violate the assumptions in Fisher's (1930) explanation for a sex ratio of 0·5 (proportion males). However, if we consider the effects of differential competition and mortality between the sexes, sex ratios other than 0·5 will be expected (Taylor 1981). Selection will now operate simultaneously on the brood size and sex ratio. Sex ratio selection is primarily a function of the behaviour of the population, making the use of models for individual behaviour (such as that just developed) difficult to employ. For simplicity we restrict brood size considerations to use of the Lack solution.

Let us drop the implicit assumption that the sexes exert and experience the same within-brood fitness effects. An individual in a brood of size c may experience different fitness penalties as the sex ratio, r, of the brood changes; $f(c)$ is replaced by $f_f(c,r)$ for females and by $f_m(c,r)$ for males. A number of authors have observed changes in sex-specific mortality over different brood sizes (Grosch 1948; Wilkes 1963; Wylie 1966; Chacko 1969) and in the majority of cases males fared better than females. Fewer studies have looked at the relative competitive effects of the sexes. Chacko (1969) found that female *Trichogramma minutum*, which produce a maximum of two parasites on their pyralid host (*Corcyra cephalonica*), have a higher fecundity and longevity if their partner is another female than if it is another male. Benson (1973) and Rotary & Gerling (1973) have evidence for a similar phenomenon in an ectoparasitic braconid.

At evolutionary equilibrium, when all hosts contain the same number and sexual composition of larvae, all males will suffer the same $f_m(c,r)$. The value of $f_m(c,r)$ does not influence the competition between males for mates and does not lead to a biased sex ratio. What about $f_f(c,r)$? Let us assume $f_f(c,r) = \exp - c(k_m r + k_f(1 - r))$ where k_m and k_f are constants representing the effects of male and female brood partners on female fitness. We can simultaneously calculate the optimal brood size and sex ratio under these conditions (see Appendix)

$$c = \tfrac{1}{2}(1/k_m + 1/k_f) \qquad r = k_f/(k_m + k_f) \qquad (3)$$

Note that if $k_m = k_f$, r becomes 0·5, but that if males have a greater effect on female fitness than other females, a female-biased sex ratio will result. As it is likely with parasitoids that k_m is normally greater than k_f, a female-biased sex ratio is predicted in gregarious species.

LOCAL MATE COMPETITION

The assumption of panmixis in the models described above may not be appropriate to many parasitoid species. Gregarious parasitoids, in particular, often mate on the host at emergence, such that the majority of matings are between siblings or at least between the progeny of a very small fraction of the parental population. In some cases, mating even occurs within the host before emergence (Hamilton 1967; Suzuki & Hiehata 1984).

Optimal sex ratios for such parasitoids are better predicted from models for local mate competition (LMC), first developed by Hamilton (1967). In Hamilton's model, n females colonize a resource patch within which their progeny develop and mate, and from which mated daughters then disperse to find new patches. The optimal sex ratio, r, for such a population may be derived by means of an ESS fitness model (Hamilton 1967; Charnov 1982) which yields the expression,

$$r = (n-1)/2n \qquad (4)$$

Hamilton (1979) and Taylor & Bulmer (1980) have shown using genetic models that the optimal sex ratio for haplodiploids like the hymenopterous parasitoids is slightly different, but the general pattern is the same. At high n, where mating on the patch approaches panmixis, a sex ratio of 0·5 is predicted. For very small n, where mating is restricted to the progeny of very few females, a very low, female-biased sex ratio is predicted. When only one female colonizes a patch, she should produce only as many sons as necessary to mate all her daughters.

Recently Wilson & Colwell (1981) and Colwell (1981) have shown that at the most basic level, the biased sex ratio associated with these conditions can be interpreted as intrademic group selection (Wade 1978; see also Wilson 1983). Other models produce the same results as they compare gene frequencies across the generations and so need not explicitly treat group productivity. Harvey (p. 59) gives a full discussion of the usefulness of this approach and its relation to the more traditional methods.

We can introduce LMC into the sex ratio and brood size models already developed (see Appendix). The simplest case is when n foundresses attack a host within which their larvae compete for food and around which their progeny mate before dispersal. Using the same within-brood density-dependent function as in eqn (3) we obtain;

$$r = k_f(n-1)/(k_m(n-1)+k_f(n+1)) \qquad (5)$$

$$c = (1/2n)((n+1)/k_f+(n-1)/k_m) \qquad (6)$$

Thus, both female competitive inferiority and LMC can generate female-biased sex ratios in gregarious parasitoids, and they tend to act in an additive manner. Note that if $k_m = k_f$, c becomes the same as the Lack solution $(1/k)$ and r becomes the Hamilton solution. The presence of LMC does not alter the brood size in the absence of sexual asymmetries.

From the sex ratio patterns which we actually see in parasitoid populations, it is often difficult to distinguish between the effects of sexual asymmetry and LMC. Thus, the general pattern that population samples of gregarious parasitoids yield more female-biased sex ratios than those of solitary parasitoids may reflect effects of LMC, sexual asymmetries, or both. It should also be remembered that most samples of population sex ratio in parasitoids give sex ratio at emergence, which may differ from the primary sex ratio as a result of differential survival from larval competition and of male mortality due to the exposure of lethal mutations in their haploid genome (Smith & Shaw 1980).

Less ambiguous evidence for the effect of LMC on population sex ratios comes from a comparison of sex ratios when foundress number per host patch varies. In the Scelionidae, solitary parasitoids of insect eggs, Waage (1982a) has found a correlation between population sex ratio and the egg mass size of the host species. Scelionid species attacking small egg masses, where one foundress will usually parasitize the entire egg mass, produce female-biased sex ratios predicted by LMC theory. Sex ratios for species attacking either isolated eggs, where wasps must disperse to mate, or large egg masses, where n is likely to be large, produce sex ratios closer to 0·5, as predicted.

For a particular species of parasitoid, experiments which vary foundress number per host patch have also revealed an increase in sex ratio with n (Werren 1983; Waage & Lane 1984). In such studies, care must be taken to eliminate the complicating effects of differential mortality, as high foundress numbers usually lead to superparasitism and high levels of larval mortality.

In gregarious parasitoids experiencing LMC and sexual asymmetries, we have seen that the decisions of how many eggs to lay and what sex ratio to produce are not independent. An interaction between these decisions also arises in the absence of sexual asymmetries, when brood sizes are small. Here, the addition of a single male or female to a brood can have strong effects on both progeny fitness and mating success. Waage & Ng (1984) have developed a simulation model for simultaneous optimization of brood size and sex ratio in the small-brooded *Trichogramma evanescens* under conditions of high LMC, and have obtained experimental support for the model's predictions.

HOST QUALITY

In nature, parasitoids will encounter hosts which vary in the amount and kind of larval resource which they contain. Small hosts, already parasitized hosts and hosts older or younger than the stage most suitable for development provide parasitoids with either less resource per larva or a lower quality of resource or both. What predictions can be made regarding progeny and sex allocation to hosts of different quality?

Consider first quality differences associated with parasitized *v.* unparasitized hosts. Superparasitism is the act of laying an egg in a previously parasitized host. The decision to superparasitize can be viewed as an optimal diet problem, an approach taken by Iwasa *et al.* (1984) and Charnov & Skinner (1984). They predict that superparasitism will be commoner when the proportion of hosts encountered which are already parasitized is high. There is much empirical support for these predictions: many parasitoid species avoid superparasitism when unparasitized hosts are abundant, but tend to superparasitize when the proportion of unparasitized hosts is low due to previous exploitation of the host population (van Lenteren 1981). When superparasitizing, some solitary wasps can even discriminate between hosts with different numbers of eggs from previous attacks (Bakker *et al.* 1972).

Superparasitism should also be commoner when recognition time is long (Hughes 1979), the rate of host finding is low and when parasitoids have high fecundity. Iwasa *et al.* (1984) have looked at superparasitism from a dynamic perspective over a parasitoid's lifetime and predict that it will become less common when the parasite is running low on eggs.

In considering the clutch size which a gregarious parasite should lay when superparasitizing, it is necessary to consider the effect that a certain probability of superparasitism will have on the number of eggs laid by a parasite in a fresh host. In the simplest case this is a two-player game and game theory techniques can be used to find the ESS strategies for the first and second wasps. The solution depends in large part on the nature of the within-brood density-dependent mortality. If, as earlier, we let $f(c) = \exp(-kc)$, both wasps should lay the same clutch size when maximizing brood pro-ductivity. However, the optimal clutch size for the second wasp may be smaller if other within-brood mortality functions apply (Suzuki & Iwasa 1980) or if travelling time considerations are included (Parker & Courtney 1984). Skinner (1984) has identified a situation where it might be advantageous for the second wasp to lay a larger clutch than the first. Smaller broods from superparasitizing wasps have been found in the pteromalid, *Nasonia vitri-pennis* (Holmes 1972), and in *Trichogramma evanescens* (N. Pallewatta, pers. comm.).

If the progeny from a single host mate together and LMC occurs, superparasitism will also alter the sex ratio of the two players. This was first discussed by Hamilton (1967) who assumed equal clutch sizes for both wasps. He found that the second wasp should lay a more male-biased sex ratio but that the sex ratio of both wasps would never be above 0·25. Werren (1980) and Suzuki & Iwasa (1980) both showed that, if the second wasp produced a smaller clutch size than the first, her sex ratio should become increasingly male-biased and ultimately all male. Werren showed that the sex ratio of *Nasonia vitripennis* varied with the ratio of clutch sizes as the theory predicted. Holmes (1972) also found superparasitizing eggs to be more frequently male.

Host size is the other aspect of host quality to have received considerable attention. The adaptive value of modifying progeny allocation with respect to host size is straightforward, and gregarious parasitoids are generally known to allocate more eggs to larger hosts (e.g. Klomp & Teerink 1962). The relationship between sex ratio and host size is less easily seen, and has been modelled in solitary parasitoids by Charnov (1979), Charnov *et al.* (1981) and Bull (1981). They make the reasonable (though still largely unsubstantiated) assumption that the marginal decrement in female fitness as host size drops will be greater than that for male fitness; small size has a more damaging effect on oviposition and host-finding ability than on mating. Under these circumstances selection will act on mothers to place male eggs in poor quality hosts and female eggs in better quality hosts. There should be a sharp threshold between these behaviours (though biological and observational factors will tend to blunt this) and the effect should depend on relative and not absolute host sizes. Overall, the sex ratio will tend to be biased towards males (Bull 1981).

It has long been known that males tend to be laid in smaller hosts (e.g. Clausen 1939) and there is empirical support for the more particular predictions of the hypothesis from several studies (Charnov *et al.* 1981).

Charnov's theory may be extended to predict that eggs laid by superparasitizing females should in certain circumstances be males, a prediction also made for quite different reasons by LMC theory. Werren (1984) has modelled a system in which both the degree of LMC and host quality varies, such that both factors contribute to sex ratio optimization. Green (1982) has developed an optimal foraging model which predicts when a solitary parasitoid should reject a host, accept it and lay a male egg, or accept it and lay a female egg, in relation to host size.

Finally, quality differences between host species have been considered in models by Iwasa *et al.* (1984). Van Alphen & van Harsel (1982) have used optimal diet models in an experimental test of selection for different host species by the braconid, *Asobara tabida*.

PATTERNS OF INDIVIDUAL PROGENY AND SEX ALLOCATION

A female parasitoid under extreme local mate competition should lay just enough sons to fertilize all her daughters (Hamilton 1967), and this calculation should include the risk of male mortality (Hartl 1971). Green, Gordh & Hawkins (1982) quantified the advantages of laying non-binomial sex ratios and found evidence for precise sex ratios in the species they studied. Owen (1983) tested for precise sex ratios in another species but found only a binomial distribution.

Waage (1982a) suggested that the distinct sequence of male and female allocation per host may be adaptive in reducing the probability of pure female broods arising by chance. *Trichogramma evanescens*, for instance, lays males early in an oviposition bout, which ensures that a patch of hosts, no matter how small, gets a son. Furthermore, as *Trichogramma* tends to avoid superparasitism, as n increases on a patch of a particular size, progeny per wasp decreases, and sex ratio increases. Thus, a simple mechanism leads to adaptive responses to variation in both patch size and LMC (Waage & Lane 1984).

Quite striking patterns of non-random sex allocation may have other explanations. Pickering (1980) found that a high proportion of broods of the gregarious ichneumonid parasitoid *Pachysomoides stupidus* contained mostly individuals of one sex, and suggested that asymmetries in relatedness may be the explanation. In the haplodiploid Hymenoptera, a male is related to siblings of either sex by 0·5, while a female is related to female siblings by 0·75 and to male siblings by 0·25. Thus, female larvae might be less tolerant of sharing resources with brothers than sisters, and a form of parent–offspring conflict arises which would select for mothers which produced broods biased towards one or the other sex.

Godfray (unpubl.) has developed a model for parent–offspring conflict in gregarious parasitic Hymenoptera which yields different predictions from those of Pickering, but points to situations where single sex broods should occur. The ecological conditions under which parent–offspring conflict will occur and single sex broods will be found are those that lead to small absolute brood sizes near the Lack solution. The best example of such segregated broods in real parasitoid systems occurs in species of the eulophid genus *Achrysocharoides* attacking leaf-mining caterpillars (Askew & Ruse 1974; Bryan 1983).

There are a number of other circumstances which may constrain a female to lay only male eggs (Godfray 1985b). Single sex broods may also arise in parasitic wasps from unmated individuals, in polyembryonic species (Hagen 1964) and as a result of cytoplasmic sex-determining factors (Werren, Skinner & Charnov 1981; Skinner 1982).

If parasitoids lay some eggs before mating (as many do, e.g. Doutt 1964) then the optimal postmating sex allocation may be a female-biased sex ratio and the parasitoid could use the length of time it took to get mated to decide the extent of the bias (Godfray 1985b). Werren & Charnov (1978) have shown that temporal differences in life-history expectations for males and females can select for biased sex ratios in parasitoids.

In the section on host quality, it was shown that a superparasitizing wasp laying few eggs should produce a male-biased sex ratio. This clutch-size relationship also applies to the original Hamilton model in the absence of superparasitism. A female laying *relatively* small broods should lay a more male-biased sex ratio than average and one laying relatively large broods a more female-biased sex ratio (Werren 1983; our unpublished models). Since clutch size is often related to parasite size (e.g. Taylor 1937), small females might be expected to lay more males than large females.

REPRODUCTIVE STRATEGIES AND
POPULATION ECOLOGY

Parasitoids make ideal laboratory subjects for the study of patterns and processes of progeny and sex allocation. As we move to examine how reproductive strategies are manifested in natural populations, however, parasitoids lose all of their advantages over vertebrate subjects, simply because they are too small, too fast and too short-lived to permit field studies of individual behaviour, lifetime reproductive success and population processes. Studies on the behaviour of field populations are scarce and concentrate on foraging, rather than reproductive strategies (e.g. Waage 1983). Therefore, what little we know of parasitoid population ecology must be inferred from samples of parasitism, laboratory experiments, and the enlightened speculation of mathematical models.

One of the most ubiquitous patterns of progeny allocation in natural parasitoid populations is superparasitism. The great majority of field studies reveal superparasitism in populations of both solitary (e.g. Varley 1947) and gregarious (e.g. Richards 1940) parasitoids. While the distribution of eggs per host is often random (i.e. Poisson), caution must be exercised in using such data to infer that parasitoids do not discriminate between parasitized and unparasitized hosts (van Lenteren *et al.* 1978), and such discrimination has been revealed in many laboratory studies (van Lenteren 1981). Furthermore, discrimination is the basis of most models for optimal foraging in parasitoids: in order to determine when to leave a patch of hosts, some measure of the rate of finding unparasitized and/or parasitized hosts must be, and apparently is, used (Hubbard & Cook 1978; Waage 1979; van Alphen & Galis 1983).

From the earliest studies on patterns of egg distribution by parasitoid populations (Fiske 1910) superparasitism has commonly been treated as a maladaptive error which reflects constraints on discrimination. While such errors may occur in parasitoid populations, we now perceive an adaptive value to superparasitism: parasitoids encountering hosts parasitized by conspecifics may increase their individual fitness by superparasitism (see Host Quality, p. 457, and van Alphen & Nell 1982), as may parasitoids encountering hosts which they have previously parasitized themselves (see Optimizing Brood Size, p. 450).

Population consequences of adaptive superparasitism have been little explored. Existing population models treat parasitoids as either rejecting or accepting all parasitized hosts (Rogers 1972) or accepting a proportion of these (Arditi 1983). Realistic models, however, must make superparasitism a function of the rate of finding parasitized and unparasitized hosts. Suzuki &

Iwasa (1980) have considered the effect of superparasitism on population sex ratios in a gregarious parasitoid where less eggs and more males are laid by the second wasp to find a host. They show that, as the density of the parasitoids increases, overall sex ratio becomes more male-biased. The magnitude of the change is related to the ability of wasps to recognize parasitized hosts and assess the overall probability of superparasitism.

Patterns of progeny and sex allocation in natural parasitoid populations often vary in a regular manner between generations, variation which may reflect adaptive responses to the distribution of parasitoids and hosts. An example is intergenerational changes in progeny allocation in bivoltine eulophids of the genus *Achrysocharoides*, where brood sizes tend to be smaller in the second generation (Askew & Ruse 1974; Bryan 1983). In the eulophid *Eulophus undulatus*, winter broods may be two to three times the size of summer broods (Parker & Smith 1933). In these species, hosts size is constant, and we suggest that changes in the parameters of the lifetime fitness model may be responsible for variation in brood size; for example, larger brood sizes in *Achrysocharoides* are associated with periods when hosts are more scarce (i.e. lower p in eqn (2)).

Sugonaev & Vu Kuang Kon (1979) found that the encyrtid *Encyrtus infidus* is solitary on the small individuals of its scale hosts in the winter generation, and produces a population sex ratio of about 0·5. As a gregarious parasitoid of older, larger scales in its summer generation, it produces a population sex ratio of about 0·25 (Fig. 27.3a). Clausen (1939) found a similar phenomenon in another encyrtid scale parasitoid, *Microterys clauseni*, which produced an average sex ratio of 0·25 on its smaller winter host and 0·10 on its larger summer host. Both host quality and LMC effects may be involved in these patterns. It must be stressed, however, that regular variations in parasitoid population sex ratios have also been associated with factors such as climate (Viktorov 1976) and disease (Zelinskaya 1981), making interpretation of field samples difficult.

Laboratory studies which consider foraging over prolonged periods shed some light on variation in population sex ratios. The parasitoid *Heterospilus distinguendus* lays male eggs in the small early stages of its beetle host and female eggs in older larvae (Charnov *et al.* 1981). In long-term studies of parasitoid–host dynamics, J.T. Addison (pers. comm.) has found that asynchrony in life cycles, which leads to a single *Heterospilus* generation attacking largely young or largely old hosts, causes intergenerational sex ratio fluctuations which are a major cause of population cycles and extinction.

Though the stability properties of parasitoid populations have been intensively investigated (Hassell 1978), only recently has the effect of including variable sex ratio been considered (Hassell, Waage & May 1983; Comins &

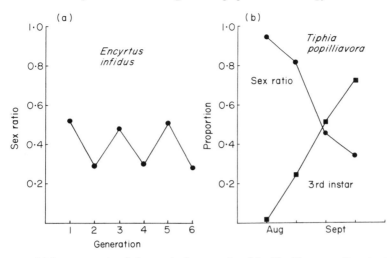

FIG. 27.3. (a) Intergenerational changes in the sex ratio of the bivoltine wasp *Encyrtus infidus* (from Sugonaev & Vu Kuang Kon 1979). (b) Field sex ratio of emerging *Tiphia popilliavora* and the proportion of its hosts in their third (and largest) instar from samples taken at different times of the season. (From Brunson 1938.)

Wellings 1984). The approach used has been to take a standard difference equation model of a host–parasitoid interaction (Hassell 1978) and to make the sex ratio (here the proportion of progeny becoming searching females) a variable.

Hassell *et al.* (1983) considered the sex ratio as a function of the absolute or relative (to the host) parasitoid density, an effect likely to occur through LMC or differential mortality of females at high host densities. Comins & Wellings (1984) in addition made sex ratio a function of host density, postulating that high host densities lead to small hosts which in certain circumstances result in a greater production of males parasitoids. They also (in an expanded model) consider the case where mating is limiting and sex ratio is a function of male density. The overall conclusion from this work is that, though sex ratio changes can be stabilizing, their effect is likely to be minor over the range of sex ratios realistically associated with LMC. Thus, sex ratio does not have the 'same pervasive stabilizing effects as some other documented factors' (Hassell *et al.* 1983).

WHERE NEXT? APPLIED BEHAVIOURAL ECOLOGY

The vast literature on parasitoid biology is valuable to the exploration of evolutionary and ecological processes discussed above, but most of it has arisen for quite a different reason: parasitoids are important agents in the biological control of insect pests. Their use poses many problems which can be clarified, and perhaps solved, by evolutionary and ecological theory (Waage & Hassell 1982).

The failure of introduced parasitoids to control exotic pests may result from many ecological factors, including factors which affect progeny and sex allocation. Thus, the poor success of the ichneumonid *Tiphia popilliavora* introduced into the US for control of the Japanese beetle was traced to a problem of sex allocation. In its native Japan, the wasp's phenology is timed to attack the third larval instar of the host, while in the US, it encounters early in the season younger, smaller larvae, on which it lays primarily male eggs (Brunson 1939; Fig. 27.3b). Similar host size effects have been implicated in the displacement of the one control agent by another: in California, the aphelinid *Aphytis melinus* accepts smaller hosts and lays a higher proportion of females on these than *Aphytis lingnanensis*, which it has displaced in most regions (Luck, Podoler & Kfir 1982; Luck & Podoler 1985).

Laboratory rearing of parasitoids presents even greater opportunities for applying the theory of sex and progeny allocation. Parasitoids for release are often reared under crowded conditions, and sometimes on less acceptable, factitious hosts, with consequent problems in sex ratio and quality of parasitoid populations (Waage *et al.* 1985). This is particularly true for *Trichogramma* spp., which are currently mass released on over 17 million ha of cropland every year. Understanding progeny and sex allocation may greatly improve methods for maximizing productivity of *Trichogramma* rearing units, even under the strict economic constraints which apply (Waage 1982b). The development of artificial diets for mass rearing is particularly exciting. Here the design of artificial hosts themselves (size, shape, density) touches on many aspects of parasitoid reproductive strategies, and gives much scope for manipulations which maximize the production of mated, fit females for release. These and other applications of fundamental research on parasitoid behavioural ecology hold much promise for practical improvements in biological control.

ACKNOWLEDGMENTS

We are deeply grateful to the following colleagues for providing much helpful advice and access to unpublished results: H. Comins, E. Charnov, M. Hassell, Y. Iwasa, N. Pallewatta, G. Parker, S. Skinner, Y. Suzuki, P. Wellings, J. Werren. We are also indebted to two anonymous reviewers for their comments on the manuscript.

REFERENCES

van Alphen, J.J.M. & van Harsel, H.H. (1982). Host selection by *Asobara tabida* Nees (Braconidae: Alysiinae), a larval parasitoid of fruit inhabiting *Drosophila* species. III. Host species selection and functional response. *Foraging behaviour of* Asobara tabida, *a larval parasitoid of* Drosophila (J.J.M. van Alphen). PhD. dissertation, University of Leiden.

van Alphen, J.J.M. & Nell, H.W. (1982). Superparasitism and host discrimination by *Asobara tabida* Ness (Braconidae: Alysiinae), a larval parasitoid of *Drosophila. Netherlands Journal of Zoology*, **32**, 232–360.

van Alphen, J.J.M. & Galis, F. (1983). Patch time allocation and parasitization efficiency of *Asobara tabida*, a larval parasitoid of *Drosophila. Journal of Animal Ecology*, **52**, 937–952.

Arditi, R. (1983). A unified model of the functional response of predators and parasitoids. *Journal of Animal Ecology*, **52**, 293–303.

Askew, R.R. (1968). A survey of leaf miners and their parasites on *Laburnum. Transactions of the Royal Entomological Society of London*, **120**, 1–37.

Askew, R.R. (1971). *Parasitic Insects*. Heinemann, London.

Askew, R.R. & Ruse, J.M. (1974). Biology and taxonomy of species of the genus *Enaysma* Delucchi (Hym.: Eulophidae, Entedontinae) with special reference to the British fauna. *Transactions of the Royal Entomological Society of London*, **125**, 257–294.

Bakker, K., Eijsackers, H.J.P., van Lenteren, J.C. & Meelis, E. (1972). Some models describing the distribution of eggs of the parasite *Pseudeucoila bochei* (Hymenoptera: Cynipidae) over its hosts, larvae of *Drosophila melanogaster. Oecologia*, **10**, 29–57.

Beckage, N.E. & Riddiford, L.M. (1978). Developmental interactions between the Tobacco Hornworm *Manduca sexta* and its braconid parasite *Apanteles congregatus. Entomologia experimentalis et applicata*, **23**, 139–151.

Benson, J.F. (1973). Intraspecific competition in the population dynamics of *Bracon hebetor* Say (Hymenoptera: Braconidae). *Journal of Animal Ecology*, **42**, 105–124.

Brunson, M.H. (1939). Influence of Japanese beetle instar on the sex and population of the parasite *Tiphia popilliavora. Journal of Agricultural Research*, **57**, 379–386.

Bryan, G. (1983). Seasonal biological variation in some leaf-miner parasites in the genus *Achrysocharoides* (Hymenoptera: Eulophidae). *Ecological Entomology*, **8**, 259–270.

Bull, J.J. (1981). Sex ratio evolution when fitness varies. *Heredity*, **46**, 9–26.

Chacko, M.J. (1969). The phenomenon of superparasitism in *Trichogramma evanescens minutum* Riley. I. *Beitrage zur Entomologie*, **19**, 617–635.

Charnov, E.L. (1979). The genetical evolution of patterns of sexuality: Darwinian fitness. *American Naturalist*, **113**, 465–480.

Charnov, E.L. (1982). *The Theory of Sex Allocation*. Princeton University Press, Princeton.

Charnov, E.L., Los-den Hartogh, R.L., Jones, W.T. & van den Assem, J. (1981). Sex ratio evolution in a variable environment. *Nature*, **289**, 27–33.

Charnov, E.L. & Skinner, S.W. (1983). Evolution of host selection and clutch size in parasitoid wasps. *Florida Entomologist*, **67**, 5–21.

Clausen, C.P. (1939). The effect of host size upon the sex ratio of hymenopterous parasites and its relation to methods of rearing and colonization. *Journal of the New York Entomological Society*, **47**, 1–9.

Colwell, R.K. (1981). Group selection is implicated in the evolution of female-biased sex ratios. *Nature*, **290**, 401–404.

Comins, H.N. & Wellings, P.W. (1985). Density-related parasitoid sex-ratio: influences on host–parasitoid dynamics (submitted).

DeLoach, C.J. & Rabb, R.L. (1972). Seasonal abundance and natural mortality of *Winthemia manducae* (Diptera: Tachinidae) and degree of parasitization of its host, the tobacco hornworm. *Annals of the Entomological Society of America*, **65**, 779–790.

Doutt, R.L. (1964). Biological characteristics of entomophagous adults. *Biological Control of Insect Pests and Weeds* (Ed. by P. DeBach), pp. 145–167, Chapman & Hall, London.

Escalante, G. & Rabinovich, J.E. (1979). Population dynamics of *Telenomus fariai* (Hymenoptera: Scelionidae), a parasite of Chagas' disease vectors. IX. Larval competition and population size regulation under laboratory conditions. *Researches on Population Ecology*, **20**, 235–246.

Fisher, R.A. (1930). *The Genetical Theory of Natural Selection.* Oxford University Press, Oxford.

Fiske, W.F. (1910). Superparasitism; an important factor in the natural control of insects. *Journal of Economic Entomology*, **3**, 88–97.

Flanders, S.E. (1950). Regulation of ovulation and egg disposal in the parasitic Hymenoptera. *Canadian Entomologist*, **82**, 134–140.

Glas, P.C., Smits, P.H., Vlaming, P. & van Lenteren, J.C. (1981). Biological control of lepidopteran pests in cabbage crops by means of inundative releases of *Trichogramma* species (*T. evanescens* Westwood and *T. cacoeciae* March): a combination of field and laboratory experiments. *Med. Fac. Landbouww. Rijksuniv. Gent*, **46**, 487–497.

Godfray, H.C.J. (1985a). The oviposition behaviour of a gregarious leaf-miner (*Pegomya nigritarsis*; Diptera, Anthomyiidae). (unpubl.).

Godfray, H.C.J. (1985b). The consequence of forced male production in parasitic wasps. (unpubl.).

Green, R.F. (1982). Optimal foraging and sex ratio in parasitic wasps. *Journal of theoretical Biology*, **95**, 43–48.

Green, R.F., Gordh, G.C. & Hawkins, B.A. (1982). Precise sex ratios in highly inbred parasitic wasps. *American Naturalist*, **120**, 653–655.

Grosch, D.S. (1948). Dwarfism and differential mortality in *Habrobracon*. *Journal of Experimental Zoology*, **107**, 289–311.

Hamilton, W.D. (1967). Extraordinary sex ratios. *Science*, **156**, 477–488.

Hamilton, W.D. (1979). Wingless and fighting males in fig wasps and other insects. *Reproductive Competition and Sexual Selection in Insects* (Ed. by M.S. Blum & N.A. Blum), pp. 167–220. Academic Press, New York.

Hartl, D.L. (1971). Some aspects of natural selection in arrhenotokous populations. *American Zoologist*, **11**, 309–325.

Hagen, K.S. (1964). Developmental stages of parasites. *Biological Control of Insect Pests and Weeds*, (Ed. by P. De Bach), pp. 168–246, Chapman & Hall, London.

Hassell, M.P. (1978). *The Dynamics of Arthropod Predator–Prey Systems.* Princeton University Press, Princeton, USA. 237 pp.

Hassell, M.P. & May, R.M. (1974). Aggregation of predators and insect parasites and its effect on stability. *Journal of Animal Ecology*, **43**, 567–594.

Hassell, M.P., Waage, J.K. & May, R.M. (1983). Variable parasitoid sex ratios and their effect on host–parasitoid dynamics. *Journal of Animal Ecology*, **52**, 889–904.

Holmes, H.B. (1972). Genetic evidence for fewer progeny and a higher percent males when *Nasonia vitripennis* oviposits in previously parasitised hosts. *Entomophaga*, **17**, 79–88.

Hubbard, S.F. & Cook, R.M. (1978). Optimal foraging by parasitoid wasps. *Journal of Animal Ecology*, **47**, 593–604.

Hughes, R.N. (1979). Optimal diets under the energy maximisation principle: the effects of recognition time and learning. *American Naturalist*, **113**, 209–221.

Ikata, T. & Suzuki, Y. (1982). Ovipositional experience of the gregarious parasitoid, *Apanteles glomeratus* (Hymenoptera: Braconidae), influencing her discrimination of the host larvae, *Pieris rapae crucivora*. *Applied Entomology & Zoology*, **17**, 119–126.

Iwasa, Y., Suzuki, Y. & Matsuda, H. (1984). The oviposition strategy of parasitoids. I. Effect of mortality and limited egg number. *Theoretical Population Biology* (in press).

Jackson, D.J. (1966). Observations on the biology of *Caraphractus cinctus* Walker (Hymenoptera: Mymaridae), a parasitoid of the eggs of Dytiscidae (Coleoptera). III. The adult life and sex ratio. *Transactions of the Royal Entomological Society of London*, **118**, 23–49.

Johannson, A.S. (1951). Studies on the relation between *Apanteles glomeratus* L. (Hymenoptera: Braconidae) and *Pieris brassicae* L. (Lepidoptera: Pieridae). *Norsk entomologisk tidsskrift*, **8**, 145–186.

Kearns, C.W. (1934). A hymenopterous parasite (*Cephalonomia gallicola* Ashm.) new to the cigarette beetle (*Lasioderma serricorne* Fab.). *Journal of Economic Entomology*, **27**, 801–806.

Klomp, H. & Teerink, B.J. (1962). Host selection and number of eggs per oviposition in the egg parasitic *Trichogramma embryophagum* Htg. *Nature*, **195**, 1020–1021.

Klomp, H. & Terrink, B.J. (1967). The significance of oviposition rate in the egg parasite, *Trichogramma embryophagum*. *Archives Neerlandaises de Zoologie*, **17**, 350–375.

Lack, D. (1947). The significance of clutch size. *Ibis*, **89**, 309–352.

van Lenteren, J.C. (1981). Host discrimination by parasitoids. *Semiochemicals, Their Role in Pest Control* (Ed. by D.A. Nordlund, R.L. Jones & W.J. Lewis), pp. 153–179, J. Wiley & Sons, Inc., New York.

van Lenteren, J.C., Bakker, K. & van Alphen, J.J.M. (1978). How to analyze host discrimination. *Ecological Entomology*, **3**, 71–75.

Luck, R.F., Podoler, H. & Kfir, R. (1982). Host selection and egg allocation behaviour by *Aphytis melinus* and *A. lingnanensis*: comparison of two facultatively gregarious parasitoids. *Ecological Entomology*, **7**, 397–408.

Luck, R.F. & Podoler, H. (1985). The potential role of host size in the competitive exclusion of *Aphytis lingnanensis* by *A. melinus. Ecology* (in press).

Maynard Smith, J. (1982). *Evolution and the Theory of Games.* Cambridge University Press, Cambridge.

Narayanan, E.S. & Subba Rao, B.R. (1955). Studies in insect parasitism. I–III. The effect of different hosts on the physiology, on the development and behaviour and on the sex ratio of *Microbracon gelechiae* Ashmead. *Beitrage zur Entomologie*, **5**, 36–60.

Owen, R.F. (1983). Sex ratio adjustment in *Asobara persimilis* (Hymenoptera: Braconidae), a parasitoid of *Drosophila. Oecologia*, **59**, 402–404.

Parker, G.A. & Courtney, S.P. (1984). Models of clutch size in insect oviposition. *Theoretical Population Biology*, **26**, 27–48.

Parker, H.L. & Smith, H.D. (1933). *Eulophus viridulus* Thoms., a parasite of *Pyrausta nubilalis* Hubn. *Annals of the Entomological Society America*, **26**, 21–36.

Pickering, J. (1980). Larval competition and brood sex ratios in the gregarious parasitoid *Pachysomoides stupidus. Nature*, **283**, 291–292.

Puttler, B. (1974). *Hypera postica* and *Bathyplectes curculionis*: encapsulation of parasite eggs by host larvae in Missouri and Arkansas. *Environmental Entomology*, **3**, 881–882.

Richards, O.W. (1940). The biology of the small white butterfly (*Pieris rapae*), with special reference to the factors controlling its abundance. *Journal of Animal Ecology*, **9**, 243–288.

Rogers, D. (1972). Random search and insect population models. *Journal of Animal Ecology*, **41**, 369–383.

Rotary, N. & Gerling, D. (1973). The influence of some external factors upon the sex ratio of *Bracon hebetor* Say (Hymenoptera: Braconidae). *Environmental Entomology*, **2**, 135–138.

Salt, G. (1961). Competition among insect parasitoids. In: *Mechanisms in Biological Competition. Symposium of the Society of Experimental Biology*, **15**, 96–119.

Sugonaev, E.S. & Vu Kuang Kon (1979). *Parasite–Host Interrelations in Insects.* Izdatel'stvo Nauka, Leningrad. 83 pp.

Skinner, S.W. (1982). Maternally inherited sex ratio in the parasitoid wasp *Nasonia vitripennis. Science*, **215**, 1133–1135.

Skinner, S.W. (1985). Clutch size as an optimal foraging problem for insect parasitoids. (submitted).

Smith, R.H. & Shaw, M.R. (1980). Haplodiploid sex ratios and the mutation rate. *Nature*, **287**, 728–729.

Suzuki, Y. & Hiehata, K. (1984). Mating systems and sex ratios in the egg parasitoids, *Trichogramma dendrolimi* and *T. papilionis* (Hymenoptera: Trichogrammatidae). *Animal Behaviour* (in press).

Suzuki, Y. & Iwasa, Y. (1980). A sex ratio theory of gregarious parasitoids. *Researches on Population Ecology*, **22**, 366–382.

Taylor, P.D. (1981). Intra-sex and inter-sex sibling interactions as sex ratio determinants. *Nature*, **291**, 64–66.

Taylor, P.D. & Bulmer, M.G. (1980). Local mate competition and the sex ratio. *Journal of Theoretical Biology*, **86**, 409–419.

Taylor, T.H.C. (1937). *The Biological Control of an Insect in Fiji. An Account of the Coconut Leaf-mining Beetle and its Parasite Complex*. Richard Clay & Sons, Ltd., Bungay, Suffolk.

Varley, G.C. (1947). The natural control of population balance in the knapweed gall-fly (*Urophora jaceana*). *Journal of Animal Ecology*, **16**, 139–187.

Viktorov, G.A. (1976). *The Ecology of Entomophagous Parasites*. Izdatel'stvo Nauka, Moscow. 151 pp.

Waage, J.K. (1979). Foraging for patchily-distributed hosts by the parasitoid, *Nemeritis canescens*. *Journal of Animal Ecology*, **48**, 353–371.

Waage, J.K. (1982a). Sib-mating and sex ratio strategies in scelionid wasps. *Ecological Entomology*, **7**, 103–112.

Waage, J.K. (1982b). The reproductive strategy of *Trichogramma*. In: *Les Trichogrammes. 1er Symposium International*, Antibes 20–23 April, 1982. I.N.R.A., Paris, pp. 155–163.

Waage, J.K. (1983). Aggregation in field parasitoid populations: foraging time allocation by a population of *Diadegma* (Hymenoptera: Ichneumonidae). *Ecological Entomology*, **8**, 447–453.

Waage, J.K. & Hassell, M.P. (1982). Parasitoids as biological control agents: a fundamental approach. *Parasitology*, **84**, 241–268.

Waage, J.K., Carl, K., Mills, N.J. & Greathead, D.J. (1985). Rearing entomophagous insects. *Handbook of Insect Rearing* (Ed. by R.F. Moore & P. Singh) (in press).

Waage, J.K. & Lane, J.A. (1984). The reproductive strategy of a parasitic wasp. II. Sex allocation and local mate competition in *Trichogramma evanescens*. *Journal of Animal Ecology*, **53**, 417–426.

Waage, J.K. & Ng Sook Ming (1984). The reproductive strategy of a parasitic wasp. I. Optimal progeny and sex allocation in *Trichogramma evanescens*. *Journal of Animal Ecology*, **53**, 401–416.

Wade, M.J. (1978). A critical review of models of group selection. *Quarterly Review of Biology*, **53**, 101–104.

Walker, I. (1967). Effect of population density on the viability and fecundity in *Nasonia vitripennis* Walker (Hymenoptera: Pteromalidae). *Ecology*, **48**, 294–301.

Weiss, A.E., Price, P.W. & Lynch, M. (1983). Selective pressures on clutch size in the gall maker, *Arteomyia carbonifera*. *Ecology*, **64**, 688–695.

Werren, J.H. (1980). Sex ratio adaptations to local mate competition in a parasitic wasp. *Science*, **208**, 1157–1159.

Werren, J.H. (1983). Sex ratio evolution under local mate competition in a parasitic wasp. *Evolution*, **37**, 116–124.

Werren, J.H. (1984). A model for sex ratio selection in parasitic wasps: Local mate competition and host quality effects. *Netherlands Journal of Zoology*, **34**, 81–96.

Werren, J.H. & Charnov, E.L. (**1978**). Facultative sex ratios and population dynamics. *Nature,* **272,** 349–350.

Werren, J.H., Skinner, S.W. & Charnov, E.L. (**1981**). Paternal inheritance of a daughterless sex ratio factor. *Nature,* **293,** 467–468.

Wilkes, A. (**1963**). Environmental causes of variation in the sex ratio of an arrhenotokous insect, *Dahlbominus fuliginosus* (Nees) (Hymenoptera: Eulophidae). *Canadian Entomologist,* **95,** 182–202.

Wilson, D.S. (**1983**). The group selection controversy: history and current status. *Annual Review of Ecology and Systematics,* **14,** 159–187.

Wilson, D.S. & Colwell, R.K. (**1981**). Evolution of sex ratio in structured demes. *Evolution,* **35,** 882–97.

Wylie, H.G. (**1966**). Some mechanisms that affect the sex ratio of *Nasonia vitripennis* (Walk.) (Hymenoptera: Pteromalidae) reared from super-parasitized housefly pupae. *Canadian Entomologist,* **98,** 645–653.

Zelinskaya, L.M. (**1981**). Sex ratio and mortality of *Anastatus japonicus* (Hymenoptera: Eupelmidae) in relation to host numbers. *Vestnik Zoologii,* **2,** 57–62.

APPENDIX

When there is differential mortality between the sexes of larval parasitoids competing in a host, sexual asymmetries arise. The following model calculates the optimal sex ratio and brood size under conditions of asymmetry, for the population structure discussed by Hamilton (1967) where a patch of hosts is colonized by n females. The model is solved for conditions of panmixis, when n is large (eqn (3) in the text) and for conditions of high local mate competition, when n is small (eqns (5) and (6)).

The fitness of a rare female laying broods with a sex ratio $\hat{r}$ in a population producing a sex ratio r has been given by Charnov (1982, p. 68). Including differential density-dependent mortality as discussed in the text we get an expression for female fitness, $W_{\hat{r}}$;

$$W_{\hat{r}} = (1-\hat{r})bf_{\mathrm{f}}(c,r) + \frac{\hat{r}bf_{\mathrm{m}}(c,r)}{(b[\hat{r}+(n-1)r])f_{\mathrm{m}}(c,r)}(b((1-\hat{r})+(n-1)(1-r))f_{\mathrm{f}}(c,r) \quad (\mathrm{A}1)$$

where n is the number of foundresses, b the number of eggs laid in a patch by one female and c is b divided by the number of hosts [$f_{\mathrm{f}}(c,r)$ is more accurately $f_{\mathrm{f}}(c,r,f,n)$ and similarly $f_{\mathrm{m}}(c,r)$]. The ESS sex ratio (r^*) is found by calculating $\partial W_{\hat{r}}/\partial \hat{r}\,|_{r=\hat{r}} = 0$ (Maynard Smith 1982; Charnov 1982) and is the solution of the quadratic;

$$\mathrm{r}^{*2}\,(2n) + r^*(2n(F-1)) - F(n-1) = 0 \quad (\mathrm{A}2)$$

where $F = -f_{\mathrm{f}}(c_1 r)/f_{\mathrm{f}}'(c,r)$, the differential with respect to $\hat{r}$. An analagous expression for a mutant brood size $\hat{b}$ can be constructed and the resultant ESS brood size is found to be;

$$b^* = -\frac{f_{\mathrm{f}}(c,r)}{\dfrac{\partial f_{\mathrm{f}}(c,r)}{\partial \hat{b}}} \quad (\mathrm{A}3)$$

Equations (A2) and (A3) can be solved simultaneously for a given $f_f(c,r)$. If $f_f(c,r) = \exp - c[k_m r + k_f(1 - r)]$ the solutions are eqns (5) and (6) which reduce to eqn (3) as n gets large. A more detailed description of this model will be published elsewhere (H.C.J. Godfray, unpubl.).

28. THE EVOLUTION OF COOPERATION AND LIFE HISTORY IN THE DUNNOCK, *PRUNELLA MODULARIS*

A. I. HOUSTON AND N. B. DAVIES

Department of Zoology, University of Cambridge,
Downing Street, Cambridge CB2 3EJ

SUMMARY

In many animals two or more individuals cooperate to raise offspring. There is evidence that each individual will work harder if others do less and will do less work if others do more. How then do cooperating individuals come to an 'agreement' on how much work each will do? To illustrate this problem, we present some data on chick feeding rates by adult dunnocks, *Prunella modularis*, who sometimes cooperate as male–female pairs and sometimes as two male–female trios. We then develop a life-history model which predicts the ESS efforts for each individual, and compare the model's predictions with the observed data.

INTRODUCTION

The evolution of life histories involves a series of trade-offs, such as those between number and quality of offspring (Lack 1954) and between reproductive effort and survival (Williams 1966; Charnov & Krebs 1974). Most recent models have emphasized how ecological factors will influence the optimal trade-offs to maximize an individual's Darwinian fitness (Gadgil & Bossert 1970; Sibly & Calow 1983). For example, food abundance and distribution, competition, predator pressure and climate will all influence the optimal life history because they will determine offspring and adult survival and also the amount of resources available for reproduction (Stearns 1976; Horn & Rubenstein 1984).

Here we suggest that a knowledge of behaviour as well as ecology is important for understanding the evolution of life histories. In many animals, two or more adults cooperate to raise offspring, the common case being a male and female cooperating as a pair. Rather than regarding cooperation as a harmonious venture in which both members of the pair have the common goal of maximizing their joint fitness, we should expect there to be conflicts of interest over how much effort each should put into the cooperation (Trivers

1972). The problem we shall address is how do two, or more, individuals reach a compromise on how hard each should work?

There is some good evidence that each member of a pair has the capacity to work harder than it actually does. Thus, when one of a pair of birds dies the remaining parent increases its rate of chick feeding, though not usually sufficiently to compensate for the loss of the other parent (Kluijver 1950; Kendeigh 1952). Increased effort in the feeding of chicks is costly for birds and leads to increased weight loss and lower survival (Askenmo 1977, 1979; Bryant 1979). Similarly a female pied flycatcher, *Ficedula hypoleuca*, who is deserted by her mate, increases her effort in chick feeding compared with females who have the full cooperation of their males (Alatalo, Lundberg & Stahlbrandt 1982). On the other hand, there is also evidence that an individual will do less work if others are prepared to do more. For example, in the grey-crowned babbler, *Pomatostomus temporalis*, a cooperative breeder, a parent puts less effort into chick feeding if there are helpers present to feed the brood (Brown *et al.* 1978). As a result of this extra help, the parents are able to have more broods per year and so increase their reproductive success (Brown *et al.* 1982).

How do cooperating individuals come to an agreement on how much work each will do? Given that each individual has the potential to work harder than it actually does, we have to consider the problem of cheating; some individuals may do less than their fair share of the work if others are prepared to work harder as a result. Clearly, in these cases the optimal reproductive effort of one individual depends on what the others are prepared to do. Natural selection should lead to an evolutionarily stable strategy, or ESS, namely a strategy which is stable against cheating (Maynard Smith & Price 1973; Maynard Smith 1982). Maynard Smith (1977) used some game theory models to specify the conditions under which it is an ESS for one or other member of a pair to desert rather than both remaining to cooperate and rear offspring. Chase (1980) has applied models from economics to derive the stable (=uncheatable) allocation of effort when two individuals co-operate.

In this paper we extend previous analyses and consider the evolution of stable cooperation in a life history context. Our ideas stemmed from an attempt to understand some data on chick feeding by a small passerine bird, the dunnock (=hedge sparrow) *Prunella modularis*. This species is of particular interest because parents sometimes cooperate in pairs (one male and one female) and sometimes in trios (two males and one female). We begin by presenting the data to help us illustrate the general problem we are considering. It will also be useful to have a real animal in mind when we come to develop the theory in the second part of the paper.

COOPERATION AMONG DUNNOCKS IN
PAIRS AND TRIOS

We have studied a colour-ringed population of about ninety breeding adults in the Cambridge University Botanic Garden since the autumn of 1980. The mating combinations were very variable and included simple pairs (monogamy), a male with two females (polygyny), a female with two or three males (polyandry) and several males sharing several females (polygynandry). The ecological factors giving rise to this variability together with the behaviour of the birds and their reproductive success in the different mating combinations have been described elsewhere (Davies 1983, 1985; Davies & Lundberg 1984). Here we give only a brief summary to provide some background to the new data we will present on the effort that adults put into chick feeding. We restrict our discussion to the two commonest mating combinations in the population, namely monogamous 'pairs' and 'trios', consisting of two males and one female.

Formation and reproductive success of pairs and trios

The ability of males to monopolize access to females depended on female range size which, in turn, was related to food distribution. Dunnocks fed mainly on small seeds and invertebrates in dense vegetation. Where these feeding patches were densely distributed, female ranges were small and they were easily monopolized by one male, hence monogamy resulted. Both members of the pair fed the chicks.

Where food was more sparsely distributed, female ranges were larger and more difficult for one male to monopolize alone. Trios usually formed when a female wandered over two neighbouring male song territories. The two males eventually coalesced their territories and came to defend the whole of the female's range together as a team. Males in trios were not close relatives. Two different outcomes could be recognized in these trios.

Only one male mated. One of the males, the alpha (usually the older one) was dominant to the other, the beta. Alpha males guarded the female closely during the egg laying period and attempted to prevent the beta male from copulating with her. If only the alpha male mated, then only he helped the female to feed the chicks. The beta male harassed the female during incubation and attempted to get access to the nest. Indirect evidence suggested that he sometimes destroyed the eggs or young chicks. Such interference would pay a beta male who had not copulated with the female because it led to the female laying a replacement clutch within a week or two, and thus hastened the day he had another chance to mate. As a result of frequent failures in trios where only one male mated, due to beta male interference, fewer young were fledged per breeding attempt compared with monogamous pairs.

Both males mated. Sometimes the alpha male was unable to guard the female sufficiently closely to prevent the beta male from copulating. Females attempted to escape the alpha male's attentions and actively encouraged the beta male to copulate. When both males copulated with her, on average the alpha male performed 60% of the matings and the beta male 40%. In trios where beta and alpha male both copulated, both helped the female to feed the chicks. Trio-fed broods received more food, weighed more, and produced more fledglings per breeding attempt, than either pairs or trios where only one male mated.

The different mating combinations may, in part, reflect the different outcomes of sexual conflict, with the female favouring cooperative polyandry (both males mating and feeding the chicks), and the dominant male favouring monogamy. The increased success of a trio-fed brood is clearly of advantage to the female but it probably does not compensate the alpha male for his loss of paternity.

Chick feeding effort by adults in pairs and trios

Total effort

Figure 28.1 shows the rate at which chicks were fed (feeds/brood/hour) during the second half of the nestling period (days 7–11), when provisioning rate was at a maximum. Provisioning rate increased with brood size but trio-fed broods received significantly more food than pair-fed broods. It is especially interesting that there was no difference between the rates at which broods were fed by monogamous pairs and by trios where only the alpha male and female fed the brood. Thus, the number of adults provisioning the brood seems to determine feeding rate rather than any differences in bird quality or territory quality between pairs and trios. The results of natural removal experiments also support this view. Some trios became pairs when either the alpha or beta male died. The provisioning rates at these nests followed the same curve as that for monogamous pairs (Fig. 28.1). Provisioning rate is probably a reasonable measure of effort by adults and benefit to chicks because differences in provisioning rate were matched by differences in nestling weights (Davies 1985).

Effort of each adult

The work rates of each adult when provisioning alone, in pairs or in trios are summarized in Table 28.1. Pair-fed broods include data from monogamous

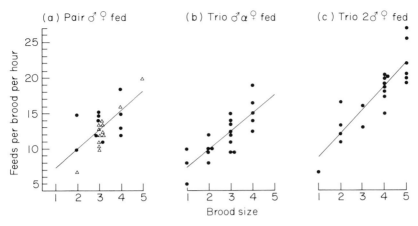

FIG. 28.1. Feeding rates (= visits to nest by adults with food in bill) of nestlings versus brood size for (a) pair-fed broods, ($y = 2\cdot678x + 4\cdot632$; $r = 0\cdot667$, $P < 0\cdot001$, $N = 24$), (b) trios where only the alpha male and female fed the brood ($y = 2\cdot556x + 4\cdot804$; $r = 0\cdot796$, $P < 0\cdot001$, $N = 21$) and (c) trios where alpha male, beta male and female all fed the brood ($y = 3\cdot336x + 5\cdot469$; $r = 0\cdot872$, $P < 0\cdot001$, $N = 21$). No significant difference between the first two lines, but feeding rates for the last case were significantly greater. In the pair-fed graph, solid circles are for normal pairs and open triangles are for 'experimental' pairs, where the mating combination was originally a trio but one of the males died thus leaving a pair. Analysis of covariance; pair versus trio where only alpha male and female fed, F slope $= 0\cdot0248$, d.f. $= 1,41$ (NS). F elevation $= 0\cdot0924$, d.f. $= 1,42$ (NS). Pair versus trio where both males and female fed, F slope $= 0\cdot709$, d.f. $= 1,41$ (NS). F elevation $= 18\cdot94$, d.f. $= 1,42$ ($P < 0\cdot001$). Trio where only alpha male and female fed versus trio where both males and female fed, F slope $= 1\cdot55$, d.f. $= 1,38$ (NS). F elevation $= 17\cdot19$, d.f. $= 1,39$ ($P < 0\cdot001$).

TABLE 28.1. Observed mean provisioning rates of nestlings by adults when working alone, in a pair or in a trio. Sample sizes in brackets

| | Mean feeds to brood per hour (N) Broods fed by: | | | | | |
| | | | | | Trio | |
Brood size	Single female	Pair Female	Male	Female	Alpha male	Beta male
1	5·2 (2)	3·9	3·8 (3)	3·4	3·1	0·3 (1)
2	—	5·6	4·6 (7)	4·1	4·8	3·3 (3)
3	9·4 (3)	6·6	5·9 (21)	6·2	4·6	5·6 (3)
4	—	6·9	8·2 (6)	7·1	6·4	5·1 (6)
5	—	8·6	11·4 (1)	8·1	8·3	6·1 (5)

pairs and trios where only one male and one female fed the chicks. The following conclusions can be drawn.

(i) Within both pair-fed broods and trio-fed broods, each adult worked harder with increasing brood size.

(ii) Within pair-fed broods, there was no significant difference between the work rates of males and females (for monogamous pairs, Wilcoxon matched pairs test for 20 broods, $T = 37.5$, NS; for trios where only the alpha male and female fed the brood, $T = 39$, data from 18 broods, NS).

(iii) Within trio-fed broods, however, there was a significant difference in the work rate of the three birds (Friedman two-way ANOVA, data on 18 trio-fed broods; $\chi_r^2 = 10.36$, 2 d.f., $P < 0.01$). Beta males worked significantly less hard than alpha males (Wilcoxon matched pairs test, $N = 18$, $T = 15.5$, $P < 0.01$) and significantly less hard than females ($T = 12$, $P < 0.01$). There was no significant difference between the work rate of the female and alpha male ($T = 72.5$, NS).

(iv) Now we compare the work rate of each bird in the different provisioning combinations. Lone females, whose mates had died, worked significantly harder than those who had help from a male (data from brood size of one is too small to test for significance but for broods of three, lone females worked significantly harder than those in pairs, Mann–Whitney U-test, two-tailed, $U = 2.5$, $P < 0.02$). Females did not, however, do significantly less work in trios compared with pairs (Table 28.1). Alpha males, on the other hand, did do less work in trios than monogamous males in pairs (sample sizes too small to test except for broods of four, where the difference is significant; Mann–Whitney U-test, two-tailed, $U = 5$, $P = 0.042$).

Summary of factors influencing effort

These data suggest that two factors influenced the effort an adult puts in to chick feeding.

Value of brood. All adults worked harder for larger broods. In monogamous pairs and trios where only the alpha male has mated both male and female have equal genetic interest in the offspring (assuming no cuckoldry by other males) and it is interesting that both worked equally hard in chick feeding. In trios, the female is again related to all the chicks and worked about as hard as she did in a pair. The two males, however, shared matings and presumably also shared paternity (enzyme polymorphism analysis is now in progress to test this). Experiments with domestic chickens have shown that, where two males mate with a female, the paternity is directly related to the proportion of copulations each performs (Martin *et al.* 1974). If this was also true for dunnocks, then the beta male, with a lower proportion of matings, would have less paternity than the alpha male. The brood would thus be less valuable to him, and his lower provisioning rate than the alpha male presumably reflects this fact. There was some evidence that beta males worked harder the more access they had to the female during the mating period (Fig. 28.2). There were not enough data to test whether increased proportion of copulations led to increased effort in chick feeding but percentage time close to the female in the mating period influenced the chances of successful copulations (Davies 1985). The lower provisioning rate by alpha males of trios compared with monogamous males may also reflect the lower value of the brood to a male when paternity is shared.

In one case, a trio fed a brood of just one chick (three of the four eggs in the clutch had failed to hatch). Obviously both males could not have fathered this chick! The fact that both, nevertheless, fed it (Table 28.1) suggests that males cannot recognize their own offspring but simply adjust their parental effort in relation to their probability of paternity.

The work others do. The second factor which influenced effort was what the other members of the team were doing. Females worked harder if their mate died and the lower provisioning rate of alpha males in trios, compared to monogamous males, may also, in part, have reflected the fact that males could do less when working in a team of three as opposed to two.

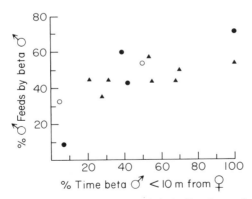

FIG. 28.2. Beta males did a greater share of the work in feeding the nestlings, the more access they had to the female in the mating period (and, by implication, the more matings they performed). Spearman rank correlation, $r_s = 0.652$, $P < 0.01$. Each of the eight solid triangles refers to a different beta male. The open circles refer to a beta male who was observed for two breeding attempts in the same trio. The solid circles refer to a male who was observed for four breeding attempts in the same trio, two as beta male (% feed values of 9 and 43) and two as alpha male (% feed values 60 and 71).

These data clearly need to be extended by removal experiments (see discussion) and more information on how provisioning rate influences both chick survival and adult survival. However, they at least provide a stimulus for considering the problem of how a stable solution is achieved among cooperating individuals and we now develop a theoretical model.

STABLE COOPERATION IN A LIFE-HISTORY MODEL

We seek the reproductive behaviour that maximizes an individual's fitness. We use the malthusian parameter, m, (Fisher 1930) as the basis of a measure of fitness (see Charlesworth, 1980, for a justification). In general, the maximization of fitness involves dynamic optimization (e.g. Schaffer 1983), but under certain conditions the problem can be simplified to the maximization in each season of

$\lambda = \exp(m) =$ number of young from a season that survive to breed + probability of a breeding adult surviving to the next season.

(Charnov & Krebs 1974; Schaffer 1974; see also Sibly & Calow 1983). Although this measure may not be completely satisfactory, it suffices to illustrate our approach in a relatively straightforward context.

We assume that each parent treats all members of the brood equally, and that the survival of each nestling as a function of total parental effort has the form shown in Fig. 28.3a. Note that there is a threshold amount of effort, A, below which survival probability is zero, and above which survival increases at a decreasing rate until an asymptote J is reached. We shall be concerned with the effort E_i that individual i devotes to each nestling. If the other individuals put in effort E_o, then individual i expects to get

$$P_i NJ[1 - \exp(-k(E_i + E_o - A))]$$

young raised to independence from a clutch of N nestlings, where P_i is the probability that individual i is the parent of a nestling. The parameter k relates chick survival to parental effort: increasing k increases the survival for a given effort, which might correspond to increasing the availability of food. When there are N nestlings, individual i's *total* effort is NE_i, and we assume that survival $S(E_i)$ to the next season decreases at an increasing rate as this effort increases (Fig. 28.3b). A convenient function to represent this is

$$S(E_i) = V_i(1 - \exp[-c(1 - NE_i)]).$$

(Note that we require an individual's total effort to lie between 0 and 1). If the effort of individual i is zero, then its survival is $V_i(1 - \exp(-c))$. Throughout this paper the V_i values will be equal for all individuals.

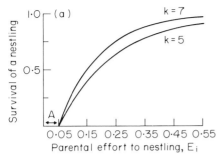
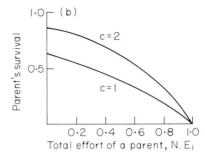

FIG. 28.3. (a) Theoretical curve for survival of a nestling versus parental effort to that nestling. (b) Theoretical curve for parent survival versus total effort put in to chick rearing by that parent.

The optimal effort of individual i as a function of the effort of the other parents can now be found by choosing E_i so as to maximize

$$\lambda_i(E_i) = P_i NJ[1 - \exp(-k(E_i + E_o - A))] + V_i[1 - \exp(-c(1 - NE_i))] \qquad (1)$$

The maximum can be found by differentiating with respect to E_i and setting the result equal to zero. Following this procedure, we find that the optimal effort, $E_i{}^*$, is given by the equation

$$E_i{}^* = (L_i - k\,E_o)/(Nc + k), \qquad (2)$$

where

$$L_i = \ln(P_i Jk/V_i\,c) + c + kA. \qquad (3)$$

We have chosen the exponential functions for brood and adult survival on the grounds of their mathematical tractability. They result in a simple relationship between the efforts of the parents. The optimal effort of one parent decreases along a straight line with slope $-k/(Nc + k)$ as the effort of the other parents is increased (Fig. 28.4). (In general the relationship will not be this simple: in fact, if the survival of the young is an 'S' shaped function of effort, then it is possible for E_i to increase with E_o when E_o is small).

Now consider two parents, whose efforts etc. are denoted by the subscripts m and f for 'male' and 'female' respectively. We expect evolution to result in an evolutionarily stable strategy (ESS). In this context we seek a Nash equilibrium, that is to say a strategy pair $(\tilde{E}_m, \tilde{E}_f)$ such that $\tilde{E}_m$ is the male's best effort given that the female's effort is $\tilde{E}_f$, and $\tilde{E}_f$ is the female's best effort given that the male's effort is $\tilde{E}_m$ (Grafen & Sibly (1978) use the same sort of procedure to analyse desertion of one parent by the other).

FIG. 28.4. Optimal parental effort for one parent in relation to the effort of the other parent. If the other does less, it pays to do more and if the other does more it pays to do less.

In our case, the ESS (if it exists) can be found from eqn (2). If each parent adopts its best behaviour against the other's behaviour, then

$$E_m = (L_m - kE_f)/(Nc + k) \qquad (4)$$

and

$$E_f = (L_f - kE_m)/(Nc + k). \qquad (5)$$

These equations determine what Chase (1980) calls the reaction curves.

Thus, an ESS pair $(\tilde{E}_m, \tilde{E}_f)$ for which both *total* efforts lie between 0 and 1 will simultaneously satisfy eqns (4) and (5). Such a solution can be found graphically by plotting both equations on the same axes, as is shown in Fig. 28.5. For our purposes we require an algebraic expression for the solution. One way to proceed is to use eqn (4) to eliminate E_m from eqn (5). This yields the following equation for the female's evolutionarily stable effort:

$$\tilde{E}_f = [L_f (Nc + k) - L_m k]/[N^2 c^2 + 2Nc \, k]. \qquad (6)$$

$\tilde{E}_m$ can be found from eqns (6) and (4).

Given that the reaction curves intersect, the intersection will be stable as long as each curve has a slope that is less than -1, i.e. $\delta E_i^*/\delta E_o < -1$. (as drawn in Fig. 28.4. We expect this condition to hold in cases where selection favours iteroparity). In such cases if one parent reduces its effort by a certain amount, then the response of the other parent is to increase its own effort but by a smaller amount insufficient to compensate for the reduction by the other, so that the total effort is reduced. Figure 28.5 shows that a sequence of smaller and smaller changes in effort converges on the ESS.

Chase (1980) gives three other possible outcomes. If the female reaction curve is completely above that of the male (Fig. 28.6a), then the male would desert and the ESS would require the female to put in all the effort. Likewise, if the male reaction curve is above that of the female (Fig. 28.6b) then the ESS involves the male putting in all the effort. The third possibility is for the reaction curves to have slopes greater than -1 at the region of intersection (Fig. 28.6c). Such an intersection is unstable; if one parent reduces its effort by a certain amount then the response of the other parent is to increase its own effort by a larger amount so as to more than compensate for the reduction by the other. Reactions then proceed by larger and larger amounts until one parent ends up doing all the work. Which parent it is depends on the initial conditions (Fig. 28.6c).

These three (Fig. 28.6) together with the stable intersection (Fig. 28.5) exhaust the basic possibilities, but if E_i^* is a non-monotonic function of E_o then the reaction curves may intersect at three points. We expect the middle intersection to be stable.

Exactly the same sort of procedure can be followed when there are three parents. We give these parents the subscripts 'f', 'α' and 'β' to indicate the

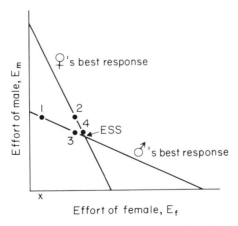

FIG. 28.5. Lines for both parents (of the form in Fig. 28.4) plotted onto the same graph. If the male works harder it pays the female to do less and if the female works harder it pays the male to do less. The stable point (ESS efforts for male and female) is where the two lines intersect. Imagine, for example, that the female plays effort x. The male's best response is 1. The female then replies with effort 2, the male with 3, the female with 4, and so on until the efforts reach the ESS. At the stable point it does not pay either individual to change its effort.

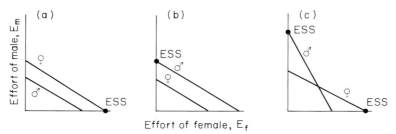

FIG. 28.6. Three other possible arrangements of the male and female reaction curves. (a) The female curve lies completely above that of the male. Here the ESS is for the female to do all the work. (b) The male curve lies above that of the female. Here the ESS is for the male to do all the work. (c) The curves intersect but the intersection point is unstable. Either 'all female work' or 'all male work' is an ESS.

female, the alpha male and the beta male respectively. Expanding eqn (2) for each parent:

$$E_f = [L_f - k(E_\alpha + E_\beta)]/(Nc + k)\qquad(7)$$

$$E_\alpha = [L_\alpha - k(E_f + E_\beta)]/(Nc + k)\qquad(8)$$

and

$$E_\beta = [L_\beta - k(E_f + E_\alpha)]/(Nc + k).\qquad(9)$$

A stable solution with all parents contributing will satisfy eqns (7)–(9). Such a solution can be found graphically in a three-dimensional space in which the optimal effort of each parent forms a plane as a function of the efforts of the other two parents. In general three planes intersect at a point. (The intersection of two planes is a line, the intersection of the third plane and the line is a point). In this case the algebraic analysis is obviously more convenient than the graphical one. E_α can be eliminated by subtracting eqn (9) from eqn (7) to yield

$$E_\beta = (L_\beta - L_f)/Nc + E_f.\qquad(10)$$

Equation (8) can then be used to eliminate E_α from eqn (9), and the resulting equation, together with eqn (10) gives us the following equation for the female's evolutionarily stable strategy:

$$\tilde{E}_f = \frac{L_f(Nc + 2k) - k(L_\alpha + L_\beta)}{N^2 c^2 + 3Nc\,k}.\qquad(11)$$

$\tilde{E}_\beta$ now can be found using eqn (10), and then $\tilde{E}_\alpha$ can be found from eqn (8). (We make no attempt to catalogue all the possible ESSs in three-dimensional space.)

The advantage of having an algebraic expression for the effort of each parent is that the effects of the various parameters, including the number of nestlings, N, can easily be investigated.

Table 28.2 illustrates how the predicted total stable efforts (i.e. NE_i) of the parents vary with N. For trios, the columns labelled F, α, β are the total efforts of the female, the alpha male and the beta male respectively, and the next column is the fitness of the female if behaviour is optimal with $E_i = \tilde{E}_f$ and $E_o = \tilde{E}_\alpha + \tilde{E}_\beta$, and $P_i = P_f = 1$. For trios, the two males' share of paternity has

TABLE 28.2. Predictions derived from the model described in text for the ESS chick feeding efforts for parents working in trios and pairs. Female fitness in trios and pairs is also given. Parameter values used in the model: $A = 0.15$, $k = 4.2$, $c = 2.4$, $J = 0.35$, $V = 0.8$. For trios, $P_f = 1$, $P_\alpha = 0.6$, $P_\beta = 0.4$. For pairs, $P_f = P_m = 1$

	Trio				Pair	
	Chick feeding effort				Chick feeding effort for female (F)	
Brood size (N)	Female (F)	Alpha $\male(\alpha)$	Beta $\male(\beta)$	Fitness of female	and male (M) (F = M)	Fitness of female
2	0·46	0·25	0·08	1·03	0·42	1·08
3	0·55	0·33	0·16	1·12	0·53	1·15
4	0·61	0·40	0·23	1·17	0·61	1·16
5	0·66	0·45	0·28	1·18	0·68	1·13
6	0·71	0·49	0·32	1·15	0·73	1·06

been assumed to reflect their share of the copulations with $P_\alpha = 0.6$ and $P_\beta = 0.4$. The final two columns concern a pair. The column headed F = M is the total effort for each parent and the last column is their lifetime number of offspring.

To test the model quantitatively we would need to know how effort influenced both parent and chick survival. The details of this are not yet known for any bird. Dunnock survival of adults from year to year is approximately 50% (Davies & Lundberg 1984) and the parameter c is scaled to give a value in this region. A and k are chosen so that from a brood of four chicks, less than one is expected to survive to breeding, which is a reasonable estimate of survival in the field. The predictions of the model do not depend on the precise values we have used in Table 28.2, and at this stage we are only concerned with qualitative predictions of trends in effort with changes in brood size and for pairs versus trios.

MODEL'S PREDICTIONS VERSUS OBSERVED DATA

The output of the model in Table 28.2 reproduced quite well the main trends shown by the observed data in Table 1, namely;

    (i) each bird works harder with increasing brood size;

    (ii) in trios, the female works harder than the alpha male who, in turn, works harder than the beta male;

    (iii) effort of the female in a pair is about equal to that in a trio;

    (iv) effort of the alpha male in a trio is less than that of a male in a pair.

In addition, the model makes a prediction concerning the optimal clutch size for the female:

    (v) in a trio, the female's optimal clutch size is 5 whereas in a pair it is 4.

Point (v) is sensitive to the parameter values in the model but the others, (i)–(iv) are fairly robust. Prediction (v) fits well the observed behaviour of the birds because females who have copulated with two males do indeed lay larger clutches than females who have copulated with just one male (Davies 1985). This makes good adaptive sense because when two males have copulated, the female can expect both to feed her young and so she receives more help with parental care. Females therefore adjust their clutch size in relation to the amount of help they expect with chick feeding.

One of the most important conclusions from the observed data is that the total effort of a trio was greater than that of a pair (Fig. 28.1). The model predicts, however, that this will not always necessarily be true. Certainly for large brood sizes the total effort of a trio is greater than that of a pair (Tables 28.2 and 28.3), but for small brood sizes a pair is predicted to work harder than a trio. The brood size at which trios come to work harder than pairs depends on the parameter values in the model. For example, Table 28.3 shows how adult survival influences total effort of pairs and trios. By increasing adult survival, the optimal clutch size for a trio is reduced from 5 to 4, while fitness is, of course, increased. When $V = 0.8$, the optimal effort for a trio is 1·40 and the optimal effort for a pair is 1·23. When $V = 0.9$, the optimal effort for a trio is 1·17 and the optimal effort of a pair is 1·18. Thus, increasing adult survival can result in the optimal effort of a pair being about the same, or even greater, than the optimal effort of a trio.

DISCUSSION

Our main conclusion is that it is useful to think of cooperation in life-history models as a game and to seek the ESS effort for each cooperating individual. Qualitatively, the output of our model gives a reasonably good description of cooperation in chick feeding by dunnocks working in pairs and trios. The next

TABLE 28.3. The influence of adult survival, V, on total effort to the brood and female fitness for trios and pairs. All other parameter values are as in Table 28.2. Total effort shown for different brood sizes with fitness of female underneath in brackets

| Brood size (N) | Total effort to brood (female fitness) | | | |
| | Low adult survival ($V=0.8$) | | High adult survival ($V=0.9$) | |
	Trio	Pair	Trio	Pair
3	1·04 (1·12)	1·06 (1·15)	0·99 (1·17)	1·02 (1·20)
4	1·24 (1·17)	1·23 (1·16)	1·17 (1·20)	1·18 (1·20)
5	1·40 (1·18)	1·35 (1·13)	1·32 (1·19)	1·30 (1·16)
6	1·53 (1·15)	1·45 (1·06)	1·45 (1·15)	1·39 (1·08)

step is to test the model quantitatively. For this we will need to know precisely how effort in chick feeding influences adult survival and chick survival. The only direct way to discover this is by experiment; for example, making parents work harder or less hard and seeing the effects this has on their own survival and that of their offspring. Experiments are also needed to investigate how hard adults will work for broods of different sizes. Observations of natural variation in work rate for various brood sizes (Fig. 28.1, Table 28.1) are difficult to interpret because they may be confounded by effects of season, food abundance and parental ability.

Although in dunnocks the total effort of a trio is greater than that of a pair (Fig. 28.1), the model predicts that this will not always be so (Table 28.3). The theoretical possibility, raised by the model, that an increase in number of adults provisioning a brood will not necessarily always lead to an increase in total effort, is supported by data from cooperative breeders, where several 'helpers' (often previous offspring) assist a pair of breeders to feed the nestlings. Although in some cases the feeding rates to the young are greater when helpers are present (e.g. in silver-backed jackals, *Canis mesomelas*, and white-fronted bee-eaters, *Merops bullockoides*; Emlen 1984), in other cases they are not (e.g. grey-crowned babblers, *Pomatostomus temporalis*, Brown *et al*. 1978). In this last example the breeders do less work as more helpers are present and the result is that the total feeding rate to the brood remains approximately the same. This emphasizes again the need for quantitative data on the parameters in the model (e.g. adult survival) to help us understand why different species may behave in different ways.

Finally, it will be interesting to discover how the stable chick feeding effort is reached. The optimal selfish solution for one member of a pair would be that individual's best response to the maximum possible effort of the other. Male and female may move towards the stable solution by bargaining, each reacting on a short time scale to the 'bids' of the other. Indeed, complex courtship displays may represent such bargaining for a stable compromise. Alternatively, we may not actually witness the bids on a behavioural time scale because the game may have been played over evolutionary time with individuals now designed by selection to play the ESS effort in relation to the role they find themselves in; for example, female, alpha or beta male.

ACKNOWLEDGMENTS

This work was supported by a SERC grant to N.B.D., for which we are most grateful. We also thank Kate Lessells, Richard Sibly and Robert Smith for their helpful comments on the manuscript.

REFERENCES

Alatalo, R.V., Lundberg, A. & Stahlbrandt, K. (1982). Why do pied flycatcher females mate with already-mated males? *Animal Behaviour*, **30**, 585–593.

Askenmo, C. (1977). Effects of addition and removal of nestlings on nestling weight, nestling survival and female weight loss in the pied flycatcher, *Ficedula hypoleuca. Ornis Scandinavica*, **8**, 1–8.

Askenmo, C. (1979). Reproductive effort and return rate of male pied flycatchers. *American Naturalist*, **114**, 748–753.

Brown, J.L., Dow, D.D., Brown, E.R. & Brown, S.D. (1978). Effects of helpers on feeding of nestlings in the grey-crowned babbler, *Pomatostomus temporalis. Behavioural Ecology and Sociobiology*, **4**, 43–59.

Brown, J.L., Brown, E.R., Brown, S.D. & Dow, D.D. (1982). Helpers: effects of experimental removal on reproductive success. *Science*, **215**, 421–422.

Bryant, D.M. (1979). Reproductive costs in the house martin (*Delichon urbica*). *Journal of Animal Ecology*, **48**, 655–676.

Charlesworth, B. (1980). *Evolution in Age-Structured Populations*. Cambridge University Press, Cambridge.

Charnov, E.L. & Krebs, J.R. (1974). On clutch size and fitness. *Ibis*, **116**, 217–219.

Chase, I.D. (1980). Cooperative and non-cooperative behaviour in animals. *American Naturalist*, **115**, 827–857.

Davies, N.B. (1983). Polyandry, cloaca-pecking and sperm competition in dunnocks, *Prunella modularis. Nature*, **302**, 334–336.

Davies, N.B. (1985). Cooperation and conflict among dunnocks, *Prunella modularis*, in a variable mating system. *Animal Behaviour*, **33** (in press).

Davies, N.B. & Lundberg, A. (1984). Food distribution and a variable mating system in the dunnock, *Prunella modularis. Journal of Animal Ecology*, **53**, 895–912.

Emlen, S.T. (1984). Cooperative breeding in birds and mammals. *Behavioural Ecology; An Evolutionary Approach* (2nd edn) (Ed. by J.R. Krebs & N.B. Davies), pp. 305–339. Blackwell Scientific Publications, Oxford.

Fisher, R.A. (1930). *The Genetical Theory of Natural Selection.* The Clarendon Press, Oxford.

Gadgil, M. & Bossert, W.H. (1970). Life historical consequences of natural selection. *American Naturalist,* **104,** 1–24.

Grafen, A. & Sibly, R. (1978). A model of mate desertion. *Animal Behaviour,* **26,** 645–652.

Horn, H.S. & Rubinstein, D. (1984). Behavioural adaptations and life history. *Behavioural Ecology: An Evolutionary Approach* (2nd edn) (Ed. by J.R. Krebs & N.B. Davies), pp. 279–298. Blackwell Scientific Publications, Oxford.

Kendeigh, S.C. (1952). Parental care and its evolution in birds. *Illinois Biological Monographs* XXII. University of Illinois Press, Urbana.

Kluijver, H.N. (1950). Daily routines of the great tit, *Parus major. Ardea,* **38,** 99–135.

Lack, D. (1954). *The Natural Regulation of Animal Numbers.* Clarendon Press, Oxford.

Martin, P.A., Reimers, T.J., Lodge, J.R. & Dziuk, P.J. (1974). The effect of ratios and number of spermatozoa mixed from two males on proportions of offspring. *Journal of Reproduction and Fertility,* **39,** 251–258.

Maynard Smith, J. (1977). Parental investment: a prospective analysis. *Animal Behaviour,* **25,** 1–9.

Maynard Smith, J. (1982). *Evolution And The Theory of Games.* Cambridge University Press, Cambridge.

Maynard Smith, J. & Price, G.R. (1973). The logic of animal conflict. *Nature,* **246,** 15–18.

Schaffer, W.M. (1974). Selection for optimal life histories: the effects of age structure. *Ecology,* **55,** 291–303.

Schaffer, W.M. (1983). The application of optimal control theory to the general life history problem. *American Naturalist,* **121,** 418–431.

Sibly, R. & Calow, P. (1983). An integrated approach to life-cycle evolution using selective landscapes. *Journal of Theoretical Biology,* **102,** 527–547.

Stearns, S.C. (1976). Life history tactics: a review of the ideas. *Quarterly Review of Biology,* **51,** 3–47.

Trivers, R.L. (1972). Parental investment and sexual selection: *Sexual Selection And The Descent of Man* (Ed. by B. Campbell), pp. 136–179. Heinemann, London.

Williams, G.C. (1966). Natural selection, the cost of reproduction and a refinement of Lack's principle. *American Naturalist,* **100,** 687–690.

29. DIFFERENCES IN THE BREEDING PERFORMANCE OF INDIVIDUAL KITTIWAKE GULLS, *RISSA TRIDACTYLA* (L.)

J. C. COULSON AND CALLUM THOMAS

Department of Zoology, University of Durham, Durham

SUMMARY

Data from a 30-year study of a marked population of kittiwakes were analysed to investigate some of the factors associated with variation in annual and lifetime reproductive success. A number of factors influence young production.

The variation in the number of chicks fledged per pair in any year arose primarily from differences in clutch size and the hatching success and not from variation in fledging success.

Breeding success in any year increased with the experience of the parents for the first 3–4 years, changed little amongst birds which had previously bred for between 4 and 9 years and declined in older birds. A small proportion of kittiwakes exhibited intermittent breeding, which was most common following the first breeding attempt and was higher amongst females than in males. Birds which nested in the 'centre' of the colony bred more successfully than those on the 'edge'. Those which retained the same mate from the previous year were more successful than those which had changed mate. The most successful group of birds were those which bred in the centre with the same mate as last year. Breeding success changed little during the first third of the season but declined thereafter.

Individual females showed year-to-year consistencies in clutch size, hatching success, fledging success and the number of chicks fledged per pair. Between 23 and 33% of the variance in breeding success can be attributed to consistent differences between individuals.

Males have a lower annual survival rate than females but the incidence of intermittent breeding was higher amongst females, with the result that the distribution of breeding life-span is similar in the two sexes.

Lifetime reproductive success is primarily determined by the number of years in which an individual breeds. There was no difference between the variation in lifetime reproductive success in males and females.

METHODS AND TERMINOLOGY

The detailed methods have been presented previously (Coulson 1968; Coulson & Wooller 1976; Coulson & Thomas 1980, 1985; Thomas 1983). The colony is situated on the window-ledges of a warehouse at North Shields, Tyne and Wear. Virtually every bird which has bred in the colony since 1954 has been uniquely marked, either when prospecting or during the year of first breeding, with the result that each can be recognized as an individual. Once a bird bred at North Shields, it rarely, if ever, moved to a new colony. As a result, it is reasonable to assume that unmarked individuals were young recruits attempting to breed for the first time and that the loss of a bird from the colony indicated that it had died.

The following parameters have been considered in this paper.

Breeding age. Breeding age is less than the true age of most birds by, on average, 3 or 4 years—the normal age of recruitment (Wooller & Coulson 1977)—and is measured in years from first breeding.

Pair status. Kittiwakes frequently retain the *same mate* from one breeding season to the next. However, approximately 45% *change mate*, either as a result of the death of last year's partner or through 'divorce' (Coulson 1972).

Nest location. Coulson (1968) showed that the colony could be divided into two areas (*centre/edge*) where the breeding biology was different. The centre is defined as that area which was occupied when the breeding population was half its maximum size.

Date of laying. The date on which the first egg of the clutch is laid (1 May = 1).

Egg volume. The length and breadth of eggs were measured to the nearest 0·1 mm and the volume calculated from the formula (Coulson 1963):

$$\text{Volume (ml)} = \text{length} \times \text{breadth}^2 \times 4\cdot866 \times 10^{-5}$$

where the linear measurements are in mm.

Breeding success. Four measures of breeding performance have been used in this paper: clutch size, the number of chicks fledged by each pair, the percentage hatching success of eggs (the proportion of eggs laid which hatch) and the percentage fledging success of chicks (the proportion of chicks hatched which fledge).

RESULTS

Annual breeding success

Age and breeding success

The number of chicks fledged per pair increased with the experience of the parents, reaching a peak amongst those which had previously bred for 4–9 years (Fig. 29.1). There is evidence of a decline in breeding success in older birds, which is significant in males (5–10 years *v.* 11–19 years; $\chi_3^2 = 8\cdot14$, $P < 0\cdot05$) but not in females ($\chi_3^2 = 2\cdot95$) (Table 29.1). Age-related variation in success is mainly caused by changes in the number of eggs laid (Fig. 29.1), although smaller differences are also found in the hatching success of eggs (Fig. 29.2). Fledging success in this colony is high (approximately 88%) (Fig. 29.2) and there is no evidence of any age-related variation in the fledging success of chicks from broods which start as one or two. Fledging success of chicks from broods which started as three increased with female breeding experience (Thomas 1983).

There was no consistent or significant difference in breeding success between males and females with similar breeding experience, in part, because kittiwakes are monogamous and tend to mate with a partner of the same breeding experience (Coulson & Thomas 1980).

Age and intermittent breeding

Once kittiwakes start to breed they usually do so every year for the rest of their lives; however, a minority of birds exhibit intermittent breeding (normally in only one year). The incidence of intermittent breeding was higher in females

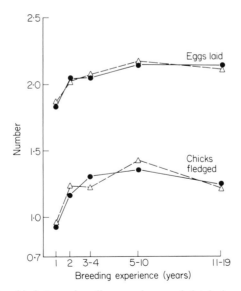

FIG. 29.1. The relationship between breeding experience and clutch size and the number of chicks fledged per pair amongst male (△ – – – – △) and female (●———●) kittiwakes.

TABLE 29.1. The relationship between breeding age and the number of chicks fledged per pair by male and female kittiwakes

Breeding age (years)	Females Chicks fledged					Males Chicks fledged				
	0	1	2	3	Mean	0	1	2	3	Mean
1	211	177	160	6	0·93	228	173	194	4	0·96
2	72	80	107	5	1·17	67	104	120	10	1·24
3–4	77	125	183	8	1·31	107	136	184	12	1·23
5–10	117	164	255	34	1·36	85	151	235	33	1·43
11–19	44	45	72	7	1·25	26	29	47	1	1·22

The decline in chick production between 5–10 and 11–19 breeding age is significant in males ($\chi^2_3 = 8 \cdot 14$, $P < 0 \cdot 05$) but not in females ($\chi^2_3 = 2 \cdot 95$).

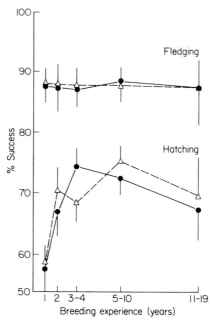

FIG. 29.2. The hatching success ($\pm 95\%$ c.l.) and fledging success of chicks ($\pm 95\%$ c.l.) from one- and two-chick broods in relation to breeding experience amongst male ($\triangle$ – – – – $\triangle$) and female ($\bullet$————$\bullet$) kittiwakes.

than amongst males, was most common following the first breeding attempt (29% of females and 19% of males) and declined in older birds (4–7% of females and 2% of males) (Wooller & Coulson 1977).

Nest location, pair status and breeding success

The number of chicks fledged per pair by birds nesting in the centre of the colony was, on average, 11% higher than that of birds breeding on the edge (Table 29.2). In addition, pairs which have remained together since the previous breeding season fledged, on average, 17% more chicks than those which had changed mate. The two effects of nest-site location and pair status are compounded such that the most successful birds were those nesting in the centre of the colony in pairs which were formed in previous years. These effects arose primarily from differences in the number of eggs laid and in higher hatching success (Table 29.3). There was no corresponding significant variation in fledging success (Table 29.3).

Date of laying and breeding success

Breeding success changed little in those pairs which laid in the first third of the breeding season. However, thereafter, the number of chicks fledged per pair declined by about 20% per week through the rest of the season (Fig. 29.3). The decline arose almost entirely from reductions in the number of eggs laid and in

TABLE 29.2. The number of chicks fledged per pair by experienced female kittiwakes nesting in the centre and on the edge of the colony in relation to the status of the pair bond

Pair status	Nest location	Chicks fledged per pair				Mean
		0	1	2	3	
Change mate	Edge	88	90	111	7	1·13
	Centre	74	106	132	6	1·22
Same mate	Edge	64	86	131	9	1·29
	Centre	73	123	207	32	1·46

Improvement by nesting at centre, $\dfrac{100 \,(\text{centre–edge})}{\text{edge}} = 11\% \,(P < 0.05)$

Improvement by retaining same mate, $\dfrac{100 \,(\text{same–change})}{\text{change}} = 17\% \,(P < 0.01)$

TABLE 29.3. The clutch size, hatching success and fledging success produced by experienced female kittiwakes nesting in the centre and on the edge of the colony in relation to the status of the pair

		Clutch size				Hatching success			Fledging success		
Change mate	Edge	26	236	34	2·03	66·0	1·93	600	84·3	1·83	396
	Centre	17	267	34	2·05	69·2	1·81	653	85·9	1·64	450
Same mate	Edge	28	224	38	2·04	71·0	1·87	590	89·0	1·53	420
	Centre	16	291	128	2·26	74·8	1·39	982	86·4	1·27	733
Effect of nest location $\frac{100 \ (centre-edge)}{edge}$			6%*			5%			−1%		
Effect of pair status $\frac{100 \ (same-change)}{change}$			5%*			8%*			3%		

*$P < 0.05$.

hatching success (Figs 29.3 and 29.4) but not from seasonal variation in fledging success (Fig. 29.4).

Egg size and breeding success

In clutches of two and three, bigger eggs have a higher hatching success (Thomas 1983). Similarly, the fledging success of chicks from broods which

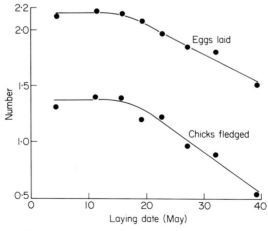

FIG. 29.3. Seasonal variation in clutch size and the number of chicks fledged per pair in the kittiwake.

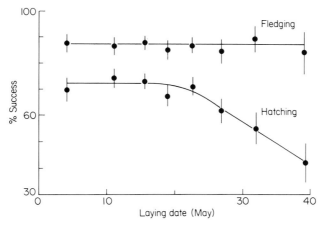

FIG. 29.4. Seasonal variation in the hatching success ($\pm 95\%$ c.l.) and fledging success of chicks ($\pm 95\%$ c.l.) in the kittiwake.

started as two or three also increased with egg volume, but no such relationship was found in one-egg clutches and one-chick broods (Thomas 1983). The effect of egg volume on hatching and fledging success of two-egg clutches and two-chick broods is presented in Fig. 29.5. On average, a 10% increase in egg volume is associated with an 11% increase in hatching success and a 5% increase in fledging success.

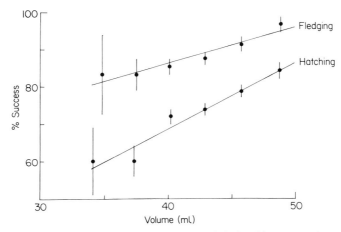

FIG. 29.5. The relationship between egg volume (ml) and the hatching success (± 1 s.e.) of eggs from clutches of two and the fledging success of chicks from broods of two (which hatched from clutches of two) in the kittiwake. (After Thomas 1983.)

Year-to-year variation in breeding success

Between 1954 and 1983, the mean number of chicks fledged per pair in each year ranged between 0·94 and 1·61. In addition to annual variations, an overall long-term trend is evident when a 5-year running mean is plotted (Fig. 29.6). The trend has arisen from changes in clutch size, hatching and fledging success (Coulson & Thomas 1985).

The comparative stability of environmental conditions at North Shields has resulted in relatively small year-to-year variation in breeding success in comparison with that reported from colonies at the northern extreme of the kittiwakes' breeding range. Using information in Barrett (1978) the mean number of chicks fledged per pair in 3 years in a colony in NW Norway was 0·89, 0·26 and 0·0. Mean clutch size over the 30 years of this study has varied between 1·88 and 2·18, whereas mean clutch size in a 4-year study reported for colonies in Arctic Russia by Belopol'skii (1961) varied between 1·53 and 2·33.

Individual variation in breeding success

There has been remarkable consistency in the reproductive performance of individual birds in successive breeding seasons. The clutch size laid in each year by ten long-lived females from the North Shields colony is presented in Table 29.4. Despite the fact that within the colony as a whole only 15% of females lay three-egg clutches in any year, one female in this study (ring no. 2044875) produced three eggs in 13 out of 14 years of breeding, and another

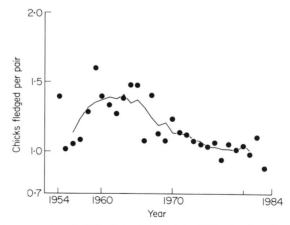

FIG. 29.6. The mean number of chicks fledged per pair by kittiwakes breeding at North Shields in each year, 1954–1983. The line is the 5-year running mean. (After Coulson & Thomas 1985).

TABLE 29.4. The number of eggs laid in each year of breeding by ten long-lived female kittiwakes from the North Shields colony

Ring number	Clutch size produced in each year																	C/1	Totals C/2	C/3	Mean clutch size	% C/2
2044875	3	3	3	3	3	3	3	3	3	2	3	3	3	3				0	1	13	2·93	7
2044067	2	3	3	3	3	3	3	3	3	3	2	3	1	2	2	2		1	5	10	2·56	31
2028368	2	2	3	3	2	3	3	3	3	2	2	2	2	2	2	2		0	10	6	2·38	63
EC11371	2	2	2	2	2	2	3	3	2	2	3	3	2	1	3	3		1	9	6	2·31	56
2020006	1	2	2	2	3	2	2	2	2	2	2	2	2	3	3	1	3	2	11	4	2·12	65
EC11605	2	2	2	2	2	3	2	2	2	2	2	2	2	3	2	2	2	0	16	2	2·11	89
2028794	2	2	2	2	2	2	2	2	3	2	2	2	2					0	13	1	2·07	93
2044874	2	2	2	2	2	2	2	2	2	2	2	2	2	2				0	14	0	2·00	100
2044892	2	2	2	2	1	2	2	2	2	2	2	2	2	2	2	2	2	1	16	0	1·94	94
2044917	2	2	2	2	2	2	2	2	2	2	2	1	2	2	2	2		1	14	0	1·93	93

(2044067) laid ten three-egg clutches in fifteen seasons. Table 29.5 shows the relationship between the number of eggs laid in consecutive years by the same female, and confirms that, within the colony as a whole, considerable individual consistency in clutch size existed. Note particularly that 54% of females which laid three eggs one year laid three in the next year also. There was no significant relationship in the number of chicks hatched from two-egg clutches laid by the same females in successive years (Table 29.6) and there was no consistency in the fledging success of chicks from consecutive broods of two produced by the same female. As a result of consistency in clutch size, females which fledged more chicks one year tended to fledge more in the next year also (Table 29.7). For example, 17% of females which fledged three chicks

TABLE 29.5. The relationship between the number of eggs laid by the same female kittiwakes in consecutive years. Data represent the percentage of females laying a particular number of eggs last year which produced 1, 2 or 3 this year. There is a significant tendency for females to lay the same number of eggs in consecutive years ($\chi^2_4 = 235$, $P < 0.001$)

		Clutch size this year				
		1	2	3	Mean	n
Clutch size last year	1	10%	82%	8%	1·89	95
	2	7%	82%	11%	2·04	1015
	3	3%	43%	54%	2·52	222

TABLE 29.6. The relationship between the number of chicks hatched from consecutive clutches of two laid by the same female kittiwakes. Data represent the percentage of females which hatched a particular number of chicks last year which hatched 0, 1 or 2 this year. There is no significant tendency for birds to hatch the same number of chicks from consecutive two-egg clutches ($\chi^2_4 = 2 \cdot 8$)

| | | No. chicks hatched this year | | | | |
		0	1	2	Mean	n
No. chicks hatched last year	0	17%	26%	57%	1·40	98
	1	18%	21%	61%	1·42	135
	2	18%	18%	64%	1·46	362

TABLE 29.7. The relationship between the number of chicks fledged in consecutive years by the same female kittiwake. Data represent the percentage of females which fledged a particular number of chicks last year which fledged 0, 1, 2 or 3 this year. There is a significant tendency for birds to fledge the same number of chicks in consecutive years ($\chi^2_9 = 22 \cdot 5$, $P < 0 \cdot 01$)

| | | No. chicks fledged this year | | | | | |
		0	1	2	3	Mean	n
No. chicks fledged last year	0	26%	29%	43%	2%	1·23	204
	1	22%	31%	43%	4%	1·30	286
	2	23%	24%	48%	5%	1·35	460
	3	14%	17%	52%	17%	1·71	35

one year did equally well in the next year also, despite the fact that within the colony as a whole, only 4% of the pairs reared three fledged young.

Similar relationships are found if data are analysed with respect to the same male in consecutive years.

Partitioning the variance in annual breeding success

Analysis of covariance* was used to partition the variance in reproductive success in the data set into (i) that which could be accounted for by consistent differences which exist between individual birds and (ii) that variation for each bird which could be accounted for by significant, independent effects of proximate factors which have been demonstrated above. The results are summarized in Table 29.8.

*Analysis of covariance was carried out using the programme BMDP2V available in the BMDP statistical package (Dixon *et al.* 1981). Appropriate transformations were carried out on non-linear proximate factors.

TABLE 29.8. The source of variation in annual breeding success in the kittiwake. Analysis of covariance was used to partition the variance in breeding success into that which arises from consistent difference among individual females and that which comes from annual variation within each bird. Data presented represent the percentage of total variance which can be attributed to individual differences and that due to the significant effects of the proximate factors studied

Dependent variable	Variance due to individual	Within-bird variation explained by proximate factors	Proximate factors involved	Number of females	Number of cases
Clutch size	33%	8%	1,2,3,4	331	1694
Hatching success	26%	3%	1,4,5	283	1354
Fledging success	23%	5%	4,5	243	1080
Chicks fledged	23%	5%	1,2,4	331	1694

Proximate factors: (1) date of laying; (2) pair status; (3) breeding experience; (4) year of breeding; (5) egg volume.

A third of the variance in clutch size was accounted for by consistent differences amongst females. Four of the proximate factors studied had significant (and independent) effects upon within-bird variation in clutch size but only explained 8% of the total variance.

Consistent individual differences amongst females contribute 26% of the variance in hatching success and 23% of the variance in fledging success with less than 6% explained by the proximate factors.

Similar results exist for males. Approximately a quarter of the variance in the number of chicks fledged per pair was attributable to consistent differences between individuals. That this value is lower than that obtained for clutch size, hatching and fledging success suggests that individuals which produce larger clutches in successive years are not necessarily the same birds which are more successful at hatching eggs and fledging chicks.

Lifetime reproductive success

The variation in lifetime reproductive success (number of chicks fledged during lifetime) amongst 310 breeding male and 271 breeding female kittiwakes from North Shields is presented in Fig. 29.7. There is no significant difference in the variance in lifetime reproductive success between the sexes even though the annual survival rate of males is lower than that of females (Coulson & Wooller 1976). The difference in survival rates is compensated by the higher incidence of intermittent breeding in females (Wooller & Coulson 1977), with the result that the distribution of the number of years in which an individual breeds is similar for both sexes. Lifetime reproductive success in the kittiwake is roughly proportional to breeding lifespan (Fig. 29.8). Breeding lifetime alone accounts for 85% of the variance in lifetime reproductive success

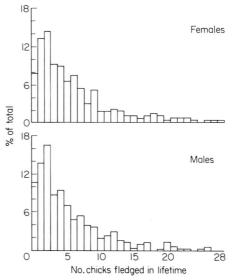

FIG. 29.7. The distribution of lifetime reproductive success amongst 310 breeding male and 271 breeding female kittiwakes.

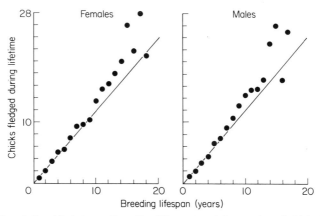

FIG. 29.8. The relationship between 'breeding life-span' and the number of chicks fledged during lifetime amongst male and female kittiwakes. The trend line corresponds to an annual reproductive output of 1·2 chicks per pair (the colony mean).

in both sexes. The reproductive output of older birds deviates progressively from the trend line in Fig. 29.8. In part, this is due to the increase in breeding success with age, but in addition, long-lived birds tended to breed more successfully when young, than birds of a similar age but which had a shorter breeding lifespan (Table 29.9).

TABLE 29.9. The relationship between breeding experience and reproductive success amongst male and female kittiwakes grouped according to 'breeding life-span'

Breeding experience (years)	Breeding years in life-span									
	Less than 10 years					10–19 years				
	Chicks fledged					Chicks fledged				
	0	1	2	3	Mean	0	1	2	3	Mean
Males										
1	70	86	94	1	1·10	3	11	14	0	1·39
2	32	64	72	5	1·29	6	7	9	1	1·22
3–4	51	70	106	8	1·30	6	19	28	2	1·47
5–10	28	59	96	7	1·43*	17	43	73	21	1·64*
Females										
1	60	82	69	4	1·08	4	12	12	0	1·29
2	31	53	58	2	1·22	7	5	14	0	1·27
3–4	36	69	94	6	1·34	11	15	30	2	1·40
5–10	49	79	86	12	1·27*	25	33	100	18	1·63*

* Significantly different ($P < 0.01$) between two groups of 5–10 years breeding experience.

DISCUSSION

The most important factor influencing the breeding success of a particular pair of kittiwakes is the quality of the individuals. Between a quarter and a third of the total variation in several aspects of the breeding success is attributable to consistent differences between female parents (and there is evidence that the males show similar variation), arising from a relative consistency in clutch size, hatching success and fledging success in individual birds throughout their life-span. This consistency accounts for a greater proportion of the variation in breeding success than all other factors which are known to influence breeding success including age, date of laying, pair status, position of the nest-site in the colony and year-to-year variation. In effect, the quality of the individual, as measured by relative consistency in breeding success, is the most important factor in determining the breeding performance of an individual. It follows that the range of quality in individual female kittiwakes is considerable. It has been shown previously that there are differences in the quality of individuals breeding in the centre and edge of a kittiwake colony and that, in males, those breeding in the centre breed for more years and are also more successful each year than those breeding at the edge (Coulson 1968). Although gaining access to the centre of the colony would appear to be a measure of the quality of kittiwakes, young reared at the centre are not more likely to recruit there when adult (Wooller & Coulson 1977). Thus, there is no strong evidence that the consistency in individuals shown in this study is inherited rather than acquired by experience.

In considering the costs of breeding, it is often assumed that there is a negative relationship between life-span and annual reproductive output; no such relationship is evident in the kittiwake. Good quality kittiwakes live longer and are also more productive each year, and a random sample of individuals tends to produce a positive correlation between life-span and annual reproductive output. This variation in the quality of individuals creates problems in assessing the cost of breeding in kittiwakes, particularly since the selection of subsets of similar quality birds would be carried out on reproductive success.

ACKNOWLEDGMENTS

Data used in the analysis for this paper have been gathered by a number of people. In particular, we thank Dr E. White, G. Brazendale, Dr A.F. Hodges, Dr R.D. Wooller, Dr J.W. Chardine and J. Porter. This research has continued thanks to the goodwill, cooperation and protection provided by Smiths Dock Co. Ltd. and in recent years by Jim Marine Ltd.

REFERENCES

Barrett, R.T. (1978). *The breeding biology of the kittiwake* Rissa tridactyla *(L.) in Troms, North Norway.* Unpublished Cand. Real. Thesis, University of Tromsø.

Belopol'skii, L.O. (1961). *Ecology of the Sea Colony Birds of the Barents Sea.* Jerusalem, Israel Program for Scientific Translation.

Coulson, J.C. (1963). Egg size and shape in the Kittiwake (*Rissa tridactyla*) and their use in estimating age composition of populations. *Proceedings of the Zoological Society of London,* **140**(2), 211–227.

Coulson, J.C. (1968). Differences in the quality of birds nesting in the centre and on the edge of a colony. *Nature (London),* **217,** 478–479.

Coulson, J.C. (1972). The significance of the pair-bond in the Kittiwake. *Proceedings of the International Ornithological Congress,* **15,** 424–433.

Coulson, J.C. & Thomas, C.S. (1980). A study of the factors influencing the duration of the pair-bond in the Kittiwake Gull, *Rissa tridactyla. Proceedings of the XVII International Ornithological Congress, Berlin,* pp. 822–833.

Coulson, J.C. & Thomas, C.S. (1985). Changes in the biology of the kittiwake *Rissa tridactyla*: A 31-year study of a breeding colony. *Journal of Animal Ecology*, **54**, (in press).

Coulson, J.C. & Wooller, R.D. (1976). Differential survival rates among breeding kittiwake gulls *Rissa tridactyla* (L.). *Journal of Animal Ecology*, **45**, 205–13.

Dixon, W.J. (Ed.) (1981). *BMDP Statistical Software.* University of California Press, Berkeley, C.A.

Thomas, C.S. (1983). The relationships between breeding experience, egg volume and reproductive success of the kittiwake *Rissa tridactyla*. *Ibis*, **125**, 567–574.

Wooller, R.D. & Coulson, J.C. (1977). Factors affecting the age of first breeding in the Kittiwake *Rissa tridactyla*. *Ibis*, **119**, 339–349.

V
SOCIAL BEHAVIOUR AND POPULATION DYNAMICS

30. POPULATION CONSEQUENCES OF
SOCIAL STRUCTURE

R. I. M. DUNBAR

Zoological Institute, University of Stockholm,
S–106 91 Stockholm, Sweden

SUMMARY

Competitive interactions among members of a population of animals invariably enforce some degree of structuring, no matter what the mating system. This structuring is reflected in both the nature of the social relationships between individual animals and the size and composition of the groups in which they live. These aspects of social structure often act in such a way as to disrupt the reproductive physiology of some females (thereby affecting birth rates) or to influence their access to resources (thereby affecting mortality rates). Changes in these life-history variables can be expected to influence population dynamics. This paper draws on data from mammals to show how social behaviour at the level of the individual can have consequences that may influence population dynamics even in the absence of classical density-dependent effects.

INTRODUCTION

In this paper, I want to draw attention to the fact that behaviour at the level of the individual cannot be dissociated from demographic considerations at the level of the population. Although this is of course a two-way process (individual level behaviour both influences and is influenced by population demography), I shall restrict my remarks to the effect that the behaviour of individuals can have on population dynamics. It is, of course, obvious that such things as territorial behaviour have consequences for the way in which a population of animals is dispersed. The question that I really want to raise goes beyond this more obvious level to ask whether the behaviour of individual animals can affect population dynamics.

  In general, I shall try to show that aspects of the social relationships between individuals in social groups can directly influence primary life-history variables (birth, death and migration rates) and, as a result, can be expected to have consequences for the future state of the population.

Present address: 33 The Grove, Linton, Cambridge, CB1 6UQ.

Few studies are so broad as to bridge the gap between the behaviour of individuals and that of populations. It is therefore rather hard to find clear examples that show conclusively how social behaviour can affect population dynamics. However, it is obvious that if life-history variables are affected by behaviour, then this must have straightforward consequences for the dynamics of the population concerned. This, of course, assumes that the relationship between fecundity and mortality rates, for example, is not self-compensating when seen from the population's viewpoint. Most mammals, however, have age-structured populations and the lag effects introduced by that fact make the relationship between present birth and death rates and future population growth rates far from simple (Charlesworth 1980).

SOCIAL STRUCTURE AND FECUNDITY

Ever since the classical studies of rodent populations by Christian (1961) and Calhoun (1962), it has been widely appreciated that stress due to overcrowding can disrupt the female's reproductive physiology. As a result, females may either fail to go through puberty or, if they are already of reproductive age, may fail to conceive or suffer increased rates of fetal loss (by spontaneous abortion or by resorbtion). This effect is largely a consequence of the fact that crowding and the resultant competition for access to food, water and nesting sites generates a great deal of fighting which not only leads to injury (and sometimes death) but also stresses the animals (thus disrupting their reproductive physiology).

The physiology of this effect is now quite well understood. The fact that physiological stress can cause ovulatory failure in humans has been of some considerable interest to fertility clinics and has therefore led to a good deal of research into its physiology.

It has not been appreciated until fairly recently, however, that aspects of social structure other than sheer density can have precisely the same effect.

Evidence that this might be so occurs widely in the literature, though its significance has often been overlooked. Zimen (1974), for example, reported that only the dominant female in a pack of wolves was likely to breed. Similar results have been reported from African wild dogs (Frame & Frame 1976). Abbott & Hearn (1978) found clear evidence for the suppression of reproduction in subordinate females in the marmoset (*Callitrix jacchus*). They found that if the monkeys were housed in groups, only the dominant male and dominant female formed a pair-bond and bred. The other females invariably had low plasma progesterone levels, indicating that they were not ovulating. As soon as the groups were broken up and the animals housed in pairs, all the subordinate females formed pair-bonds with their females and most ovulated within 30 days. One clear implication of this is that if female offspring remain in their natal groups, they will not go through puberty. This was indeed found to be the case in the marmosets. Reproductive suppression in female offspring seems to be widespread in monogamous species of mammals, including gerbils (Payman & Swanson 1980), canids (Macdonald & Moehlman 1982) and small antelope (R.I.M. Dunbar, unpubl.). This may help to reduce population growth rates when food is in short supply, while at the same time providing the demographic flexibility to respond as soon as conditions improve.

Reproductive suppression has also been found to act in a continuous rather than a step-wise fashion in some species. Birth rates have been shown to be inversely correlated with dominance rank within groups of rhesus macaques (Drickamer 1974; Sade *et al.* 1976) and at least two species of baboons (Dunbar 1980a; Wasser & Barash 1983). Although there is evidence to suggest that this kind of relationship can be due to the fact that high-ranking females interfere in the copulations of lower ranking individuals, e.g. prairie chickens (Robel & Ballard 1974), sticklebacks (Li & Owings 1978), this is not the only possible explanation. There is now clear cut esperimental evidence to demonstrate that, in some primates at least, it can be due to increasing frequencies of anovulatory oestrous cycles caused by stress generated by harassment (Bowman, Dilley & Keverne 1978).

Birth rates have also been found to be inversely related to the ratio of adult females to adult males within breeding groups in marmots (Downhower & Armitage 1971) and *Papio* baboons (Dunbar & Sharman1983). In the latter case, it seems that females form coalitions with males that buffer them against the physiological stresses created by harassment from higher-ranking females. Obviously, as the sex ratio becomes increasingly biased towards females, proportionately fewer of them will be able to have male allies to protect them from harassment. These will consequently suffer increased rates of ovulatory failure, which will be reflected in lowered overall birth rates. It is important to note that in this particular case the size of the female cohort can be ruled out as a possible cause of reproductive suppression. In other words, it is not the density of females relative to the space occupied by the troop that is important, but their density relative to the number of adult males (i.e. pure sex ratio).

DeLong (1978) obtained rather similar results from a study of captive mouse populations in which he experimentally varied the adult sex ratio. Removal of males resulted in reduced frequencies of pregnancy among parous females and delayed maturation among prepuberty females, while removal of parous females had the opposite effect.

The distribution of births over time may also be affected by social factors when these lead to the synchronization of reproductive cycles and a consequent tendency for births to occur in pulses. This is particularly likely to happen in those species where the females live in small stable groups, each of which is held by a single breeding male for a limited period of time. When the harem-holder is ousted by a competitor, this new male may practise infanticide, killing off most of the small infants present in the group at the time. Such behaviour has been reported from species as diverse as lions (Bertram 1975), lemmings (Mallory & Brooks 1978), apes (Fossey 1976) and at least three species of Old World monkeys (Hrdy 1977; Struhsaker 1977; Marsh 1979). Mice are known to undergo spontaneous abortion following the appearance of a strange male (Bruce 1959) and a similar phenomenon has been reported in the meadow vole (Mallory & Clulow 1977), *Papio* baboons (Pereira 1983) and gelada baboons (Mori & Dunbar 1984). In addition, gelada and patas monkey females may come into oestrus prematurely when a new male takes over their unit, even though infanticide does not normally occur in these two species (Dunbar 1980b; Rowell 1978). In the case of the gelada, a female will come into oestrus providing her previous infant is at least 6 months old (i.e. anything up to a year earlier than she would normally do: see Dunbar 1980b, figure 6). In this case, the cause seems to be due to the general excitement generated by a takeover, or by what Rowell has termed the 'Hoo Haa' effect.

It is also worth noting that group-living females may synchronize their oestrous cycles spontaneously. McClintock (1971) found that women living together in close physical proximity tended to synchronize their menstrual cycles, and she has since experimentally demonstrated the same phenomenon in rats (McClintock 1978). More importantly perhaps, she was able to show that the rats synchronized their oestrous cycles purely by means of airborne chemical communication: so long as they shared the same air supply, they did not need to be living in the same cage. Although these results relate only to the synchronization of oestrous cycles, it is not too great a leap to suggest that females might be able to synchronize their reproductive cycles as well. Indeed, there is evidence from patas monkeys to suggest that one female returning to reproductive condition tends to stimulate other females to do so too, with the result that reproduction within patas groups is closely synchronized (Rowell & Hartwell 1978).

SOCIAL STRUCTURE AND MORTALITY

That crowding and a shortage of resources can increase mortality rates is too well known to require further comment. Of greater interest is the fact that a number of recent field studies have found that the mortality often falls differentially on individuals of different status.

Wrangham (1981), for example, found evidence to suggest that water shortage resulted in higher mortality for low-ranking than for high-ranking vervet monkey females. In addition, Cheney, Lee & Seyfarth (1981) found that mortality due to illness and associated conditions was highest among low-ranking females in this population, but that mortality due to predation was highest among high-ranking females, though they have no explanation as to why this should be so. Dittus (1977) found that, during periods of severe environmental stress, the highest mortality rates were suffered by the infants and by juvenile females of his *Macaca sinica* population. He argued that this is because these individuals are the ones least able to defend themselves; as a result, their access to the limited food supplies tends to be restricted by the larger and more dominant members of the group. Stuhsaker (1973) also found that juvenile females carried the brunt of the mortality when his population of vervets underwent rapid decline due to changing environmental conditions.

Silk (1983) has presented evidence from captivity studies of macaques showing that survival to 24 months was lower among females than among males under conditions of environmental and social stress. She found that this effect was mainly due to increased mortality among the female offspring of low-ranking females. In addition, Silk found evidence for differential neonatal sex ratios in this species, with low-ranking females consistently producing a higher proportion of male offspring than female offspring. Similar results have been reported for at least two other species of primates (Altmann 1980; Simpson & Simpson 1982). Neither the functional significance nor the mechanism by which females achieve this are understood at present (Clutton-Brock 1982), though this does not negate the fact that it can occur. It has been suggested that the females are acting in such a way as to capitalize on the different reproductive potentials of the two sexes of offspring under different conditions.

From a population viewpoint, the significant fact about these differential survival rates is that the local population's complement of females may often be hit particularly hard. If recruitment of young females is greatly reduced as a result, the numbers of infants born into the population in succeeding years will fall when these cohorts mature and join the reproductive component of the population. The decline in the birth rate will then be much greater than if the mortality had been spread evenly throughout the population. Moreover, the age distribution of the female complement will be shifted upwards by the poor recruitment and, since fecundity usually declines with age in most species, the mean birth rate will tend to fall dramatically. Thus, a behaviourally determined effect can influence subsequent population growth rates in an exaggerated way, leading to a much more rapid decline in the population than would be predicted by the more traditional models. Strum & Western (1982) give data that suggest that changes in the age structure of the female complement of their *Papio anubis* population made some contribution to the variance in the birth rate over time.

In many species that have highly competitive mating systems (such as those that form leks), a reproductively active male may be effectively prevented from feeding throughout the period in which he holds a territory or harem. Consequently, males often loose weight dramatically during the mating season. As a result, they become increasingly susceptible to predation or disease, e.g. antelope (Gosling 1974; Jarman 1979), feral goats (Dunbar, Buckland & Miller 1984), deer (Gibson & Guinness 1980), and frogs (Wells 1978). This necessarily results in sex differences in survivorship, and hence an increasingly biased adult sex ratio. The degree of bias, however, may vary from year to year, depending on the levels of competition and the environmental conditions in previous years. In contrast, competition for access to mates is much less fierce in monogamous species, and there may be little difference in the survivorship curves of the two sexes in these cases. Consequently, a species' characteristic life-history pattern will in part reflect its mating system and in part be influenced by year-to-year variations in the level of competition among members of one sex for access to members of the opposite sex.

SOCIAL STRUCTURE AND BEHAVIOUR

In this section, I want to consider some ways in which the demographic structure of the population may affect the behaviour of individuals in ways that are likely to have consequences at the population level. I shall concentrate on three specific phenomena: migration rates, rates of aggression and the extent to which a population's demographic structure may be influenced by the behaviour of the constituent animals.

In most species of mammals, males migrate from their natal groups, whereas females remain in theirs throughout their lives (Harcourt 1978). Patterns of male migration, however, are seldom random: often they are directed at population units of particular demographic structure. Packer (1979), for example, found that male baboons tended to transfer into troops that had more cycling females than the one from which they had come (see also Hausfater 1975; Rasmussen 1979). Non-random dispersal may also occur either because males tend to transfer to groups into which male relatives have previously migrated (*C. aethiops* Cheney & Seyfarth 1983) or to migrate as groups of closely related kin (Meikle & Vessey 1981).

The timimg of dispersal is likewise seldom random and often reflects the need to find conditions that are more conducive to successful reproduction (Moore & Ali 1984). Boelkins & Wilson (1972), for example, found that rates of transfer between groups by male rhesus monkeys were significantly higher during the mating season when there were large numbers of cycling females around than at other times of the year. Harcourt (1978) found that a female gorilla was more likely to leave her natal group and move to another is she had been unable to reproduce successfully. Thus, migration need not always be a consequence of high population densities in relation to available food resources. Rather, it may reflect mating success (or the lack of it), particularly in those cases where the social system constrains one sex's access to the other. As a result, population units that are already living at high ecological densities may be as likely to receive immigrants as to lose emigrants.

In those species that live in closed social groups, as many primates do, ecological densities can only be reduced in the absence of high mortality by the mass emigration of whole sections of a group following group fission (see for example Nash 1976; Sade *et al.* 1976; Koyama, Norikoshi & Mano 1975; Ohsawa & Dunbar 1984). Of particular interest in the present context is the fact that, when a group does undergo fission, it often does so along what may be termed lines of 'least genetic resistance'—in other words, relatives stay together, so that the mean degree of relatedness among the members of each half is greater than that in the group as a whole (see Chepko-Sade & Sade 1979). This is of significance from the point of view of population genetics since it means that groups will not necessarily be a random sample of the population as a whole.

The traditional Christian–Calhoun syndrome centred around increased rates of aggression when migration is prevented and the population density rises. However, density may not be the only cause of increased levels of aggression. Studies of a number of species have shown that levels of aggression often reflect the level of competition for access to members of the opposite sex, and this usually means that sex ratio is the more important variable (Dunbar 1982). Hausfater (1975), for example, presents evidence from *Papio* baboons showing that the frequency of wounding and the frequency of rank changes among males were highest when there was a single female in oestrus in the group, and declined progressively as the number of females simultaneously in oestrus increased. Rates of fighting are, of course, known to increase dramatically during the mating season in many species and often lead to increased mortality among males as a result of injuries, e.g. caprids (Nievergelt 1974; Dunbar *et al.* 1984), and primates (Jolly 1966; Wilson & Boelkins 1970). The consequences of differential mortality in the sexes have been discussed from a population point of view in the preceding section.

Competition for access to breeding females can be expected to act in different ways depending on the structure of the social system. Among harem-forming gelada baboons, males acquire their own harems either by taking over the units of other males (in which case the defeated harem-holder remains in the unit) or by entering a unit as a submissive follower and picking up one or two peripheral females with whom to form an incipient harem (Dunbar 1984). It is perhaps not surprising to find that the frequency of units that contain more than one mature male is inversely related to the adult sex ratio (Ohsawa & Dunbar 1984): the fewer the number of females per male in the population, the more frequent will be the rate of entry into reproductive units by males trying to acquire harems, and the higher the proportion of units with two or more males. Thus, the demographic structure of the population (the way it is divided up into groups) is in part a consequence of the interaction of male reproductive strategies with particular demographic parameters.

In addition to this, there is another demographic effect at work that is the result of purely behavioural considerations. Because of the particular nature of female reproductive strategies in the gelada, the ease with which a male can take over a unit depends on its size: units with fewer than five reproductive females are too cohesive and the females too 'loyal' to their male for an outside male to take over successfully, but the likelihood of takeover increases steadily thereafter (for details, see Dunbar 1984). Not only does the rate of takeovers increase with increasing mean harem size in a given local population, but so does the proportion of males entering units by way of takeover (as opposed to follower-entry). Note that these effects are purely consequences of the way in which the local population happens to be divided up into reproductive units: it bears no relationship to the size of the population or its density. Moreover, the size of the reproductive units has nothing whatsoever to do with food availability since the reproductive units are not ecological units (see Dunbar 1984).

These changes in the absolute and relative frequencies of the two different male reproductive strategies can have knock-on effects. Takeovers lead to a temporary increase in the birth rate as a result of the premature return to oestrus of many of the females. On the other hand, the entry of a follower into a unit will eventually lead to that unit undergoing fission. Since that results in two harems of smaller size, the adverse effects of low dominance rank on female fertility (see Dunbar 1980a, 1984) are greatly reduced; as a result, the mean birth rate for the constituent females increases dramatically. However, there is a lag built into this component of the system, since fission does not occur until about 2 years after the follower has joined the unit (Dunbar 1984). Thus, while a high proportion of takeovers results in an immediate rise in the overall birth rate, a high proportion of follower entries results in a sudden increase in the birth rate 2 years later.

SOCIAL STRUCTURE AND STATISTICAL SAMPLING EFFECTS

If a population is divided up into relatively small discrete units (as it often is in many species of primates) or occurs at low densities, then statistical sampling effects are likely to arise. This means that demographically extreme events such as neonatal sex ratios that depart significantly from the norm are likely to occur. In most species of primates, for example, neonatal sex ratios approximate 50:50 males:females, but this is only true for samples taken from very large populations. Within individual groups (which are rarely larger than eighty animals), the neonatal sex ratio can vary widely (see Table 30.1).

TABLE 30.1. Variance in neonatal sex ratios within groups of monkeys over time

| Species | Sample | Percentage males | | Source |
		Minimum	Maximum	
Macaca fuscata	1 troop over 7 years	25·0	75·0	Mori 1975
Macaca sinica	2 troops over 4 years	36·4	60·0	Dittus 1975
Theropithecus gelada	2 bands over 4 years	25·0	61·0	Dunbar 1980b
Papio hamadryas	1 band over 7 years	7·1	60·0	Sigg *et al.* 1982
Pan troglodytes	1 community over 16 years	0·0	100·0	Goodall 1983

Whereas the likelihood of a birth cohort consisting entirely of one sex is negligibly small over the whole population, it is a far from improbable event where individual groups are concerned. This means that the levels of competition for social and sexual partners may vary widely from group to group and from year to year, with the result that birth, death and migration rates will be radically affected for reasons that are quite independent of any environmental factors that may normally affect them.

These effects become important at the population level when they begin to introduce apparently random fluctuations into life-history processes and hence into population dynamics. These effects would normally be written off as statistical error, but they may in fact be the deterministic consequences of bona fide components of the biological system.

CONCLUSIONS

Ecologists have traditionally been inclined to ignore behaviour as a trivial irrelevance. To some extent, this view has been justified. What may be described as the emergent properties of population ecology are not often influenced by the kinds of behaviour that ethologists have traditionally studied. In the last decade, however, the interests of ethologists have shifted from pure behaviour in this sense to the functional consequences of behaviour. Ultimately, those functional consequences are concerned with reproduction and at this point behaviour begins to impinge more directly onto population processes.

Nonetheless, it might still be fair to argue, as many population biologists have implicitly done, that any behavioural idiosyncrasies at the individual level will be ironed out statistically at the population level and can therefore be ignored. This is very probably true for most of the classical ecological species like insects that form very large, dense populations, many of which are virtually unstructured. Most mammals, however, do not live at the kinds of densities where statistical sampling biases are averaged out. Moreover, the much greater degree of structuring in their societies imposes its own costs on the individuals who live in them. At least some of these costs have consequences for birth and death rates, and therefore are likely to influence the future dynamics of the population as a whole. Since there may often be lags of several years between behavioural cause and population effect, it will not always be easy to identify the relationships when they occur.

I have tried to show how and why this should be so. My main concern has been to argue that we shall only be able to achieve an adequate understanding of these species' population dynamics if we take behaviour into account. Of course, the converse is equally true: we will never fully understand behaviour if we fail to take demographic processes into account. In general, species that occur at low densities in highly structured groups are not noted for their willingness to adhere to classical population models. Our ability to predict their population dynamics will be much greater if the behavioural and demographic levels are integrated more closely.

REFERENCES

Abbott, D.H. & Hearn, J.P. (1978). Physical, hormonal and behavioural aspects of sexual development in the marmoset monkey, *Callithrix jacchus. Journal of Reproduction and Fertility*, **53**, 155–166.

Altmann, J. (1980). *Baboon Mothers and Infants*. Harvard University Press, Harvard (Mass.).

Bertram, B.C.R. (1975). Social factors infuencing reproduction in wild lions. *Journal of Zoology (London)*, **177**, 463–482.

Boelkins, R.C. & Wilson, A.P. (1972). Intertroop social dynamics of the Cayo Santiago rhesus (*Macaca mulatta*) with special reference to changes in group membership by males. *Primates*, **13**, 125–140.

Bowman, L.A., Dilley, S.R. & Keverne, E.B. (1978). Suppression of oestrogen-induced LH surges by social subordination in talapoin monkeys. *Nature (London)*, **275**, 56–58.

Bruce, H.M. (1959). An exteroceptive block to pregnancy in the mouse. *Ecology and Systematics*, **9**, 123–156.

Calhoun, J.B. (1962). Population density and social pathology. *Scientific American*, **206**, 139–148.

Charlesworth, B. (1980). *Evolution in Age-Structure Populations* Cambridge University Press, Cambridge.

Cheney, D.L. & Seyfarth, R.M. (1983). Nonrandom dispersal in free-ranging vervet monkeys: social and genetic consequences. *American Naturalist*, **122**, 392–412.

Cheney, D.L., Lee, P.C. & Seyfarth, R.M. (1981). Behavioural correlates of non-random mortality among free-ranging female vervet monkeys. *Behavioural Ecology and Sociobiology*, **9**, 153–161.

Chepko-Sade, B.D. & Sade, D.S. (1979). Patterns of group splitting within matrilineal kinship groups. *Behavioural Ecology and Sociobiology*, **5**, 67–86.

Christian, J.J. (1961). Phenomena associated with population density. *Proceedings of the National Academy of Sciences, USA*, **47**, 428–449.

Clutton–Brock, T.H. (1982). Sons and daughters. *Nature (London)*, **298**, 11–13.

DeLong, K.T. (1978). The effect of the manipulation of social structure on reproduction in house mice. *Ecology*, **59**, 922–933.

Dittus, W.P.J. (1975). Population dynamics of the toque monkey, *Macaca sinica*. *Socioecology and Psychology of Primates* (Ed. by R.H. Tuttle), pp. 125–151. Mouton, The Haque.

Dittus, W.P.J. (1977). The social regulation of population density and age-sex distribution in the toque monkey. *Behaiour*, **63**, 281–322.

Downhower, J.F. & Armitage, K.B. (1971). The yellow-bellied marmot and the evolution of polygamy. *American Naturalist*, **105**, 355–370.

Drickamer, L.C. (1974). A ten-year summary of reproductive data for free-ranging *Macaca mulatta*. *Folia Primatologica*, **21**, 61–80.

Dunbar, R.I.M. (1980a). Determinants and evolutionary consequences of dominance among female gelada baboons. *Behavioural Ecology and Sociobiology*, **7**, 72–87.

Dunbar, R.I.M. (1980b). Demographic and life history variables of a population of gelada baboons (*Theropithecus gelada*). *Journal of Animal Ecology*, **49**, 485–506.

Dunbar, R.I.M. (1982). Intraspecific variations in mating strategy. *Perspectives in Ethology*, Vol. 5 (Ed. by P.P.G. Bateson & P.H. Klopfer), pp. 385–431. Plenum Press, New York.

Dunbar, R.I.M. (1984). *Reproductive Decisions: An Economic Analysis of Gelada Baboon Social Strategies.* Princeton University Press, Princeton (N.J.).

Dunbar, R.I.M. & Sharman, M. (1983). Female competition for access to males affects birth rate in baboons. *Behavioural Ecology and Sociobiology*, **13**, 157–159.

Dunbar, R.I.M., Buckland, D. & Miller, D. (1984). The feral goats of Rhum. *Rhum: Ecology of an Island* (Ed. by T.H. Clutton-Brock & M. Ball). Edinburgh University Press, Edinburgh (in press).

Fossey, D. (1976). *The Behaviour of the Mountain Gorilla.* Ph.D. thesis, University of Cambridge.

Frame. L.H. & Frame, G.W. (1976). Female African wild dogs migrate. *Nature (London)*, **263**, 227–229.

Gibson, R.M. & Guinness, F.E. (1980). Differential reproduction among red deer (*Cervus elaphus*) stags on Rhum. *Journal of Animal Ecology*, **49**, 199–208.

Goodall, J. (1983). Population dynamics during a 15 year period in one community of free-living chimpanzees in the Gombe National Park, Tanzania. *Zeitschrift für Tierpsychologie*, **61**, 1–60.

Gosling, M. (1974). The social behaviour of Coke's hartebeest (*Alcelaphus buselaphus cokei*). *The Behaviour of Ungulates and its Relation to Management* (Ed. by V. Geist & F.R. Walther), pp. 488–571. IUCN Publications, Morges.

Harcourt, A.H. (1978). Strategies of emigration and transfer by primates, with particular reference to gorillas. *Zeitschrift für Tierpsychologie*, **48**, 401–420.

Hausfater, G. (1975). *Dominance and Reproduction in Baboons (Papio cynocephalus)*. Karger, Basel.

Hrdy, S. (1977). *The Langurs of Abu*. Harvard University Press, Cambridge (Mass.).

Jarman, M.V. (1979). *Impala Social Behaviour: Territory, Hierarchy, Mating and Use of Space*. Advances in Ethology, Vol. 21. Paul Parey, Hamburg.

Jolly, A. (1966). *Lemur Behavior*. University of Chicago Press, Chicago.

Koyama, N., Norikoshi, K. & Mano, T. (1975). Population dynamics of Japanese monkeys at Arashiyama. *Contemporary Primatology* (Ed. by M. Kawai, S. Kondo & A. Ehara), pp. 411–417. Karger, Basel.

Li, S.K. & Owings, D.H. (1978). Sexual selection in the three-spined stickleback. I. Normative observations. *Zeitschrift für Tierpsychologie*, **46**, 359–371.

McClintock, M.K. (1971). Menstrual synchrony and suppression. *Nature (London)*, **229**, 244–245.

McClintock, M.K. (1978). Estrous synchrony and its mediation by airborne chemical communication (*Rattus norvegicus*). *Hormones & Behaviour*, **10**, 264–276.

Macdonald, D.W. & Moehlman, P.D. (1982). Cooperation, altruism and restraint in the reproduction of carnivores. *Perspectives in Ethology*, Vol. 5, (Ed. by P.P.G. Bateson & P.H. Klopfer), pp. 443–467. Plenum Press, New York.

Mallory, F.F. & Brooks, R.J. (1978). Infanticide and other reproductive strategies in the collared lemming, *Dicrostonyx groenlandicus. Nature (London)*, **273**, 144–146.

Mallory, F.F & Clulow, F.V. (1977). Evidence of pregnancy failure in the wild meadow vole, *Microtus pennsylvanicus. Canadian Journal of Zoology*, **55**, 1–17.

Marsh, C.W. (1979). Female transfer and mate choice among Tana River red colobus. *Nature (London)*, **281**, 568–569.

Meikle, D.B. & Vessey, S.H. (1981). Nepotism among rhesus monkey brothers. *Nature (London)*, **294**, 160–161.

Moore, J. & Ali, R. (1984). Are dispersal and inbreeding avoidance related? *Animal Behaviour*, **32**, 94–112.

Mori, A. (1975). Signals found in the grooming interactions of wild Japanese monkeys of the Koshima troop. *Primates*, **16**, 107–140.

Mori, U. & Dunbar, R.I.M. (1984). Changes in the reproductive condition of female gelada baboons following the takeover of one-male units. *Zeitschrift für Tierpsychologie* (in press).

Nash, L. (1976). Troop fission in free-ranging baboons in the Gombe Stream National Park, Tanzania. *American Journal of Physical Anthropology*, **44**, 63–78.

Nievergelt, B. (1974). A comparison of rutting behaviour and grouping in the Ethiopian and Alpine ibex. *The Behaviour of Ungulates and its Relation to Management* (Ed. by V. Geist & F.R. Walther), pp. 324–340. IUCN Publications, Morges.

Ohsawa, H. & Dunbar, R.I.M. (1984). Variations in the demographic structure and dynamics of gelada baboon populations. *Behavioural Ecology and Sociobiology*, **15**, 231–240.

Packer, C. (1979). Intertroop transfer and inbreeding avaoidance in *Papio anubis. Animal Behaviour*, **27**, 1–36.

Payman, B.C. & Swanson, H.H. (1980). Social influences on sexual maturation and breeding in the female Mongolian gerbil (*Meriones unguiculatus*). *Animal Behaviour*, **28**, 528–535.

Pereira, M. (1983). Abortion following the immigration of an adult male baboon (*Papio cynocephalus*). *American Journal of Primatology*, **4**, 93–98.

Rasmussen, D.R. (1979). Correlates of patterns of range use of a troop of yellow baboons (*Papio* *cynocephalus*), I. Sleeping sites, impregnable females, births and male emigrations and immigrations. *Animal Behaviour*, **27**, 1098–1112.

Robel, R.J. & Ballard, H.B. (**1974**). Lek social organisations and reproductive success in the greater prairie chicken. *American Zoologist*, **14**, 121–128.

Rowell, T.E. (**1978**). How female reproductive cycles affect interaction patterns in groups of patas monkeys. *Recent Advances in Primatology*, Vol. 1, *Behaviour* (Ed. by D.J. Chivers & J. Herbert), pp. 489–490. Academic Press, London.

Rowell, T.E. & Hartwell, K.M. (**1978**). The interaction of behaviour and reproductive cycles in patas monkeys. *Behavioural Biology*, **24**, 141–167.

Sade, D.S., Cushing, K., Cushing, P., Dunaif, J., Figueroa, A., Kaplan, J.R., Lauer, C., Rhodes, D, & Schneider, J. (**1976**). Population dynamics in relation to social structure on Cayo Santiago. *Yearbook of Physical Anthropology*, **20**, 253–262.

Sigg, H. Stolba., A., Abegglen, J.-J. & Dasser, V. (**1982**). Life history of hamadryas baboons: physical development, infant mortality, reproductive parameters and family relationships. *Primates*, **23**, 473–487.

Silk, J.B. (**1983**). Local resource competition and facultative adjustment of sex ratios in relation to competitive abilities. *American Naturalist*, **121**, 56–66.

Simpson, M.J.A. & Simpson, A. (**1982**). Birth sex ratios and social rank in rhesus monkey mothers. *Nature (London)*, **300**, 440–441.

Struhsaker, T.T. (**1973**). A recensus of vervet monkeys in the Masai-Amboseli Game Reserve, Kenya. *Ecology*, **54**, 930–932.

Struhsaker, T.T. (**1977**). Infanticide and social organisation in the redtail monkey (*Cercopithecus ascanius schmidti*) in the Kibale Forest, Uganda. *Zeitschrift für Tierpsychologie*, **45**, 75–84.

Strum, S.C. & Western, J.D. (**1982**). Variations in fecundity with age and environment in olive baboons (*Papio anubis*). *American Journal of Primatology*, **3**, 61–76.

Wasser, S.K. & Barash, D.P. (**1983**). Reproductive suppression among female mammals: implications for biomedicine and selection theory. *Quarterly Review of Biology*, **58**, 513–538.

Wells, K.D. (**1978**). Territoriality in the green frog (*Rana clamitans*): vocalisations and agonistic behaviour. *Animal Behaviour*, **26**, 1051–1063.

Wilson, A.P. & Boelkins, R.C. (**1970**). Evidence for seasonal variation in aggressive behaviour by *Macaca mulatta*. *Animal Behaviour*, **18**, 719–724.

Wrangham, R.W. (**1981**). Drinking competition in vervet monkeys. *Animal Behaviour*, **29**, 904–910.

Zimen, E. (**1976**). On the regulation of pack size in wolves. *Zeitschrift für Tierpsychologie*, **40**, 300–341.

31. GROUP TERRITORIES OF CARNIVORES: EMPIRES AND ENCLAVES

HANS KRUUK[1] AND DAVID MACDONALD[2]

[1]*Institute of Terrestrial Ecology, Banchory, Scotland and*
[2]*Department of Zoology, University of Oxford, Oxford*

SUMMARY

Many species of Carnivora live in group territories. Within several such species, highly variable numbers of individuals form groups which inhabit territories of widely different sizes. Two mechanisms are discussed which may partly explain this intraspecific variation as alternative ways of exploiting limited resources.

Expansionists are animals that tend to increase the size of their territories, with larger groups inhabiting larger ranges. Contractors are animals that maintain the smallest economically defensible area, living in larger groups if resources within this area allow. Examples are given of species in each of these categories.

Implications of this dichotomy are discussed, experiments are suggested and a number of predictions are made which help identify the two strategies.

INTRODUCTION

Animals belonging to species which are territorial and live in groups may adjust the sizes of their groups and home ranges in several different ways with different effects on the exploitation of available resources. In this paper we will discuss two such strategies, and suggest predictions arising from them and give examples of species to which these predictions apply.

We restrict ourselves to the order Carnivora, although the arguments should also apply more widely; in this order there is much variation in social organization between species, with some participating in cohesive, intricately structured groups whereas others live alone. Moreover, within several species, different populations show a marked variation in social organization, for example with respect to group size and range size (Kruuk 1975; Macdonald 1983). The question arises as to what environmental factors underlie this variation; we will discuss this question for intraspecific differences, in the hope that the answers will also throw some light on variation between species. Understanding intraspecific variation is fundamental to understanding the evolution of groups of carnivore communities and, furthermore, it is important for predicting the consequences of management of these species and their habitats.

Probably, members of most species of carnivore are solitary, with single females defending territories against other females, and single males using larger areas which overlap the ranges of several females but exclude other males. Where such species are food limited it is likely that the size of the female territory is related to food availability, while that of the male may be dependant on food indirectly—through the size of female territories—as well as directly: little is known about this. The existing evidence indicates that this single-sex territorial system typifies most members of the Ursidae, Procyonidae, Mustelidae, Viverridae and Felidae. Most Canidae live in pairs whose members share a territory. Here, however, we will be concerned especially with those species which tolerate other adult conspecifics of the same sex in their territories, of which examples are found in almost all families of carnivore (examples in Macdonald 1984a). For instance, spotted hyaenas, *Crocuta crocuta*, live in 'clans' of 8–80 animals, occupying territories of 15–1500 km² (Kruuk 1972; M.G.M. Mills, pers. comm.). Lions, *Panthera leo*, form prides of 4–15 members, ranging over 30–400 km² (Schaller 1972). The coati, *Nasua narica*, forms bands of 1–38 members, ranging over 13–300 ha (Kaufmann 1962; Kaufmann, Lanning & Poole 1976). Among canids, coyotes, *Canis latrans*, form groups of 2–7 members ranging over 8–20 km² (Bowen 1982) and wolf, *C. lupus*, packs of 2–15 animals have home ranges of 60–350 km² (Mech & Frenzel 1971; Mech 1977). Silver-backed jackal, *C. mesomelas*, groups vary from 2 to 5 in 1·5–5 km² territories (Moehlman 1983), while red foxes, *Vulpes vulpes*, with groups of 2–6 adults hold the record for variation in territory size of 0·1–20 or more km² (Macdonald 1981). Several authors have argued that such variation is related to the dispersion of resources (Macdonald 1981; Kruuk & Parish 1982; Mills 1982) and these arguments are reviewed for carnivores by Macdonald (1983). Similar ideas have been applied to other mammalian orders, e.g. Clutton Brock (1974), Jarman (1974), Bradbury & Vehrencamp (1976). One expression of these ideas, which Macdonald (1983) termed the resource dispersion hypothesis (RDH), is that the smallest home range with an economically defendable (Brown 1964) configuration which will reliably support a pair of animals will sometimes support additional group members. In an environment where food is patchily available, RDH predicts that group sizes are determined by patch richness, whereas territory sizes are determined by the dispersion of these patches. These predictions have been supported by several studies, for example Kruuk & Parish (1982). Here, we want to consider the mechanisms underlying this variation in order to suggest how a carnivore could adjust its use of space to resource dispersion.

There are many hypothetical courses of action which an animal might follow to simultaneously regulate the sizes of group and home range, but we will try to restrict ourselves to those which appear to have a foundation in observation. Our approach derives from an apparent dichotomy in the observed territoriality of carnivores. There are species, e.g. coyotes, amongst which members of some populations appear to strive for larger territories. In contrast, members of some populations of other species, such as Eurasian badgers, *Meles meles*, seem to decline opportunities to occupy larger territories. We will argue that these species illustrate two different strategies, which are affected by the benefits of group living and by the impact of the structure of their habitats on the economics of territoriality.

GROUP SIZE AND TERRITORY SIZE

Carnivores use their territories for foraging as well as reproduction. In the following discussion of strategies in relation to territory size we make four assumptions. Firstly, we will confine ourselves to populations whose members we assume to be limited by food, although much of the argument will still apply where other resources are limiting.

Secondly, we suppose that territories adjoin one another and that the degree of overlap between adjoining territories is not correlated with territory size. Usually, in fact, neighbouring territories overlap little or not at all, e.g. wolves (Mech 1970), coyotes (Bowen 1982), lions (Schaller 1972), spotted hyaenas (Kruuk 1972), Eurasian badgers (Kruuk 1978), red foxes (Macdonald 1981), but sometimes overlap is substantial, e.g. wild dogs, *Lycaon pictus* (Frame, Malcolm & Frame 1979) and some populations of spotted hyaenas (Kruuk 1972).

Thirdly, we are addressing ourselves to what is probably the majority of species: those that have relatively few long-term non-residents in the population (transients or nomads; refs as above). In these species, population density should approximate group size divided by territory size, where group size is defined as the number of adults inhabiting a territory. Group members may use the territory separately or as a pack.

Finally, we assume that all or many of the group contribute to the defence of the territory, although not necessarily to equal extents. Therefore, larger groups can muster proportionally greater strength from their members during agonistic encounters with outsiders. There is evidence that larger groups are victorious during clashes with smaller packs in coyotes (Bowen 1982), golden jackals, *Canis aureus* (Macdonald 1979), spotted hyaena (Kruuk 1972), dwarf mongoose, *Helogale parvula* (Rood 1983a) and coalitions of male lions (Bygott, Bertram & Hanby 1979). In each of these cases, members of groups sometimes travel as a cohesive group, but even those groups whose members never operate together nevertheless accrue greater corporate strength with increasing group size, in that more individuals are available to intercept or invade.

In populations where the group size is a constant (e.g. one for many mustelids, two for many canids) the population density is a direct, inverse function of territory size. Under our assumptions, in facing the 'decision' of how big a territory to defend, each occupant has to balance the costs of defence and exploitation against the yield of surviving offspring and other kin. Such a territory owner might be expected to defend as large an area as possible, up to the point at which further territory ceases to increase inclusive fitness (Davies & Houston 1984). In contrast, for those species which can form groups of variable size the 'decision' regarding optimal territory size is complicated by the interacting consequences of variation in either or both of group size and territory size (e.g. Brown 1982). This is because a shifting balance of advantages and disadvantages is associated with different group sizes.

Living in larger groups may bestow a number of advantages on some individuals among carnivores. In several species sexually mature animals help others with the rearing of offspring (review in Macdonald & Moehlman 1983), and it is likely, but largely unproven, that this enhances the survival of the beneficiaries. Group members may tend to an ailing companion (Kühme 1965; Rasa 1984). Communal hunting may increase hunting success and also the size of prey which may be taken (Kruuk 1972, 1975; Lamprecht 1978; Bowen 1981; van Orsdol 1981) and larger packs may be more successful at repelling scavengers (Lamprecht 1981; Bowen 1981) and territorial intruders. As another advantage, living in a group may enable a young animal to remain in its native home range whilst it prospects for a vacancy elsewhere or until it inherits its parents' territory. Members of larger groups may also be better able to detect predators, and to escape from them either due to safety in numbers, confusion or intimidation (Gorman 1979; Rood 1983a,b).

Disadvantages of living in groups may include an increased likelihood of direct competition over food items or feeding sites, and because of this the size of prey items could have an important affect on group size (e.g. Kruuk 1972, 1975; Zimen 1976). There is evidence, too, that reproduction is inhibited in some (low status) individuals as a consequence of their group membership (e.g. Kruuk 1978; Kruuk & Parish, unpubl.; Packard & Mech 1980; Macdonald 1983; Moehlman 1983). Membership of a group may increase the likelihood of contracting a contagious disease (Bacon & Macdonald 1980; Ball, in press). The balance of advantages and disadvantages may differ between group members (of different sex and status), so that there is no one group size that is optimal for all members.

Since territory size ultimately sets limits upon group size, the benefits of defending a territory of a given size are clearly affected by the existence of this varied suite of advantages and disadvantages of group living. Our argument in this paper is that in species where several individuals may occupy a range, a territory owner follows one of two different courses which will determine the size of its range and the number of its cohabitants:

(a) *An expansionist* tends to increase the size of its territory ('empire'), in excess of minimal requirements for breeding. Expansionists would therefore increase their territory sizes up to an asymptote at a species- or habitat-specific optimum. Therefore, all else being equal, the territory owners who can draw on the greatest corporate strength (e.g. the strongest or largest group) will occupy the largest range.

(b) *A contractor* will maintain the smallest economically defensible area ('enclave') which will encompass sufficient resources for reproduction. This does not require that group size for contractors be restricted to a single animal or breeding pair. For instance, in habitats where resources are patchy in availability (i.e. where various food patches are productive at different times) a contractor's territory may support additional residents. These will be tolerated as resources allow, and balancing the costs and benefits of their presence against the expense of expelling them (the resource dispersion hypothesis, RDH; Macdonald 1983). For example, the territory shown in Fig. 31.1 accommodating four animals, may be the smallest economically defensible territory which embraces each of several necessary foraging zones. The figure also shows how the occupants might partition the range while maintaining individual access to each patch; however, partitioning into such convoluted territories would be uneconomic.

Thus, the same wide range of group and territory sizes could result from either strategy. In seeking analyses that will distinguish expansionists from contractors it is necessary to disentangle the effects of resource dispersion on strategists of each type. It is important to remember our assumptions, most notably that the populations in question are limited by food, or other resource, availability.

PREDICTIONS

(A) The expansionist strategy

Within one habitat, range size is a function of the relative strength of the defending occupants; and for a population of expansionists we predict that:

(A.i) Since larger groups will be stronger than smaller ones, group size will correlate positively with territory size.

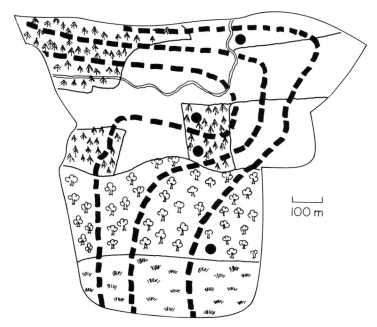

FIG. 31.1. Map of the territory of a clan of four Eurasian badgers radio-tracked in Scotland. The clan territory embraced pasture, deciduous and coniferous woodland and moorland. The badgers foraged in patches of each of these vegetation types. Dots indicate burrows used by all members of the clan. The dotted lines are hypothetical partitions of the real territory into individual territories which would give access to the same vegetation types. (data: H. Kruuk & T. Parish, unpubl.)

(A.ii) Territory sizes will fluctuate from year to year with changes in relative group size, even in the absence of changes in the pattern of resource availability.

(A.iii) If group size is experimentally manipulated there will be concomitant change in territory size.

Prediction (A.i) derives simply from the assumption that larger groups can muster greater strength. If data are drawn from similar habitats the relationship should be especially clear, because differences in resource availability increase variance in the group-size : territory-size relationship and, especially with small sample sizes, this 'noise' might obscure the overall relationship.

The manipulation, (A.iii), would be conclusive if removal of group members resulted in reduction in territory size. An alternative experiment, provisioning with food, is less straightforward since it alters the habitat; therefore the simple prediction that provisioning would sustain larger groups (probably through reduced emigration) and thereby facilitate range expansion, could be difficult to control. For example, the results might be ambiguous if the extra food led to increased defence costs due to extra trespassing.

In planning an experiment involving reduction of group size, one would have to consider that the tendency for one group to expand at the cost of another would be affected not only by the inequality in their strength (and hence the risks of combat), but also by the advantage of expansion, and therefore by differences between prevailing and optimal group size. We will return to the importance of optimal group size, and other functional considerations, in the Discussion.

(B) The contractor strategy

Since a contractor occupies the smallest economically defensible territory (Brown 1964), a group of contractors can only develop where distribution or availability of resources are such that this smallest range can, at least sometimes, support a larger group (viz RDH). There may be many ways in which these conditions arise. It may well happen most commonly where the availability of food is patchy (Macdonald 1981; Kruuk & Parish 1982; Mills 1983), but there are also cases where purely temporal variations in availability (Lindstrom, Poulson & von Schantz, 1981; von Schantz 1984b,c) or the pattern of renewal of resources (Waser 1981; Davies & Houston 1984) might create conditions where a contractionist range could sustain larger groups. The same principle is illustrated by the possibility that the territory size of spotted hyaena is determined by the average distance over which they chase prey, such as wildebeest, *Connochaetus taurinus*; the smallest territory which allows even one hyaena the space needed to overhaul a wildebeest supports sufficient prey to sustain many hyaena. In all these cases the effect is that the occupants' group size will be limited by the availability of resources (e.g. food) within the range (often in patches), and territory size by their dispersion. Therefore, assuming that there is no correlation between patch productivity and patch dispersion, we predict that a population of contractors would have the following qualities:

(B.i) There will be no correlation between group size and territory size, because underlying mechanisms regulating either one are independent. A regular pattern of either patch richness would yield uniform group sizes, and regular patch dispersion would produce uniform territory sizes.

(B.ii) Where the dispersion of a resource varies less with time than does the richness of the resource, as seems often to be the case, the size of territories will be relatively stable, irrespective of short-term variations in resource availability. This is because the size of the smallest sustainable territory is that which will allow the dominant individual or pair to survive periods of minimum resource availability. Amongst the disadvantages of premature adjustment of territory size to short-term changes in food availability is the increased future likelihood of dangerous, escalating territorial conflicts, as argued by von Schantz (1984a).

In a patchy environment two aspects of resource availability may change, i.e. the richness and the dispersion of patches. Variation in one or other of these quantities leads to the following predictions:

(B.iii) Group size may vary with changes in food availability within patches, but there will be no concomitant change in territory size. Similarly, reduction of group size will have no effect on range size. Reduction of patch richness will result in the shedding of (lower status) group members until only one or a pair is left (further reduction would then require territories to enlarge). If the availability of food in patches is manipulated (without changing patch distribution) then there will be a concomitant effect on group size, but not range size.

(B.iv) Removal of a key foraging patch will make the territory unsustainable and it will therefore collapse, since it cannot shrink.

For the purposes of such experiments it is obviously important to be able to identify the role of different foraging patches. For example, consider carnivore groups which are structured by a dominance hierarchy which affects access to numerous patches which fall on a continuum of fruitfulness, and provide different and mixed types of prey, e.g. red foxes (Macdonald 1981). In this case the minimum territory size which sustains the optimal reproduction of a single pair may encompass some low quality feeding patches where the dominants rarely forage, but which provide vital supplement to a subordinate's diet. Fencing one such patch might therefore not precipitate territorial collapse (although it might cause the expulsion of a subordinate).

Since contractors strive to minimize the defence costs of their territories, it may happen that a contractor alters, or temporarily expands, its range following the death or removal of a neighbour. A territorial vacancy could provide the opportunity to realign the neighbouring boundaries, perhaps taking over a vacated patch and relinquishing a less easily defensible one (such a process would tend to produce hexagonal ranges). However, a long-term addition to the previous range would not be in keeping with contractionism, if resource dispersion had remained unaltered.

EXAMPLES

Clearcut cases of expansionism are found amongst canids. In a study of coyotes in Canada, Bowen (1981) found that their food consisted largely of rodents and young deer in summer, but of adult mule deer and elk in winter. The elk were mostly scavenged, but mule deer were hunted by packs of coyotes; there was a significant correlation between pack size and percentage of mule deer in the diet, suggesting greater hunting efficiency for larger packs. There was some, but not much, overlap between adjacent territories and larger packs were at an advantage during clashes over elk carcasses near these borders. Bowen (1982) found a high correlation between home range size and pack size (Fig. 31.2), in which 87% of the variation in range size was explained by variation in pack size. There were considerable changes in home range configurations from one year to the next, and on both occasions when a reduction in pack size occurred, it was followed by a reduction in range size within a year.

Similarly, Fritts & Mech (1981) described variation in wolf pack membership from 2 to 9 in the Superior National Forest of Minnesota. This was significantly correlated with the size of the ranges of these packs; moreover, several changes in numbers of wolves in particular packs were paralleled by changes in the territory sizes of these packs.

Eurasian badgers provide an apparently clearcut example of contractors. They live off small food items, mostly earthworms, but also various insects,

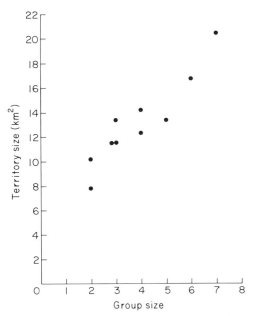

FIG. 31.2. Group and territory sizes of coyotes in a woodland area of Jasper National Park, Alberta (Bowen 1982).

rabbits, and vegetable foods such as fruits, cereals and tubers (Skoog 1970; Kruuk & Parish 1981). In Scotland the most important food, earthworms, occurs in pastures and some woodlands, with a very heterogeneous distribution, and is accessible in the various patches at fairly unpredictable times (dependent, amongst other things, upon weather and grazing by livestock (Kruuk & Parish 1981)). Badgers forage alone, but they live in clans which defend well defined territories, and there is no correlation between clan size and territory size in any or all of several study areas (Kruuk & Parish 1982; Fig. 31.3). The size of territories is closely correlated with the distance between feeding patches. The number of badgers per clan is correlated with the biomass of earthworms per territory and with the biomass of earthworms per field or patch (Kruuk & Parish 1982). Over a 6-year period, territory size and configuration were quite stable, as was the distribution of worm pastures. A decline in clan size of badgers in one part of a study area (caused by human interference) did not affect the territory size (H. Kruuk & T. Parish, unpubl.). Elsewhere, the complete removal of neighbouring badger clans did not affect neighbouring clan boundaries, even over a period as long as 6 years, despite the fact that the numbers in the cleared area were not back to their original levels (in three different areas the populations were back to 38% after 6 years, 86% after 5 years and 13% after 4 years, respectively; C. Cheeseman, pers.

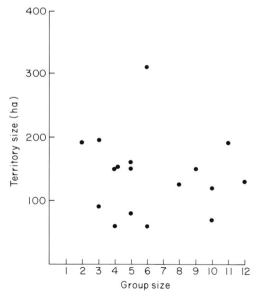

FIG. 31.3. Group and territory sizes of Eurasian badgers from various populations in Scotland (Kruuk & Parish 1982).

comm.). The colonizing badgers, however, had larger ranges than the original occupants, and the number of clans was only about half, so presumably it takes a very long time for a new spatial organization to develop.

Red foxes are found in a wide variety of habitats, in some of which they live as pairs (e.g. Storm *et al*. 1976) and in others they form groups of one male and up to five females (Macdonald 1981). Home range sizes vary widely from local means of 45 ha to more than 2000 ha. Although overlap between neighbouring home ranges varies, most populations studied to date appear to be territorial (e.g. Sargeant 1972; Lindstrom 1979; Nieuwold 1980; Macdonald 1981). Study areas differ greatly in patterns of both resource dispersion and mortality, so it is difficult to resolve the respective effects of these two factors upon variation between populations regarding groups and range sizes. In a study area where food was patchily distributed there was no correlation between group size and territory size (Macdonald 1981). There, despite a threefold variation in territory size, each territory encompassed a similar number of houses and gardens. These human residential areas were the most productive foraging habitat, although houses differed in quality (for example in the amount of food scraps they produced). These rich patches tended to lie at territory borders and it therefore appeared that territory size and configuration were determined by the dispersion of these patches. Lower status group members were seen to forage more frequently away from these rich patches than were dominant foxes (Macdonald 1980). The mosaic of patch productivity, combined with the omnivorous habits of the fox and the indications that individuals of high status foraged more than subordinates in rich patches all complicate the relationship of group size and patch productivity. It may be important that the estimated production of human food scraps per territory ranged from 4·7 to 8·9 (mean 6·4) kg per week and that a pair of foxes eating nothing else was calculated to require 6·3 kg per week of such food (Macdonald 1981). Elsewhere, in two different habitats in Sweden, red foxes have been found to maintain rather constant territory sizes whereas group sizes varied with fluctuating prey abundance (Lindstrom 1979; von Schantz 1984b), these findings are compatible with the resource dispersion hypothesis (von Schantz 1984c; Macdonald 1984b).

Arctic foxes, *Alopex lagopus*, have a social system similar to that of red foxes. Three adjacent groups of Arctic foxes studied in Iceland occupied territories which varied from 8·6 to 18·5 km², but each comprised three adults (one male and two vixens), so for three neighbouring groups there was apparently no relationship between group size and range. They fed principally on carrion washed ashore on those beaches favoured by the drift of the tide. This food was very patchy in its availability, depending on where carrion happened to be washed up. Despite their disparate areas, each territory encompassed an equal length of 'productive coastline' onto which flotsom was washed. Local farmers gathered driftwood for fenceposts from the coastline and each territory yielded a similar number of fenceposts annually. By implication, each also yielded an equal availability of carrion (Hersteinsson & Macdonald 1982) which, since the group sizes were constant at three, is compatible with RDH and contractionism.

Dwarf mongooses forage in packs, in exclusive ranges in fairly open savanna habitat (Rood 1983a). They are territorial, with territory size varying from 28 to 160 ha, and pack sizes anywhere between 3 and 27. There was no correlation between range size and pack size, which is compatible with prediction (B.i). Furthermore, although both pack size and range size changed between years, there is no correlation between the amount of change in pack size and that in range size (data from Rood 1983a), indicating a contractor strategy. In zones of range overlap, neighbouring packs may well meet, whereupon smaller packs avoided larger ones. Within a pack only one pair usually reproduces, and the other animals assisted with rearing offspring even if they were not related. Unfortunately, there are no data on the dispersion of food.

DISCUSSION

The distinction between contractors and expansionists is important in so far as it may help in understanding the processes underlying the adjustment of population density, group sizes and range sizes to the availability of resources. It leads to predictions about the relation between parameters of spatial organization and resources such as food supply, and we have suggested experiments to test these relations.

On a more practical level, knowledge of the processes involved allows prediction of the outcome of the management of carnivore populations. As an example, the Eurasian badger is frequently removed from farmland in SW England, in an attempt to limit its role in infecting cattle with bovine tuberculosis (Zuckerman 1980). It is important to know how badgers living adjacent to eradication areas will behave, e.g. what will happen to the territory sizes of those groups adjoining an eradicated group. Since it appears that badgers are contractionists, we would have predicted that the neighbours of evacuated territories will continue to cover the same range, contacting the same herds of cattle as before. This has, indeed, been shown to be the case (C. Cheeseman, pers. comm.). Also, the effects on carnivores of fencing off part of the habitat (von Schantz 1984c) would depend on not only the spatio-temporal properties of the food supply (and thus which patch was fenced) but on whether the population was composed of contractors or expansionists.

While we have discussed variations in group and territory sizes as if they had no limit, it is obvious that this is so over only a certain range; presumably there are asymptotes to the values of each of these variables, which are species- and habitat-specific.

In considering the stability of the two strategies it is useful to speculate on the consequences for a population of either strategist of invasion by an individual or group adopting the alternative strategy. For instance, what would be the effect if a group of contractors arose in a population of expansionists and sought to restrict their empire to an enclave? Since the key to expansionism is strength of numbers one would predict that the contractors would be swamped. Conversely, if a group of expansionists arose within a population of group-living contractors, or an individual expansionist in a group of contractors, their progress would be affected by the patchiness of their environment (patchy environments being those most likely to give rise to group-living contractors). In a patchy environment we would predict that the would-be expansionists' attempt to increase their range size might be thwarted by the very substantial increase in range size required to encompass the extra patches needed to support one (or several) new group members. Therefore, the advantages of expansionism might be equally real in both homogeneous and patchy environments, but the costs of obtaining an enlarged territory could differ greatly between the two. Also, there are potential disadvantages to a predator occupying a greatly expanded territory, for instance the difficulty of knowing it intimately.

We have suggested that some species or populations behave in an expansionist manner, while others are contractors, but we have not presented any functional arguments as to why such differences should occur. The functional advantages of expansionism are the classical ones advanced for the evolution of larger groups of carnivores as discussed above. In contrast, in some extreme forms of contractionism, groups may be an epiphenomenon of resource dispersion, without an optimal size, and additional members tolerated so long as the costs of doing so remain less than that of expelling them. Such group members are effectively 'sitting tenants', and major benefits they derive from their tenancy may be the postponement of dispersal and the chance to await an opportunity to acquire a neighbouring territory or elevated status in their present range (Macdonald 1983). Amongst unrelated individuals, such a system would amount to social parasitism, and one may expect groups to protect themselves against this. Individuals in groups of this sort may not derive benefits from sociality *per se*, but they could be quite different from transient aggregations in that their membership could be structured and limited proximately by social factors. Macdonald (1983) argued that patchy environments which supported sitting tenants could thereby create conditions of familial and social relationships where large groups with functional advantages would readily evolve. The evolution of groups of cooperating individuals could presage a transition from contractionism to expansionism if these groups developed optimal sizes greater than that sustainable by the richness of patches in their environment. In some apparently contractionist species, such as red and Arctic foxes, black-backed jackals, dwarf mongooses and others, there is evidence of a considerable individual benefit to living in groups, because of alloparental behaviour (Macdonald & Moehlman 1983), cooperative hunting (Kruuk 1975), joint predator defence (Rood 1983b) etc. It is therefore possible that while populations in patchy environments behave as contractors, they might, in an homogeneous environment, behave as expansionists, at least to the extent necessary to secure resources for one or two additional group members. However, we have no evidence that this occurs.

It is likely that the dispersion of resources is important to the contractor versus expansionist dichotomy. An expansionist strategy is more likely to be cost-effective where the distribution of the limiting resource (e.g. food) is rather homogeneous. On the other hand, contractors may live successfuly in groups under conditions where territory and group sizes vary independently, such that the minimum defensible territory can sustain additional members. There are diverse advantages and disadvantages to larger group size among carnivores, and the balance between these, plus the degree of heterogeneity in availability of the limiting resource, could well determine the merits of defending an empire or an enclave.

ACKNOWLEDGMENTS

We are grateful to Geoff Carr, and Drs David Jenkins, Robin McCleery, Robert Moss and Ian Patterson for their helpful criticism of an earlier draft, and to members of Oxford Animal Behaviour Research group for stimulating discussions.

REFERENCES

Bacon, P.J. & Macdonald, D.W. (1980). To control rabies: vaccinate foxes. *New Scientist*, **1980**, 640–645.

Ball, F. (in press). Spatial models for the spread and control of rabies, incorporating group sizes. *Population Dynamics of Rabies in Wildlife*. (Ed. by P.J. Bacon), Academic Press, London.

Bowen, W.D. (1981). Variation in coyote social organisation: the influence of prey size. *Canadian Journal of Zoology*, **59**, 639–652.

Bowen, W.D. (1982). Home range and spatial organisation of coyotes in Jasper National Park, Alberta. *Journal of Wildlife Management*, **46**, 201–216.

Bradbury, J.W. & Vehrencamp, S.L. (1976). Social organisation and foraging in Emballonurid bats. II. A model for the determination of group size. *Behavioural Ecology and Sociobiology*, **2**, 1–17.

Brown, J.L. (1964). The evolution of diversity in avian territorial systems. *Wilson Bulletin,* **76,** 160–169.

Brown, J.L. (1982). Optimal group size in territorial animals. *Journal of Theoretical Biology,* **95,** 793–810.

Bygott, J.D., Bertram, B.C.R. & Hanby, J.P. (1979). Male lions in large coalitions gain reproductive advantage. *Nature,* **282,** 839–841.

Clutton-Brock, T.H. (1974). Primate social organisation and ecology. *Nature,* **250,** 539–542.

Davies, N.B. & Houston, A.I. (1984). Territory economics. *Behavioural Ecology* (Ed J.R. Krebs & N.B. Davies), pp. 148–169. Blackwell Scientific Publications, Oxford.

Frame, L.H., Malcolm, J.R. & Frame, G.W. (1979). Social organisation of African wild dogs, *Lycaon pictus,* on the Serengeti plains, Tanzania, 1967–1978. *Zeitschrift für Tierpsychologie,* **50,** 225–249.

Fritts, S.H. & Mech, L.D. (1981). Dynamics, movements and feeding ecology of a newly protected wolf population in North Western Minnesota. *Wildlife Monograph,* **45,** 1–80.

Gorman, M.L. (1979). Dispersion and foraging of the small Indian mongoose, *Herpestes auropunctatus* (Carnivora: Viverridae) relative to the evolution of social viverrids. *Journal of Zoology (London),* **187,** 65–73.

Hersteinsson, P. & Macdonald, D.W. (1982). Some comparisons between red and arctic foxes, *Vulpes vulpes* and *Alopex lagopus,* as revealed by radio tracking. *Proceedings of the Symposia of the Zoological Society of London,* **49,** 259–288.

Jarman, P.J. (1974). The social organisation of antelope in relation to their ecology. *Behaviour,* **48,** 215–267.

Kaufmann, J.H. (1962). Ecology and social behaviour of the coati, *Nasua narica,* on Barro Colorado Island, Panama. *University of California Miscellaneous Publications in Zoology,* **60,** 95–222.

Kaufmann, J.H., Lanning, D.V. & Poole, S.E. (1976). Current status and distribution of the coati in the United States. *Journal of Mammalogy,* **57,** 621–637.

Kruuk, H. (1972). *The Spotted Hyaena.* University of Chicago Press, Chicago.

Kruuk, H. (1975). Functional aspects of social hunting by carnivores. *Function and Evolution in Behaviour* (Ed. by G. Baerends, C. Beer & A. Manning), pp. 119–141. Clarendon Press, Oxford.

Kruuk, H. (1978). Spatial organisation and territorial behaviour of the European badger, *Meles meles,* L. *Journal of Zoology (London),* **184,** 1–19.

Kruuk, H. & Parish, T. (1981). Feeding specialisation of the European badger, *Meles meles,* in Scotland. *Journal of Animal Ecology,* **50,** 773–788.

Kruuk, H. & Parish, T. (1982). Factors affecting population density, group size and territory size of the European badger, *Meles meles. Journal of Zoology (London),* **196,** 31–39.

Kühme, W. (1965). Freilandstudien zur Soziologie des Hyänenhundes, *Lycaon pictus lupinus,* Thomas, 1902. *Zeitschrift für Tierpsychologie,* **22,** 495–541.

Lamprecht, J. (1978). The relationship between food competition and foraging group size in some larger carnivores. *Zeitschrift für Tierpsychologie,* **46,** 337–343.

Lamprecht, J. (1981). The function of social hunting in larger terrestrial carnivores. *Mammal Review,* **11,** 169–179.

Lindstrom, E. (1979). The red fox in a small game community of the south taiga region in Sweden. *The Red Fox* (Ed. by E. Zimen), pp. 177–184. Biogeographica 18. W. Junk, den Haag.

Lindstrom, E., Poulson, O. & von Schantz, T. (1981). Spacing of the red fox, *Vulpes vulpes (L),* in relation to food supply. T. von Schantz, thesis, University of Lund, Sweden.

Macdonald, D.W. (1979). Helpers in fox society. *Nature,* **282,** 69–71.

Macdonald, D.W. (1980). The red fox, *Vulpes vulpes,* as a predator upon earthworms, *Lumbricus terrestris. Zeitschrift für Tierpsychologie,* **52,** 171–200.

Macdonald, D.W. (1981). Resource dispersion and the social organisation of the red fox, *Vulpes*

vulpes. Proceedings of the Worldwide Furbearer Conference, Vol. 2. (Ed by J.A. Chapman & D. Pursley), pp. 918–949. University of Maryland Press.

Macdonald, D.W. (1983). The ecology of carnivore social behaviour. *Nature*, **301**, 379–384.

Macdonald, D.W. (1984a). *The Encyclopaedia of Mammals*, Vol. 1. George Allen and Unwin, London.

Macdonald, D.W. (1984b). Reply to von Schantz. *Nature*, **307**, 390.

Macdonald, D.W. & Moehlman, P.D. (1983). Cooperation, altruism and restraint in the reproduction of carnivores. *Perspective in Ethology*, 5 (Ed. by P.P.G. Bateson & P. Klopfer), pp. 433–466. Plenum Press, New York.

Mech, L.D. (1970). *The Wolf: Ecology and Behaviour of an Endangered Species.* Doubleday, New York.

Mech, L.D. (1973). Wolf numbers in the Superior National Forest of Minnesota. *USDA Forest Service Paper NC-97*, 1–10.

Mech, L.D. (1977). Productivity, mortality and population trends of wolves in Northern Minnesota. *Journal of Mammalogy*, **58**, 559–574.

Mech, L.S. & Frenzel, L.D. (1971). Ecological studies of the timber wolf in north-eastern Minnesota. *USDA Forest Service Research Papers, NC-52*, 1–34.

Mills, M.G.M. (1982). Factors affecting group size and territory size in the Brown Hyena, *Hyaena brunnea*, in the southern Kalahari. *Journal of Zoology (London)*, **198**, 39–51.

Moehlman, P.D. (1983). Socioecology of the silverbacked and golden jackals (*Canis mesomelas* and *Canis aureus*). *Advances in the study of Mammalian Behaviour* (Ed. by J.F. Eisenberg & D.G. Kleiman), pp. 423–453. American Society of Mammalogists, Pittsburgh.

Nieuwold, F.J. (1980). Aspects of the social structure of red fox populations: a summary. *The Red Fox* (Ed. by E. Zimen) pp. 185–193. Biogeographica 18. W. Junk, Den Haag.

Orsdol, K. van. (1981). *Lion predation in Rwenzori National Park, Uganda.* Ph.D thesis, University of Cambridge.

Packard, J.M. & Mech, L.D. (1980). Population regulation in wolves. In: *Biosocial Mechanisms of Population Regulation* (Ed. by M.N. Cohen, R.S. Malpass & H.G. Klein), pp. 135–150. Yale University Press, New Haven.

Rasa, O.A.E. (1984). A case of invalid care in wild dwarf mongooses. *Zeitschrift für Tierpsychology*, **62**, 181–268.

Rood, J.P. (1983a). The social system of the dwarf mongoose. *Advances in the study of mammalian behaviour* (Ed. by J.F. Eisenberg & D.G. Kleiman), pp. 454–488. American Society of Mammalogists, Pittsburgh.

Rood, J.P. (1983b). Banded mongoose rescues pack member from eagle. *Animal Behaviour*, **31**, 1261–1262.

Sargeant, A.B. (1972). Red fox spatial characteristics in relation to waterfowl predation. *Journal of Wildlife Management*, **36**, 225–236.

Schaller, G.B. (1972). *The Serengeti Lion.* University of Chicago Press, Chicago.

von Schantz, T. (1984a). Spacing strategies, kin selection and population regulation in altricial vertebrates. *Oikos*, **42**, 48–58.

von Schantz, T. (1984b). 'Non-breeders' in the red fox, *Vulpes vulpes*: a case of resource surplus. *Oikos*, **42**, 59–65.

von Schantz, T. (1984c). Carnivore social behaviour—does it need patches? *Nature*, **307**, 389–390.

Skoog, P. (1970). The food of the Swedish badger, *Meles meles*, L. Viltrevy, **7**, 1–120.

Storm, G.L., Andrews, R.D. Phillips, R.L., Bishop, R.A., Siniff, D.B. & Tester, J.R. (1976). Morphology, reproduction, dispersal and mortality of midwestern red fox populations. *Wildlife Monographs*, **49**, 1–82.

Waser, P.M. (1981). Sociality or territorial defense? The influence of resource renewal. *Behavioural Ecology and Sociobiology*, **8**, 231–237.

Zimen, E. (1976). On the regulation of pack size in wolves. *Zeitschrift für Tierpsychologie*, **40**, 300–341.

Zuckerman, Lord, (1980). *Badgers, cattle and tuberculosis.* HMSO, London.

32. VARIATIONS IN THE SOCIAL STRUCTURE OF RABBIT POPULATIONS : CAUSES AND DEMOGRAPHIC CONSEQUENCES

D. P. COWAN[1] AND P. J. GARSON[2]

[1]*Ministry of Agriculture, Fisheries and Food, Worplesdon Laboratory,*
Tangley Place, Worplesdon, nr Guildford, Surrey GU3 3LQ, and
[2]*Department of Zoology, University of Newcastle,*
Newcastle-upon Tyne NE1 7RU

SUMMARY

The social behaviour and population dynamics of two free-living populations of wild rabbits were compared and related to differences in the distribution and abundance of potentially limiting resources.

Animals living on a chalk hill shared their home ranges extensively, but with relatively few conspecifics. Those living on sand dunes shared their ranges less extensively but with a large number of conspecifics. On both sites aggression was predominantly intrasexual and aggression between females was less common in the sand dune population. Discrete social groups could be defined on the basis of shared access to burrow systems only on the chalk hill site.

In the chalk hill population females competed for access to burrows. On both sites males competed directly for females. However, male territorial behaviour was only apparent within the chalk hill population, probably because of a more clumped pattern of female dispersion there.

The growth rates of juvenile rabbits in the sand dune population were negatively correlated with population density and were lower than those on the chalk hill site.

The patterns of density-dependent mortality and population stability were consistent with 'scramble' competition for food on sand dunes and 'contest' competition for burrows and mates on chalk hills.

INTRODUCTION

Contest competition, involving some form of social interaction (Lazarus 1982), occurs when a limited resource is economically defendable (Brown 1964): the costs of defending the resource being less than the benefits accruing through its monopolization. For instance, if food is evenly and predictably distributed and limited it may be defended by territiorial behaviour but not if it is clumped unpredictably in space and time (Horn 1968). Both social structure and social organization, as defined by Rowell (1972), may be viewed best as the resultant of individual competitive interactions. Thus dominance hierarchies, for example, reflect a series of individual compromises over priority of access to some limited resource (Williams 1966; Clutton-Brock & Harvey 1976).

Competition between individuals for limited resources will impose density-dependent constraints on the rate of population growth. The form which this competition takes should in theory influence the nature of these effects. At one extreme 'scramble' competition, acting on survivorship, is supposed to be destabilizing because of catastrophic mortality at some threshold density. In contrast, 'contest' competition implies an unequal division of limited resources between individuals arising from despotic defence (Fretwell & Lucas 1970), and tends to lead to population stability (Bellows 1981). Thus, the nature of social competition observed can be used to predict population dynamics, and *vice versa*. Entomological ecologists in particular have often adopted the second approach (e.g. Varley, Gradwell & Hassell 1973; Hassell 1976), but the first has rarely been employed, even by vertebrate ecologists able to individually mark and observe the behaviour of their study animals (e.g. Krebs 1971).

An opportunity to predict the type of dynamics to be expected in two populations of a species has arisen from our parallel field studies of the European wild rabbit (*Oryctolagus cuniculus* L.) living in contrasting habitats. Both studies were initially intended to extend our understanding of rabbit social behaviour, derived to date mainly from studies of enclosed populations (Mykytowycz 1959, 1960, 1961; Lockley 1961; Myers & Poole 1959, 1961, 1962). A prime aim in both cases was to determine how social behaviour influences the division of resources within populations.

Rabbits require access to three principal resources: food, burrows and mates. In this paper we document variation in rabbit social behaviour and relate this to differences in the nature of the limiting resources. The type of competition observed between individuals is then used to predict, qualitatively, the form of the relationships between mortality, population density and population stability at each site.

METHODS

The chalk hill ('Chalk') site worked by D.P.C. at Aston Rowant National Nature Reserve, Oxfordshire consisted of an 8·2 ha valley in chalk hills surrounding a 2·6 ha field of winter cereal. The 8 ha coastal sand dune site

('Sand') worked by P.J.G. was on Holy Island, Northumberland, within Lindisfarne National Nature Reserve. More detailed descriptions of both sites will be published elsewhere.

On both sites most rabbits were caught by using cage traps (Henderson 1979), supplemented by the use of ferrets in winter, and by 'spotlighting' (netting rabbits as they move in the beam of a torch) at Sand in autumn and winter. Rabbits aged less than 9 months were identified by external examination of the tibial epiphyses (Watson & Tyndale-Biscoe 1953). All animals were weighed, sexed and given numbered ear-tags; a unique combination of large coloured tags was used on adults and large juveniles.

Observations of behaviour were made from hides at both sites using 15–60 × 50 zoom telescopes, from March to December on Chalk and March to September on Sand. Winter observations were limited primarily by low levels of daytime rabbit activity. On Chalk the entire study site was viewed from a single position and all observations were made during the 4 hours prior to dusk. On Sand behavioural observations were made from a single position overlooking a flat, moist productive 'slack' and the surrounding dunes (an area of approximately 1 ha), primarily during the 4 hours following dawn. Mykytowycz & Rowley (1958) found dawn and dusk periods of rabbit activity to be similar. A population census over the whole of the Sand site involved repetitive counting of all rabbits in view, and identification of marked ones from a variety of positions: an observer could not view the whole site from any one place.

Individual home ranges were plotted as minimum convex polygons, from all observations of identifiable adults made each year. Since the extent of range overlap between individuals may be influenced by population density, and the proportion of marked adults in the population, the analyses of range overlap presented here are confined to years when the adult densities and proportions marked were comparable within and between sites: 1982 and 1983 at Sand and 1978, 1979, 1980 and 1982 at Chalk.

On Chalk, 75–85% of the adult population was marked throughout the study, except in 1977 when only 31% was marked. The number of marked and unmarked adults counted at the beginning of each breeding season was in close agreement with overwinter capture–mark–recapture estimates of the overwinter population (Cowan, in press). The minimum number of juveniles alive each month, estimated from direct observation and by using weight at first capture to assign a birth month to those trapped, was summed with the number of adults known to be alive that month to give a minimum population estimate. The peak monthly population estimate thus does not include a substantial number of juveniles which died without being caught or survived undetected.

On Sand between 22% (1979) and 91% (1983) of adults were tagged. The total number of adults alive each summer was calculated using a simple Lincoln Index on the data from scans (see below), each sighting of a marked animal being regarded as a recapture. On Sand the breeding season is short (young emerging late April to late June compared with February through to August on Chalk) and most young are produced early in the season. The sum of the number of adults known to be alive and the number of juveniles tagged during each season was therefore used as a minimum peak population index. This index is an underestimate because appreciable proportions of the young were never captured in all years. Directly comparable estimates were not made between sites because of the short breeding season on Sand and the greater age at first capture on Chalk (annual median initial capture weight 310–450 g) than on Sand (annual median 230–305 g) which would have led to relative underestimates of the Chalk population.

All active burrows were mapped at the beginning of each breeding season. On Sand the areas covered by the major habitat types (slack, dune slopes adjacent to slacks, and other dunes) were measured.

RESULTS

Social behaviour and organization

We have compared three different aspects of social behaviour in an attempt to define the major differences between our populations: (i) the nature and extent of home range overlap between individuals; (ii) the extent of refuge sharing between individuals; (iii) the tendencies of individuals to associate closely with members of their own and the opposite sex and the frequency and context of agonistic interactions within and between sexes.

Ranging patterns

Figure 32.1. shows the extent to which individual ranges overlapped. Many ranges were extensively shared on Chalk, but relatively few on Sand, suggesting that each sex lived in spatially discrete groups on Chalk but not on Sand. Moreover, both males and females shared ranges with more members of their own sex on Sand than on Chalk (Fig. 32.2). Taken together these results suggest that on Chalk males and females tended to form small groups, whereas on Sand the ranges were more dispersed but each overlapping with a relatively large numbers of conspecifics.

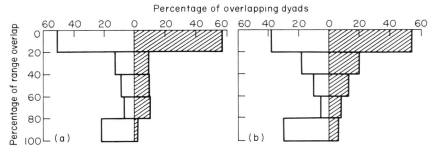

FIG. 32.1. Frequency distributions for the proportion of each adult's range overlapped by any other on Chalk during 1978–80 and 1982 (unshaded) and on Sand during 1982 and 1983 (shaded) for (a) all male–male overlapping dyads: $n_C = 194$, $n_S = 148$; Kolmogorov–Smirnov $D = 0.19$ $P < 0.01$; and (b) all female overlapping dyads: $n_C = 304$, $n_S = 391$; Kolmogorov–Smirnov $D = 0.24$ $P < 0.001$.

Refuge sharing

Given the above contrasts in the spatial distribution of home ranges between the two sites it might be predicted that more individuals would share refuges on Chalk than on Sand. On Chalk, refuges consisted of complex, discrete systems of interconnected burrows with multiple entrances (warrens). The numbers of individuals which were known to share each warren (i.e. observed entering, leaving or sitting at a burrow entrance) in each year on Chalk are shown in Fig. 32.3a. Social groups on Chalk were recognized on the basis of shared access to warrens (Cowan 1983). These groups were characterized by strong site fidelity amongst females and different relationships amongst males within and between groups (see below).

Little is known about burrow interconnection on Sand, although the movement of ferrets between nearby entrances suggested that warrens were much smaller and simpler than those on Chalk, with few interconnections between entrances more than 5 m apart. The extent of burrow entrance sharing (see above) by rabbits living on Sand in 1983 (Fig. 32.3b) was much less than the warren sharing on Chalk, although the shared units are not strictly comparable because of the differences in refuge structure.

Associations and interactions

Animals with overlapping ranges may potentially associate together and interact socially. Data on between- and within-sex associations are shown in Table 32.1 for males and females seen during scans at both sites. Comparable data from Sand could not be included from years other than 1983 because of

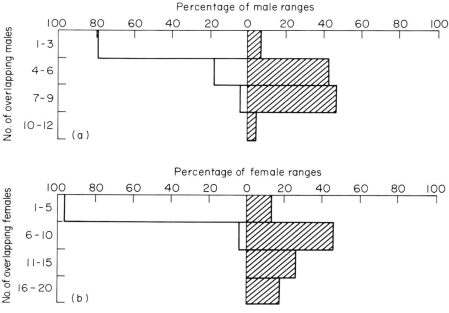

FIG. 32.2. Frequency histograms for the number of individuals of the same sex which overlapped part or all of each individual's range on Chalk during 1978–80 and 1982 (unshaded) and on Sand during 1982 and 1983 (shaded) for (a) males: $n_C = 70$, $n_S = 24$ Mann-Whitney $Z_{corr} = 6·00$, $P < 0·0001$; and (b) females: $n_C = 119$, $n_S = 42$ Mann-Whitney $Z_{corr} = 9·02$, $P < 0·001$.

the high frequencies of association involving at least one untagged individual. On both sites males associated more frequently with females than with males; however, males spent more time alone and less time with other males on Sand than on Chalk ($\chi^2 = 54·3$, 2 d.f., $P < 0·001$). Thus, the social relationships between males in the same social group on Chalk were different from those amongst males whose ranges overlapped on Sand. Females were seen more frequently in association with other rabbits of both sexes, and less frequently alone on Chalk than on Sand ($\chi^2 = 61·59$, 1 d.f, $P < 0·001$).

Male–female associations were more frequent than intrasexual associations at both sites, except amongst females on Sand. This could be a direct result of more aggression within than between sexes. Seventy-two overtly aggressive interactions were seen on Sand in 1983, and 130 during all the years on Chalk. Each aggressive interaction involved the active participation of two individuals defined as the 'chaser' and 'chased'. Only 14% (10) and 15% (20) of aggressive interactions were intersexual on Sand and Chalk respectively.

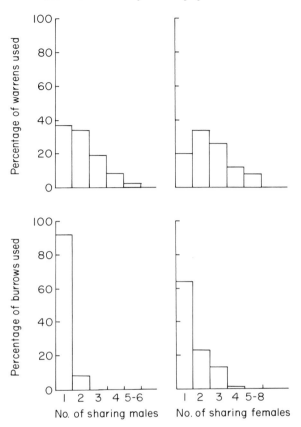

FIG. 32.3. (a) The precentages of active warrens ($n = 170$) on Chalk that were used by different numbers of males and females during all years of the study. (b) The percentages of active burrows on Sand that were known to have been used by different numbers of males ($n = 37$) and females ($n = 80$) during 1983.

Table 32.2 shows the frequencies of intrasexual aggression expressed both as proportions of male and female observations, and as rates relative to the association frequencies shown in Table 32.1. The first of these measures indicates that males spent a similar amount of time interacting with one another at the two sites, whilst females interacted more than twice as often on Chalk than on Sand. The second index shows that males interacted more per same sex association on Sand than on Chalk. This effect probably results from males being less aggressive within groups than between adjacent groups on Chalk (D.P. Cowan, unpubl., see below).

TABLE 32.1. Associations within and between sexes. Figures in the tables are the numbers of occasions (row %) when the focal animal had a male, a female, an unsexed individual or no adult rabbit as their nearest adult neighbour within 5 m

| Focal Animal | Nearest adult animal within 5 m | | | | Total |
	Male	Female	Unsexed	None	
Chalk					
All years					
Males	188	455	6	605	1254
	(15)	(36)	(<1)	(48)	
Females	495	220	12	815	1542
	(32)	(14)	(<1)	(53)	
Sand					
1983					
Males	20	224	5	333	582
	(3)	(38)	(<1)	(57)	
Females	218	228	85	1059	1590
	(14)	(14)	(5)	(67)	

TABLE 32.2 Association frequencies and aggressive interaction rates between adults of the same sex

| | Chalk | | Sand | |
	♂–♂	♀–♀	♂–♂	♀–♀
Number of associations (from Table 32.1)	188	220	20	228
Number of interacting individuals	142	78	62	32
% of all observations of that sex	11.7	5.1	10.7	2.0
Interactions per association	0.76	0.35	3.1	0.14

Competition for limited resources

Competition for food

No attempt was made in either study to measure directly the availability or quality of food, but both are likely to influence the post-weaning growth rates of juveniles. Lower growth rates at higher population densities can be interpreted as circumstantial evidence for food being a limited resource.

Growth rates were calculated for all juveniles weighing between 200 and 1000 g when recaptured after initial tagging. Rabbit growth rates are approximately constant between these weights (Southern 1940; Dunnet 1956), so these data were pooled to give a mean growth rate (g day^{-1}) for each season at each site. The relationship between population density and growth rates (Table 32.3) was positive but not statistically significant ($R_s = 0.70$) on Chalk. However, there was a negative correlation ($R_s = -0.90$, $P = 0.05$) on Sand. The annual mean growth rates on Sand were significantly lower than those for each year

TABLE 32.3 Juvenile growth rates (SE) in relation to population density (between-year variation: $F_{4,279} = 1.65$, $P = 0.16$; on Chalk; and $F_{4,513} = 2.49$, $P = 0.043$ on Sand)

Year	Chalk		Sand	
	Mean growth rate (g day^{-1})	Minimum peak population density ha^{-1}	Mean growth rate (g day^{-1})	Minimum peak population density ha^{-1}
1978	10·2 (0·53)	29·8	—	—
1979	8·9 (0·70)	18·0	9·4 (0·94)	20·9
1980	9·7 (0·36)	23·3	8·9 (1·12)	45·1
1981	9·8 (0·40)	27·4	6·4 (0·59)	75·8
1982	11·0 (0·35)	26·5	7·8 (0·60)	58·5
1983	—	—	6·5 (0·35)	44·3

on Chalk, with the exception of 1979 ($t_{236} = 2.34$, $P < 0.02$ to $t_{156} = 5.29$, $P < 0.001$). These lower growth rates may have led to the reduced adult size on Sand ($\bar{x} = 1394$ g, SD 161, $n = 214$) compared with Chalk ($\bar{x} = 1664$ g, SD 204, $n = 461$) ($t_{673} = 17.07$, $P < 0.001$).

The Sand site is very heterogeneous with respect to food, especially in summer, when the slacks are at their most productive. The dunes themselves are dominated by the extremely fibrous marram grass *Ammophila arenaria* L. If the distribution of burrows approximates to the distribution of rabbits over the whole study site, at any time, the distribution of burrows can be used to estimate how rabbits partition themselves over the site. Table 32.4 shows that the density of burrows was always greater on dune slopes next to slacks than it was elsewhere and that the ratio of the densities in any one year did not vary appreciably between years after 1979, despite a sustained increase in the total population of burrows. This pattern is that predicted by the ideal-free model (Fretwell & Lucas 1970) of 'scramble' competition (Hassell 1976).

Table 32.4. The number of burrows at the start of each breeding season and their distribution between the two principle habitat types on Sand (1979–1983)

Year	Number of burrows	Burrow density ha^{-1} in: dunes next to slacks (a)	elsewhere on dunes (b)	ratio (a/b)
1979	96	37·3	7·3	5·11
1980	275	80·0	23·0	3·48
1981	574	151·1	48·8	3·10
1982	625	175·1	53·3	3·29
1983	743	208·9	62·2	3·36

Competition for burrow space

There are several reasons for suggesting that burrow availability was a limiting resource on Chalk. First, there was a significant positive correlation between female group size and the number of burrow entrances available to a group using one or more adjacent warrens ($R_{74} = 0.81$, $P < 0.0001$). Second, 72% (28) of female–female agonistic interactions on Chalk took place within 5 m of a burrow entrance. Third, females were seen on five occasions to thwart attempts by others, who were carrying nesting material in their mouths, to enter a warren. Fourth, the number of burrows used each year varied very little (range 314–337) and did not correlate with adult population size (r_s 0·25 NS). Finally, of the twenty-nine warrens present in 1977, only one had fallen into disuse and disrepair by 1983, and only one new warren had been constructed. A dispersion index (Elliot 1971) (variance/mean for the number of burrow entrances in 36 m^2 quadrats) had values in the range 3·69–4·27 over the study period, demonstrating that burrows were highly clumped ($P < 0.001$).

In contrast, female–female aggressive behaviour on Sand was not associated with burrow defence and animals seemed capable of digging a usable burrow in 1–2 days. The number of burrows increased during the period of the study (see Table 32.4) as the population increased. Consequently burrows cannot have been limiting in all years at this site. Burrow entrances were significantly clumped ($P < 0.001$) in all years but the dispersion index (see above) had relatively lower values in the range 1·20–1·47. This reflected the unequal distribution of burrows between units of uniform habitat on Sand (see Table 32.4) rather than clumping within such units caused by the presence of large warrens as on Chalk.

Competition for space above ground

The patterns of female range overlap shown in Table 32.1 and 32.2 might have resulted from the defence of warrens by group-living females on Chalk. Males, however, were not seen defending burrows but still exhibited similar patterns of range overlap. Two forms of behaviour were suggestive of territorial defence by males which belonged to adjacent social groups. Nine (28%) male–male aggressive chases ended abruptly at a point where the chased male remained, rather than moved away as was typical of other chases, and then 'paw-scraped' by raking the ground repeatedly and rapidly with his forepaws. The resulting horeshoe-shaped scrapes were at a higher density within areas of intergroup male range overlap than elsewhere (Cowan 1983). The second behaviour consisted of the two protagonists running parallel with each other, approximately 1 m apart, for 5–25m. They would then stop and both paw-scrape. Generally the sequence would be repeated a number of times interspersed by periods of vigilance. Fifteen such interactions (21% of all male–male interactions) were seen on Chalk. By contrast overt space defence was never seen on Sand.

Competition for mates

Male rabbits should be under much stronger selection pressure to compete for access to females than *vice versa* (Trivers 1972). On both sites males defended their access to females directly. Males approaching male–female dyads were chased away by the associating males (e.g. in all 13 approaches in 1983 on Sand). Intergroup space defence by males on Chalk might also reflect competition between males for access to females. An analysis of group composition on Chalk shows that although there was a positive correlation between male and female group size ($R^2 = 0.69$) there was considerable variation in the group sex ratios (0.33–3 females per male). (Cowan 1983), which implies despotic behaviour (Fretwell & Lucas 1970) by some males in the population.

Males on Sand cannot have been associating with particular females in the same way that the existence of social groups allowed on Chalk. One method of inspecting how males partitioned their access to females on Sand is to compare the number of male and female ranges overlapping that of each male (an index of their potential for sexual access). A positive correlation, however, would only indicate a functional relationship if the numbers of male and female overlappers were independent of male range size. This condition only holds in 1983, and the relevant data are therefore plotted for this year alone in Fig. 32.4. The slope of this line reflects the population sex ratio of 1·95 females per

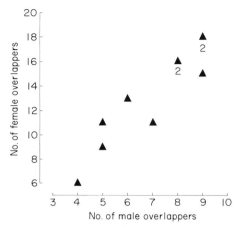

FIG. 32.4. Number of males and females overlapping each male's range on Sand during 1983, $y = 1.88x - 0.07$; $n = 11$; $r_{10}0.94$, $P < 0.001$.

male in this year, and the relatively high R^2 of 0.88 can be interpreted as evidence that males conform to an ideal-free distribution implying scramble competition for access to females.

Population processes

The resource-related differences in social behaviour should give rise to different population dynamics on Chalk and Sand. Despotism amongst females for access to burrows and amongst males for mates on Chalk suggests contest competition while the rabbits on Sand apparently scrambled for both food and mates. If this was so then density-dependent mortality would be expected to occur at lower densities on Chalk than on Sand.

K values for mortality (Varley *et al.* 1973) were calculated from the numbers of animals alive at the time of the minimum peak population estimate each year (N_t) and the number of these that survived to enter the following breeding season (N_s). These have been plotted against $\log_{10} N_t$ in Fig. 32.5 which shows that density-dependent mortality is indeed acting powerfully at relatively lower densities on Chalk than on Sand. If competition on Sand was closer to scramble than contest then the maximum slope of the relationship shown in Fig. 32.5 should be higher there than on Chalk (Bellows 1981). Without more data it is not possible to test this prediction by fitting realistic values to Hassell's (1975) model of this relationship.

Contest competition should lead to greater stability in the size of the Chalk

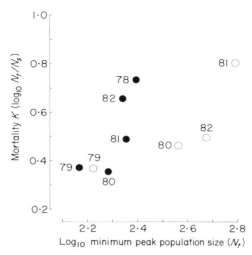

FIG. 32.5. K values, log (N_t/N_s) where N_t is the peak population size during each year and N_s is the number of these individuals which survived to enter the following breeding season, plotted against log N_t for each year on Chalk ($\bullet$) and Sand ($\bigcirc$).

population. This prediction is supported by the ratio of the maximum to minimum breeding population estimates being higher on Sand than on Chalk ($185/32 = 5 \cdot 8$ and $92/61 = 1 \cdot 5$ respectively).

DISCUSSION

The behaviour of individuals

On the evidence presented in this paper there appear to be major differences in the social structure of our two populations. To what extent, at least in retrospect, are these differences explicable in terms of the behaviour of individual animals competing for limiting resources?

On Chalk there was very little change in the availability of warren space from year to year, over a period including at least one significant population fluctuation (1981). Observations of female–female aggression concerning access to nest sites implied that burrow space was in short supply and that breeding females competed amongst themselves for its use. This finding, together with the positive correlation between burrow availability and female group size, suggests that the subdivision of the breeding female population on Chalk into warren-based groups was a result of female–female competition.

This conclusion is similar to that reached by Armitage (1962) for female yellow-bellied marmots *Marmota flaviventris* Audubon and Bachman, in which there is also evidence of a spatially clumped and limited supply of refuges. Furthermore, there is a tendency for the average *per capita* female reproductive success to decline as group size increases in these marmots (Downhower & Armitage 1971) and amongst the rabbits on Chalk (Cowan 1983). Thus, females of both species seem to form groups because this gives each individual at least some opportunity to breed, not because group formation itself carries any mutualistic advantages for all participants (Altman, Wagner & Lennington 1977; Bertram 1978; Garson 1982). The important costs of group living (Alexander 1974) will include increased interference, competition and transmission of density-dependent diseases such as coccidiosis (Bull 1958). The clumped burrow distribution on Chalk probably results from the difficulty of digging into the hard substrate to a sufficient depth to avoid nest predation by the red fox *Vulpes vulpes* L. (Wood 1980) and the European badger *Meles meles* L. New nesting sites are created by the expansion of existing burrows, at or below a safe depth, rather than by initiation of new warrens.

The spatial organization of females on Sand does not consist of obvious groups, nor did burrows seem to be in short supply. New burrows were created frequently and rapidly, most especially when the population expanded in each of the first three summers of the study. The lower rate of female–female aggression, and the lack of a clear context for these interactions, reinforces our view that the extent of any contest competition between females for burrow space on Sand was minimal.

As male rabbits are unable to contribute substantially to the care of their young they are expected to behave in such a way as to maximize the rate at which they achieve matings with oestrus females (Williams 1966; Trivers 1972; Wittenberger 1979). The exclusive defence of a group of females by a male for mating purposes, so-called harem defence polygyny (Emlen & Oring 1977), is only likely to be economic if females live in spatially discrete groups during the mating period, as do red deer *Cervus elaphus* L. (Clutton-Brock, Guinness & Albon 1982). However, any pronounced tendency for females living in groups to combine a short oestrus period with reproductive synchrony will both increase the costs of defence against intruding males and decrease the benefits to owning males as a result of opportunistic matings by other males (e.g. Leboeuf & Peterson 1969). This latter point is apparently very relevant to the rabbit case because studies of groups in enclosures have shown that females enter a behavioural oestrus for perhaps as little as 12 hours *post partum*, or every seventh day in non-pregnant individuals (Myers & Poole 1961, 1962; Lockley 1961). Consequently, it was not surprising to find males guarding females and repelling single intruding males from such sexual associations at both our sites in a similar way to that described by Bell (1983).

The males' habitat on Chalk of defending space containing warrens used by certain females, as well as much of these females' home ranges, whilst often sharing space with other adult males, may be seen as a rather conservative tactic. However, a study using allozymes to determine the paternity of young in a similarly organized rabbit population in Australia indicated widespread promiscuity which was not predicted on the basis of observed associations (Daly 1981). Daly's observations were made exclusively during daylight when ranges may be smaller than at night (Gibb, Ward & Ward 1978). The mating system of the rabbits on Chalk may thus resemble overlap/hierarchial promiscuity (Wittenberger 1979) more than polygyny, as exemplified by male yellow-bellied marmots defending harems (Armitage 1974), and 'coterie' based males in the black-tailed prairie dog *Cynomys ludovicianus* Ord (Hoogland 1981). In both these species allozyme studies failed to detect promiscuous matings and implied that social grouping reflected mating allegiences (Schwartz & Armitage 1980; Foltz & Hoogland 1981).

The more scattered dispersion pattern of females on Sand completely precludes the defence by a male of a territory which contains most of the space used by a few females (Clutton-Brock & Harvey 1978; Wittenberger 1980). The lack of space defence and apparently opportunistic attention to receptive females by males (P.J. Garson & A.M. Rosser, unpubl.) suggests a promiscuous mating system resembling those found in ground squirrels *Spermophilus* spp. (Dunford 1977; Michener 1979; Sherman 1980, 1981; Hanken & Sherman 1981), the eastern chipmunk *Tamias striatus* L. (Yahner 1978), and the European hare *Lepus europaeus* L. (Holley & Greenwood 1984).

In summary, the warren-based groups on Chalk, similar to those seen in both enclosed populations (see Garson 1982 for review) and some free-living ones (Myers & Schneider 1964; Parer 1977), reflect competition between females for a clumped and limited supply of nest sites. The resulting aggregated distribution of females leads to territorial defence amongst males. The more dispersed pattern of female distribution on Sand is a consequence of the lack of competition for burrows. Males there adopt an opportunistic strategy of guarding oestrus females when they are present within their ranges because they only have to be present for a relatively short and particular period to ensure paternity, but share only part of the range of each of a large number of females and thus cannot monopolize matings with any of them through territorial defence against other males.

Population dynamics

On Sand there was a negative correlation between the growth rate of juveniles and the population density of rabbits in different years; adults there were lighter than on Chalk. This would be expected of a population ultimately limited by food, although it does not necessarily imply that a lack of food was the direct cause of mortality. In order to meet its energetic requirements the rabbit has to spend a high proportion of its time feeding (Gibb, Ward & Ward 1978). The territorial defence of areas containing the necessary food supply would progressively reduce the time available for feeding with increasing density. In Australia it is known that the social structure of group-living populations breaks down during periods of extreme food shortage (Myers & Poole 1961). Thus, the economics of resource defence dictate that rabbits faced with a limited food supply should compete by consuming as much of the available food as quickly as they can, primarily be spending more time active above ground (Gibb 1979). Consequently the Sand population should exhibit the relationship between mortality and population density (Bellows 1981) and the population instability (Hassell 1976) expected from scramble competition. The data are sparse but the results are suggestive that this is so.

On Chalk, there is evidence of space defence within both sexes, and it may be that despotic behaviour limits the breeding density of each sex, leading to the mortality-density relationship shown in Fig. 32.5 and the relatively stable breeding population density. This is consistent with contest competition being important in determining the dynamics of this population. The alternative extreme case of scramble competition assumes that all individuals are of equal competitive ability. This assumption is not met properly, even in the Sand population, where adults survived better than juveniles and females better than males (P.J. Garson & I.C. Macdonald, unpubl.).

Overall we have obtained quite good qualitative agreement between the population dynamics we have observed and what might have been predicted if the data on social behaviour had been collected alone. Furthermore, the essential differences between the populations, both in terms of social structure and population processes, are adequately explained in terms of the economics of limiting resource defence by individuals.

ACKNOWLEDGMENTS

We thank the Nature Conservancy Council for permission to work within Lindisfarne and Aston Rowant National Nature Reserves. The Natural Environment Research Council provided a postgraduate studentship for D.P.C. and a research grant (GR3/4534) to P.J.G. P.J.G. acknowledges additional support from Royal Society and Newcastle University, and thanks Alison Rosser and Ian Macdonald, in particular, for much help in collecting, collating and analysing field data. D.P.C. thanks Graham Christer for extensive help in the field during the latter stages of his study. We also thank Peter Diggle, Gordon Beaks and Les Huson for statistical and computing advice. Richard Brown, Andy Hart, Richard Sibly and two referees gave us helpful comments on earlier drafts.

REFERENCES

Alexander, R.D. (1974). The evolution of social behaviour. *Annual Review of Ecology and Systematics*, **5**, 325–383.

Altman, S.A., Wagner, S.S. & Lenington, S. (1977). Two models for the evolution of polygyny. *Behavioural Ecology and Sociobiology*, **2**, 397–410.

Armitage, K.B. (1962). Social behaviour of a colony of yellow-bellied marmots *Marmota flaviventris*. *Animal Behaviour*, **10**, 319–331.

Armitage, K.B. (1974). Male behaviour and territoriality in the yellow-bellied marmot. *Journal of Zoology*, **172**, 233–265.

Bell, D.J. (1983). Mate choice in the European rabbit. *Mate Choice* (Ed. by P.P.G. Bateson), pp. 211–223. Cambridge University Press, Cambridge.

Bellows, T.S. Jr (1981). The descriptive properties of some models for density dependence. *Journal of Animal Ecology*, **50**, 139–156.

Bertram, B.C.R. (1978). Living in groups: predators and prey. *Behavioural Ecology: an Evolutionary Approach* (Ed. by J.R. Krebs & N.B. Davies), pp. 64–97. Blackwell Scientific Publications, Oxford.

Brown, J.L. (1964). The evolution of diversity in avian territorial systems. *Wilson Bulletin*, **76**, 160–169.

Bull, P.C. (1958). Incidence of coccidia (Sporozoa in wild rabbits *Oryctolagus cuniculus* (L) in Hawke's Bay New Zealand. *New Zealand Journal of Science*, **1**, 289–329.

Clutton-Brock, T.H., Guinness, F.E. & Albon, S.D. (1982). *Red Deer: Behaviour and Ecology of Two Sexes.* Edinburgh University Press, Edinburgh.

Clutton-Brock, T.H. & Harvey, P.H. (1976). Evolutionary rules and primate societies. *Growing Points in Ethology* (Ed. by P.P.G. Bateson & R.A. Hinde) pp. 195–237. Cambridge University Press, Cambridge.

Clutton-Brock, T.H. & Harvey, P.H. (1978). Mammals, resources and reproductive strategies. *Nature*, **273**, 191–195.

Cowan, D.P. (1983). *Aspects of the behavioural ecology of a free-living population of the European wild rabbit (Oryctolagus cuniculus L.) in Southern England.* Unpublished Ph.D thesis, University of London.

Cowan D.P. (in press). The use of ferrets for the study and management of the European wild rabbit (*Oryctolagus cuniculus*) *Journal of Zoology* (*London*).

Daly, J.C. (1981). Effects of social organisation and environmental diversity on determining the genetic structure of a population of the wild rabbit (*Oryctolagus cuniculus*). *Evolution*, **35**, 689–706.

Downhower, J.F. & Armitage, K.B. (1971). The yellow-bellied marmot and the evolution of polygyny. *American Naturalist*, **105**, 355–370.

Dunford, C. (1977). Social system of round tailed ground squirrels. *Animal Behaviour*, **25**, 885–906.

Dunnet, G.M. (1956). Growth rates of young rabbits, *Oryctolagus cuniculus*. *CSIRO Wildlife Research*, **1**, 66–67.

Elliot, J.M. (1971). *Some methods for the statistical analysis of benthic invertebrates*. Scientific publication 25. Freshwater Biological Association, Great Britain.

Emlen, S.T. & Oring, L.W. (1977). Ecology, sexual selection and the evolution of mating systems. *Science*, **197**, 215–223.

Foltz, D.W. and Hoogland, J.L. (1981). Analysis of the mating system in the black-tailed prairie dog (*Cynomys ludovicianus*) by likelihood of paternity. *Journal of Mammalogy*, **62**, 706–712.

Fretwell, S.D. & Lucas, H.L. (1970). On territorial behaviour and other factors influencing habitat distribution in birds. I. Theoretical development. *Acta Biotheoretica*, **19**, 16–36.

Garson, P.J. (1982). Social organisation and reproduction in the rabbit: a review. *Proceedings of the World Lagomorph Conference 1979* (Ed. by K. Myers & C.D. McInness), pp. 256–270. University of Quelph, Canada.

Gibb, J.A. (1979). Factors affecting population density in the wild rabbit, *Oryctolagus cuniculus* (L.) and their relevance to small mammals. *Evolutionary Ecology* (Ed. by B. Stonehouse & C.M. Perrins), pp. 33–46, Macmillan, London.

Gibb, J.A., Ward, C.P. & Ward, G.D. (1978). Natural control of a population of rabbits, *Oryctolagus cuniculus* (L.), for ten years in Kourarau enclosure. *New Zealand Department of Scientific and Industrial Research Bulletin No. 223*. Wellington, New Zealand.

Hanken, J. & Sherman, P.W. (1981). Multiple paternity in ground squirrel litters. *Science*, **212**, 351–353.

Hassell, M.P. (1975). Density dependence in single species populations. *Journal of Animal Ecology*, **44**, 283–295.

Hassell, M.P. (1976). *The Dynamics of Competition and Predation*. Edward Arnold, London.

Henderson, B.A. (1979). Regulation of the size of the breeding population in the european rabbit, *Oryctolagus cuniculus*, by social behaviour. *Journal of Applied Ecology*, **16**, 383–392.

Holley, A.J.F. & Greenwood, P.J. (1984). The myth of the mad March Hare. *Nature*, **309**, 549–550.

Hoogland, J.L. (1981). Nepotism and co-operative breeding in the black-tailed prairie dog: *Cynomys ludoviciamus*. *Natural Selection and Social Behaviour: Recent Research and New Theory* (Ed. by R.D. Alexander & D.W. Tinkle), pp. 283–310, Chiron, New York.

Horn, H.S. (1968). The adaptive significance of colonial nesting in the Brewer's Blackbird (*Euphagus cyanocephalus*). *Ecology*, **49**, 682–694.

Krebs, J.R. (1971). Territory and breeding density in the Great Tit *Parus major*. *Ecology*, **52**, 2–22.

Lazarus, J. (1982). Competition and conflict in animals. *Cooperation and Conflict In Humans and Animals* (Ed. by A.M. Colman), pp. 26–56 Nostrand Reinhold, United Kingdom.

Leboef, B.J. & Peterson, R.S. (1969). Social status and mating activity in elephant seals. *Science*, **163**, 91–93.

Lockley, R.M. (1961). Social structure and stress in the rabbit warren. *Journal of Animal Ecology*, **30**, 385–423.

Michener, G.R. (1979). Spatial relationships and social organisation of adult Richardson's ground squirrels. *Canadian Journal of Zoology*, **57**, 125–139.

Myers, K. & Poole, W.E. (1959). A study of the biology of the wild rabbit, *Oryctolagus cuniculus*, in confined populations, I. The effects of density on home range and formation of breeding groups. *CSIRO Wildlife Research*, **4**, 14–26.

Myers, K. & Poole, W.E. (1961). A study of the biology of the wild rabbit, *Oryctolagus cuniculus* (L.), in confined populations, II. The effects of season and population increase on behaviour. *CSIRO Wildlife Research*, **6**, 1–41.

Myers, K. & Poole, W.E. (1962). A study of the biology of the wild rabbit, *Oryctolagus cuniculus* (L.), in confined populations, III. Reproduction. *Australian Journal of Zoology*, **10**, 225–267.

Myers, K. & Schneider, E.C. (1964). Observations on reproduction, mortality and behaviour in a small free-living population of wild rabbits. *CSIRO Wildlife Research*, 9, 138–143.

Mykytowyz, R. (1959). Social behaviour of an experimental colony of wild rabbits, *Oryctolagus cuniculus* (L.), I. First breeding season. *CSIRO Wildlife Research*, 4, 1–13.

Mykytowycz, R. (1960). Social behaviour of an experimental colony of wild rabbits, *Oryctolagus cuniculus* (L.), III. Second breeding season. *CSIRO Wildlife Research*, 5, 1–20.

Mykytowycz, R. (1961). Social behaviour of an experimental colony of wild rabbits, *Oryctolagus cuniculus* (L.), IV. Conclusion, outbreak of myxomatosis, third breeding season and starvation. *CSIRO Wildlife Research*, 6, 142–155.

Mykytowycz, R. & Rowley, I. (1958). Continuous observation of the activity of the wild rabbit, *Oryctolagus cuniculus* (L.), during 24-hour periods. *CSIRO Wildlife Research*, 3, 26–31.

Parer, I. (1977). The population ecology of the wild rabbit, *Oryctolagus cuniculus* (L.), in a mediterranean type climate in New South Wales. *Australian Wildlife Research*, 4, 171–205.

Rowell, T.E. (1972). *The Social Behaviour of Monkeys*. Penguin, Harmondsworth.

Schwartz, O.A. & Armitage, K.B. (1980). Genetic variation in social mammals: the marmot model. *Science*, 207, 665–667.

Sherman. P.W. (1980). The limits of Ground Squirrel nepotism. *Sociobiology: Beyond Nature/Nurture* (Ed. by G.W. Barlow & J. Silverberg), pp. 505–544. Westview, Boulder.

Sherman. P.W. (1981). Reproductive competition and infanticide in Belding's ground squirrels and other mammals. *Natural Selection and Social Behaviour* (Ed. by R.D. Alexander & D.W. Tinkle), pp. 311–331, Blackwell Scientific Publications, Oxford.

Southern, H.E.N. (1940). The ecology and population biology of the wild rabbit (*Oryctolagus cuniculus*). *Annals of Applied Biology*, 27, 509–526.

Trivers, R.L. (1972). Parental investment and sexual selection. *Sexual Selection and the Descent of Man* (Ed. by B. Cambell), pp. 156–179, Aldine Chicago.

Varley, G.C., Gradwell, G.R. & Hassell, M.P. (1973). *Insect Population Biology: an Analytical Approach*. Blackwell Scientific Publications, Oxford.

Watson, J.S. & Tyndale-Biscoe, C.H. (1953). The apophyseal line as an age indicator for the wild rabbit, *Oryctolagus cuniculus* (L.). *New Zealand Journal of Science and Technology. B*, 34, 427–435.

Wittenberger, J.F. (1979). The evolution of mating systems in birds and mammals. *Handbook of Behavioural Neurobiology, 3. Social Behaviour and Communications* (Ed. by P. Marler & J.C. van den Bergh), pp. 271–350. Plenum, New York.

Wittenberger, J.F. (1980). Group size and polygamy in social mammals. *American Naturalist*, 115, 197–222.

Williams, G.C. (1966). *Adaptation and Natural Selection: a Critique of Some Current Evolutionary Thought*. Princeton University Press, Princeton, New Jersey.

Wood, D.H. (1980). The demography of a rabbit population in an arid region of New South Wales, Australia. *Journal of Animal Ecology*, 49, 55–80.

Yahner, R.H. (1978). Adaptive nature of the social system and behaviour in the Eastern chipmunk, *Tamius striatus. Behavioural Ecology and Sociobiology*, 3, 397–427.

33. COMPETITION AND POPULATION REGULATION IN SOCIAL MAMMALS

T. H. CLUTTON-BROCK AND S. D. ALBON

Large Animal Research Group, Department of Zoology, University of Cambridge, Cambridge

SUMMARY

The breeding system typical of a species is likely to influence many aspects of its population demography. Where females live in groups, competition for food is common between group members and dominant females typically have priority of access to resources and show superior breeding success to subordinates. As group size increases, reproductive success declines but dispersal does not necessarily increase. As a result, population regulation may commonly occur at the level of the group, rather than at the level of the population, and this may affect both population stability and the competitive strategies of group members.

Female sociality also has a profound effect on males since it permits the development of polygyny, which is commonly associated with sexual dimorphism in body size. In sexually dimorphic species, males are more likely to die during periods of food shortage than females, both as juveniles and adults. This raises the intriguing possibility that sexual selection is commonly associated with asymmetries in scramble competition which favour females.

Since social behaviour affects most aspects of competition there may be little value in attempting to distinguish between species that are regulated by behaviour and those that are regulated by food availability directly. Instead, it may be more useful to investigate how different behavioural mechanisms contribute to population regulation.

INTRODUCTION

Research on rodents over the last two decades has produced extensive evidence that behaviour can limit population density through changes in social behaviour and dispersal (Krebs 1964, 1971, 1979; Gaines & McCleneghan 1980; Tamarin 1983). In apparent contrast, demographic research on large mammals indicates that many populations are resource limited and there is little evidence that behavioural mechanisms regulate population density (Caughley 1970, 1976a,b; Sinclair 1977; McCullough 1979; Fowler 1981).

Recently Caughley & Krebs (1983) have suggested that while population density in small mammals is regulated by intrinsic mechanisms 'built into the population and transmitted by its genes', population regulation in large mammals is extrinsic—'a mechanical consequence of interaction between the population and the organisms providing its food'. Their explanation for this contrast is based on the argument that, on account of their high potential rate of increase, small mammals are more likely than large ones to drive their prey to extinction. Consequently, intrinsic mechanisms for regulating density are more likely to have been favoured by group or individual selection.

Unlike Caughley & Krebs (1983), we believe that the paucity of evidence that behavioural factors play an important part in regulating population density among large mammals is probably a consequence of the reliance of demographic studies on count and carcass data. Field studies of carnivores, primates and ungulates which have been able to identify individuals and to examine the effects of age, social rank and genealogy on reproductive success and survival typically emphasize the importance of social behaviour in affecting demographic processes (Bertram 1975; Zimen 1976; Dittus 1979, 1980; Clutton-Brock *et al.* 1982a,b, 1984a). Although no single study of a large mammal fulfils all the conditions necessary to demonstrate that population density is regulated by social behaviour (Watson & Moss 1970), there is abundant evidence that behavioural mechanisms play an important part in most demographic processes and can operate in a density-dependent fashion (see below). It would be surprising if they did not also play a part in population regulation.

By this, we do not intend to suggest either that behavioural factors operate independently of food availability or that the mechanisms regulating population density are similar in all mammals. We suspect that the usual effect of behaviour is to concentrate the effects of food shortage on particular individuals. Species differences in the size and structure of female groups influence the frequency of female dispersal and this may have profound effects on the way in which population density is regulated. In many large mammals, females live and breed in the matrilineal groups where they were born and female dispersal is uncommon, even when local population density has increased to a point at which reproductive success is depressed (see below). In these species, it appears unlikely that dispersal regulates population density and reproductive suppression or mortality *in situ* may be more important. In other species—including those where females are solitary or monogamous—the majority of daughters disperse from their mothers' home ranges and dispersal associated with reduced fecundity or increased mortality among dispersers may play a more important role in regulating density.

The relationship between social organization and dispersal may help to explain the apparent difference in population regulation between large and small mammals for the available data suggest that closed and cohesive matrilineal groups and low rates of female dispersal are more commonly found in large mammals than small ones (Gaines & McClenaghan 1980; Greenwood 1980; Wrangham 1980; Eisenberg 1981). Our contention—that it is the species' typical pattern of social organization rather than body size *per se* that affects the frequency of dispersal—is supported by evidence of infrequent female dispersal among small mammals living in cohesive matrilineal groups (Hoogland 1981) and of frequent dispersal among large species where females are solitary or monogamous (Zimen 1976; Geist 1974a; Tilson 1981).

However, even if female dispersal proves to be comparatively unimportant in regulating population density in many large mammals living in close-knit matrilineal groups, other behavioural mechanisms may be involved. Grouping can be expected to intensify local competition for resources (Alexander 1974) and to provide individuals with a variety of opportunities for increasing their own access to limited resources at the expense of other members of the same or neighbouring groups (Wynne Edwards 1962; Clutton-Brock & Harvey 1976; Wrangham 1980, 1981; Macdonald 1983; Houston & Davies, p. 471). Among social mammals there is extensive evidence of reproductive suppression of subordinate females and of socially-induced mortality among juveniles or adults.

In this paper, we review some of the demographic consequences of female sociality on females and males. Though we rely principally on published studies, we also draw on information collected between 1972 and 1984 on the red deer population of the 12 km² North Block of Rhum where the annual cull was terminated in 1972 and an initial population of 57 hinds and 124 stags changed to 165 and 107 respectively (Clutton-Brock, Guinness & Albon 1982b). During this period, all animals regularly using the study area could be recognized as individuals and records were kept of their habitat use, social behaviour and reproductive success (see Clutton-Brock *et al.* 1982b).

FEMALE SOCIALITY AND COMPETITION BETWEEN FEMALES

The costs of sociality to females

Direct competition for resources between females belonging to the same group is common in social vertebrates (Alexander 1974). For example, female vervet monkeys regularly compete for food and water, and dominant individuals consistently displace subordinates from preferred feeding sites (Wrangham 1981; Whitten 1983). Feeding competition for food and stable individual differences in resource access are found in a wide variety of social vertebrates including other primates (Southwick 1967; Dittus 1977, 1979), carnivores (Lamprecht 1978; Macdonald 1980) and ungulates (Clutton-Brock, Greenwood & Powell 1976).

Subordinate females commonly show lower reproductive success and survival than dominant animals, e.g. gelada baboons (Dunbar 1980b), toque macaques (Dittus 1980), dwarf mongooses (Rood 1980), elephant seals (Reiter, Panken & LeBoeuf 1981), and red deer (see Table 33.1), though this is

TABLE 33.1. Measures of breeding performance in hinds above median rank versus those below it (from Clutton-Brock *et al.* 1984a). Data from cohorts born between 1967 and 1978. The analyses control for the effects of age as well as for geographical variation in reproductive performance within the study area. All *P* values are for two-tailed tests

	Subordinate	Dominant	Significance level
Median age of first breeding (years)	3·90	3·48	$P < 0.05$
Fecundity rate (calves/year²)	0·65	0·68	NS
% conceiving before median conception date	38	58	$P < 0.05$
% changing into winter coat before 1 November	35	62	$P < 0.02$
Median weight of calves at birth (kg)	6·4	6·8	$P < 0.001$
% male calf mortality	41·5	21·7	$0.1 > P > 0.05$
% female calf mortality	25·0	31·3	NS
% male yearling mortality	29·2	8·5	$0.1 > P > 0.05$
% female yearling mortality	12·5	11·1	NS
Mean life-span (years)	9	11	$P < 0.05$
Median lifetime reproductive success (calves reared to 1 year old)	2·3	6·0	$P < 0.05$

not always the case (Fedigan 1983). The offspring of subordinate mothers may inherit their mothers' low rank and inferior reproductive performance, e.g. primates (Silk 1983), and red deer (Clutton-Brock, Albon & Guinness 1984a; see Table 33.1).

Group size and competition between females

Rising group size increases both direct and indirect competition between females. Although in some social vertebrates, the area occupied by a group increases with its size (Chivers 1969; Wolfenden & Fitzpatrick 1978; Takasaki 1981; Macdonald 1983) group size and population density typically increase together (see Mittermeier 1973; Hoogland 1981; Dittus 1980).

As might be expected, the frequency of aggressive interactions at feeding sites also rises with group size (Wrangham 1977; Waser 1977; Clutton-Brock *et al.* 1982b). The effects of increasing group size on feeding competition may be most intense among carnivores and frugivores where preferred food sources are clumped (Clutton-Brock & Harvey 1978) or where breeding females depend on food brought to them by other group members (e.g. Malcolm & Marten 1982), but increasing group size may also be important in herbivores. In red deer, members of large social groups spend less time feeding and more time moving than members of small ones and feed less on preferred plant communities and more on less heavily used areas where standing crop is greater but food quality is inferior (see Table 33.2).

TABLE 33.2. Feeding behaviour of red deer hinds belonging to matrilineal groups below average size (5 animals) versus those above it. Estimates based on 24 full-day watches of hinds > 2 years old belonging to large groups and 24 belonging to small groups in March and April 1983. A matrilineal group is the total number of related females sharing a common home range (Clutton-Brock *et al.* 1982a)

	%daytime spent:		
Activity	members of large groups	members of small groups	Significance level
Feeding	63·5	72·8	$P < 0.05$
Moving	3·9	2·6	$P < 0.01$
On herb-rich and *Agrostis/Festuca* grasslands	30·6	59·8	$0.1 > P > 0.05$
On *Calluna* and *Molinia* dominated communities	35·1	17·7	$P < 0.05$
On seaweed and litoral debris	10·8	1·8	$P < 0.01$

Group size and female reproductive success

Recent studies of social mammals provide evidence that the average reproductive success of group members declines with increasing group size. In black-tailed prairie dogs, females live in matrilineal groups (coteries) and both fecundity and offspring survival decline with increasing group size (Hoogland 1981). Both in elephants and social primates, the ratio of juveniles to adults declines in large groups (Laws, Parker & Johnstone 1975; Schaik 1984). And in red deer, hinds belonging to matrilines of above average size breed later and less frequently and produce lighter calves which are more likely to die than animals belonging to small matrilines (see Table 33.3). In the red deer study, it was possible to exclude the alternative possibility that reduction in breeding success in large groups was a consequence of increased intergroup competition, for the extent to which the breeding success of different matrilines

TABLE 33.3. Effects of matrilineal group size on reproductive success in red deer hinds on Rhum. A matrilineal group is the total number of related females sharing a common home range (from Clutton-Brock. *et al.* 1982a)

	Members of large groups	Members of small groups	Significance level
Median number of calves born per individual per year	0·695	0·847	$P < 0·05$
Median number of calves reared to 1 year old per individual per year	0·500	0·675	$P < 0·01$
% male calves dying in first year of life	36·4	16·2	$P < 0·001$
% female calves dying in first year of life	22·1	24·1	NS
% male yearlings dying	22·7	6·5	$P < 0·01$
% female yearlings dying	9·1	9·3	NS

declined over a 12-year period was correlated with the extent to which matriline size increased (Clutton-Brock *et al.* 1982a). In addition, a multiple regression of reproductive success on the frequency with which relatives versus unrelated animals were seen in their home range showed that only the first measure was inversely correlated with matriline size.

Reproductive suppression

Though competition between females may usually influence female breeding success through its effect on food access, sociality can have direct effects on reproduction. In naked mole rats, some females never breed and reproductive suppression appears to be irreversible (Jarvis 1981). In many social carnivores, subordinate females are inhibited from breeding by the presence of dominant females and any offspring they produce are likely to be attacked (Zimen 1976; Frame *et al.* 1979; Malcolm & Marten 1982; Packard & Mech 1980; Rood 1980; Macdonald 1980).

Similar but less complete suppression of reproduction in subordinate females occurs in other social mammals. In some species, dominant females harass subordinates when they come into oestrus, increasing the frequency of anovulatory cycles and amenorrhea, e.g. marmots (Downhower & Armitage 1971; Wasser & Barash 1983), gelada baboons (Dunbar 1980a,b), and yellow baboons (Wasser 1983). In others, dominant females attack the offspring of subordinates, either killing them directly as in elephant seals (LeBoeuf, Whiting & Gantt 1972; Reiter, Panken & LeBoeuf 1981) and Belding's ground squirrel (Sherman 1981), or increasing mortality through starvation as in toque macaques (Dittus 1977) and bonnet macaques (Silk 1983). Attacks by female conspecifics can represent an important source of juvenile mortality: for example, in Belding's ground squirrels, conspecifics kill 8% of all pups born and infanticide is the single largest cause of juvenile mortality in most years (Sherman 1981).

Where competition occurs principally within groups, females living in matrilineal groups might increase their fitness by eliminating the daughters of other mothers since they represent the future competitors of their own offspring (Silk 1983). Increased harassment of female juveniles by adult females, associated with reduced survival compared with that of juvenile males, occurs in toque and bonnet macaques (Dittus 1977, 1979; Silk *et al.* 1981). In pigtail macaques there is even some evidence that dominant females are more likely to attack and wound subordinates carrying female fetuses than those carrying males, leading to an increase in the frequency of abortions.

Group size and dispersal

Where reproductive success declines with group size, females born into large groups might be expected to disperse (Clutton-Brock & Harvey 1976; Macdonald 1980; Hoogland 1981). In species where breeding females are solitary or monogamous, young females commonly leave their birth site (Tilson 1981; Moore & Ali 1984) though they may not move as far as males (Greenwood 1980) and sometimes adopt ranges overlapping those of their mothers (Lockie 1966; Montgomerie & Sunquist 1978). In group-living species where a single dominant female is responsible for virtually all breeding attempts, dispersal of females is also common, e.g. red fox (Macdonald 1980), Cape hunting dog (Frame *et al.* 1979) and dwarf mongoose (Rood 1980). However, where social groups consist of matrilineal relatives, female dispersal often appears of be uncommon, even from groups which have reached the point at which reproductive success is depressed. For example, in Hoogland's (1981) population of prairie dogs, 90% of females (but less than 5% of males) were still in their natal coterie in their second year of life and emigration by adult females was infrequent. In the red deer population of Rhum, only two females dispersed from their natal area in 12 years, though some groups changed or extended their ranges (Clutton-Brock *et al.*1982b).

Dispersal is known to be associated with high mortality rates in many mammals, e.g. musk rats (Errington 1963), rodents (Christian 1970), white-tailed deer (Hawkins 1971) and red fox (Macdonald 1983), but may have particularly high costs in species that live in matrilineal groups because group members behave nepotistically towards relatives and are intolerant of unrelated animals, e.g. lions (Bertram 1976), primates (Clutton-Brock &

Harvey 1976; Wrangham 1980), rodents (Sherman 1980; Hoogland 1981) and ungulates (Clutton-Brock et al. 1982b). In species that live in matrilineal groups, dispersing females may not be allowed to form resident groups and may be unlikely to find unoccupied habitat (Hoogland 1981; Clutton-Brock et al. 1982b). It is interesting to note that where female dispersal occurs in matrilineal species, it commonly involves either movement by two or more animals at the same time or group splitting, e.g. prairie dogs (Hoogland 1981), Japanese macaques (Sugiyama & Ohsawa 1982; Furuya 1973) and that the frequency of both increase with group size and population density (Furuya 1968, 1969; Masui et al. 1973; Koyama, Novikoshi & Mano 1975).

FEMALE SOCIALITY AND MALE MORTALITY

Polygyny and the energetic costs of sexual dimorphism

Female sociality also has important effects on males. The aggregation of females in defensible groups permits the development of polygyny (Bradbury & Vehrencamp 1977; Emlen & Oring 1977; Clutton-Brock & Harvey 1980) and is typically associated with intense competition between males for access to females (Geist 1971, 1974b; Clutton-Brock et al. 1979). Direct consequences of intense competition between males include a high frequency of fighting and injury (Geist 1971), reduced food intake by adult males in the breeding season (Kay & Staines 1981) and poor body condition at the onset of winter (see Mitchell, McCowan & Nicholson 1976).

The evolutionary consequences of polygyny include sexual dimorphism in adult body size (Clutton-Brock, Harvey & Rudder 1977; Alexander et al. 1979) and in juvenile growth rates (Clutton-Brock et al. 1982b). As a result, the absolute nutritional requirements of adult males commonly exceed those of females (e.g. Coelho 1974) while, among juveniles, requirements per kilo also exceed those of females (Glucksman 1974; Fiala 1981). For example, Morrison (1948) calculates that young rams must be fed 15% more nutrients than ewes of similar age and weight while studies of wild ungulates show that juvenile males suck more than females, e.g. red deer (Clutton-Brock et al. 1981) and feral goats (Pickering 1983).

In most dimorphic species, the greater body size of adult males gives them priority of access to food resources over females (Schaller 1972; Kleiman 1977; Clutton-Brock et al 1982b). However, this will not compensate for the greater nutritional requirements of males among species where the rate of food intake is not at least proportional to body weight$^{0.75}$ (Clutton-Brock &

Harvey 1983). In addition, this advantage is not shared by juvenile males which are usually subordinate to females and their high nutritional requirements may be a severe disadvantage in times of food shortage (Case 1978).

Sex differences in adult mortality

Increased mortality and shorter life-spans in adult males compared with females have been documented in a wide variety of mammals (Ralls, Brownell & Ballou 1980). In part, increased mortality is a direct consequence of injuries resulting from breeding competition; for example, in polygynous ungulates, between 5 and 10% of breeding males may be injured or killed each year, e.g. mountain sheep (Geist 1971), red deer (Müller-Using & Schloeth 1967; Clutton-Brock *et al.* 1979), reindeer (Bergerud 1973, 1974a,b) and musk ox (Wilkinson & Shank 1979). Males are also more likely to die than females during periods of food shortage in dimorphic mammals, e.g. red deer (Ahlen 1965; Sobanskii 1979), elk (Anderson 1958; Flook 1970), reindeer and caribou (Bannfield 1954; Klein 1968) and wildebeest (Talbot & Talbot 1963), and a similar tendency has been found in dimorphic birds (Latham 1947; Lack 1954; Howe 1977). In one island population of reindeer which fell from over a thousand to 42 in the course of a year, only one of the survivors was a male (Klein 1968).

Several reviews have suggested that sex differences in adult mortality among mammals increase with the degree of sexual dimorphism (Stirling 1975; Ralls *et al.* 1980; Clutton-Brock *et al.* 1982b). Among birds, a significant correlation between male mortality and sexual dimorphism in body weight has recently been demonstrated across different species of Icteridae (Searcy & Yasukawa 1981).

Sex differences in juvenile mortality

Sex differences in survival are also found among juveniles. In most social mammals, adolescent males disperse from their natal group (Greenwood 1980) and consequently show higher rates of mortality (see above). Higher mortality among male juveniles also occurs before dispersal (Clutton-Brock *et al.* 1982b) as well as in captive populations (Glucksman 1974; Widdowson 1976; McClure 1981). Sex differences in juvenile mortality are most pronounced in strongly dimorphic species (Clutton-Brock, Albon & Guinness 1984b) and increase during periods of harsh weather or food shortage, e.g. Soay sheep (Grubb 1974), wildebeest (Child 1972), wapiti (Flook 1970) and caribou (Bergerud 1971). For example, one experimental study of wood rats

(*Neotama* spp.) which maintained breeding females on *ad lib* or restricted diets, showed that food shortage had a greater effect on the growth and survival of males than females and that the sex ratio of pups born to food-restricted mothers fell from 50% at birth to 29% by 20 days, while that of controls remained at 50% (McClure 1981). Stressful conditions may also cause sex differences in mortality before birth: for example, female laboratory mice reared on low fat diets show reduced fecundity and produce relatively few male pups (24% male) compared with those reared on adequate diets (Rivers & Crawford 1974; see also Lane & Hyde 1973; Moriya & Hiroshige 1978).

Two other explanations of increased mortality of male juveniles have been suggested. First, Myers (1978) argues that increased male juvenile mortality in mammals results from the fact that males are the heterogametic sex and may consequently suffer from the effects of deleterious recessive alleles on the X chromosome. Second, Trivers & Willard (1973) have suggested that where parents conceive an offspring of the more expensive sex but cannot invest enough resources to give it a reasonable chance of breeding successfully, they should terminate investment rather than waste it (Trivers & Willard 1973). However, neither provides a completely satisfactory explanation: the first because increased mortality of juvenile males also occurs in birds where males are the homogametic sex (Trivers 1972; Howe 1977); the second because, when food is short, differential mortality also occurs among juveniles housed separately from their parents (MacArthur & Baillie 1932; Widdowson 1976).

Differential mortality and population density

In several species, there is evidence that food shortage is associated with increased male mortality (Klein 1968; McClure 1981) but the relationship between population density and differential mortality has rarely been investigated. In the red deer population of Rhum, the mean age at death of stags that reached the age of 3 years fell from 14 to 9 years, as female numbers increased from 57 to 165, while the mean age at death of hinds remained constant (Clutton-Brock *et al*, 1982b). Sex differences in juvenile mortality also increased with population density (Fig. 33.1). Moreover, they were particularly pronounced in large matrilines (Table 33.3) and among the offspring of subordinate animals (Table 33.1). As a result of the relationship between population density and differential mortality, the adult sex ratio became progressively biased as density increased. High population density is also commonly associated with an excess of adult females in other deer populations (Clutton-Brock *et al.* 1982b) as well as in other ungulates (Cowan 1950).

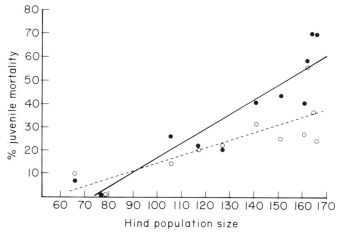

FIG. 33.1. Changes in mortality during the first 2 years of life among males (●) and females (○) born between 1971 and 1982 in the red deer population of the North Block of Rhum (Regression equations. Males: $Y = 0.662x - 45.45$, $r = 0.913$; $F_{1,9} = 43.8$, $P < 0.001$. Females: $y = 0.328x - 18.487$, $r = 0.788$; $F_{1,9} = 12.69$, $P < 0.01$: Difference in slopes: $F_{1,18} = 4.96$, $P < 0.05$).

DISCUSSION

The involvement of behavioural processes in most aspects of female competition among social species suggests that behaviour is likely to play an important role in most demographic processes. Consequently, it may often be impossible or unprofitable to attempt to distinguish between populations that are regulated by behaviour and those that are regulated by resource availability directly. The original interest in this dichotomy stemmed largely from the suggestion that group selection had produced behavioural mechanisms specifically adapted to regulating population density (Wynne Edwards 1962). However, there is little evidence that this is the case and it is now appreciated that classical group selection theories of adaptive population regulation face formidable obstacles, especially in species where the frequency of group extinction or disbanding is low (Maynard Smith 1964), as in most social mammals. Like so many juxtapositions, the contrast between intrinsic and extrinsic limiting mechanisms masks other, more important questions about population regulation.

First, at what level does population regulation occur? Several studies of social species suggest that regulation may occur through density-dependent processes operating at the level of the social group rather than at the level of the population as a whole (Furuya 1969; Zimen 1976; Dittus 1977, 1979) and, if so, this may have important repercussions both on individual strategies (Silk 1983) and on population stability (Lomnicki 1982). In practice, the distinction between the effects of group size and those of overall population density reflects the relative importance of intra- versus intergroup competition, and this probably varies between species. Intragroup competition may be most important where the home ranges of neighbouring groups overlap little and average range size is unaffected by increasing group size or population density (see Kruuk & Macdonald, p. 521). Conversely, intergroup competition may be most important where range overlap is extensive (as in many herd-forming ungulates) or where rising population density is associated with a marked reduction in average range size.

Second, to what extent do different behavioural mechanisms contribute to population regulation in different species? In many rodents, dispersal evidently plays a key role in regulating density (Krebs 1978; Gaines & McClenaghan 1980; Caughley & Krebs 1983). We suspect that female dispersal may also be important in many solitary, asocial and monogamous large mammals—including both large animals such as moose (Geist 1974b), tigers (Sunquist 1981) and orangs (Rodman 1977)—as well as in those social mammals where males remain in their natal area and females disperse, such as the African wild dog and the red colobus (Greenwood 1980). Conversely, reproductive suppression and food limitation *in situ* may have a greater effect in social species living in cohesive matrilineal groups (see Hoogland 1981; Rood 1980). Several different mechanisms may be involved in these species, including aggression directed at adolescent females, infanticide and socially-induced adult mortality (see above). The extent to which these events increase in frequency with rising group size or population density and their relative importance in regulating animal numbers are topics that still need to be examined.

Third, how are male numbers regulated? In no species do we know much about the regulation of male numbers. The prevalence of male dispersal in mammals (Greenwood 1980) suggests that immigration and emigration may be important, but few studies have yet been able to examine the effects of population density on these processes or their contribution to population regulation (see Redfield, Taitt & Krebs 1978a,b). Where males defend feeding territories, territorial behaviour may limit male numbers but, in many social mammals, males only defend females or mating territories during the breeding season (Owen Smith 1977; Eisenberg 1981). In these species, it may be that male density is regulated by resource access outside the breeding season. In sexually dimorphic species (which include the majority of large mammals), the greater susceptibility of juvenile and adult males to food shortage raises the intriguing possibility that, like competition between species (Lawton &

Hassell 1981), competition between the sexes may often be asymmetrical and male recruitment may be influenced principally by female density (Clutton-Brock *et al.* 1982b; Clutton-Brock & Harvey 1983). In contrast, in species where the sexes rely on different resources (e.g. Gautier-Hion 1980), competition for food may occur mainly among members of the same sex and the resources limiting population density may differ between males and females.

Though, in this paper, we have concentrated on the effects of social behaviour on population demography in group-living species, complex social interactions may also have a profound effect on population dynamics in species where females spend much of their time alone. A growing number of studies are reporting that females commonly adopt home ranges overlapping those of their relatives (see Krebs, p. 295; Moss & Watson, p. 275) and that apparently homogeneous populations in fact consist of a number of clusters of related females sharing overlapping home ranges. In such cases, social interactions may well exert an important influence on demographic processes, too. We suspect that many of the unsolved problems in vertebrate demography (see Krebs, p. 295, Moss & Watson, p. 275) will only be resolved when it is possible to examine density-dependent changes in the behaviour of recognizable individuals.

ACKNOWLEDGMENTS

We are grateful to the Nature Conservancy Council for permission to work on Rhum; to Fiona Guinness, C. M. Thouless, Glenn Iason, Callan Duck and Martin Major, our collaborators in the Rhum deer project, for their respective parts in data collection and analysis; and to NERC, SERC and the Royal Society for support.

REFERENCES

Ahlen, I. (1965). Studies on the red deer, *Cervus elaphus* L. In Scandinavia. III. Ecological investigations. *Viltrevy*, **3**, 177–376.

Alexander, R.D. (1974). The evolution of social behaviour. *Annual Reviews of Ecological Systematics*, **5**, 325–383.

Alexander, R.D., Hoogland, J.L., Howard, R.D., Noonan, M. & Sherman, P.W. (1979). Sexual dimorphism and breeding systems in pinnipeds, ungulates, primates and humans. *Evolutionary Biology and Human Social Behavior: An Anthropological Perspective* (Ed. by N.A. Chagnon & W. Irons), pp. 402–435, Duxbury Press, North Scituate, Mass.

Anderson, C.C. (1958). The elk of Jackson Hole. *Wyoming Game and Fish Commission Bulletin*, **10**, pp. 84.

Banfield, A.W.F. (1954). Preliminary investigation of the barren ground caribou, Part 2. Life history, ecology and utilization. Canada Dept. Northern Affairs and Natural Resources, National Parks Branch, Canadian Wildl. Serv., Ottawa. *Wildlife Management Bulletin*, Series 1, No. 10B, 1–112.

Bergerud, A.T. (1971). The population dynamics of Newfoundland caribou. *Wildlife Monograph*, **25**, 1–55.

Bergerud, A.T. (1973). Movement and rutting behaviour of caribou (*Rangifer farandus*) at Mount Alberta, Quebec. *Canadian Field Naturalist*, **87**, 357–369.

Bergerud, A.T. (1974a). Rutting behaviour of Newfoundland caribou. *The Behaviour of Ungulates and its Relation to Management* (Ed. by V. Geist & F. Walter), pp. 395–435. IUCN, Morges, Switzerland.

Bergerud, A.T. (1974b). Decline of caribou in North America following settlement. *Journal of Wildlife Management*, **38**, 757–770.

Bertram, B.C.R. (1975). Social factors influencing reproduction in wild lions. *Journal of Zoology*, **177**, 463–482.

Bertram, B.C.R. (1976). Kin selection in lions and in evolution. *Growing Points in Ethology* (Ed. by P.P.G. Bateson & R.A. Hinde), pp. 281–301, Cambridge University Press, Cambridge.

Bradbury, J.W. & Vehrencamp, S.L. (1977). Social organization and foraging in Emballonurid bats. III. Mating systems. *Behavioural Ecology and Sociobiology*, **2**, 1–17.

Case, T.J. (1978). On the evolution and adaptive significance of postnatal growth rates in terrestrial vertebrates. *Quarterly Reviews of Biology*, 53, 243–282.

Caughley, G. (1970). Eruption of ungulate populations, with emphasis on Himalayan Thar in New Zealand. *Ecology*, **51**, 53–72.

Caughley, G. (1976a). Wildlife management and the dynamics of ungulate populations. *Applied Biology, Vol. I*, (Ed. by T.H. Coaker), pp. 183–246. Academic Press, London.

Caughley, G. (1976b). Plant–herbivore systems. *Theoretical Ecology: Principles and Applications* (Ed. by R. May), pp. 94–113. W. B. Saunders, Philadelphia.

Caughley, G. & Krebs, C.J. (1983). Are big mammals simply little mammals writ large? *Oecologia*, **59**, 7–17.

Child, G. (1972). Observations on a wildebeest die-off in Botswana. *Arnoldia*, **31**, 1–13.

Chivers, D.J. (1969). On the daily behaviour and spacing of howling monkey groups. *Folia primatologia* **10**, 48–102.

Christian, J.J. (1970). Social subordination, population density and mammalian evolution. *Science*, **168**, 84–90.

Clutton-Brock, T.H., Albon, S.D., Gibson, R.M. & Guinness, F.E. (1979). The logical stag: adaptive aspects of fighting in red deer (*Cervus elaphus* L.). *Animal Behaviour*, **27**, 211–225.

Clutton-Brock, T.H., Albon, S.D. & Guinness, F.E. (1981). Parental investment in male and female offspring in polygynous mammals. *Nature*, **289**, 487–489.

Clutton-Brock, T.H., Albon, S.D. & Guinness, F.E. (1982a). Competition between female relatives in a matrilocal mammal. *Nature*, **300**, 178–180.

Clutton-Brock, T.H., Albon, S.D. & Guinness, F.E. (1984a). Maternal dominance, breeding success and birth sex ratios in red deer. *Nature*, **308**, 358–360.

Clutton-Brock, T.H., Albon, S.D. & Guinness, F.E. (1984b). The fragile male: sex differences in juvenile mortality in birds and mammals. *Nature* (in press).

Clutton-Brock, T.H., Greenwood, P.J. & Powell, R.P. (1976). Ranks and relationships in Highland ponies and Highland cows. *Zeitschrift für Tierpsychologie* **41**, 202–216.

Clutton-Brock, T.H., Guinness, F.E. & Albon, S.D. (1982b). *Red Deer: Behavior and Ecology of Two Sexes.* University of Chicago Press.

Clutton-Brock, T.H., Guinness, F.E. & Albon, S.D. (1984). Individuals and populations. *Proceedings of the Royal Society of Edinburgh.* **82** B, 275–290.

Clutton-Brock, T.H. & Harvey, P.H. (1976). Evolutionary rules and primate societies. *Growing Points in Ethology* (Ed. by P.P.G. Bateson & R.A. Hinde), pp. 195–237. Cambridge University Press, Cambridge.

Clutton-Brock, T.H. & Harvey, P.H. (1978). Mammals, resources and reproductive strategies. *Nature*, **273**, 191–195.

Clutton-Brock, T.H. & Harvey, P.H. (1980). Primates, brains and ecology. *Journal of Zoology*, 190, 309–323.

Clutton-Brock, T.H. & Harvey, P.H. (1983). The functional significance of variation in body size among mammals. *American Society of Mammalogy spec. publ.* 7, 632–663.

Clutton-Brock, T.H., Harvey, P.H. & Rudder, B. (1977). Sexual dimorphism, socionomic sex ratio and body weight in primates. *Nature*, 269, 797–800.

Coelho, A.M. (1974). Socio-bioenergetics and sexual dimorphism in primates. *Primates*, 15, 263–269.

Cowan, I. McT. (1950). Some vital statistics of big game on over-stocked mountain range. *Transactions of the North American Wildlife Conferences*, 15, 581–588.

Dittus, W.P.J. (1977). The social regulation of population density and age–sex distribution in the toque monkey. *Behaviour*, 63, 281–322.

Dittus, W.P.J. (1979). The evolution of behaviors regulating population density and age-specific sex ratios in a primate population. *Behaviour*, 69, 265–301.

Dittus, W.P.J. (1980). The social regulation of primate populations: a synthesis. *The Macaques* (Ed. by D.G. Lindburg), pp. 263–286. Van Nostrand, New York.

Downhower, J.F. & Armitage, K.B. (1971). The yellow-bellied marmot and the evolution of polygamy. *American Naturalist*, 105, 355–370.

Dunbar, R.I.M. (1980a). Demographic and life-history variables of a population of gelada baboons (*Theropithecus gelada*). *Journal of Animal Ecology*, 49, 485–506.

Dunbar, R.I.M. (1980b). Determinants and evolutionary consequences of dominance among female gelada baboons. *Behavioural Ecology and Sociobiology*, 7, 253–265.

Eisenberg, J.F. (1981). *The Mammalian Radiations*. University of Chicago Press, Chicago.

Emlen, S.T. & Oring, L.W. (1977). Ecology, sexual selection and the evolution of mating systems. *Science*, 197, 215–223.

Errington, P.L. (1963). The phenomena of predation. *American Scientist*, 51, 180–192.

Fedigan, L.M. (1983). Dominance and reproductive success in primates. *Yearbook of Physical Anthropology*, 26, 91–129.

Fiala, K.L. (1981). Parental investment and the sex ratio in red-winged blackbirds. *Natural Selection and Social Behaviour* (Ed. by R.D. Alexander & D.W. Tinkle), pp. 198–216. Chiron Press, New York.

Flook, D.R. (1970). A study of sex differential in the survival of wapiti. *Canadian Wildlife Service Report Series no. 11*. Ottawa: Department of Indian Affairs and Northern Development.

Fowler, C.W. (1981). Comparative population dynamics in large mammals. *Dynamics of Large Mammal Populations* (Ed. by C.W. Fowler & T.D. Smith), pp. 437–456, Wiley-Interscience, New York.

Frame, L.H., Malcolm, J.R., Frame, G.W. & van Lawick, H. (1979). Social organisation of African wild dogs (*Lycaon pictus*) on the Serengeti Plains, Tanzania, 1967–1978. *Zeitschrift für Tierpsychologie*, 50, 225–249.

Furuya, Y. (1968). On the fission of troops of Japanese monkeys, 1. Five fissions and social changes between 1955 and 1966 in the Gagyusan troop. *Primates*, 9, 323–350.

Furuya, Y. (1969). On the fision of troops of Japanese monkeys, 2. General view of troop fission of Japanese monkeys. *Primates*, 10, 47–69.

Furuya, Y. (1973). Fissions in the Gagyusan colony of Japanese monkeys. *Behavioral Regulators of Behavior in Primates* (Ed. by C.R. Carpenter), pp. 107–114. Bucknell University Press, New Jersey.

Gaines, M.S. & McClenaghan, L.R. Jr (1980). Dispersal in small mammals. *Annual Reviews of Ecological Systematics*, 11, 163–196.

Gautier-Hion, A. (1980). Seasonal variations of diet related to species and sex in a community of *Cercopithecus* monkeys. *Journal of Animal Ecology*, 49, 237–269.

Geist, V. (1971). *Mountain Sheep: A Study in Behavior and Evolution*. University of Chicago Press, Chicago.

Geist, V. (1974a). On the evolution of reproductive potential in moose. *Naturaliste Canadiene*, **101**, 527–537.

Geist, V. (1974b). On the relationship of social evolution and ecology. *American Zoologist*, **14**, 205–220.

Glucksman, A. (1974). Sexual dimorphism in mammals. *Biological Reviews*, **49**, 423–475.

Greenwood, P.J. (1980). Mating systems, philopatry and dispersal in birds and mammals. *Animal Behaviour*, **28**, 1140–1162.

Grubb, P. (1974). Population dynamics of the Soay sheep. *Island Survivors: The Ecology of the Soay Sheep of St Kilda* (Ed. by P.A. Jewell, C. Milner & J.M. Boyd), pp. 242–272, Athlone Press, London.

Hawkins, R.E. (1971). Dispersal of deer from Crab Orchard National Wildlife Refuge. *Journal of Wildlife Management*, **35**, 216–220.

Hoogland, J. (1981). Nepotism and cooperative breeding in the black-tailed prairie dog (Scuridae: *Cynomys ludovicianus*). *Natural Selection and Social Behaviour* (Ed. by R.D. Alexander & D.W. Tinkle), pp. 283–310, Chiron Press, New York.

Howe, H. (1977). Sex ratio adjustment in the common grackle. *Science*, **198**, 744–746.

Jarvis, J.U.M. (1981). Eusociality in a mammal: cooperative breeding in naked mole-rate colonies. *Science*, **212**, 571–573.

Kay, R.N.B. & Staines, B.W. (1981). The nutrition of red deer (*Cervus elaphus*). *Nutrition Abstracts and Reviews*, **51**, **601–622**.

Kleiman, D.G. (1977). Monogamy in mammals. *Quarterly Reviews of Biology*, **52**, 39–69.

Klein, D.R. (1968). The introduction, increase and crash of reindeer on St Mathew Island. *Journal of Wildlife Management*, **32**, 350–367.

Koyama, N., Norikoshi, K. & Mano, T. (1975). Population dynamics of Japanese monkeys at Arashiyama. *Proceedings of the Fifth International Congress of Primatology*, pp. 411–417, Karger, Basel.

Krebs, C.J. (1964). The lemming cycle at Baker Lake, Northwest Territories during 1959–1962. *Arctic Institute for North America Technology, paper No. 15*: 1–104.

Krebs, C.J. (1971). Genetic and behavioural studies on fluctuating vole populations. *Proceedings of the Advanced Study Institute on Dynamics of Numbers in Populations* (Ed. by P.J. den Boer & G.R. Gradwell), pp. 243–256, Oosterbeek 1970.

Krebs, C.J. (1978). A review of the Chitty Hypothesis of population regulation. *Canadian Journal of Zoology*, **56**, 2463–2480.

Krebs, C.J. (1979). Dispersal, spacing behavior and genetics in relation to population fluctuations in the vole *Microtus townsendii*. *Fortschr. Zoologie*, **25**, 61–77.

Lack, D. (1954). *The Natural Regulation of Animal Numbers*. Clarendon Press, Oxford.

Lamprecht, Jürg (1978). The relationship between food competition and foraging group size in some larger carnivores. *Zeitschrift für Tierpsychologie*, **46**, 337–343.

Lane, E.A. & Hyde, T.S. (1973). The effect of maternal stress on fertility and sex ratio: a pilot study with rats. *Journal of Abnormal Psychology*, **82**, 73–80.

Latham, R.M. (1947). Differential ability of male and female game birds to withstand starvation and climatic extremes. *Journal of Wildlife Management*, **11**, 139–149.

Laws, R.M., Parker, I.S.C. & Johnstone, R.C.B. (1975). *Elephants and their Habitats: The Ecology of Elephants in North Bunyoro, Uganda*. Clarendon Press, Oxford.

Lawton, J.H. & Hassell, M.P. (1981). Asymmetrical competition in insects. *Nature*, **289**, 793–796.

LeBoeuf, B.J., Whiting, R.J. & Gantt, R.F. (1972). Perinatal behaviour of northern elephant seal females and their young. *Behaviour*, **34**, 121–156.

Lockie, J.D. (1966). Territory in small carnivores. *Symposia of the Zoological Society of London*, **18**, 143–165.

Lomnicki, A. (1978). Individual differences between animals and the natural regulation of their numbers. *Journal of Animal Ecology*, **47**, 461–475.

Lomnicki, A. (1980). Regulations of population density due to individual differences and patchy environment. *Oikos*, **35**, 185–193.

Lomnicki, A. (1982). Individual heterogeneity and population regulation. *Current Problems in Sociobiology* (Ed. by King's College Sociobiology Group), pp. 153–167. Cambridge University Press, Cambridge.

MacArthur, J.W. & Bailie, W.H. (1932). Sex differences in mortality in Abraxas type species. *Quarterly Review of Biology*, 313–325.

McClure, P.A. (1981). Sex-biased litter reduction in food-restricted wood rats (*Neotama floridana*). *Science*, **211**, 1058–1060.

McCullough, D.R. (1979). *The George River deer herd: Population ecology of a k-selected species.* University of Michigan Press, Ann Arbor.

Macdonald, D.W. (1980). Social factors affecting reproduction amongst red foxes (*Vulpes vulpes* L., 1758). *The Red Fox* (Ed. by E. Zimen) pp. 123–175. Biogeographica, 18. W. Junk, The Hague.

Macdonald, D.W. (1983). The ecology of carnivore social behaviour. *Nature*, **301**, 379–384.

Malcolm, J. & Marten, K. (1982). Natural selection and the communal rearing of pups in African wild dogs (*Lycaon pictus*). *Behavioural Ecology and Sociobiology*, **10**, 1–13.

Masui, K., Nishimura, A., Ohsawa, H. & Sugiyama, Y. (1973). Population study of Japanese monkeys at Takasakiyama. I. *Journal of the Anthropological Society of Japan*, **81**, 236–248.

Maynard Smith, J. (1964). Group selection and kin selection. *Nature*, **201**, 1145–1147.

Mitchell, B., McCowan, D. & Nicholson, I.A. (1976). Annual cycles of body weight and condition in Scottish red deer, *Cervus elaphus*. *Journal of Zoology (London)*, **180**, 107–127.

Mittermeier, R.A. (1973). Group activity and population dynamics of the howler monkey on Barro Colorado Island. *Primates*, **14**, 1–19.

Montgomerie, G.G. & Sunquist, M.E. (1978). Habitat selection and use by two-toed and three-toed sloths. *The Ecology of Arboreal Folivores* (Ed. by G.G. Montgomery), pp. 329–360. Smithsonian Institution, Washington.

Moore, J. & Ali, R. (1984). Are dispersal and inbreeding avoidance related? *Animal Behaviour*, **32**, 94–112.

Moriya, A. & Hiroshige, T. (1978). Sex ratio of offspring of rats bred at 5°C. *International Journal of Biometeorology*, **22**, 312–315.

Morrison, F.B. (1948). *Feeds and Feeding* (21st edn). Morrison Publ. Co., Ithaca, New York.

Müller-Using, D. & Schloeth, R. (1967). Das Verhalten der Hirshe, Kükenthal, *Handbuch der Zoologie*, **10**, 1–60.

Myers, J.H. (1978). Sex ratio adjustment under food stress: maximization of quality or numbers of offspring? *American Naturalist*, **112**, 381–388.

Owen Smith, N. (1977). On territoriality in ungulates and an evolutionary model. *Quarterly Reviews of Biology*, **52**, 1–38.

Packard, J.M. & Mech, L.D. (1980). Population regulation in wolves. *Biosocial Mechanisms of Population Regulation*, (Eds. by M.N. Cohen, R.S. Malpas & H.G. Klein), pp. 135–150. Yale University Press, New Haven.

Pickering, S.P. (1983). *Aspects of the behavioural ecology of feral goats* (Capra domestica) Unpubl. Ph.D. thesis, University of Durham.

Ralls, K., Brownwell, R.L. & Ballou, J. (1980). Differential mortality by sex and age in mammals, with specific reference to the sperm whale. *Report of the International Whaling Commission Special issue 2*, 223–243.

Redfield, J.A., Tait, M.J. & Krebs, C.J. (1978a). Experimental alteration of sex ratios in populations of *Microtus townsendii*, a field vole. *Journal of Canadian Zoology*, **56**, 17–27.

Redfield, J.A., Taitt, M.J. & Krebs, C.J. (1978b). Experimental alterations of sex-ratios in populations of *Microtus oregoni*, the creeping vole. *Journal of Animal Ecology*, **47**, 55–69.

Reiter, J., Panken, K.J. & LeBoeuf, B.J. (1981). Female competition and reproductive success in Northern elephant seals. *Animal Behaviour*, **29**, 670–687.

Rivers, J.P.W. & Crawford, M.A. (1974). Maternal nutrition and the sex ratio at birth. *Nature*, **252**, 297–298.

Rodman, P.S. (1977). Feeding behaviour of orang-utans of the Kutai Nature Reserve, East Kalimantan. *Primate Ecology* (Ed. by T.H. Clutton-Brock), pp. 383–413. Academic Press, London.

Rood, J.P. (1980). Mating relationships and breeding suppression in the dwarf mongoose. *Animal Behaviour*, **28**, 143–150.

Sackett, G.P., Holm, R.A., Davis, A.E. & Fahrenbruch, C.E. (1974). Prematurity and low birth weight in pigtail macaques: incidence, prediction and effects on infant development. *Symposium of the Fifth Congress of the International Primate Society*.

Schaik, C. (1984). Does primate group size increase reproductive success? *Behaviour* (in press).

Schaller, G.B. (1972). *The Serengeti Lion: A Study of Predator–Prey Relations*. University of Chicago Press, Chicago.

Searcy, W.A. & Yasukawa, K. (1981). Sexual size dimorphism and survival of male and female blackbirds (Icteridae). *Auk*, **98**, 457–465.

Sherman, P.W. (1980). The limits of ground squirrel nepotism. *Sociobiology: Beyond Nature/Nurture?* (Ed. by G.W. Barlow & J. Silverberg), pp. 505–544, Westview Press, Boulder.

Sherman, P.W. (1981). Reproductive competition and infanticide in Belding's ground squirrels and other animals. *Natural Selection and Social Behavior: Recent Research and New Theory*, (Ed. by R.D. Alexander & W.D. Tinkle), pp. 311—331, Chiron Press, Concord.

Silk, J.B. (1983). Local resource competition and facultative adjustment of sex ratios in relation to competitive abilities. *American Naturalist* **121**, 56–66.

Silk, J.B., Clark Wheatley, C.B., Rodman, P.S. & Samuels, A. (1981). Differential reproductive success and facultative adjustment of sex ratios among captive female bonnet macaque (*Macaca radiata*). *Animal Behaviour*, **29**, 1106–1120.

Sinclair, A.R.E. (1977). *The African Buffalo: A Study of Resource Limitation of Populations*. University of Chicago Press, Chicago.

Sobanskii, G.G. (1979). Selective elimination in the Siberian stag population in the Altais as a result of the early winter of 1976/77. *Soviet Journal of Ecology*, **10**, 78–80.

Southwick, C.H. (1967). An experimental study of intragroup agonistic behaviour in rhesus monkeys (*Macaca mulatta*). *Behaviour*, **28**, 182–209.

Stirling, I. (1975). Factors affecting the evolution of social behaviour in the Pinnipedia. *Rapports et Procès-verbaux des Réunions du Conseil International pour l'Exploration de la Mer*, **169**, 205–212.

Sugiyama, Y. & Ohsawa, H. (1982). Population dynamics of Japanese macaques at Ryozenyama; III. Female desertion of the troop. *Primates*, **23**, 31–44.

Sunquist, M.E. (1981). The social organisation of tigers (*Panthera tigris*) in Royal Chitawan National Park, Nepal. *Smithsonian Contributions to Zoology*, No. 336, Smithsonian Institution Press, Washington.

Takasaki, H. (1981). Troop size, habitat quality, and home range area in Japanese macaques. *Behavioural Ecology and Sociobiology*, **9**, 277–281.

Talbot, L.M. & Talbot, M.H. (1963). The wildebeest in Western Masailand. *East Africa Wildlife Monograph*, **12**, 88 pp.

Tamarin, R.H. (1983). Animal population regulation through behavioural interactions. *Advances in the Study of Mammalian Behaviour* (Ed. by J.F. Eisenberg & D.G. Kleiman), pp. 698–720. American Society of Mammalogists. Special publications No. 7.

Tilson, R.L. (1981). Family formation strategies of Kloss' gibbons. *Folia primatologie*, **35**, 259–287.

Trivers, R.L. (1972). Parental investment and sexual selection. *Sexual Selection and the Descent of Man* (Ed. by B. Campbell), pp. 136–79. Aldine, Chicago.

Trivers, R.L. & Willard, D.E. (1973). Natural selection of parental ability to vary the sex ratio of offspring. *Science*, **179**, 90–92.

Waser, P. (1977). Feeding, ranging and group size in the mangabey *Cercocebus albigena*. *Primate Ecology: Studies of Feeding and Ranging Behaviour in Lemurs, Monkeys and Apes*. (Ed. by T. H. Clutton-Brock). Academic Press, London.

Wasser, S.K. (1983). Reproductive competition and cooperation among female yellow baboons. *Social Behaviour of Female Vertebrates* (Ed. by S.K. Wasser), pp. 350–390. Academic Press, New York.

Wasser, S.K. & Barash, D.P. (1983). Reproductive suppression among female mammals: implications for biomedicine and sexual selection theory. *Biology*, **58**, 513–538.

Watson, A. & Moss, R. (1970). Dominance, spacing behaviour and aggression in relation to population limitation invertebrates. *Animal Populations in Relation to their Food Resources* (Ed. by Adam Watson), pp. 176–220, Blackwell Scientific Publications, Oxford.

Whitten, P.L. (1983). Diet and dominance among female vervet monkeys (*Cercopithecus aethiops*). *American Journal of Primatology*, **5**, 139–159.

Widdowson, E. (1976). The response of the sexes to nutritional stress. *Proceedings of the Nutritional Society*, **35**, 1175–80.

Wilkinson, P.F. & Shank, C.C. (1977). Rutting-fight mortality among musk oxen on Banks Island, Northwest Territories, Canada. *Animal Behaviour*, **24**, 756–758.

Woolfenden, G.E. & Fitzpatrick, J.W. (1978). The inheritance of territory in group breeding birds. *Bio Science*, **28**, 104–108.

Wrangham, R.W. (1977). Feeding behaviour of chimpanzees in Gombe Stream National Park, Tanzania. *Primate Ecology: Studies of Feeding Behaviour in Lemurs, Monkeys and Apes* (Ed. by T.H. Clutton-Brock). Academic Press, London.

Wrangham, R.W. (1980). An ecological model of female-bonded primate groups. *Behaviour*, **51**, 262–299.

Wrangham, R.W. (1981). Drinking competition in vervet monkeys. *Animal Behavioural*, **29**, 904–910.

Wynne-Edwards, V.C. (1962). *Animal Dispersion in Relation to Social Behaviour*. Oliver and Boyd, Edinburgh.

Zimen, E. (1976). On the regulation of pack size in wolves. *Zeitschrift für Tierpsychologie*, **40**, 300–341.

34. BEHAVIOURAL ECOLOGY AND POPULATION DYNAMICS: TOWARDS A SYNTHESIS

R. H. SMITH AND R. SIBLY*

Department of Pure and Applied Zoology, University of Reading, Reading RG6 2AJ

SUMMARY

The population biology of animals has three strands: evolutionary genetics, population dynamics and behavioural ecology. We give a brief historical overview of population biology, noting that behavioural ecology has previously been linked mainly to evolutionary genetics. The links stressed at the 1984 symposium are between behavioural ecology and population dynamics. We note the pervasiveness of individual variation within age–sex classes and consider possible reasons for individual variation, both adaptive and non-adaptive. Finally, we note that individual variation has important implications for population dynamics and we consider some possible consequences for population growth and stability.

INTRODUCTION

In their introduction to the first edition of *Behavioural Ecology: an Evolutionary Approach*, Davies & Krebs (1978) define population biology as population genetics, evolution and ecology and say of their book that it 'explores areas in which ethology and population biology overlap.' The first great strides in this area were made by D. Lack and R.H. MacArthur who developed the population geneticists' idea that evolution is a fitness-maximizing process (Fisher 1930), subject to constraints which vary between species, and tested the idea of fitness maximization with many fine experiments and biogeographical data. For example, Lack (1947) applied the fitness-maximizing principle to the study of clutch and egg size, and MacArthur & Pianka (1966) applied the principle to the study of foraging. The continuing use of population genetics thinking in considering the evolution of behaviour and life history has been immensely fruitful, revolutionizing our understanding of social behaviour (Hamilton 1964) and animal conflict (Maynard Smith & Price 1973; Maynard Smith 1982).

---

*The order of authors is arbitrary, as is the order of editors of the symposium. Both the editing and this paper represent joint and equal efforts.

Until recently, population biology incorporated population dynamics and evolutionary genetics, the theory of which describes changes in the genetic structure of populations under the influence of natural selection. Previous symposia of the British Ecological Society on *Population Dynamics* (Anderson, Turner & Taylor 1979; see also den Boer & Gradwell 1971) and *Evolutionary Ecology* (Shorrocks 1984) have dealt with these two aspects of population biology. The 1984 *Behavioural Ecology* symposium completes the new population biology triad although, unlike the other two symposia, *Behavioural Ecology* concentrates almost entirely on animals.

The theme defined for the 1984 symposium of the British Ecological Society was that there are ecological consequences of the new evolutionary understanding of behaviour and life history, in particular for the dynamics of populations (see also Klomp & Woldendorp 1981). In contrast, the emphasis of the approach pioneered by Krebs & Davies (1978, 1984) is on how behaviour is influenced by natural selection in relation to ecological conditions. The two approaches are complementary; the 'evolutionary approach' of Krebs and Davies emphasizes the link between behavioural ecology and evolutionary genetics, while the 'ecological approach' emphasized in this symposium stresses the consequences of adaptive behaviour for population dynamics.

HISTORICAL BACKGROUND TO POPULATION BIOLOGY

Evolutionary genetics

The theory of population genetics provides the formal description of evolutionary change in population structure expressed as frequencies of alleles and of genotypes. With Mendel's Laws as its foundation, population genetics theory is better established than, for example, theories of animal population dynamics. Controversies that do arise (e.g. the selectionist–neutralist debate, reviewed by Gale 1980) are less about the correctness of different theories than about their relative importance in real populations, and it is the matching up of theory with data that presents the problem. Natural selection acts directly on phenotypes, and therefore indirectly on genotypes and genes. However, it is seldom possible to measure the fitness of a particular genotype; data on the average fitness of individuals of known genotype are hard to come by and require long-term studies of genetics and ecology, exploiting for example genotypic differences in colour (e.g. arctic skua; O'Donald 1983). However, quantitative genetics may often provide a practical way of investigating selection in relation to complex traits, and to life-history evolution in particular (Rose & Charlesworth 1981; Lande 1982). Quantitative genetics theory, which was developed in the practical context of plant and animal breeding, uses an approximate, statistical model whose main assumption is that genes and environmental influences affecting a character act additively in producing the phenotype of an individual. Because the predictions depend on attributing variation in a population to genetic and environmental effects, much larger sample sizes are required to estimate components of variance precisely than are needed to compare means. In long-term field studies, it is sometimes possible to estimate heritabilities of and genetic correlations between ecologically important traits in wild populations (van Noordwijk *et al.* 1980). Thus, although it is accepted that it can be useful to postulate the existence of genes affecting characters without direct evidence that such genes exist (Dawkins 1982), predictions about genetic variability, genetic correlations and responses to selection can often be and therefore ought to be tested.

An important prediction from population genetics theory is that chacteristics evolve according to a fitness-maximizing process by which one allele is selected for at the expense of another. In models of population genetics, fitness is defined as the per capita rate of increase of a genotype. Fitness is not an absolute quantity but is defined with reference to the population carrying the associated genes and the environment in which the population occurs. A new character is only expected to spread if its fitness is higher than that of its competitors; similarly, when a character has become fixed in a population, only a character with higher fitness can invade the population. Thus, evolution is a maximizing process in which characters move towards their locally optimal values (which maximize fitness; Falconer 1981, p. 305).

Fitness may be frequency-dependent or density-dependent, which can complicate matters in several ways (Charlesworth 1980). As a character moves towards fixation, its fitness approximates the per capita rate of increase of the entire population. If fitness depends on the frequency of alternative characters, a game theory analysis may be appropriate and the evolutionarily stable outcome can be a polymorphism (Maynard Smith 1982); Maynard Smith's important concept of the evolutionarily stable strategy (ESS) as the solution to an evolutionary game has opened up possibilities of answering evolutionary questions which conventional genetic theory has been unable to address. There is an important distinction between frequency-dependent and density-dependent selection (Charlesworth 1980). In frequency-dependent selection, the fitness of a phenotype depends on the relative proportions of different phenotypes in a population. In density-dependent selection, fitness depends on numbers of individuals per unit resource, although phenotypic variation between those individuals present may affect the definition of population density. Parker (p. 33) has explored some of the consequences of frequency- and density-dependent selection acting together.

Population dynamics

Like population genetics, the basic theory of population dynamics (Lotka 1925; Volterra 1926) was developed before many data were available, although theories of population dynamics are less generally accepted than those of population genetics because population dynamics lacks the firm foundations of meiotic segregation and random fertilization. The most celebrated controversy in population ecology concerns the relative importance of density-dependent and density-independent population regulation. The concept of density-dependent regulation of populations was expressed mathematically by Lotka (1925) and Volterra (1926). Lack (1954) supported the idea that density-dependent regulation by food shortage and by predation was of overriding importance in natural populations with a wealth of data, taken mainly from studies of birds and mammals. In the same year, Andrewartha & Birch (1954) expressed the contrary opinion, rejecting generalizations about the importance of density-dependent factors and competition as being based on peculiar logic and few data. Andrewartha & Birch argued that results of laboratory studies (e.g. Gause 1934; Park 1948) cannot be directly related to natural populations, and that attention should be focused on environmental factors affecting the rate of increase. Andrewartha & Birch considered that population numbers were limited in three ways:

(i) shortage of resources such as food or nesting sites;
(ii) inaccessibility of resources relative to the animals capacity for dispersal and searching;
(iii) shortage of time when the rate of increase is positive.

Fluctuations in the rate of increase were thought by Andrewartha & Birch to be caused by extrinsic factors (such as weather or predators) rather than intrinsic factors (density-dependent regulation of births, deaths or migration rates); their arguments were influenced by their own long-term study of annual fluctuations of an insect pest, *Thrips imaginis*, whose numbers were determined largely by climatic variations, while Lack had studied wild birds with a life-span extending over more than a single year. The divergent views were aired and discussed at the 22nd Cold Spring Harbor Symposium on Quantitative Biology (1957), and later reviewed by Lack in the appendices to his 1966 book on bird population studies. The general consensus now is that both density-dependent and density-independent factors are expected to play a role in the dynamics of natural populations. Morris's (1959) concept of a key factor and the development by Varley & Gradwell (1960 and later) of analytical methods to separate out the roles of different mortality factors have enabled ecologists to identify some factors which reduce fluctuations and regulate populations, and others which contribute to population fluctuations (e.g. McCleery & Perrins, p. 353).

A second great controversy in population ecology was generated by the exciting and provocative book on *Animal Dispersion* by Wynne Edwards (1962). Wynne Edwards suggested that the ultimate constraints of food shortage were seldom applied in nature because 'autoregulation' through social behaviour kept populations below their carrying capacities, as a consequence of group selection. The arguments for and against auto-regulation are well known (see section II of Williams 1971), and in general the group selection arguments relating to population regulation have been rejected (Maynard Smith 1976; Wynne Edwards 1978). However, the contribution of Wynne Edwards to the development of population biology should not be underestimated.

Because debates in population dynamics have not always taken full account of other aspects of population biology, arguments have not always been based on the Darwinian tenet of selection acting on individuals. Following the important theoretical contributions of May (1973), the concept of stability became something of a fetish in population dynamics, and ecologists have sometimes used arguments implicitly based on different versions of group selection when discussing the evolution of stability. Without some form of group selection, stability (which is clearly a property of groups and not individuals) may or may not evolve as an indirect consequence of selection acting on the life-history characteristics of individuals. Explicit reference to group selection (e.g. Gilpin 1975) does at least encourage consideration of the assumptions required for the process to operate. More sophisticated versions of group selection have arisen recently, and their value is reviewed by Harvey in this volume (p. 59).

Behavioural ecology and life-history theory

Underpinning behavioural ecology and life-history theory is the idea derived from quantitative genetics that evolution is a fitness-maximizing process, so that behaviours seen in long-established environments are likely to produce higher fitness than plausible behavioural alternatives. Optimization theories based on this premise have been developed to cover a wide variety of situations (see e.g. Krebs & Davies 1984). In some cases it is possible to examine the effect of behaviour on fitness directly, as when the number of eggs fertilized by a male depends directly on his mating behaviour (Parker 1978). In other cases it is necessary to use an index assumed proportional to fitness, such as 'net rate of energy intake' which is generally taken as the optimized variable in foraging studies. If resorting to the use of an index is a weakness in the approach, the assumption that an index is proportional to fitness is often very plausible, as with energy intake, and there is a powerful compensating advantage accruing from the predictive power of optimization theory which has been exploited in particular by a series of elegant experimental studies carried out to test optimal foraging theory. Optimal foraging theory was developed by MacArthur and his co-workers in North America in the 1960s (see e.g. MacArthur & Pianka 1966) but was firmly established as a discipline in its own right by a series of elegant experimental tests of Charnov's (1976) marginal value theorem (Fig. 34.1) by J.R. Krebs and others (see Krebs & McCleery 1984 for a recent review). Although optimal foraging studies are of special importance within behavioural ecology because of the number of experimental tests that have been made of clear theoretical predictions, the links with population dynamics have received relatively little attention (but see Comins & Hassell 1979). The present consensus is that optimal foraging theory provides insight and accurately predicts some outcomes but does not yet make adequate allowance for sampling the environment (Kacelnik & Krebs, p. 189) or individual variation (Partridge & Green, p. 207, and see below).

Theories about how groups of animals, that feed and perhaps live in patchy environments, should be distributed are of central importance to this symposium, in particular in Part III. If the foraging success of individuals is a decreasing function of the number of conspecifics feeding in the same patch,

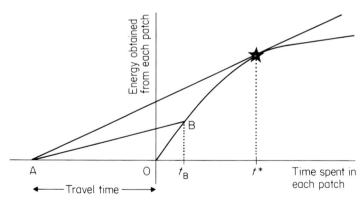

Fig. 34.1. Illustration of the marginal value theorem, which calculates the optimal time to spend in a patch if the travel time (between patches) is fixed. The curve represents the energy obtained from a patch in relation to the time spent exploiting it (i.e. a pay-off curve). The patch illustrated yields returns at a diminishing rate. The slope of the line A–B is equal to (energy obtained by spending time t_B in each patch)/(travel time + t_B), i.e. rate of obtaining energy. Hence rate of obtaining energy is maximized by the steepest line from A to the curve (starred).

and if the individuals are each maximizing energy intake and are assumed to be equally capable, then the distribution of individuals should mirror the profitability of the patches, this being the 'ideal-free distribution' (Fretwell & Lucas 1970; Fretwell 1972). Indeed, in the simple case that the foraging success of individuals is inversely proportional to the number of conspecifics feeding in the same patch, then the numbers in each patch should be linearly proportional to patch profitability. A similar model would apply to a territorial system in which territories were equally divided between the animals of breeding age, with the result that reproductive success was an inverse function of population density (Fig. 34.2a).

In contradistinction to the above cases in which all individuals were assumed equally capable, it may happen that some individuals (despots) through differences in strength, ability or behaviour are able to monopolize more than their share of the competed-for resource with the result that they

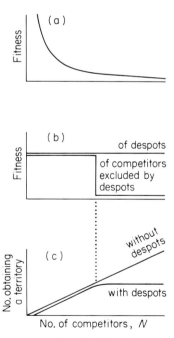

FIG. 34.2. Two possible consequences of territorial behaviour. In (a) every competitor gets an equivalent territory, so if there are more competitors territory size and fitness decrease. By contrast in (b) some competitors are despots and maintain territory size and fitness irrespective of how many competitors there are, and excluded competitors get nothing. The population consequences are shown in (c). See Davies (1978), Maynard Smith (1974) and O'Connor (p. 105) for further discussion.

occupy the better areas, and are more reproductively successful that the others (Fig. 34.2b). This is presumably the process by which territoriality evolved (Brown 1964), and the idea underlies many fine studies of territoriality by behavioural ecologists (for reviews see Davies 1978; Patterson 1980; Davies & Houston 1984; O'Connor, p. 105). As the population increases, the number obtaining a territory reaches an assymptote (Fig. 34.2c).

In the above case, the success of a particular tactic depends on the behaviour of other animals and the appropriate development of optimality theory to deal with such cases is the game theory approach (see p. 579). Although game theory models have only come into general use in recent years, they have nevertheless received a lot of experimental interest e.g. Brockman, Grafen & Dawkins 1979; Houston & Davies, p. 471).

If a particular behaviour affects the growth, survivorship or reproductive success of a relative then the definition of fitness must be extended to 'inclusive fitness'. The adoption of this wider definition underlies the modern understanding of sociobiology, though the subject still suffers measurement problems, e.g. in estimating the degree of relatedness of animals in the field (Grafen 1984).

THE SIGNIFICANCE OF INDIVIDUAL VARIATION

If evolution is a maximizing process in which beneficial alleles are successively selected for and give rise eventually to optimal strategies, then one might expect the end-product to be the same alleles occurring in all individuals in a population (subject to qualifications discussed below), so that individuals would all be the same, identically optimal 'wild type'. This classical view of evolution has provided part of the theoretical basis of a whole generation of studies in behavioural ecology, including the theories of optimal foraging and ideal-free distributions, but has frequently been shown to be incorrect. Many contributions to this symposium document the types and extent of individual variation in behaviour and fitness, tackle the question of why so much variation should exist, and discuss some of the ecological consequences.

Variation is found within populations in parameters affecting fitness directly, e.g. breeding success and survivorship, and in parameters affecting fitness indirectly, e.g. foraging success, obtaining a territory, dominance and migration. Some variation is simply related to age, for example juveniles are very often less successful than adults, and there are often differences between the sexes, but even when age and sex are accounted for, there remains variation within age–sex classes. Why is there so much variation between individuals?

Evolution of individual variation

We begin by listing possible evolutionary reasons for differences between sex- and age-classes. Differences between the sexes probably stem from differences in the resources they supply to their gametes (the evolution of which is discussed by Parker, Baker & Smith 1972). Given that females invest more resources in gametes and males invest more in finding mates, then males may compete for access to females. Male–male competitions may take many forms, from seizing and guarding to fighting for access to females in the period before they ovulate (see Vehrencamp & Bradbury (1984) for an extended list). Selection may then act directly to improve male competitive ability.

In addition, there may be selection for females to choose between males: either on the basis of fighting ability, or on the basis of resources offered to prospective mates, or on demonstrated parental ability. If females are choosey, then male attractiveness to females may also be selected for. As a side-effect of such processes males may dominate females in non-breeding interactions with the result that during seasonal migration, for example, females may be forced to migrate further because the preferred areas are occupied by males. On the other hand, if there is no seasonal migration, juvenile males may be forced to leave if older animals are better fighters.

Within-sex differences between age-classes probably stem from differences in size and experience. Juvenile mortality generally declines with age (Ito 1980) probably because older, bigger animals are better at avoiding predation and starvation. Size also affects energy acquisition and expenditure and affects allocation of energy between growth, maintenance, defence and reproduction. First breeding is generally less successful than later; possible reasons are that experience helps animals find and retain food, territories and mates and improves parental care.

Functional reasons for differences between sex and age-classes, as outlined above, are well documented in particular cases. Brought to the forefront in the examples in this book are differences within sex–age classes. Why should there be differences between individuals within sex–age categories? Such differences may be genetic or non-genetic, adaptive or non–adaptive.

(a) Adaptive genetic differences occur if morph A is fitter than morph B in environment/population A but less fit in environment/population B. A and B may be separated in space, in which case allopatric speciation may eventually occur unless there is migration between environments, or in time if there are environmental cycles (e.g. seasonal cycles) lasting at least several generations. Or morph A may be fitter than morph B at low population density, but less fit at high population density (density-dependent selection). Another possibility is that fitness is frequency-dependent, which can also lead to a genetic polymorphism in, e.g. various kinds of fighting behaviour (Maynard Smith 1982). Adaptive genetic differences also occur if heterozygotes are fitter than homozygotes, or if there is a negative genetic correlation between traits involved in fitness trade-offs such that a range of genotypes have similar fitness overall (Lande 1982).

(b) Non-adaptive genetic differences occur through random drift, deleterious mutation and change of environment.

(c) Non-genetic adaptive differences between individuals within age–sex classes can represent contingent responses to accidents of birth, development or environment. For example, individuals born in resource-rich environments may grow faster and larger and, as a result, have options in terms of feeding, mating and fighting not available to individuals born in resource-limited environments; they may therefore have a genetically-coded but phenotype-limited strategy (Parker 1982). Consequent differences between individuals would be adaptive but could be labelled non-genetic by quantitative geneticists because breeding studies would not reveal heritable differences between individuals.

(d) On the other hand, non-genetic differences between individuals may simply be responses to unusual accidents of environment which have no adaptive value.

Ecological consequences of individual variation

Although there may be some consequences for community structure (e.g. Mann, p. 227) and nutrient cycling, the main ecological consequences of individual variation are seen in population dynamics, affecting in particular the per capita rate of increase at a given density, which affects the equilibrium level of a population, and the stability or otherwise of an equilibrium. The extreme example of individual variation in Fig. 34.2b shows despotic animals holding a territory and so surviving and breeding while excluded competitors get nothing. Despotic behaviour therefore reduces the carrying capacity of an area below its potential if territories were smaller and animals distributed themselves equally (Fig. 34.2c). However, individual variation in feeding specializations might allow animals to exploit more of the available resources and hence increase equilibrium population levels.

An immediate consequence of individual variation is that animals are not distributed randomly through an environment, either because of some sort of specialization (e.g. feeding specialization) or because of despotic behaviour by animals able to exclude other individuals (e.g. territorial behaviour). Non-random distributions of animals may also arise not as a consequence of individual variation but because animals concentrate feeding and reproduction in suitable patches of an heterogeneous environment. What are the effects on population dynamics of non-random distributions of animals? Hassell & May (p. 3) conclude that aggregation tends to enhance stability whether it results from interspecific competition within patches (de Jong 1979, 1981; Atkinson & Shorrocks 1981) or predators foraging between patches (Hassell & May 1974; Comins & Hassell 1979). Hence, it is tempting to suggest that clumped distributions, whether they reflect an heterogeneous environment or the consequences of individual variation, may generally act to stabilize population dynamics.

Lomnicki's (1978, 1980) theoretical models incorporating genetic differences between individuals in competitive ability also suggest it is generally true that individual variation and spatial heterogeneity generally stabilize population dynamics.

The contrast between the two extremes where all individuals are equivalent (Fig. 34.2a) or despotic individuals obtain a disproportionate share of resources (Fig. 34.2b) is enshrined in Nicholson's (1954) terms 'scramble' and 'contest' (see Smith & Lessells, p. 423, for discussion of the use of these terms). Using the terms scramble and contest to imply outcome (as in Fig. 34.2) rather than behavioural process, it is generally believed that the population dynamic consequence of scramble competition (Fig. 34.2a) tends to be oscillatory because everybody obtains inadequate resources, and therefore density-dependent mortality overcompensates when population size exceeds the carrying capacity. By contrast, contest (Fig. 34.2b) tends to stabilize population size because, when population size exceeds the carrying capacity, despots alone obtain adequate resources and therefore mortality (of excluded competitors) compensates relatively quickly (cf. Fig. 2.11 of Varley, Gradwell & Hassell 1975; Chapter 3 of Maynard Smith 1974).

TOWARDS A SYNTHESIS

The argument for bringing population dynamics and behavioural ecology closer together is a powerful one, since comprehensive study of behavioural ecology provides the information needed to deduce the dynamics of the population (Hassell & May, p. 3). The direct link is that behavioural ecology is the study of the relationship between fitness and behaviour and other variables, including population density, N, where fitness of a phenotype is defined as the rate of increase per individual $(1/N) \cdot dN/dt$. But the dynamics of a population depend on its rate of change dN/dt in relation to N and other variables. Therefore, a behaviour study which actually relates fitness to behaviour and density necessarily provides the information needed to calculate the rate of change of the population in relation to its density, and thus the population dynamics.

The above account presupposed a population of identical individuals, but what emerges in the present symposium is the importance of individual variation. On detailed investigation almost every study population is seen to be composed of individuals in different classes—breeders/non-breeders, residents/migrants, adults/juveniles, male/female—and while individuals in each class at any time may seem to be doing the best they can (maximizing inclusive fitness), success varies very strikingly between the classes. Moreover, the proportion of individuals in each class varies dramatically with population density, with the common result that the proportion of non-breeders increases and juvenile survivorship falls as population density increases. Naturally there is an important, direct and calculable effect on population dynamics. By investigating the fitness of the observed behaviour of a particular category of individuals in relation to possible alternatives, behavioural ecologists can test whether observed behaviour maximizes fitness given the constraints imposed by environment and individual capability (phenotype). Thus, from a knowledge of the behavioural ecology one understands the reasons why individuals in different categories are limited in the fitnesses they can achieve, and knowing the fitnesses achieved by its subgroups it is possible to calculate the population's dynamics (Charlesworth 1980). Thus, behavioural ecology reveals the mechanisms that limit population increase or enforce population decrease and hence determine the carrying capacity of the environment in which the population lives. Behavioural ecology therefore has the potential to explain differences in dynamics between populations.

Furthermore, although the relationship between N and dN/dt has always been seen as the starting point in a study of population dynamics, the relationship has not been particularly easy to establish in the field; and where data have been obtained, they can often be described equally well by a variety of statistical curves. Behavioural ecology can sometimes guide our choice between these curves by indicating which would maximize fitness. For example, in a discussion of filter feeding, Lehman (1976) points out that different mathematical curves have been used to describe essentially the same empirical data, with unfortunate consequences when the curves were incorporated into simulation models of trophic dynamics and into theoretical discussions of stability in aquatic communities, since the curves differed most strikingly at low food densities where the effect of grazing has a strong effect on the predicted stability of the plankton. There may therefore be considerable practical value in a unifying theory which gives guidance in choosing between equally good statistical descriptions of data; because of its evolutionary basis, the optimality approach is well equipped to fill this role.

REFERENCES

Anderson, R.M., Turner, B.D. & Taylor, L.R. (1979). (Eds) *Population Dynamics.* Blackwell Scientific Publications, Oxford.

Andrewartha, H.G. & Birch, L.C. (1954). *The Distribution and Abundance of Animals.* University of Chicago Press, Chicago.

Atkinson, W.D. & Shorrocks, B. (1981). Competition on a divided and ephemeral resource: a simulation model. *Journal of Animal Ecology,* **50,** 461–471.

Brockmann, H.J., Grafen, A. & Dawkins, R. (1979). Evolutionarily stable nesting strategy in a digger wasp. *Journal of theoretical Biology,* **77,** 473–496.

Brown, J.L. (1964). The evolution of diversity in avian territorial systems. *Wilson Bulletin,* **76,** 160–169.

Charlesworth, B. (1980). *Evolution in Age-Structured Populations.* Cambridge University Press, Cambridge.

Charnov, E.L. (1976). Optimal foraging: the marginal value theorem. *Theoretical Population Biology,* **9,** 129–136.

Comins, H.N. & Hassell, M.P. (1979). The dynamics of optimally foraging predators and parasitoids. *Journal of Animal Ecology,* **48,** 335–351.

den Boer, P.J. & Gradwell, G.R. (1971). (Eds) *Dynamics of Populations.* Centre for Agricultural Publishing and Documentation, Wageningen.

Davies, N.B. (1978). Ecological questions about territorial behaviour. *Behavioural Ecology: An Evolutionary Approach* (1st edn) (Ed. by J.R. Krebs & N.B. Davies), pp. 317–350. Blackwell Scientific Publications, Oxford.

Davies, N.B. & Houston, A.I. (1984). Territory economics. *Behavioural Ecology: An Evolutionary Approach* (2nd edn) (Ed. by J.R. Krebs & N.B. Davies), pp. 148–169. Blackwell Scientific Publications, Oxford.

Davies, N.B. & Krebs, J.R. (1978). Introduction: ecology, natural selection and social behaviour. *Behavioural Ecology: An Evolutionary Approach* (1st edn) (Ed. by J.R. Krebs & N.B. Davies), pp. 1–18. Blackwell Scientific Publications, Oxford.

Dawkins, R. (1982). *The Extended Phenotype.* W.H. Freeman, Oxford.

de Jong, G. (1979). The influence of the distribution of juveniles over patches of food on the dynamics of a population. *Netherlands Journal of Zoology,* **29,** 33–51.

de Jong, G. (1981). The influence of dispersal pattern on the evolution of fecundity. *Netherlands Journal of Zoology,* **32,** 1–30.

Falconer, D.S. (1981). *Introduction to Quantitative Genetics* (2nd edn). Longman, Harlow, Essex.

Fisher, R.A. (1930). *The Genetical Theory of Natural Selection.* Oxford University Press, Oxford. (Second edition 1958, by Dover, New York).

Fretwell, S.D. (1972). *Populations in a Seasonal Environment.* Princeton University Press, Princeton.

Fretwell, S.D. & Lucas, H.L. (1970). On territorial behaviour and other factors influencing habitat distribution in birds. *Acta biotheoretica,* **19,** 16–36.

Gale, J.S. (1980). *Population Genetics.* Blackie, Glasgow.

Gause, G.F. (1934). *The Struggle for Existence.* Williams and Wilkins, Baltimore. (Reprinted 1964, by Hafner, New York.)

Gilpin, M.E. (1975). *Group Selection in Prey–Predator Communities.* Princeton University Press, Princeton, New Jersey.

Grafen, A. (1984). Natural selection, kin selection and group selection. *Behavioural Ecology: An Evolutionary Approach* (2nd edn) (Ed. by J.R. Krebs & N.B. Davies), pp. 62–84. Blackwell Scientific Publications, Oxford.

Hamilton, W.D. (1964). The genetical evolution of social behaviour. *Journal of theoretical Biology,* **7,** 1–52.

Hassell, M.P. & May, R.M. (1974). Aggregation in predators and insect parasites and its effect on stability. *Journal of Animal Ecology*, **43**, 567–594.

Ito, Y. (1980). *Comparative Ecology*. Cambridge University Press, Cambridge.

Klomp, H. & Woldendorp, J.W. (1981). *The Integrated Study of Bird Populations*. Centre for Agricultural Publishing and Documentation, Wageningen.

Krebs, J.R. & Davies, N.B. (1978). (Eds) *Behavioural Ecology: An Evolutionary Approach* (1st edn). Blackwell Scientific Publications, Oxford.

Krebs, J.R. & Davies, N.B. (1984). (Eds) *Behavioural Ecology: An Evolutionary Approach* (2nd edn). Blackwell Scientific Publications, Oxford.

Krebs, J.R. & McCleery, R.H. (1984). Optimization in behavioural ecology. *Behavioural Ecology: An Evolutionary Approach* (2nd edn) (Ed. by J.R. Krebs & N.B. Davies), pp. 1–121. Blackwell Scientific Publications, Oxford.

Lack, D. (1947). The significance of clutch size. *Ibis*, **89**, 302–352.

Lack, D. (1954). *The Natural Regulation of Animal Numbers*. Clarendon Press, Oxford.

Lack, D. (1966). *Population Studies of Birds*. Oxford University Press, Oxford.

Lande, R. (1982). A quantitative theory of life-history evolution. *Ecology*, **63**, 607–613.

Lehman, J.T. (1976). The filter feeder as an optimal forager, and the predicted shapes of feeding curves. *Limnology and Oceanography*, **21**, 501–516.

Lomnicki, A. (1978). Individual differences between animals and the natural regulation of their numbers. *Journal of Animal Ecology*, **47**, 461–475.

Lomnicki, A. (1980). Regulation of population density due to individual differences and patchy environments. *Oikos*, **35**, 183–197.

Lotka, A.J. (1925). *Elements of Physical Biology*. Williams & Wilkins, Baltimore. (Reprinted 1956, by Dover, New York.)

MacArthur, R.H. & Pianka, E.R. (1966). On the optimal use of a patchy environment. *American Naturalist*, **100**, 603–609.

May, R.M. (1973). *Stability and Complexity in Model Ecosystems*. Princeton University Press, Princeton, New Jersey.

Maynard Smith, J. & Price, G.R. (1973). The logic of animal conflict. *Nature (London)*, **246**, 15–18.

Maynard Smith, J. (1974). *Models in Ecology*. Cambridge University Press, Cambridge.

Maynard Smith, J. (1976). Group selection. *Quarterly Review of Biology*, **51**, 277–283.

Maynard Smith, J. (1982). *Evolution and the Theory of Games*. Cambridge University Press, Cambridge.

Morris, R.F. (1959). Single-factor analysis in population dynamics. *Ecology*, **40**, 580–588.

Nicholson, A.J. (1954). An outline of the dynamics of animal populations. *Australian Journal of Zoology*, **2**, 9–65.

Noordwijk, A.J., van Balen, J.H. & Scharloo, W. (1980). Heritability of ecologically important traits in the Great Tit, *Parus major*. *Ardea*, **68**, 193–203.

O'Donald, P. (1983). *Arctic Skua: Study of the Ecology and Evolution of a Sea Bird*. Cambridge University Press, Cambridge.

Park, T. (1948). Experimental studies of interspecific competition. I. Competition between populations of the flour beetles, *Tribolium confusum* Duval and *Tribolium castaneum* Herbst. *Ecological Monographs*, **18**, 265–308.

Parker G.A. (1978). Searching for mates. *Behavioural Ecology: An Evolutionary Approach* (1st edn) (Ed. by J.R. Krebs & N.B. Davies), pp. 214–244. Blackwell Scientific Publications, Oxford.

Parker, G.A. (1982). Phenotype-limited evolutionarily stable strategies. *Current Problems in Sociobiology* (Ed. by King's College Sociobiology Group), pp. 173–201. Cambridge University Press, Cambridge.

Parker, G.A., Baker, R.R. & Smith, V.G.F. (1972). The origin and evolution of gamete dimorphism and the male–female phenomenon. *Journal of theoretical Biology*, **36**, 529–553.

Patterson, I.J. (1980). Territorial behaviour and the limitation of population density. *Ardea*, **68**, 53–62.

Rose, M.R. & Charlesworth, B. (1981). Genetics of life history in *Drosophila melanogaster*. *Genetics*, **97**, 173–196.

Shorrocks, B. (1984). (Ed.) *Evolutionary Ecology*. Blackwell Scientific Publications, Oxford.

Varley, G.C. & Gradwell, G.R. (1960). Key factors in population studies. *Journal of Animal Ecology*, **29**, 399–401.

Varley, G.C., Gradwell, G.R. & Hassell, M.P. (1975). *Insect Population Ecology*. Blackwell Scientific Publications, Oxford.

Vehrencamp, S.L. & Bradbury, J.W. (1984). Mating systems and ecology. *Behavioural Ecology: An Evolutionary Approach* (2nd edn) (Ed. by J.R. Krebs & N.B. Davies), pp. 251–278. Blackwell Scientific Publications, Oxford.

Volterra, V. (1926). Variations and fluctuations of the numbers of individuals in animal species living together. (Reprinted, 1931, in R.N. Chapman, *Animal Ecology*, McGraw-Hill, New York.)

Williams, G.C. (1971). (Ed). *Group Selection*. Aldine Atherton, Chicago.

Wynne-Edwards, V.C. (1962). *Animal Dispersion in Relation to Social Behaviour*. Oliver and Boyd, Edinburgh.

Wynne-Edwards, V.C. (1978). Intrinsic population control: an introduction. *Population Control by Social Behaviour* (Ed. by F.J. Ebling & D.M. Stoddart), pp. 1–22. Institute of Biology, London.

AUTHOR INDEX

Page numbers shown in italics indicate lists of references.

SUBJECT INDEX